THE
TENNIS
PLAYER'S
HANDBOOK

A BUYER'S GUIDE AND SERVICE DIRECTORY

THE TENNIS PLAYER'S HANDBOOK

A BUYER'S GUIDE AND SERVICE DIRECTORY

BY THE EDITORS OF TENNIS MAGAZINE

A TENNIS MAGAZINE BOOK

Published by
Tennis Magazine
A New York Times Company
495 Westport Avenue
Norwalk, Connecticut 06856

Trade book distribution
by Simon and Schuster
A Division of Gulf & Western Corporation
New York, New York 10020

First Printing
ISBN: 0-914178-32-6
Library of Congress: 79-65033
Manufactured in the United States of America

ACKNOWLEDGEMENTS

The publisher is indebted to the following whose collaboration was indispensable to the production of this book:

TENNIS Magazine

Founder: Asher Birnbaum; Editor: Shepherd Campbell; Managing Editor: Jeffrey N. Bairstow.

Editors, Contributing Editors and Staff Members, past and present: Louise Ackerman, Charlene Cruson, Robert Cubbedge, Cheryl Davis, Patricia de Jongh, Donna Doherty, Teresa Girgasky, Kathy Jonah, Robert LaMarche, Tracy Leonard, Marven Moss, Karen Salling, Barry Tarshis.

Contributing Authors: Bernard Bartzen, Bjorn Borg, Vic Braden, Dave Bushnell, Bill Clark, Morris Edwards, James Fixx, Carol Cooper Garey, Harry Hopman, A. Paul Lawrence, Chris Evert Lloyd, John K. Lovitt, Gail Matsumoto, Robert P. Nirschl, M.D., Jim Pons, Dennis Ralston, Joan Ramey, J. H. Slogar, Fred Weymuller, Gus White, M.D., Ward C. Williams.

TENNIS Magazine Instruction Advisory Board, past and present: Julie Anthony, Margaret Court, Roy Emerson, Ron Holmberg, Billie Jean King, George Lott, Bill Price, Vic Seixas, Stan Smith, Tony Trabert.

Alexander McNab, TENNIS Magazine Assistant Editor, who organized the material.

Marven Moss, for research, updating and editing.

Steve Sjurlej, TENNIS Magazine Staff Photographer.

"The Types of Rest All Players Need" (page 189) by Jim McManus is reprinted with permission of the Association of Tennis Professionals from the association's official newsletter, "International Tennis Weekly."

"Twenty Ways to Tone Up Your Body" (page 170) is reprinted with permission of Armour-Dial, Inc.

"The Way a Racquet is Strung" (page 30) and "How to Regrip Your Own Racquet" (page 34) are adapted from "A Manual for Racquet Stringers" by A. Paul Lawrence (Ektelon, San Diego).

Manufacturing facilities, pages 16–17, courtesy of Bancroft Sporting Goods.

Airport facilities, page 239, courtesy of American Airlines.

Tennis club facilities, pages 100, 143, 149, 157, 215–217, 255, courtesy of The Four Seasons Racquet Club, Wilton, Conn.

Tennis clothing and equipment, pages 50, 59, 61, 70, 73, courtesy of Sport Mart of Westport (Conn.), Inc.

ILLUSTRATION CREDITS

PHOTOS

Courtesy Avco Community Developers, Inc. (Rancho Bernardo), 248A

Beauchamp, Bob, 107, 109

Bilbao, Joseph, 176

Braden, Melody, 212, 213, 214

Courtesy Vic Braden Tennis College, 146, 256

Braverman, Stan, 286

Courtesy Callaway Gardens, 136

Courtesy Chase, Ltd., 220

Courtesy Cushman & Associates, 94

Delphia, Fran, 56

Courtesy Doral C.C., 249A

Courtesy Eastman Kodak Corp., 163, 164, 166

Courtesy East Side Tennis Club, 160

Fox, Jeffrey, 134, 202–203, 234, 239, 245

Gaines, Leslie, 184

Courtesy John Gardiner's Tennis Ranch, 248B

Goldstrom, Steve, 274

Henczel, Zoltan, 12, 43, 45, 46, 49, 50, 62, 63, 64–65, 70, 73, 113, 204, 227, 294, 304–305, 306–307, 308, 309, 310

Courtesy The Homestead, 249B

Courtesy Hutchins Photography, 92

Courtesy Don Kerbis Tennis Ranch, 267

Lovitt, John, 312–313

McIntyre, Bob (Broadmoor Hotel), 122, 126

Mecca, Jack & Peter, 16–17

Newcomb, John, 99, 168, 187

Courtesy Newks Tennis Ranch, 259

Courtesy Pinehurst Tennis Club, 141

Courtesy Polaroid Corp., 162

Rabinowitz, Barry, 210

Courtesy Sea Pines Plantation, 273

Szurlej, Steve, 59, 61, 100, 139, 143, 149, 157, 193, 215–217, 233, 255

Tenin, Barry, 182

Courtesy 3M Corp., 277, 278

Courtesy Wayne Racquet Club, 253

ILLUSTRATIONS

Courtesy Armour-Dial, Inc., 171–175

Duggan, Laura, 68

Harbaugh, David, 290

Keeler, Susan, 53, 54

Kohfield, Dick, 29, 30–31, 77, 79, 80, 82, 86, 88, 151, 152, 153, 230

Luft, Jim, 222, 242

Nirschl, Robert P. M.D., 196

Porges, Peter, 271

Staepelaere, Barbara, 74, 155

Vebell, Ed, 206–207, 264

Wexler, Elmer, 14, 18–19, 22, 24, 33

TABLE OF CONTENTS

FOREWORD

As the popularity of tennis has grown during the last decade, so has the number of how-to books about the sport. Until now, virtually all those books have dealt with how to hit the ball. "The Tennis Player's Handbook" is different. It deals with everything *but* stroking instruction.

The growth of tennis has meant a growth in ways to spend your money on tennis-related goods and services—equipment, clothes, courts, lessons, indoor time, practice devices, tennis vacations, tennis camps. This handbook will help you make your choices when you search for a new racquet, shop for a new pair of shoes, scout around for an indoor club or plan a trip to a resort. It will tell you what the differences are between similar goods and services, how to choose the one appropriate for your game and how to get the most out of what you choose.

"The Tennis Player's Handbook" also will help you stay fit, avoid injuries, organize tournaments and parties, work tennis into your business schedule and enjoy off-court tennis-related activities. It contains everything the tennis enthusiast needs to know about the sport.

Compiled by our TENNIS editors, the Handbook features advice from the experts—top tour professionals, renowned teaching professionals and industry leaders. You'll find diet tips from Chris Evert Lloyd, suggestions on staying mentally sharp from Bjorn Borg and advice on running from James Fixx.

We have purposely avoided lists of brand names—racquets, clothes, strings, resorts, camps, shoes, TV or board games. The turnover in the tennis market is so rapid that any list would be outdated too quickly to be useful. However, regular updates on many of these items can be found month-to-month in the pages of TENNIS magazine. For example, the January issue annually carries a complete directory of tennis camps and clinics, and December gives you the yearly lowdown on the latest in racquets.

In short, all the information you need about tennis is here, at your service. Once you read the Handbook, you'll find it will be your advantage!

BOW
The circular part of the frame. The bow and the shaft are fashioned from the same piece of material.

CROWN
The top part of the bow, reinforced on some racquets.

FACE
The flat part of the racquet formed by the strings.

SWEET SPOT
The central area of the strings where the most controlled and powerful hits are made.

STRING HOLES
Holes drilled through the frame for the string. Typically, there are 64 holes on a conventional wood racquet.

STRINGS
About 33 feet of nylon or gut are used to string a normal-sized racquet. There are usually 18 horizontal (cross) strings and 21 vertical (main) strings.

YOKE
The center section of the throat between the two sides of the shaft and the bow.

OVERLAY
Thin sections of fiberglass or other reinforcing material bonded to the bow and shaft for extra strength.

THROAT
The section where the shaft and bow join. Usually reinforced with overlays on wood racquets.

FLAKE
A panel added to the shaft for extra strength. The longer the flake, the stiffer the racquet.

SHAFT
The handle of the racquet from the butt to the throat.

GRIP
A long strip of leather or synthetic material wound around the end of the shaft and secured with tacks and adhesive tape.

BUTT PLATE
A small plastic cover for the end of the shaft.

CHOOSING THE RIGHT EQUIPMENT

Everyone who plays tennis needs at least three items of equipment: a racquet with strings, tennis balls and tennis shoes.

However, you don't have to run out and buy the same kind of racquets and shoes that Bjorn Borg uses, nor should you get your racquet strung as tightly as his.

What's right for a Wimbledon champion is not necessarily right for you. Instead, you should tailor your choice of equipment to your own game: how you play, when you play and where you play. Using the right equipment will help you to improve your game and make tennis more enjoyable.

WHAT'S AVAILABLE IN RACQUETS

Until 1978, the only mention of racquets in the rules of tennis was a vague reference to the "instrument used to strike the ball." If it tickled your fancy, you could, legally, have used an old piano leg or a lacrosse stick.

The new definition, passed by the International Tennis Federation (ITF) in the wake of a controversy over double-strung or so-called "spaghetti" racquets, says: "The racquet shall consist of a frame and a stringing . . . The frame may be of any material, weight, size or shape."

That's quite a bit of leeway and in the past few years racquet manufacturers have developed an array of space-age racquets with names right out of "Star Trek." Despite all the new technology, these racquets trace their roots back to the traditional wood model.

WOOD RACQUETS: Like the faithful old rocking chair, the wood tennis racquet has changed remarkably little in the past 50 years. And, like the rocking chair, the wood racquet is a classic example of an aesthetically pleasing form performing a nearly optimum function. Wood racquets do their job so well, in fact, that they hold a substantial share of the market against the newer

THE WOOD RACQUET

A wood racquet is made from a dozen or more wood strips called laminations that are bonded together and bent to form the frame. A high-grade white ash is the best lamination for resilience and light weight. The outside lamination is often birch or maple, both of which are hard and resist scuffing. The more laminations, the stronger and livelier the racquet; but the higher the price. Wood composite racquets have added laminations of graphite, fiberglass or other extra-strong materials.

metal, fiberglass, graphite or composite (racquets that combine two or more of these materials) models.

The design of a racquet is actually a rather nifty compromise between weight and strength, just like the bentwood chair. A racquet must be strong enough to withstand the battering of the balls and the pull of the string tension. Yet it can't be so heavy that it will feel like an iron weight after five gruelling sets.

The earliest tennis racquets were quite heavy since they were made from a single cut of wood, usually ash or hickory, which was steam-bent to form the handle and the bow in one continuous piece. Around the time of World War II, new wood bonding techniques allowed racquet-makers to use several thin laminations to form the bow and the shaft. The result was a racquet that was immediately stronger and lighter than its predecessors. Except for the addition of fiberglass reinforcement, the construction of modern wood tennis racquets is still similar to the early laminated models.

The dimensions of a wood racquet are dictated largely by the need to keep the weight down and maintain the stiffness. Consequently, virtually all the laminated racquets have similar dimensions. A typical racquet is about 27 inches long and weighs between 12 and 14 ounces unstrung. The shaft is generally about 15 inches long, while the bow is about 12 inches long and 9 inches wide.

When metal racquets began gaining popularity in the late 1960's—and later fiberglass and composite materials—some tennis observers predicted that the end was near for the wood racquet. They thought metal racquets would offer such superior and radically different designs that the wood racquet would become so much kindling. That, obviously, has not happened. In fact, wood racquets still have about half of the racquet market.

METAL RACQUETS: Most metal racquets have a "trampoline" effect that catapults the ball off the strings with more power than a conventional wood racquet. Because metal racquets usually have an open throat design which causes less wind resistance, they can be moved through the air faster. The result is that most metal racquets offer a power advantage over wood racquets.

Of course, there is a price to be paid. Many players notice a distinct loss of control with some metal racquets. To get the most from a metal racquet, you should be a good enough player to be able to hit the ball accurately in the center of the strings most of the time. Hitting the ball off center drastically reduces control over direction.

Because metal racquets are more difficult to manufacture, a good metal racquet also generally costs more than an equivalent wood model. It may also cost a little extra to string a metal racquet because some of them have unusual wire or plastic string suspension systems that require more of a stringer's time.

Initially, apart from the open throat, metal racquets were made in the same

THE MAKING OF A WOOD RACQUET

1. *A modern wood racquet is made from six to 12 long thin strips of ash and maple, which run in a continuous length from the handle around the bow and back down the other side of the handle. This machine bends the strips, already coated with glue, to form the basic racquet shape. Still clamped together, the strips are then baked in an oven for several hours. Later, reinforcing overlays of maple, fiber or fiberglass are added.*

2. *After the excess glue has been cleaned off and the racquet sanded to its basic shape, this monster machine drills the string holes in the bow (the racquet is below the operator's left hand).*

4. *Looking distinctly like a completed frame, the racquet is now given a final sanding before it is weighted and balanced. Although many racquet sanding operations can be handled by a machine, this final finishing work is best done by hand. It's one reason that no two wood racquets are exactly alike.*

3. *Next, the handles are built up to the proper size using short strips of basswood called flakes. This operator glues the flakes on batches of six racquets at a time; they're held together by a large clamp. When the glue is dry, another operator bevels each flake to give the handle its usual octagonal shape.*

5. *When the woodworking is complete, each racquet is checked for balance (as shown here) and for weight (on the scale at left). A hole is drilled in the racquet handle and leaded rubber plugs are inserted until the weight and balance are correct. The hole is then closed with a wooden plug.*

6. *The racquets are next sealed and sprayed with up to four coats of a tough, clear lacquer. Decorative and "signature" decals are pasted on the racquets after the first coat of lacquer.*

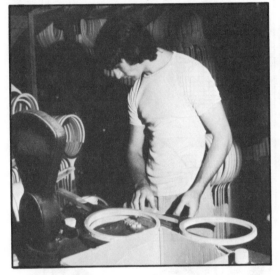

7. *This operator puts the butt cap on the end of the racquet and then uses a lathe-like device to turn the racquet for winding on the grip.*

8. *Finally, the racquet may be strung by the manufacturer or offered unstrung on the retail market. All that remains is for the cover to be zipped on.*

general size, shape and weight as their wood counterparts. Then advancements in technology led to the introduction of over-sized models which have proved popular, by and large, with players who feel more confident with an expanded hitting area.

Steel, aluminum, titanium and various alloys are the basic metal racquet materials. The racquets are usually made from a single piece of metal bent to form the two sides of the shaft and bow in one continuous piece. At the throat, a wedge-shaped section called a "yoke" is inserted to complete the arc of the bow.

At the outset, metal racquets posed certain stringing problems. The string would snap if fed directly through the sharp-edged holes in the bow. To minimize string breakage, manufacturers employ a variety of unconventional stringing patterns.

THE NEW GENERATION OF RACQUETS: If you are actually tempted to turn your back when you first confront the wide selection of space-age racquets, don't. This new generation of racquets represents a genuine improvement in racquet design. These racquets can be divided into four different groups.

The largest group is the graphite fiber racquets. Most people think of graphite as the substance used in lead pencils. And that hardly seems the kind of material which could be used successfully to strengthen a tennis racquet.

It's not. Actually, the new graphite composites that are being applied to tennis

THE METAL RACQUET

Metal racquets are made from hollow tubes bent to form the frame and fastened at the throat with a plastic yoke. The handles are foam or plastic sections bonded or screwed to the frame. Metal racquets are less easily damaged than wood models and can often be repaired without difficulty. Some metal racquets have a wire strip around the bow for the strings while others have holes drilled through the frame with plastic inserts (called grommets). Early metal racquets were made from steel, but current designs also use aluminum, magnesium and titanium alloys for strength, yet with light weight.

racquets are made from millions of tiny graphite fibers, each about three-ten-thousandths of an inch in diameter.

The graphite fibers are made from synthetic textile fibers which are heated to such high temperatures (around 5,000 degrees Fahrenheit) that everything is burned off except the carbon which forms graphite. This carbonizing is done with the fibers under tension so that the graphite molecules align themselves and, thus, produce fibers of remarkable strength and stiffness. They are embedded in a plastic base formed out of nylon or epoxy (which is a hard, glue-like resin). Like steel rods in concrete, the graphite fibers reinforce the base to make a composite material which is strong and stiff, but it is also extremely light because both the fibers and the plastic weigh relatively little.

As a result, graphite frames typically vibrate less and have more resistance to twisting on off-center shots than conventional racquets.

A graphite racquet, consequently, is well-suited to more powerful players. They will find that they can hit the ball hard with good control. However, a graphite racquet can be tough on a player with a history of tennis elbow since it will transmit shocks more easily to the wrist and elbow.

A second grouping of racquets is the wooden composite models. These are essentially wood designs that have been improved by reinforcement with graphite or other fibers, such as boron. They are generally higher priced than conventional

THE COMPOSITE RACQUET

Composite racquets are made from a variety of non-wood materials including graphite, fiberglass and aluminum alloys. There are two types: the hollow-core designs, usually of fiberglass, and the foam-core designs which have a polyurethane foam core with graphite fibers or fiberglass wrapped or molded around the core. The foam cores provide excellent shock absorption and plenty of power with no loss of playability. The hollow-core designs offer uniform flexibility and also provide exceptional power for the hard hitter.

wood racquets, but not as expensive as graphite racquets.

The third group of racquets is the fiberglass models, made from fiberglass laminations over a plastic core. Most fiberglass racquets are not noticeably different in design and description from wood racquets, but their playing characteristics vary widely.

Although fiberglass racquets have been on the market for some time, there are some new designs around that seem to represent a considerable improvement over the earlier versions. Most are, incidentally, about half the price of graphite racquets.

The fourth group of racquets are made from "sandwiches" of aluminum alloys and fiberglass, sometimes with graphite or boron reinforcement. In many ways this kind of construction resembles that of modern skis, and, indeed, most of these racquets are made by ski manufacturers.

Some of the new generation of racquets differ in shape from the more conventional models. Already mentioned were metal racquets with oversized heads. Other novel racquet head designs include a near-diamond shape, extra-long and/or extra-wide traditional elliptical shapes and variations on circular shapes.

New racquets come on the market almost every month. But don't hold your breath waiting for the perfect one. The chances are that there already are plenty of racquets around to fit your game. The se-lection of a tennis racquet is so subjective that California coach Bob Harman, when queried about racquets, is fond of telling this story:

"A famous pro ordered a batch of racquets from his sponsor. When they came, they all felt too heavy. The pro, furious, sent them back and demanded replacements. A week later, the company representative arrived, profusely apologetic, with a new batch of racquets. The pro, feathers smoothed, tried them and pronounced them all 'just perfect.' The rep knew better than to tell the famous pro that these new racquets were the same ones which had felt too heavy a week earlier."

HOW TO BUY THE RIGHT RACQUET FOR YOUR GAME

Buying a new racquet—and especially switching to a new type—is a decision to be approached with care and forethought. A racquet, needless to say, is your most important piece of tennis equipment. The wrong one can damage your game. The right one can help improve it.

Stepping into a pro shop or a sporting goods store to select a new racquet can be an overwhelming experience. The wall is lined with several dozen different models of various materials, shapes and sizes. They all look good—and they probably are. But that's the problem: There's such an abundance of quality among racquets today that it's difficult to know which one is best.

There's no one answer because every tennis player has his or her own special needs.

That's not to say that expert advice won't help you. Consult with a knowledgeable teaching professional before you start looking for a new racquet. If you are a member of a tennis club with a good pro or regularly take lessons from a pro, then you already have a person from whom you can get advice. If not, ask around among your tennis-playing friends for the name of a teaching pro who knows his racquets.

The pro will be able to analyze your needs and suggest a few racquets you might try. He should start by looking at the racquet that you are now using. Maybe all you need is a new string job and, perhaps, a new grip. However, if you do need a new racquet or want to make the switch from, say, wood to a fancier composite model, your pro should be able to loan you demonstrator racquets that you can play with a couple of times to help narrow down your choices.

And that is what racquet selection is all about. You must test a racquet in your own hands before you buy. Get out on the court with your regular practice partner and hit the complete range of strokes—forehands and backhands, serves, volleys, lobs and overheads. If the racquet feels wrong, try to analyze that feeling by comparing it to your old racquet and telling your pro what it is that you don't like. Then he can suggest another racquet that might be closer to your needs.

There are three important properties to consider when buying a new racquet—weight, balance and stiffness. Cost may also be an important consideration to you, but that's strictly between you and your pocketbook.

WEIGHT: Tennis racquets weigh between 12 and 14½ ounces unstrung (strings add about ¾ ounce to a racquet's weight). In recent years, there has been a decided trend toward the lighter racquets —those around 12½ ounces.

Generally, lighter racquets are easier to swing and will place less stress on your arm muscles. A heavier racquet is harder to swing but, in the hands of a strong player, can put extra power on the ball. Try a lighter frame if you are considering a non-wood racquet, and either a light or a medium frame if you are looking for a wood racquet.

BALANCE: You can check a racquet's balance by supporting it on a straightedge at the racquet's midpoint. An evenly balanced racquet will rest horizontally, while the head will rise on a head-light racquet and dip on a head-heavy racquet.

Just as there has been a trend to lighter racquets, there is also a trend toward racquets that are head-light, especially among the non-wood frames. A head-light racquet will move faster through the air than a head-heavy racquet. Head-light racquets are also quicker when volleying at the net. Therefore, it's a good idea to consider only racquets that are evenly balanced or head-light.

THE WEIGHT AND BALANCE OF A RACQUET

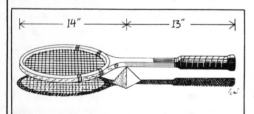

Scale weight is less important than the way the weight is distributed throughout the frame. This swing weight, or balance, greatly influences the performance of a racquet and how it feels in your hand.

You can check the balance of a racquet by putting it on a fulcrum; if the racquet isn't strung, don't forget to add a weight to simulate the strings. Now, measure the distance from the balance point to the butt of the racquet (see drawing above left). If this distance is less than half the racquet's length, it is head-light (and vice versa for head-heavy).

Another test for balance is to hold a racquet in your hand and let the head drop (see the drawing below). A head-heavy racquet will feel heavy as it drops and you attempt to slow it down. Most club players perform best with a racquet that is either evenly balanced or slightly head-light. Such a racquet will swing easily in the hand.

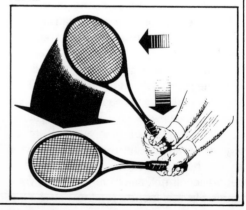

STIFFNESS: Much of that elusive factor tennis players call "playability" is determined by the stiffness of a racquet. In general, a flexible racquet will give an average player added power, sometimes at the expense of a little loss of control. By contrast, a stiffer racquet will let a powerful player hit hard, controlled shots. If you do not hit the ball hard, you should look for one of the more flexible racquets. If you hit the ball hard and your game is improving, then you should consider a racquet that is a little stiffer than the one you are using now. However, if you have ever suffered from tennis elbow, do not move up to a stiffer frame. A more flexible frame will be more forgiving of off-center shots that might trouble your elbow muscles.

YOUR TYPE OF GAME: If you are a beginner, chances are you've started with an inexpensive wood racquet, just to see if the game has any appeal for you. You've probably seen metal, fiberglass, graphite and composite racquets on the courts and have asked yourself if you should switch to one of them.

The answer most experts give is "No." For example, Billie Jean King thinks inexperienced players develop sounder strokes using wood racquets. "You must put more effort into hitting a ball with a wood racquet," she says. "As a result, the follow-through is better, as are your stroking concepts." So the improving beginner should use a better wood racquet, perhaps one with a stiffer frame to gain more control.

But what if you are an improving intermediate player? If you have been using the same racquet for a year or more and that racquet has been restrung a number of times, you should certainly be thinking about a new model.

You may find that a change to a metal or composite racquet will help your game. If you are a good player with a competitive style and get out on the court several times a week, you might like to invest in a fiberglass, graphite or composite racquet. The term "invest" is appropriate, because a good racquet of these types will cost at least twice as much as a good wood racquet. Only you can decide if the benefits from these racquets are worth the extra expense, so be sure to try a demonstrator for several sets.

If you are a good player who has always used a wood racquet but who might like a change, look for a wood composite racquet. You should expect racquets in this group to have the usual characteristics of wood but to be made somewhat livelier by the addition of the graphite or boron reinforcement.

In general, the newer fiberglass models possess a whippy action that can add considerable power to your shots. But they appear to give better overall control than previous fiberglass racquets.

Although it's hard to generalize, most of the sandwich composites tend to play like metal racquets but with more control. So if you are already using a metal racquet, you might consider switching to a sandwich composite.

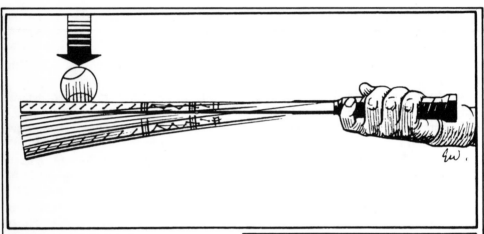

THE FLEXIBILITY FACTOR

A tennis racquet can bend along its length (longitudinal flex) or the head can bend about the axis of the shaft (torsional flex). The degree of longitudinal flex (see drawing above) will determine the liveliness and shock-absorbing qualities of your racquet.

Torsional twisting (see drawing center right) is caused by off-center hits. If you tend to meet a lot of balls off center, then you'll need a racquet that is stiffer in the head.

There are no easy ways for you to check a racquet's torsional flex but you can check the longitudinal flex by trying to pick up a ball by tapping it with the racquet (lower right). The stiffer the racquet head, the easier it is to pick up a ball this way.

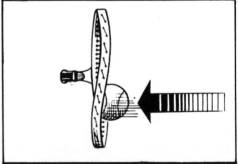

Finally, you may want to change to a racquet with an oversized head. These racquets are usually the same length, weight and balance as conventional racquets, but the hitting area can be as much as 50 percent larger. Also, the jumbo models now come in wood, wood composites, graphite and fiberglass as well as the original aluminum ones. Some of the aluminum models have been criticized as having too much vibration, and all of them are strung a little differently than conventional-sized racquets (obviously you need more string, for starters). But thousands of players have bought oversized racquets, so there's no question the design concept is a valid one.

The oversized racquet can do at least three things for your game. First, it can help you volley better. Second, it can give you increased power on your ground strokes. Third, it can boost your confidence to the point where you'll successfully hit shots you might not normally make. This psychological factor is particularly evident on volleys, where beginning and intermediate players often have trouble hitting shots with control and direction.

Advanced players may find the racquet makes serving more difficult at first, because of the size. But the larger head has a sweet spot (the area of the strings with very high ball response) that's much bigger than the sweet spot on a conventional racquet. That means a player who does not always hit the ball close to the center of the racquet will still be able to hit powerful and accurate shots. If you are content with your own conventional-sized racquet, you probably should stick with it. But if you'd like to try something different, play a while with an oversized racquet.

Today you need not go the full route to the jumbo. You may have noticed that your local pro shop is beginning to stock racquets that are bigger than the conventional designs yet smaller than the jumbo-sized racquets. They're the new midsized racquets and they represent both a reply to the competitive success of the jumbo model and a distinct step forward in racquet design. That is, the midsizes are more than a compromise dictated by the patent protection of the jumbo design; they are attempts to realize the advantages of the oversized racquet design without the disadvantages.

The midsizes generally have heads that are between 70 and 85 square inches in area as opposed to the normal racquet head size of 65 to 70 square inches. By comparison the jumbo has a head area of 109 square inches.

So the midsized racquets have moved in to fill a special niche in the tennis market by aiming to provide the discriminating intermediate and advancing player with all of the advantages of a larger sweet spot and hitting surface without limiting racquet maneuverability or control. And unlike most jumbo-sized racquets, they are easy to wield on the serve.

Of course, as with any new racquet, some adjustments are required with the midsizes. They all hit the ball farther and with a higher trajectory. But once you get

the range with these racquets, you consistently hit a deeper ground stroke.

Simply go to your local pro shop and check out a couple of midsized demonstrators. Take time to give them a fair test, and then decide whether bigger is better.

Most quality racquets are sold unstrung, so your first order of business after making your purchase will be to have your racquet strung properly.

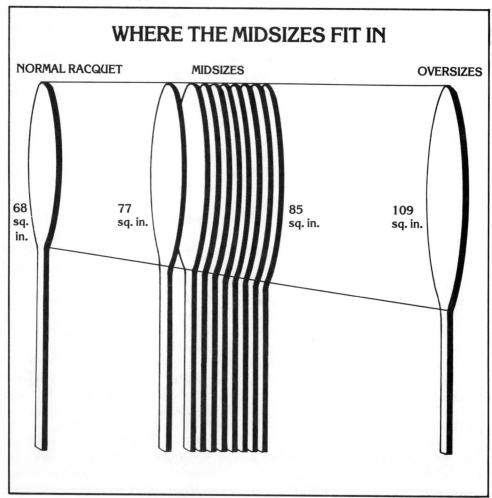

WHERE THE MIDSIZES FIT IN

NORMAL RACQUET   MIDSIZES   OVERSIZES

68
sq.
in.

77
sq. in.

85
sq. in.

109
sq. in.

HOW TO GET YOUR RACQUET STRUNG

Have you ever stopped to think how dependent your tennis game is on a piece of string—string that can stretch or shrink or break, string that's affected by heat and cold and dampness? Of course, it's a rather special piece of string. It's long enough to reach almost all the way across a tennis court (a conventional racquet has 33 feet of string). And it's strong enough to deflect a tennis ball at speeds of more than 100 m.p.h.

If you are like most players, your first racquet was probably a pre-strung model. But once you decide to invest in a quality racquet, stringing becomes vital, for it can make a world of difference in the way you play.

How should you have your racquet strung?

The easiest way—and probably the best way—is to ask your club pro, or someone else whose judgment you respect, for the name of a good stringer, and then place yourself and your racquet in his hands. But to help your stringer do his job right, there are a few basic facts about stringing you should know.

TYPES OF STRING: The first thing you need to know about string is that you can have your racquet strung with nylon, with gut or with synthetic gut.

What's the difference? Price—and playability.

Nylon is the most popular string because it's inexpensive and durable. A nylon string job should cost you between $10 and $15, depending on the quality of the string used. There are several types available. The cheapest is the monofilament nylon which is the kind you find in racquets made in the Far East and sold in your local five-and-ten. Avoid it. You'll be better off with the most common form of nylon, the multifilament type (if you cut a piece of multifilament you'll be able to see the many strands inside it). Multifilaments are not expensive and generally wear quite well. Most beginners and intermediates will be happy with a racquet strung with multifilament nylon.

Some nylon strings come with an extra added ingredient: oil. One type impregnates multifilaments with the liquid. The other has a hollow, tubular center which is filled with oil. The claim for each is that the oil enhances the playing characteristics of the string. Some players, though, have found that the oil-filled strings generally don't wear as well as multifilaments. Finally, there is a steel-reinforced nylon string which is said to wear well but lacks the flexibility of the other types of nylon.

Choose one of the nylon strings unless you're a pretty good player. Gut is more expensive than nylon—you can expect to pay about $25 or more for a gut stringing

job—and it's more fragile, which means you'll need to have your racquet strung more frequently. Gut is worth the extra money only if you're an advanced player who can take advantage of the better "feel" and ball control it offers.

Another consideration for some players is the fact that conventional gut is made from the intestines of sheep or steers. You may be one of those who feel squeamish about that.

If that's the case, you might want to consider one of the so-called "synthetic guts" now available. They are actually made from nylon, but the filaments are twisted in such a way that the end product resembles animal gut in appearance and play, although there is some disagreement about how close a synthetic gut comes to a good animal gut in playability. Synthetic gut is tough and inexpensive, like nylon (from $15 to $25 per stringing job).

STRING THICKNESS: Whatever material is used, the majority of tennis racquets are strung with 15-gauge string (about one-fifteenth inch in diameter). Some players prefer the thinner 16-gauge string, which is sometimes called "tournament" gauge. The thinner string is a little livelier and, as a result, can add an extra zip to a good player's shots. However, there's a trade-off: The thinner string is more prone to breakage and will not last as long as the conventional 15-gauge string.

However, if you're a tennis elbow sufferer, you may find that the 16-gauge string transmits less vibration to your sore muscles. Some sports medicine experts recommend that tennis-elbow victims use 16-gauge string with a reduced tension. That's worth a try if it allows you to play with tennis elbow.

STRING TENSION: How tight should your racquet be strung? The best the experts can do is give you some very general guidelines. If you are a beginner, there's nothing to be gained by having your racquet strung very tightly; the balls will simply pop off your racquet. At the same time, you won't be able to take advantage of the extra control offered by a loosely strung racquet, either. So something around 50 pounds for a start would make sense.

If you are an aggressive player who hits a powerful serve and deep volleys, then you'll benefit from a more tightly strung racquet. You should try a racquet strung five pounds tighter than the one that you are currently using—or at least 60 pounds.

On the other hand, if you play a more controlled game, you should try a relatively loosely strung racquet—perhaps around 45 pounds. The slacker tension may help you put a little extra spin on the ball since you'll be able to keep the ball on the racquet for a fraction of a second longer.

In some cases, the racquet itself may have specific instructions for stringing and tension. For example, certain oversized racquets come with manufacturer's recommendations that the racquet be strung with a certain type and gauge of string at a certain tension. When the International Tennis Federation introduced its new racquet defi-

THE ANATOMY OF A STRINGING MACHINE

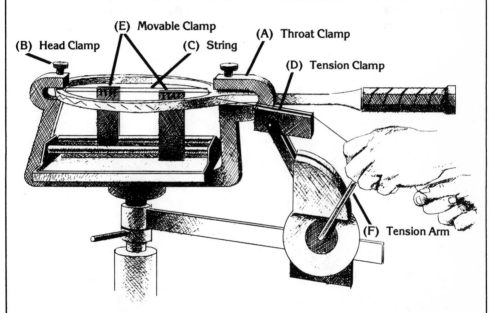

(E) Movable Clamp

(B) Head Clamp

(C) String

(A) Throat Clamp

(D) Tension Clamp

(F) Tension Arm

Although stringing machines differ in design and appearance, they all have certain essential parts in common. Typically, the racquet is held by two clamps, one at the throat (A) and one at the top of the head (B). Tension is applied to the string (C) by a clamp (D) that is moved to tighten the string to the desired tension. After the string is tensioned, smaller movable clamps (E) hold the strings until the loose end of the string is fed through the racquet and tensioned again. In this particular machine, the tension arm (F) can be rotated around the racquet as the stringing progresses. In other designs, the racquet head is rotated around a fixed tensioning device.

THE WAY A RACQUET IS STRUNG

The simple act of stringing a tennis racquet doesn't take that much skill; it's nowhere near as complex an operation as you might be led to believe by looking at the knobs, vises and clamps on the stringing machine. What does take skill is making sure that there is a consistent tension on all of the strings—which is one reason you should always go to an expert when you want a racquet strung.

The method shown here is the most common technique used for stringing racquets in all of the various racquet sports. It takes an expert about half an hour to do the job. For a tennis racquet, he starts with 33 feet of string divided into two pieces of 16½ feet each — one for the main (or vertical) strings and one for the cross (or horizontal) strings. He then follows these steps:

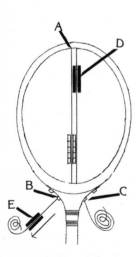

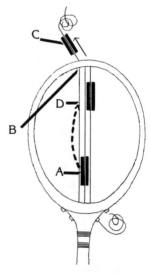

1. *After the racquet is clamped at the head and throat, the main string is fed through the two center holes at the top of the bow (A) and out through the two holes closest to the throat (B and C). One of these main strings is then held by a movable clamp (D) near the head and the end pulled tight by tension arm (E).*

2. *The tensioned string is now held by the second movable clamp (A). Next, the end of the string is fed back through the bow and out again at head (B). The tension arm is rotated so that it can again pull the string to the desired tension (C). The string is then held by moving a clamp to the head (D).*

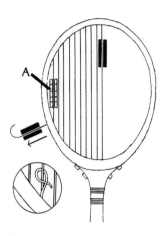

3. The process of threading and clamping continues moving out from the center until each hole has been strung. After the last string is tensioned and clamped (A), the loose end is then pulled tight and pushed through the fifth hole from the center and is tied off around one of the main strings (inset drawing).

4. Now the other half of the main strings can be threaded and tensioned. Again, the loose end is tied off in the fifth hole from the center on that half of the racquet. Why the fifth hole? The idea is to avoid knotting at the corner because three strings would have to pass through one hole and that's too tight a squeeze.

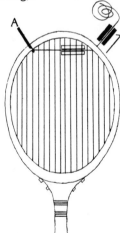

5. The cross strings are started by tying one end (A) around the fifth main string (from the center), feeding it back through the racquet, over and under the main strings and out on the other side of the head. Tension is applied and the string clamped.

6. After the 20 cross strings are threaded and tensioned, the loose end is pulled tight, fed back through an adjacent hole and tied off around the sixth main string from the center. The stringing is now complete and the racquet is ready for play.

nition in 1978, most of it dealt with specific guidelines on strings, so you won't see many of the fancy string patterns (such as used on the spaghetti racquet) that were fads a few years ago.

COURT SURFACE: Finally, there is one other consideration to take into account when you are having a racquet strung. What kind of surface do you normally play on? If the courts are relatively slow, then even if you're an aggressive player you might benefit more from a racquet with slightly looser strings. Conversely, if the courts are very fast, favoring the serve-and-volley game, then a more tightly strung racquet will pay off in terms of added power on the serve and, to a lesser extent, on the volley.

So you may have to experiment to find the right tension for you. If your teaching professional knows your game, he's the one to ask for advice. And you'd probably be smart to let him do the stringing rather than trust the job to the kind of large store where you can't speak to the stringer personally. If the stringing job isn't quite right, you can always show the pro what's wrong and he ought to be prepared to make good.

Stringing a tennis racquet is not a particularly complicated task, but it is extremely hard to get the strings at the same tension. So although you may ask your pro to string a couple of racquets at a specific tension, the two might differ considerably. That's because there are differences in the way the string stretches, in the way the stringer clamps and unclamps each string

as the work progresses, in the way he ties off the ends of the string, and so on. And there will be differences in the tension of the main string and the cross strings because of the friction created as the cross strings are threaded. Each time a cross string comes in contact with a main string, the friction reduces tension. Thus, although the stringing machine tensioner may be set at, say, 60 pounds, the actual tension in the string may be as low as 40 pounds.

You may be tempted to string your own tennis racquets or even to set up a basement business stringing racquets for friends. A good stringing machine can be quite an expensive proposition, however, and there isn't much of a market for used machines should you decide that stringing is not for you. A few suppliers do produce inexpensive table-top machines, but the more expensive machines are better suited to stringing as a commercial enterprise.

How long will new strings last in a racquet? For the player who's on court once a week, they should be good for a season of at least six months. The life expectancy, of course, depends partly on what type of player you are and what surface you use. For instance, a hard hitter who plays on clay, where grit from the surface can erode strings, will have to get new strings a lot sooner than a soft stroker who plays on hard courts.

A lot also depends on the care you give your racquet.

WHAT YOU SHOULD KNOW ABOUT GRIPS

When you go into a pro shop to buy a new racquet, apart from the frame and the weight, shape, balance and stiffness of the racquet, you should also closely consider the grip.

SIZE: The simplest and most accurate method for measuring your grip size is to take a ruler and measure the distance from your long palm crease (the second one down from your fingers) to the tip of your ring finger. If the measurement comes out to 4¼ inches, for example, then that's your correct grip size.

MATERIAL: Most racquets now come wrapped with a smooth leather grip, so you don't have much choice in the matter at purchase time. But it may surprise you to learn that your pro probably has several different kinds of grips that he can quickly, easily, and fairly inexpensively install on your racquet. And each has certain characteristics that can greatly affect your hand's comfort during play—and, thus, your overall game.

The basic grips you can choose from include: four types of leather grips (smooth, perforated, raised and suede-like); several synthetics, the most successful being a rev-

YOUR GRIP SIZE

The The easy way to determine which grip size is best for you is to lay a ruler between your ring and middle finger. Measure the distance from your "lifeline"—the long crease across your palm-to the tip of your finger (see the drawing above). Make sure you use the hand that actually grips the racquet.

You can check the fit of a grip by holding the racquet as you would hit the ball and asking a friend to twist the racquet quickly both forward and backward to simulate an off-center hit. If you can keep a firm hold on the racquet it is correctly fitted to your hand.

olutionary new fabric-type grip (called Supreme Grip), and rubber slip-on grips.

Leather grips, of course, have been universal in the sport since the era of wooden handles ended in the 1930's. Through the years, advancements have been made to improve the durability and feel of leather grips. Still, they do have one drawback that you must consider: During play, they become slippery from hand perspiration if you don't care for them properly.

The problem is that the natural oils of the leather—combined with the tanning and dyeing oils used to give it color— impede the absorption of perspiration. Many leather grips absorb moisture (a quality that's known as their "wicking rate") quite well. But because of the oils, they can't dissipate it quickly enough to prevent a buildup of moisture on the grip surface, making it slippery.

That's why many of the touring pros carry rosin or sawdust with them onto the court—to eliminate or counteract that excess moisture. The wicking rate can also be temporarily improved by cleaning a leather grip with a mild detergent and water, or with lighter fluid. Both methods help open the surface pores of the leather.

In recent years, the smooth-type leather grip has become the most widely used by manufacturers of racquets. Many players like its fine surface because it provides excellent feel when making contact with the ball. Perforated leather offers the advantage of being able to absorb perspiration quickly; that's because the pattern of holes punched in the leather draws off the moisture from the surface with a higher efficiency than the smooth grips.

On the other hand, the raised leather grip, which has an extra, thinner rib of leather stitched onto its surface, seems to be disappearing for a couple of reasons. First, the stitching comes unraveled with heavy use. And second, the raised rib is abrasive and can produce blisters on the hands of players with tender skin.

The suede leather grip has also been on the market for a while, and although it has an exceptional ability to absorb perspiration, it becomes hard and abrasive if not cleaned frequently.

If none of the leather grips seem to work or feel right to you, there are several synthetics you can choose from, including terry and rubberized tape grips.

A new, fabric-type of grip, marketed under the name of Supreme Grip, has a wicking rate that's about 100 times greater than leather and the ability to dissipate accumulated amounts of perspiration very quickly, according to the manufacturer.

The third type of grip available is the rubber, slip-on variety. It resembles rubber golf grips in feel and texture. A couple of firms have tried to market these grips, but none seem to have caught on with tennis players. That's largely because the rubber grips don't absorb moisture very well and can become quite abrasive with continued use.

HOW TO REGRIP YOUR OWN RACQUET: If your grip is worn and needs re-

placing, or if you just want to try out a different type of grip, you can do the wrapping yourself. The job will take only a few minutes of your time and doesn't require any special skills.

To regrip your racquet, you'll need a hammer and a couple of small tacks, a roll of three-eighth-inch vinyl tape, a bottle of white glue, a sharp knife or a single-edged razor blade and, of course, a new grip. Most pro shops and sporting goods stores offer a selection of new grip materials.

Once you have the grip and the tools at hand, here's how to install the grip:

1. *Take off the old grip.* Start by removing the vinyl tape at the throat end of the grip. Then remove the tack, holding the leather to the handle (the tack will be hidden under the vinyl tape). Slowly unwind the old leather grip, trying to make sure that as much leather as possible comes off the handle. When you reach the butt of the handle, remove the tack that is holding the leather to the handle. If you have been careful, and not bent either of the tacks, you can probably reuse them when installing the new grip.

2. *Clean and prepare the handle.* If any dirt, glue or old leather is still on the handle, make an effort to remove as much of it as possible. Start by scraping away the large chunks and then use some medium to rough sandpaper first to remove any fine debris, and then to "rough-up" the surface of the entire handle. That will make the glue adhere better to the new grip. Then, take a cloth and clean all the dust from the handle.

3. *Install the new grip.* Start at the butt end of the handle with the tapered end of the new grip. Practice putting the grip on before you put the glue and nails in place. Starting at the spot where the old grip ended, place the tip of the tapered end of the grip against the butt end of the handle. The edge of the grip that has been tapered (or slanted) should be toward the butt of the handle.

As you start wrapping the grip around the handle, you will notice that the angle caused by the taper will cause the grip to advance up the handle. If everything looks like it will fit without any problems, you can install the grip permanently.

Begin by placing the tapered end of the new grip against the butt of the handle. Place a tack about one-quarter inch from the end of the grip, then hammer the tack into place in the handle. If the handle of your racquet is made of plastic, use a little contact cement to attach the start of the grip.

With the end of the grip fixed to the handle, but with the rest of the grip hanging free, apply a medium amount of glue to the entire surface of the handle. Too little glue won't hold the grip and too much will ooze out onto the grip. Allow about a minute for the glue to become tacky.

Next, hold the racquet either between your legs or in a vise and begin to wrap the new grip around the handle. Apply a moderate amount of tension to the grip so there is no slack. That will prevent ripples in the leather when the grip is in place. As you

wind the grip up the handle, each turn should overlap the previous one by between one-sixteenth to one-eighth of an inch. Look at the amount of feathering on each edge of the new grip to get a feel for how much overlap would be used. Continue winding the new grip onto the racquet until you have installed at least as much grip as was present with the old grip.

When enough grip has been installed, hammer a tack into the leather and handle just below the level where you want to cut the grip. Use a razor blade to cut a clean ring in the leather around the entire handle. This cut should be placed just to the throat side of the tack.

Finally, finish the grip by putting about two wraps of vinyl tape around the throat edge of the leather. The vinyl tape should lie half on the throat and half on the leather. It should also cover the tack at the throat end of the grip.

Let the glue dry overnight and your racquet will be ready for play. Take care of your new grip by washing it occasionally in water that contains some mild detergent.

ADJUSTING GRIP SIZE: If your racquet handle is not the right size for your hand, you can either build up or cut down the size of the handle before rewrapping your grip.

Two warnings, though. First, don't attempt a change of more than one-eighth inch because anything above that will upset the balance of the racquet. Second, don't try to do it yourself unless you're a fairly competent handyman.

But if you feel you can handle the job yourself, here's how to go about it.

Wood racquets are simpler to modify than metal or composition models. First, remove the grip itself as well as the butt cap found on most models.

To build up the handle, use masking tape. One manufacturer says that two layers of tape will provide about a one-eighth inch increase, but adds that "a superior though more time-consuming method is to use one-thirty-second-inch thick balsa wood."

To reduce the handle's size, a plane or file or razor blade contained in a safety holder device is recommended. Be sure to work carefully, pushing away from the body so as not to cut too deeply; mistakes could mean ruin. If your goal is simply to reduce the grip size, be sure to plane or file each flat surface to reduce them proportionately.

If your intent is to make the handle flatter or more nearly round, the procedure is different. For a flatter handle, plane the two sides that are at right angles to the ground when the racquet is held in the hitting position. To achieve a more rounded feel, try to equalize all eight planes.

When the work is completed, be sure all surfaces are smooth. Then rewind the gripping and reattach the butt plate.

If your racquet is a metal or composition model, you probably should turn the job over to your pro, or send the racquet back to the manufacturer with detailed information about what you want modified.

However, a few of them have wooden

pallets which can be modified. Others have metal or plastic pallets which, although they can be purchased and interchanged, do not lend themselves readily to planing and filing. Some others have sleeves that fit over the end of the handle and are held in place by recessed screws. Still others have molded or foam handles that can be shaved down fairly conventionally.

The main word here is caution. When in doubt, let a pro do it.

HOW TO TAKE CARE OF YOUR RACQUET

Like any finely tuned instrument, a tennis racquet requires a certain amount of care to keep it operating at peak efficiency. Here, then, are some pointers on how to take care of your racquet so that it—and you—can both perform better and longer.

WOOD RACQUETS: The greatest enemy of this kind of racquet is intense heat, which will deaden its strings, at least, and can cause it to warp. Never store your wood racquet in the trunk of your car, in direct sunlight or anywhere else that's apt to prove exceedingly hot or steamy.

Where should you keep your racquet? Almost any place that's cool and dry will do. If you can hang it on wall pegs—or from the small loop at the top of your head cover, if you have one—so much the better. But standing it up against a wall on its butt end is almost as good.

When storing your racquet, you should also make sure your strings are clean and dry. "If they're gut strings," says racquet consultant Warren Bosworth, "you should put just a little bit of baby powder or talcum powder inside your racquet cover and tap it a few times. That will absorb any excess moisture."

In the old days, it was thought that you should always keep your racquet in a press when it was not in use. Most industry experts agree, though, that a press is passé.

METAL RACQUETS: These should be kept clean and covered, the same as wood racquets, to keep the metal from pitting. They should also be hung up or stood up to prevent them from "oil-canning," or developing a cant to one side or the other.

"Another thing to remember," says Bosworth, "is that metal and plastic are affected by extreme cold more than wood. A plastic yoke in a metal racquet can become brittle and easily subject to fracture. And very often when people play outside in the winter, they'll get cracks in their string strips (around the outside of the racquet head), and the string will fracture."

If a metal racquet has an Achilles heel, though, it's really in its handle. These are usually made of foam; if you bang them around, they can become dented. Should that happen, you'll probably need the help of a pro to set things right again.

COMPOSITE RACQUETS: These are the most care-free of all racquets, within reason. They're affected comparatively little by either heat or cold, strings excepted, of course; they're virtually impervious to warping, and they're so strong they seem almost indestructible.

The only problem is that many, if not most, composite racquets are finished off with a final coat of paint. If not given the same tender, loving care as any other racquet, they can easily develop chips.

HOW TO SHOP FOR TENNIS BALLS

If Major Walter Clopton Wingfield can be called the "father of modern tennis," Christopher Columbus must surely be rated the godfather. It was Columbus who, in the 15th century, brought home from Haiti a remarkable new plaything, a ball made of a seemingly solid substance called rubber, which actually bounced right back at you when you threw it or hit it against a hard surface.

That first rubber ball was only a beginning, of course. In fact, it really didn't bounce all that well.

Enter Major Wingfield—and with him the first true tennis ball—a hollow, rubber sphere he had imported to England from Germany. This ball would bounce on grass, so lawn tennis was then not only feasible— it was an idea whose time had come. British technology soon got hold of the ball, went to work on it, pressurized it and perfected it. The device has since changed amazingly little in size, shape and weight. In appearance and performance, though—and in the way it's made and tested for reliability— the modern tennis ball is constantly changing and, it's to be hoped, getting better all the time.

How can you make sure the ball you get is the newest and the best there is—the ball that's just right for you?

The answer, for some, is easy. They simply pick up the first can of balls they see—or the one that's on sale—as long as it bears a U.S. Tennis Association (USTA) stamp of approval. Indeed, the USTA currently sanctions the use of some three dozen different balls in tournament play across the nation. With a selection that large, it's hard to miss.

But if you want to take the time and trouble, you can select a ball to meet your specific needs. It could help your performance on the court. In making your choice, here are some of the factors you ought to consider.

COLOR: Color may seem a frivolous consideration; it isn't. Probably 99 percent of tennis balls sold in America are now yellow in color, partly because they're ophthalmologically "gentle" on the eye but more important because on most surfaces and against most backgrounds, they can be seen better than balls of any other color. The first rule of the game is still: "Keep your eye on the ball." On grass, however, as at Wimbledon, white is still the preferred color. Same reason: it's easier to see. Yellow and green are complementary colors; when a yellow ball gets stained with grass it tends to blend in with the green of the court. The white ball is more visible—for players and officials alike.

If neither yellow nor white is just right for you—say, when you're playing indoors

or outdoors at night under artificial light— you might want to try some of the new orange or gold balls which seem at times to be almost luminescent.

DURABILITY: On clay, grass and most synthetic surfaces, regular-type balls should be all you'll ever need. If, however, you play mainly on abrasive hard courts (such as cement or asphalt), you should probably be using one of the new heavy-duty balls. These have covers made largely of wool, the same as regular balls, but they contain a highter proportion of synthetic fibers—usually Dacron or nylon or both— to resist tears, abrasions and premature aging.

Which is best? You'll have to decide for yourself; the USTA cannot help. "We're obviously looking for longer-life tennis balls " says a USTA spokesman. "But there are no wear characteristics in the rules, and it would be almost impossible to set any."

PERFORMANCE: To gain USTA approval, a tennis ball must bounce 53 to 58 inches in the air when dropped from a height of 100 inches onto a hard surface. That allows for a variance of nearly 10 percent between regular, lively balls and slower, seemingly "soggier" heavy-duty balls. In a game of inches, as tennis is, that's a sizable amount.

If you're smart, you can use that difference to your advantage. If, for example, you're a big hitter who employs a lot of topspin, by all means go with the lively one. If, however, you're a player who specializes in soft shots, who hits with underspin, who

tries to keep the ball in play until your opponent makes an error on the other side of the net, the less-lively ball may be just your meat.

COST: A few years ago when tennis started zooming out of sight, ball manufacturers were unable for a time to keep pace with demand. Shortages developed in a number of areas and prices began to climb. But production schedules have since been stepped up, new plants have been built both in the U.S. and abroad, and there is now a definite glut of tennis balls. Prices generally run from just under $2 to more than $4 for a can of three balls; but discounting is rife, so shop around.

If you should get a bad can of balls—one that doesn't "hiss" when you open it—or a bad ball in an otherwise good can, take it back to the store where you bought it. Most reputable dealers will replace balls that are clearly defective, assuming you haven't already played a dozen sets with them.

WHEN TO REPLACE TENNIS BALLS: How long will your new tennis balls last? Longer, probably, if they're heavy-duty balls. But the longevity of a tennis ball depends to an even greater extent on the treatment it receives both before and after it's removed from the can. "Balls that were stuck in a railroad car during severe winter weather," says an industry spokesman, "are not going to perform as well and last as long as balls that are fresh from the factory."

It is also true that people who play with the same can of balls week after week cannot expect to get the same consistency of performance as those who open a new can every time they go out to play. "Frankly," says Tony Trabert, a member of the TENNIS Magazine Instruction Advisory Board (IAB), "I wouldn't want to play with a week-old can of balls. If you open a can, play three or four sets and then throw the can in the trunk of your car, those balls will bounce noticeably less the following week."

Playing with balls that have been whapped until the fuzz falls off does nothing good for your game, unless you relish digging up ankle-high bouncers in the backcourt. The problem with denuded balls is that once the fuzz is gone, there's nothing for the racquet strings to grip at impact. The result is loss of control.

But the precise point at which a ball should be retired from play is "a matter of personal preference," says Tim Heckler, a USPTA teaching pro. "It depends on the caliber of the player and the money he wants to spend buying new balls."

It does no good, incidentally, to replace the plastic lid over the can after opening. "The minute you open the can, air comes out," comments one manufacturer's representative. And the gradual depressurization of the balls from then on is irreversible. "Balls," says the representative, "are a consumable item that go downhill as you use them."

PROPER CARE: There are some basics of ball care that should be observed to prolong the life of this most crucial, if dis-

posable, piece of tennis equipment.

Most important, a ball should be kept dry. "Moisture is going to shorten the life of a tennis ball," warns one industry executive. "If a ball gets wet and you put it back in the can, it's going to lose its bounce as it dries out." So always be sure to place balls that are dry in a can that is dry.

Temperature can also have a lot to do with whether a ball zips off your racquet strings or plops over the net with a yawn. Heat makes tennis balls lively; cold makes them sluggish. That's why the balls at Wimbledon and other summer tournaments are stored in coolers maintained at 70 degrees or so. It keeps them out of the heat and sun and means no players will have the edge of playing with warmed-up super-bouncy balls.

When the weather gets cold, on the other hand, it's wise to keep the balls at room temperature or thereabouts. Don't leave them in the garage or the trunk of a car because chilly air works to reduce the resiliency of the rubber used in tennis balls. And whatever the climate, it will help the nap if you give a ball a light brushing with a stiff brush after playing with it.

When the nap's gone, the pressure's disappeared and the ball just won't bounce, chuck it. "In comparison with the dollars shelled out for other tennis equipment like racquets and clothes, you're not saving that much money trying to get by with worn-out balls," remarks Ron Holmberg, also of TENNIS' IAB. "You're better off just opening a new can and enjoying the game."

PRESSURELESS TENNIS BALLS: If your concern for long life is paramount, you might consider switching from a pressurized ball to one of several varieties of "pressureless" balls. These originated in Europe a few years back, gained a great deal of popularity there and since have been introduced to the U.S. market.

What's the difference between pressurized and pressureless balls? Plenty. The pressureless variety is made with a thicker core than a pressurized ball; it is packed in a box rather than a pressurized can (usually four to a box), and it is said to have a longer shelf life and to last longer. U.S. players have generally found to their dismay, however, that the pressureless ball tends to fly more slowly through the air, seems to have a lower bounce and is far "heavier" to the touch. To Americans with tender elbows, that last point can be crucial.

"It doesn't matter whether you are playing championship tennis or not," says Roy Emerson, another TENNIS IAB member. "When you go to Europe, you've got to do more with your serve and your arm is going to get sore. It's simply because you've got a heavier ball and your arm is not conditioned for the work it has to do."

QUALITY CONTROL: Whatever type of ball you do get, your chances of getting a bad one have been greatly reduced in the last few years because of the advanced quality control methods instituted by most major ball-makers. For example, General Tire, probably the world's biggest maker of balls, has an electronic gadget that scans

each carton of ball cans before it leaves the factory and instantly pinpoints any unpressurized cans. The USTA has been a driving force in bringing about the introduction of such safeguards.

"Our primary interest," says a USTA official, "is to ensure that tournament directors can select balls that will give consistent performance throughout a tournament. We have some 4,000 USTA-sanctioned tournaments every year, so the choice of balls is no small matter. As it happens, we rarely receive complaints. But if we do, then we test some of the balls used in that event and, if necessary, retest a larger sample.

"If it turns out the ball is a total failure, we may withdraw approval. If the manufacturer makes an effort, though, to come together with the committee, find out what's wrong and make changes—why, then we might place him on temporary approval (probation). If he straightens out, fine. If not—well, we've rarely had companies that went to temporary approval and off in the last 10 years. That's a tribute to the manufacturers, I believe, and to us. After all, we're not in the business of trying to limit the number of ball manufacturers. We're in the business of approving tennis balls and making sure there's an adequate supply for all of our members."

Next question: Will the industry ever come up with what comedian and tennis nut Bill Cosby calls "intelligent tennis balls —those that go over the net, not into it"? Maybe—in an aeon or two.

SHOULD YOU BUY A TENNIS BALL PRESERVER?

There are a number of devices on the market designed to help you retain the bouncing properties of your latest can of tennis balls. They are called ball preservers and they're designed to reduce the loss of pressure that occurs after balls have been used. Some also claim to restore the pressure that originally existed in the ball when it was in a virgin can.

Most preservers simply stop a used ball from losing any more pressure after it has been played with on court. In other words, most of these devices will prevent your tennis balls from losing any more pressure between sessions on the court. For the occasional player, that can be very useful in extending the playing life of a can of balls.

Tennis balls are made from a hollow rubber core covered with a mixture of nylon, Dacron and wool. Some manufacturers pressurize balls by first putting small amounts of an easily vaporized chemical into them before the two halves of the core are sealed together. Later, the balls are heated and the resulting vapor provides the pressurization. Other makers inject air during manufacture. Finally, under either sys-

tem, the balls are sealed under pressure in metal cans to keep them factory fresh. In play, the air in a ball leaks out slowly until so little is left that the ball is "dead."

Ball preservers offer the chance of extending the life of a ball for those who play only once a week or so.

Are ball preservers worth the money? All the devices appear to go some way toward extending the life of tennis balls. If you are the type of player who demands new balls every time you go out to play, then obviously you'll never need a ball preserver. If you play only once a week, you might find that a preserver would save you money by prolonging the playing life of your balls.

HOW TO GET YOUR MONEY'S WORTH IN TENNIS SHOES

Not much more than a decade ago, buying a tennis sneaker was a simple operation. Like the old Model T Ford, sneakers came in one style and one color—and if the shoe fit, you wore it.

Now, tennis shoes resemble those flashy cars so loaded with options that you sometimes wonder if they are actually intended to be driven. Tennis shoes are available in an almost endless medley of colors, styles and tread patterns. They look great, sure, but can you really play tennis in them?

You'd better believe it. Despite all the flashy logos and plush paddings, today's tennis shoes are vastly better to play in than the models of yesteryear—just as today's autos leave the Model T standing at the stoplight. A pair of properly fitted, comfortable tennis shoes can do almost as much for your game—and a lot more for your feet—as a new tennis racquet. So it will pay you to give a little thought to your next purchase.

WHEN YOU NEED NEW SHOES: If you really care about your feet, though—and especially if you've had foot problems in the past—proceed with utmost caution. The best place to begin buying your new

tennis shoes is not in a store at all but in your locker room or in the privacy of your own home.

Take off your old shoes and look at them carefully. Are your toes starting to come through along the tips of your uppers (the top of the shoe)? Are there signs of excessive creasing—or excessive wear— on either the inside or the outside of either foot? Turn your shoes over. Are your heels worn unevenly? When you lay your shoes flat, upside down, do the soles seem to toe in or toe out? Look inside and check your "cookies," or arch-supportive features. Have your cookies crumbled? What about your tongue—has it become twisted or perhaps torn? And think about it a minute —have your feet been acting up lately after a hard day on court?

If the answer to any of these questions is yes, you may need new shoes.

A tennis shoe has to cushion, grab and protect—all at the same time. It has to stand up to the stress and strain of quick starts and quicker stops. It has to be pliable enough to conform to the contours of your foot, yet strong enough to give you the support you need. It has to have the feel of foam, but wear like iron. It has to do all these things—and it has to look attractive so people will want to buy it.

Before you go into a sporting goods store or a tennis pro shop, you ought to have some idea of what you're looking for in terms of tread design and style of upper.

TYPES OF SHOES: There are four basic sole tread designs and the one you should select depends largely on the surface on which you normally play.

For a clay-court player with a sliding style, nothing beats the traditional flat, rubber-soled shoe because it puts lots of sole in contact with the court and the fancy cushioning of a nubbed tread isn't needed on relatively soft clay.

Many hard-court players favor the traditional herringbone design which provides excellent traction and has some cushioning effect. Herringbone designs do tend to pick up grit from clay courts and that can cause the shoe to wear quickly.

If you play on a variety of surfaces, you might prefer a shoe with a ribbed sole. It is commonly found on a shoe with a synthetic rubber or polyurethane sole. Ribbed soles are an attempt to combine the advantages of flat and herringbone tread shoes with harder wearing materials.

For play on concrete courts that are especially hard on the legs, many players prefer a nubbed tread design. The "nubs" look like the ends of pencil erasers stuck to the underside of the shoe. They produce a cushioning effect that eases jarring starts and stops, and may improve traction on slick cement or synthetic indoor courts.

Soles come in polyurethane, gum rubber and rubber composite—each of which provides longer tread life than shoes of just a few years ago. In general, polyurethane soles are harder wearing and longer lasting than gum rubber but may not offer as much traction—particularly on synthetic indoor surfaces. Gum rubber soles are

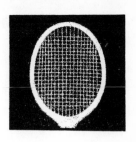

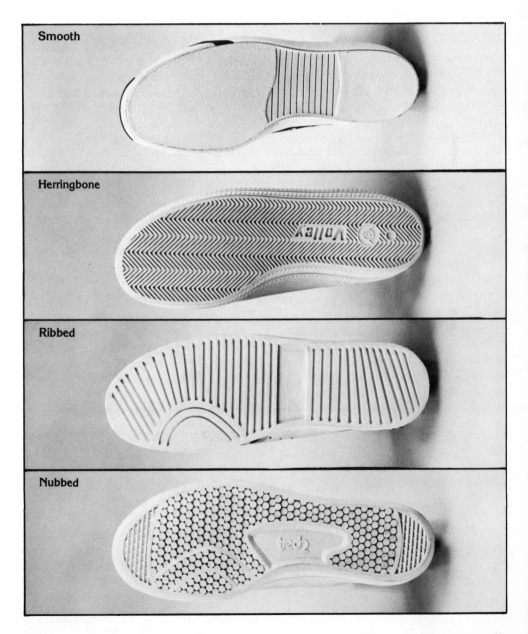

Smooth

Herringbone

Ribbed

Nubbed

45

usually softer and have excellent traction on most surfaces.

You'll find there are as many styles of uppers as there are ways to blow a match. Here are some of the points to keep in mind when picking an upper:

First, decide whether you'd prefer a canvas or leather model. Leather shoes are popular, look nice, are easy to clean and will also wear longer than a canvas shoe. Canvas shoes on the other hand, are less expensive, adapt quickly to the shape of the wearer's feet and allow the feet to breathe easily.

Your second decision involves the type of lacing. Probably the most common form is the lace-to-toe style. It allows the wearer to get a good fit easily, although some lace-to-toe shoes can squeeze your small toe.

A popular style among women's shoes is the circular vamp. It often allows more room for the toes to move, but may be harder to fit to irregularly shaped feet.

A style that attempts to combine the lace-to-toe and circular vamp features is the U-throat design. It is said to give a better fit than most circular vamp styles and still avoids compressing small toes unduly.

One intriguing attempt to solve the problem of fit is the double-laced shoe. The maker claims that this lacing allows for a more exact fit both across the toes and over the arch.

A knowledge of the types of shoes that might be right for you is only half the battle. When you're in the store, take the time to check out your selection so you get the shoe that fits you best. Here are some pointers to follow so you get your money's worth:

TIPS FOR BUYING: The best time for fitting any kind of shoe, but especially a sports shoe, is the end of the day when your feet are fatigued and maybe even a little swollen. A shoe that fits you then is going to be a good fit on a hot day after a couple of tough sets.

• Wear the kind of socks that you'll

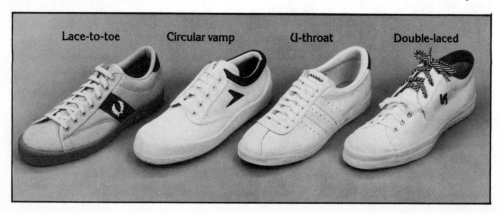

Lace-to-toe   Circular vamp   U-throat   Double-laced

have on when playing in your tennis shoes. Many experts recommend two pairs of socks to prevent blisters; use one thinner pair next to your feet.

• When you try on a shoe, kick the heel against the floor to seat your foot before you tie the laces. If the shoe feels loose after lacing, kick your heel again and relace the shoe.

• Your tennis shoe size may be different from your street shoe size, especially if you are trying on foreign-made styles. Try a half-size larger if your normal size seems tight. Most tennis shoes come in half sizes except for the very largest men's shoes.

• Make sure that a shoe is wide enough, and that the widest part of the shoe comes at the widest part of your foot. Many manufacturers make shoes in medium and narrow widths, but only one or two make wide shoes. Women with wider feet should try men's shoes (but one-and-a-half sizes smaller than your usual women's size).

• Don't buy a tennis shoe that puts even the slightest pressure on either your big toe or your smallest toe. Any pressure on your big toe can soon lead to "tennis toe" (a rupturing of the blood vessels which can keep you off the court for quite a long time). Pressure on your smaller toes can easily lead to very painful blisters.

• Walk around in both shoes (don't buy in a store where they'll only let you try on one at a time). If wrinkles appear across the top of the upper, try another shoe. The wrinkles could irritate the top of your foot.

• Jog briefly around the store—you'll just have to steel yourself for the stares of the other customers—and make a few rapid starts and stops. If the shoe is too big, you'll feel your foot slide inside the shoe. If the shoe is too small, you'll feel pressure on your toes which could lead to blisters.

• Don't let a salesman tell you the shoes will stretch to accommodate your toes. They won't. A too-short shoe may cause "tennis toe." Buy shoes that are a half-inch longer than your longest toe.

• Accept nothing less than a perfect, comfortable fit.

What if you do all this—or try to—and you still can't get a shoe that feels just right?

Your problem may be simply a hard-to-fit foot. Try another store, another brand, another style. If that doesn't help, you may have a congenital foot problem and have to check with a podiatrist. Don't panic, though. Except in extreme cases, he won't advise you to give up your sport. What he will probably do is to fit you with padding or wedging to alleviate the problem and get you back on court as soon as possible.

THE CASE FOR BUYING EXPENSIVE SHOES: A lot of the decision-making process when buying tennis shoes depends on the status of your budget. But if you are considering top-of-the-line tennis shoes, they can make good economic sense in the long run for a number of reasons.

If you're a serious player who takes to the court a few times a week and you use fairly inexpensive shoes, you probably wear them out after about two months of play—

THE ANATOMY OF A TENNIS SHOE

A. UPPER

Top parts of the shoe which are stitched and glued together before being fastened to the sole. Generally canvas or leather, but synthetics are beginning to be used on some models.

B. LINER

Inner layer of the upper. Usually found only on more expensive shoes. Covers inside seams and makes the shoes more comfortable. Generally made from a light cotton or synthetic material.

C. TONGUE

Strip of the upper covering the foot underneath the facing. Frequently padded on higher-priced shoes. A rough seam around the tongue can cause blistering on top of the foot.

D. TOE STRIP

Reinforcement of the toe area where the outsole and upper are joined. Essential if you have a toe-dragging style of serve that can open up the foxing. Not needed in molded shoes.

E. OUTSOLE

Bottom side of the shoe which determines the traction you get on court. Usually made from rubber, although some newer shoes employ polyurethane—a light, hard-wearing synthetic material.

F. INSOLE

Inside sole of shoe, often (as here) composed of two parts: a hard but flexible layer of material on top of a base of foam rubber. Some shoes have terry cloth liners laid over insole for extra comfort.

G. VENT EYELETS

Holes, often reinforced by metal, to allow ventilation. (Not visible here.) Necessary on leather shoes and on canvas styles with liners and extensive heel padding.

H. HEEL COUNTER

Reinforced area inside the heel. On better quality shoes, it's padded and extends around the back of the heel. Should have at least a cover over its seams to prevent chafing.

I. ARCH CUSHION

Raised layer of foam rubber between the outsole and the insole to provide extra arch support. Often combined (as here) with a heel cushion to elevate foot slightly at that point.

J. FOXING

One or more strips of rubber running around outside of shoe. Function is to join upper to sole. Not used on shoes that have soles molded to upper.

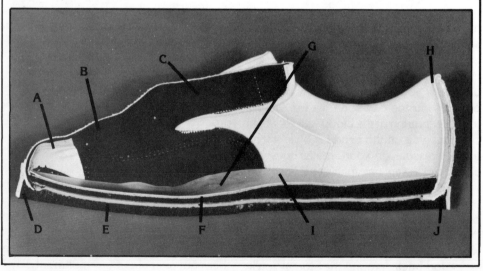

even sooner if you're a toe-dragger or hard court regular.

So, let's say you spend $15 every two months for a new pair of shoes. Wouldn't it make more sense to spend about $30 on an expensive pair that will last at least two, and maybe even three or four times, longer?

Besides the financial considerations, there's also the important factor of shoe quality. That is, how do the shoes feel and perform on the court when you make those foot-punishing starts, stops, turns and leaps?

If cared for properly, a leather upper can last for years. And with the new soles that can be installed on leather shoes (but not canvas models), a $30 investment can keep paying off for a good long time.

The extra foam padding and high heel "counters" around the ankle area, moreover, mean you get more comfort and support in expensive shoes. And everyone knows that the less you think about foot blisters and soreness, the better you can concentrate on your game.

On the other hand, you may be one of those players who'd probably be just as well off in a pair of less-expensive canvas shoes. If you play a great deal, for instance, you might prefer to buy several pairs of cheaper shoes so you have a dry pair available each time you play. Or if you have irregularly shaped feet, you may find that canvas shoes adapt more easily to the contours of your feet.

But by and large, it can be said that, yes, expensive tennis shoes are worth it. They're better made and better looking, more comfortable and more durable.

Your feet come in for an awful lot of punishment as you pound around the court. So take the time and trouble to buy the right shoes. They'll carry you a lot further in the game.

TENNISWEAR

Like everything else in the sport, tenniswear has come a long way from the days of all-white everything with a little flora or fauna emblem on the left breast of the shirt. Today sporting goods stores and pro shops carry pastels with pinstripes, European designer outfits and color-coordinated costumes for the whole family, along with the more traditional togs.

Although you might be able to play in cutoffs and a T-shirt at some public courts, you'll feel better, look better and perhaps play better if you dress in proper tenniswear. It's designed for the type of movement you'll be making on the court. Dresses, shirts, shorts, skirts and socks are the basics.

No fabric does it all in warm weather or during a hot game of tennis. In fact, cloth-ing interferes with the efficient physics of cooling: the evaporation of perspiration.

Cotton generally is considered the best fabric for active sportswear because it readily sops up body perspiration and sends it to the fabric's surface, where it is evaporated away. However, as cotton works its wicking miracles, it *wilts*. The bottom line on fabrics for summer play: If comfort is your goal, cotton is your choice. If you'd prefer to remain crisp-looking through your first match, you'll probably be satisfied with a blend of cotton and polyester. Either way, look for fabrics that are also lightweight, perforated or paneled in sheer fabric to encourage air circulation and, if you're playing under the sun, they should be light in color. These characteristics are as important to coolness as the fiber itself.

THE ESSENTIAL TENNIS WARDROBE

If you play two or three times a week or more, you should set up a basic tennis wardrobe that's small enough so it won't break the family budget, but flexible enough so you can create a variety of tennis outfits with just a few pieces. That way you'll be able to maintain your on-court appearance without using your off-court time to do laundry or hocking the family jewels for more tenniswear. Here's what you'll need.

If you're a woman, pick up a skirt, a pair of shorts and about three different styles of tops. Then you'll be able to mix and match them for a half-dozen different looks. Sometime during the course of the season, you might buy a basic white tennis dress for a change of pace. And it will come in handy if you visit a club where the "whites-only" rule still holds.

If you're a man, a couple of pairs of shorts with three coordinating shirts of any style you like—plus maybe one basic white outfit—will see you through a busy schedule of matches.

Both men and women will need several pairs of socks—(at least four) to recycle in the season. Both should have a warm-up suit or sweater to keep from getting chilled before, after and sometimes even during play. You may also need one or more accessories, such as a wristband, hat or glove. Finally, to carry all your gear to and from your club, an equipment bag is a must.

Well-made tenniswear can be a bit expensive. But in the long run, you'll find that it's worth the investment because with the minimal care that most tennis apparel requires, your basic wardrobe should last through many tennis seasons. And, of course, it can be expanded—as your budget permits.

FOR MEN

1 warm-up suit

3 shirts

2 pairs shorts

1 sweater　　　1 white shorts and shirt　　　4 pairs socks

FOR WOMEN

1 warm-up suit

3 tops

1 skirt

1 pair shorts

1 white dress

4 pairs socks

1 sweater

HOW TO SHOP FOR A TENNIS DRESS

When you buy a tennis dress, you should look for a garment that's both fashionable and functional.

The fashion part of your bargain begins and ends with you. Only you can determine if some of the colors, for instance, are right for you.

Function, however, is something else. Certain construction points can help or hinder your game. If you don't consider how that gorgeous dress you've been eying at the pro shop will move and feel on court, you may not be getting your money's worth in comfort and wear when you do buy it. So choose a dress that appeals to you and is practical as well.

Top tenniswear designers will tell you, first of all, that the most practical tennis dress silhouette is the sleeveless A-line skimmer with a low neck. Boring? Hardly. Some of the most smashing looks around are simple shapes brought to life with details.

When features are added to this basic shape, constriction, chafing and even weight become potential problems. Belts, for instance, can be flattering. The chief designer for a major sportswear company says that belts lend proportion to a tennis dress. But if you opt for a belt, avoid possible discomfort by choosing an elasticized waist or a flexible fabric belt in a stretch material.

If you want a sturdier belt, your best bet from a comfort standpoint is a narrow, lightweight, adjustable one. Check for strong loopholes securing the belt at the waist. When you try on the dress, stretch your arms over your head as you would when serving to make sure that the belt doesn't restrict your movement or ride up too high.

Some players feel constricted in sleeves, even if they are well constructed. When choosing a dress with sleeves, look for a short cap sleeve in a stretch fabric that just covers the shoulder. A raglan sleeve or one cut deep into the front of the bodice are also good choices, since the seam will not be felt as readily in the active shoulder area. Finally, a sleeve cut high in the armhole is freer than a loose sleeve; the excess fabric in the loose model tends to restrict shoulder movement.

In sleeveless styles, check that the armhole follows the contours of your body. "I find that many tennis dresses are not anatomically shaped and tend to bunch at the armhole," says British-born designer Ted Tinling. When trying on a tennis dress, take a swing and check for gapping or constriction.

The most popular dress length for a size 10 is 29 to 30 inches as measured from the bottom of the neck. A tennis dress

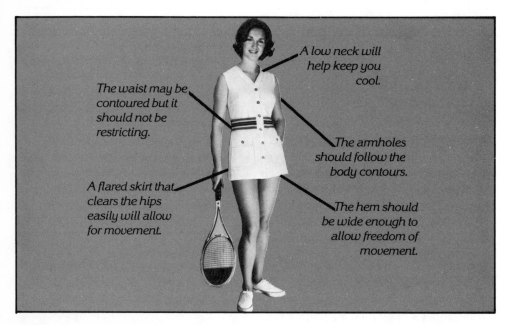

A low neck will help keep you cool.

The waist may be contoured but it should not be restricting.

The armholes should follow the body contours.

A flared skirt that clears the hips easily will allow for movement.

The hem should be wide enough to allow freedom of movement.

should cover the top part of the thigh, especially if the player is heavy. Designers say a woman should choose a dress about an inch longer than she thinks she needs, since it will rise when she serves and bends and will shrink a small amount. Tinling notes that the beginner, who will bend a lot, should add two inches.

How much should you pay for a tennis dress? With few exceptions, tennis dresses on the U.S. market range in price from $20 to $50, with most concentrated in the $20 to $30 bracket.

Tenniswear prices are determined by the same factors that apply to every kind of apparel. An inexpensive dress, thus, will usually cost less because it cost less to manufacture; the fabric may be light and

the seams may be held by a long, weak stitch without reinforcement at the stress points. This dress will probably not wear well, which is all right if it is bought for just one tennis party. If you are a regular player, however, one of the better-made dresses could well be more economical in the long run. These offer a life expectancy of three or four seasons for the moderate player and about two seasons for the frequent player.

A discussion of wear is immaterial, however, if you relegate your dress to the back of your closet because it's uncomfortable. So try to shop sensibly. And most important, don't just stand at the mirror in the fitting room. Bend, stretch, serve and swing. You don't want any surprises on court, do you?

HOW TO BUY TENNIS SHIRTS AND SHORTS

SHIRTS: "Why should I buy a shirt especially for tennis," you ask, "when I have a closet full of short-sleeved shirts I could wear on court?"

It's a good question, especially with the prevalence of color and the trend to higher collars in tenniswear. Indeed, at first glance, the casual shirts in your closet don't differ much from the newest styles in active sports shirts.

To conclude that the two types are interchangeable, however, is premature. While they may look similar to the average consumer's eye, there are design differences between the two models which can have a real bearing on your comfort on court.

The major difference between the casual shirt and the true active-wear shirt is in the size and cut. If you wear a medium shirt in a casual or dress shirt, you would probably need a large in that same shirt for tennis. Manufacturers of tennis clothing allow for the extra room needed in active wear by cutting the shirt about five percent larger than dress shirts; in other words, a medium in a tennis shirt should provide ample room for the medium-sized player.

Armholes are cut larger and deeper in tennis shirts for ease of movement at the crucial area; shirts designed for dress or casual wear may bind at the shoulder during the swing. Tennis shirts must also be long enough to stay tucked in when the player serves and bends over for the ball. Some tenniswear makers will, therefore, cut the back of the shirt, which rides up when a player bends, longer than the front. A quick test for acceptable length is to tuck the shirt into your slacks, then bend and twist at the waist several times. If the shirt stays tucked in, it will most likely do the same during a game.

If the armhole and sleeve are roomy enough, the type of shoulder on the garment is inconsequential. The raglan sleeve presents a smooth line at the shoulder, making it more popular in active than in dress shirts. Models with shoulder seams, however, are just as comfortable if the armhole is cut large enough. Gusset inserts— extra material set in under the arm— provide extra room for movement and, if made of reinforced cotton, absorb perspiration. Few casual shirts feature gusset inserts.

The traditional tennis shirt is the placket-front model with a full-fashioned collar that lies flat against the shirt. This collar has been adopted for active wear for two reasons: its flat lines preclude possible chafing of the neck and it doesn't have long, stiff points which could curl during washing.

Although it doesn't seem very func-

tional, the cut-and-sewn stand-up collar with long points has become popular for tennis. Tenniswear makers offering this style, however, make sure the collar is kept low and that there's a wide neck opening for comfort. Most casual and business shirts, on the other hand, tend to have high collars.

Tenniswear manufacturers pay close attention to these comfort and easy-care features because they are what make a shirt really practical, and usually comfortable, for tennis. The price tag that accompanies a tennis shirt is usually low; you can expect to pay a minimum of about $12 for a well-made tennis shirt. That's probably less than what you paid for any of those casual shirts in your closet—and it's a small price to pay for comfort on the court.

SHORTS: Tennis shorts are walking out of the store in ever-increasing numbers these days because, as one manufacturer admits, "About half of all tennis shorts sold never see a tennis court. They're popular as streetwear. They're chic." That's why bona fide players should take a few seconds to check over potential tenniswear purchases: Some pieces won't stand up to more than use as loungewear.

Your first check should be for sufficient leg room. "The proper leg dimension is critical," says the tenniswear merchandise manager for a major apparel firm. "You want a minimum of two inches of room at each leg. And it's smart to choose a stretch fabric because it will give even more. It won't resist your movements."

If you're eying one of those abbre-viated running-short styles for tennis, look for side vents—slits at the seams that provide extra room to move. And whatever the style, look for more length from waist to crotch—a longer rise—than you normally wear in your jeans and flannels. As you stoop and stretch and run crosscourt, you don't want uncomfortable binding and chafing at the legs and in the rise. That swimsuit-tight pair of shorts may make you look like Bjorn Borg in the mirror, but it's going to make you sore on court.

Look for tennis shorts that have an "action back"—elastic banding at the back or at the sides. Elastic banding holds the shorts securely to the waist as you turn, serve and lunge. Yes, those adjustable tabs at the sides serve the same purpose—just not as well as elastic banding does. At this point in the evolution of tennis gear, adjustable tabs are more fashionable but less functional.

About pockets: You'll want them whether you're a serious player or a hacker. Everyone faults on his first serve once in a while. Go for two side pockets and one back pocket as well.

If you tend to soil your tennis gear with sweaty palms, look for shorts that have pockets lined in terry cloth or have terry cloth panels at the sides. Terry cloth absorbs perspiration faster than Jimmy Connors can drive a crosscourt forehand.

Your choice of fabric is probably going to be a compromise between crisp appearance and comfort. If you really heat up during a match or play tennis in a warm

Knit, full-fashioned collar for comfort

Armholes cut large and deep for freedom of movement

Fabric: polyester (easy care) and cotton (coolness) blend, or all-cotton

WHAT YOU SHOULD KNOW ABOUT BUYING TENNIS SOCKS

No longer are tennis socks just simple white socks: They come in a flurry of styles and colors and a range of fabrics and construction that will make both your feet and your sense of fashion happy. Purists can always resort to the traditional wool numbers that provide the ultimate in absorption but most require traditional hand washing, too.

Easier to care for are the acrylic/nylon blends that make up in wear endurance what they lack in wool's qualities of moisture absorption. But for the best of both worlds, cotton or wool blended with a synthetic fiber offers a happy medium.

For the fastidious player, some manufacturers now market a tennis sock that works on the same principle as the Pampers baby diapers, with acrylic on the inside and cotton out. The acrylic layer next to your foot draws perspiration away and into the cotton layer, where it is absorbed and keeps your foot drier and freer from bacteria and foot odor.

If your brand of tennis involves a lot of frantic runs to the net and crosscourt dashes, your feet will appreciate a full-

climate, opt for a high percentage of cotton in your clothing. The trend today is to stretch fabrics of cotton blended with polyester plus a small amount—five percent, say—of Lycra. Lycra is the ultimately stretchable fiber that puts the snap in bathing suits and bras and, now, tennis shorts.

Expect to pay from $10 to $45 for tennis shorts: the popular range $17–$19.

cushion sock which features extra layers of fabric. A half-cushion covers only the sole of the sock, but the full cushion coddles the entire foot. And don't overlook the support socks which offer uplift to your feet and calves, if not your form.

Whatever the fabric, color or style, most tennis socks have a partial nylon content which makes them stretchy and validates manufacturers' "one-size-fits-all" claims. So unless your foot size is less than a woman's 4½ or bigger than a man's 12, the standard 8½–11 women's and 10–11 men's sizing should fit—if not like a glove, then at least like a sock.

A SHOPPER'S GUIDE TO WARM-UP SUITS

The tennis warm-up suit used to have all the panache of dad's old flannel bathrobe. Baggy and rumpled, it ranked right up there with long johns for sartorial pizzazz.

No more. They've stripped it down and spruced it up by adding chromatic cotton velours, racy trim striping and flared slacks. Today, in fact, the tennis warm-up suit has acquired a certain glamour. It's been adopted by some who wouldn't know a racquet from a roulette wheel—much like the polo shirt that's worn to the laundromat, the safari jacket that never sees game bigger than a roast peahen or the aviator glasses that have never left the ground.

"People are buying training suits for more than tennis," observes the president of a major sportswear firm. "They want fashion clothing for just kicking around in."

Still, the manufacturers have had the interests of the tennis player at heart as they've moved to modernize the old baggies. While the pegged leg with an ankle zipper is passé, practicality demands a pant leg that fits over a tennis shoe. Makers, therefore, are styling suit pants with both flared and straight legs.

Nor has the jacket (suits are usually

sold as one unit, not as separates) escaped the designer's sketch pencil. While the old bag-bellied sweatshirt styling has been abandoned, the lines of the warm-up jackets still follow function sufficiently to allow for plenty of elbow room.

You can pick up a suit for anywhere from $20 to $150, but a cheap garment is liable to reward you with an unproportioned fit, wavy seams and thin fabric. Whatever your price range, look for a stretch knit, either single, double or triple knit, each a little warmer and sturdier than the next—and check that the seams stretch, too.

The warm-up customer basically has two fabric choices: synthetics (acrylic, acrylic/nylon blends and polyester) or cotton and cotton blends. The synthetics offer durability, easy cleaning and reasonable cost, but tend to snag easily and aren't very absorbent. Cotton, strong in the velour and terry cloth warm-ups, tends not to snag, but it will bag more than its inorganic cousins.

One warning: fleece backing in some suits can be deceptive. Acrylic models often have backings that look and feel like flannel but are really acrylic brushed up to look fluffy. Often this fleeting fleece will disappear in the washer, partially destroying the bulk and warmth of the fabric. Cotton backing, often found with the polyester models, is more reliable.

The fit of a warm-up should fall somewhere between that of a dancer's leotard and that old bathrobe of dad's: loose, with room to move, but not baggy. If possible, try

Sturdy stretch fabric

Fit: cozy but not cramped

Seams: should stretch and hang straight

Pant legs: should fit comfortably over tennis shoes

the suit on over your tennis clothes, checking especially that the jacket cuffs allow lots of room for your swing.

Ball pockets are sometimes found in warm-up slacks, and the jackets in women's suits are coming in longer lengths to cover a tennis dress.

61

Instructions for making the woman's tunic and man's shorts shown above are found on the following pages.

HOW TO MAKE YOUR OWN TENNIS CLOTHES

You may think it's a lot of bother to make your own tennis clothes when it's so easy, after all, to pick something off the rack at your favorite pro shop. But when you consider that many sew-it-yourself tennis outfits take very little time to make and cost a fraction of ready-made apparel, it's definitely worth the effort.

Most pattern makers offer a variety of tenniswear styles for both men and women. In the large pattern books available at most fabric stores, you can find anything from simple, basic outfits to more complex warm-up suits. And all patterns come with complete, step-by-step instructions and diagrams.

So next time you're stuck in the house on a rainy day, you needn't forget about your tennis completely. Try your hand at making a new outfit for your next court date.

WOMEN'S TUNIC: 1. Pattern instructions offer several suggestions on how to lay out the design. The method shown here for the tunic on the left—folding the edges of the fabric toward the center rather than folding it in half—may not appear on the layout diagrams, but it saves both work-

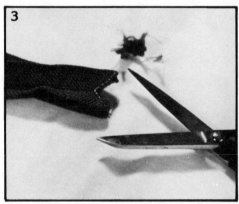

2. For buttonholes or an opening for a drawstring such as this tunic requires, baste a piece of bias seam tape over the area on the inside of the fabric. That will secure the material and will reduce any stretching at the opening. Once the slit is in place, the contrasting basting thread may be removed.

ing space and material.

If you're working with knit material, stitch along the edges using a small zigzag stitch—or a stretch stitch if your machine has one. It may seem to be an extra and unnecessary step, but stitching along the edge will prevent the material from stretching out of shape as you work with it. And it finishes seams nicely as well.

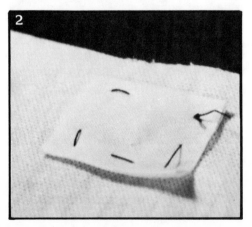

3. The trim on a V-neck looks formidable to finish but it is quite simple. With a washable tailor's chalk, mark the trim where the pattern indicates and then stitch according to the directions. The stitching will prevent the trim from unraveling and will hold the shape of the V. Cut out the V, following the chalk lines, close to the stitching as shown here, but be careful not to cut any of the threads. You might find it easier to use contrasting thread for this stitching so that you'll be able to see clearly how close you're cutting. And don't worry, the different color won't show on the finished product.

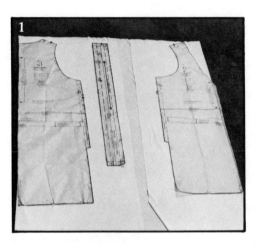

4. Turn the trim right side out and pin it in place to the neckline of the garment. Stitch the trim to the fabric using a small zigzag, this time selecting thread that matches the color trim you chose.

Snip off any stray threads and finish off the outfit according to the directions.

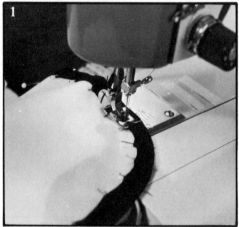

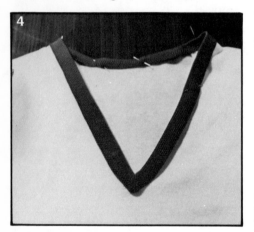

2. When you're ready to sew the seams, pin the material into place to match the trim properly.

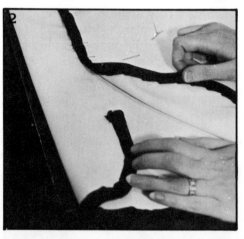

MEN'S SHORTS: 1. The trickiest step in making men's pull-on shorts is probably stitching the trim. But if you take your time, you'll find it's not that difficult.

First, pin all the trim down to the material, fitting it carefully at the corners or easing it around the curved edges of jogging-style tennis shorts. As you sew, make sure that the material is sandwiched between the edges of the trim. And work slowly around curves and corners where the material or the trim is most likely to bunch. Using a zigzag for this step allows you to stretch and ease the sewing threads on curves.

3. Both men's and women's shorts require reinforced stitching on all seams Don't neglect this step; otherwise, the shorts may split.

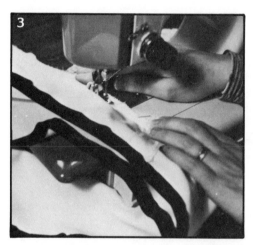

the elastic won't get caught as you guide it through the casing.

At the opening in the back, draw the two ends of the elastic together and gather the waistband material neatly until the shorts fit comfortably. Then, tack the two ends of the elastic together securely, tuck it in place under the waistband casing and close the back with a slip stitch.

4. For pull-on shorts, the waistband is simply elastic drawn through a casing. Iron all seams and fold the top of the waist over according to the instructions. Press it with a hot iron to keep the fold in place; then pin and stitch, leaving an opening at the back seam as shown here. Since you've pressed the seams open, the material will lie flat and

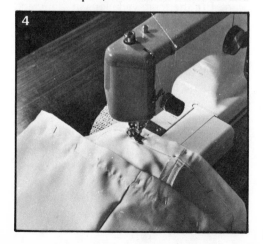

WHAT WRIST-BANDS AND GLOVES CAN DO FOR YOUR GAME

WRISTBANDS: The history of the tennis wristband is shrouded in the mists—gauze, really—of time. It seems that prior to the 1950's or so, players who felt the need for a sweat-stopper simply wrapped bandage gauze around their wrists. And they could have chosen any color as long as it was white.

Today, the player with an eye for style as well as need can slip his hand into a rainbow of hues and come up with a band to match his shorts, his eyes or his Scotch plaid racquet cover. And he may have college basketball to thank for it. "The tennis wristbands as we know them may have started with basketball players in the late 1950's," says a New York manufacturer of wristbands.

One big step toward color was made when a manufacturer produced bands for basketball teams in hues to match their college colors. It was only a short step from there to the retail tennis counter. Now, you can add even more flash to your flamingo bands with silk-screened or personal names.

Even though the Bicentennial is over, red, white and blue are the standard best-

sellers, reports another industry representative. Stylish as it has become, though, the wristband has just one function: to absorb stray perspiration before it reaches your palm. Most of the top pros wear them and recommend their use. Virginia Wade, Britain's 1977 Wimbledon champion, says the accessory "should be part of everyone's tennis equipment. You need to keep your hands dry so you can grip the racquet firmly."

And sporting a band on your non-racquet wrist isn't just an exercise in color coordination: Cliff Drysdale, the South African star, notes that players with two-handed backhands need bands on each wrist and that, "indoors or outside, the second wristband is good for mopping your brow."

It seems like such a simple item, you'd think the only thing you have to decide when shopping for a set is the color you want. But there are variations in fabric and construction. The one-piece stretch terry cloth models are the most familiar, followed by cotton and elastic combinations and knitted numbers.

Machine laundering will cut down a wristband's life span slightly, and machine drying takes a big toll in stretchiness. Hand rinsing in mild soap and water, followed by drip-drying, is the best way to make it last.

At about $1 to $1.25 per pair, wristbands are at the bottom of the tennis equipment cost list, but don't confuse them with wrist supports, which are another item entirely. "Some people do buy bands tight for

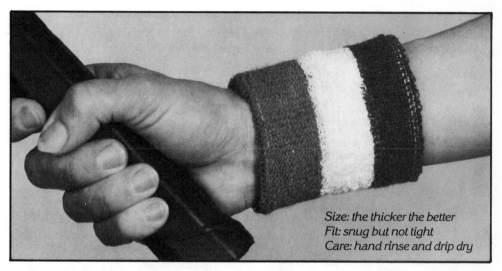

Size: the thicker the better
Fit: snug but not tight
Care: hand rinse and drip dry

support, but that's not what they're made for," says a manufacturer. "When a wristband fits properly, it should feel like it's not even on."

GLOVES: If your racquet hand takes a beating when you play or the grip tends to slip and twist in your hand, a tennis glove might be the antidote to your problem.

A glove will prevent blisters and calluses. It aborbs moisture from a perspiring hand, thereby ensuring a firmer grip. "Players who don't wear a glove in warm weather are always wiping their hands on their clothing or a towel," says Drysdale. "That's an aggravation I don't need."

Like most top players who use gloves, Drysdale favors the half-finger model shown on p. 68. This style covers the palm and the top of the hand but leaves the fingers exposed, allowing the sensitive fingertips to contact the racquet handle di-

rectly. The full glove is generally recommended for beginners or those who blister particularly easily.

Quality tennis gloves retail for about $4.50 to $6. Most have a leather palm to aid in gripping and a stretch terry cloth top to absorb perspiration. The better gloves carry an extra layer of terry cloth on the inside for extra absorption and feature tiny holes in the leather for added ventilation. They can be gently hand laundered and should last most, if not all, of a season.

The closure of a glove is especially important; it determines whether or not the glove will slip comfortably onto the hand. The Velcro closure is adjustable to the wrist size, while the elasticized top with a snap often doesn't give as precise a fit. So a buyer should be sure this last type is snug at the wrist.

A player who decides to experiment

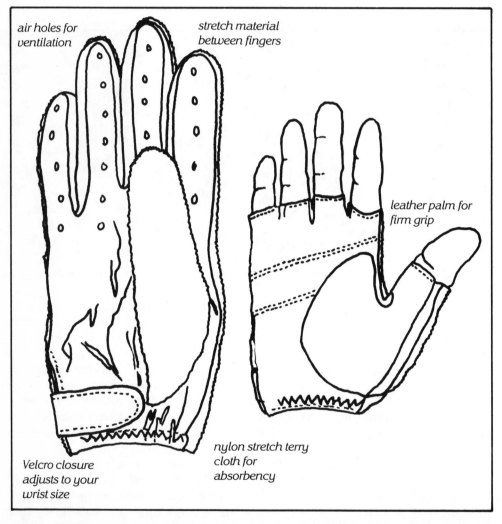

air holes for
ventilation

stretch material
between fingers

leather palm for
firm grip

Velcro closure
adjusts to your
wrist size

nylon stretch terry
cloth for
absorbency

with a tennis glove should give it a chance. Drysdale occasionally urges other competitors on the pro circuit to try a glove, but he admits they usually toss it aside quickly. "They blame their first bad shot on the glove," he says. "It does take time to get used to the feeling of wearing one. It took me about three months, for instance, but now I can't play without one."

HATS AND VISORS: HELP OR HINDRANCE?

Who needs a tennis hat or a visor? You may—if you frequently play under a hot sun, if you burn easily or if you find you're losing sight of the ball in the glare of a bright day.

Tennis headgear can be as fashionable as it is practical. Both hats and visors come in a range of styles, colors and materials—all designed to help you play as coolly as you look.

HATS: The tennis hat has long been more of a fixture abroad than it has been in the United States—particularly in Australia. A lot of the popularity of tennis millinery Down Under has to do with the searing temperatures that come with the Australian summer. The mercury can hit 110 degrees on occasion and anyone who's keen enough to play under those conditions obviously needs protection.

It's not surprising, then, that the style of hat most associated with tennis is the soft, brimmed model known as the "Aussie." Usually made of absorbent cotton or a cotton/polyester blend, the modern-day Aussie hat often has air holes for ventilation and a small brim that shades the eyes and neck without impairing vision.

The pros who play day after day in the sun also recognize that it's not only the face that is in danger of getting burned; the tender back of the neck is, too. Australian great Margaret Court, as a result, prefers a small, floppy hat and stipulates that it must have a long back brim to protect the neck. She also likes an adjustable or elasticized hat—a practical idea for women who wear different hairstyles on court.

Her fellow Australian, Rod Laver, also dons a hat when it's hot to protect both his face and neck. "I get fried if I don't wear a hat," Laver says. "I like the floppy Aussies that have a green underbrim to ward off glare from the court. But getting a good Aussie hat in the States isn't easy. I used to have mine sent from Australia."

Because his skin is so sensitive to the sun, Laver also covers all the exposed parts of his body with lotions. And to help him keep cool on stifling days, he has this little gimmick: He puts wet handkerchiefs in an ice cooler and wraps a fresh one around his neck at each change of courts. Jimmy Connors sometimes does the same.

For women in particular, and some men, a hat also keeps the hair out of their eyes when it is at an awkward length.

For some pros, hats are as much a psychological boon as a practical accessory. Kerry Reid of Australia, for example, rarely starts a match wearing one. So when she does put one on during a game, she feels as though she's really getting down to business. She thinks that her opponents now recognize this "get tough" signal and

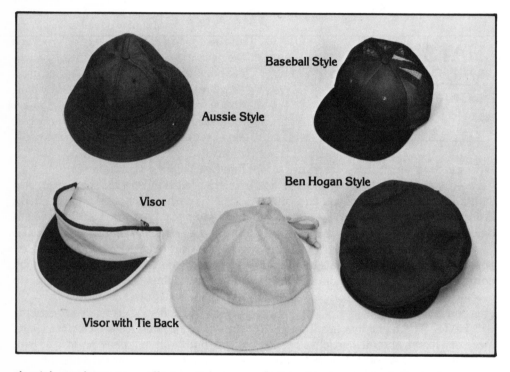

Baseball Style

Aussie Style

Visor

Ben Hogan Style

Visor with Tie Back

that it has at least some effect on them.

There is one world-class player who has made a hat his trademark: South Africa's Frew McMillan seldom appears on court without his distinctive British golf cap, which he orders from Dunn & Co. in London. "I've worn a cap since I was a youth in South Africa where they are compulsory at many schools," he explains. "I used to wear one when I played cricket, so it seemed natural also to have it on for tennis—especially under the South African sun. Now, I just feel more comfortable that way."

Some top players, moreover, have been known to try to improve on their hats.

Quite a few bore extra holes in them to get more ventilation. But perhaps the most novel innovation was used by Laver in Australia during his second Grand Slam run in 1969. Playing countryman Tony Roche in the semifinals of the Australian Open, Laver put cabbage leaves that had been soaked in cold water inside his hats. The theory was that the cold, wet leaves not only kept the head cooler but also provided another barrier against the sun's rays. Laver wore out three hats in the five-set match, which lasted four hours in 105-degree heat.

VISORS: Another common form of headgear is the visor. Years ago, the jaunty

headpieces were almost as much a part of court attire as long whites and ankle-length skirts. The classic visor was white with a 3¼ inch peak and that was held in place by an elastic band. It was also about as exciting as a flubbed forehand.

But designers have spruced up the old visor with a dash of color and flair that's revolutionized so much else in tenniswear. They come in a rainbow of colors and in materials that range from droopy terry cloth to rigid plastics to poplin interfaced with a stiff fabric. They tie at the back in a bow (for women only, please) or attach with two Velcro strips. Some even have sweatbands built in.

Actually, the visor is most closely associated with women players—such as the great Helen Wills Moody Roark, who made it her trademark during her reign as the game's top woman player a half century ago. "Visors were quite in fashion in California when I was 15 or so," she recalls. "I always wore one, first, because it kept my hair in place and, second, because it protected my eyes and my complexion, depending on just where the sun was. And because I wasn't squinting, I didn't develop those squint lines so many tennis players have. People didn't know back then that the sun could be harmful—but my father was a doctor, and he knew. He told me to protect myself."

Today, professional players who wear anything on their heads usually opt for hats. Some players complain that a visor blocks vision overhead—particularly when they are tracking lobs. But the brims on tennis hats also protrude out over the face. And in any case, visors didn't hamper the games of Helen Roark and her contemporaries. "You could always find some that didn't block vision," she says.

Besides checking on visibility when buying a visor, it's a good idea to make sure the fit is correct. Most models stretch or adjust to accommodate any size head (like the "one-size-fits-all" pledge on some socks). But it pays to be certain. If a visor's too loose, you'll be peering out from under it. If it's too tight, it can give you as much of a headache as that flubbed forehand.

HOW TO BUY A TENNIS EQUIPMENT BAG

Are you the spartan type of player who carries your tennis gear to and from the courts in a scruffy briefcase or a tattered shopping bag?

Aesthetics aside, there's nothing wrong with that. But in recent years, luggage manufacturers have begun providing special bags for tennis players that will enable you to make the round-trip between home and the courts by car—or home and a resort by jet—with a lot more comfort, convenience and style.

Some bags come with a handle or a shoulder strap or both. Some are soft and crushable, some are hard-sided. Some have outside pockets for one or two racquets, others accommodate racquets inside. Some have locks. All have clothing compartments, but some feature two or three separate compartments. And many are waterproof.

Most tennis bags are made of either leather, vinyl or canvas. The leather models are the most expensive; a basic leather bag with one outside racquet pocket will run you about $45. The same bag in vinyl costs about $20.

Leather looks great, of course. But it doesn't hold its shape as well as vinyl. And it can't be cleaned as easily as vinyl, which can be tidied up with a household liquid cleaner.

A vinyl bag—or one with vinyl or plastic lining—is best if you'll be toting damp tennis clothes and towels home after a match. Wet gear can spot leather or canvas. Shoes of leather or canvas can suffer the same fate, one reason some bags provide two or more clothing compartments; they permit shoes to be stored separately.

In shopping for a tennis bag, here are some other pointers to keep in mind:

• Be certain that your racquet fits in the racquet pocket. The wide-throated and round-faced racquets won't make it in the standard tear-drop-shaped racquet covers and pockets.

• Check that the handle is firmly secured to the bag. The strongest handles are riveted.

• If you fancy a large, heavy bag with a shoulder strap, be sure that there's a shoulder pad for the strap. This extra strip of material distributes the bag's weight more comfortably over the shoulder.

• Test out any zippers to make certain they work smoothly. Big, heavy-duty zippers are best.

If you buy a bag that leaves the racquet handle exposed, don't check the bag through as luggage when you travel by air. Take the bag on board with you and stash it under the seat or in the carry-on luggage compartment. If you send it into a plane's cargo hold, the handle can get nicked or

even snapped off as it comes down the conveyor belt or as other luggage is piled on top of it. Touring pros have long since realized that. And that's why most of them carefully remove their racquets, which they carry aboard personally, before they check their tennis bags through as luggage.

One of the great assets of tennis bags, of course, is that they can be used for so many things other than tennis. Who knows, if you get one, you might never again use your old briefcase or shopping bag.

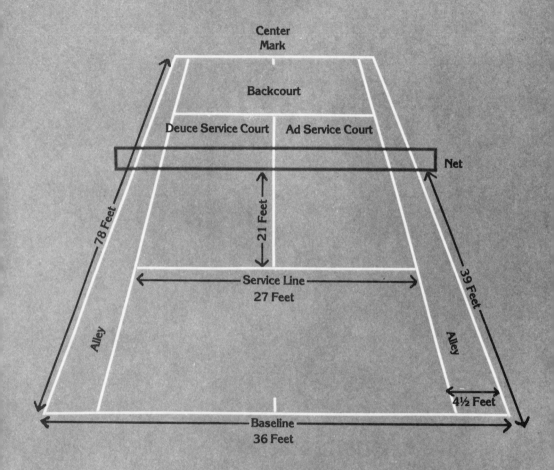

COURTS, COURT SURFACES AND TENNIS CLUBS

All tennis courts are alike, yet all are different. The dimensions as shown in the illustration remain consistent. The lines that border the court—baselines, sidelines, etc. —are common to all courts, but they are just the beginning in determining how a court affects your tennis. Court surfaces vary from place to place, and even two adjacent courts with the same surface can have individual characteristics that affect play. For example, when the U.S. Open was played for the first time at the USTA National Tennis Center in Flushing Meadow, N.Y., many players reported that the stadium court was faster than the outside courts, although all the courts had the same cushioned surface.

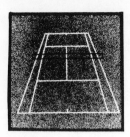

HOW COURT SURFACES DIFFER

To a Bjorn Borg and a Martina Navratilova it doesn't matter all that much what type of court surface they're playing on. They are so accomplished at the game that they can play and win on courts set up anywhere.

But if you're like most players, you're not that skilled. The surface on which you're competing does make a difference. You may play on maybe two or three different surfaces a year. When you visit another club or a tennis resort, the surface may be another type. If you play indoors, it's likely that the surface is different from the one you're familiar with outdoors.

A different surface is no insurmountable problem if you know how to adjust to it.

There are five general types of court surfaces, categorized by their playing features, rather than their methods of construction. In a few instances, a particular surface may fall between groups with characteristics of each. But the category headings are those most commonly used by the majority of average tennis players.

The categories are: 1) clay-type granular or composition courts found mainly in the East; 2) hard courts of the cement and asphalt variety, mostly with plain, painted surfaces; 3) cushioned courts, built with a resilient layer over a base of cement or asphalt; 4) grass courts, the original surface for lawn tennis, and 5) special indoor surfaces made from synthetic materials.

When you venture onto an unfamiliar surface, your timing may be off and you may experience initial problems with your footwork. It's rather like taking the wheel of a new car for the first time; you may stall the engine and step too hard on the brakes. But if you're prepared for the differences and proceed cautiously, it shouldn't take too long to acclimate yourself to a new court. You should take the extra time to practice and to become accustomed to the bounce of the ball and the speed of play.

Remember, too, as Rod Laver says, "The conditions are the same for you and your opponent. Don't let him see that you're bothered. Let him think you grew up playing on furrowed fields in hailstorms."

CLAY-TYPE COURTS: If you live in the Northeast, Florida or the Midwest, the chances are you've played on one of the dark red or green, grit-like courts that are often called "clay" or "composition." Whatever name is used, this type of court plays very slowly; that is, the ball bites into the gritty surface, slows down and then sits up waiting for a player to hit it.

Their slow-playing characteristics make clay-type courts popular with beginners and intermediate players. With top players, though, they can produce interminable rallies because it's so tough to hit an outright winner. A serve-and-volley play-

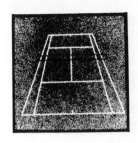

CLAY COURTS:
The greatest test of tennis
Moderate installation cost
High maintenance cost
Slow playing
High bounce
Easy on feet
(unless dry
and hard)

Granular
Surface

Crushed
Stone

Base

er can't blast away on his serve, rush the net and then put away a volley. The surface blunts the speed of his serve and the high bounce of the ball gives his opponent plenty of time to line up a passing shot if the player charges the net. So most players stay back on these surfaces, trading ground strokes from the baseline.

Still, clay courts are often referred to as the greatest test of tennis ability because a good clay player must have an all-court game. To play well on clay, you need a consistently deep serve, preferably with spin. Your ground strokes must be solid, your return of service must be reliable and you must be able to go to the net when the occasion demands it. Significantly, in 1975 when U.S. Open officials decided to abandon grass for their tournament still at Forest Hills, N.Y., they chose as the new surface a clay-like composition—Har-Tru.

The best strategy on clay is to play from the backcourt and wait for your opponent to make the errors. Bob Harman, one of the game's top coaches, sums up clay-court tactics by saying: "Try to outsteady your opponent. The steadier player, not the harder hitter, usually wins on clay."

Traction is relatively good on clay-type courts and the loose surface allows a player to slide to a stop without jarring the legs as can happen on hard courts. The gritty surface, though, can be tough on shoes, especially for a slider. In addition, the balls and

racquet pick up dust easily.

Clay-type courts have other disadvantages. The surface is easily disturbed by heavy use or by non-tennis playing activities. So they are best suited for locations where access is carefully controlled and where they can get constant maintenance. Older clay courts also often suffer from drainage problems because the clay binds into a solid mass which doesn't permit water to drain properly.

Most clay-type courts are now constructed from a granular fine-crushed stone, usually green in color, which allows the water to drain and the courts to dry quickly.

Even the new courts require daily watering, brushing and rolling. Frequently, during a day's play, the lines will be obscured by dust kicked up by players' feet and will need cleaning. And at the beginning of each season of use, the court must be top-dressed with a ton or more of new surface and a special binder. The tapes will need replacing or repositioning at the same time. Thus, clay-type surfaces are usually found only on private courts or at country clubs where adequate maintenance can be provided and the courts are not likely to be abused by non-tennis playing use as they might well be at public facilities.

Some clay-type court brand names include: Har-Tru, Fast-Dry, Tenico, En-Tout-Cas and Stade Rouge.

HARD COURTS: It's often said the reason so many top-level players have come out of California is that the fast ce-ment courts of that state breed a slugging, serve-and-volley type of performance. On a hard court, the prevailing style is usually a booming serve followed by a dash to the net and a quick put-away volley. It's a style that was popularized a generation ago by Jack Kramer and Pancho Gonzalez, two former greats who grew up playing on the cement courts of the Los Angeles Tennis Club.

Not too long ago, hard courts—whether cement or asphalt—always had solid, slick surfaces. The ball glanced off those surfaces as fast as it did on grass, although the bounce was higher because a ball doesn't skid as much on a hard court as on grass. Now, however, a variety of top surface coatings are available and they slow down hard cement or asphalt courts to a degree that makes them playable by players without strong serve-and-volley games. But even then a hard court will still be faster than a clay court and will call for a different playing style.

The best way to handle a fast, hard court is to copy the pros and develop a powerful serve and a good net game. Get your first serve in and follow it to the net where you should try to put away your first or second volley. If you are used to clay courts, you'll have to sharpen your reflexes for hard-court play. Swing your racquet a little faster to catch the rapidly moving ball. Shorten your backswing and consciously keep it short until your timing improves.

If you lack confidence in your ability to rush the net after your serve, stay back for

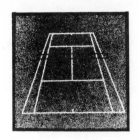

HARD COURTS:
The surface for sluggers
Moderate installation cost
Low maintenance costs
Usually fast playing
Medium bounce
Hard on feet

Concrete
or Asphalt

Crushed
Stone

Base

your opponent's return and wait for a short ball that will allow you to approach the net at your own pace. If you do stay back—as you might, for example, after a weak second serve—hit your ground strokes deep so your opponent doesn't get a short ball and come storming to the net. On a hard court with an abrasive surface which slows down the ball, you'll be able to use more of an all-court game.

You won't be able to slide on a hard court, so you'll have to be more careful about footwork than on clay courts. The unyielding surface, moreover, is tough on your feet and legs. Experts recommend that you wear a pair of soundly built tennis shoes with firm arch supports.

Toughness, though, gives hard courts a major advantage: low maintenance. Provided that the court is constructed soundly to resist the elements, the only upkeep required is an occasional washing and brushing. Every few years or so, the top surface will need repainting, but that is not usually an expensive item.

Unlike the granular clay-type courts, water will not drain through cement or asphalt, so hard courts must be built with a slight slope to encourage rapid draining after a rainstorm. Unfortunately, asphalt courts in particular tend to settle in time and develop shallow depressions, often called "birdbaths," which collect rainwater. If you play on a court with birdbaths, you may

CUSHIONED COURTS:

The wave of the future?
High installation cost
Low maintenance costs
Slow playing
Easy on feet
High bounce

Concrete
or Asphalt

Crushed
Stone

Base

have to brush the water off before you can play.

The easy maintenance of hard courts makes them ideal for public and school courts. Besides, the surfaces are unlikely to suffer much damage from such non-tennis playing use as bicycling or roller-skating.

Some hard court surface brand names include: Action-Seal, Color Court, Decoralt, Laykold and Plexipave.

CUSHIONED COURTS: This new type of surface combines the slow playing characteristics of clay courts with the durability and low maintenance costs of hard courts. A cushioned court is made by putting an extra layer of resilient material on top of a concrete or asphalt base. The result

is a court that feels slightly spongy underfoot and plays appreciably slower than a conventional hard court. Cushioned courts are a delight to the player, but expensive and relatively difficult to install.

The U.S. Tennis Association's National Tennis Center in Flushing Meadow, N.Y., where the U.S. Open moved in 1978, has cushioned courts—DecoTurf II. The pros can play serve-and-volley tennis, as they did on the grass courts at Forest Hills prior to 1975, or they can rally from the baseline, as they did on the clay-type courts at Forest Hills in '75 through '77.

On a cushioned court, the speed of play is slower than hard courts because of the resiliency of the surface and because

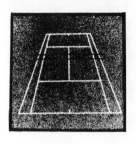

the ball will bite into the textured surface just as it does into a clay-type surface. Consequently, rallies will tend to be longer than on hard courts, and the advantage of a powerful server will be somewhat reduced. If you are used to playing on a clay-type surface, you'll adapt quickly to a cushioned court—although you will not be able to slide your feet.

If you're a hard-court player, you should use a little more caution on your shots. If you rush to the net after a poor serve, you may find that the slower court gives your opponent plenty of time to hit a winning passing shot. When you do go to the net, you'll have to place your volleys deep and away from your opponent, because the surface will cause the ball to sit up longer than on a hard court.

Cushioned surfaces are so expensive that they are unlikely to be found at public courts. You will see them at some of the more affluent private clubs or at indoor tennis facilities. Although recently developed, cushioned courts appear to wear well and require little maintenance other than occasional scrubbing and brushing.

Despite their high cost, cushioned courts are fast gaining popularity. In fact, Alfred Alschuler, a tennis court planning consultant, sees cushioned surfaces as the wave of the future—especially for clubs. "As tennis players become more sophisticated," he says, "they'll demand cushion-type surfaces for both indoor and outdoor use."

Some cushioned court brand names include: Dynaturf, Plexicushion, Grass-tex, Latex-ite, Cushion-Kote and DecoTurf.

GRASS COURTS: "Nothing can quite compare to playing on grass," says Bill Talbert, a former champion who is director of the U.S. Open at Flushing Meadow. "The smell, the pleasant footing and the pace of play sum up tennis for me."

Unhappily for Talbert and other traditionalists, the surface on which lawn tennis was first played is now on the way out. There are still a few among the opulent country clubs and private estates in the eastern U.S. But each year, more and more grass courts are replaced by other surfaces. Indeed, Talbert himself presided over the transition from grass to clay-like Har-Tru for the U.S. Open in 1975.

The reasons for the demise of grass are principally the escalating costs of maintenance, an unevenness that gives bad bounces and an inability to withstand hard use.

If you ever have the opportunity to play on grass—beware! Not only are the bounces uneven, but the conditions will change from day to day and even hour to hour, depending on the dampness of the grass. The bounce is fast and, on top of that, the ball will skid so low that your forehand will seem more like a half volley. The only answer to the problems of grass play is to have a strong serve and a good net game so the ball does not get a chance to bounce.

On the other hand, a grass court is a delight for your feet. Its soft sponginess will make you feel as if you could play all day,

GRASS COURTS:
The ultimate luxury
High installation cost
High maintenance costs
Fast playing
Low bounce
Easy on feet

Grass

Soil

Crushed Stone

Base

and the footing is quite good unless the court is damp from rain or dew.

The overwhelming disadvantage of a grass court is, of course, the upkeep. It must be watered, rolled and mowed almost every day. New court lines also have to be chalked regularly. And as the season progresses, the lines have to be moved periodically to spread the wear on the court— especially at the service lines. Before the season opens, the topsoil and grass must be carefully nurtured by a team of experienced groundskeepers.

When the high costs of maintenance are added to the limited playing time and short season for grass courts, it's easy to see why they have virtually disappeared.

INDOOR SURFACES: Three of the surfaces described previously—clay, hard and cushioned courts—can be used for indoor play. But in recent years, several new types of artificial surfaces have been developed specifically for indoor facilities— although the manufacturers say they can be used outdoors, too.

The group of special indoor surfaces in most widespread use are carpets— manufactured textile or plastic mats which can be laid on top of almost any surface. The textile carpets, such as Bolltex or Sport-Eze, are synthetic fiber, felt-like materials, about a quarter of an inch thick. They come in wide rolls which are glued to a concrete or asphalt surface. In play, the

textile carpets are quite slow, due to the resilience of the fibers. So an all-court, clay-style game is best.

The plastic carpets, such as Uni-Turf, are laid down much like the textile mats. But they offer a wider choice of playing speeds. Thus, some plastic carpets are quite slow and find favor with beginning and intermediate players, while others are so fast they are preferred by professional players.

All plastic carpets have a consistent bounce and give excellent traction. Indeed, the traction is often so good that a clay-court player will have difficulty moving unless he learns to pick his feet up smartly. The plastic carpets require only an occasional brushing or vacuum cleaning. They have proved to be durable, and while some carpets have tended to become slightly tacky with use, manufacturers now appear to have that problem in hand.

A less common group of indoor surfaces are the plastic decks and artificial turfs that are put down in interlocking blocks or seamed rolls. Their playing characteristics vary widely, ranging from a clay-like slowness to the speed of grass. However, they are all relatively easy to install and appear to be very long-wearing.

Several surfaces in this group are suitable for outdoor use. In fact, one grass-like artificial surface was tested for a year on one court at Forest Hills and now is in regular play and works well.

HOW TO BUILD YOUR OWN COURT

Ever had this dream? One sunny spring morning, instead of phoning futilely for a court reservation, you eat a leisurely breakfast, put on your tennis gear and then saunter out onto your own backyard court and play until it's time to shake the martinis. Of course, you have. Is there a tennis player who hasn't?

Ah, but tennis courts cost big money you say. And what with the orthodontist's fees, the college bills and keeping the house in one piece, you don't have that kind of money. But didn't old Frampton build his own tennis court? Maybe you could, too. Well, friend, it's a very big maybe.

Building a tennis court isn't like finishing your basement. It's a major construction project which calls for plenty of time, lots of effort, some very special skills and more than a little money—five thousand dollars, at least. You'll want help from friends and neighbors, just at the time when they all want to play tennis. You'll have to put in hours of back-breaking work, and you may run into problems that call for expensive specialist assistance.

Is it all worth it? Only you can answer that yourself. Here's what's involved in con-

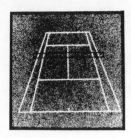

structing a typical home-built court. It is not intended to be a complete guide to tennis court construction, but should give you enough information to decide if building a backyard court is realistic for you.

The first thing you have to determine is whether you have enough room for a court. The actual dimensions of a tennis court are 36 feet by 78 feet but, to allow for running room outside the baselines and sidelines, you should have an area of 60 feet by 120 feet. And there should be an extra 10 feet beyond that on all sides to give a bulldozer room to maneuver.

To find out how a court would fit into your property, get a copy of the plot plan of your house and land. Then, cut out a paper rectangle representing your court, using the same scale as your plot plan, and try positioning it on your plan. If you have lots of space, the long axis of the court should run 22 degrees west of true north so that the players will not be troubled by looking directly into the sun when it's low in the east or west. If you can, find a spot for the court where as little as possible excavation and filling will be required to make the court level.

When you have satisfied yourself that you do indeed have room for a court, start reading everything you can lay your hands on about building one. The best place to begin is a booklet called "Tennis Courts," published by the USTA Facilities Committee (it's available from the USTA Education & Research Center, 729 Alexander Rd., Princeton, N.J. 08540 for $5). Other infor-

mation booklets can be had for free from such surface suppliers as the Binghamton Brick Co., Inc. (Box 1256, Binghamton, N.Y. 13902), Malott Peterson Renner, Inc., (1375 West Alameda, Denver, Co. 80223), Robert Lee Co., Inc. (Box 1909, Charlottesville, Va. 22903) and the Har-Tru Corp. (Box 569, Hagerstown, Md. 21740). Detailed court specifications are available from the U.S. Tennis Court & Track Builders' Association (1800 Pickwick Ave., Glenview, Ill. 60025).

The construction procedure described here is for a clay-type fast-drying court since that is the variety most suited to do-it-yourself builders. Asphalt or cement courts are too difficult for most home builders and, indeed, often for conven-tional paving contractors. They are best left to court building professionals.

GETTING STARTED: Most communities require that you obtain a building permit before you start your court. In some towns, that is a simple formality; in others, zoning board approval may be needed. Draw up a plan showing your property, your house and your proposed court. A sketch of your existing plot plan will probably be suffi-cient. However, your plan should show how any heavy machinery can gain access to the court area and demonstrate that the placement of the court will not interfere with drainage or septic systems. If the court re-quires a variance from zoning laws, you may have to hire an attorney to advance your case; and be prepared for some delay.

Building permit in hand, you can now

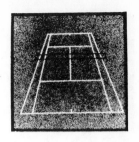

start on the site preparation and excavation. Your first step is to stake out on area of about 140 feet by 80 feet and remove all trees and shrubs. Small trees 10 feet or shorter may be dug out and replanted. Larger trees should be cut down leaving stumps 2½ feet high so that a bulldozer can push them over and pull out most of the roots at the same time.

To remove the tree stumps and the topsoil, you'll have to hire a bulldozer and an operator. Depending on the terrain and the skill of the operator, this preparation and rough grading stage may take three or more days. Bulldozers can cost $300 and up per day, but there is a bonus: You can sell the topsoil to a builder for $2 to $3 per cubic yard and you'll probably excavate 100 cubic yards.

The tree stumps and roots can be burned or buried in a large hole off the court. The earth taken out when the hole is dug can be used to fill any low places on the excavated area. After excavation and filling, you should allow the ground to settle for about six weeks. While you're waiting for that to happen, you can install curtain drains around the perimeter where water is likely to run onto the court. That will involve digging a trench into which you lay perforated pipe and stone, and then cover with salt hay and top with soil.

If your land is extremely hilly, you may also have to dig a "swale," or open ditch, to prevent runoff water from getting to the court. You can dig curtain drains and swales by hand with sufficiently enthusi-astic labor; but it's simpler and easier to hire a backhoe and an operator for a day to dig the trenches.

PREPARING FOR THE BASE: After the sub-base has had enough time to settle, it must be fine-graded and preparations made for a crushed stone base. Here is perhaps the most critical stage of court construction since mistakes made at this point will be expensive to fix later on. So be ready to put in time and care in fine-grading —it will pay you back later.

For drainage, the court should slope one inch in every 24 feet from side to side. Sloping the court from end to end may make one end wetter after a heavy downpour. Using a surveyor's level (a "transit") and a measuring rod, calculate the contours of your sub-base at about 10-foot intervals and make a grid plan so you can determine where to add or remove material to grade the surface.

If you are not sure how to use a transit, you may be able to find a local engineering student who will assist you for a small fee. You can level the sub-base by hand with a pick, shovel and wheelbarrow, but the work will go much faster if you hire a small grader or bulldozer. Tamp down or roll the fill that you have added (don't do more than a six-inch depth at a time) and check that it is sloping for proper drainage.

Next, construct a brick curb around the perimeter to contain the base and the top surface. A single line of bricks, placed on their sides, should be laid on a three-inch deep by six-inch wide wedge-shaped

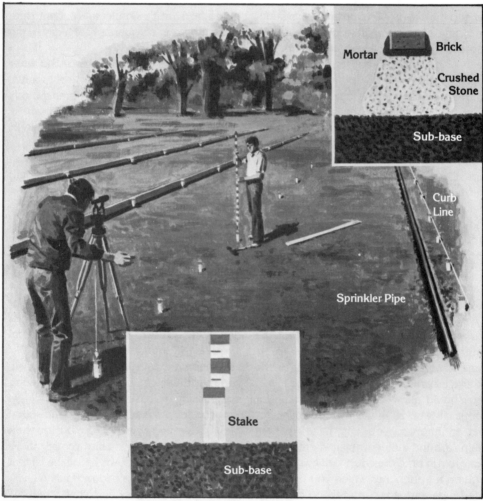

Mortar · Brick

Crushed Stone

Sub-base

Curb Line

Sprinkler Pipe

Stake

Sub-base

pile of crushed stone, held together by mortar. The bricks should be placed with the top of the brick line four inches above grade so they will be a little below the finished surface when the court is completed. Leave a section of the curb uncompleted at one end of the court so trucks can enter later with the stone base and surface material.

If you want to have a sprinkler system for watering the court, the sprinkler lines (but not the sprinkler heads) should be in-

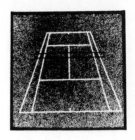

stalled in shallow trenches and covered. Mark the intended head locations with small stakes.

Finally, you should again use the transit and surveying rod to place stakes six feet apart in 12-foot wide lanes. These stakes will support the furring strips that will house each section of the stone base as it is laid. The top of each stake should be adjusted until it is precisely at the desired level of the stone base. The one-inch by four-inch furring strips are nailed to the side of the stakes. The court is now ready to receive the stone base.

LAYING THE BASE: The base of a fast-drying court should consist of four inches of processed stone mixed with stone dust. You'll need between 150 and 200 tons of three-quarter-inch crusher-run stone—that is, stone ranging from chips no larger than three-quarters of an inch down to stone dust. Get yourself plenty of manual labor—high-school students are often looking for part-time work—and be prepared to spend several weekends laying the base.

When the first truck arrives with its 20-ton load of stone, have your work gang ready with steel rakes and heavy shovels, plus a 14-foot straightedge made from two-inch-by-12-inch board with a steel bottom. You'll also need to rent a half-ton power roller to help compact the gravel as work proceeds. You might consider investing in a new or used power roller since you'll need one to finish and maintain the surface.

If the site permits, the stone truck should back down the first of the lanes that you've prepared with furring strips. It should then drive slowly back down the lane, emptying the truck ("tailgating") along the way. Not all drivers are skilled at emptying an even flow of material, so you should tell the quarry company that you'd like the stone delivered in this way. Be warned, though: you may have to pay extra for this service. If you can't arrange to have the stone tailgated, rent a front-end loader or "bobcat" to spread the stone. Stone costs vary considerably, but you can expect to pay between $6 and $12 per ton delivered to your site.

Use the straightedge to level off each lane as the truck progresses, fill in any low spots and then roll the stone to compact it. After that, cover the stone and fill in any remaining low spots with a layer of stone screenings. Level the base again with the straightedge and roll. If any slight depressions develop, don't allow the truck to come back to fill them; it will create ruts in your base. Instead, use a wheelbarrow and a couple of your willing assistants. Putting in the base is backbreaking and dusty work —definitely not for the weakhearted.

When the base is laid, the furring strips and stakes should be removed and the resulting holes filled and compacted by hand. Finally, the entire base should be rolled.

SURFACING THE COURT: The choice of a top surface for most home-built courts really boils down to dirt, clay or a fast-dry material. Whichever you select depends on your own personal preference,

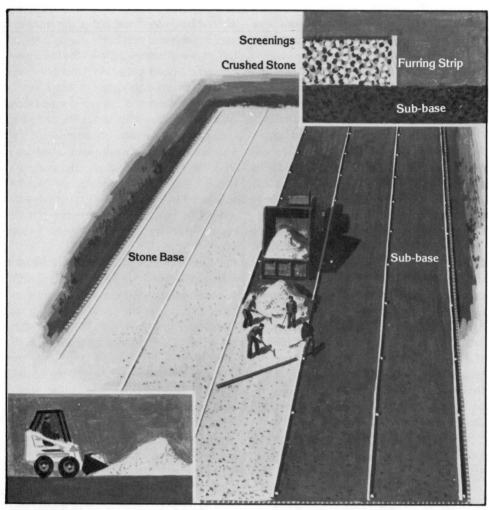

Screenings

Crushed Stone

Furring Strip

Sub-base

Stone Base

Sub-base

your budget and what's available locally. All three types will require constant maintenance but, as the name suggests, fast-dry surfaces dry quickly after rain.

Until recently, fast-dry materials were available only in the East and Midwest, part-ly because the two major suppliers are in the East and partly because Westerners have, in the past, shown a preference for cement or asphalt courts. Clay-type courts, though, are now gaining some popularity in the West.

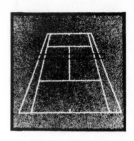

Whichever material you choose, the method of laying the surface is the same. Wooden screed strips (1¼ inch by 4 inch redwood board) are set up 12 feet apart down the length of the court. The surface material is placed between the screed strips and leveled with a straightedge. After one lane is complete, the surface is thoroughly watered to its full depth and allowed to soak for at least 15 minutes.

Next, the surface is rolled and compacted. Since the surface is very loose at this point, some experts recommend using a hand roller for the first stage—although a power roller of less than 1,000 pounds can be used with great caution. After compaction, the surface should be a little over one inch thick.

When one lane is complete, remove the screed strip and set it down to make another 12-foot lane. Fill in the lane with surface material and use the straightedge to make the second lane level with the first. A sheet of tin placed on the previously completed surface will prevent the straightedge from damaging that surface.

If you use a fast-drying material, you'll need 40 tons at about $45–$50 per ton plus shipping. The cost of clay varies considerably from one part of the country to another. So it's not possible to give even an approximate cost; you'll have to check building contractors in your locality. Just make sure the clay you get is suitable for a tennis court surface.

PUTTING ON THE FINISHING TOUCHES: When the surface is finished and you've filled in the sections of the brick curb left open for the heavy machinery, you can start working on the accessories—the net posts and net, the tapes and the fencing.

For the net posts, you will have to dig two holes about three to three and a half feet deep. Put a concrete base into the hole and set a pipe sleeve into the concrete—taping the bottom of the sleeve before you put it in the concrete. The post itself should push into the sleeve so that the height of the net is exactly 3 feet 6 inches at the post. The posts should be 42 feet apart for a standard doubles court. A net anchor should be set into the court at the center of the net for the center strap. It's not necessary to cement the anchor in place—just hammer it in. You can figure on paying at least $75 for a pair of net posts and about $100 for a rot-proof nylon net.

The marking tapes can be either leaded or an acrylic-coated fabric. They should be two inches wide and fixed in place with special aluminum nails. Anchor the tapes at one corner first, stretch them and then fasten down from the midpoint to the corners with nails at three-inch intervals. A set of tapes and nails will cost about $10.

The backstop fencing should be 10 to 12 feet high, although it can be lower in the middle of the side fences. Public courts normally use chain-link fencing, but that's expensive and not necessary for the home-built court. An alternative is to use vinyl-covered home and garden wire. The wire can be mounted on treated 4-inch by 4-

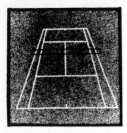

inch posts or on galvanized steel poles. The posts should be set in concrete at 10-foot intervals. Fencing will cost you at least $500 for minimum coverage.

Now you can go out and play on your brand-new court. However, the work doesn't stop here. To keep your clay or fast-dry court in tip-top shape, it should be watered and brushed each day it is used. The court must also be rolled about every week, and once a year it should be top-dressed with about two tons of surface material. Protect your investment and it will repay you with unlimited hours of tennis— and make that dream come true.

CHOOSING THE RIGHT INDOOR CLUB

Not too many years ago, when the thermometer dropped and the evenings darkened, a tennis enthusiast outside the sun belt either had to toss his racquet into the closet or resort to stumbling around in a dingy armory or a drafty school gymnasium if he wanted a game. Tennis, in most of the country, was strictly a warm-weather sport. It was meant, they used to say, to be played only in the great outdoors. But they used to say that about baseball, too, before the Astrodome, and about swimming before the advent of the modern filtration system.

Today, all the old constraints and clichés about indoor play have been firmly laid aside. Indoor tennis has blossomed out across the U.S. like mountain laurel on a wintry hillside. In 1965, there were just 100 indoor courts in the country. As the 1973 winter season started, there were some 7,200 in operation. In 1978, the USTA put the total number of indoor courts at 9,000.

The growth of indoor clubs has been nationwide, too, not just restricted to the northern regions where the opportunity to play during cold weather gave the new indoor trend much of its initial impetus. In-

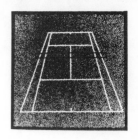

door facilities are now thriving in Florida, Texas, New Mexico and southern California —places where they were once given no hope of catching on. But instead of warmth, they offer air-conditioned comfort that makes tennis possible on the most unbearably sweltering days.

Some indoor clubs have a "no-frills" approach in providing merely courts and rudimentary locker rooms. Others have luxurious facilities that make the Waldorf-Astoria look pale by comparison.

To a degree, of course, as an indoor player you will get what you pay for. It is just as possible to play fine tennis in the least expensive air-bubble-covered court as it is in an architecturally beautiful air-conditioned building with cushioned courts, glare-free lighting, luxurious lounges and sybaritic locker rooms with saunas, exercise machines and whirlpool baths. How do you decide on the club that's right for you? Let's begin by looking at a typical facility.

The normal suburban indoor club is housed in a barn-like steel structure and offers from four to 12 courts under one roof. Its off-court facilities include a reception area, locker rooms and a pro shop, at the very least.

The plushest of the indoor clubs come with luxuriously carpeted and appointed locker rooms, often with relaxing saunas, steam rooms, sun rooms and whirlpool baths. There is a comfortable lounge with color television and a nursery where you can leave your pre-schoolers. An extensively stocked pro shop provides all you need for the game in terms of equipment and apparel. For your pre-game warm-up, you'll probably find a fully equipped exercise room. Some clubs now have squash and badminton courts and even offer facilities for playing table tennis. There may be an indoor pool and, as part of the clubs that operate year round, an outdoor swimming pool.

The courts themselves are generally spacious and well lit, heated in winter and probably air-conditioned, if the club also operates during the summer. Most clubs have at least one full-time teaching professional who gives private and group lessons. The pro may also oversee the formation of tournaments and tennis leagues.

Indoor tennis, it's clear, has come a long way since the first national indoor championships were held in New York's Seventh Regiment Armory in 1900. Indoor courts were a rarity then. But in the 1920's and 1930's, some die-hards managed to play during the winter months in the gloom and grime of armories, old gyms or county fairground buildings.

These days, the winter tennis player no longer has to survive the horrors of the armory or the school gym because a host of comfortable and brightly lit commercial clubs has spread across the land.

Indeed, the overall quality of indoor tennis facilities today is such that many tennis players—those, at least, who can afford it—would rather play tennis indoors than outdoors, even during warm weather.

Basically, there are two types of indoor

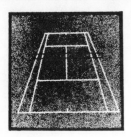

The striking architecture of the Hazel Hotchkiss Wightman Tennis Center in Weston, Mass., is a sharp departure from the hangar-like appearance of most indoor tennis clubs. The center offers tennis, squash and swimming.

facilities—the air-pressure-supported plastic bubble and the prefabricated steel building.

AIR BUBBLES: These are usually erected over outdoor courts and are taken down for summer play at the same site. Since the initial cost of a bubble is considerably less than that of a permanent structure, the cost of play in a bubble is usually less than for a permanent club.

However, bubbles do have some disadvantages. Noise can be quite considerable, both from the players inside the bubble and from traffic on the outside. "I was completely spooked the first time in a bubble," says one New Englander. "This bubble was close to a busy highway and conversation across the net was impos-

sible." The lighting is often dimmer in a bubble than in a permanent court. The compromises required for lights that have to be removed when the bubble is taken down for summer play may result in poor positioning or dark spots on the court. But bubbles are generally translucent so that the lighting will be much improved during daylight hours.

The bubbles are quite fragile, of course, and some Eastern bubbles have been damaged in winter storms. Fortunately, repairs are quite simple, rather like patching the inner tube of a tire. So the court can usually be reinflated within a day or two.

PERMANENT STRUCTURES: The metal-framed year-round building may

cover up to six tennis courts under one roof without inner pillars. A large club may have two of these buildings on either side of the lounge and office area so all the courts can be supervised simultaneously.

The chances are that the clubs in your area contain a variety of extra facilities other than the courts and the locker rooms that are the basic necessities of the indoor player. Don't ignore the frills but take a close look at the basics first.

SPECIFICS TO LOOK FOR: Start with the courts themselves because, when you get right down to it, that's what you're really paying for. Arrange a tryout of the courts with the people who will eventually make up your playing group. Most club owners will allow you to knock a ball around for 30 minutes or an hour to get the feel of the court's surface and the effectiveness of the lights.

Many experienced players reckon that the *lights* are the most important factor in choosing a club. "I like to see plenty of lights down the sides between the courts," says one seasoned indoor player. "If anything, I prefer indirect lighting to avoid the possibility of losing the ball on an overhead." So in assessing a club, look out for badly positioned lights—particularly as you receive service and prepare to hit an overhead.

As you play, compare the *surface* with the kind of outdoor surface that you've used regularly. Many indoor clubs opt for synthetic surfaces because these pose fewer maintenance problems. However,

synthetic surfaces often have quite different characteristics from most common outdoor courts. "The artificial surfaces tend to have a high bounce and play slowly," notes the same player. "Frankly, the ball is kept in play too long for the experienced player. On the other hand, slow surfaces might be better for the beginner or the social tennis player."

Some clubs do have clay-like surfaces, but these tend to be hard and dusty unless they are well maintained. Since the clay-like courts have to be watered, the atmosphere can get cool and damp. Still, many indoor players feel that's a minor inconvenience in return for the advantages of being able to play on the same type of court both indoors and outdoors. Asphalt or cement surfaced courts tend to be harder on the feet and legs than cushioned or clay surfaces, and that can be a telling factor, especially if you're playing singles.

When sizing up a club, it's also well to note the *space between the courts.* Can you take an angled shot without running into the next court or into the divider curtains? Divider curtains are a useful feature, particularly if the next court happens to be occupied by a group of erratic players.

Ideally, according to the USTA, there should be a playing area of 120 feet by 60 feet for each court, which would mean 21 feet behind each baseline and at least 12 feet between the courts, or 20 feet if divider curtains are used. It's equally important that the court roof be high enough to permit lobbing. The USTA recommends that the

Lights that are high-powered but not distracting are vital for indoor play. Lighting systems may be direct (as shown above at the Nassau Tennis Racquet Club in Montgomery Township, N.J.), with the lights shining onto the court from the sides and sometimes the rear of the court as well. Or the lighting can be indirect, with the lamps aimed at the ceiling of the club (as shown below at the Northbrook, Ill., Racquet Club).

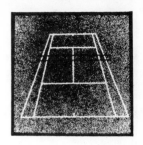

ceiling be 16 feet high at the walls behind the courts and 35 feet high at the center above the net.

It's wise to have a few words with the management of the club and with players who are already members. The club owners should be happy to give you the names of a few members with whom you can discuss the club.

Don't be afraid to ask how the club handles *court etiquette* problems, such as noisy players, hackers who constantly interfere with the play on other courts, disputes over changeovers at the end of time periods, and so on. One Midwestern club uses the public address system to embarrass slow-playing members. Your prime concern should be that the club is operated as a club, that is, for the benefit of the members.

Look into the *teaching program.* An indoor teaching program is not just a professional who gives lessons for $20 a half hour. ("Well, you're not just paying for me, you're paying for the court, too.") Any club today that doesn't offer group lessons of one kind or another hasn't really kept up with the times. And while you may not feel at the beginning of the season that you want to take lessons, who knows how you'll feel come mid-year after you've gone through three straight sessions of doubles without having hit a single good serve? If you have a family and the club has a junior development program, so much the better.

If you are a parent with pre-school children a club with a *nursery* has obvious appeal. Most of the newer indoor clubs that cater primarily to suburban players offer baby-sitting services, sometimes at no extra cost; that's one less hassle to think about. So even if these places charge a little more for court time, you may end up spending less overall by the end of the year.

Depending upon how serious you are about your tennis, you may want a club that runs several *tournaments* throughout the year. Not all of the clubs do, and fewer still have ladders and the like. The best clubs have a wide variety of tournaments; different age groups, different levels of play. Usually—but not always—clubs with active tournament programs cater to the better players in a particular area, while clubs that feature tennis parties as extracurricular activities cater primarily to intermediates.

As far as plushly carpeted locker rooms and saunas and exercise rooms and all that other jazz—well, who can knock it? Given the choice, probably everyone would much rather shower and dress in a palace than in a hovel, but there is a point at which luxury becomes redundant. It's ultimately a question of price. Some indoor tennis players do not make abundant use of saunas and exercise rooms and the like, and unless you're going to use them, why pay extra for them?

After all your preliminary inspections and research, if you're satisfied that a club is for you, you can always plunk down your membership fee and take your chances on being able to line up partners and a court whenever you want to play. Demand is so great for indoor courts in some places,

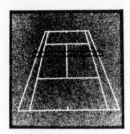

though, that you may have to reserve a court for the same time each week during the season, which usually runs 37 weeks. And you'll probably have to pay in advance —an average of $500 for a one-hour session. Many players lighten the financial burden by putting together a weekly doubles group to share the costs.

Unless you have a very new club in your area, you may have difficulty in reserving a court at the time that you'd like. Prime evening hours are jealously guarded from year to year by already established doubles groups. Even daytime hours are hard to get in some suburban areas. If you're an early riser, the breakfast hours are the easiest to come by and the cheapest, naturally.

A major problem for many prospective indoor players is *assembling a group to play* each week throughout the indoor season. Most indoor veterans agree that there should be six persons in a doubles group to guarantee a game each week. Even with six, though, there will be times when the group is one short for doubles. Usually it isn't too difficult to find a substitute, and most clubs are able to suggest players who can fill in on a moment's notice.

If you already play at an outdoor facility, you're probably way ahead in getting a group together from your acquaintances there. Or you may find several groups already in existence at the indoor club and one will almost certainly have a vacancy. An alternative is to ask the indoor club operator to help place you—making clear to

him the standard of the group that you'd like to join. See if you can arrange a couple of quick sets to test your mutual acceptability before committing yourself to a group.

Before you sign up for a season of indoor tennis, take a careful look at the *costs.* Indoor tennis clubs are operated to make a profit for the owners, and it's expensive to provide all those opulent facilities which often occupy a valuable piece of suburban real estate. The clubs usually charge a membership fee ranging from $35 to $175; it's higher in the Midwest than in the East. An hour of court time permanently reserved throughout the season will cost from $200 to $800 depending on the time of day, the location and the size of the club.

A recent change in indoor tennis is in the greater flexibility of *playing times.* Today, many tennis clubs are concentrating more on open-time bookings and some tennis players are giving up their regular weekly games in favor of round robins, leagues and weekly parties. One woman, for instance, has figured out that by paying the $6 entry fee every Tuesday morning at a local club's intermediate round robin, she gets in nearly twice the tennis she would if she were in her regular weekly game, and at less cost. "And the best part," she says, "is that I don't feel obligated to go all the time, the way I used to when I'd paid for the court in advance."

Some clubs, of course, operate on an open-time-only basis, charging a yearly

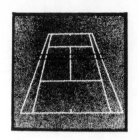

membership fee in addition to an hourly fee. Whether such a club is better for your situation will depend almost entirely upon how flexible your schedule is and how much money you're willing to spend.

If you do decide to form a group and sign up for a full season of weekly play, it's helpful to work out the total cost and then divide it among the members of your group.

For example, for a group of five players who reserve an hour and a half during prime evening hours at a suburban club, the finances go like this: five memberships at $35 each plus an hour and a half of court rental at $500 per hour (for a 37-week season) totals $925 or $185 per person. Over a full season, that represents an outlay of $6.38 per person per session for the two who play 29 weeks and $6.17 per session for the three who play 30 weeks.

One other thing you may want to find out about if you're comparing price is whether the indoor club has a coordinated *year-round plan,* whereby you can get a sharply reduced rate in the summer by paying a little extra during the normal indoor season. Clubs vary considerably in their policies on summer play, but frequently if you make your deal early in the season, you can secure yourself a considerable amount of low-cost indoor time during the summer as well. The point is not to be shy. Most indoor tennis operators are willing to negotiate, particularly when it comes to courts that are going to be open anyway.

Of course, there is a way of avoiding these expenses: become a tennis bum. An experienced tennis bum can get plenty of winter tennis, mostly for free. You simply hang around in the lounge of the club and wait for those groups that are one person short. Generally, a short-handed group is so pleased to have a fourth available that they will not ask for a contribution toward the playing costs. The management may ask you to pay a membership or guest fee, of course.

At its best, the indoor game is an immensely rewarding form of tennis. Clean and climate-controlled courts that are well lit and well maintained can make for tennis that is superior in some ways to the outdoor variety. "You know," says one indoor club member, "I play more tennis indoors in the winter now than I do outdoors in the summer. The only thing that keeps me from the court is a blizzard."

HOW TO ADAPT TO INDOOR CONDITIONS

The adjustments that you'll have to make for indoor play are relatively minor. Indoors, the conditions are so consistent that you can concentrate solely on playing tennis. Outdoors, you have to cope with sun and shadow, wind and dusty courts, even rain. But with the unfamiliarity of the conditions, some players have a hard time adjusting to indoor play after a summer season outdoors. Here are some suggestions on how to make that adjustment by former No. 1-ranked U.S. player and Davis Cup captain Dennis Ralston:

I personally feel that the problems some players have playing indoors are more mental than anything else. For years, for instance, Arthur Ashe was convinced he couldn't play well indoors. He didn't feel that he saw the ball as well indoors. Eventually, though, he reached a point where he played some of his best tournaments inside. Roy Emerson is another player who used to complain about seeing the ball indoors, and yet I've watched Emmo play some terrific tennis there.

All things considered, it probably is a little more difficult to see the ball indoors, especially for players who wear glasses or contact lenses, which can produce problems with glare. But it's the sort of problem you can overcome, so long as you don't let it get the best of you. If you're having trouble seeing the ball, the thing to do is concentrate harder. And then stop thinking about it. The minute you start worrying too much about match conditions—whether it's the light indoors or the wind outdoors—you can very easily psych yourself out.

To my mind, a more important consideration in indoor tennis than the lighting is the amount of space between the baseline and the back partition, as well as the amount of space between courts. In some indoor facilities, these dimensions are less than regulations call for. With too little room between the courts, angled shots become troublesome to deal with. If you're playing someone who is using these angles to his advantage, try not to give him too many wide shots. The more you can keep the ball toward the center, the tougher you make it for your opponent to hit sharply angled shots. If he has a wide serve, take the ball early before it takes you into the divider curtain between courts.

On a court that doesn't have much back space, high, deep lobs can cause you problems. If the ball bounces deep enough, and has enough topspin, you won't be able to retrieve it. The best way to deal with this shot is to line up fairly close to the ball before it bounces and try to make contact on the overhead before the ball bounds over your head.

balls will get heavier and move slower. So you'll have to put a little more zip into your shots if you want the ball to go anywhere. If you're playing for fun, I would recommend that you choose heavier balls for cool and dry conditions and lighter balls when the air is warmer and heavier.

All in all, however, your basic game should not undergo that much of a change when you move from outdoors to indoors. The overall playing conditions indoors are, if anything, better than the playing conditions outside, which means that your game should get better, not worse. If you're having problems indoors, it may well be that the problems are in your head more than on the court. If you look hard enough, you can always find excuses for not playing well, but these will rarely make you a better tennis player.

Dennis Ralston

Then again, lobs may not be a problem, because the ceiling may be too low. Players who like to lob very high are at a disadvantage when the ceiling is somewhat lower than average, while a player with a good, low offensive lob has a slight advantage.

The atmospheric conditions inside an indoor tennis facility—how cool it is or how hot and humid—can have an effect on your shots. But the only time it's going to make any real difference to the average player is when the conditions are extreme. The cooler and drier the atmosphere, the faster the balls will travel and the more important it is for you to really hit through the ball. When there's a lot of moisture in the air, the

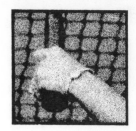

YOUR PLAYING TIME

The most important aspect of tennis for anybody is enjoying your playing time. It doesn't matter what kind of racquet or clothes you have or what kind of court you are playing on, unless you are having a good time.

In 1979, one of the final stumbling blocks to finding a suitable opponent was removed with the introduction of a nation-wide tennis rating system. Because the system allows players to identify the quality of their play instantly, you are now able to avoid mismatches, which makes for better and more enjoyable tennis.

There are other things that can help you get more out of your precious court time. Proper etiquette tops the list. Establishing a compatible doubles group is another.

You will also enjoy tennis more if your club has a good program, including club tournaments. If you want competition outside a club, tennis leagues are the answer. Finally, an excellent way to make tennis fun without an overdose of competition is by throwing a successful tennis party.

HOW TO RATE YOUR PLAYING ABILITY

It's happened to you; it's happened to practically everyone who's ever been stuck for a tennis partner.

You agree to a pick-up game—at your club, at a resort or on a business trip, almost anywhere—and quickly discover that your opponent, who calls himself a B player, can hardly get the ball back across the net. Or, worse, he's so good that you can hardly get the ball back.

Another tennis date shot! And why? Because until recently tennis has never had a definitive system for rating its players.

Ask a golfer his handicap and you can tell instantly whether your games are compatible. Ask a bowler his average, and you know without question how you compare. Ask a tennis player, except at the highest levels of play, and he'll tell you he's either an A or a B or C level player—any one of which can mean almost anything, depending on who's doing the rating and where in the nation he's doing it.

Confusing? Obviously. A drag on the game? Most certainly. But that is changing, thanks to a new concept in the measurement of comparative ability on court. It's the long-awaited National Tennis Rating Pro-

gram (NTRP), developed over a period of years by the National Tennis Association (NTA) in cooperation with the USTA and the U.S. Professional Tennis Association (USPTA). It was introduced in the spring of 1979 in clubs, recreational programs and tennis resorts across the country.

What makes the new rating program so special? Why is it expected to succeed where all other rating proposals have failed?

"An important point," say the three sponsoring groups, "is that for the first time a single program has the approval and backing of the three leading tennis organizations: the NTA, representing commerical club owners; the USTA, speaking for thousands upon thousands of member players; and the USPTA, the organization of teaching professionals . . . For the first time, players everywhere will have a common denominator, a tennis language that each can speak and each can understand."

Equally important, add the three groups, "is the purity and simplicity of the program itself: It's free, it's self-administered, it's easy and there are no strings."

The program, in fact, is so uncomplicated that it's fully explained in a three-page, 3½-by-6-inch brochure, about a million of which were distributed in a first mailing to tennis centers everywhere. Each is a self-contained, self-rating guide, complete with a rating card that a player can fill out, remove and carry in his wallet once he's determined his comparative standing.

And how does he do that? By ranking

himself on a scale of 1 to 7 based upon the performance requirements which comprise the heart of the new rating system.

If you're a rank beginner, for example, your rating is a 1.

Getting a little better at keeping the ball in play? Then you're probably a 1.5.

Beginning to feel a little more comfortable on court? Taking a few lessons? Starting to play matches? You're probably a 2, and well on your way to becoming a tennis aficionado.

To qualify for 2.5, though, your strokes will have to be "more dependable."

To make it to 3, moreover, you'll have to be able to "place your shots with moderate success . . . (and) sustain a rally."

And to qualify for 3.5, halfway up the rating scale, your forehands and backhands will have to get even better—as will your serve and volley.

Are you past that stage? Have you developed a dependable lob? An overhead? Can you place your first serve and "force some errors?" Nice going; you're probably a 4.

Have you begun to hit with power and spin? Can you rifle in your first serve but place your second, when necessary? Can you rush the net with speed and confidence? O.K., you're a 4.5.

Can you do all the foregoing and more? Can you hit placements, force errors, execute drop shots and half volleys, serve with spin and smash "with above average success?" That's a 5; plus it's time to think about entering some tournaments.

When you reach the quarters or semis of "the highest level club or park championships," that's still another step up the ladder—to 5.5.

Have you won a ranking in a major city or USTA district? If so, take a bow; you're a 6.

Are you capable of earning a USTA sectional ranking? That's even better—6.5.

Have you competed widely? Are you ranked nationally? Congratulations, you've hit the top; you're a bona fide 7.

As you can see from the capsule summaries above—and as you'll note from studying the full text of the rating guidelines that appear here—the ranking you ascribe to yourself will be based arbitrarily on generalizations relating to specific skills. It's also quite likely that your game will have matured more quickly in some areas than in others. So the sponsoring groups advise you to try to be honest with yourself and, "if you're uncertain between two categories, place yourself in the lower one."

You can also double-check yourself, if you wish, by having your rating verified by a teaching pro, a coach or some other expert. But the real test of your rating will come, of course, in actual competition.

"You may find," the sponsors say, "that you actually play above or below the category, which best describes your skill level, depending on your competitive ability. [But] the category you choose is not meant to be static and may be adjusted as your skills change or as your match play demonstrates the need for reclassification

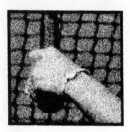

THE NATIONAL TENNIS RATING PROGRAM: WHERE DO YOU STAND?

1.0 This player is just starting to play tennis.

1.5 This player has played a limited amount but is still working primarily on getting the ball over the net; has some knowledge of scoring but is not familiar with basic positions and procedures for singles and doubles play.

2.0 This player may have had some lessons but needs on-court experience; has obvious stroke weaknesses but is beginning to feel comfortable with singles and doubles play.

2.5 This player has more dependable strokes but is still unable to judge where the ball is going; has weak court coverage; is still working just to keep the ball in play with others of the same ability level.

3.0 This player can place shots with moderate success; can sustain a rally of slow pace but is not comfortable with all strokes; lacks consistency in serving.

3.5 This player still lacks stroke dependability, depth and variety but has improved ability to direct shots away from opponent; rarely double faults but does not usually force errors on the serve; hits forehand and backhand volleys with consistency if the ball is within reach.

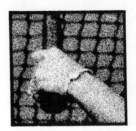

4.0 This player has dependable strokes on both forehand and backhand sides; has the ability to use a variety of shots including lobs, overheads, approach shots and volleys; can place the first serve and force some errors; is rarely out of position in a doubles game.

4.5 This player has begun to master the use of power and spins; has sound footwork; can control depth of shots and is able to move opponent up and back; can hit first serves with above average power and accuracy and place the second serve; is able to rush net with some success on serve against players of similar ability.

5.0 This player has good shot anticipation; is able to overcome some stroke deficiencies with outstanding shots or exceptional consistency; will approach net at opportune times and is often able to force an error or make a winning placement; can execute lobs, drop shots, half volleys, and overhead smashes with above average success; is able to vary the spin on the serve.

5.5 This player is able to execute all strokes offensively and defensively; can hit first serves for winners and second serves to set up an offensive situation; maintains a winning level of play in social tennis and can reach at least the quarterfinals or semifinals of the highest level club or park championship.

6.0 This player has mastered all of the above skills; is able to hit both slice and topspin serves; can vary strategies and styles of play in competitive situations; is capable of being ranked in a major city or USTA district.

6.5 This player has developed power and/or consistency as a major weapon; has all of the above skills as well as the concentration necessary for successful tournament play; is capable of earning a USTA sectional ranking.

7.0 This player is highly skilled in all of the above categories; is a polished tournament player who has traveled extensively for sanctioned competitions; has been ranked nationally by the U.S. Tennis Association.

... Remember, there is no substitute for on-court performance as a measure of playing ability. The new rating method is simply an initial step in achieving better competition, on-court compatibility, new goals to pursue and, in short, more tennis enjoyment."

The basic for this system was a self-rating concept originated by Chicago pro Dan Olson in 1975 and later adopted, following a number of modifications, by the Chicagoland Indoor Tennis Association. The Chicago system worked so well that it was picked up in a number of Midwestern cities, then found its way to Boston and finally to western New York State, with additional refinements along the way. But it was Jack Aldworth, executive director of the NTA, who spearheaded the final revisions that cleared the way for universal acceptance.

"I became convinced about four years ago," says Aldworth, "that this sport for the masses absolutely required a rating system, so that tennis players at La Costa or the Wall Street Racquet Club or wherever all had a lingua franca. Now you can walk in anywhere and say you're a 4.5 or a 5.5 and it means something. It's a marvelous system because it makes for a lot of fun.

"But the real beauty of these ratings is that they can be plugged into a computer and converted into a handicapping system for individual play and for inter-club, inter-league and even inter-city competition. We haven't tried to do that yet; one step at a time. But let's say I'm a 4 and you're a 5.

That means you'd probably give me a point at the start of each game. If you were a 6, you'd probably give me two points at the start of each game."

"We're very excited about this program," adds Eve Kraft, the USTA's education and research director, "because we feel there's a good combination here. You have the teaching pros who have developed it; you have the club owners who have promulgated it and with whom we've worked very closely and respect very highly; and then you have the USTA which has the players who are using it. For once, we're all working together."

The USPTA is also sold on the value of the rating program as a spur to the creation of more and better tennis players.

"This is essentially a self-rating system," one of its officials notes. "You don't need a pro to verify your rating, unless you want him to. But if a pro knows your game —because you're in a club league or you've taken some lessons and he's seen you play —he can easily verify your rating with no charge.

"The bottom line is simply this: For the first time it'll be possible for a player to find a compatible match anytime he wants one— not only at his home club but throughout the country."

COURTESY ON THE COURT

Newcomers and veterans alike should be aware, if they are not already, that there is more to a tennis match than hitting the ball back and forth. In recent years, tennis has shed its reputation as a prissy kind of sport played by affluent snobs mincing around in whites and being desperately polite to each other, hissing "sssh" at those who dare to open their mouths.

Tennis is, and has been, a keenly competitive and grueling sport, even when played for fun. Nevertheless, it's a game that requires a fair amount of plain civility to other players if it's to be enjoyable for everyone. One reason is the common courtesy that should apply in any activity. Another is that tennis demands intense concentration which can all too easily be broken by thoughtless interruptions or needless distractions.

All players—whether veterans or novices—should be familiar with the basic, generally accepted manners and customs of tennis. It makes the game more pleasant for themselves, other players and, if any, spectators.

Good tennis manners begin before you get onto the court. Make certain that your equipment is in good order so you won't be tempted to use it as an alibi should you lose. Dress appropriately; public courts may not require an immaculate all-white outfit, but some private clubs have quite rigid dress codes. There's little point in parading colors at a stuffy country club— you'll merely feel uncomfortable and your play may suffer.

DO: *Wear the proper attire.*
DON'T: *Show up in jeans.*

KNOW THE RULES: Before you even go out on the court, be quite sure that you are familiar with the rules of the game. Nothing is more likely to sour a match than a dispute about, say, striking the net with the racquet.

If you've never actually looked through the official rules, the USTA (51 East 42nd St., New York, N.Y. 10017) will sell you a

copy for 10 cents. The USTA also publishes a code of ethics for tennis players (USTA, 729 Alexander Rd., Princeton, N.J. 08450; 50 cents). There's no virtue in becoming a carping courtside lawyer, but a knowledge of the basic rules will allow you to concentrate more on the game at hand.

WAITING FOR A COURT: When you get to the courts, you may have to wait for a match to be completed. Don't make a nuisance of yourself by impromptu umpiring or volunteering gratuitous advice. You can occasionally make yourself useful by retrieving balls that are hit out of the court so that play can continue there without any undue interruption.

When a court becomes vacant, don't walk to it by crossing the middle or even the end of an intervening court while play is in progress. Wait at least until the end of the point and then hustle across the back of the court.

One of the biggest problems at unsupervised facilities are the players who hog the courts for themselves. That's not only selfish, it can be shortsighted, too; the players you keep waiting too long this weekend might well retaliate next weekend. So out of common courtesy when others are waiting their turn to play, try to limit yourself to 45 minutes for singles and one hour for doubles.

KEEP NOISE TO A MINIMUM: Since tennis demands concentration, loud noise can disrupt the timing and rhythm of players on an adjoining court. So whether you and your friends are playing a match or waiting on the sidelines for a court to clear, try to keep your voices low. Don't whoop it up after an exciting or frustrating point. And don't shout to each other from baseline to baseline; if you want to talk, go to the net where you can do it quietly.

ALWAYS GIVE YOUR OPPONENT THE BENEFIT OF A DOUBT: Very few tennis matches are played with officials, so the chances are that you will have to make your own calls on shots landing in your half of the court. The unwritten rule here is that you should *always* give your opponent the benefit of a doubt.

Unfortunately, the temptations to disregard this rule are strong and players may, at one time or another, be guilty of breaking the rule. Of course, everyone will make mistakes from time to time. However, try not to question your opponent's calls and he surely will give your calls the same courtesy.

Line calls should be made promptly and clearly. Any ball that is hit without a call is presumed to be good and play should continue. If a serve is clearly out, say so and don't hit the ball unless you wish to prevent it from going into an adjoining court.

SERVICE TIPS: It's generally considered rude to return a service that is obviously out of the service box. Of course, it's tough to call a very fast serve and the receiver may have hit the ball before he can call. Good practice says that the receiver has taken the chance and played the ball whether that point is won or lost. Similarly, if, as server, you fail to play a return because you thought the serve was out, then you

DO: *Wait off-court to retrieve a ball.*

DON'T: *Charge in during mid-point.*

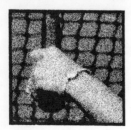

should surrender the point, gracefully.

In the case of a delayed or misunderstood service call, it is customary for the receiver, not the server, to offer a replay of the point. Don't ask for a replay just to give your opponent a break. If there is any doubt in your mind, the point should be his.

When it's your turn to serve, make quite sure that the receiver is ready before you begin your motion. You are expected to offer a replay of the serve if there's any doubt about that. If your first serve is a fault, then check that the receiver is ready for your second delivery. If the receiver makes any attempt to return serve, then you can presume he was ready.

In a doubles game, you should not serve until both your opponents are ready. But it is the responsibility of the receiver to check that his partner is ready and not to signal to the server until assured both are prepared. It isn't fair to expect the server continually to check both opponents.

ANNOUNCE THE SCORE REGULARLY BEFORE YOU SERVE: The responsibility for keeping track of the score during a game rests with the server. It is his duty to call out the point score before the beginning of each point and the game score before the start of each game. That eliminates confusion and uncomfortable disagreements.

When you return the balls to your opponent for his serve, do it promptly without stalling. And hit the balls so each reaches the server easily, preferably on one hop. Never roll the ball on the court. The receiver

is not normally expected to retrieve a distant third ball while a game is in progress, nor should the server go and get a distant ball himself. Balls that are way out of court should be retrieved at the end of the game, keeping in mind the rules for not crossing other courts while play is in progress. Some servers like to have three balls in hand before serving and the receiver should comply with this request whenever it is possible.

KEEP PLAY MOVING SMOOTHLY: After the completion of each point, get back into position to serve or receive as promptly as possible. Don't stall in an attempt to take a breather or to disrupt your opponent with gamesmanship. It cuts unnecessarily into your court time, to say nothing of the ill feeling it can generate in your opponent.

If a ball comes into your court from an adjoining court during play, then you have the basis for claiming a let. Don't hit the stray ball back right away, however. Wait until the point has finished on the other court and then direct it to one of the players there so the ball reaches him on the first bounce. Always return balls at the first break in your play.

Should you happen to lose a ball on an adjoining court, don't ask for the ball until the other players' point has been completed and don't go behind another court to retrieve a loose ball. If the other players have not seen your ball, a simple "Thank you" will generally bring it back to you.

CONTROL YOUR TEMPER: The player tantrums that are so unattractive at the professional level are just as offensive, if

not more so, up close at the club level of the game. Indeed, nothing can sour the fun of a tennis match faster than outbursts of anger. And they can cost you dearly in terms of concentration and friendships. Keep your temper under control—and always shake hands with opponents at the end of a match.

If you keep some of these suggestions in mind when you're on court, you should find tennis not only more enjoyable, but you will be able to spend more time concentrating on your game.

FORMING A COMPATIBLE DOUBLES GROUP

Everybody knows that good marriages are made in heaven, but what about compatible doubles foursomes? On the surface, it would seem easy enough to get together for a regular weekly game four or five players who play at the same general level and get along pretty well off the court. Yet judging by reports from many facilities, the only thing higher than the divorce rate is the rate at which doubles foursomes switch players from season to season.

Does it have to be that way?

Probably not. True, some "breakups" are inevitable. People move, change their work patterns, go on to a higher level of tennis. On the other hand, much of the acrimony that occasionally permeates a doubles foursome during the course of a season can easily be avoided, providing your group adheres to some basic guidelines. Here are a few of them.

GETTING THE GROUP TOGETHER: Organizing a foursome that can stand the test of a season is no mean achievement, and it would be nice to report that there's a simple way to do it. There isn't.

Most foursomes (and fivesomes, etc.) originate as twosomes. Two tennis players

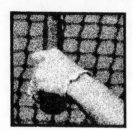

who get along well decide to get a doubles group together and, as if they were on the membership committee of an exclusive club, begin to run down the virtues and faults of all the tennis players they know.

At the risk of sounding sexist, it's been reported that women, in most instances, handle this selection process somewhat differently from men. As a rule, women players do not take their games with the same desperate seriousness that men do. The main qualification that women seem to look for is whether a prospective member is "nice." Men, on the other hand, generally subscribe to the notion that a backhand is a backhand is a backhand even if it belongs to Jack the Ripper.

This is a risky generalization and, indeed, among good women players, the selection process is probably more rigorous than among men players. What happens on occasion is this: You get a call from one of the women known to be a top player in the area. You think you are receiving an invitation to play in a friendly game of doubles. Actually you're being invited to a tryout, and how well or poorly you acquit yourself on the day of your match will determine whether you will be invited to join the fall foursome.

There is no way, unfortunately, of knowing for sure if you are being evaluated, but there are certain signs to look for. The presence of a videotape machine, for instance. Or an extra player or two on the sidelines, taking notes! Or the sort of questions they ask you: how old your children

are, how much traveling you do and who does your hair.

If you happen to be one of the original twosome who's doing the "screening," remember there is more to a regular doubles partner than a dependable serve and a pleasant smile.

Reliability, friends, that's the key. So what if a person plays like Chris Evert Lloyd or Bjorn Borg. Don't get involved if he frequently arrives late ("Sorry, everybody, I couldn't find my sneakers, the car wouldn't start and there was a 22-car collision on the freeway . . .") or isn't conscientious about providing a suitable substitute when he can't make it ("Well, he told me he'd taken lessons from Don Budge. . .") or, in the case of a young mother, can never find anybody to take care of the kids ("She won't bother anybody if we just let her sit there by the net. . .").

There's also the matter of attitude. Probably the principal cause of ill feeling among doubles foursomes is not so much uneven playing levels, but the fact that one or two players are taking the whole thing much more seriously than the others.

It's always possible, of course, that you'll have trouble finding enough players, in which case the best procedure is to talk to the manager of the club where you intend to play. At many clubs, there are bulletin boards on which players looking to hook up with foursomes leave their names and general playing levels.

There's nothing wrong with getting a group together for a trial run with the ex-

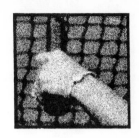

press idea of seeing how well you all play together. Such sessions can get sticky, though, particularly when one player is clearly beneath the level of the other three; usually, however, the player in this position will recognize that he's in over his head and, unless he's a masochist, will bow out on his own without peer pressure.

SETTING UP A SYSTEM: The first thing is to get more than four players. There are any number of ways of structuring a more-than-four system. You may have four "regulars" and one or two "alternates" (the alternates to pay a small percentage or to pay, proportionately, each time they fill in). Or you may have all regulars, in which case everyone takes a turn sitting out. The big

advantage to having more than four is that in the event somebody can't make it, you don't have to scour the universe rounding up a fourth.

It's usually a good idea to appoint a leader or "captain." This person should assume the responsibility of getting four healthy bodies on the court every week. In some groups of more than four, a schedule is usually drawn up before the season starts. It lists those who play and those who sit out that week.

The system works well enough, except when a person who is scheduled to play one week can't make it and attempts to negotiate with a person sitting out ("I'll trade you Christmas week for Thanksgiving

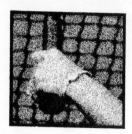

week . . ."). If everyone gets along well and is reasonable, you can usually work out these complications without much trouble. In the event one of the regular four can't make it, the captain should assume the responsibility of finding a substitute. Countless players have arrived at the request of a regular doubles player only to find that somebody else has asked a substitute as well. Keep it simple. Imbue whoever is responsible with absolute power.

An alternate to the captain system is to have each player be responsible for his own substitute. This type of system works best if a list of spare players is agreed upon by all so that the substitutes will be compatible in playing ability with the group.

ARRANGING THE FINANCES: Generally speaking, indoor foursomes pay the seasonal court fee in advance—a system that works well enough, except in cases when somebody has to drop out and wants his money back. One way to avoid that problem is to make it clear, in the beginning, that in the event one player has to drop out, it's his or her responsibility to find a replacement and make his own financial arrangement.

Another problem can arise in situations where the group pays its fee on an installment basis. Frequently, it is the captain of the group who assumes the responsibility to the facility, but it's wrong to expect one person to foot the bill when somebody else can't meet the installment date. Granted, this doesn't happen often, but when it does, it can get sticky. Best

advice: work out all financial arrangements as early and as completely as possible.

BALLS: This could be a possible source of friction—particularly if your foursome includes the super finicky ("O.K., we've played nine games. Time for a new can!") or the super cheap ("Whaddya mean, dead? I just bought them last month!"). There are two frequently practiced systems that work pretty well.

The easiest method is for everyone to kick in equal money on the evening you play and to take turns carting home the once-used can. An even less complicated system is to figure in the cost of the balls at the time you sign up for the season, and let one player pay proportionately less but be responsible each week for the balls.

CHOOSING SIDES: Since there are only three combinations of teams that you can come up with out of four players, you would think that the whole business of who plays with whom would be of minor consequence in most foursomes. Generally speaking, that is the case. But there are foursomes in which the choosing of sides frequently takes on the atmosphere of SALT II negotiations.

The whole idea behind establishing teams is to have a reasonably even and competitive game. But a tennis player's vanity invariably exceeds his judgment, and it usually takes three straight 6–0 sets to convince the losers that luck alone has not played the pivotal part in the result.

A good system seems to be one in which the teams change after every set,

regardless of how the set turns out. If the set has been a cliff hanger, then it's frequently a nice idea to keep the same sides. But the switch-after-every-set system invariably works better when everyone is more or less equally matched. For one thing, it allows the man or woman who cares about such things to keep a running account of how many games his or her team has won over the course of the time spent on court.

MAKING IT MORE FUN: There are two bits of advice which—if followed by most doubles groups, particularly intermediates—should make a noticeable and welcome difference in the quality of the tennis and in the amount of fun everyone has.

The first thing is to give yourself at least 10 to 15 minutes of warm-up before you start to play for keeps. Ask any tennis authority and he will cite the failure to warm up properly as one of the main reasons intermediates play so inconsistently. "You have to get into a groove," says former Davis Cup captain Dennis Ralston. "Sometimes you can do it in a few minutes. Sometimes it takes you a half-hour. But if you start to play and you're not grooved, you're going to be struggling throughout the match."

A second important reason for warming up is to avoid an arm injury. One of the easiest ways to pull a muscle is to start serving hard or hitting out before your arm is sufficiently limber.

Now, for the second bit of advice: keep the ball in play. Time and again in club doubles play, fewer than half the points ever get beyond the serve or return of serve. The server—more in men's play than in women's—will blast the fuzz off the ball and hit as many double faults as winning serves. The returner will blast the ball back with similarly inconclusive results. As a result, more time is spent in retrieving balls between serves than actually playing.

To quote Australian great Roy Emerson: "Doubles is an entirely different game from singles. You don't win by blasting the ball. It's a game of position and finesse. You don't serve as hard, you don't try for as many outright winners and you lob a lot more. When the game is played the way it's supposed to be played, it's more interesting than singles, and much more fun."

HOW TO IMPROVE YOUR CLUB'S TENNIS PROGRAM

Maybe it has something to do with the nature of the breed, but it's hard to meet a tennis player who doesn't have some complaint about the tennis club where he or she is a member. The biggest complaint comes from players who have trouble securing court time on weekends, but there are players who complain about there not being *enough* players around during certain times of the week. Some tennis players speak in homicidal terms of the kids who play at their clubs, and some gripe that their tennis-playing children are discriminated against.

That's not even to mention the complaints about groups of players who hog the courts. At one club, for example, just about everybody—the good players and the mediocre players, the women and the men—thinks that everybody else "dominates the courts." It's the same club at which the teaching professional moans about not giving enough lessons, while the members complain that he monopolizes too many courts for his clinics.

All of which is another way of saying that there is probably no such thing as the "perfect" tennis club, and there will proba-bly never be one as long as there are players of different playing abilities, competitive outlooks, sex, backgrounds, schedules and psychological needs.

On the other hand, it seems safe to say that most tennis clubs could do a lot more to satisfy the special needs of their members—provided, that is, that the members themselves get involved.

It isn't as difficult as you may imagine to make changes in procedures and policies. There's only one hitch: you have to stand up and be counted. So here is a list of frequently voiced complaints and some suggestions on how the club you belong to might deal with them.

1. COURT TIME IS TOO DIFFICULT TO GET. If court time is inordinately hard to come by at your club, it means one of two things: Either you have too many members in relation to courts, or your system of court assignment needs revamping. Unfortunately, there is no accepted standard in the tennis club field for what the member-to-court ratio should be.

The problem with establishing such a standard is that you have no way of determining ahead of time how often a player is going to use the courts. There are crowded clubs where the ratio of members to courts is less than 20 to 1 and clubs where getting an open court is never a problem despite the fact that the member-to-court ratio is twice that figure. Short of assassinating 30 percent of your present members, here are some measures that might help you ease the crowding problem:

• Set a "doubles-only" policy for your busiest times or limit the number of "singles-only" courts.

• If your normal playing time is more than one hour, shorten it. When people are waiting, some clubs limit singles play to 45 minutes.

• Set aside certain periods on weekends for members who can't play during the week.

• Divide your courts into two categories—reserved and open—and let people use the open courts on a first-come, first-served basis.

• Limit the number of times a day a player can use a court when others haven't yet played.

2. I CAN'T FIND ANY SUITABLE OPPONENTS WHEN I WANT TO PLAY. Any club worth its salt should be able to fix you up with an opponent, provided you give some advance notice. Some clubs keep a list of "players looking for games" on hand and will have somebody in the pro shop do the calling for you. The National Tennis Rating Program will aid clubs in their pairing of players of comparable abilities.

Another system is to offer reduced rates or complimentary memberships to pretty good players (solid high school players, for instance) who get court privileges in exchange for making themselves available as opponents to club members when the need arises.

3. THE SAME PLAYERS KEEP WINNING THE TOURNAMENTS. In addition to regular tournaments (all of which, by the way, should be double-elimination or else have a consolation bracket), try staging some handicap events. The simplest way is to make the better players start each game at minus 15, or minus 30, which means they have to win not just four points to take a game but as many as seven or eight.

4. THERE ISN'T A CLUB ATMOSPHERE. PEOPLE JUST COME AND GO. The only way you can create an atmosphere that keeps people around a club is to have enough courts available on an open basis so players will have a reason to be there. It's more work to run a club that doesn't operate strictly on a reservation basis, but few, if any, clubs that operate on a reservation-only basis generate any sort of clubby atmosphere.

The presence of a snack bar or lounge is another way of cultivating a club-like atmosphere. And a lot, too, has to do with the personality of the pro and the pro shop personnel. It's up to the pro to generate the positive vibrations that make a tennis club a nice place to frequent.

5. THE CLUB HAS TOO MANY CLIQUES. Cliques are as indigenous to tennis as tennis elbow. The only thing you can do is to hold special tournaments (A & B doubles, for instance) that will help players who wouldn't normally be together on the court to get to know each other.

6. THERE ARE TOO MANY KIDS AND THEY MAKE TOO MUCH NOISE. Here, a lot depends on the sort of club you have (some people like having lots of kids around). But in the better-run clubs, non-

playing children are not allowed to hang around the courts and play ball boy or ball girl for Mommy and Daddy. If there are members who say they can't afford to play tennis unless they bring their tots along, see about setting up a babysitting service at the club. An alternative is to set aside certain times of the day for parents who have no other option but to bring the little ones.

7. NOT ENOUGH IS DONE FOR THE KIDS. If there are a good number of younger families at your club, there's no reason that children shouldn't have a chance to use the courts, too. At one club, the courts are reserved for children every day (except weekends) during the summer from noon to 2 p.m. At other times, adults have first crack. If there are enough young players, your club should have a genuine children's program—complete with clinics, tournaments and inter-club matches. But don't put it all in the lap of the pro. Have a member assume the prime responsibility.

This list probably doesn't cover all the complaints you may encounter about your club, nor does it propose all the possible remedies. But by incorporating some of these suggestions into your club's program, you may be able to make the tennis more enjoyable for all the members.

PREPARING FOR YOUR CLUB CHAMPIONSHIP

If your club's big season-end tournament is just a few weeks away and you're starting to dread putting your game, your good name and your pro's reputation on the line in front of an audience, take heart. There are ways to point toward a club trophy that can make the whole affair less traumatic than a root canal—and maybe even fun.

At the risk of overstating the obvious, you can best prepare for a match by playing the game. "The one thing most club players don't do enough is play competitive matches," says one Texas teaching pro. "Two or three weeks before the tournament you should play really competitive matches about three times a week."

Echoes the head pro at a California club: "If you've been playing regularly before the tournament, you're tougher when the score gets to 6–5. It's that old confidence factor." At a recent championship event at his club, the pro reports that "the teams that did well were the teams that had played heavily a month before the tournament. And some of our better club players who hadn't been practicing didn't do too well."

Most pros agree that a few brush-up

lessons before the big event will help, but not if you try to learn or change too much at the last minute. "It's a good idea to take a few extra lessons before the tournament, as long as the pro doesn't try to change anything drastically; then you'll get too stroke-conscious," warns a Tennessee club pro.

While you're getting match-ready on court, you should be taking especially good care of yourself off court to be at your best on the big day. Proper rest, a balanced diet (if you've got time, one that will help you shed excess pounds) and regular stretching and conditioning exercises are recommended by pros around the country for pre-match preparedness. As a Florida pro notes: "Those great-looking strokes will soon disappear if you're out of shape."

For the tournament day itself, there are a few more tips offered by teaching pros to help give you an edge. All concur that tournament day is not the occasion to show off new equipment. "This is not the time to try new shoes or a new racquet," advises one, for the sake of both your feet and your strokes. "Stick to the equipment you're familiar with," he adds. If you have a back-up racquet, of course, it's wise to bring it along in case of string breakage (and it might help intimidate your opponent, too).

The intimidated party could turn out to be you, though, if you misjudge your abilities at "scouting"—checking out your opposition in action before your match. While many pros give their blessing to the practice, there are pitfalls. "If you can analyze someone else's strokes and come away with useful information about his game, then scouting is helpful," says a knowledgeable tournament player.

Some pros advise against the practice altogether. "You'll just worry about your own game, and it can really put you off," one pro feels. So, if you can scout with a calm, analytical mind, go ahead. Otherwise, spare your nerves.

And what if, despite all your preparation and strategy, you get knocked out in the first round? "Remember," cautions another tournament veteran, "tennis is a sport, not a life-and-death battle." And, there's always next year.

HOW TO
RUN A CLUB
CHAMPIONSHIP

If you think playing in your club championship is enough to lead to ulcers, wait until you supervise one. It's not really a thankless job, it just seems that way at times.

Times like when the club president tries to enter his wife in the women's singles at the last minute and you've already completed a seeded drawsheet. Times like when the guy who promised to order trophies at a discount from his friend in the business reports that they won't arrive till the weekend after the finals. Times like when your 8-year-old daughter says, "Daddy, the weatherman on TV says the forecast is for rain this weekend." Times like when the defending champ demands a change in the draw to make him the No. 1 seed and beneficiary of a bye in the first round, although the best player in the club, and this year's top seed, wasn't in the tournament a year ago.

Are you to become another disillusioned director? Will your tourney sprout unhappy, even unsportsmanlike, feelings among the usually cordial club members? Is it all really necessary? Can't clubs just have friendly tournaments and let the best man and woman (and/or junior) win?

Nobody can guarantee a perfect tournament. But maybe your club can benefit from pointers gleaned from tournament-wise players and pros. Every club has its own character and personality and its unique, local problems. You can accept or reject any of the points brought out, depending upon your situation.

THE KIND OF TOURNAMENT: There are at least a dozen different types of tourneys your club can stage—all the way from a Junior Novice Play Day to Invitational Doubles. The major points presented here apply to all kinds of events but with emphasis on the three major club championships—singles, doubles and mixed doubles.

THE TOURNAMENT DIRECTOR: In case Henry Kissinger doesn't happen to be a member at your club, look for the next best diplomat around. You'll be happy to have a director skilled in the art of getting along with people.

There's universal disagreement as to what his official title should be, so right off let's make an arbitrary distinction. The Tournament Chairman is the person designated by the club to head up the year-long slate of tournaments and all major details connected with them. The Tournament Director—the official with whom we are mainly concerned here—is responsible for running one or more specific tournaments.

In some clubs, the chairman and the director are one and the same individual—handling the entire season's program as well as each separate contest. The disad-

vantage of giving so much responsibility to one person for a whole year is that he will inevitably wear himself out and, when his year is up, swear "he's done his duty to the club" and henceforth and forevermore remove himself from tournament chores. That would be a pity, because what you really need is continuity and experience among your committee members, not a succession of untried chairmen who have a whole new group of volunteers every year.

Most tournament chairmen serve for a year. It can be a separate job or it can be performed by the club's vice president. One club rotates the job every six months, with the retiring chairman staying on the committee and indoctrinating incoming personnel. Considering that tennis players are a busy lot anyway, this idea has much merit: spread the load around.

Another club appoints a separate director or co-director, e.g., husband and wife, for each tourney. The latter combination is excellent; it recognizes the true contribution of the committee member's spouse, who generally serves behind the scenes as an ex-officio co-chairperson handling the burden of phoning, contact and detail work, or filling in while the other is away.

So for your chairman, choose a good organizer, delegator and seasoned competitor who knows, as an insider, what tournaments are all about. Your director, who is really a coordinator, should have the same qualities, plus guts to say "no" and mean it when the situation calls for it. A wide ac-

quaintanceship among the rank and file members and a knowledge of their playing talent will mean the chairperson can better help seed the draw and fit doubles partners together.

GETTING HELP: The director will need willing bodies to staff the desk and score sheets, to hand out balls, to shepherd players onto their assigned courts and to double-check with them on next-round matches. These volunteers need not be experienced competitors; the main need here is reliability—you don't want someone running off and vacating the command post.

A big help is a "runner" volunteer who moves around the club to advise where the open courts are to keep them fully occupied.

Don't overlook the assistance the club pro can provide, either. At the very least, he can help with the seeding and scheduling. At most, he can run your tournaments for you. Says the head pro at a California club: "My staff and I control the sign-up of entries, make the draw, handle notification of players and run the desk and score sheets on tournament days. We strive for a good turnout of entrants; we know the players quite well and can handle the draw and other aspects of the tournament in an impartial way. We also draw up our schedule at the first of the year and avoid conflicts with other events in the area ... I even take pictures of the winners."

CATEGORIES: If your club is large enough, you'll probably want to have tournaments for players of various levels of abil-

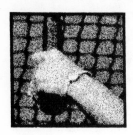

Trophies being presented to the winners of the Broadmoor Family Invitational Tennis Tournament, Colorado Springs, Colorado.

ity. But whether or not you do that, don't forget to include a consolation bracket composed of first-round losers, since that will assure everyone of at least two matches. But watch your scheduling problems. Don't attempt a consolation round if you cannot control the court usage situation; otherwise, the screams will be loud and long.

Just make sure you get each player in his proper group and, remember, trophy hunters tend to underrate themselves around entry time!

SPREADING OUT THE DATES: "The one-weekend club tournament is almost extinct," says another California pro. "It just ties up too many courts over a two-day stretch and freezes out the recreational

players. It's better to spread out the play more and open the courts for social tennis as soon as the tournament matches are finished."

A three-day weekend may be sufficient, providing enough players are going to be on hand to assemble a proper draw.

If there are 32 players—or more—in any one draw, though, it's just not feasible in one weekend (1) to work in the required number of matches or (2) to expect players to engage in so many (three, possibly four) matches on a single day. That's not going to help their health or quality of play.

Two weekends may be required, but that should be the limit. Interest wanes after that and, during the summer, people usually won't commit themselves to sticking

around that many days. (An exception is the club in a resort area where the members come and go all season long but are never all on hand on a given weekend; the format here is for members to schedule their own matches before the finals deadline.)

BALLS: Balls constitute the single biggest expense of a tournament. By all means, order them through the club pro. He will not use your tournament as a big chance to get rich; you might be able to get the balls at cost. Don't feel sorry that the pro is not making a profit; the advantage is that it adds to his clout in volume buying in competition with the chain and discount stores who buy by the boatload. Also, afterward, he can use the balls for teaching.

Each early-round match warrants two new balls; semifinals and finals rate three. If the final match is a marathon affair, be prepared to break out a new can for the gladiators, just like Flushing Meadow!

Your distinguished colleagues who go into consolation can be content with playing with used balls, except for their finals, where they get two new ones.

A time-honored method for holding down the entry fee is to have everyone bring a new can of balls. The winner of each match gets to keep the unopened can, right down to the finals, while each loser gets to take home the used ones. Although some club players view this practice as somewhat bush league, it's commonly accepted in many events. But if you try it, be warned: someone will probably show up on Court 17, a half mile from the pro shop, and find

he forgot to bring a new can of balls.

AWARDS/TROPHIES: If your treasury can afford it, it's best to buy your trophies early in the year, because trophy prices escalate like everything else in today's marketplace.

Your pro can line you up with a supplier. Stick with your pro for the whole season's buying and you'll be treated right. Often the trophy firm will throw in free engraving if it can count on your business. One club has used the same source for 18 years and has no trouble staying within the budget on purchases.

Most players prefer trophies over merchandise—they want the emblem of supremacy staring down from the shelf, especially those individuals who've never won anything in their lives.

Trophies should go to the winners and runners-up in each category and to the consolation winners. Some clubs stretch it a little and award the consolation runners-up a trophy, but this is one you can cut out in the name of economy. After all, does a double loser really merit a prize?

Names of champs and runners-up earning major club titles should go onto plaques on the perpetual trophies kept at the club. Your grandchildren will be proud of you circa 1995.

It adds interest and fun to give out other awards, too, such as a sportsmanship award, with the recipient chosen by the tournament committee on the basis of attitude, playing spirit and kindness displayed. Also, pick out perhaps a little Snoopy cup

for the "Most Unimproved Player" and another for the "Goat" of the tourney. Handle it with taste and a touch of humor and you'll help build interest for the future and involve more club members.

"There are alternatives to the typical metal trophy," says one pro. "I like to see something usable. At one club, they give out free sailing and water ski lessons. Free dinners at a good restaurant make for something different. Wheels of cheese are great prizes. For major club championships, the perpetual trophy is the way to go. I believe a lot of the repeat winners get tired of collecting more and more hardware."

If it's a junior tourney you're staging, consider medallions for every entrant; buy them by the gross and the cost will be low.

JUNIORS—YES OR NO? Should club tournaments be open to juniors as well as adults? For the championship events, the answer is an emphatic "Yes." But for purely adult or social tournaments, perhaps not.

Newer, smaller clubs want juniors in the contests to provide more competition. Many adult members see the value of the youngsters competing in serious club matches since, for many aspiring juniors, it's one of the few shots they'll get at tournament play.

The clubs are now strongly emphasizing junior tennis development, and the pros and proud parents like to see the young people compete in club events. If a junior is on a men's or women's ladder, he or she certainly ought to be welcome to partici-

pate in the club tourneys.

One pro recommends that when there are A, B and C categories in the club championships, the better juniors and any who are on the A ladders should go into the A's, not into the B's and C's.

"In our club, the main thing about juniors is that we want them to feel welcome," is one stand on this question. "If they're good enough to enter, we want them."

There's one exception: Juniors should not be invited to participate in purely social adult tournaments, such as the Mystery Mixed Doubles or Calcutta Mixed Doubles or Invitational Doubles, which are usually held in conjunction with receptions, dinners or parties.

OTHER RESTRICTIONS ON ENTRANTS: How about your club's superstars? A man or woman player who clearly outclasses the field or is ranked in USTA regional listings should be welcome to enter. But the chances are he or she won't be around anyway. Even if such top-notch players are on hand, they probably won't be interested or they may prefer to let the rank and file slug it out for the trophies.

That doesn't necessarily apply to doubles or to those ranked in senior or junior categories. If your club has several luminaries, though, and they all enter, that's a real boon because it means the later rounds will see some exciting and close matches.

There's wide agreement that the tournament director should be permitted to enter his or her own event. He may, how-

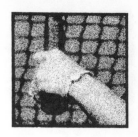

ever, count himself out if it's an exceptionally big draw and there are numerous problems (particularly due to weather or other extenuating circumstances). The theory is that he has things so well organized, he certainly ought to play, and in smaller clubs, the director's playing ability may be eagerly desired to raise the level of competition.

As the pro at one club says: "A good director should be freer than anyone else. He's lined up his co-workers and done his advance groundwork. His tournament should run itself. Sure, I say let him play."

Invitational doubles pose an entirely different problem about who can play. That's because some ordinary players like to slip in a "ringer" for a partner who proceeds to drill holes through all opposition in a category well below his usual level. What fun he gets by wiping out inferior players match after match!

The problem can be countered by printing on the entry blank this trio of choices: "My invited partner is (a) below my ability, (b) above my ability or (c) about the same." Another good rule is that a doubles team must enter the category of the better of the two players.

Of course, the invitational event is definitely designed to bring in excellent outside players in the Open or A classes, as well as just good hacker friends. But you risk the everlasting enmity of fellow club members by inviting your "long-lost-cousin" who steps into the nearest phone booth only to emerge as his true self—a three-time Big 10 champ and the current head pro at Purple Pines Island in the Caribbean.

PUBLICITY: The idea is to get as many players into your tournament as you can. To do that, you've got to publicize the events. Employ every device you can to spread the word; it's amazing how many people forget or don't hear about club tournaments.

Send out entries to all club members. Use your club newsletter, bulletin boards, posters, postcards—everything you can to excite interest. "We even phone the defending champion to make sure he gets his entry in on time," one director says.

HANDLING ENTRIES: All entrants must send in their fees *with the entry blank*; you may have a problem getting their money after they've played.

In a big club, after all the publicity that's put forth, late entries should not be accepted. There are simply too many people involved to consider all the special (and hardship) cases that arise. Late entries often wreck the draw, especially where seeded players are involved. If you must bend a little, be prepared to tell a late entry that *if* there is a bye slot open, he'll have to play a seed right off the bat.

A clearly explained and understood "waiting list" is acceptable. Thus, if someone drops out, you have a reservoir of substitutes, and can keep the draw up to strength.

Small clubs can stretch the deadline because they probably need all the players they can get to make a decent draw. Also, fewer problems are apt to surface.

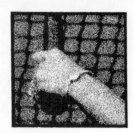

Make your semifinals and finals important events, complete with linesmen and ball boys.

If you do announce a serious deadline, stick to it. Otherwise, you'll soon get boxed into a corner trying to decide just which late entrants to accept and whom they're going to play. But don't make your club tourney too inflexible. After all, it is for the members.

For doubles, make it clear that you will refuse to accept "and partner" entries. Either two players enter as a team or not at all. However, here's a chance for the club and committee really to perform a service to the new member or to an old member who suddenly finds himself partnerless. Let it be known that the committee will help line up partners for members seeking them; that should be done informally and in ad-

vance of the tournament, not at the last minute.

THE DRAW: Make your draw as soon as you can following the deadline for entries. Some clubs call on a few experienced members familiar with all the players to handle this task. But some ask the club pro to do it. One advocate of that system says: "The pro should do the draw because he knows everyone better than any of the members. He's in the best position to be impartial and he's got to be a good diplomat to hold his job in the first place."

Whoever takes on the job should follow USTA guidelines for making up draw sheets. Last year's winner usually gets the

top seeding as defending champ, but not always. And as soon as the sheets are completed, they should be posted prominently in the clubhouse.

NOTIFICATION OF PLAYING TIME: Publicize and include on every entry blank this type of statement: "Play will begin at 8:30 on Saturday morning unless you are otherwise notified."

Then, on the draw sheet have a date, time and court for every match (figure about 20 minutes a set, plus warm-up and transition time). This makes it the responsibility of each contestant to check the draw sheet for upcoming matches. Only in the case of a change will it be necessary to phone the players; however, it doesn't hurt to confirm the times of the semifinals and finals with those players.

SCORING: Conventional two-sets-out-of-three matches and the 9-point tie-breaker are universal. The 1–2–3–4 no-ad scoring can be used in early rounds, if necessary, to save time, but should be discarded for the quarterfinals and beyond. Since the USTA has approved no-ad as optional for tournaments, it will gain more adherents, and perhaps will become standard.

BIG DAY—THE FINALS: The finals rate top billing and prime time on the club's "Center Court." The challenge is to make the finals an exciting—and well-attended—occasion.

Some American clubs over-organize their tournaments to the point where the finals become an anticlimax. In Europe, clubs really make a field day out of the finals. In fact, one stresses the semifinals as much as the finals and, as a result, draws an excellent gallery. At one Swiss club play on the other courts ceases and non-participants attentively sit sipping their drinks on the terrace overlooking center court as the semifinals begin. They treat it as an important occasion.

For their tournament finals, some clubs enlist linesmen and ball boys and install a microphone so the umpire can be clearly heard when he calls out the scores. These may seem to be unnecessary frills, but they do enhance the occasion.

Ideally, you should line up the officials and ball boys in advance—no calling for volunteers at the last second or pushing Good Old Bill onto the court following his third beer to call lines in the hot sun. The minimum number of officials is three: one person calling the service line, one calling the far sideline away from the umpire and the ump sitting high in his chair where he can see all the rest of the court well. Calling lines not only makes a better player out of the club member who volunteers for that chore, but also adds a touch of class to the finals.

Ball boys aren't just for class, however; they facilitate prompt and better play. And consider those who play a three-and-one-half-hour match in the broiling sun—ball boys would be a blessing for them and the gallery. When the finals are played, it is always outlandish to see the club's top two players marching all the way across an ad-

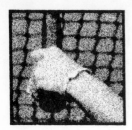

jacent vacant court—and back—to retrieve a ball many times in a match.

EXHIBITION MATCHES: "Tying in an exhibition with your club tournament is an excellent idea," says a seasoned pro. "People like to see another quality of tennis. It makes a good show. One pro set is enough, though—don't let the match drag or everyone becomes bored. And don't forget—it's good exposure for the club pro if he's asked to be one of the players. He gets to be seen by the club members in another pose besides just standing at the net hitting the ball to beginners."

A well-executed exhibition match can lend interest and distinction to your club tourney. The best format is doubles, selecting a foursome from ranked local players, your own club's pros, and visiting pros, with an eight-game set.

Hold it between the semis and the finals. Build up interest and bring out a crowd.

This is a capsulized course in tournament organization and execution. Follow it and you'll find tournament organizing as rewarding as playing.

CAN YOU HAVE MORE FUN WITH A TENNIS LEAGUE?

A weekly tennis game with a group of congenial and roughly comparable players should be one of the good things in life—fun, athletic, healthy and sociable. But sometimes it isn't. The logistics of phoning around every week to arrange playing times that are acceptable to all can be, frankly, one big pain. And for all the camaraderie, a weekly group can lack the kind of competitive edge you can get in other sports where league play and team battles are involved.

Happily, though, there is a way to correct those shortcomings and make group tennis play every bit as rewarding as it should be. It's a system that has been developed and refined in recent years in the Southeast. It's a sound method to revitalize routine play, since sessions can become rather sporadic and somewhat bothersome to arrange. It's a tennis league, which involves drafting a schedule and a standings sheet to tighten things up.

It sounds like a good idea, but can it be kept simple? Will it efficiently handle both singles and doubles? Who will draw it up and distribute it?

Here's how a Florida group came up with answers to those questions and gave

themselves a workable, challenging tennis arrangement that can be helpful to any group.

For simplicity, the group wanted a system that could have both schedules and standings for singles and doubles on one sheet of paper. Singles was easy enough. They decided to use a simple ladder where any player could challenge any other without having to work his way up. If the higher-ranked player wins, the ladder is unchanged. If the lower-ranked player wins, he moves to the rung of the defeated player and the loser moves down one rung.

For example, if player No. 7 beats No. 2, then No. 7 moves to the second rung, No. 2 moves to the third rung and the players in standings 3 through 6 move down a rung. They also keep a cumulative win-loss record for each singles player as another way to stimulate interest.

Doubles proved to be somewhat more difficult. They didn't want permanent doubles teams—that would be too rigid and there was a good chance of one or two teams becoming dominant. So they decided initially to schedule doubles play with random partners for each match. They kept doubles standings by giving a win or a loss to each player after every match, without trying to keep records of particular teams.

For example, let's suppose players A and B play and beat players C and D. A and B would each be credited with a win while C and D would be charged with a loss. Standings were drawn up on the basis of a win-loss average. If player A lost his next match,

no matter who his partner, or opponents, his average would be .500.

As you might expect, a pattern began to emerge after a few matches. The group then scheduled matches to balance the competition and give more closely contested matches. For example, players ranked 1 and 4 might play numbers 2 and 3. Or 5 and 12 might play 6 and 11, and so on.

The key to the smooth execution of the system is the schedule-maker, who must perform faithfully each week to keep things rolling. The Florida players rotate the job every few months unless someone likes to do it and retains the post longer. The schedule-maker must enter the scores, update the win-loss records and order of standings and arrange the next week's matches—all of which takes less than an hour a week.

This group plays on Tuesdays and Thursdays, although some players opt for only one or the other of those days. The schedule sheet is drawn up on Friday and a copy is mailed or delivered to each player by noon the following Tuesday. To simplify the schedule-maker's job, there is a prearranged guide which indicates each player's desired playing days. Ideally, that never changes so that the matches can be scheduled from week to week without personally contacting each player every week.

But a player must call the schedule-maker by the Friday noon deadline if he wishes to depart from his normal playing pattern. And any player who can't get to the

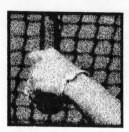

courts after the schedule is issued must arrange a substitute—either from the group list or from outside. If he can't find a substitute for doubles, he notifies the other players and they decide among themselves if two of them want to get together for a singles match instead.

Some players like doubles one day and singles the next, and the schedule-maker tries to honor these requests whenever possible. Players can arrange their own matches, which often occurs when the competition between particular pairs is especially keen. They do that simply by calling the schedule-maker prior to the deadline.

The winners of all matches must notify the schedule-maker of the results before the deadline, so they can be entered on the schedule. The scores of previous matches and the schedule for the next week both appear on the mailed sheet.

The system has been both efficient and fun, with everyone eagerly anticipating the release of the schedule and standings sheet each week. This interest has kept everyone playing on a regular basis and with an exceptional degree of enthusiasm. As a policy, the record is wiped clean each year and started anew.

The Florida league is an intermediate-level group and new players—generally within their skill range—are added at the invitation of any one of the existing members. Occasionally, players above or below their level have been taken on, with mixed results. They encourage experienced novices to join them to help them develop their games; and by appropriate pairings, they attempt to make competitive matches for them. But a number of them have gotten discouraged and dropped out voluntarily.

Expert players, too, have moved on because of dissatisfaction with the caliber of competition. And there have been a few cases where members have improved so much they've graduated to a circle of better players.

Apart from the accepted rules of tennis, the group has no complex regulations to govern play, only the rules listed at the bottom of each schedule sheet to remind each player of his responsibilities.

The system has virtually eliminated the nuisance factor in arranging group play, while at the same time providing competition and an ever-shifting ladder ranking to keep interest high. The key ingredients for the league's success are: 1) the routine issuance of a printed schedule; 2) a playing schedule that is automatic, requiring phone calls only for changes, and 3) the stimulation of interest by maintaining records.

The specifics can easily be tailored to any group's needs. Why not try it for yours? Also, look for other leagues in your area. The USTA is becoming increasingly involved in league play, and some cities, such as Atlanta, have leagues for players of all levels and ages. If you don't have access to a club or if your club wants a way to compete with others in your area, leagues may be the answer.

HOSTING A SUCCESSFUL TENNIS PARTY

If you are a tennis player who enjoys the company of similarly inclined individuals, then you are prime material for a tennis party. But don't wait for someone else to throw one; make a bid for social acclaim and throw one yourself. Be careful, though. Done badly, a tennis party can rank right up there on the thrill meter with a root canal job. But if you heed the advice of those who have given and attended dozens of such affairs, you can almost guarantee that a splendid time will be had by all.

Your first impulse may be to just phone up a few courtsful of tennis folks, buy some booze, rent a few courts and wait for magic to happen. Resist that impulse. "The worst tennis party I ever attended," recalls one woman-about-tennis-society, "had no schedule, no organization. People just walked into the club, wandered around and asked other people: 'Can I join you?' Sometimes they could, and sometimes they couldn't."

Much as you might favor the idea of spontaneous merriment, a tennis party must have a plan, a schedule, some organization to make it work. Round-robin play seems to be the most popular at tennis

parties, and part of your advance planning should include drafting a firm, inviolable playing schedule so everyone will know exactly when, and whom, they play.

ROUND ROBINS: A round robin lets everyone play the same amount of tennis and can provide good competition even when the playing abilities within the group differ. Some party-givers limit each doubles match to four games so each player can serve once. A disadvantage of that method is that some matches may take longer than others and, thus, may throw the schedule off. This problem can be reduced by insisting on no-ad scoring (1, 2, 3, game). An alternative is simply to establish a time limit for each round of matches. That can range from 15 to 30 minutes or so, depending on the number of rounds to be played.

Pencils and copies of the table of play should be provided at each court so guests can enter their results at the conclusion of each round. At the end of the evening, each couple or individual totals up the number of games won—or their winning percentages, if a time limit was used. Prizes are usually given for the highest and lowest scores.

Round robins, though, do have two problems: Some mathematical ability is required to work out the order of play, particularly if there is an odd number of players. And for a large party, many rounds are required if every team is to play every other team.

However, there are published tables of round-robin play that you can probably match to your group.

Below is a sample table for a five-team round robin for use when two courts are available.

You can also run round robins that have changing partners and opponents in every round. Round robins can be used for groups of all sizes by creating divisions with playoffs between division winners to see who is best.

MATCHING: Democracy has no place in a tennis party, so if you want your guests to enjoy themselves, make sure they're of roughly comparable stroking ability. "The key factor separating a good party from a bad one," says the editor of a social newsletter in New York City, "is a host who makes sure everyone's matched well in a competitive game." That means no beginners, unless all people you're inviting are novices. It can be embarrassing for everyone, especially the beginner himself, to have one guest flailing away haplessly against his betters in what is supposed to be a fun situation.

One Rhode Island group that specializes in tennis parties has organized things to such a point that they've evolved two different tennis party formats—one social and one tournament.

The group has found the distinction necessary. "It's very important to have the two formats," a spokeswoman from Rhode Island says, "because a real competitive person can destroy a tennis party. The competitive types in our club limit themselves to tournament-type affairs, which we have about once a month. They're not happy at a straight party."

"In a social situation," offers the general manager of a Michigan club, "you've got to be careful of making it too competitive, particularly with regard to the stronger men. The biggest complaint I hear after parties is from the women grumbling

ROUND	COURT 1	COURT 2	SCORES				
			A	B	C	D	E
1	A vs. B	C vs. D					bye
2	A vs. C	B vs. E				bye	
3	A vs. E	B vs. D			bye		
4	A vs. D	C vs. E		bye			
5	B vs. C	D vs. E	bye				
		Totals					

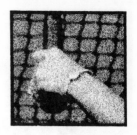

about the stronger men getting out of hand."

For just that reason, the Rhode Island spokeswoman says, a typical Saturday night social affair should feature two or three sets of mixed doubles, and two or three sets of men's and women's doubles. "People can't stand playing only mixed doubles," the spokeswoman says. Most tennis party organizers agree, which is why they generally see to it that the men get a chance to have at each other at some point in the affair. "By the end of the evening," says one organizer, "the men are itching to play together and it's a good idea to let 'em do it."

RESERVING COURTS: Once you know how many tennis buddies you'll be mustering for your party, you can reserve the courts. That needs to be done well in advance—especially for holiday periods. Lead times of anywhere from one to six months are often required to book Saturday night courts, and even more time should be allowed for monster holidays like New Year's or the Fourth of July.

How many courts should you book? That depends on the number of guests you'll have and the playing format you'll be using. But a rough rule of thumb is to figure at least four people per court at almost all times. One party-giver rents four courts for 20 people, so that while most are playing, a handful are snacking and socializing. Some hosts count on eight people per court, but that's the most you can hope to squeeze in and, if you try it, you'd better have at least a four-hour party to be sure everyone gets in a reasonable amount of play. Since the per-person tab for most tennis parties is about $10, you don't want to send anyone away feeling cheated.

COSTS: For the financial peace of mind of those who have no experience with tennis parties, it should be comforting to learn that the host is not expected to mortgage his home to foot the bill; each guest pays a set admission fee that includes court time, balls and usually food and drink (some parties operate on the bring-your-own basis).

REFRESHMENTS: If you're responsible for lining up the refreshments, what should you provide? As Donna and Bob Casciano observe in "The Tennis Party Book": "Feeding your tennis players can run the entire gamut from having a fully catered affair complete with bartender to bringing your own box lunch. Both can be fun."

The most popular route seems to be something in between—i.e., platters of cold cuts, bowls of chips and dip, beer, wine and soda. Stay away, though, from liquor; most players won't touch it during play and few really feel like it afterward. "The majority of people at a tennis party are there to play tennis," notes one organizer, "so we serve things like fried chicken or a big submarine sandwich, as well as beer, wine and soda." For a 32-person affair at one club, the bar will include four 12-packs of beer, three half-gallons of wine, four eight-packs of diet soda and two eight-packs of regular soda.

At an Illinois club, the general manager reports that things get a bit more exotic. "People enjoy nibbling, so we try to have two or three types of hot hors d'oeuvres. And then we usually have a theme to our parties ... Oriental night (sweet and sour pork), Italian (lasagna) and then, in addition, something like fried chicken for those who don't want the other dishes. We put the hors d'oeuvres out early and then serve the main dish around 11 p.m."

If your site has the facilities for hot food, and you know that everyone will be off the court by a certain time, then it can be a nice touch to serve chop suey, pizza or whatever strikes you. Most tennis party givers, though, have found that serving cold foods that enable guests to eat when and what they like is easier. It might be the more practical option, too.

If you've got a spare body around, incidentally, it can be helpful to have one person in charge of setting out the food while another supervises all that carefully organized play.

Now that you know most of the do's about tennis parties, there are a few important don'ts to watch out for:

• Don't ask people to show up at 7:30 p.m. and expect the tennis to start at 7:30. Many of the guests will be late, so invite people for 7:00 to insure a 7:30 starting time.

• Don't necessarily pair husbands and wives together. Often spouses want to get away from one another at these parties. And try to be tactful with all pairings. At one memorable court party, a couple fresh from divorce court found themselves partnered, to their mutual distress.

• Don't let persuasive guests alter your playing schedule. Remember, a good tennis party is an organized one and, once the format goes, so does the party—right down the tubes.

With planning, foresight and the company of some friendly tennis folks, a tennis party can be a great way for people to meet, play and socialize.

TENNIS LESSONS

The best equipment, the latest tenniswear and your own court will not improve your strokes, but a teaching pro will. If you are new to tennis, a teaching pro can help you build some fundamentals. If you've been playing for some time, he can help you refine your strokes and help you with tactics and strategy. Even the best players have coaches. When Jimmy Connors, for example, wants to tune up his game, he consults either his mother, Gloria, a teaching pro who taught her son the basics, or Pancho Segura, who helps Connors with strategy and tactics. Choosing a teaching pro and getting the proper instruction are extremely important. If you make a mistake, both your tennis game and your pocketbook will be the victims. But if you make the right choices, you'll get more enjoyment and exercise from tennis than ever before.

WHAT TO LOOK FOR IN A TEACHING PRO

When it comes to selecting the right tennis professional, sometimes a player doesn't have a real choice: there's only one club with one pro in his area and he has to take what he gets.

But where there is a choice, take the time to check out the various pros available to locate the one who seems to be the most qualified and compatible. The best way to do that is to ask a few questions of the club members who've had experience with the pro's teaching. Here are the key questions you should ask:

1. IS THE PRO A MEMBER OF A REPUTABLE ORGANIZATION OF TEACHING PROFESSIONALS? There are two such groups in the United States— the U.S. Professional Tennis Association (USPTA) and the newer Professional Tennis Registry. To become a member of either organization, a pro has to pass written and practical examinations on knowledge of the game and ability to teach it. In choosing a pro who is affiliated with one of the groups, you can be sure that his teaching techniques have been checked out by his peers.

That's particularly important these days because it's an unpleasant but inescapable fact that as tennis has boomed, so has the number of unqualified persons trying to hustle a share of the action by passing themselves off as teaching professionals. The danger of studying with an unqualified pro, especially for a beginner, is the hard-to-change bad habits which can become ingrained.

2. WHAT ARE THE PRO'S PERSONAL CHARACTERISTICS? Like any other teacher, a tennis pro should be patient, interested in his work, have a pleasing personality and take pride in his appearance. If your pro can barely drum up the enthusiasm to drag himself onto the court or if he looks like he just fell off a boxcar, the lesson will probably be equally boring and sloppy.

3. WHAT IS THE PRO'S EXPERIENCE? Question the pro on his teaching philosophy to find out if his goals match yours. If not, look elsewhere. Check with the club members to find out how well the pro teaches at the beginner, intermediate and advanced player levels. If you can find one, select a pro who teaches well at all three levels since he will be able to move you through these levels as you improve.

4. HOW WELL DOES THE PRO PLAY? The better the player, the better his tennis knowledge. However, some excellent players have difficulty in communicating with players at a lower level. Wide teaching experience is often a better indicator of a pro's ability than his tennis game.

5. IS THE PRO GOOD WITH

GROUPS? Even if you wish to take private lessons, look for a pro who is a good group teacher. Group lessons force a pro to work harder and be more observant, characteristics that will carry over to his private lessons.

6. HOW DOES THE PRO RELATE TO HIS STUDENTS? A good pro will be flexible in teaching technique so that anyone can learn to hit the ball. No two people have the same athletic abilities, so a good pro will adjust his methods to each student.

7. DOES THE PRO MAKE HIS LESSONS INTERESTING? If the pro works hard to do that, the lessons will also be fun and you will want to continue. If the lessons are fun, then you will be able to relax and your game will progress faster.

8. DOES THE PRO RESPOND TO STUDENTS? Your pro should progress with you. He should respond to your specific problems so you can become proficient with each stroke before moving onto the more difficult aspects of the game. Your pro should not dismiss a student's own reactions and problems, whether real or imagined. If you feel you are having problems with your serve, the pro should not ignore your comments and work only on, say, your forehand.

9. DOES THE PRO ENCOURAGE PRACTICE? After a lesson, your pro should tell you how to practice the points that were emphasized in the lesson. He ought to be able to think of ways to help you even when you are not taking a lesson. For example, he should be able to give you pointers for practicing in front of a mirror or with a backboard.

Once you get all or most of these questions answered, you'll have a pretty good idea whether or not the pro is for you. In the final analysis, only a lesson will tell you whether you have made the right decision. Chances are that, if you checked the pro first, the lesson will be interesting and fun. You'll be able to relax, knowing that you made the right decision and your game will be on its way to improvement.

PRIVATE VS. GROUP LESSONS: WHICH ARE BEST?

You don't know the difference between a lob and a volley?

There's safety in the numbers of a group lesson, for your ego, your game and your wallet.

You're the terror of the weekend doubles courts? The luxury of having a teaching pro all to yourself may be the way to go.

Whether you pick group or private tennis lessons depends on a couple of things —the state of your game, your pocketbook, the teaching pro and how well you relate to him or her.

But, generally, people whose business is tennis agree that the novice is probably better off in a group, and the advanced student can get the most out of a one-on-one situation.

Vic Braden, the California teaching pro familiar to many television tennis watchers, is a fan of group lessons for the newcomer.

"Tennis is a people game," says Braden. "We've developed just as many champions from groups as from private lessons. But matching the skills in a group is important because each student is a motivator for the others."

That motivator effect is especially im-portant for novices of any age, particularly children, who may get discouraged trying to copy, without success, their pro's picturebook backhand in a private lesson. With four or more equally struggling students on a court, the pressure to perform is diluted.

There are also more partners to play with once the lesson ends. An Alabama pro finds that, in private instruction, some students tend to report for their weekly sessions with a mournful, "Gee, I haven't had a chance to practice since the last time."

More adamant about the virtues of group lessons for the novice is Dennis Van der Meer, founder of the Professional Tennis Registry. "The only way you can learn to play tennis is in a group," he declares.

Not that learning in multiples is always the most prudent method.

Most teaching pros agree that a one-on-one teaching situation is best for a student. In some areas, however, there are not enough qualified pros to go around, and everywhere price is a major consideration. An hour-long private lesson can cost anywhere from $12 to $50 and more, depending on what part of the country you're in and how famous the pro is. Group rates can be substantially less per person.

The economics of spreading the gospel in groups are not lost on either the students or the pros. The ranks of the die-hard one-on-one instructors are steadily losing ground to the "learn-in-numbers" camp, and Eve Kraft, director of the USTA Education and Research Center in Prince-

A group lesson in progress at Pinehurst Tennis Club, Pinehurst, North Carolina.

ton, N.J., offers a convincing why: "If a student cancels a private lesson, the pro loses that hour, but with groups frequently being a pre-paid series, the pro is covered."

Is the private lesson, then, headed for the same fate as grass courts—out-moded and available only to the gifted and/or well heeled?

California pro Paul Xanthos, though not putting it quite so dramatically as that, does remark that there are "so many people now who want to learn, and the pro can make more money" in group lessons, that one-on-one instruction isn't as practical as it once was.

Van der Meer sums up: "The private lesson is passé. Even when I'm teaching Billie Jean King, I have a third person on court to help speed things. If a group is good enough for Billie Jean, I guess it's good enough for everybody."

HOW TO PREPARE FOR YOUR LESSON

To get the most out of your lesson time and money, you have to be prepared—and that means more than just showing up on time. A sampling of teaching pros around the country reveals several keys to insure that you're as ready as you can be when you step onto the lesson court.

Two items—practice and telling the pro just what it is you want to work on—crop up most frequently in the pros' tips on lesson preparation. "The best practice-to-lesson ratio is five to one," offers USPTA pro Kenneth McAllister.

"If you take a half-hour lesson per week, you should devote about two and one-half hours practice time to what you learned."

Most players, the pros agree, neglect a very important stroke—the serve—and the teachers polled offer two simple corrections for the neglect. "Most people just don't practice their serve," says North Carolina coach Jim Leighton. "Take a bucket of balls, get out there and practice that serve," he exhorts, noting that a partner isn't even needed.

But you don't even need a court to hone what USPTA pro Sally Payberg finds is the trickiest part of serving for many: the ball release. "For a few minutes each day," advises the Florida pro, "just practice the release, making sure to let go of the ball only when your arm is fully extended. For many students, this is the hardest part of the serve, and you don't want to waste your lesson time on something that you can practice at home."

An important part of lesson preparation, many pros agree, is to have a definite idea in mind when you go on court about just what you want to work on. "With many intermediates, I've almost got to drag out of them what they want to work on," comments Andy Briant of California. "The student should ask questions and bring things out in the open," he urges. "A game plan is important. The student should be able to review for a few minutes what he learned in the last lesson."

Being in adequate physical shape is also important for lesson preparedness. If you're stiff and creaky, you won't be able to execute the moves your pro is teaching. "Stretching exercises, skipping rope, making big circles with the arms—all these are good to get the muscles used to working," says Barry Andrews, another California teaching pro. "Good muscles are necessary for good tennis," he believes, and recommends an isometric-type exercise for use at home. Assume your normal backhand stance beside a wall and press the racquet against the wall, making the forearm and shoulder muscles work.

Dennis Grainger, a Maryland instruc-

tor, recommends an all-around calisthenics program, including running, jumping rope and sit-ups. Grainger's own exercise program with the juniors he teaches includes swinging the racquet with the cover on, and bouncing the ball (both up from the racquet face and down to the ground) to develop coordination.

Just as important as practice, conditioning and communicating, pros feel, is a student's attitude on the lesson court. "Ideally, you should clear your mind of all outside interests so you can understand what your body is doing and what the instructor is saying," says Andrews.

Preparation, then, means practice, physical condition, communicating, attitude and, of course, a willingness to learn. Oh, and don't forget to show up on time.

WHEN SHOULD YOU GO BACK TO YOUR PRO?

Chris Evert Lloyd does it. So do Bjorn Borg and Virginia Wade. In fact, all of the world's top players—and probably the guy at your club who's always beating you—do it from time to time, too. They go back to their teaching pros or coaches.

Everyone who doesn't have a weekly lesson needs to return to the instructional fold occasionally. But how do you know when it's time?

Your game will tell you. "When an area of your game is consistently off—say, your usually dependable forehand falls apart—then it's time for some brushing up," advises USPTA pro Jack Michalko of Arizona. "You don't want to run to your pro the moment you don't hit a perfect forehand," he cautions. But it's dangerous to let a faltering stroke deteriorate indefinitely; the worse it gets, the longer it will take to correct.

If you suspect that something somewhere is off, but would like to pinpoint it more, try what pro Deborah Welsh Smith of Pennsylvania suggests: keep track of your percentages. "I emphasize to my students that they keep track of how their shots are going, actually noting the percentage of

crosscourt backhands, for example, that are good. Then, if you hit a slump, you can see exactly where the problem is.

"Finding a percentage is an objective thing," Smith adds. "Without charting your stroke performance, all you'll know is that something just 'feels' off."

Florida pro Donald Kaiser has a simple test for slipping shots: "Are you willing to bet on your shot? That's the key. If not, if you know you don't have the knowledge, ability and confidence to hit a good volley, for example, then you need help. If you don't see a pro a few times a year, you get complacent with your game, and then you just perfect your mistakes."

There's another, more serious way to discover that it's lesson time again, and your body will let you know right away. Says Smith: "If you develop tennis elbow, shoulder strain or pulled muscles, any of these warning signs tells you it's time to go back to your pro. But I'd hate to see anyone delay it to the point that they were getting injured."

Problems with strokes alone needn't propel you back to the teaching court; if you've got the shots but not the scores, it could be your strategy that needs work. "When you feel that you're losing more points than your opponent is winning, when you're beating yourself, then the problem may be half stroke production and half strategy," says Michalko.

It doesn't always take a slump or an injury or ingrained bad habits to warrant a return to your pro, however. As Michalko points out, it can be a positive step, signaling a player's arrival at a new stage of development. Says Michalko: "When a beginner progresses to the point where he has the basics down pretty well and wants to go for bigger things, like a twist serve or a half volley, then, too, it's time to see his pro."

How often you go back to your pro will depend, of course, on how often you need it, and that's a purely individual matter. As Texas pro Don Fuller notes: "Everyone ought to go back once in a while. Just time itself tends to cloud things." According to which pro you consult, "every once in a while" can range anywhere from once a month to once a year, from private lessons to a series of group clinics.

The important thing is to go often enough to keep you on top of your game, to forestall injury and to prevent bad habits from getting entrenched. Just ask Chris Evert Lloyd.

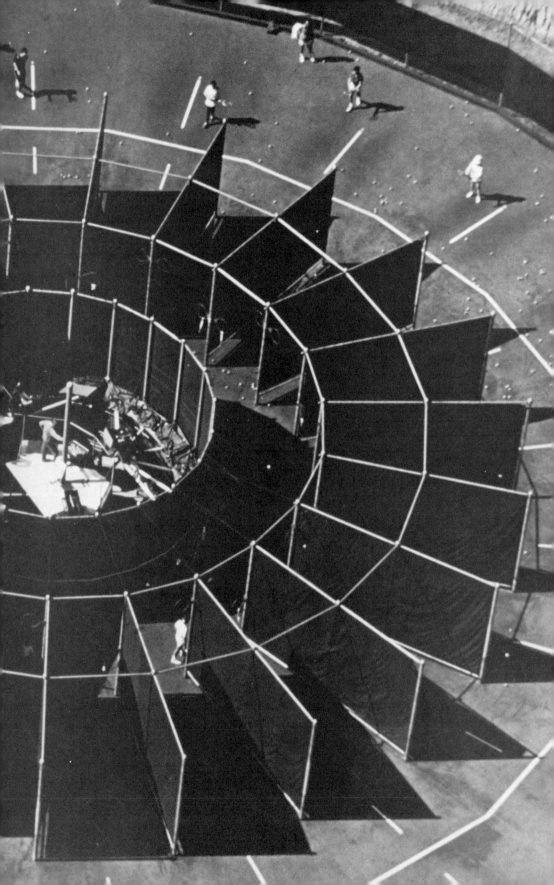

PRACTICE DEVICES

Nothing will help you improve your tennis game like practice. Once you have begun to learn the fundamentals of stroke-making, practice is the one thing that will help them become second nature to you. You can practice with one or more partners, but you can also practice effectively alone—by using backboards, rebound nets, ball machines and practice alleys. You can also help your game by making use of film—both still and moving. Seeing yourself hitting a ball can aid you in identifying and correcting problems with your strokes. By using these practice devices, you will be well on your way to improving your game by using one of the best resources you have—yourself.

HOW TO IMPROVE BY USING A BACKBOARD

Hitting against a wall of any sort—be it a backboard, the side of a building, an outdoor handball court or a garage door—is the simplest and most convenient way to practice. Many great players, from the French star of the 1920's, René Lacoste, to the Polish star of the 1970's, Wojtek Fibak, have either gotten started in tennis or worked on their strokes during their careers by playing against a backboard. Here the famed former coach of the Australian Davis Cup team, Harry Hopman, tells how to use a board to develop all your strokes:

Put me in front of a board, a wall, a packing case or even a slab of cement at least six feet wide and six feet high and I will never lack for a way to improve my game and my form. The backboard always gives me consistent returns and—with a little imagination—it can be used to practice a variety of strokes from the beginner to the championship level.

GROUND STROKES: The most obvious use of the backboard is for practicing the ground strokes, but I prefer to employ it for working on volleys, half volleys, overheads and serves. Those shots are harder than the ground strokes, of course, but that's my point: You shouldn't use the backboard just for the strokes you like best. Use it to practice your weaknesses, too.

You can start your backboard practice by warming up with your ground strokes. Stand well away from the board, remembering that the net is 39 feet from the baseline, and hit the ball so it strikes the board well above the net line. That way, the ball will come back to you so you can hit it after one bounce—just as you would in actual play.

Practice hitting forehands and backhands alternately and angle some of your shots so you have to run to reach the ball on the next rebound. Anticipate the direction of the ball to give you time to set up properly with your racquet back well before the ball comes to you. Keep your eyes sharply focused on the ball at all times. It will make your session more meaningful if you see how many shots you can hit in a row with the ball bouncing only once after coming off the wall.

VOLLEYS: For your volleys, you should stand much closer to the backboard; about 12 feet is best, I find. Drop the ball and hit it so it rebounds a few feet to your left. Leap and lunge for the ball as though you were intercepting it with a backhand volley at the net. Then do the same thing on the forehand side. Try to keep any ball from getting past you; remember that you are trying to improve your reflexes as well as your stroking.

Low volleys and half volleys can be practiced by standing about 15 feet from

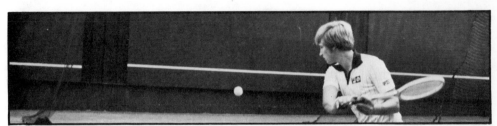

the backboard so the ball comes back to you either close to the ground for half volleys or about two feet high for low volleys. Get down low for your half volleys and use a shorter stroke than you would use for a normal ground stroke.

Your low volley should be a firm blocking shot with, perhaps, a little slice on it. Angle your low volleys to the side, if you can, since that's the way you'll have to hit them in match play. As with the half volley, get down to the ball and keep a firm wrist as you hit the ball.

SERVES: When you practice your serve at the backboard, it's best to stand a full half-court away from the board. If your space is limited, however, you can still work on your serve. Aim about 18 inches above the usual net line if you have only about half the usual distance available. The first thing to do is practice your ball release without hitting the ball. When you have achieved a consistent release, try a few flat serves and run for the ball as it ricochets off the wall. Then work on developing or improving the slice and kick serves.

OVERHEADS: To practice your overhead smash at the backboard, you first have to get the ball to loop up in the air as a lob does. To do that, stand about 12 feet

from the wall and hit the ball down sharply so it bounces on the ground just in front of the wall. The ball will bound up, graze the backboard and continue upward and outward with a lob-like trajectory. Now, you can run back and hit the ball in the air with an overhead. Smash the ball down so it again bounces on the ground just in front of the wall and, once again, rises like a lob. Keep this exchange of lobs and smashes going until you get tired.

Don't neglect the backhand smash, either. Hit an occasional ball to your backhand side and experiment with the shot. Try to get your arm up high and watch the ball carefully.

You can also hit the ball so the lob goes deep, forcing you to run back and take the ball after the bounce, either as a smash or as a forehand drive. The possibilities are endless.

If you approach backboard practice the right way, it can be both profitable and fun. There are so many strokes and combinations of strokes you can try out that you should easily be able to keep it entertaining. And, at the very least, spending time at the backboard beats hanging around idly waiting for a court or an opponent.

BUILD YOUR OWN BACKBOARD IN FOUR EASY STEPS

In these days of busy lifestyles and crowded local courts, few social tennis players can take the time to practice enough so they make real progress in the sport. But there is a practical alternative: a do-it-yourself backyard backboard.

A backboard may not be as convivial as a human practice partner, but it has a number of compensating advantages. It is *always* available, it *always* returns the ball and it *never* criticizes a flubbed shot. A few minutes a day at a backboard, moreover, can quickly put a new sharpness in your game, as many top players will attest.

If you follow the construction plan described here, you'll wind up with a substantial unit that should last for many years. It can be built by anyone who can use simple woodworking tools, and it can be assembled and erected in less than a couple of weekends.

But because it's designed to last, the board is not cheap. In fact, depending on the cost of lumber in your area, you'll probably have to pay something in the neighborhood of $160 for the necessary materials. Still, it's an investment that will repay itself over the years and, thus, should be

worthwhile—especially when you compare it with the cost of tennis lessons or court rentals.

You'll need a lot of room for both the backboard and the playing area in front of it. Ideally, you should have a space that is about half the size of a normal singles court (27 feet by 39 feet)—although you could manage with an area of only 16 feet by 20 feet. The playing area should be flat and paved with either asphalt or concrete.

The siting of the board should be done with care. If you have a strong fence, the board could be bolted to the fence supports. However, your neighbors might object to stray balls whistling by as they sip cocktails on their patio. An alternative might be to attach the board to the side of your garage or house. Nearby windows or fragile siding around the board should probably be protected with strong chicken wire fencing.

Noise can also be a problem with backboards. Not only do the balls often make a loud "thwack!" as they bounce off the board, but your yard may become a social attraction for all the tennis players on your street. So consider the possible noise pollution before you erect the board.

The backboard described here consists of four 8-foot-by-4-foot sheets of three-quarter-inch exterior grade plywood held together by construction grade 2 by 4's (see list of materials). If the board is to be self-supported, then you'll also need some 4-by-4 posts. You can put the board together by using basic woodworking hand

tools, although you'll find that the work will go faster with a small circular saw and an electric drill. Assembled, the board is quite heavy so you'll need an extra hand or two to erect it.

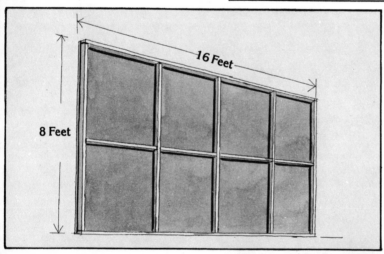

1. Start by sawing all the lumber to size (see the dimension drawing directly above). It's helpful to lay the sheets of plywood on the floor and put the bracing on top as a check on the dimensions. The center horizontal cross braces will each be about 3 feet 8 inches long.

2. Lay the framing on the floor and assemble it by toe-nailing (see inset). Start with the outside sections, then insert the vertical braces and finally the center cross braces. You'll need a friend to help keep the assembly square during nailing.

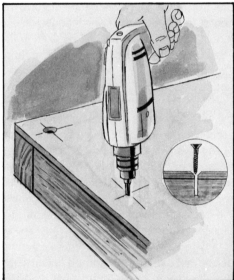

3. Drill and countersink (see inset) holes of each plywood sheet for the wood screws that will attach the sheets to the frame. The holes at the corners of each sheet should continue right through the frame because they will be needed for bolts that will attach the board to its supports.

4. Screw each plywood sheet to the frame. Pinning each sheet lightly with nails first will help you keep it firmly butted to the adjacent sheets. Each screw should be countersunk below the surface of the sheet and the tops filled with plastic wood filler.

SHOULD YOU SPRING FOR A REBOUND NET?

Many players prefer to work out by batting the ball around with a friend or fellow club member. Others like the very real benefits of spending time in front of a backboard to smooth out the rough spots. They either ignore or are put off by the idea of using a rebound net. And to be sure, the rebound net is not an inexpensive practice tool. The cost runs from about $20 to almost $200 for a net that has extra features and is suitable for the heavy use it would get at a school, club or camp practice area.

Still, the rebound net represents an excellent investment for every player or tennis facility that can afford one. Looking something like a trampoline tipped up on its side, the rebound net can be used by a beginner as well as an advanced player. And it's hard to beat for versatility.

It doesn't require much space, it can be used outdoors or inside and it gives a return that more nearly resembles a ball struck by a racquet than a backboard does. By changing the tension and degree of inclination of the net, moreover, it can be used for practicing ground strokes as well as volleys, overheads and serves. A player can even set some nets so he receives high,

low, shallow, deep, hard or soft rebounds.

The basic rebound net consists of a nylon net strung on a sturdy metal frame about eight feet by seven feet or larger. The net's tension is adjustable by tightening or slackening the straps that secure the net to the frame. Most have a tape across the center to simulate the conventional top of a tennis net. A simple net will be fixed in the vertical postiton at a slight angle. The more expensive nets can be tilted to vary the height or distance of the returns.

The larger rebound nets can be used by two players for doubles practice and some can be used by several people from both sides at the same time. You'll find that an area of around 10 feet by 20 feet will provide ample room for rebound-net practice. In use, the net is almost silent, unlike the backboard which can produce an unpleasant booming sound.

Some teaching pros prefer the rebound net over the backboard because the net allows you more time to get ready for the next shot. That's because the net lengthens the rebound interval by giving slightly and literally absorbing the ball before it is returned. And it does that without greatly reducing the velocity. It gives the player the time he needs to prepare himself for the next shot. It also provides the hitter with a "set-up ball"—one which is returned at a constant speed and height.

You'll find the rebound net a useful tool in many ways, particularly for following up a tennis lesson with practice and drill. By using the rebound net to work on a stroke

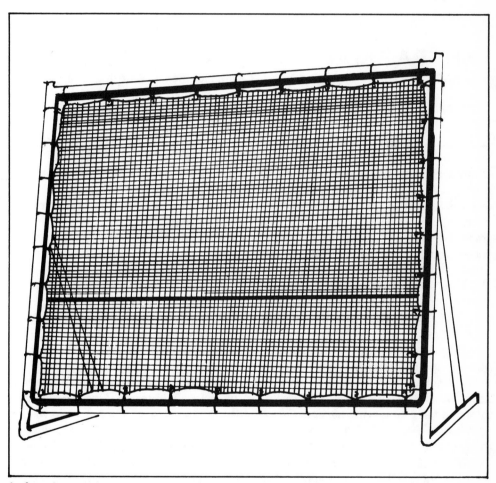

before the next lesson, you'll start to establish the stroke in your neuromuscular system.

And, you can play against yourself by trying to establish your own records for consecutive forehands and backhands. It's not too difficult to achieve more than 50 hits; in one camp, the record for the fore-

hand is more than 1,000.

To get the most out of your rebound net, you should employ some specific drills to follow up on your lessons and groove your strokes. You can turn some of these drills into games with other club or family members. Indeed, practice at the rebound net can be fun as well as quite hard work.

WHAT A BALL MACHINE CAN DO FOR YOUR GAME

Given a choice, most players will opt for playing a few sets rather than feeding balls to a friend who wants to work on his backhand or his overhead. It's not easy to find someone who can consistently hit balls to you so you can develop the rhythm that is so essential in tennis.

One solution to the practice problem is to buy one of those mechanical gadgets that will tirelessly hurl balls over the net more or less at your command.

Buying a ball machine is rather like purchasing a car. You can choose an economy model for only $50 that serves up a short lob repetitiously, as if the pro was tossing a ball to you underhanded. Or you can invest up to $7,500 for sophisticated models with built-in retrieval systems, micro-computers that program patterns of up to 99 shots or that can even provide a strong or weak game plan and an infinite number of shot variations of varying velocities.

If you're a beginner, then a simple machine will probably suit your purposes. If you're an advanced player, you'll probably get more out of a machine that offers variable spin, that alternates balls to your forehand and backhand and that can produce a pattern of short and deep shots. As with the purchase of an automobile, there's no substitute for the test drive. If you can, try out a machine before you purchase it to see if it can produce the complexity of shots your game needs.

There are three basic types of ball machines. The simplest machines replicate the action of a racquet; that is, they have a throwing arm that sends the ball to you with the desired trajectory. Most of these simpler impact machines do not oscillate (throw balls alternately to either side of the court) and do not have the ability to add spin. Some, however, may have an inherent slight topspin action.

The second type of machine is slightly more sophisticated, using two contra-rotating wheels to squeeze the ball and shoot it out in the desired direction. These rotary machines are often available with an oscillating action and different degrees of spin can be obtained. One machine will deliver a preset pattern of shots to various points in the court. The rotary machines are often quite heavy—150 pounds or more—and are more expensive than the impact type. But they are generally quieter in operation.

The third type of ball machine uses compressed air to shoot the ball in the same way as an air rifle. The air machines don't put much spin on the ball, but they usually offer an oscillating option and are relatively light in weight. One such machine, the Prince, offers an extension pipe

Compressed Air Ball Machine

that allows the machine to simulate serves. Since the air machines have few moving parts, maintenance is said to be less of a problem than with the mechanical throwers.

When you start checking into the ball-machine market, you may have difficulty finding machines to examine. Only the largest sporting goods stores are likely to have one in stock and it's not probable that they'll have enough room for you to try it out. Many manufacturers sell their machines through teaching pros. Naturally, an agent who is a pro will be able to demonstrate the machine on his court, and you should be able to hit a few with the machine. Make an appointment for a demonstration, though, because teaching pros often have pretty tight lesson schedules.

Ask about the options available and their cost. If you intend to use the machine alone, some form of remote control is necessary. Some manufacturers offer tiny radio controls that can be carried in your pocket. Others have foot switches that require a cable connection with the machine.

For all except the outright beginner, most pros recommend an oscillating machine. The stationary type is fine for grooving the basic strokes, but eventually you'll want to practice your footwork also. Even better than the oscillating machine is the type that not only delivers balls to either side of the court, but will also produce a preset pattern of short and deep balls.

You should ask about ball capacity. Fifty balls at one loading may not be enough for an intermediate or advanced player. On the other hand, you won't want to risk possible injury from running about on a tennis court that is littered with several hundred balls. A capacity of 150 balls should be plenty for the non-professional user.

See if the machine can be moved easily by one person. Most have wheels and some have convenient lifting handles. Look

also for too-small wheels and sharp projections that might damage your court surface.

After you have settled on a machine that meets your needs, question the supplier about maintenance. Find out if the manufacturer has any arrangements for service in your area. It may be difficult to obtain parts rapidly unless the local agent maintains his own supply. You may even have to take the machine to some central location for repairs. If you do, weight and the ability of the machine to fit in your car become important factors.

When you get your machine and have it assembled and working properly, practice slowly at first. Put the machine on its slowest speed and set it at a stationary action. Adjust the trajectory so the ball bounces about two or three feet beyond the service line of the opposite half of the court. Then practice your ground strokes. When you feel confident with the machine, you can experiment with different speeds and with the oscillating facility.

You'll find the machine very useful for practicing volleys, but don't start volleying until you've learned the idiosyncrasies of your machine from the ground-stroke practice. When you start on volleys, have the machine on a slow speed again and have the shot clear the net sufficiently high so you can volley easily. As you become more confident, you can speed up the action and lower the trajectory.

Although most inexpensive machines do not have a service action, you can simulate the service by making the machine toss balls into the appropriate service court. If your machine has adjustable spin, experiment with the settings for topspin and sliced serves.

Your new ball machine can also help you get plenty of practice on overheads. Start by setting the machine to toss easy lobs you can hit from a position at the net. Then gradually increase the depth of the lobs, but have a long interval between the shots so you can return to your net position after each overhead. In this way, you'll get used to running back to return the deep lob.

A daily half-hour of practice with a ball machine will probably do more for your tennis than several sets of tennis each day. There is a danger that you might use the machine to ingrain bad habits as well as good, so supplement your practice with lessons from your pro occasionally. You'll probably find that he will be able to suggest ways of getting even more out of your ball machine practice.

USING A PRACTICE ALLEY

Your own ball machine can help you improve, but for many people the idea is impractical for space and for financial reasons. It's also difficult to get a pro to give you access to his machine, for which you'll also need valuable court time. While backboards are tremendously useful practice devices, they do have some limitations. So do practice partners. It's not always easy to find someone with the time or the patience to spend hours helping you work on the deficiencies in your game.

A newer solution to the practice problem may well be a practice alley. Hundreds of them have been established around the country in recent years, and they're offering players a handy and efficient way to hone their strokes.

What is a practice alley, or tennis lane, as it is also called?

Basically, it's a narrow, confined area (usually less than half the width and at least half the length of a normal tennis court) separated from adjoining courts or alleys by some type of screen. Within this area, a player can practice his or her strokes by using a ball-machine system.

Although most alleys are rectangular in design, there is an interesting alternative type that's known as the geometric practice lane. Pioneered and first built by famed tennis instructor Vic Braden in 1970 at his Tennis College near San Diego, the geometric lane makes the most of the available space. About 20 alleys can be constructed side by side around a circular core. The geometric alleys, when completed, resemble wedges of a huge pie, with ball machines located at the narrow ends of the alleys (see pp. 146 and 160).

Some facilities solve the time-consuming problem of picking up balls with ingenious ball-retrieval systems that use mesh screens, sloping wood ramps and even a bowl-shaped court construction. For example, a typical system might use a nylon mesh curtain, hung about five to 10 feet behind the net; it catches balls hit by a player and drops them onto a ramp which feeds them back into the machine for refiring. Under another system, there is a large, bowl-shaped depression in the middle of the court on the ball machine's side of the net; balls roll down the slope and are channeled back to the base of the machine where a special mechanism scoops them up to be used again.

No one knows for sure how long alleys have been around. But a couple of crude lanes may have been built in the New York City area in the 1930's, according to Braden, who's generally recognized as the leading authority in the field. Braden had a simple, straight lane constructed at the Toledo (Ohio) Tennis Club in 1952, and it

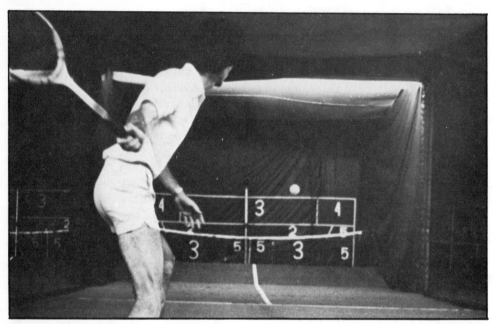

Lanes at the East Side Tennis Club in New York City have target areas for improving placement.

was his innovative design of the geometric alleys several years ago that touched off the nationwide trend in tennis alleys.

Since then, many new clubs have capitalized on the idea, installing several of the lanes instead of constructing an extra court in the hope of satisfying members who want to practice but don't have the time and/or the money to rent a court and an instructor for a couple of hours. Generally, use of practice lanes is quite economical, with typical rates averaging about $5 for each half-hour. That may not sound all that reasonable, until you take into consideration the fact that, with the advanced ball machines and the even more advanced

ball-retrieval systems, you'll probably get to hit about 300 to 400 shots in your half-hour—that is, if your arm and legs hold out.

Where can you find a practice alley if you haven't heard of one in your town or seen one advertised? The best course is to pick up your phone and start calling local tennis clubs. If you don't have any luck at one facility, ask if they can direct you to another club that does offer alleys. There are even a few clubs that are devoted entirely to practice lanes, so check if any are in operation near you by asking around or consulting the telephone yellow pages.

Once you find an alley, though, be careful. Just like any other training device,

the practice lane can be used improperly. And you could end up hurting your strokes instead of honing them.

Your attitude when you first enter a practice alley should be focused on developing proper stroke production. If you're a beginner, be sure to have a professional instructor with you. He can tell you how to stroke the ball properly. Without that kind of professional guidance, the chances are you'll be grooving incorrect strokes and developing bad habits which will be tough to break later.

Advanced players can also use practice lanes to their advantage, especially if they're having problems with particular shots. In these cases, the alleys provide a controlled environment for experimentation. But here, too, it would be wise to enlist the assistance of a trained teaching pro.

When you use a lane, your first move should be to adjust the ball machine for the type of shot you want to practice. You can set it to regulate speed, direction and elevation. With a couple of the more advanced machines, you can even program a number of different shots to be fired consecutively. But, if you're new to the game, don't complicate things by varying the speed and spin on the ball.

After the machine is adjusted, assume your ready position on the other side of the net. Then, simply follow the directions of your instructor. Or, if you're working by yourself, you can aim for target areas that are clearly marked in many lanes.

To get the most out of your time at the alley, resist the temptation to "cheat" against the machine because you know its firing pattern. If you're practicing moving to the right for forehands, for example, position yourself well away from the contact area. Don't try to get an extra jump on the shot by inching toward the area where you know the ball will land before it's even been fired from the machine. You're defeating your purpose in practicing and wasting your money as well. And don't think the ball machine can do all of the work in solving your problems. Make it tough on yourself—you'll get more out of your practice session.

You should recognize, though, that a practice alley can take you only so far in the game. As Braden notes: "If a player has really fine strokes and he still can't win, he needs match play under stress, not lanes. Some people become so good on the alleys, it looks like they can do almost anything, like beating Jimmy Connors or Bjorn Borg. But then, they get on a real court and fall apart.

"Although lanes can be very beneficial, it's important that students don't get tied down with them. The personal element in competitive play is extremely important. In other words, the practice lane is not a panacea for the tennis player. Remember, you'll never have to play a big match in an alley. A lot of people are champions of the lanes, but not the tennis courts!"

Still, a practice lane can be of immense value to players who are developing their strokes or trying to correct them. So try one. It could be right up your alley.

HOW TO ANALYZE YOUR STROKES WITH A CAMERA

In their dogged efforts to improve their games, most tennis players overlook one obvious and simple aid which they may already possess or can easily acquire: the home camera. Intelligent on-court use of photographs and/or movies is one of the quickest ways to upgrade your game.

U.S. Davis Cup captain and TENNIS Magazine Instruction Advisory Board member Tony Trabert likes to use instant photography to spot his pupils' stroking weaknesses and correct them. Here he describes how he does it:

In the years I've been teaching tennis, I've noticed that many players don't have a good mental picture of themselves hitting a tennis ball. I can tell a student what to do and get an enthusiastic nod of agreement, but the player will then go right on doing the same thing wrong.

INSTANT CAMERAS: Videotape is an excellent way to overcome that problem, because the player himself can actually see his mistakes. But it's too expensive for use by individuals. I've found you can get many of the same benefits through the use of instant cameras. They'll take fine pictures

for immediate critiques on the court.

To use an instant camera for tennis analysis, all you need are a court, a relatively bright day and someone to feed balls to the player. If you're taking the pictures, position yourself about 15 feet from your subject and to one side so you are facing the player at about a 45-degree angle to the baseline. That way, you'll get the shot you want and

A student's ground stroke captured on film by TENNIS Magazine Advisory Board member Tony Trabert.

minimize the risk of being hit by the ball.

Before you start taking pictures, have the subject act out the stroke in slow motion while you look through the viewfinder to be sure you are covering the whole range of the stroke. The person who's feeding balls to your subject should be stationed at the net and asked to throw or hit a succession of balls, preferably to the same point on the court. You should then take a series

A tennis pro films a side view of a pupil's two-handed backhand.

of photos of each part of the stroke—the ready position, the backswing, the forward swing, the contact and the follow-through.

Study the pictures to see if the player is hitting the ball properly. If you'd like further assistance in this analysis, I suggest you show the pictures to a teaching professional or compare them with the high-speed photo sequences in TENNIS Magazine's Instruction Portfolio series.

Because the speed of an instant camera is relatively slow (about one two-hundredth of a second on a bright day), you will probably see some blurring of the hand and racquet. That can be an advantage, though, since the blurring will tell you if contact is being made when the racquet is moving fastest.

Once you see the errors in your strokes, you should work deliberately at correcting them through practice. Then, after you feel you've made progress, take more pictures to check on how you're coming along. Keep this process up and before long, who knows? Your game may become picture perfect.

MOVIE CAMERAS: A super-8 movie camera can work as well as Trabert's instant photography. Many tennis families

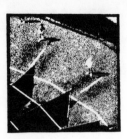

What films reveal about these forehands.

The strip on the left shows a faulty stroke with a racquet preparation that's too high (top frame), weight on the back foot with contact too close to the body (center) and a backward lean on the follow-through (bottom).

The later strip on the right indicates that the student is now beginning to lean into the shot (top frame), is making contact ahead of the front hip (center) although the ball could have been hit at a higher point in its flight, and is following through completely.

own home movie cameras, but perhaps relatively few have ever thought of using them to film their strokes and pinpoint the faults in their game. They won't see the results right away as they will with instant photo cameras (unless they have one of the new instant movie cameras). But they will capture the entire motion of the swing and, if their projectors have still features, they can examine a stroke frame by frame.

It's even possible now to take tennis movies at an indoor court without lights by using such cameras as the Kodak XL series. Indoors or out, bring along a couple of cartridges; each one is good for three minutes and 20 seconds, which should be enough for about 50 strokes.

If you'd like to use a movie camera for stroke therapy, you need three people: a cameraman, someone to feed balls and, of course, a subject. The cameraman should film from these three positions:

- At the net on the side where the player hits the ball for front views.
- Directly opposite the point of racquet contact for side views.
- Behind the players to show racquet and ball contact.

Have the ball-feeder stand just on the other side of the net and toss or hit balls to the same spot each time. On ground strokes, record the subject hitting several of the balls from each of the three positions. You should also film the player hitting alternate forehands and backhands by having the ball-feeder toss one ball to the player's forehand and then another ball to the backhand. Keep the camera running continuously so you can see the player recover from forehand to backhand.

FUNDAMENTALS TO WATCH FOR ON FILM

Ground stroke checklist
1. Body turning sideways?
2. Racquet well back?
3. Watching the ball?
4. Contact made ahead of front hip?
5. Weight moving forward?
6. Follow-through completed?

Service checklist
1. Releasing the ball forward of the baseline?
2. Watching the ball?
3. Ball lifted to maximum reach?

4. Racquet head "scratching" your back?
5. Wrist snap on contact?
6. Follow-through complete on other side?

Volley checklist
1. Upper body turned?
2. Short backswing?
3. Watching the ball?
4. Contact made out in front?
5. Weight forward?
6. Follow-through completed?

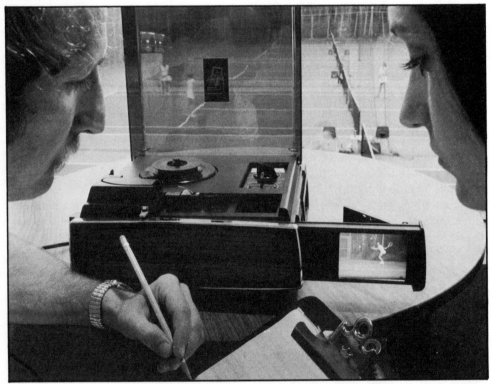

The screening. *Once films are developed, they should be reviewed on a projector which allows movies to be reviewed with slow-motion and stop-action.*

Follow the same procedure for the volleys. Get several takes of forehand and backhand volleys from all three positions, then record alternate forehand and backhand volleys.

With two cartridges, you should have enough film to record ground strokes, volleys, the serve, overhead and lob.

The principles involved in filming tennis strokes are no different than those that apply to any other kind of movie photography. But keep these points in mind:

● Hold the camera firmly with one eye pressed to the viewfinder. Keep the other eye open so you can see the ball coming.

● Start shooting the moment the player moves his racquet and continue until the swing is completed.

● Be sure that the player stays completely in the light or completely in shade throughout the stroke so the exposure control adjusts to the subject and not the back-

ground area.

• Keep the player centered within the viewfinder markings. On the serve, angle the camera so you can catch the ball at the peak of its rise.

• Focus extra carefully if you are using telephoto or wide-angle lenses.

If you have a movie camera with several speeds, use the highest one for filming tennis strokes so you will get a slower motion when you project the developed film. Remember, though, that you'll use more film at the higher speed.

After your film has been developed, watching it on a projector can be almost as exciting as playing tennis. However, don't run the film merely for the pleasure of seeing yourself (or others) in action on the screen. Examine it carefully to pick out any weaknesses in your stroking. Again, you can compare your technique to the high-speed photo sequences that appear in TENNIS Magazine's Instruction Portfolio series. List your weaknesses and then concentrate on remedying them during practice sessions.

When you feel that your game has improved, have more films taken and compare them with the original set. If you can't see an improvement, the time has come to take some tennis lessons. But you should see an improvement after each time you watch films of yourself hitting on court, because the mental pictures you carry of your strokes will be stronger in your mind. You'll be better able to eliminate your mistakes because you've seen them happen.

PHYSICAL AND MENTAL CONDITIONING

Tennis is a great way to get a lot of exercise in a small amount of space in a short amount of time. But don't kid yourself. Just smacking the ball around the court a couple of times a week doesn't give your body all the exercise it needs for you to be in top playing shape.

To play the best tennis of which you're capable—and to feel your healthiest—you should supplement your playing sessions with a sensible combination of conditioning exercises and a proper diet. You might also want to build up your endurance with a running program and check out other sports which may benefit your tennis as well. Moreover, you should not ignore mental fitness, which often provides the winning edge you need in crucial moments.

TWENTY WAYS TO TONE UP YOUR BODY

A daily conditioning program will keep you from feeling creaky the day after a hard-fought singles match. And you'll find yourself making those shots you used to miss, even though you thought you ought to be able to get to them in time.

There are no instant routes to becoming a fleet-footed, flat-bellied dynamo of the deuce court. But the exercises shown here can be done by most weekend players. It would be a good idea for you to consult your physician before you begin them—particularly if you have any history of muscular injuries. Start the exercises slowly and gradually increase the number of times you repeat them. To all or any of these exercises, you can add such endurance-building activities as jumping rope or cycling if you are a non-runner.

Isometric Conditioners: These isometric exercises (so called because the muscles push against each other constantly) can be done anytime you have a few minutes to spare and anywhere—watching TV, at the office, when your car is stopped in traffic or while you're waiting for a court. Hold each exercise for a count of five and then relax. Gradually increase to 10 times.

Tennis Muscle Strengtheners: These exercises are designed to strengthen those muscles that get the most use when you are playing tennis. The broomstick, ball squeezing and shadow-stroking exercises will strengthen your arm and wrist muscles, while the sit-ups and powerhouse pivots will build your stomach muscles.

Daily Tone-Up Exercises: These exercises can help increase your flexibility and therefore your range on court. The better your range, the better your chances will be of returning those hard-to-reach shots with less risk of injury. Each exercise requires stretching the muscles to a maximum without causing pain.

Do these exercises in a passive, slow manner. Do not jerk, bounce or otherwise force the muscles to stretch beyond the limits of comfort. Hold the stretched position for 10 to 60 seconds for each exercise. The longer the position is held, the better.

ISOMETRIC CONDITIONERS

Hand Pull. *Curl the fingers together. Take a deep breath and try to pull the hands apart.*

Shoulder Press. *Place the palms together in front of the right shoulder with the right arm bent at a 45-degree angle from the waist. Pressing down with the left hand, try to raise the right arm into an upright position. Repeat with the opposite arm and shoulder.*

Palm Press. *Place the palms together in front of the chest, with the fingers pointed straight up, and the elbows elevated parallel to the floor. Take a deep breath and press palms together.*

Grand Prix Press. *While stopped in traffic, place the hands on either side of the steering wheel with the palms facing and the elbows extended. Take a deep breath, grip the wheel firmly and push the hands together on the opposite rim of the wheel.*

TENNIS MUSCLE STRENGTHENERS

Powerhouse Pivots. Stand tall, legs wide apart, knees straight, feet firmly on the floor and raise both arms in a boxer's stance. Slowly twist the trunk to the right looking directly behind you. Hold, and punch the arm directly 180 degrees behind you. Return slowly to the center. Repeat the full twist to the left and return after the hold and punch. Twist only at the waist. Begin with 10 full repetitions and work up to 50.

Shadow Stroking. Add weight to your racquet by slipping one or more tennis balls inside the cover. Stand at an imaginary baseline and stroke smoothly, alternating between backhands and forehands.

Wrist Twister. Tape a weight onto the straw end of a broom. Place it between the legs and squat. Lift the broom handle slowly, bringing it from the floor to a position even with your hand, about knee level. Brace the elbow on the knee and twist the broom slowly—first to the left, then to the right. After 60 seconds, shift hands. Practice the exercise for five minutes three times a week.

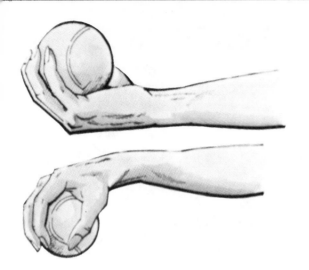

Ball Squeeze. *Squeeze a tennis ball in a palms-up position for a count of five. Relax and repeat 10 times. Next, grip the ball with the hand down, repeating as before. Then switch hands. A hole punched in the ball will make it easier to start.*

Sit-ups. *Lie on your back with your legs bent at the knees, feet spread 12 inches apart and your hands behind your head. Lift your body into a seated position, twist and touch the left elbow to the right knee. Then lie back. Repeat, twisting to touch the right elbow to the left knee.*

Broomstick Twists. *Attach a rope to a broomstick and a brick with a hole in it. With both palms up, slowly roll the entire rope into the stick handle. Then slowly unwind. Alternate by turning palms down and repeating the exercise. Start with three daily, building to a total of eight in each position.*

DAILY TONE-UP EXERCISES

Butterfly. *Stretches the groin area, important in side-to-side tennis moves. With the knees bent, grasp the feet and bring the trunk forward.*

Back Arch. *Stretches the abdominal muscle group. Do a push-up, keeping the pelvis against the floor. Look at the ceiling.*

Side Trunk Stretch. *Stretches the side muscles, important in serves and backhands. Standing straight, with both feet flat on the floor, extend one arm along the side of the leg as far down as possible. Repeat with the other arm.*

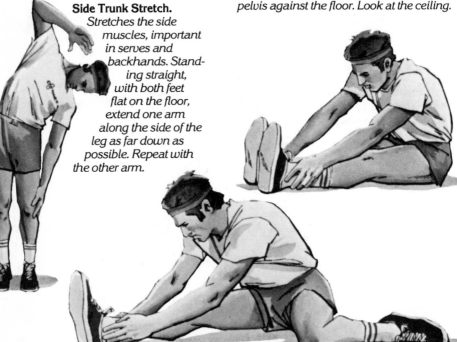

Hurdler's Stretch. *Stretches the hamstring, the muscle that's most commonly pulled in tennis. For the single stretch (above) extend one leg forward and grasp the ankle. With the other leg bent back, bring the trunk forward. For the double stretch (above right), keep the legs together and extended. Grasp the ankles and bend the trunk forward.*

Arm Stretch. *Increases the range of motion in the arms and shoulders. Try to hold hands with yourself behind your back.*

Calf Stretch. *Stretches the calf and Achilles' tendon. Stand with your hands against a wall. Place one foot in back of you and push against the wall to keep heel flat against the floor. Repeat with the other foot.*

Back Stretch. *Increases the back's range of motion. Recline on back and bring the legs overhead.*

Side Quad Stretch. *Stretches the front of the thigh, a major running muscle. Recline on the right side, grasp the left ankle and pull gently. Repeat on the left side.*

Inner Thigh Stretch. *Stretches the inner thighs and lower back. In a sitting position, grasp the ankles of outstretched legs and bend the trunk forward between them.*

James Fixx

HOW RUNNING CAN HELP YOUR TENNIS

The tennis boom of the early 1970's was followed by the jogging boom. Jim Fixx's "The Complete Book of Running," one of the publishing phenomenons of the decade, was one of the bibles of that boom. Here Fixx talks with the editors of TENNIS magazine about the benefits of running for the tennis player and the intelligent way to go about it.

TENNIS: Let's start by establishing whether there is a difference between running and jogging.

Fixx: Although some might argue the point, I don't think there's any particular speed at which jogging turns to running. If you feel that you're running—no matter how slow you're going—no one can say you're not.

How much running do you do? I run 10 miles a day, every day. Sometimes, for a treat, I do 15.

Do you play tennis? Only infrequently now. But I used to be a regular and enthusiastic player. As a kid, I lived in Jackson Heights, N.Y.—that's the stop before Forest Hills on the subway line—and I worked as a ball boy at the U.S. championships. I played

No. 1 on my high school tennis team. And when I was in the army in Korea, we had a tennis court and I played all the time. I became a fairly good player.

How can jogging or running help the tennis player? Running will build up your cardiovascular system, which means your endurance. You'll be able to perform at a higher level longer. You'll cover more ground. And you won't find it so difficult to continue bending your knees. When you get tired, you tend to straighten up and you know how disastrous that is for your ground strokes and volleys.

Aside from your heart and lungs, running is helpful mostly for your legs. It doesn't do much for the upper body and the upper body is extremely important in tennis. To stroke the ball properly, you've got to twist your trunk. So you should do other kinds of exercises to develop flexibility in the upper body—sit-ups, push-ups, torso-twisting, calisthenics of that nature.

Is the technique for distance running the same as you would use on a tennis court? No, and the disparities are significant. In distance running, the foot works like part of the circumference of a wheel. You come down first on the heel and roll forward to the front part of the foot, while in tennis, you're trying to stay on the balls of your feet—making as little contact as possible with the surface—so you can move fast and cat-like. You don't have time to lope like the distance runner.

There is no reason, however, why you can't occasionally incorporate the tennis

foot action into distance running and get the benefits of both techniques. For example, at various intervals in your distance running, you can take quick steps on the balls of your feet for 30 or 40 yards. You can run sideways, switching lead sides, and even backwards, interspersing the tennis techniques at appropriate points on your route.

What procedures would you recommend to someone who wants to start running? First, determine in your own mind how far you think you can run and how fast—and then start by doing half as much. If you don't have any concept at all of your capacity, you might reasonably begin by running 300 or 400 yards, walking the same distance and then running 300 or 400 yards, no more than that the first time out. In all, that's less than half a mile of running. The next day, if you're not wiped out from that first workout, you might step up to three-quarters of a mile with interspersed walking.

You shouldn't allow yourself to get to the point where you feel very, very fatigued. After you take your shower and get dressed, you should feel refreshed, not destroyed. If you find yourself sitting there with your head in your hands, you've done too much. If you want a goal, you might think of building up to three miles a day, or a total of 20 miles a week put together whatever way you fancy. You could run five miles four days a week or perhaps shorter distances on weekdays and longer distances on weekends, as many people prefer.

The important thing is to total 20 miles. The most recent study—an excellent one— concludes that 20 miles of running a week makes an enormous improvement in your general health. The study showed, for example, that people who run 20 miles have 60 percent less chance of having a heart attack compared with those who don't run 20 miles.

Wouldn't running 20 miles a week severely cut into a tennis player's court time? Not if you look for convenient opportunities to run. You don't have to run formally, wearing the proper apparel. For example, if you wear crepe sole shoes and your place of work is a mile or so from your home, there is no reason you can't run the distance on a crisp, fall day when you won't perspire and need a shower afterward.

Or if you need to take your car to a garage for servicing, instead of having your wife or someone else drive over in another car to transport you back, you can drive over alone, run home and then run back to the garage to pick up the car. Or let's say you're going to a friend's house. If you know that person well, it might not be too presumptuous for your wife to drive over with a change of clothes for you so you can shower there after your run is over.

Also, when I've had appointments in Manhattan, I've run from Grand Central Station to wherever I was due. I know I arrived there faster than I would have by taxi. I blaze past the cross-town traffic on foot. If you're on the lookout for running opportunities like that, you'll find all kinds of

them. You don't need to run your daily allotment of miles at one time.

How should you dress to run? Any old way. Above all, don't worry about what you look like. In running there is a kind of reverse chic. The good runners are the ones who dress the grubbiest. In fact, they snicker at those in expensive attire. So you can wear your old tennis garb or anything else you happen to have around—a T-shirt and shorts, an old sweat suit.

In colder weather, and there are practically no days in winter that you can't go out and run, the secret is to dress in layers. Don't, for example, bundle yourself into a down jacket. You'll be much warmer if you start with thermal underwear, add a T-shirt that will trap the warm air next to your body and put a wool sweater over that. Wool is the only material that will retain heat even when it gets wet. In extreme cold, you could also put on a sweat shirt and finally a nylon rain jacket. That type of layering will keep your body warm in just about any sort of weather conditions you will encounter in North America.

On your feet, you should wear wool socks, one pair. Again, wool will keep you warm even if it gets wet. You can run in slush if need be. In winter, when I get back to the house, I sometimes find that I've lost the feeling in my feet because of the cold. But it comes back. Because your feet are so active, you're generating a rich blood supply and I've never heard of any runner getting frostbitten feet.

What about footwear? At the outset, you can run in your tennis shoes. It's not harmful if you don't do much of it. But you shouldn't try to do a lot of running in tennis shoes because they are designed to withstand the stress of the foot going in any direction. That's why they have a heavy edge around the perimeter. And that means that tennis shoes are heavier than running shoes have to be.

Running shoes are made for only one kind of stress—forward stress. I like nylon uppers because nylon dries fast and wears well. If you're running three miles a day, nylon shoes should last you the better part of a year. To get a good shoe, plan to spend between $30 and $40 a pair. It may sound like a lot of money, but it's certainly well worth the expenditure.

I'd also like to add that if you're a woman, you'll want something with a good heel. Because women wear high heels a lot, their Achilles tendons are shorter. So they need something with extra support for the heel.

Do you need any other accessories? For chilly weather, yes—a hat and gloves. A hat is essential because you lose about 40 percent of your body heat through the head. The best type of hat is a wool tuque that you can pull down around your ears to keep them warm, too. And because your blood supply is going mainly to the working parts of the body, your extremities like your hands will get cold unless you wear gloves.

Oddly, the best gloves for running are not ski mitts. I've found the most practical are the white cotton gardening gloves that you can buy for about $1 a pair. Your hands

don't get sweaty in them. If your hands are sweaty when you're running, you'll feel really uncomfortable.

Is there a style for distance running that's less taxing on the body? Don't be misled by the picture you get of the sleek-looking sprinter on television. That isn't the way you want to run distances. In fact, you really shouldn't be thinking too much about style. The main thing is to be relaxed. Let the hands flop easily. If you want to work on something, then keep your forearms parallel to the ground. That way your arms are going to rock back and forth naturally. You won't have to think any more about it. But the body should be upright, not leaning forward. Leaning forward is strictly for sprinting.

Can you give examples where running has helped a tennis player to improve? For years running has been a part of the training routine of world-class players. Going back more than a decade to the era of Tony Roche, running has been incorporated into the training of the great Australian players. Running has helped Scandinavia's marvelous Torben Ulrich to play top level competitive tennis into his 40's. And today no less than Bjorn Borg is a regular runner. I also know of a 59-year-old man who runs and his only trouble, he confides, is that he's in such good shape he becomes impatient in doubles and has great difficulty finding opponents his own age in singles. He ends up hitting with players half his age.

Personally, I can recall being pitted against an opponent a short while after I started running 10 miles a day. He was thin, wiry, seven or eight years younger than myself and in the warm-up it was obvious that he had better strokes than I did. We began playing and he won the first set 6–3. In the second set, I stayed with the same strategy—going to the net whenever I could—and I noticed we seemed to be getting closer. He wasn't going for balls as briskly. I got encouraged and won it 7–5.

By the third set, he wasn't running for anything and I was still going after everything. I won it 6–1. It was clearly a match I won because of superior conditioning. My opponent had much greater physical potential and stronger techniques. But he wasn't a runner.

What reaction do you have to the complaint that running is boring? When people say that, I think they're asking for a lot more out of running than running has to give. You never hear anyone say they went for a walk and found it boring. People don't expect a walk to be terribly exciting. When I run, I'm not looking for excitement. In fact, from that perspective I think running has been oversold. You hear all this talk about a runner's high. I expect to hear any day now about a runner's orgasm.

The reality is that it's not anything like taking a drug. You don't get high every time you run. You feel good because you're using your body efficiently and the blood is flowing through you and you feel alive. When people say running is boring, I say fine. Try something like bike-riding or swimming or a high intensity activity you

might like better.

What do you think about when you're running? Some of my running friends have told me they've composed paragraphs and solved problems while running. But I don't concern myself with anything when I'm out there. I'm just glad that the phone isn't going to ring and nobody is going to harass me. I just let my mind float. There might be images on my mind but it's nothing of value, nothing I want to write down when I get back.

I run because running is good for me. It refreshes me and has a cleansing effect on my mind. And it's good for my body. When I'm finished, I feel like a newborn baby. That's what it does for me and that's what it can do for you.

DO OTHER SPORTS HELP OR HURT YOUR TENNIS?

You may not realize it, but the other sports you played as a youth—and maybe still play today—can have a significant influence on your tennis game. Sometimes they help it, sometimes they hurt it. Most of the time, though, they help—if only because experience in any sport furthers the development of the coordination and other basic skills that are the foundation of all athletics.

Nonetheless, there are elements of some sports which are detrimental to success in tennis. The important thing is to recognize these negative carry-overs and, where necessary, unlearn certain things and learn to do other things differently. It may be difficult for you, on your own, to spot these points where you need to make adjustments. But an experienced teaching professional probably can. So if you seem to be having trouble mastering one or more of the rudiments of tennis, let a teaching pro cast a knowing eye at your game. The root of your problem may be something you conditioned yourself to do in playing another sport.

Let's examine nine other sports in terms of how they help or hurt performance in tennis and what can be done to correct

any problems they create on the court.

BASEBALL: Fortunate is the tennis player who has a good background in baseball. Baseball players must train their eyes to follow a fast-moving ball in the field and at bat. They learn, thus, one of the first basics of good tennis: watch the ball. They also acquire a batting swing and follow-through that is almost identical to the natural forehand and backhand motions. Finally, the overhand baseball throw is quite similar to the proper movement of the arm for the tennis serve. It's little wonder some persons maintain that baseball is probably the best preparation a youngster can have for tennis.

BASKETBALL: This is another sport with excellent carry-over benefits for tennis. A basketball player must develop the same kind of reflexes and footwork that are essential in tennis. The quick, short steps, the need to "shadow" an opponent, the timing that's necessary on jumps—all these are positive assets when it comes to building a good tennis game.

On top of that, a basketball player must have an ability to follow the ball and anticipate angles when shooting, passing or rebounding. That's something invaluable in tennis. Have you ever wondered why some players are always at the right spot to return the ball, why they almost seem to be mind readers? They have learned to follow the ball and anticipate the possible angles of shots on the court. They know there are only certain angles at which an opponent can hit the ball from any one position on the

Rod Laver

court. Basketball is marvelous for teaching that skill.

FOOTBALL: This sport is not complementary with tennis because of its emphasis on weight and strong, thick muscles. But a fast running back or split end can have the quickness and versatility to do well at tennis. And the passing motion in football involves the same upward shoulder thrust that's necessary for a strong serve. A

few football players—such as Stanford's former star quarterback Jon Douglas—have also excelled at tennis. But it's an uncommon combination. To adapt to tennis, football players should consider cutting out heavy muscle-building exercises and working on their agility.

GOLF: Although golf strokes are completely unlike those of tennis, golf will give you a good understanding of the mechanics of hitting a ball and the laws of flight. For example, a golfer will know about hitting through a ball, which is one of the fundamentals of good tennis ground strokes. A golfer should also have a good feel for spins and slices, controlling distance and body positioning.

On the negative side, golf will not help your footwork simply because a golfer has all the time in the world to line up for a shot and to address the ball. And because golf strokes are so different from those of tennis, a golfer will often unintentionally use a golf-like body or arm motion in hitting a tennis ball. Former golfers have a tendency to drop the racquet head on the backswing. Dropping the racquet head makes for a looping stroke which usually produces an unintentional lob. The cure is to keep your racquet waist-high on the backswing.

In teaching converted golfers, pros often notice an unconscious wiggle of the hips in the ready position as though the player is about to dig into the turf. It probably helps the player feel more comfortable on the tennis court. But it's a habit that soon disappears.

OTHER RACQUET SPORTS: Almost all the other major racquet sports—badminton, paddleball, paddle tennis, platform tennis, squash, racquetball and table tennis—can be useful in developing tennis skills. After all, each involves stroking a ball. But they each also have their drawbacks.

Paddle tennis is very similar to conventional tennis except that it's played on a smaller court and mostly with a punctured tennis ball. There are lots of rallies and the game calls for some fast footwork. So paddle players usually become good tennis players. However, the underhand serve of paddle tennis isn't much good for normal tennis.

Platform tennis—so-called because it's played on a small tennis-like court atop a raised platform—is a scrambling game that sharpens the reflexes for tennis. But the smaller court makes for shorter strokes than in conventional tennis. Thus, platform-tennis players are apt to make their backswings too short and their follow-throughs too abbreviated.

Squash, racquetball and paddleball—games all played off walled courts with hard rubber balls—are excellent sports for keeping in shape for tennis. But they require wristy strokes that are too tough to execute with the heavier racquet and ball used in tennis.

Similarly, badminton players often have very wristy tennis strokes since most badminton shots require a sharp wrist flick. Very few players have wrist muscles strong enough to permit them to flick a tennis

racquet. So badminton players must remember to grip the tennis racquet very firmly, which will tighten the wrist muscles and prevent floppy strokes.

Table tennis players often have excellent reflexes, which are an asset in tennis. But the strokes of table tennis aren't much help; there's less body movement and less power required for most shots.

SKIING AND WATER-SKIING: For reasons that may have a lot to do with their individuality and a fondness for outdoor activities, skiers are often also tennis players. Unfortunately, though, there's little carry-over from skiing to tennis—except that both sports require a reasonably high level of conditioning for the enthusiast.

Most skiers are acutely aware of the balance of their bodies, but the proper balance for fast and safe skiing does not encourage the rapid forward transfer of weight that's essential for tennis. In skiing, most of the weight is balanced over the feet with only slight shifts necessary, mostly up and down, for control of the skis. In tennis, your body must move forward, almost as though you are leaving your backside behind. Your shoulders must shift forward with your weight moving onto your front foot while your rear foot stays back in contact with the ground. That last point is a problem for skiers who have been taught to keep their feet together for parallel skiing.

Although water-skiing calls for different body movements from those of downhill skiing, water-skiers also have a tendency to keep their weight to the rear. A water-skier has to lean back against the pull of the towrope, a position that is disastrous when hitting a tennis ball. So water-skiers must put extra effort into moving forward and getting their weight onto the front foot as they hit through the ball.

SWIMMING: Since it is a fine all-around conditioner and helps build long, firm muscles, swimming is a good background for tennis. In fact, competitive swimming at an early age can be first-rate training for a championship tennis player. Such a program has a reward system incorporated into it. It is easy to check improve-

Stan Smith

ment on the stopwatch. A trained swimmer knows the benefits of regular practice. A competitive swimming program, in sum, develops the body and the mind as well as the discipline and the endurance necessary for tennis.

TRACK AND FIELD: Running or jumping of any kind is beneficial for tennis. They don't do anything for the mechanics of stroke-making, of course, but they develop the agility and stamina that are so essential on court. The legs and wind of a track-man are highly desirable in tennis.

WEIGHT LIFTING: Like football, this activity is not compatible with tennis. In fact, too much weight lifting can be a liability on the court because it develops muscles at the expense of agility. One of the problems physical education teachers wrestle with is why obviously athletic and well-developed weight lifters can't execute a correct service motion. The answer, they discover, is that the muscle mass which is built up in the shoulders from weights prevents them from getting the arm extension necessary for the serve. Too many push-ups can have the same effect. If a person wants to play tennis well, he has no option but to curtail or stop these forms of training.

As we've seen, there are more positive than negative carry-overs from other sports to tennis. But even when experience in another sport proves to be a handicap in tennis, it's not too difficult to overcome the problem. An experienced instructor can help identify the trouble spots and point to the solutions.

THE PROPER DIET FOR BETTER TENNIS

Most people realize that the amount and kind of fuel they pump into their car's gas tank has a lot to do with how far and fast the car will go. Few of us would be so foolish as to try to make a high-performance sports car run on low-octane ethyl; likewise, we shouldn't expect our bodies to operate at their peak, on the tennis court or anywhere else, on a fuel mix of potato chips and soft drinks.

To keep our bodies running as efficiently as our cars, of course, takes daily servings of the old "basic four" food groups: dairy products; bread and cereals; meat, fish and poultry; and vegetables and fruits. These have traditionally been the building blocks of a sound nutritional program.

There are diet variations to give your game extra firepower while helping you shed pounds, and certain guidelines to follow about fluid intake. But before looking at those, here is how Chris Evert Lloyd eats to keep herself in championship form:

A few years ago, I was the chubbiest I've ever been in my life. I have tennis to blame for it—and tennis to thank for help-

185

ing me lose the extra pounds and keep them off.

I was 17 my first year on the European circuit in 1971, and the older players warned me: "When you go to Europe, you're going to gain weight because you don't get to practice that much. You get bored and you eat." I shrugged them off, said, "Naah, it'll never happen to me," under my breath, took off for Europe—and proceeded to add 15 pounds to my 5-foot 5-inch frame. I came home to Fort Lauderdale, Fla., tipping the scales at 135, the heaviest I've ever been, and I knew I had to get that weight off—fast.

There was really nothing magical about how I did it, even though it did take me only three days, and I know most doctors wouldn't recommend such a rapid loss for their patients. For me, three days of intensive court training, running and saying "no" to certain foods pared off those European pounds.

Since then, I've gone up and down slightly on the scales. But, generally, I manage to keep my weight in my ideal range of 115 to 120 pounds by knowing what to avoid, how much of certain foods I can take without getting into trouble, and what works best with my metabolism and my court performance.

I try to eat two good meals a day—a brunch-type meal about 11 a.m., and then something more substantial around 4 p.m. I'm a real meat person, and I love chicken and steak, but lamb is really my favorite with maybe a baked potato and butter (not every day, though) and a vegetable and salad.

When I play a match around 5 p.m. I'll come back to the hotel and, if I eat anything at all, it'll be some yogurt or an apple. I say "if anything at all" because if I don't eat after I've played in the evening—especially if I've been in both singles and doubles—then I'll drop two or three pounds the next day. My metabolism is such that I can eat pretty much anything, in moderation, and whenever I see the scale indicator creeping up I just stop eating after matches. Then I'm fine.

Just cutting out the night eating isn't enough, though. When I decide it's time to drop a few pounds, the first thing I cut out is sugar (I never eat table sugar and always use an artificial sweetener). And I cut out bread and desserts, too. Those are the killers, right there. Although I can take or leave most desserts, I do have a weakness for chocolate ice cream. I can pass up bread, and I can turn down a piece of chocolate cake, but if that ice cream is in front of me, then I'll eat it.

I don't believe in fad diets, for me or anybody who wants to lose weight, and I know from experience that sometimes they can do more harm than good. I've never been so heavy that I've had to consult a physician, but I did take up a low-carbohydrate diet (no bread, spaghetti, cereals or fruit) some years ago and I lost close to 10 pounds in the first four days. But I had practically no energy, so that rapid weight loss wasn't worth the side effect. I've never tried appetite depressants or diet pills, but I

Chris Evert Lloyd

have taken diuretics (water-reducing pills) once or twice. They gave me cramps, however, so I've never fooled with them since; they're just not healthy for me.

Basically, I try to get foods from each of the basic four food groups: dairy products; bread and cereals; meat, fish and poultry; and fruits and vegetables. It may sound old hat and unexciting, but it is important to eat balanced meals. I can say that I've never taken vitamins, and it's because I don't have to. Two balanced meals a day give me all the energy I need for my game.

Like most people, I'll snack occasionally. And the biggest temptation to do that is when I'm staying in a private home while playing a tournament or when I'm home. You might think that the biggest temptation to nibble comes in being in hotels and restaurants much of the year, but I've disciplined myself to the fact that I only order two meals a day. Period. It's just too much of a hassle to call room service and say, "Could you please send up a piece of apple pie?" That makes it easier for me to keep trim when I'm staying at a hotel. In a private home, though, the refrigerator is right there, and it's such a temptation that I could nibble all day.

Many of the players on the pro tour, men and women, go in for oranges or fruit juices when they're playing a match, but I stick pretty much to two things: diet cola and water. I used to drink fruit juices, but I found that they made me gain some weight because of their natural sugar. I'm a firm believer in diet drinks because regular soft drinks just have too much sugar.

As for eating during a match, I find I don't need to anymore. I used to take honey when I was younger, but I didn't have the stamina then that I have now, so I usually don't feel the need to eat anything when I'm playing. That includes salt tablets, too, because they upset my stomach. Of course, if I play a three-set singles match, then have to play doubles shortly afterward, I'll eat something like a chocolate bar as energy insurance.

I don't think most social players can go too far wrong by confining snacks to fruits, salads and cheese (my favorite nibble foods), especially something like a low-calorie cheese, which is lower in fat than regular cheese.

I try to allow lots of time between eating and going on court. It's never a good idea to start to play when you're feeling full of food, and I would rather go on court feeling thin, as if my stomach's empty, than feeling loaded down. When I've got a match coming up, I try to allow as much as three to four hours between a major meal and the ready call. If I get really hungry an hour or so before I'm to play, I'll have some cheese or fruit.

Food alone, of course, isn't all that's involved in keeping in shape for tennis—or for any other sport. I think those who are interested in losing weight or maintaining their present weight, shouldn't depend on just a regular social game to keep them fit. I don't do any special calisthenics while I'm on the tour because I'm playing three to

four hours a day and that's plenty. When I'm not on the tour, though, I will jog to build up my legs, and I usually log two miles a day.

I don't ever intend to let myself get up to 135 pounds again, the way I did on that first trip to Europe, and a careful eye on what I eat, plus all my tennis and exercising, will help me keep that scale indicator where I want it.

Pro trainer Bill Norris adds, for the average player, "I like to see players drink small amounts of liquid throughout the course of a match—especially on a very hot day. Water is fine. Some of the electrolyte drinks, like Gatorade, are good. But I don't think drinking soda during a match is a good idea at all. The carbonation doesn't do anything for you and you could get a gas attack. Don't overdo the liquids, but you want to replenish what you're losing. One of the things that happens when you lose certain nutrients through perspiration is that you become much more susceptible to a cramp.

"As for salt tablets," he adds, "they're O.K. for a professional who travels a lot and isn't always careful about what he eats. But for the club player, salt pills don't really mean anything. If you eat a normal diet, you don't need them."

THE TYPES OF REST A PLAYER NEEDS

Tennis is an exercise in destruction in certain ways. Each time you practice or play a match, your body is torn down. Blood sugar levels drop, metabolic wastes accumulate, dehydration occurs and muscle tissue is torn. Ligaments and tendons are strained and stretched. You become overheated and muscle glycogen is depleted. The greater the duration or intensity of the match or workout, the more pronounced the damage becomes.

The body tries to recover and rebuild from this punishment, but far too often the body is not allowed to complete the rebuilding phase for lack of rest (some physicians say that at least 40 hours are needed to rebuild the body after a tough match).

Rest can be divided into three types: passive, active and mental.

PASSIVE REST is simply inactivity. Many people do nothing to promote passive rest (sleeping, napping and sitting), but rather give nature time to run its course, healing and rebuilding the body. Passive rest is important and has a place in regenerating your body.

ACTIVE REST includes the things you can do to enhance the regeneration of your

body and multiply the effectiveness of rest. There are many things you can do to utilize more effectively the rebuilding processes of rest. For example, sauna and steam baths clean the body and produce intense relaxation and relief of tension.

Swimming and massage have a relaxing effect, relieve muscle tension and promote deep circulation. Whirlpools and therapeutic pools promote relaxation, circulation and help rest tired, sore and stiff muscles.

Stretching exercises have been shown to stimulate circulation in all areas of the body, but particularly in the exercised area. Stretching also enhances tissue oxygenation. A variety of researchers have found meditation to be an intense form of rest and relaxation for the body. Liberal doses of these activities can quicken and deepen

John Newcombe finds a game of billiards to be a good source of mental relaxation.

healing, thereby promoting the rebuilding of the body after a destructive workout.

MENTAL REST is something most players neglect. You can regenerate the psyche by using the same positive approach you should take in healing the body. Take a departure from tennis for a few days, a week, a month, long enough to refresh the mind and give you renewed interest and stimulation.

Do something unusual or different. Take a walk, sightsee, go to a movie, go on a safari, go fishing, visit a zoo, do some sort of handicraft or read. It is just as important to have a fresh, healthy mind in your tennis activities as it is to have a sound body.

With some thought and good planning, you can incorporate rest into your schedule. Plan ahead for that "rest week" or that time when rest will be needed most. Don't condemn rest or take it lightly. Rest will make you more aware of your own needs and your approach to tennis will be more comprehensive and more intelligent. Put rest into your schedule.

HOW TO STAY MENTALLY SHARP ON COURT

Being in shape mentally is just as important to good tennis as being in shape physically. Bjorn Borg never displays erratic emotions on court. One reason is that he works to stay in control of his mental faculties. His coach and companion, Lennart Bergelin, says that the important thing Borg does in preparing for major championships is to get mentally fresh for the pressure involved. That means pacing himself during the weeks leading up to Wimbledon or the U.S. Open. When Borg goes into an important tournament, his mind as well as his body are primed for the effort and concentration needed to succeed. During a tournament, Bergelin helps Borg retain that peak of interest by shielding him from outside distractions—reporters' phone calls, getting racquets strung, and the like. Here Borg gives his own prescription on how to stay mentally sharp:

Everybody recognizes that when you are physically tired, it's almost impossible for you to do your best in a tennis match. But what many tennis players don't often recognize is that being tired mentally can hurt your game just as much.

191

It's difficult to define exactly what being "mentally tired" really means. But mainly, I think, it's the inability to stay interested in the match—really interested. What usually happens when you go into a match mentally tired is that it's difficult to sustain concentration over long periods of time. I'm sure you've noticed in yourself, or maybe in observing tournament matches, that a player can be playing very well and suddenly go through two or three games in which he makes several errors and loses.

It happens to me. It happens to every player. And very often, in a very close match, it's that brief letdown—caused, I believe, by mental fatigue—that makes the difference between a win and a loss.

You're always going to make errors in a match, of course, whether you're mentally tired or not. But the errors you make when you are not mentally keen affect you differently than the errors you make when your mind is as fresh as it should be. I know from my own experience that if I'm not keen mentally, I become much more irritated with myself when I make errors than I do otherwise, and it's much harder for me to take the necessary steps to avoid those errors the next time.

Some people insist that it's good to get angry at yourself or lose your temper in a match because that helps your concentration. But I don't believe it. As a younger player, every time I lost control of myself—even briefly—it usually cost me the match. It took a lot of work on the part of my parents and a lot of experience to teach me

that it's next to impossible to be angry and to concentrate at the same time.

Recognizing mental fatigue in yourself is not too difficult. First of all, if you find your mind wandering in a match for no apparent reason, the chances are pretty good that your mind is simply tired of tennis. I can usually tell how mentally keen I'm going to be as soon as I wake up on the morning of a match. If I find myself eager to get out of bed and to get to the tennis court, I know when the match starts I'm going to concentrate well. But if I feel like staying in bed the whole day (and sometimes, after a long match the day before, you feel that way) and if I don't feel like going down to the court early to warm up or practice, I'm pretty sure that when the match does begin, I'm not going to be that mentally alert.

What causes you to become mentally tired in the first place? Well, for me it has a great deal to do with how physically tired I am. It's difficult to look forward to a match when you don't feel physically like playing and, if you don't feel like playing the match physically, it stands to reason that you're not going to be eager mentally, either.

A lot depends, too, on the things you have on your mind apart from tennis. All of us who play tennis professionally are very much aware of the fact that if our minds are involved with too many things other than tennis, it's very hard to maintain concentration in a match. That is why, for instance, I prefer to remain rather quiet before I go out on the court. It's not that I'm antisocial or anything like that. It's simply that I don't

Bjorn Borg

want to get my mind working on things that have nothing to do with the game.

The best way to deal with mental fatigue, I think, is to do your best to prevent it from occurring in the first place. Being fit physically is very important in this respect because, as I've already said, physical fatigue will almost always produce mental fatigue.

Another way of preventing mental fatigue is to get completely away from tennis every now and then. Some people think that if they don't play for a week or two or more, their games will suffer greatly. But if you have been playing tennis for any length of time and you take off for a while, it shouldn't take you more than a day or two on the courts to regain your timing. In the meantime, what you'll gain in mental attitude will more than make up for what you may have lost in timing.

I can give you a good example in my own case of how a long layoff helped me win an important match.

In 1976, I decided to put away my racquet for the entire month of December, mainly because I had played so many tournaments throughout the year that I was losing my enthusiasm for the game. I thought very little about tennis the whole month and I didn't even train. I have to admit that when I finally did start to practice again in the early part of January my timing was off, and I was a little nervous about whether I would be able to do my best in the first tournament I was scheduled to play: the 1977 Pepsi Grand Slam.

Well, I wouldn't say that I played my best tennis in that tournament. I came very close to losing to Adriano Panatta in the first match I played and if you saw the match I played with Jimmy Connors in the finals, you saw that I had to struggle very hard to win that one, too.

The Connors match was especially interesting in light of what we're talking about here, because it was one I had not been very keen to play and had I not been away from the game for a month I might not have won. It was obvious to everyone who watched the match that when I lost the second set to Connors (after having three match points in my favor), I was angry with myself and discouraged.

Fortunately, I was able to collect myself during the break between the last game of the second set and the first game of the third. Because my mind was fresh, I could think clearly and didn't allow the disappointment I felt with myself to go too far. Instead of criticizing myself for having let the match out of my hands—something I might have done as a younger player under different circumstances—I was able to see that I had come very close to winning and that there was no reason, so long as I didn't beat myself, that I couldn't beat Connors in the third set. So I went out and played a very good game on my serve, and that gave me the confidence to play well for the rest of the set.

Once you are in a match and you feel yourself getting mentally tired, there isn't much you can do to regain your alertness.

You can tell yourself to concentrate more, but that doesn't always work. The best advice I can give from my own experience is to try not to press too much. Getting angry with yourself doesn't solve anything; it just makes matters worse.

After Manuel Orantes won the fourth set in our quarterfinal match at the U.S. Open in 1976, I remember that I made a strong effort not to press too hard. He was playing very well, making sensational shots and the crowd was obviously behind him. But I thought to myself that there's no way he can continue to make the same kind of shots, and I wasn't going to change my game to force the issue. As it turned out, my feelings were right. I won the match because some of the shots that Orantes was making in the fourth set were missing in the fifth, and that was the difference in the outcome.

What it all comes down to in the end is just how eager you are to play and to win. Normally, if I'm well rested it is never a problem for me to stay keen throughout a match. Even when I'm not playing that well, I can hold my game together enough so I don't beat myself.

Like everyone else, it's sometimes a problem for me to stay interested in a match against a player whom I know I'll have no trouble beating. But I find that as long as I'm comfortably ahead, I can still maintain an interest by working on parts of my game that need improving.

These things work for me today at this stage in my career, because I love tennis and—with the exception of the traveling—I can't think of any aspect of the game I don't like. Whether I'll feel the same way five years from now or not is something else again, but I can tell you that the day I stop enjoying myself on the court is the day that whatever mental keenness I bring to the game is going to start to disappear.

TENNIS ELBOW

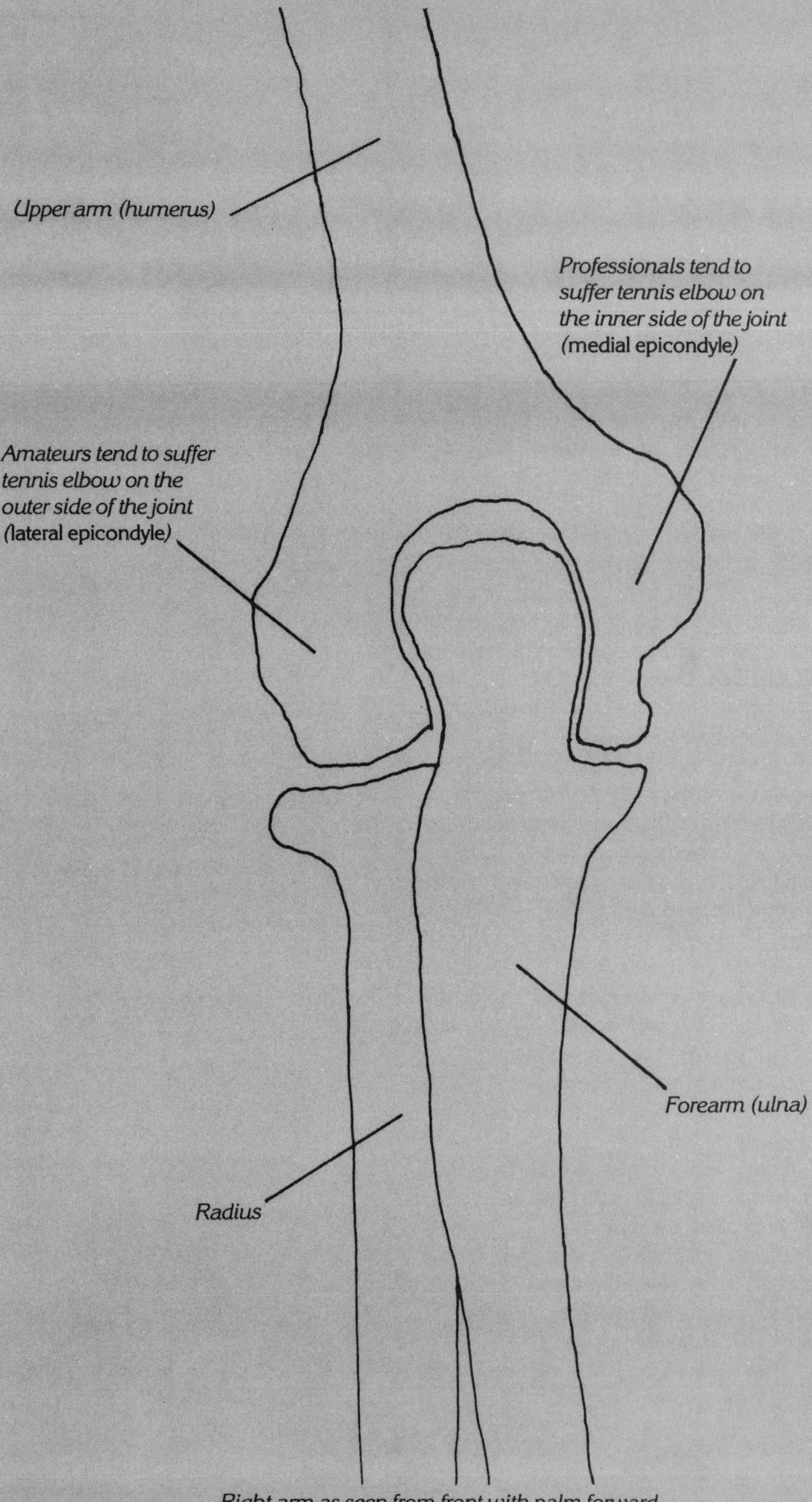

Upper arm (humerus)

Professionals tend to
suffer tennis elbow on
the inner side of the joint
(medial epicondyle)

Amateurs tend to suffer
tennis elbow on the
outer side of the joint
(lateral epicondyle)

Forearm (ulna)

Radius

Right arm as seen from front with palm forward

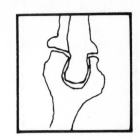

COMMON COURT INJURIES

Some players never suffer a serious injury during their entire tennis lives. Others seem almost injury-prone. But almost nobody who plays tennis remains completely unscathed.

Blisters often crop up at the start of a new season. A nasty spill can lead to cuts and bruises. Some players pull muscles, some sprain ankles, some suffer from cramps. Unfortunate or careless players might incur eye injuries. All of these ailments can be avoided and can be cured.

The injury that all players dread is named after the sport they love—tennis elbow. Tennis elbow has destroyed professional careers and made weekend players switch to sailing. But like other injuries, it, too, can be avoided and remedied.

Sooner or later, chances are you are going to fall victim to a tennis injury. If you work hard to avoid it, it may not occur. But when you do suffer one, don't give up. Inevitably there is a cure.

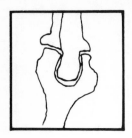

HOW TO AVOID INJURIES ON THE TENNIS COURT

One side effect of the tennis boom of the past decade has been a rise in the number of injuries that players—particularly beginners—are suffering on the court.

What are these injuries and how can they best be avoided?

Improper warm-ups are the biggest source of sprained ankles, torn muscles and similar injuries. The club player, who probably hasn't played much during the week, is itching to start a set as soon as he hits the court on Saturday morning. So he usually doesn't warm up properly. "The warm-up is where aggravation begins," says Ray Mitchell, a Florida teaching pro. "People hit the ball too hard to begin with. They get out there, murder the ball three times and then want to start playing."

Mitchell says each player's warm-up procedure will vary, but he recommends that everyone do some stretching exercises, particularly knee bends, to begin with. Then, as you begin to rally, hit the ball easily at first, working up to harder strokes. And go through your service motion smoothly and slowly at least 15 to 20 times before actually serving a ball.

Know your capabilities, too. Trying the impossible shot is another good way to pull muscles or develop back pains. "Jimmy Connors can hit a jumping-running forehand and feel no effect," Mitchell says. "He is used to doing it." Those of us who are mere mortals, however, cannot. So take it easy.

When you must scramble for a difficult shot, try to run with your racquet back so you're ready for the ball when you get to it. Don't get there and then try to react. That's the easiest way to hurt an arm. Mitchell suggests a lesson or two solely on methods of running to assist you in chasing down difficult shots.

Playing when you are tired is also dangerous. If you're fatigued but still want to play, let the "hard-to-get" shots go by. Or seek out an easier game. Be aware, too, Mitchell adds, that "you can't perform the same way late in the match that you did in the beginning. Many ligaments are torn at the end of weekend matches because players are trying to do the same things they did an hour and a half before. Accidents occur when the body is not moving the way it should because it's tired."

If you do get tired in a competitive match, but must continue to play hard, adjustments can be made. Go for more putaways so points are shorter. When rushing net, don't come in quite so fast and pull up a couple of feet before the service line. Your opponent will no doubt be a bit tired by this point, too. So he'll be swinging slower, giving you more time to get to net and react to his shot.

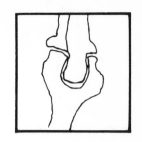

Want to improve your wind so you don't get tired so easily? Do whatever exercise you want, Mitchell says, but do it every day. Skipping rope is tops on his list. Knee bends are good, too. Even more tennis—as long as you can play every day.

Mitchell's suggestions boil down to knowing what you can and can't do, knowing when you've had enough and generally being aware of your physical condition. Just don't overdo it or you'll suffer the cruelest blow of all for a tennis player—an enforced layoff.

HOW TO TREAT COMMON COURT INJURIES

No one expects to get hurt or become ill when he goes out to play tennis. After all, you're supposed to be having fun—relaxing. But accidents do happen and illnesses do occur. So a familiarity with first-aid treatment for tennis-related ailments can often ease a painful—or possibly dangerous—situation.

The first thing to remember is that first aid is just that —initial and immediate primary care. Anything more should be left to trained, medical personnel. There are, however, certain basic first-aid facts every tennis player should know, for his own benefit as well as that of others. Here are the fundamental ones.

SPRAINS, PULLS AND OTHER MUSCLE PROBLEMS: The most common injuries in tennis are sprained ankles or knees, usually caused by a failure to warm up properly or an attempt to start playing again before an old injury has had sufficient time to heal. A sprain involves damage to a muscle, tendon or ligament—or all three—that can range from the tearing of a few fibers to a complete rupture.

If you have a history of muscle problems, says pro trainer Bill Norris, you

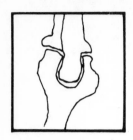

should try to take a hot shower before you play—or at least get some hot water on the area that gives you trouble. You should always try to do some stretching and bending exercises before you start to hit, and never try to hit the ball hard until you're fully warmed up.

"If you have an arm or a leg muscle that's bothering you a lot, I don't think you should play," says Norris. "Usually you only aggravate it, and rest is really the only treatment for most muscle inflammation. If the pain is minor, play, take it easy and try to get some ice on it afterward."

To treat ankle and knee sprains, immobilize and elevate the injured leg. Then, pack it in ice, if some is available, or wrap it tightly with an elastic bandage—but not so tightly that you cut off circulation. The next stop should be a doctor's office for a definitive diagnosis and a prescribed program of treatment.

BLISTERS: Anyone who has ever tried to play tennis for any length of time in ill-fitting shoes knows how painful a foot blister can be. If your shoe fits, though, you can usually avoid blisters by powdering your feet before play and wearing a thin pair of socks under a heavier pair.

As for your hand, Norris says, "Blisters are most likely to develop in very dry conditions. A good moisturizer helps to prevent them. But if you play a lot and your hands are sensitive, there isn't too much you can do. The important thing to remember about a blister is not to lance it until it's ready. If you're going to lance it yourself,

make the puncture on the outer edge and with a sterilized needle. Once you get the water out, keep the outer skin covering as intact as possible because the skin beneath it is very raw and sensitive."

If you get a foot blister treat it by cushioning the area around the blister (not over it) and wait until it heals before you try to play again.

CUTS AND BRUISES: Tripping or skidding, especially on a concrete surface, can produce a nasty scrape. If it happens to you—if you skin an elbow or a knee or any other part of your body—cleanse the area thoroughly with soap and water and, if necessary, cover it with a light dressing. If you should run into a net post or some other obstacle and a bruise develops, put a cold compress on it. For minor cuts, a tape bandage will probably do. In cases of serious bleeding, however, apply direct pressure on the wound to stem the flow of blood and take the victim immediately to a hospital emergency room.

HEAT PROBLEMS: Playing tennis in hot weather under a relentless sun can lead to serious consequences, most of which can be avoided by limiting play and by wearing a hat and heat-reflecting white clothing. Fail to take these precautions and you could end up with heat exhaustion or, worse, heat stroke. Which is which? It's important to know; it could mean, in fact, the difference between life and death.

The player suffering from heat exhaustion will probably complain of weakness and dizziness; he may even faint. His skin

will be wet and clammy, his pupils dilated. His pulse rate will be rapid and faint and his breathing will be shallow. Should a player demonstrate any of these symptoms, have him lie down immediately in a cool or shady place and loosen any tight clothing. He should recover in a short period of time but *should not* return to the court. If you have any doubts about his condition, the best advice is to take him to the nearest emergency room.

Heat stroke is less common than heat exhaustion but far more serious, and it can be fatal if not treated promptly and properly. Heat stroke is caused by excessive dehydration. The skin becomes hot and dry. The victim has stopped perspiring; he is unable to control his own body temperature by sweating, and so must be cooled *immediately* with ice or cold towels and taken to a hospital as soon as possible.

Excessive playing in hot, humid weather can also lead to so-called "stomach" cramps (they're really in the lower abdomen) which, though temporary, can be extremely painful. To prevent such cramps, you can drink one of the commercial beverages heavy in salt, such as Gatorade, or take one or two salt tablets per hour of strenuous play, although, as Norris says, you really don't need them if you eat a normal diet. If you do get cramps, you may think that you can resume play when they go away. Don't. You're only inviting another attack.

MUSCLE CRAMPS: These can be caused by a direct blow, by exhaustion from too much play, by a sudden change in temperature or, as with stomach cramps, by an excessive loss of salt and fluid through sweating. If that last reason is the cause, replacing lost salt and sugar is a must. All muscle cramps should be treated immediately, though, by massaging the affected area and gently manipulating the affected muscle until it returns to normal. Heat, whirlpool and professional massage can also help to prevent a recurrence.

EYE INJURIES: A lightning-like volley, a mis-hit tennis ball or a racquet thrown in anger or frustration—any of these can cause a serious injury.

A ball that hits the eye directly can cause scratching of the cornea (the outer surface of the eyeball), bleeding within the eye or a tear in the retina (the tissue lining the back of the eye). If it's left untreated, a torn retina could lead to some loss of vision and require surgery to repair.

How can you protect your eyes from possible injury while playing tennis? For starters, you should follow some common-sense precautions out on the court to reduce the likelihood that you or others will get smacked by the ball unawares.

The oldest maxim in the sport—watch the ball—will not only help your game but guard your eyes, too. Unless you concentrate on hitting the ball in the center of your racquet, it may deflect off the rim up into your face. Keep your racquet well up in the ready position whenever you're at the net. That way, you'll be much better able to defend yourself against a hard-hit shot that

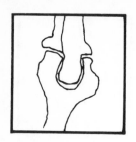

HOW TO PROTECT YOUR EYES ON COURT

READY OR NOT: Right

Wrong

EYES RIGHT: Right

Wrong

flies unexpectedly toward your eyes.

When you're at the net while your partner is serving, look straight ahead into your opponents' court. If you turn to watch your partner put the ball into play, his serves will pose a serious threat to your eyes.

When you're watching a match from the sideline or walking back to position after a point, always be sure to be alert. A ball could suddenly come zinging your way

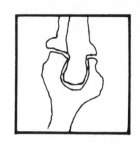

DOUBLES JEOPARDY: Right   Wrong

PAY ATTENTION: Right   Wrong

when you least expect it.

Beyond these measures, you might want to wear some sort of protective eye-guard. Some are just frames that will deflect hard-hit tennis balls, while others have lens-es like eyeglasses.

Should you or a fellow player be struck in the eye, the best thing to do is to leave it alone. Compresses, ice or heat could turn a slight injury into a major problem. But if

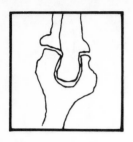

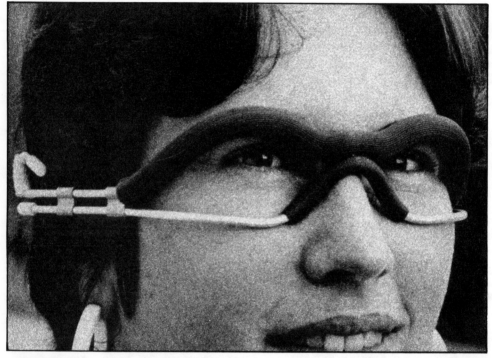

your vision does not clear up quickly, see an eye doctor immediately. Even if normal vision returns quickly, it might be wise to have the eye checked anyway, just in case.

If you wear contact lenses and get hit in the eye, carefully remove the lens that's been struck if it's still on the eye in order to prevent any possible scratching of the cornea. If your vision returns to normal shortly after impact, there's generally not too much likelihood of serious damage—although it's wise to have the eye checked, anyway. But if there's any loss of vision at all, you should seek medical care.

Whatever the outcome of an examination after an eye injury, follow it up with another visit in three or four months because a tear in the retina may not show up immediately. And if there's any change in your vision—at any time—notify your doctor at once.

HEART ATTACKS: Tennis, by its very nature, is a natural preventive against heart disease. With luck, you will never see or even hear of a case of cardiac arrest during the course of normal play. For the older player in particular, though, the possibility of a heart attack cannot be ignored. Typical symptoms include severe chest pains which often radiate to the left shoulder and

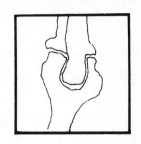

left arm, shortness of breath and difficulty in breathing, apprehension, nausea and sweating.

What should you do when a fellow player displays these symptoms? According to the American Heart Association, your first step should be to get help immediately. Call for an ambulance or, if you can get the victim to the hospital faster by car, drive him yourself. Loosen his clothing and try to relax and reassure him. Do not, however, give him any fluids or drugs, except on the advice of a physician.

If the victim faints or stops breathing, lay him out flat on a firm, level surface and, if you know how, begin to administer mouth-to-mouth resuscitation. Keep it up until the victim revives or until trained medical personnel arrive on the scene.

While some injuries are unavoidable, most can be prevented with common sense and a little forethought. A regular conditioning program is one of the best ways of heading off trouble—and improving your game at the same time. Above all, if you do get injured and your doctor advises you to stop playing until your injury heals, do it. Better to wait and play another day than to throw away a whole season.

TENNIS ELBOW: CAUSES, PREVENTION, CURES

Woodchoppers get it. Javelin throwers get it. So do hand-shaking politicians, fencers, carpenters, polo players, golfers, scrubwomen, baseball players, oarsmen and even violinists.

In medical circles, it's a painful ailment known formally as *epicondylitis,* since it is essentially an inflammation of the epicondyle of the humerus—the knob of the bone of the upper arm which protrudes at the elbow. But because it occurs most commonly, and perhaps most insidiously, among tennis players, it is popularly known as "tennis elbow."

The agony of what we call tennis elbow has probably been plaguing mankind in one form or another since the days when a prehistoric ancestor wrenched his elbow while dragging his mate back to his cave. But it was first described medically by a German physician, Dr. Herman Runger, in 1873—which, coincidentally enough, happened to be the very year when lawn tennis was invented.

Today, all the evidence indicates that close to 50 percent of all tennis players who

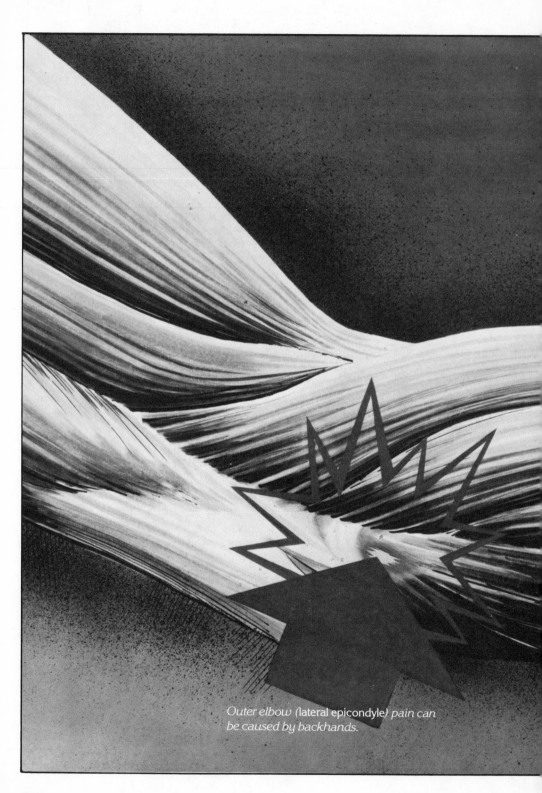

Outer elbow (lateral epicondyle) pain can be caused by backhands.

Inner elbow (medial epicondyle) problems can be caused by forehands or serves.

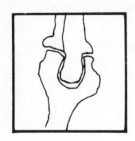

are 30 or older suffer from tennis elbow at some point in their playing careers. It remains, in some way, a mysterious malady: its causes aren't entirely clear, and the available cures are many and varied. But tennis elbow can be overcome—and almost always is. No one cure is universally successful, but almost every case is curable. What is universal is that tennis elbow produces more anguish than anything else in tennis —more even than a consistently errant backhand.

Anyone determined to get rid of tennis elbow—or avoid it entirely—should encounter many fewer confusing distractions and dissenting opinions than he or she would have faced 10 years ago. At that time, before lightning struck the tennis scene, few medical people had much experience in treating the ailment. Afflicted players often sought remedies from their tennis professionals, and for every pro who recommended heat, a smaller racquet grip, a lighter racquet and tighter stringing, there was a second instructor who believed in cold, larger grip, heavier racquet and looser stringing. Improper stroking rarely was discussed as a causal factor. But the need to acquire more information about effective treatment was felt to any considerable extent by the medical profession only after doctors' offices were inundated with aching elbows, some of them attached to professional players whose income depended on effective treatment.

It's pretty safe to say that you'll know if you've developed tennis elbow. Usually, the elbow area starts to hurt a little bit. The pain then increases sharply with continued use of the arm. Rest for a few days tends to improve the situation. But further strenuous use of the arm muscles brings back the pain rather quickly. Not only is there pain where the muscles of the forearm are attached to the outside of the elbow joint, but the tissue in that area will also be painful to the touch. However, major nerve problems rarely if ever occur with tennis-elbow sufferers.

When things get really bad, a mere handshake becomes an ordeal. Simple acts like brushing teeth or reaching across a table to pick up an object or turning a doorknob send twinges of pain shooting through the forearm. And hitting a tennis ball with a racquet—especially if the ball is off center—brings on an immediate pain that some players liken to being struck on the elbow with a hammer.

The root of tennis-elbow pain is a partial rupture at the elbow joint of those muscles which straighten and extend both the fingers and the wrist. The rupture is apparently brought on by the shock to the arm of many jarring meetings between ball and racquet. At the point of this rupture, there is an internal outpouring of fluid and blood plasma with resulting irritation and pain, usually on the outside of the elbow. The amount of bleeding and the pressure of the escaping fluid will determine how painful the elbow becomes.

To some extent, the very nature of the elbow joint and its associated muscles

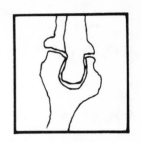

means that it is a problem area. For the wrist and hand to be able to grip and twist strongly, there must be a concentration of forces where the muscles attach to the elbow, particularly on the outside of the joint. The price to be paid for structural strength in the grip is a relative weakness in the elbow.

COMMON CAUSES: Not all of the ways you can get tennis elbow are an outgrowth of playing tennis. For most players, though, the basic cause is putting too much stress on those forearm muscles that allow the extension of the wrist and fingers. That can happen when you curl your wrist while hitting a backhand or when you try to roll your racquet over while attempting a pronounced topspin forehand. The same thing can happen, incidentally, when you twist a screwdriver too vigorously.

Even if you don't use excessive wrist rotation on your strokes, you can still be a candidate for tennis elbow if you have less than adequate muscle tone due to lack of exercise. If your arm muscles are weak, it's easy to strain them and so cause tennis elbow.

Many sports medicine specialists who have studied the affliction feel that improper stroking of the backhand is primarily at fault. For example, Dr. Robert P. Nirschl, chairman of the Committee on Medical Aspects of Sports for the Medical Society of Virginia, estimates that 90 percent of all tennis-caused elbow problems are triggered by what many doctors term a "leading-elbow" backhand.

A properly stroked backhand, the experts agree, generates its power from body weight transfer and arm rotation from the muscles at the back of the shoulder. The trunk leans toward the net with the front shoulder down, the elbow and wrist firm. The forearm and hand provide control, not power.

A dangerously improper backhand is characterized by the trunk leaning away from the net, front shoulder raised. The elbow and wrist absorb the force overload as the forearm awkwardly attempts to supply power rather than control. Frequently, this type of player will also hit the ball off center on his racquet, causing additional strain to the wrist and arm. The result, very often: *lateral epicondylitis*—tennis elbow on the outer side of the elbow.

Forehands and serves also can create elbow problems, usually of the medial (inner elbow) variety. Similar to the frequently seen improper backhand, the improper forehand is hit with the trunk leaning away from the net, weight on the back foot and the front shoulder raised, probably because the ball is being contacted late—behind the body. As in the case of the culprit backhand, the forearm is used for power rather than control. Body weight should move forward, with power originating from the front shoulder muscle and body weight transfer. Contact with the ball should be made opposite the front hip.

Topspin should be imparted by a forward and upward motion. When it is attempted, instead, by rolling over the arm,

HOW POOR STROKING CAN CAUSE TENNIS ELBOW

BACKHAND

Right

Wrong

Faulty backhand tries to generate power from forearm, with elbow leading and weight back. The correct stroke is powered by body weight transfer and arm rotation.

FOREHAND

Right

Wrong

Incorrect forehand places stress on forearm. The correct stroke generates power from weight transfer and arm rotation, with ball contact opposite leading hip.

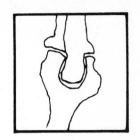

medial epicondylitis may not be far behind. The exaggerated topspin lob should be shunned by players deliberately avoiding motions that might affect the elbow.

Of course, even top-level players with textbook forehands and backhands can suffer from tennis elbow. But when professionals do get it, the reason usually is that they've put too much strain on their arm muscles while serving.

The serve very often places the forearm in an unnatural position. Careful trial and error should help you determine which motions you can safely employ.

Many top players use the backhand grip when serving, whether the serve is to be flat or sliced. For a flat serve with a backhand grip, the forearm must be rotated; and that means the wrist snap at the point of impact puts considerable pressure on the forearm muscles. The American twist serve pulls the forearm (as well as the back) into an even more exaggerated position than the flat serve. The pros who use this serve are more prone to tennis elbow than more conventional servers. Club players would be well advised to forgo this serve, says Nirschl. But because top players normally have good muscle tone, the incidence of tennis elbow among them is relatively low.

In addition to improper stroking, there are other factors that can have a bearing on tennis elbow. One is age. As a tennis player gets older, his or her muscles tend to lose their resiliency and become less able to withstand the shock that comes with hitting a tennis ball. Age does begin to take its toll after 30, so the most common age category for the tennis elbow sufferer is 30 to 50.

Tennis elbow can also be induced by playing with improper equipment. An overly heavy racquet or heavy-duty tennis balls only add to the pressures on the elbow. A grip that's the wrong size or a racquet that's improperly strung can be bad, too. And players should be aware that when they play on fast surfaces or face hard-hitting opponents, the danger of tennis elbow will increase because their arms will have to absorb more shock.

Susceptibility to tennis elbow can be forecast to a certain extent, according to Dr. John L. Marshall, director of the Department of Sports Medicine at the Hospital for Special Surgery in New York City. Marshall—who has been testing this concept for several years with skiers, football players and, more recently, with tennis players—uses three basic test procedures: a musculoskeletal profile, a fitness profile and a specific motor-skills profile.

The musculoskeletal profile determines whether a player is tight-jointed or loose-jointed. Marshall recommends that loose-jointed players concentrate on developing strength to avoid sprains. Tight-jointed persons should concentrate on stretching and flexibility to reduce the likelihood of muscle pulls.

To determine whether you are tight or loose, hold your racquet hand in front of the body with fingers pointing up. Using your second hand, apply pressure to the thumb

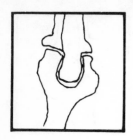

to lower it as far as it will go. If you achieve no more than a right angle to the forearm, you are tight-jointed; if your thumb touches your forearm, you are loose-jointed.

Tight-jointed players are much more likely to do well in tennis than those who are loose-jointed. That's the good news for tight-jointed players; the bad news is that they are more susceptible to injury than loose-jointed persons, says Marshall.

The good news for loose-jointed folks, apart from less susceptibility to injury, is that this theory does not pretend to be all inclusive. Marshall makes this point very effectively: Chris Evert Lloyd tests out as loose-jointed. Despite her remarkable success on court, says Marshall, she is not a natural athlete; but intensive training and practice served as more than adequate compensations. So, if you are tight-jointed, your chances for tennis success are greater than if you are loose-jointed. But remember Chris Evert Lloyd!

PREVENTING TENNIS ELBOW: Since incorrect stroking is the major cause of tennis elbow, it's obvious that the most effective way to prevent it or at least relieve it is simply to learn to hit the ball properly. By doing that, you'll develop a stroking style which reduces the stress placed upon the elbow or increases the elbow's capacity to withstand stress or redistributes the stress to new and stronger areas.

There's another dividend, too: it should all make you a better player. The professional tennis player looks smooth because his body and arm move into the

ball in a synchronized and fluid manner. The less effective player often looks rather comical because there seem to be isolated body and arm movements which have little or no relationship to each other. If you know that improper strokes are your problem, you ought to assign top priority to developing correctly hit ones. Any competent teaching professional should be able to help you make the change.

Here are some specific ways to lessen the stress on your elbow and, very probably, improve your game at the same time, as demonstrated by Vic Braden.

1. When running for shots, turn your shoulders to take the racquet back rather than using only your arm in an isolated movement. You can't uncoil a body which

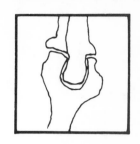

hasn't been previously coiled. Moving your arm without turning your body will create rapid and jerky swings which often cause excessive wrist action.

tennis elbow. Try keeping the racquet head vertical while swinging forward with a low to high motion. Hit softly at first and watch the results closely.

2. Always try to hit the ball in the center of the strings. Off-center hits create stress overloads on the elbow. You can practice watching the ball by rallying with a friendly opponent. As soon as one of you hits the ball without watching it hit the racquet, he must admit his mistake, the rally is stopped and a new one begun.

3. Forget the notion that topspin is achieved by rolling the face of the racquet up and over the top of the ball. That causes excessive wrist rotation, a prime cause of

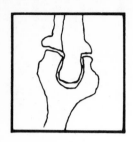

4. On your forehand follow-through, allow the "vee" of the thumb and the index finger of your hitting hand to fall toward your opposite shoulder. On the backhand, allow the "vee" on the hitting hand to fall toward the shoulder of your hitting arm. If you can't do that comfortably, you are probably guilty of forcing excessive wrist roll.

5. When serving, your throwing arm on the toss should be held parallel to the baseline rather than point toward the net. The reason is simple: If you turn your shoulder back on the ball toss, you'll achieve much greater shoulder rotation and rhythm on the swing. More shoulder rotation usually means more power and far less stress on the arm.

6. When serving, toss the ball well in front of your body to allow your synchronized shoulder and arm movement to move gracefully through the ball. If you throw the ball behind your head, you'll restrict your shoulder rotation and force your arm to move alone. That will create stress on the elbow.

Equipment: There is less authoritative information available about how equipment affects a tennis player's elbow, but here are some widely accepted guidelines for those who seek to avoid or alleviate tennis elbow.

• Racquets range in flex from flexible to very stiff. Avoid very stiff or stiff racquets. Look for racquets that are described by their manufacturers as flexible or average.

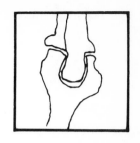

• Avoid racquets that are too heavy for you. When in doubt, consult a competent tennis professional or sports medicine specialist.

• Avoid any racquet, regardless of total weight, that is "head-heavy." Use an evenly balanced racquet or one that is "head-light."

• Avoid tight stringing. Try to get your racquet strung accurately in the 50 to 55 pound range. You may temporarily find it helpful to use a racquet strung at lower tension, but avoid extreme minimums because that can provide another type of problem. Make certain that you are dealing with a stringer who takes seriously such specific tension requests and has proven himself capable of meeting them.

• Try to get an accurate measurement of your correct grip size. If your measurement falls between available sizes, it is better to use a slightly large grip rather than a slightly small one, but your professional can increase or decrease racquet grip size to fit your needs.

• If you are determined to cover all bets, have your racquet strung with 16-gauge gut. The material is more delicate than other stringing and wears out more quickly. But it could well be worth it.

• Avoid worn-out tennis balls both for practice and competition. In selecting new balls, avoid brands which are heavier than the norm.

Physical fitness is another important preventative measure. As mentioned earlier, weak arm muscles can lead to tennis elbow. The following seven exercises recommended by Dr. Nirschl are designed "to increase strength, endurance and flexibility in the wrist, elbow, forearm and shoulder."

• Shoulder shrug. Shrug shoulders toward ears; repeat several times. Shrug shoulders in circular motion; repeat several times.

• Rhomboid isometric. In standing position, place arms down at sides with palms facing front. Pull arms behind the back and squeeze shoulder blades together. Hold for three seconds. Repeat three times; gradually increase to 10 repetitions.

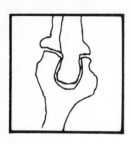

• Military press. Stand erect. Lift three-pound weight to fully extended position above head. Progress gradually to 30 repetitions. Then, gradually increase weight to 10 pounds for women, 20 pounds for men.

• From standing position, bend at waist to 90 degrees. Place non-exercising hand on same side knee. With other hand, swing five-pound weight across front of body to overhead position. Progress gradually to 30 repetitions.

• Stand erect. Using two-pound weight, lift arm to horizontal in front of body; hold for five seconds. Move arm to side; hold for five seconds. Drop arm slowly to side. Progress gradually to 30 repetitions. Gradually increase weight to five pounds for women, 10 pounds for men.

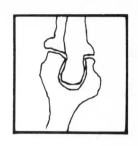

• Hold arm extended close to horizontal in front of body. Squeeze tennis ball; hold for five seconds. Progress gradually to 50 repetitions.

• Hold arm extended close to horizontal in front of body. Actively pull fingers and wrist into fully extended position; hold for five seconds. Progress gradually to 50 repetitions.

CURES: Some players, when they get tennis elbow, simply elect to tough it out— that is, they do nothing, play with the pain and pray that it eventually goes away. It's a trying way of dealing with the injury, but there is at least one sufferer who claims it does give him one advantage on court. "When I hit a backhand," he says cheerfully, "I often scream so loudly that my opponent is disconcerted and misses his return."

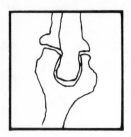

For those who are interested in solutions that are usually prompter and less painful, however, the medical profession offers a selection of treatments.

Most of the medical people who treat large numbers of elbows are involved in sports medicine, a young discipline (the American College of Sports Medicine was founded in 1944). Doctors entering this field generally first qualify as orthopedic surgeons. Some of them serve as team physicians, usually for football squads or tennis teams at the professional, college or high school level.

If you do develop tennis elbow, the symptoms are likely to persist for about a year unless positive steps are taken to improve the quality of muscle and tendon through progressive, resistive exercises; improve playing skill and form to eliminate improper stroking; and replace playing equipment with alternates better suited to this particular situation, as discussed.

Strengthening and stretching exercises for the arm and upper torso receive primary emphasis from most physicians.

One New York sports physician often prescribes a simple strengthening exercise using rubber bands of varying resistance placed over the fingertips. "Stretching out the fingers against the rubber bands provides exercise for intrinsic muscle groups," he explains. This exercise can be done almost anywhere. Because it is so convenient, some patients may tend to overuse it. All exercises, including this one, should be done in moderation.

Dr. Nirschl recommends the home exercises mentioned here for some of his tennis elbow patients. In those cases where extensive rehabilitation of the arm and upper torso is required, possibly due to inactivity, both Nirschl and Marshall prescribe supervised workouts on Nautilus exercise equipment. They report very good results with tennis-elbow patients who have utilized the equipment. Among the increasing number of tennis professionals who have trained on Nautilus equipment are Billie Jean King, Arthur Ashe and Sandy Mayer.

Specific exercises. Besides working on upper-torso conditioning, etc., the tennis-elbow victim should do the following exercises before playing, according to Marshall.

1. Upper extremity stretch. Grasp a towel in both hands. Raise arms in front of body, hands spread as far apart as possible; pull. Raise arms overhead; move arms to right as far as possible, then to left; repeat three times. Bring towel over the head, with one hand close to head and the other outstretched; hold towel behind shoulders and pull. Lower towel to buttocks and pull. Repeat three times.

2. Forearm stretch. Raise racquet arm to horizontal position with wrist raised; pull back wrist with second hand until you feel pressure on underside of forearm and elbow. Release. Repeat three times. Lower the wrist; push down with second hand until you feel pressure on outer side of forearm and elbow. Repeat three times.

3. Back stretch. Sit on edge of chair.

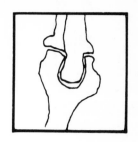

Drape head and shoulders forward and down. Bend the back and attempt to touch the floor between your feet with folded elbows. Relax; hold position for five seconds. Repeat three times.

4. Back and hamstrings. Stand erect, bending right knee. Reach down as far as possible across bent knee to grab left leg with both hands, keeping left knee straight. Stand erect; repeat three times. Bend left knee, reach for right leg. Repeat three times.

5. Groin muscles. Sit on floor with knees to the side and soles of the feet touching. Push down knees as far as you can. Release knees. Repeat three times.

6. Calf muscles. Stand on step with only toes touching so that heels can drop below level of the step. Raise body as far as you can; hold. Lower body as far as you can (to stretch the calf and heel cord); hold. Repeat three times.

Proper warm-up and cool-down. If you suffer from tennis elbow, take the following steps to warm up properly before playing and to cool down following play:

1. Take two aspirin or some other analgesic about 15 minutes before going on court.

2. Prior to play, massage the elbow with a topical analgesic containing methyl-salicylate, such as Ben-Gay. Some players are helped by various creams which contain aloe vera, an old folk remedy.

3. Allow a few minutes for exercise as described above before going on court and discipline yourself to follow this regimen regularly. If necessary, keep your playing partners waiting a few minutes, rather than run the risk of injury.

4. Keep the elbow warm with a sweater or jacket at least until you have hit for several minutes. You may want to try one of the commercially available products that covers the elbow; or you can do it with an old sock and a bit of imagination.

5. Restrain yourself when you start to hit the ball. Concentrate on smooth stroking. Don't attempt any demonstration of power until your body has warmed up (even on a hot day). If you've had a recent history of *lateral epicondylitis*, start with forehands; if you've had *medial* elbow problems, start with backhands. Don't rush this practice period. If your opposition is ready to play before you're fully prepared, ask for—and get—a few more minutes. Try only for control on your early overheads and serves. Gradually increase the pace if your elbow feels comfortable. Don't be pressured by the addlebrained example of an opponent, or even your doubles partner, to start serving in a game with an inadequate number of practice serves or none at all.

6. When you have completed play, apply ice to a tender elbow, no longer than 20 minutes at a time.

Other cures. Heat and massage are also helpful with tennis elbow. Nirschl finds that heat is best applied with a whirlpool bath, but ultra sound devices are useful, too. Massage, with one of the patent medicines containing methylsalicylate, is often

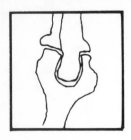

quite comforting. After massage, the player should take aspirin, jog for several minutes and stretch the sore parts gently before picking up a racquet.

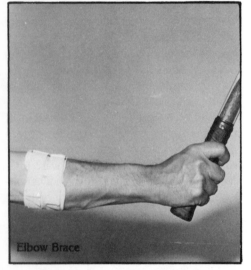

Elbow Brace

Many tennis-elbow sufferers find that an elbow brace helps them to continue playing. Some are of adjustable fabric, covering the forearm. Others are more like splints, some of them sold commercially. The most common brace (adjustable fabric) is worn on the forearm just below the elbow crease. The wider the brace, the more effective it will be in spreading—and thereby reducing—the forces that cause tennis elbow. It should be worn only during play.

When you seek medical help for an ailing elbow, the chances are that your treatment will include one or more of the following: muscle relaxants, anti-inflammatories taken by mouth; anti-inflammatory injections in or around the affected area; heat; ultra sound, possibly utilized under water; massage; whirlpool and electrogalvanic stimulation. One of the more well-known treatments is cortisone shots. Contrary to popular thought, cortisone injections are not necessarily painful. They can, moreover, be very effective. Relief can last as long as six months. And provided that the player does not subject his arm to further stress, the relief obtained from cortisone can be permanent.

If none of these proves effective, surgery may be suggested. In about 90 percent of these cases, Nirschl says, surgery will permit the player to return to full tennis activities without any major difficulty.

The surgical procedures involve the lifting and replacement of muscle tendons to change the leverage forces that are causing the pain. About four months will be needed for a full recovery.

There's another method of treatment that's been tried in recent years by a number of sufferers: acupuncture. Based on the ancient Chinese treatment, one or two stainless steel needles about as long as sewing needles are inserted about one inch into the elbow while others are sometimes put in the hand. They are left in for 10 or 15 minutes and, occasionally, are rotated.

A New York acupuncturist concedes there is as yet no solid explanation about why the technique should work. He contends that relief is usually achieved after only one or two treatments. Others remain

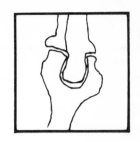

skeptical about the value of acupuncture.

Some of the measures listed above are capable of producing undesirable side effects, particularly if overused. Anyone whose tennis elbow lasts for an extended period may, for any number of reasons, find it necessary to be treated by more than one person. Whether you are able to stay with one doctor or are treated by several, the best precaution against carelessness is to maintain your own records of treatment and take them along to the doctor's office each time.

When elbow injury limits or prevents your normal tennis game, consider some alternative measures that might well keep you on court during your period of rehabilitation. Chances are that one or more of the following measures will enable you to maintain your overall fitness and your feel for the game without interfering with your recovery. Do not follow any of these suggestions if they cause physical pain; do not be surprised if, at the beginning, they cause some mental anguish.

1. Two-handed backhand. If your problem is pain on the outside of the elbow, aggravated by backhands, try using a two-handed backhand. During this period of tenderness around the elbow, you may deliberately try to have the opposite hand do most of the work. Some sports medicine people report no incidence of tennis elbow among players who have always used two-handed backhands.

2. Backhand serve. If your problem is pain on the inside of the elbow, aggravated by serving, you may find that you can manage to hit ground strokes but that serving causes pain, or, if you are playing with a brace or splint that permits ground strokes but prevents serving, you'll find that you can put the ball in play with a backhand serve.

Simply bring the racquet over your left shoulder (for a right-hander). Drop it behind your back if you can do it without pain (that is not an essential step). With your left hand, release the ball forward of the body and to the left side. Bring the racquet forward, up and across the body. With a bit of practice, you'll have a fairly slow-paced, but accurate, serve. If circumstances permit a wrist snap, your backhand serve becomes more potent. With or without wrist snap, if you're looking for a way to play tennis while recovering from an injury, this can help.

3. Shift hands. If tennis elbow entirely prevents your playing tennis, shift to the opposite hand; if you are right-handed, play with your left hand. All it takes is patience. While a high school athlete might be expected to adapt to such a change more quickly than a 50-year-old whose primary exercise is tennis, many players of all ages have successfully made this adjustment. Special agility is less crucial than determination and patience.

In fact, those two qualities—determination and patience—are what are required to overcome tennis elbow. It's an aggravation in every way, to be sure. But just remember that there are steps you can take and specialists you can consult to help you conquer it permanently.

PROTECTION FROM THE ELEMENTS

In addition to staying fit and protecting your body against tennis-related injuries, you should also take care while you play to avoid ailments and discomforts caused by the natural elements. The chief culprit here is the sun, which can damage your hair, your eyes and your skin. Wind can also create problems if you are not careful. But difficulties can be avoided with proper care.

HOW TO PROTECT YOUR SKIN FROM THE SUN

Ask most players to describe their optimum conditions for tennis and they'll probably muse about a cloudless, windless, bright sunny day when their only cares are the court, their opponent and pursuit of victory. What's wrong with this picture? Plenty, if the players value their hides, literally, and haven't done anything to protect them.

What's wrong, you ask, with some good old, healthy sunshine? What could be more beneficial to the body than to soak up some rays while you're giving your muscles and tissues a good workout on the court? Nothing, for the player who's aware of the dangers of the sun and takes steps to protect himself before he plays a couple of sets. Everything could be wrong, though, for players who expose themselves to those rays.

Despite the continued warnings of medical experts that repeated overexposure to the sun can dry skin, age it prematurely and even lead to skin cancer, America's tan-conscious society keeps chasing that golden glow at its own peril. The result is that more people may be destroying their skins on tennis courts than at any other place except the beach. And de-stroying is not too strong a word.

The penalties of excessive sun exposure without adequate protection are not pleasant. You can look forward to "sunburn, freckling, premature aging, development of growths in the skin and, possibly to those susceptible, skin cancer," warns one skin expert.

But do you have to give up your tennis to literally save your hide? No—there is a wealth of sun preparations on the market that are designed to protect you, to help you tan or just to keep your skin from drying out. Armed with a tube of goo carefully selected for your skin type and condition, some common sense and some other precautions, you can enjoy your game without worrying. The main thing is just to be careful.

Sunburn is no stranger to most of us; we know it hurts, that it makes the skin tight and dry and, since it's only a first-degree burn, that it will go away after a few days. Dermatologists get a lot of business from players who plunge into marathon matches without adequate protection and come away a painful shade of crimson. Repeated exposure to the sun without benefit of protection can lead to dry and flaky skin, a common complaint of tennis players, according to dermatologists.

The next step in sun damage is leathery skin, great for racquet grips or the Marlboro man, but not so nice for women *or* men. While overexposed skin is turning tan and leathery, dry and wrinkled, it can also develop freckles, which may or may not

strike you as pleasing.

From there, more serious sun-inflicted problems develop: pre-cancerous lesions and skin cancer itself. A premalignant lesion is often a rough, reddish-brown spot when it first appears, and at this stage is usually treatable. Some teaching pros in southern areas, for example, regularly have whole patches of affected skin removed.

"About 95 percent of skin cancers can be cured with early detection," says the American Academy of Dermatology. When an actual cancer develops, the treatment can get drastic; it was nothing out of the ordinary when a male social player, who was just 43, came to a dermatologist with a dangerous cancer on his lower lip. A chunk of the lip had to be removed surgically.

Skin cancer is indisputably linked with the sun. The AMA notes that the affliction occurs more than 90 percent of the time on such exposed areas as the face, ears, hands or neck; that it occurs more frequently in light-skinned persons than in their swarthier peers; and that it strikes more often in the southern and southwestern parts of the U.S. than in the northern sections.

Skin cancer, premature aging or dry skin are often the result of that warm, friendly sun beating down on your doubles game and emitting, among other things, ultraviolet light rays which are capable of producing both tans and burns. Which one you get depends on a number of factors, such as your skin type and the length of exposure.

Skin, to give it its due, tries to protect itself from the sun. Tanning is not a happy benefit of sunning; it's a defense against attack. Tanning is "a response to injury to the skin," notes the dermatology academy and to understand why, it's necessary to soak up a little biology.

The outer layer of skin, the epidermis, is itself composed of several layers, including the outer (or "horny") layer. Several layers below the epidermis is where the skin musters its defenses. As the sun's ultraviolet rays strike the outer layer, they disperse melanin (pigment) already found in the skin. Penetrating deeper, the ultraviolet rays stimulate the production of more melanin, which absorbs the rays. It is this melanin, migrating to the outer surface of the skin, that produces what we call a tan. It takes as long as two weeks for enough melanin to be produced, however, to protect the skin adequately.

That's why you should increase your exposure time gradually and not try to turn nut-brown in one day. The body needs time to build up its sun defenses and, if you rush things, your poor, non-acclimated skin just burns. And a burn does *not* change to a tan, especially if there's blistering and peeling involved. You just lose some of the darkened melanin already near the surface and have to start all over again.

How dark you tan depends on how much natural protection (melanin) you have in your skin and, on this basis, dermatologists classify skin into three types: fair, moderate and dark.

Fair, or pale-skinned persons, usually

have blue or green eyes, little pigment in their skins and rarely tan. Players with this skin type, exemplified in pro circles by such stars as Rod Laver and Dianne Fromholtz, need to be especially careful about exposure to the sun. The moderate skin types can tolerate more sun—Chris Evert Lloyd is an example here—but still need protection and moisturizing. Dark-skinned persons, like Evonne Goolagong, can bronze at the mere mention of the word sun, but even they have to exercise some caution since it is possible to burn through a tan. Goolagong, for one, makes it a point always to wear a moisturizer on court to counter the drying effects of the sun.

Once the skin has been aged, wrinkled or otherwise damaged by excessive, repeated exposure, there's no turning back. Once the skin's elastic tissues have been affected by years of overexposure, the leathery texture, the wrinkles and the sagging folds are there for keeps.

You don't have to make an either/or choice between your tennis game and your skin, though, if you follow some common-sense rules.

WHAT YOU CAN DO: 1. Know your skin type and act accordingly. If you just don't tan, admit it and don't bare yourself to any more sun than is necessary. If you tan moderately, take your time. If you get tan just walking on court, you still need moisturizers to offset drying and a sun screen product the first few times out.

2. Avoid the peak ultraviolet ray period of 10 a.m. to 2 p.m. Earlier or later in the day, the rays are weaker and burning is less likely to occur.

3. Use a sun preparation before and during court time, and a moisturizer afterward.

4. Don't be misled by hazy days. "You can do a fair amount of damage" even on dull days, warns a professor of dermatology at Stanford University. Ultraviolet rays are hardy devils and can penetrate clouds, haze and fog.

5. Build exposure time gradually. Start with 15 or 20 minutes and increase by 15 minutes or so daily. It takes about two weeks before a tan reaches its maximum protection level.

SUN-PROTECTION AIDS: When you walk into your local pharmacy in search of a skin product to keep you from broiling, to help you tan or simply to moisturize sun-fried skin, you should know which products do what. Otherwise, the glut of lotions, gels and creams on the shelves is apt to leave your wallet empty, your head spinning and your skin at the mercy of slick packaging.

There are basically two types of sun protection—sun blocks and sun screens. Tanning aids, a third type, do not protect against the hazards of the sun but do offer some benefits. What's the difference? Mainly, the presence or absence of a chemical which will let in all, some or none of the sun's ultraviolet, burning rays. This protective screening action is very important for fair-skinned persons, and less so for those with darker complexions or those who are already tanned.

The chemical often recommended by dermatologists is PABA (para-aminobenzoic acid), and if a product contains this screening agent or something similar, the label will usually trumpet that fact prominently.

Sun blocks, aptly named, will block out virtually all of the sun's burning and tanning rays. If you need this maximum protection because of your skin type or if your first exposure of the season will be a prolonged one, these are the friends you need—especially on vulnerable areas such as the nose and ears. Periodic reapplication is necessary to combat perspiration wash-off.

Sun screens offer protection against burning and allow some tanning; the degree depends on how much screening agent they contain. The form—whether lotion, spray or gel—is a matter of personal preference. Persons of almost all skin types should use a screen during their first major sun exposure and continue to apply it even after tanning.

As with sun blocks, most sun screens can be washed away by perspiration, al-

though those with an alcohol base tend to stay on longer. To get the maximum benefit, apply before and during a match.

Even some of the better sun screens on the market may leave an oily film on the skin, which could cause some grip problems on the court. Others may stain light-colored clothing. If the first application is made about two hours before playing, though, the preparations will have time to sink in fully.

Tanning aids include the butters, oils and lotions which claim little or no screening or blocking powers because they have very few. They don't have much to do with tanning, either, except to help keep the skin smooth and moist while your own body chemistry does the work of tanning. These products are strictly for those who can tolerate a lot of sun, either because of their natural coloring or a deep, slowly acquired tan.

After you get out of the sun, it's a good idea to apply some sort of moisturizer to the body to offset the sun's drying effects and to reduce the chance of peeling. It could be anything from baby oil to moisturizing gel to the fancy lotions packaged by cosmetic companies. But don't confuse moisturizing with protecting against the sun. Another good after-sun idea is a warm, not hot, shower or bath.

What if you want to make your season's debut in skin that's already tanned, but you don't have the time to sunbathe? There are so-called "instant tan" products on the market that may be instant but, according to skin specialists, they don't truly tan. Most get their effectiveness from a chemical which produces a tan color on the skin, but they're not recommended for tennis players. Playing five games down in the second set, if your golden "tan" is evaporating with your perspiration, any psychological edge you thought your color gave you will evaporate, too.

If you should suffer a burn, most dermatologists favor treating it as soon as possible with cool, wet compresses and lotions to ease dryness. Skin specialists aren't enthusiastic about the anesthetic sunburn sprays on the market, chiefly because some contain chemicals which can irritate certain persons' skins. For many, though, they can give temporary relief.

What if you've already burned, but don't want to abandon the great outdoors? Cover up as much as possible; use a hat to protect your face; wear long, loose sleeves and protect areas still exposed with a sun block or screen. If you've acquired a severe burn, doctors advise against going out in the sun at all.

If, after all the experts' cautions, you're still tempted to ignore their warnings and let your skin fend for itself, you should bear in mind this excerpt from a medical journal editorial: "Your skin never forgets an injury ... The eventual condition of the skin results from a summation of all the injuries it has received."

The player who values his hide will have the skin to show for it.

WHAT SUN-GLASSES CAN DO FOR YOUR GAME

Should you wear sunglasses on court?

Sunglasses are designed to ease strain by cutting down on the amount of light that gets through to your eyes. That's why you'll rarely see the pros wearing sunglasses in actual competition. They need every speck of visibility they can get; their livelihoods depend on it.

For the rest of us, though—those of us who don't have to face 120-m.p.h. serves, who can afford a slight loss of acuity— sunglasses can be a godsend. They can ease the glare from a blazing sun at noon on a concrete court; they can block out reflected light from passing cars, trucks or buses; they can help you play better in the early morning or in the early evening when you may have to glance head-on into the sun; they can prevent splitting headaches and, most important perhaps, they can prevent the loss of night vision that so often results from extended exposure to bright sunlight.

O.K., you've decided to try a pair of sunglasses specifically designed with the tennis player in mind. Which kind should you get?

First of all, you'd better make sure they're the kind that are going to stay on. Sunglasses that fail to fit properly, that are more decorative than functional, have their place, of course, but not on a tennis court where they're liable to go sailing into space the first time you lunge to save a match point. You'll also want them to fit the size and shape of your face.

As for the type of lenses you choose, that will depend to a great extent on the conditions under which you expect to wear them most. For normal use in bright sunlight, the experts say gray optical quality lenses are probably best. Why? Because they can absorb anywhere from 70 to 85 percent of the sun's harsh rays with little or no color distortion whatsoever. If, however, your problem is mainly reflected glare, you'd probably be better off with polarized sunglasses, which are especially designed to reduce that. In and out of the sun all day? You might try the new photochromatic lenses that lighten and darken automatically, as needed.

Whatever lenses you choose, make sure they're impact-resistant for safety. If you do, you'll be less prone to eye injury from a speeding ball than the player who wears no glasses at all. In a way, it's like wearing a catcher's mask in baseball.

Sunglasses are prettier, though. And not the least of their charm is that you can pop them up on your head when the match is over, just like Telly Savalas or Jackie Onassis. How's that for instant chic!

SOME TIPS ON SELECTING SUNGLASSES

Sunglasses can be fun glasses—and they can help you to look better, too. The trick lies in choosing a style or shape that most flatters your own natural features.

If your face is heart-shaped, geometric frames will probably flatter you most.

If your face is triangular, try a rectangular frame with rounded corners for a gentler look.

If your face is square, round frames will help to ease and soften the sharp angles.

If you have a Miss America-type oval face, so-called "aviator sunglasses" may be just right for you.

If you have a round face, try sunglasses with boldly angular or geometric frames.

HOW TO KEEP YOUR HAIR LOOKING GOOD

During the outdoor tennis season, a tennis player's hair is assaulted by sun, wind and sweat, the three biggest enemies of healthy hair. But by taking careful care of your hair, and armed with tips from tennis pros and hair-care experts, you can keep yours looking good.

"Dryness is a big problem on the tour," says Julie Anthony, a member of TENNIS Magazine's IAB. "You're washing your hair a minimum of once a day and blowing it dry, so you need to compensate." Anthony applies a rinse-off conditioner to her hair every day, takes it easy with blow-drying ("I only blow-dry bits of it") and uses a ph (acid)-balanced shampoo, rather than an alkaline (detergent) product. A permanent gives her naturally straight hair body and curl, while a professional trim once a month maintains the style's shape and eliminates split ends.

A good, professional cut, of course, is the building base of hair for active players, and it's important that your style follow natural partings or waves. Beyond that, how great a toll sun, wind and sweat exact on your court look is up to you.

"The sun is the biggest enemy for ten-nis players," says one professional hair stylist. "Sun can bleach and dry hair, so if you're on court a couple of times a week outdoors, it's really best to cover the hair with a cap or kerchief." Sun exposure is especially harmful for color-treated hair, and hair that gets submerged in chlorinated pools.

Adds a chemist of a major hair-care products company: "Sun damage is perhaps the worst thing that can happen to hair." Ultraviolet radiation from the sun can actually destroy hair, says the chemist, who also advocates covering hair outdoors.

If headgear isn't your court style, at least give your hair a break by recognizing the problems that outdoor tennis can pose for untended hair.

First, it helps to know a bit about hair structure to understand how and why it can be damaged. "A single hair is like a tree trunk," says a hair-care industry research supervisor. "It's covered with a cuticle scale that has anywhere from seven layers in fine hair to 10 layers in thick Oriental hair." Pulling or tugging hair, improper brushing, careless dryer styling and failure to replenish texture lost in the great outdoors can all chip away at this cuticle scale and cause breakage, split ends and dullness.

That summer breeze skimming across the courts isn't in itself a foe of your follicles, but what it carries along with it is. "The soot, pollen and grit that can be carried by wind all contribute to the task of keeping the hair clean in summer," notes the chemist.

And that task is further magnified because of a by-product of all that summer running and dashing on court: sweat. Profuse perspiration activates the sebaceous (oil) glands in the scalp, so the salt deposits left on the hair shaft by sweat are accompanied by extra oil. The result is that hair gets dirtier faster.

Naturally, you'll be shampooing more frequently in hot weather to purge the dirt. But be careful: overshampooing can aggravate summer dryness, especially in longer hair. Experts recommend only one lathering and rinsing per wash, instead of the conventional two, if you're stepping up your playing time and your scalp's activity.

It might be a good idea, if you usually use a shampoo for oily or normal hair, to switch to a dry-hair formula for the duration of your heavier court schedule. That will help cut down the chances of overcleaning when your shampoo and tennis time increase.

"The main thing is to keep the hair clean, and put back the condition it loses because of exposure and frequent shampooing," says a New York stylist who is a consultant to a hair-care products firm. "Conditioning the hair is like taking sunglasses with you to the court so you won't wrinkle from squinting." Except for those with oily hair, a treatment of instant, rinse-off conditioner after every shampoo isn't a bad idea. And dry or color-treated hair benefits from a once-a-month deep conditioning treatment.

It should be remembered, in all these cautions and corrections, that men as well as women are subject to the hair horrors that can arise from too much summer play and not enough attention to the scalp. To a degree, many men don't suffer hair problems as severely as women because their generally shorter, frequently cut styles head off split ends and frizziness sooner. But certainly the need for keeping the hair and scalp clean and conditioned is just as important for men as for women, and particularly for those males who favor longer locks.

"Men are getting many hair problems similar to women because of the longer styles," notes the director of research and development for a firm which markets a number of hair-care products. He believes that men "do need to condition their hair, and since men's hair often lacks body, sometimes hair sprays are helpful."

Just like fingerprints, "no two heads of hair are the same," he says, "and active people need to take more care than others."

The attentiveness must extend to what's done to hair after shampooing and conditioning, lest all that conscientiousness be washed down the drain.

"After you shampoo," suggests one stylist, "pluck a single wet hair and work it between your fingers. See how far you can stretch it without breaking it, and then try the same routine with a dry hair." The wet strand will stretch far more than the dry one, and too much stretching can weaken and break hair. That helps explain how a hair

brush applied to wet hair can uplift that cuticle scale. That's why hair experts advocate using a wide-toothed comb on wet, tangled hair, working always from the ends, up to the roots—not vice versa—to avoid intensifying tangles and snagging hairs.

Many post-match styles are fashioned in locker rooms with blow-dryers, and while the devices themselves are a boon to quick presentability, misusing them can be bad news.

"The problem in blow-drying," says the chemist, "is not with the blow-drying itself, but with the styling that goes along with it. Excessive combing and brushing can strip the cuticle from the hair shaft." Eventually, this will increase the rate of hair breakage, and you'll get split ends and straggles."

Not surprisingly, most pros opt for shortish styles to cut down on fuss as much as split ends and frizzies. Notable exceptions are Bjorn Borg, Vitas Gerulaitis and Guillermo Vilas. Some years ago, when Chris Evert Lloyd shed her long pony-tail style for a shorter bob, she said with relief, "It's lots easier to look after this way. I wash it, blow-dry it and walk out on the court. When it was longer, it was much more of a production."

Similarly, Virginia Wade's shoulder-length, pulled-back style gave way to her flattering "Winner's Shake" in 1977, and Julie Anthony is another whose long hair is a thing of the past. "A lot of the girls— Martina Navratilova, Betty Stove, Wendy Turnbull—have short hair," observes An-

thony. "They opt for pragmatism."

Of course, that doesn't mean that you —male or female—have to sacrifice a tumbling mane for success on court. Headbands—a la Vilas, Borg and Rosie Casals— can keep longer hair in its place, as will strategically placed barrettes, combs and pins. Just be sure you don't compress the hair too tightly or pull it back under such constant tension that it reaches the breaking point.

And, for your tresses' sake, stay away from rubber bands; almost nothing is more effective at ripping hair, especially when yanked out.

With an eye toward your hair's special hot-weather needs, you can easily prevent stepped-up court time from turning your crowning glory into a dunce cap.

Wendy Turnbull

TENNIS VACATIONS

About five years ago, the idea of a tennis vacation was a relatively new thought in the minds of tennis players and travel agents. But now the combination of tennis and travel is commonplace, and the tennis traveler is better off for it. By asking the right questions as you plan your tennis getaway, you can come up with a trip that will satisfy both your tennis and tourist instincts.

There are some specifics you'll need to think about. First on the list is the value of tennis resort package deals. Next is what to do when you get to your vacation site. Then there's that unavoidable element, the weather, and how to cope with it. Finally, you need to know how to take the kids on a tennis holiday—and enjoy it.

HOW TO PLAN A TENNIS VACATION

Today, it's safe to say, there isn't a major resort or major resort area that doesn't have at least some capability of catering to the needs of the tennis addict. There are now dozens of places where, if you go at the right time, you can play tennis for as long as your arm and legs can hold out.

That's the good news. The bad news is that the old problem of picking the place that's right for you remains. Too many people are not having as good a time on tennis vacations as they might—not because the places they've chosen to go to are not "good," but because these people haven't done a good enough job of coordinating what they really want out of a tennis vacation and what the resort they choose has to offer.

With this problem in mind, here's a list of questions you can ask yourself to come up with criteria that will help you to make a happy choice. If you go through these questions and follow up on the suggestions, your chances of going to a place that will satisfy you are much better than if you relied on brochures or a travel agent.

1. WHAT KIND OF TENNIS VACATION AM I LOOKING FOR? If you're look-ing for a great pastrami sandwich, you don't go to a Chinese restaurant—and that same principle applies, more or less, to tennis vacations. Generally speaking, there are three types of tennis places (although some resorts fall into more than one category): places that are almost entirely instruction-oriented; places that feature tennis as the chief recreational inducement, and places at which tennis is but one of many activities offered. (There is a possible fourth category—resorts that have tennis courts but don't offer much in the way of a tennis program.)

The "instruction-only" places are designed for people who want to do little else but concentrate on getting better, which is not necessarily the same thing as relaxing. Usually, but not always, there isn't too much going on at night in these places and not much in the way of "social tennis." But some people love this while others find it tedious and boring.

Know thyself. If you're the sort of person who isn't particularly receptive to instruction ("I've always hit my backhand with my eyes closed and I refuse to change"), you're better off not going to one of these places. If, on the other hand, getting better is important—more important than just hitting balls or getting a tan or falling in love—you're better off here than at the more vacation-oriented sites.

Places that specialize almost exclusively in tennis tend to attract a more social-minded crowd than the instruction-only places, but a more tennis-minded crowd than resorts where there

are many other things to do besides tennis.

What's nice about these places is that you can mix instruction with a lot of social playing, and do it in an atmosphere that is almost ubiquitously tennis. What can be taxing, however, is that tennis is sometimes the only thing ever talked about. ("Oh, yes. Anwar Sadat. Well, to be honest, I've never see him play.")

The final category is the full-service resort in which tennis is but one of a slew of recreational activities; places where you can play tennis in the morning, fire a round of golf after lunch, shoot skeet before dinner, then take a horseback ride at night.

The real appeal of these places is that, even if you don't exercise it, you still have a wide choice of what you'd like to do. The disadvantage of the "big" facilities is that the courts often get filled with people who've never really played tennis before and don't really care about it—the kind of guys, for instance, who arrive on the court dressed in baggy bermudas, an orange golf shirt and a baseball cap, and who think they're being charitable when they meet you later in the elevator and invite you to "volley" the next morning.

2. HOW DEPENDABLE IS THE WEATHER? Unless you have celestial connections, there is no way you can guarantee yourself ideal weather on your tennis vacation. But with a little bit of research, you can find out about weather patterns and at least tilt the odds in your favor. Don't be misled by the term "average daily temperature." If

a place has a lot of humidity, 78 degrees can feel like a steam room.

And don't overlook the wind factor. Unfortunately, nobody talks much about the wind in the resort business and it isn't until you get out on the court and discover that your serve goes over the net even when you don't hit it that you recognize the problem. One of the things to do in talking to resort operators is to pretend that tennis is only a secondary interest and you're primarily interested in being comfortable.

"I hope it's not too still where you are," you might say. "I really like a breeze." And if the guy says, "Well, if it's breezes you like, you're coming to the right place," then you know it's the wrong place.

3. HOW IMPORTANT IS THE FOOD AND LODGING? How comfortable you are when you're off the court and how much you look forward to—or dread—meals is going to vary enormously from tennis place to tennis place. But there's very little to say, apart from talking about each resort individually, that will help you make choices in these areas. The brochures can be cruelly deceptive, often promising a life of sybaritic excess when the prospect of Dickensian privation would be far more accurate.

Price tends to be a fairly accurate barometer of how well a tennis place does in food and lodging. The more expensive a place, the better looking it tends to be and the more elaborate its menu.

Here are two other factors to remember. First, places that are far removed from urban centers—and that means sources of

food supplies—tend to have more trouble in the kitchen than more conveniently located places. Second, places that offer villas where you can buy your own food and cook in tend to concentrate less on food than places where the restaurant is a key element in the overall vacation deal.

4. WILL I LIKE THE PEOPLE WHO GO THERE? How can anyone answer this question? Some people are so gloomy they would spread mass depression at a convention of card-carrying optimists, and it doesn't matter where they go, their response is usually the same: "I didn't like the crowd." There are other people who, no matter where they go, manage to get on famously.

Certainly, there are patterns to look for. Some of the older-line resorts, where you are expected to dress for dinner and which still provide an orchestra for dancing, will likely attract a somewhat older, more conservative group. Other resorts project a decidedly "family" atmosphere, and to be there without children is like being at a loud party without a drink.

5. WILL I BE ABLE TO GET GAMES WITH PLAYERS AT MY LEVEL? The number of players you'll meet at your level of play will depend, naturally, on your own level of play. Generally speaking, advanced players have a much tougher time picking up games at most tennis resorts than intermediate players. That's why an "A" player who's going on a tennis holiday should bring along a suitable partner.

The better resorts have a match-making system that goes beyond a list of names and numbers on a bulletin board and will make sure that a player of every level is matched up. In some places, too, there are good young players around who will hit with you for a couple of bucks.

6. WILL I BE ABLE TO PLAY ENOUGH TENNIS? Weather conditions apart, the amount of time you can figure to log on the courts each day will depend not only on the number of courts at the resort, but the ratio of courts to tennis-playing guests. You're better off at a place where there are four courts to 100 guests than a place with eight courts to 500 guests.

Once the ratio of players to courts gets higher than 20 to 1, crowding can become a definite problem, although there are other factors (maybe not all the guests are tennis players) that have to be considered, too.

One of the best ways to tell ahead of time if a resort's courts are reasonably available is to ask about their sign-up policy. If a resort is adamant about limiting daily court time to one hour per room, there's a good chance you're not going to be able to play much more than that.

7. WILL I BE BORED AT NIGHT? Talk about loaded questions. The usual reply to questions regarding night life at many tennis resorts is that the people play so much tennis during the day nobody even thinks about night life. Would that it were true. No matter how much tennis you play during the day, chances are you're going to want to do something at night, even if it's nothing more than sitting around

a lounge telling everybody how tired you are from all the tennis you played that day.

For some reason, tennis resorts, as a genre, are not notably strong when it comes to night life, and if you don't care, then don't let this question even concern you. On the other hand, if you suspect that come 9 p.m., you may want to do more than go back to your room to soak your aching feet, try to pick a place that either

239

has some night life or else is near enough to a large city so you have some options—should you choose to exercise them.

8. WILL THE VACATION BE WORTH THE MONEY? That is the toughest question of all. You'll never really be sure until you've tried it. But here's a tip to help you evaluate your answer.

The surroundings, the accommodations, the service, the food, the crowd—in short, the overall atmosphere—should all be so appealing that even if you are playing the worst tennis of your life you can still get up the next morning and proclaim, like Browning's Pippa, "God's in his heaven. All's right with the world."

All of which is another way of suggesting that if you're going to institute economies, why not stay a day or two less at a place you're likely to enjoy, rather than risk a place that's cheaper but suspect.

SHOULD YOU SIGN UP FOR A TENNIS RESORT PACKAGE DEAL?

Tennis packages have been around for several years. Like tennis resorts themselves, they are better planned and smoother operating than when they first hit the scene; but it still takes some close study to decide if a tennis package is right for you.

Some tennis "packages" offered by a number of resorts are not really packages in the true sense of the word and, in fact, offer you almost nothing you couldn't get for the same money—even less—if you were going to the same place but not on a package deal. Why should this be?

"It's simple," explains a person in the resort business. "The basic philosophy behind tennis packages is more psychological than economic. There are a lot of travelers who feel comfortable knowing ahead of time what everything is going to cost, even if they can do it cheaper on their own. The reason some packages cost more is that commissions to travel agents are built in—simply added to the bill."

Fortunately, however, there are some tennis packages worth unwrapping, and there are ways to differentiate Granada from Asbury Park, without actually going to either place. One way is to be wary of pack-

ages that offer nothing more than a lot of little "extras," like free cocktails, hats, a can of balls, etc., none of which really mean anything when it comes to the bottom line.

How, then, do you evaluate tennis packages? Here are several criteria.

LODGING AND MEALS: Generally speaking, the lodging and meals segment of most tennis packages ends up costing roughly the same as it would outside the package. The more generous packages do offer a reduction of 10 percent. As a rule, however, "package" guests do not receive prime accommodations—although it's different in some resorts. For the most part, you take what they give you.

Tennis package or not, you'll always pay less for a room out of season than you will in season. And you'll always pay less, on a proportional basis, when you are sharing a room with someone than when you're bunking down alone.

As for meals, one could debate for years the economic advantages or disadvantages of American plan (meals included) versus European plan (meals not included). But most packages seem to be built around a modified American plan (no lunch), which can be either good or bad depending upon (1) how good the food is, and (2) how much less (or more) it would cost you to eat at other restaurants.

A veteran tennis traveler recommends the European plan, except in situations where the resort eating facilities represent the only game in town. It isn't so much that you save any money—he's pretty much

convinced that for most people it works out the same—but it frees you from the guilt you may experience if, for some unforgivable reason, you should miss a meal for which you're already paying.

A second advantage is that the European plan allows you to pursue the culinary side of your vacation with a little more flexibility so that when all the American-plan people are sitting down to dine, you can be out on the tennis courts. Then, again, the cheapest way is to go to a place with a lodging mix that includes tennis facilities and, in a manner of speaking, "brown-bagging" it.

AIRFARE AND OTHER TRANSPORTATION COSTS: Unless you're part of a group that has chartered a plane or part of a smaller group of 40 or more persons that qualifies for group fares on scheduled flights, the airfare portion of the standard tennis package—when airfare is part of the price—is no less than it is normally.

Actually, the only way you, as an individual, can save on airfare when you're taking a scheduled flight is to qualify for one of those super-saver fares. And charter flights do offer some intriguing possibilities. But on regular packages, the best you can hope for is a break on the limo fare from the airport to the resort.

INSTRUCTION: Most resorts sweeten their package deals with education-oriented offerings which vary from a "complimentary lesson" to "clinics daily" to "supervised play," etc., none of which, unfortunately, tell you very much. Among other

things, what you want to find out first is: Is the "complimentary lesson" private, an hour or half-hour, with the head pro (if he's a name)? Second, are the "clinics" genuine group lessons or do you stand around watching college players hit forehands? Three, if the clinics are genuine, do they divide you according to ability? Probe for details.

COURT TIME: The manner in which court time is arranged and charged for is, in most cases, the chief factor that will determine whether the tennis package you're looking into is genuinely worthwhile. You may not be aware of it, but most resorts (particularly the multi-sports resorts) zing you with a court fee for every hour you play.

This fee usually runs around $2 or more per person per hour (more for indoor time) which may seem like peanuts until you get your bill at the end of the week and discover that the two or three hours of tennis you logged in with your mate added close to $80 to your final bill, not to mention the money you may have squandered for balls, lessons, drinks afterward and long-distance telephone calls to your home pro to find out if you left your backhand beside the pro shop soda machine.

All of which is to say that the inclusion of "free" court time in a tennis package is not to be sneezed at, although there should be certain conditions. The first condition, obviously, is that the place have enough courts so the nettlesome phrase "when available" doesn't haunt you when you come back from your first hour of tennis and discover the reservation list completely filled. Some resorts will "guarantee" you a certain number of hours, usually two, but even this guarantee may not mean all that much if you're going to a place where the heat makes it suicidal to play during the afternoon.

In any event, the amount of tennis you expect to play, coupled with the court fees under normal circumstances and compounded by the availability of court time are the main variables in the formula you can work up on your own to see whether or not a tennis package makes sense. If the most you figure to be playing is an hour a day, you're probably going to lose a little money on a package inasmuch as most resorts, when they're costing out packages, usually do their computations on the basis of two hours of play. If, on the other hand, you have the stamina to spend three or four hours on the court and you're visiting a place that charges $3 an hour, a package that includes all of your court time makes sense.

Certain packages for certain people at certain times makes eminently good sense. Just don't automatically assume, simply by the term "package," that you're going to save yourself some money.

Before you invest in any tennis package, figure out what it would cost you to get the same fun and games from the same resort but on an "a la carte" basis.

HOW TO GET THE MOST OUT OF YOUR TENNIS VACATION

Once you've made definite plans to take a tennis vacation, there are some other things you should do before you go—and things you should plan on doing once you arrive—to get the most out of your trip. Here is a list of items, to which you may be able to add even more.

START GETTING IN SHAPE BEFORE YOU GO: If your tennis routine in the past has been an hour or two of doubles a week and you think you're going to increase that overnight to three hours a day for six or seven days, you're asking for trouble—particularly if you're past 40. At least two weeks before you actually leave, try, first of all, to increase your playing time gradually (even if it means taking some playing lessons from a pro). It's not a bad idea, either, to start doing some jogging and light calisthenics.

PLAN TO TAKE SEVERAL LESSONS AND BOOK THEM IN ADVANCE: Every tennis vacation budget should have built into it enough money for at least two or three lessons. Try to book these lessons ahead of time and arrange them for early in your stay. By doing that, you accomplish several things. First, you get to know the pro

and he gets to know you, and he can then be in a better position to arrange games for you. Second, taking lessons early in the vacation gives you specific things to think about while you're playing more than you normally do and is a fine chance to reinforce good habits. The reason for booking lessons is that it's often three or four days after your arrival before you can get an open hour.

TAKE ENOUGH CLOTHING AND EQUIPMENT: If you intend to play more than an hour or two of tennis, you should bring along extra playing apparel (or else be prepared to buy it at the pro shop). The chances are—and this is especially true if you're playing in a hot climate—that you're going to be playing at different times of the day—early morning and late afternoon—which means you'll need two changes of clothing instead of one. An extra racquet is insurance against breakage, but isn't all that necessary in resorts that operate pro shops (although in many foreign countries, it's always a good idea to have an extra racquet). And make sure the shoes you bring along are *not*—repeat *not*—new. The simplest way to get blisters is to break in a new pair of tennis shoes while you're on a heavy playing vacation schedule. Another good idea is to bring along some extra cans of new balls if you have room in your suitcase. Finally, ask ahead of time if the resort has an all-white rule. Some still do.

GO EASY AT FIRST: Asking a typical club or public-park player to exercise restraint the first day or two of his vacation is

like expecting an evangelist to forgo the mention of God in his next sermon. But there's no easier way to ruin a tennis vacation totally than to overdo it the first or second day. The point is to increase your court time gradually, keeping in mind how often and how intensely you played at home.

HANG AROUND THE CLUBHOUSE: The fact that the reservation sheet is completely filled on a particular day doesn't necessarily mean you won't be able to get more than an hour's play. There are always cancellations—even at resorts. People get eaten by sharks. They wake up hung over. Or they simply don't choose to play. Just by hanging around the clubhouse, you can usually "fill in" a lot of games and, at the same time, get an idea of the kind of players with whom you'd like to arrange games.

One of the most ticklish aspects of tennis is just how do you go about arranging a game with a stranger? Some resorts —the better ones—take the embarrassing guesswork out of this problem by arranging games on their own, based on their (not your) assessment of how well you play. (This system, by the way, is murderous on your ego, but highly workable.) Barring this sort of divine intervention, it's best to be candid and, if anything, to underplay your assessment of your skills.

Usually, if a stranger (a stranger, by definition, is someone whose tennis skills are unknown to you) asks you to play, chances are he is an intermediate. Beginners are generally too shy to ask, and advanced players are usually too wary to ask. You should always accept graciously —with one exception: If you happen to be a beginner yourself, let the other person know you're not exactly Bjorn Borg or Chris Evert Lloyd and then let him or her make the decision.

RELAX: It's difficult to relax when it's costing you $50 a day to play lousy tennis, when your wife or husband keeps saying, "But, dear, it's only game," and when the teaching pro tells you that you've been hitting your forehand (your money shot) all wrong. Remember, the point of a vacation is to have a good time. If you're going to get depressed, why not do it on your home court—just think of all the money you would save.

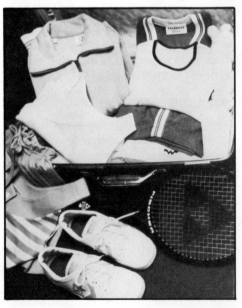

HOW TO BEAT
THE WEATHER

Mark Twain once observed that weather is the one thing everybody talks about but nobody can do anything about. But you can do more about the weather you encounter on a tennis vacation than you may think.

To say that the weather you run into when you're on a tennis vacation has an effect on how much you enjoy yourself is a little like saying that a net is important for a proper game of tennis. Paris may be lovable in a drizzle and London romantic in a fog, but when you go somewhere mainly to play tennis and the weather is either too cold or too hot or too wet or too windy to make for pleasant playing conditions, it's tough not to get depressed about it.

What usually happens when you run into a spell of rotten weather on a vacation is that you start out being mature and philosophical by telling yourself it's unrealistic to expect perfect weather. You remind yourself that if the worst thing that ever happened to you in your life was that because of the weather you couldn't play tennis one day, you should consider yourself fortunate. That is called keeping things in perspective.

Unfortunately, however, perspective becomes a tricky thing to keep if the rotten weather persists for more than a day or two. Oh, you try to adjust. You read magazines. You play video games until you hear the bleep-bleeping in your sleep. You hang out in the hotel shops. You linger a little longer at meal times. You strike up commiserating conversations with other guests. But then the fact that you are spending $80 a day to do all of that begins to dominate your consciousness, and you suddenly find yourself behaving as if you were a Michelin Guide critic, determined to build a case that will result in a three-star demotion.

You find the food increasingly rubbery and you're convinced somebody is pouring vinegar in the wine. The maid isn't cleaning your room the way she should and you're sure, by the way the front desk clerk keeps smiling, that he's enjoying the fact that all the guests are miserable. And who, in God's name, does the paperback buying for the gift shop? Is Zane Grey the only author he's ever heard of?

No need to bludgeon the point. A tennis vacation without good weather is like a disco record you can't dance to. But the question remains: Is there anything you can do about it? There is. Sort of.

The main thing you can do about the weather is to do some research ahead of time about the meteorological patterns in a particular resort area. And "research" does not mean just a phone call to a travel agent or a perusal of travel brochures, whose photos and prose would lead you to believe that weather is never a problem.

Get thee to your local library and check out any of the numerous weather reference books for information on what the weather is apt to be like at the place you want to go, when you want to go.

Granted, you have no way of knowing that the week or so you go off to a particular place will bring "typical" weather for that time of year. But it's certainly useful to know that in Puerto Rico, for instance, the average monthly rainfall is three times as heavy in May as it is in March. It's helpful to know, too, that Acapulco averages something like 11 inches of rain per month from June to September but less than one-half inch per month from December through April.

Weather information on file at most libraries can also tell you things like the average number of clear or cloudy days in a given month, wind patterns and humidity. Were you aware, for example, that probably the best month to play tennis at the growing number of resorts in the Virginia area is October? Why? Because, according to the U.S. Weather Almanac, both the average temperature and humidity are in the 60's, but, more important, the average number of clear and sunny days is 14, as compared to seven in June and July.

October also appears to be the best month from a weather standpoint to go tennis vacationing in Arizona. The average temperature then is in the low 70's, the average monthly rainfall is less than one-half inch, and there are only two months (June and September) when the statistics relating to clear days are more propitious. In January, by contrast, the average temperature during the day over the past 25 years has been in the low 60's and the average number of clear days 14, one third less than in October. Oddly enough, however, January is a much busier month for most Arizona resorts than October.

Which brings up one of the more curious aspects of weather as it relates to resort operations: the connection between weather and seasonality. Most resorts adjust their rates according to the season, but don't you confuse seasonality with weather conditions. At one time, there was a direct connection between weather and a resort's seasonal rates, but that was before air-conditioning. Today, seasonality has as much to do with sales patterns as it does with weather patterns.

A case in point is Florida. A lot of vacationers refuse even to consider Florida as a place to go in the summer. It's simply too hot, too humid, right? Yet, resorts in South Carolina and Georgia are busiest in July and August despite the fact that the weather patterns are quite similar to those of Florida, the difference being only a point or two in temperature and humidity.

What explains the differences in public attitude? Probably the fact that most of the resorts in South Carolina and Georgia were built after the advent of air-conditioning and, unlike the older Florida resorts, they don't carry with them the stigma of being too hot and humid to visit in summer. Not that you should neglect Georgia or South

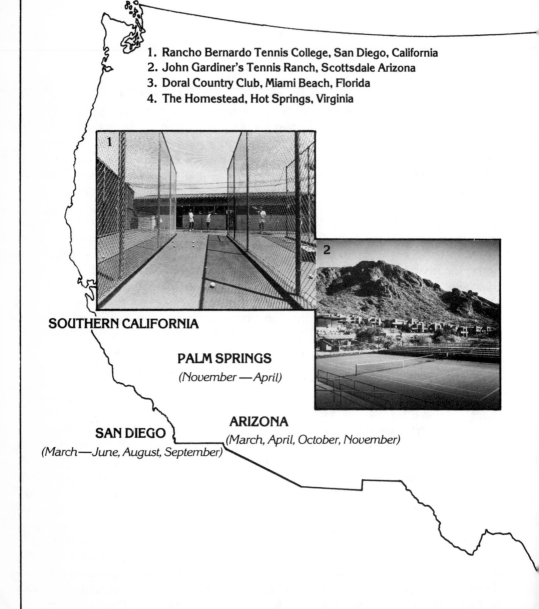

1. Rancho Bernardo Tennis College, San Diego, California
2. John Gardiner's Tennis Ranch, Scottsdale Arizona
3. Doral Country Club, Miami Beach, Florida
4. The Homestead, Hot Springs, Virginia

SOUTHERN CALIFORNIA

PALM SPRINGS
(November —April)

ARIZONA
(March, April, October, November)

SAN DIEGO
(March—June, August, September)

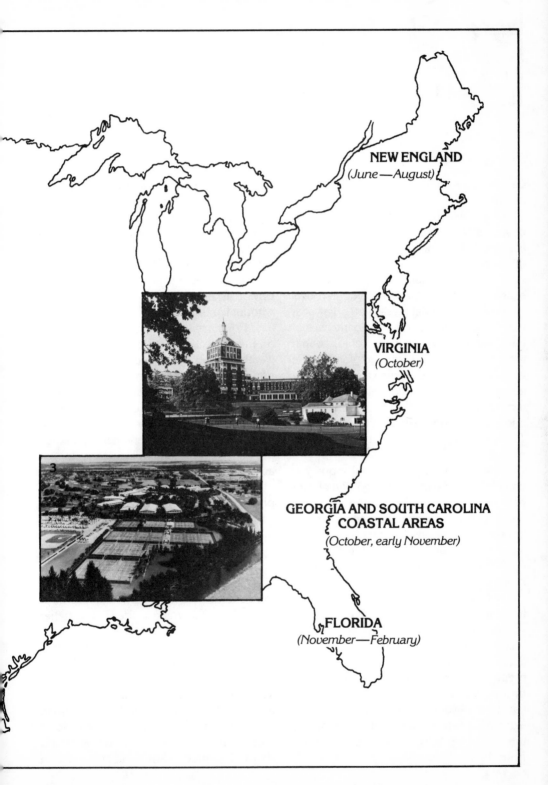

NEW ENGLAND
(June — August)

VIRGINIA
(October)

GEORGIA AND SOUTH CAROLINA COASTAL AREAS
(October, early November)

FLORIDA
(November — February)

Carolina as a summer vacation destination in favor of Florida. It's just that you shouldn't assume because one area is charging "high" season rates and another area isn't, that the weather is necessarily different.

There are other ways, apart from researching on your own, that you can deal with the weather that awaits you on a vacation trip. One thing you can do in cases of bad weather is to cash in your chips sooner than you'd planned and go somewhere else. People have been known to go to Florida and, after two days of below-50-degree temperatures, spend an hour on a phone and make arrangements to go to St. Thomas, where the temperatures are in the mid-70's.

Even if you've prepaid your room, you can usually get back a good portion of your payment, if you handle it in the right way. Many tennis places that run week-long clinic programs will, in the case of really bad weather, charge you only for the days you've been there and refund the rest of the money.

Another thing you can do if you're really paranoid about the weather is to choose a resort that is close to a city or an area that has a sizable number of non-tennis attractions. And a final thing you can do is to prepare for the weather—pack at least one or two pieces of clothing you may have to use in the event temperatures vary in the extreme. Keep in mind that the temperature in many places fluctuates considerably from day to night.

Remember, too, that the kind of court surface a resort has is something to consider. Generally, surfaces like clay and Har-Tru are easier to play on in very hot and sunny weather than the hard surfaces which reflect the heat and sun more. And hot-climate resorts that have lighted courts obviously enjoy an advantage over those without lights.

Forecasting, even in the short term, is an inexact science at best. Looking at the weather map published in most newspapers is helpful, but only to a point. You can tell whether a high-pressure system (a sign of good weather) or a low-pressure system (uncertain weather) is headed in the direction of your resort and can usually tell if a serious situation—a hurricane, for example—is in its embryonic stages. But any number of things can happen in the atmosphere to change the situation by the time you arrive. That's particularly true of mountain areas, where the weather can change by the hour.

Following is a list of the more heavily trafficked resort areas in the country and the general weather patterns that prevail in each place, according to the U. S. Weather Almanac.

FLORIDA: The weather patterns here vary slightly from coast to coast and north to south. The west coast of Florida—Sarasota, etc.—tends to be a little colder than Miami and northern Florida in the summer. In the winter months, the southern tip of Florida, including the Miami area, is a good six to 10 degrees warmer on average than

areas to the north and west, such as Jacksonville, Orlando and Tampa.

Florida's rain patterns are interesting. The driest months throughout the state are November through February, but there are some sectional differences. Miami, for instance, averages more than eight inches of rain in October, while Tampa averages less than three inches in the same month. Tampa, on the other hand, tends to get more rain in the summer months.

Rain patterns in the summer months, moreover, tend to be fairly predictable, consisting mainly of afternoon showers. Summer temperatures throughout Florida tend to average in the low 80's, but it's the relative humidity, usually in the low 70's, that makes for discomfort.

GEORGIA AND SOUTH CAROLINA COASTAL AREAS: The best tennis months for the resorts in this area are October and early November. Temperatures usually range in the mid-70's and rainfall averages half the amount that falls in September, when the temperature and humidity levels are about the same as in October.

June through August are the wettest months, but the rain tends to come in short squalls and usually at night. If you go to any of the resorts in this area from December through March, your chances of finding warmish weather are about 50/50. Winter temperatures tend to average in the 50's, except in March when the average climbs to near 60 degrees.

ARIZONA: This state's best months for tennis are March, April, October and November. The summer months are fine if you're a bedouin and don't mind average daily temperatures in the mid to high 90's. December through February can get a little chilly—warm-up suit weather, to be sure. The big attraction in Arizona, of course, is the sunshine. Phoenix receives less rainfall in a year than Miami gets in August, and the wettest month is August, when you wouldn't want to go there anyway.

SOUTHERN CALIFORNIA: Except for the inland and desert areas like Palm Springs, southern California is pretty much an all-year tennis vacation place. San Diego's coldest months, for instance, are December and January, when the average temperature is in the mid to high 50's. And in the summer months, it's rarely warmer than 80 degrees. On the other hand, San Diego can be a sticky place in July, when the humidity averages in the high 70's, and there is quite a bit of fog to contend with from October through February, although it generally burns off by late morning or early afternoon.

Palm Springs? It's dependably dry throughout the year but extremely hot in the summer months. The wind can be troublesome, but it's tough to predict. Palm Springs' season runs from Christmas through Easter, but November and late April are good months to go, not only because of the weather, but because of the off-season rates.

NEW ENGLAND: The resorts in this region keep lengthening their tennis sea-

sons, but June through August remains your safest bet. August tends to be wetter than June or July, but not by much. September is drier than all three summer months but a good 10 degrees cooler on average than the other months. (The foliage, however, makes up for it.) Showers are common in the mountain resorts, but long rainy spells are rare.

ENJOY A TENNIS VACATION WITH YOUR CHILDREN

Some tennis players would rather undergo open-heart surgery than take their children with them on a tennis vacation. It is not easy to enjoy yourself on a tennis vacation when you have children who: (1) station themselves outside your court, like bodyguards for a Latin dictator, and interrupt your game every five minutes to find out when you are going to be finished playing; (2) demonstrate their disenchantment with the luncheon menu by pouring salad vinegar into the water pitcher; (3) choose to stay in the hotel room watching reruns of "Get Smart," "Mr. Ed" and "My Little Margie" rather than participate in the children's tennis clinic for which you have prepaid $50.

But does it have to be this way? Do children who don't play tennis belong on a tennis vacation? Do children who *play* tennis belong on a tennis vacation? Do children belong, period?

Many parents think children should vacation with them, even if it's the sort of vacation in which the chief priority for the adults is to play as much tennis as possible. Some parents don't like the idea of leaving their kids at home alone with a sitter for more than a day or two. Others who do

Adults and children alike can enjoy lessons and clinics on tennis-playing vacations.

travel without their children invariably cross paths with happy families traveling together and end up spending their whole vacation berating themselves for having deprived their own kids of the trip.

On the other hand, some children have a tendency to reenact World War II every time they travel with their parents, so that taking them on a trip is not without its special challenges. As Robert Benchley once said: "Traveling with children is like traveling third class in Bulgaria." Still, it is possible to work things out. It takes a little

planning, a little imagination and a lot of patience. Here are some suggestions.

Most tennis resorts "welcome" children, but not every place is firmly oriented to the same degree. So rule No. 1 when you're planning a tennis vacation with the children is to choose a resort that holds special appeal for them. For example, there are some resorts that offer structured daily children's programs. Day camps, really. This means that if your kids are too young to play tennis, you don't have to chain them to the bedpost or drag them down to the

courts whenever you're playing. The quality of these programs depends pretty much on the counselors but most of the resorts offering the service do a pretty good job of administering it.

In the absence of a genuine children's program, it's prudent to look for a place that offers a fairly large spectrum of activities —more than just courts and a swimming pool. Most kids adore beaches—provided they haven't seen"Jaws"—but don't overlook such amenities as a game room, horseback riding, bike riding or a bowling alley. None of these non-tennis activities may mean anything to you if your key purpose is to develop a second serve, but they can keep the children occupied while you're developing it.

Another thing to think about when you're choosing a place is the type of accommodations available. All things being equal, villa-style accommodations are more suitable—and usually cheaper—for families than typical hotel or motel rooms. There's more space, more privacy. What's more, the presence of kitchenettes enables you to be more flexible with meal schedules.

Air transportation for a family vacation can swallow up most of the budget, so some people motor to vacation destinations despite energy costs. Depending on the sort of kids you have, a long motor trip can either be a fine opportunity for a family to get to know one another better or an instant replay of Dante's "Inferno." Having survived dozens of long motor trips, one veteran parent traveler offers the following advice.

1. Try to limit each day's driving to six or seven hours and break it up into two halves, a meal in between.

2. Get an early start or drive early in the evening, but try to avoid the afternoon heat.

3. Buy a ton of comic books, games, activity cards, etc., to keep the kids occupied.

The idea of establishing a schedule on a vacation may strike you as ridiculous and self-defeating. But your kids will enjoy themselves a good deal more and give you a lot less trouble if you spell things out for them every day. Let them know, for instance, that after you play your two or three hours of tennis in the morning, everyone is going to have lunch at the beach or pool, at three o'clock go on a hike or a horseback ride, at five come back to the room for a rest and at seven go to dinner. One family distributes a written daily schedule that all members carry with them throughout the day. It has a remarkable psychological effect.

The amount of time you spend playing tennis with your children will obviously depend on how advanced they are. Beginners pose a problem, so it might not be a bad idea to spring for some lessons. (And it would be nice, incidentally, if more resorts offered clinics especially for kids.) But even if the kids are only beginners, be a sport and set aside some of your own court time for them.

Don't worry about instruction. Just

have some fun. Try to play a couple of games. The important thing here is to give the kids a sense of participation. You'd be surprised at how much more tolerant they'll be about your own playing schedule if they can look forward to a hitting session later in the day with Mom and Dad.

One of the more common mistakes that some couples make when they take children with them on vacation is to expect the kids to adjust to adult routines—particularly when it comes to evening meals. A nine o'clock dinner with candlelight and wine is romantic and continental but generally intolerable for the typical 8-year-old. Compromise. If you're going to be away for six nights, figure on eating at least four evening meals at a reasonable hour with the kids. The other two nights you can arrange for a babysitter and go off by yourselves. There's no law, of course, that says you can't go off by yourselves every night and leave the kids with a sitter. But most children resent being left behind every night, and some of them have intriguing ways of showing it, like spilling maple syrup on your newly strung racquet the next morning.

One final tip. It may involve bringing along an extra suitcase, but try to take with you as many little games, books and activity booklets as you can manage. Kids, remember, have low boredom thresholds and can be particularly bothersome during those periods of the day when you and your mate, having played tennis for three hours in 90 degree temperatures, simply want to relax. So bring checkers, crossword puzzles, some jigsaw puzzles—anything that can keep the kids reasonably absorbed.

Television is a help, too, but not all resorts have sets in the rooms, and not all the sets in the rooms get good reception. One couple never goes anywhere with their kids without a portable TV set. Another man, moreover, taught his daughter to play chess during the course of a tennis vacation. He's prouder of that than he is about anything else that happened on the vacation, other than the fact that he spent a week with his kids and still likes them.

TENNIS CAMPS AND CLINICS

If you took the money it costs to go to a tennis camp (and the average is at least $600 per person) and handed it over to your local pro, you could probably get twice the amount of actual instruction time you receive at most camps and be able to spread it out over several weeks, too. But this argument doesn't really relate to the way things are in recreational tennis.

Not many people spend $600 on private lessons with their local pro. And if they do and cannot show markedly improved strokes and results because of it, they'd be subject to their own self-doubts as well as ridicule from their tennis-playing friends.

Realistically speaking, you're highly unlikely to devote yourself as single-mindedly to tennis on your own as you are obliged to do at a tennis camp. If you choose the right one, a tennis camp will help your game. There are different types of camp programs which you should evaluate before making your final choice. Once you get there, you should follow some simple guidelines to make sure you get the most out of the experience. You may find later that you want to go back for a second time. Finally, while you may decide to skip the camp routine entirely, one or more of your children might ask to go, in which case, it will be important to choose the right one.

WHAT A TENNIS CAMP CAN DO FOR YOUR GAME

The fun of going to a tennis camp actually begins several weeks before you take flight, when you begin to notice a subtle change in your outlook about the game. Whereas before, the act of missing an easy overhead at a critical point in a match might have inspired fantasies of self-immolation on the center court of Wimbledon, you now absorb errors with professional nonchalance, filing the experience away in that portion of your mind now specifically designated for PROBLEMS TO BE IRONED OUT WHEN I GET TO TENNIS CAMP.

You don't even boil inside when the snobs at your club perform their look-away-from-you number the minute you come into the clubhouse in search of a partner. For you are secure in the knowledge that once you get back from tennis camp, they will be clawing at your feet for the privilege of having you in their foursome.

But is it true? That is, can you really improve that much in a single week? Perhaps not, but that's not the purpose of a tennis camp. Let's see how a camp actually operates.

There is a lot of confusion surrounding the various terms used in the description of tennis facilities that specialize in structured lessons for adults. Some tennis executives don't like the term "camp," their feeling being that it conjures up the wrong sort of image: water fights and overnight hikes and being chewed to death by mosquitoes in a dank bunk. Hence some camps refer to themselves as clinics, while still other instructional facilities prefer the more Ivy-league sounding term "academy."

No matter. A tennis camp, for our purposes, is any tennis facility that offers an organized instructional package running anywhere from three to six days. A clinic is usually for a shorter period of time, such as a Friday afternoon through Sunday afternoon weekend session.

Within this definition, though, are two specific categories of camps. Category I takes in all those places that operate out of colleges, private schools and children's camps. In these the emphasis is almost entirely on tennis with little in the way of night life or other activities. Category II takes in those camps that operate out of true resorts where the lodging is fancier, the food more elaborate, the night life spicier and generally there is a broader range of non-tennis activities after you're finished on the court. More and more standard resorts are instituting tennis camp programs of a sort, and they fall into this category.

(There is another classification that falls under category II. These are the so-called "celebrity camps," places that bear the names of well-established tennis figures. Many of these have disappeared re-

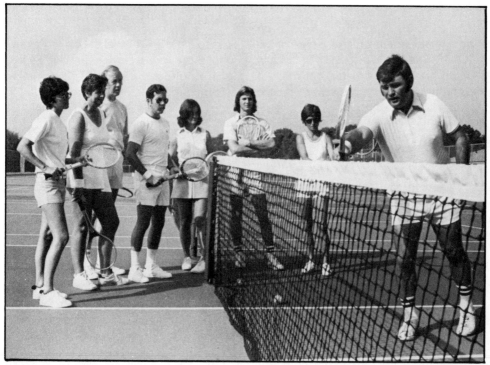

Clinic participants listen avidly to their instructor at Newks Tennis Ranch, New Braunfels, Texas.

cently for economic reasons. Most established professionals can earn more money by signing autographs in a shopping center than a tennis camp can afford to pay them for a week's work without putting the price of the week beyond the reach of the average camper. Leave your autograph book at home.)

As you might well imagine, you pay considerably more for the camps in category II than you do for category I. And what you're paying for, mainly, are the non-

tennis trappings, all of which may or may not be important to you. The instructional format and the actual tennis aren't all that much different from one category to another and, in some instances, actually better in the more Spartan-like camps. Unfortunately, there are so many variables—not the least of which is the personalities of the instructors—that it's impossible to generalize as to which type of camp offers the best all-around value.

Nearly all instruction at tennis camps

is done in groups: four or five to a group, on one court with one instructor. Some of the time, of course, you're getting individual attention from the instructor, but most of the time the regimen consists of practice drills specifically designed for four players.

All things considered, the four-to-a-court system works reasonably well. But it's far from perfect. At some camps, where the ratio of campers is 5 to 1 or higher, you might spend at least 20 percent of the time standing around with nothing to do except fret about the money you've spent to stand around.

A more nettlesome problem arises when you find yourself the only player in a foursome who can hit the ball over the net more than three consecutive times—a situation roughly analogous to being a claustrophobic on a crowded elevator. Tennis camps do their best right from the start to segregate the better players from the out-and-out beginners, but their best is frequently not good enough.

The only foolproof way of making sure this never happens to you is to arrive at the camp with your hand-picked foursome already established. Otherwise, if you don't like your foursome, you can always issue a discreet complaint to the head pro, who will usually try to figure out some means of accommodating you even if it means some individual instruction (at no extra cost) after the regular session is over.

The increased competition in the field of tennis camps in recent years has led to improvements in the instruction offered. In the past it would have been stretching a point to describe most of the camp instructional programs as having any true educational basis. But as the level of players going to camps rose, the organizations began to perfect their knowledge about techniques and sound instruction.

More changes are coming—like shorter instructional days. Most tennis camps are finding that the average player, regardless of how much he or she *says* he wants to play, doesn't fare all that well on a six- or even five-hour-a-day instructional regimen. Four hours a day—two in the morning and two in the afternoon—is becoming more and more the norm throughout the field. Many places are opting for a three-hour instructional set confined to either the morning or the afternoon.

Finally, the individual instructional programs are a lot more varied than ever before. More intelligent use of video; a greater emphasis on strategy and "supervised play." At some camps, you get running drills. Other places offer "station"programs during which you pick and choose the strokes you want to work on.

All of which pretty much takes care of the good news. The bad news—or, at least, the troublesome news—is that still too few camps have spent enough time thinking about either the quality of the instruction they offer or the effectiveness of their overall programs. There are far too many indifferent and unqualified persons working as teaching professionals throughout the tennis camp field (alas, the money isn't that

great and many places rely on young college players, many of them lacking experience and desire). And certainly there is too little organization in some programs if the one thing you do most is stand in line waiting for a turn to hit.

There is an underlying reason for most of these problems. It is that many tennis camps haven't really made up their minds about what exactly they are trying to accomplish during the three or four or six days you spend at a camp.

Not that it's easy. The dilemma that every tennis camp faces is whether to do something for you that will institute immediate improvement or something that will produce a temporary decline but noticeable improvement two or three months down the pike.

What makes this such a dilemma is that while many players profess to want the latter, most are psychologically equipped to deal only with the former. Vic Braden puts it as well as anybody when he tells his Tennis College students, "Everybody in tennis just wants to beat one other person, the one who beats you 6-3, 6-3 every Saturday. Well, when you leave here, if you do what we say, you will go back home and get beat 6-1, 6-1 because you will be uncomfortable. Most of you will then go back to what you were doing before so you will only get beat 6-3, 6-3 every week for the rest of your life."

Recognizing this tendency in human nature, many camps—the majority, certainly—do not try to do too much in the way of overhauling your game. Rather than outfit you with a new chassis, they'll smooth out the dents in the old one. Rather than waste your time with a lot of technical details you are likely to leave behind with your room key, they stress a few basic stroking fundamentals—footwork, eye contact, hitting through the ball—and try to get you to hit as many balls as possible. The function of the pro who feeds you balls on each court is to point out "little things," but mainly to ply you with encouragement and maintain an upbeat atmosphere. You don't get nagged. "Whatever else we want our people to get out of our camps," John Newcombe says, "it's enjoyment. We want them to learn, but have fun doing it."

Others in the field more than echo Newcombe's sentiments. The operating philosophy of the John Gardiner camps, for instance, has long been that it is unwise and unfair to try and teach an old tennis dog new tricks. "We build on what you already have," Papa John himself likes to say. And at the All American Sports Camps, the key phrase is "accelerated improvement." "It's impractical to think that you can rebuild somebody's game in a week," says All American's Gil deBotten. "What we try to do instead is accelerate the normal improvement process. We figure that after a week at one of our camps, you'll be playing as well as you'd be playing four or five months from now if you hadn't come."

Even as solid a fundamentalist as Harry Hopman has resigned himself to overlook the little quirks and idiosyncrasies

in the stroking styles of many of the intermediate players who come to his International Tennis Camp at Bardmoor in Largo, Fla. "You have to be realistic," says the Australian coach. "Most people come to a tennis camp to improve. They want to see improvement when they leave. So I am very careful about making changes in a person's game.

"Take a woman in her late 30's who has been playing the game for 10 or 15 years and has been using a flat serve with a forehand grip. If you try to get that woman to change to a spin serve with a different grip, she probably won't be able to make the change unless she is willing to really work at it. And you're likely to give her a shoulder problem. My approach is to take that flat serve with the forehand grip and show the woman how to use it more effectively—how to place the ball better or how to balance the pace better between her first and second serves."

There is nothing at all wrong with this outlook and it unquestionably suits many, many players. But there is the player who really wants to get his game overhauled, has an armored tank for an ego and is willing to spend whatever time and endure whatever pain is necessary to remold his game. Too often, players who fall into this category feel they're being patronized.

"There is a very subtle game that goes on at some of the camps I've been to," says Bill Cosby, one of the most intense buffs on the celebrity tennis circuit. "They think you don't really want to do what's necessary to get better, but they know you want them to think you do, so you spend a lot of time doing things that give you the illusion you're learning but aren't really helping you much at all."

There are certain camps, to be sure, about which this criticism cannot be made, and they include those where the prime focus is on the mechanics of stroke production. What distinguishes these camps isn't so much the methods of stroke production they teach, but the degree to which detailed stroke instruction and analysis dominate the program.

You don't run or rally as much at these places as you do at others. The pace is slower, there is less emphasis on socializing and hardly any supervised play as such. For better or worse, the instructors make a definite attempt to reshape your strokes. Not all of them are equally successful and some campers find the regimen boring. But the seriousness of purpose is here.

"I do not believe the old cliché that you can't change the strokes of somebody who's been playing for years," insists Dennis Van der Meer, whose TennisUniversities are among the most mechanically oriented and structured in the business. "What does it take to get a stroke regrooved? A few thousand balls? Hell, you can do that in a few days. The reason many camps have been unsuccessful at changing people's games is that the instructors at a lot of them don't know how to teach."

The average player is more receptive to change than many camps are willing to

recognize, agrees another camp director who says, "Technique is everything. And part of the job of a teaching pro is to be able to isolate those few important things in a player's stroke that will make a difference. I agree, there are some players whose games you wouldn't attempt to reconstruct, but I wouldn't say that these players are in the majority."

Fred Stolle, the resident pro at a Florida club, is another top teacher who believes a player's game can be rebuilt. Says Stolle: "Our attitude is that it's our job not only to recommend changes, but to motivate the people to keep these changes in mind when they leave the camp. I always give a speech on the next-to-last night when I suggest to the campers that they not play any matches for the next couple of months, but practice instead. I tell them frankly that if they don't do this, they've wasted their time."

All things being equal, a beginner would be better off at a camp that lays it on very heavy when it comes to the fundamentals of stroke production. Supervised play is of no use if you can't hit the ball over the net. Videotape is nice, but not essential. Look for a place that has a well-organized program and a definite philosophy of teaching.

As for intermediate and advanced players, it all boils down to exactly what you want to get out of a tennis camp. If you are one of those players who is genuinely committed to getting better and you are willing to put in the time and endure the frustration of rebuilding your game, you would obvi-

ously be better off at a place that is willing and able to perform the necessary surgery.

But if you're simply looking for a tennis vacation that has an instructional flavor or are interested in solidifying what you already have—shaky as it may be—don't mess up your mind by worrying about it too much. Pick a place that's within your price range, that has a good reputation and offers non-tennis features—lodging, location, etc.—that appeal to your non-tennis tastes.

Harry Hopman: "You have to be realistic."

264

TEN COMMANDMENTS FOR SURVIVAL AT A CAMP

Before you take off for tennis camp, you should make sure your racquet and clothes are ready, the instructional format is what you want, the number of courts and instructors in relation to the number of campers is large enough (one teacher and one court per four students is fine, one to five is so-so), there is time for free play after instruction and the price and amenities fit into your budget and lifestyle.

After you've finished with this checklist, you can start getting ready for the actual camp experience. To survive there—and get the most out of it—you have to be able to cope with a sudden and dramatic increase in the demands you make on your body, your brain and your psyche.

The 10 commandments for survival at a tennis camp offered here are an attempt to reduce and possibly eliminate the suffering—to leave you free to concentrate on developing a Tanner-like serve, a Borg-like forehand, an Ashe-like backhand or whatever it is you seek at a camp or clinic. If you follow these commandments and still don't make it—well, at least you'll know you gave it your best shot.

The first thing you have to realize about a tennis camp is that it's a place where you're going to play *a lot* of tennis— maybe more than you've ever played before in a concentrated period. You'll be running, stopping, starting, volleying, stroking for an average of about four hours a day each day of your stay. That's a lot of running, stopping, starting, serving, volleying and stroking. And your body may rebel— unless it's ready for it.

Hence, the first commandment: *Thou shalt prepare thyself before going to a tennis camp.* The best way to do that is to start exercising at a moderate pace and then build up to approximately the same level of activity you expect to experience at camp. Hard to do? Sure. But the extent to which you prepare yourself—by doing push-ups, sit-ups, jogging, sprinting and weight-lifting—is the extent to which you'll minimize your aches and pains and maximize your fun and learning.

What if for some unavoidable reason you can't prepare yourself completely? Second commandment: *Thou shalt pace thyself as much as possible.*

For example, the mind may say: "Well, I was a star halfback in high school (not mentioning that it was 20 to 30 years ago), so with my talent and guts, I can handle whatever they throw at me." It is not so. You must pace yourself, not try so hard every second of the day and sublimate your ego when it threatens to pose a health hazard. If you find yourself suddenly breathless—or experience a twinge of pain in the chest— just say: "I'm going to have to drop out for a

minute or so."

Which brings us to the third commandment: *Thou shalt not overeat or overindulge and then attempt to bust a gut on court.*

In other words, you can't expect to stuff yourself at breakfast or lunch, then go out and play up a storm. Even more important, you can't expect to party into the wee hours of the morning, imbibing more than you should, and then get up early the next day and cavort about like a frisky all-American. Unless you're young and fit enough for that kind of action—and few of us are—you just can't withstand it for even so short a period as a week.

Taking it easy on the bubbly, though, does not mean you shouldn't drink a lot. You should. The fourth commandment says: *Thou shalt replace thy body fluids adequately.*

And that's one of the most important commandments of all, especially if you're heading into a warmer climate. Drink plenty of water, fruit juices and/or bottled thirst-quenching beverages. Indeed, if you get thirsty at anytime on court, don't keep on playing. Stop and get some water immediately. You could be heading off a bad case of heat exhaustion or even a stroke. And, anyway, you're supposed to be having fun, not torturing yourself.

The fifth commandment: *Thou shalt honor thy racquet hand and thy feet.* Self-explanatory—a little thing like a blister on your racquet hand or either of your feet can easily spoil what should be a holiday.

How can you prevent it from happening? By wearing a tennis glove if your gun hand isn't up to hours of play; by checking your racquet hand and your feet each day for potential blisters, and covering up the trouble spots with tape bandages; by making sure that your shoes fit properly and are well broken in before you go to camp; by always wearing two pairs of socks.

A blister is bad enough, but a sprain or break can be a disaster. Thus, the sixth commandment: *Thou shalt keep an eye out for stray balls on court.*

This one's a "must" rule—on a par with "never play with fire" or "look before you leap"—and most coaches are very conscientious about seeing that it's observed. Tennis campers, though, should take it upon themselves before they begin to run on court to make sure there are no stray balls lying about that they might trip on. If they don't they'll possibly risk serious falls.

Injuries aside, a certain amount of soreness is inevitable—the kind that almost always accompanies a sudden burst of physical exertion. Nevertheless, a pain of any kind, especially an acute pain, is a warning signal and should not be ignored.

Or as the seventh commandment instructs: *Thou shalt tend thy sore parts with heat, aspirin or rest, as necessary.* Heat can be applied perhaps most pleasantly by means of a steam bath, a sauna or a whirlpool, but a long soak in a hot tub will do in a pinch. A massage, if it's available, is even better. A couple of aspirin will also

help to reduce soreness.

If, however, the pain is caused by a severe strain or a sprain of any sort, and it persists in spite of routine care, you may have to lay off for a day or two; either that or risk a more serious injury that could blow your whole camp experience.

Eighth commandment: *Thou shalt protect thy skin.* From what? From the sun. The reasons are obvious. A bad case of sunburn can be very painful at worst and unsightly at best. And, really, there's no reason for it. All it takes to protect yourself from the sun is a liberal application of any of a number of commercial protective ointments containing PABA (para-amino-benzoic acid) to block out some of the ultraviolet rays. You'd better take along a hat, too.

Ninth commandment: *Thou shalt protect thyself from insects.* Bugs can be a terrible nuisance. So pack some insect repellent and you won't be bothered—it's as simple as that. And be sure to use it the first day; afterward may be too late.

As for the tenth commandment: *Thou shalt give thyself a rest before going back to a busy work schedule.* Easy—and, thus, easily overlooked. If you're smart, though, you'll give yourself at least a half-day or a full-day's rest after you return home before you plunge back into the workaday grind. That's to allow your "wounds" to heal so you won't return to work from a vacation as so many of us do—dead tired.

This camper-to-be is avoiding potential aches and pains by observing the first commandment.

WHAT'S IN STORE THE SECOND TIME AROUND

There is a case to be made for the second time around. You already know about love and marriage. The question is whether you know about tennis camps.

You may have been to a tennis camp once and there's a possibility you're not that anxious to repeat the experience. Possibly, you were victimized by one of the following experiences:

• You went to a tennis camp with the impression you would spend a week under the personal tutelage of a tennis superstar, but the chief claim to fame of the person actually running things was the fact that, as a ball boy during the 1968 U.S. Open, he developed a foot blister and had to be replaced in the middle of a five-set semifinal match.

• Your best shot—the forehand that carried you to your club championship last year—was found to be lacking in certain crucial elements, according to the pros who analyzed it. And thanks to their suggestions it became, in the course of a week, your *worst* shot.

• The day after you got back, you played a match with your regular tennis partner who, while you were at camp, had met and had a brief affair with a movie star and, of course, had not played tennis once in the interim. You lost 6-0, 6-0. "I hate to tell you this," your partner said, "but I think you wasted your money."

But why dwell on the past? You've probably changed since your last tennis camp experience. And because tennis camps have changed since that time, too, maybe it's time to think in terms of another visit. Except that this time, you can benefit from your past mistakes.

Let's start with what you did wrong the last time.

Your biggest mistake was going away with the idea that a week at a tennis camp was going to revolutionize your game. Nonsense. If we are to believe Bill Tilden's observation that it takes 10 years to become a champion, you can't very well expect five or six days to produce a quantum jump.

The point of a tennis camp isn't the degree of improvement you notice between the day you arrive and the day you leave. It's the opportunity it gives you to consolidate: to get a fix on where your game needs work and how you can go about improving those areas. Yes, you could achieve the same thing at home with your local pro, but a tennis camp enables you to think about nothing but tennis during the time you're there.

The second mistake you may have made was being much too passive about the entire experience, as if your mere presence at a tennis camp was enough to assure giant strides. The people who get the

most out of a camp experience are those who really throw themselves into it, who aren't bashful about asking questions and getting the pros to give special advice.

And the third mistake you may have made was picking the wrong kind of camp.

If luxury is important to you, pick a place that's selling luxury and be prepared to pay extra for it. If you're looking for companionship, find a place that draws a lot of singles. In short, research a tennis camp the same way you would research any vacation place.

Having reviewed your mistakes, let's briefly explore what you can do to make your second camp visit much more productive and enjoyable.

Remember that many camps are upgrading their instruction, tailoring it more for the intermediate and advanced player. There is more emphasis on actual playing situations than on strict hitting.

But even after you've chosen a camp that seems to fit your needs, there are still some things you can do to help assure you a good time. If possible, for example, try to put together your own foursome (ideally, everyone should play about the same level) and, when you get to the camp, don't let anybody split you up. You can do even more: Decide ahead of time just what it is you want to work on, and get the pro to set up the week's instruction schedule to meet the requirements you set.

Another thing you can do that you probably didn't do the first time is to spend a few weeks beforehand making a genuine attempt to get into reasonable shape. There is no way you can enjoy a tennis camp experience or really learn from it unless you come to each day's drills with a fresh mind and body.

Of course, if you follow this advice the first time around, you may not need to go back at all.

HOW TO CHOOSE A TENNIS CAMP FOR YOUR CHILD

The most important difference in choosing a tennis camp for yourself and choosing one for your child has nothing to do with tennis. It has to do with off-court supervision. Presumably, you are mature enough to stay happy, not get homesick and not get into trouble. Even if you are not, as an adult you should know how to deal with such problems. But your child is different.

Here's how one official of the American Camping Association puts it:

"The problem with some specialty camps, tennis included, is that they are not really camps in the way we view the term. They do a very good job of whatever it is they specialize in, but they have a tendency to let the kids fend for themselves too much during the non-instructional hours. Some kids can do all right under these conditions, but the average parent would much rather have the child be under more supervision."

Not that the American Camping Association (ACA) is necessarily the last word in the camping business. Only about half of all the camps in the U.S. have ACA accreditation, and ACA representatives are quick to note that there are any number of superbly run camps which have never even sought the ACA seal of approval. Still, it's significant that there are only a few tennis camps listed in its guide. There are, of course, a large number of general camps with good tennis programs, but only a small number of ACA-accredited camps want to be known, above all, as tennis camps.

Which, incidentally, is a good point to dwell upon. For any number of reasons, many general camps are going to great lengths to project a visible tennis profile. But what that means, in short, is that as the years go by, it becomes harder and harder to differentiate tennis camps per se from camps that simply offer good tennis programs.

Unfortunately, there is no organization overseeing tennis camps that has established operating standards. And if there were such a body, what should those standards be? Pretty much what the better tennis camps are offering today: a solid instructional program run by qualified instructors; a minimum of about four hours each day of instruction; a camper-to-court and camper-to-instructor ratio of no more than five or six to one; and a program that doesn't penalize the kid who isn't a budding John McEnroe.

There are any number of tennis-oriented factors that may affect your choice of camps one way or the other, but don't be overly swayed by some of the window dressing that fills many of the camp brochures.

Consider video replay equipment, for instance. More camps than ever incorporate video in their instructional programs

and make a point of boasting about it in their promotional material. "I'll be honest with you," confides one Connecticut camp director. "We have some of the equipment, but it doesn't really mean all that much in the final analysis. The important thing isn't the equipment you have, but the sort of people you have dealing with the kids. And not just how good they are, but how much they really care."

Another thing to be wary about when you're checking out tennis camps is the precise role a "name" player may have in the running of the camp that bears his or her name. Risky though generalizations may be, it's the rare celebrity tennis player who is going to spend more than a couple of hours a day (if that) with a bunch of 10-year-olds who are looking to learn top-spin lobs before they've mastered the basic forehand. This is not to knock the involvement of name players in children's camp enterprises. Indeed, the fact that a young-ster can spend even a few minutes with a player of stature can have a long-lasting effect. What you don't want to do is make your decision solely on the basis of name. There are simply too many other factors that count.

And what are those factors? Again, number of courts and instructors versus students, type of program, etc. But there are other, less tangible, factors that may be even more important. Chief among these is the philosophy of the camp director. If there is one common complaint about tennis in-structors in general, it isn't that they work

you too hard (or not hard enough) or that they put too much (or too little) emphasis on winning; it's that they don't possess a vision of tennis that goes beyond the tennis court.

With adults, an instructor with "tunnel vision" will have a minimal effect, at worst. But with kids, it's different. "The experience a child has at a tennis camp is going to shape his attitude toward tennis more than anything else in his life," says Neil Chase, a lanky New Englander who has been in the golf and tennis camp business for more than 20 years.

"My philosophy, and the philosophy of any good tennis camp," says Chase, "is that your principal obligation is to the total child. That's why we devote so much effort to our evening programs, like drama, photog-raphy and music."

It might be argued that if you want your child to learn photography and fiddle around with crafts, why send him to a tennis camp? Why not a regular camp instead? For one thing, most regular camps operate on either a one-month or two-month cycle and, by and large, are a little more expen-sive than the typical tennis camp. Second, regardless of how good a tennis program is at a regular camp, the program is unlikely to be either as intense or as professional as the tennis program at a genuine tennis camp.

Your choice of camp has to be based largely on what sort of child you have: how much he really loves tennis (as opposed to how much *you* would like him to love

tennis); how anxious he is to go to tennis camp, and what sort of aptitude he has for the game. Generally speaking, most camps do as good a job with beginners as they do with more advanced players (although a common complaint among some parents is that the better players get "favored" treatment). But if you have a child who simply doesn't like tennis and isn't very well coordinated to start with, a tennis camp is probably going to put him under tremendous psychological pressure. With general camps, at least, a kid has an opportunity to excel at *something*.

So when you're investigating the subject of tennis camps for your child, ask about more than just the tennis program. The personnel (if there are a lot of repeaters on staff, it's a good sign that they not only know what to teach, but how to communicate it), general facilities (including medical care) and references are all worth looking into. If a camp director is reluctant to give out references or doesn't answer your questions thoroughly, look for another camp.

A final word about age. If you look hard enough, you can find a tennis camp that will take a child as young as seven and as old as 17. Most camp directors, though, advise against sending a child to a tennis camp before the age of 9 or 10, unless he happens to be super-gifted. The same goes for kids who are too old. As one camp director puts it: "Once the average kid reaches 16 or 17, unless he's really serious about tennis, he has other things on his mind besides his backhand."

Budding tennis buffs eagerly participate in a children's clinic at Sea Pines Plantation, Hilton Head Island, South Carolina.

COMBINING TENNIS WITH BUSINESS

Not only has tennis turned into a business itself during the last decade (witness the total amount of prize money on the pro tours and the millions of dollars spent on equipment each year), but it has also joined golf as the sport of business. Where deals once were consummated during an 18-hole round, now many are finalized after a few brisk sets. Tennis takes less time than golf, it's far easier to carry equipment on a tennis-included business trip and it's easier to grab a court hour than to arrange for a starting time convenient to all on the course.

At home, businessmen find them-selves involved with tennis in many ways. Some companies go so far as to build their own courts. Others elect to sponsor tournaments. And some people make the big switch from their old job into some aspect of the tennis business.

On the road, many businessmen like to arrange informal games while traveling alone. And when the company holds an out-of-town meeting or there's a convention going on, a likely venue these days is one of the resorts that cater to corporate get-togethers.

SHOULD YOUR COMPANY HAVE ITS OWN COURTS?

When employees of the Permanent Magnet Co. in Indianapolis want to squeeze in some tennis after work, they don't have to fight the rush-hour traffic to get to the country club, nor do they have to stand in line at some overcrowded municipal facility. They simply walk to the back of Permanent's plant to get in a couple of sets on the company's own court.

Permanent employees are among the lucky ones. A number of U.S. companies, ranging from multi-billion-dollar conglomerates to small, family-owned businesses, do provide their employees with tennis courts. But unfortunately for the millions of tennis-playing employees in the nation, these companies are all too rare.

A 1978 survey by the National Industrial Recreation Association (NIRA) showed 37 of 200 representative companies operated tennis courts for their employees. Yet, according to the NIRA, at the time of the survey, some 50,000 private American companies were investing more than $3 billion a year in industrial recreation programs.

Many firms, evidently, are still reluctant to build luxurious tennis or other sports facilities for their workers for fear stockholders might object to them as some sort of corporate boondoggle. And, indeed, it's almost impossible to put a "bottom-line" figure on the value of employee recreation. Still, as one Midwestern executive notes, "leisure programs develop loyalties and a team spirit among employees."

Does your company exhibit its concern for your physical and spiritual welfare by providing or subsidizing off-hours recreation? If it doesn't, maybe the time is right for starting a movement for company-owned tennis courts at the place where you work. If a tennis court is too expensive, how about a platform tennis court or a squash court? Or you might have to begin with just a room big enough for a table tennis group to meet and play. But if you can get some activity started, you'll probably find that the momentum will carry you from table tennis to tennis courts in a surprisingly short time.

Unless your company wants to build a super-deluxe set of tennis courts and a clubhouse, you can generally get an outdoor court built and fully equipped for around $15,000—depending on the area of the country and the type of surface you prefer.

The demand for company-owned tennis courts and other recreational facilities is likely to continue to grow as leisure time increases. A century ago, American workers spent an average of 53 hours each week, on their jobs. This figure is now down to less than 40 hours (including overtime and extra shifts) and, the experts feel, it will

Tennis facilities at 3M Company.

shrink to 30 hours by 1984. Not only will the next five years bring a shorter working week, but vacations will be longer and many companies are expected to shift to the four-day, and even the three-day, week.

Beyond that, many workers—particularly the younger ones—are urging that corporations place a stronger emphasis on their social activities. As the late anthropologist Margaret Mead said a few years ago: "Where once it was wrong to play so hard that it might affect one's work, now it is wrong to work so hard that it may affect one's family life."

Of course, some U.S. corporations have been sponsoring recreation programs for years. For example, 3M Co., the manufacturer of Scotch tape and a great many other products including tennis-court surfaces, has poured millions of dollars into recreation. The company owns a 483-acre

recreational park near its St. Paul headquarters and it leases the facility to the employee-run 3M Club for a mere $1 per year.

At the park, the firm has set up an opulent clubhouse, a lush 18-hole golf course and 12 tennis courts. Membership in the club costs only $3 per year and 90 percent of 3M's 14,000 employees in the Minneapolis/St. Paul area belong to it. The rest of the club's expenses are met by special dues and the profits from the bar and vending machines. The club has a budget of approx. $1,000,000 annually and employs about 80 persons.

Although 3M's facilities are decidedly plush, similar facilities are offered by other companies such as International Business Machines, Johnson Wax, Owens-Corning Fiberglas, Timken and Westinghouse.

A company doesn't have to be the size

...Even a small company can often squeeze in a good tennis court.

of 3M to provide tennis courts for its employees. Lawry's Foods, Inc., a California food processor, employs about 300 people at its Los Angeles headquarters, where it offers not only courts but also once had a pro who gave lessons at the company's expense.

But companies like 3M and Lawry's are the exception. It seems that some of America's largest companies feel they are too big and have too many employees to even attempt building enough facilities to take care of their workers' leisure hours.

Surprisingly, even some of the recreation-minded companies have doubts about spending company cash on employee rec-

reation. One Los Angeles manufacturer with 2,500 workers feels that recreation programs and facilities do "little to help management." And a spokesman for one New Jersey firm, which spends more than $100,000 annually on recreation programs, said it sees "no effect on recruitment, contentment or productivity."

Some company executives are puzzled by these attitudes. An Illinois firm employing only 800 persons has an indoor swimming pool, lagoons where employees can fish and swim, tennis courts, a gym and facilities for many other sports. The president of the company observes that recreation facilities do not have to be expensive,

provided that "the employees really want them and put their ingenuity to work to get them." His company's swimming pool cost $90,000, but it substitutes for a water tower, necessary for fire prevention at the plant, that would have cost $160,000.

How and when should a company start developing a tennis program? "There are no guidelines for determining when it's time for the company to invest in its own tennis courts," says the head of a national recreation management firm. "I think corporations should perform a thorough recreation audit before making the first move."

Even if your company seems willing to examine its recreational needs, the message seems to be that the demand for tennis facilities has to come from the workers who are likely to benefit most from them. Provided that management is not openly hostile to recreational facilities, employees can find ways to raise funds, with some company help, to get started. The more you can get your company involved, the greater the benefits for the individual employees and for the company.

"Value from our recreational activities shows up in our financial statements," says a spokesman for 3M. "It shows up directly in the quality of the employees we attract, train and retain. It shows up in the productivity of our workers and in the attitudes of their families and the community."

HOW TO START A CAREER IN TENNIS

"What makes men happy is liking what they have to do. This is a principle on which society is not founded."—Claude Adrien Helvetius, 1715–1771.

Although Citizen Helvetius uttered this profundity over two centuries ago, it is a notion that has not withered with age; if anything, it's gotten stronger as the American worker increasingly demands more from his or her work than a paycheck every week and a company picnic every summer.

For a real dyed-in-the polyester tennis freak, any occupation that doesn't involve the game in some way will likely be less than fulfilling. If, on a workday morning, all you look forward to are your after-hours sessions on court or the weekend matches on tap, then you've got a job satisfaction problem. But there's no law saying you have to sell insurance or bring up babies or stamp widgets for the rest of your life.

Why not work where your interests lie? Not even an expanded industry like tennis can offer every Tom, Dick and Mary a dream job, of course, but there are job opportunities in fields related to the game—teaching, selling, managing—for people with good brains, sometimes next-to-no

experience and a strong identification with tennis.

As with any career switch, though, it calls for some self-assessment, research and planning prior to making a move. "Explore it very, very carefully," cautions Eve Kraft, director of the USTA's Education & Research Center, before you try to jump into tennis.

What has to be weighed most heavily, after all the fantasizing has been done about organizing tournaments or designing racquets, is what do you have to offer a future employer? Perhaps you're a solid player with a knack for getting along with people and a yen to work outdoors. Teaching could hold a niche for you. Or maybe you've been clerking in a local department store and you'd like to be pushing tennis shoes instead of tots' toys. A pro shop or sporting goods store might be able to use you.

If you have the itch to switch, consider the career possibilities described below. You could be reading your next job description.

TEACHING PROFESSIONAL: "How do I get to be a teaching pro?" is the inquiry heard most often in the tennis job world. It looks easy enough, you get to be outdoors and all you have to do is show eager students how to hit the ball. Right? Not exactly. That's the trouble. Too many self-proclaimed "pros" hang out a shingle, snag a court and wait for the lesson fees to roll in.

"One of the problems with the game today is the lack of requirements to be-

come a pro," says Tony Trabert, the U.S. Davis Cup captain and a member of TENNIS Magazine's Instruction Advisory Board. "And because everyone who wants to can become a teaching pro, the game is being hurt."

Unlike law or medicine, no one is apt to come after a teaching pro with a summons for practicing without a license, so the field is ripe pickings for fast-buck artists who want to cash in on the tennis craze. But the places for people who are seriously interested in becoming competent pros are the U.S. Professional Tennis Association and the Professional Tennis Registry, which offer professional certification for those who can pass written and on-court tests and background checks.

Here's a quick rundown of the qualities most looked for in tennis teachers:

1. Personality. A tennis pro must be able to get along with his or her students before any learning can take place. He should be patient and able to relax students during a lesson.

2. Technical Skill. "A little more than, say, a weekend or after-work player would have," says one USPTA pro. "To be a good pro, you have to be a good player—not a great one, but a good one."

3. Motivation (desire, ambition, etc.). This means wanting to teach—above all else.

Assuming you've got these qualities, how do you actually get a job as a teaching pro?

"We get a lot of inquiries from guys

who want to change jobs," says John Gardiner, who runs a string of highly regarded tennis camps in the West. "My recommendation to job-seekers is to try to find a position as an assistant professional at a good club and work up that way, or go to the local recreation department and look for a job. You may have to do volunteer work and donate your time, but something like that will at least give you a degree of teaching experience."

More than experience, though, is needed at some facilities. The tennis centers that have sprung up all over the country look for qualified pros who bring other skills to the job, too. These days, the person who has some college education and some knowledge in accounting, management or marketing is very attractive to employers. "There are so many top players from college teams who are going to instructional schools, wanting to become pros, that this has changed the educational level of the professional drastically," Kraft notes. "It's not just the ex-tennis player who does nothing else but play who is becoming a pro," she adds, citing the growing flow of applicants from top universities into the teaching field.

For those just starting out as assistant pros, the pay in tennis teaching isn't fantastic—just as it isn't on the lower levels of any other industry. An assistant pro can expect to make about $8,000 per year to start by giving lessons, sweeping courts, helping out with clinics and so forth. A head pro, on the other hand, can pull in anywhere from $15,000 to $80,000 at some of the world's chichi resorts. But the median income seems to be about $25,000 to $30,000, including whatever percentage of the pro shop revenues he pulls in.

In seeking a job, one of the teaching pro organizations can be a big help—if you're a member. They run the best employment agency in the field by regularly letting members know what clubs, facilities and resorts need personnel on their staffs.

RETAIL SALES: If there's any tennis field where interest and attitude count more than nuts and bolts experience, this is it. To help people pick racquets or accessories, of course, demands a solid knowledge of the game, but you don't have to have labored in Gimbel's or Macy's for five years to work in retailing; it doesn't hurt, of course, but it's not a prerequisite.

"To sell equipment in a retail store, the person must have an interest in the game as well as a knowledge of the equipment," observes a tennis buyer for Herman's Sporting Goods, a chain of outlets on the East Coast and Midwest. "But then, too, we've found that people who are avid sports fans, but don't have any business sense or experience, don't make good sales people. Just liking the game isn't enough. It doesn't outweigh business sense."

A different view comes from another sporting goods executive who contends that, although experience is always a plus, "We do hire a number of people right out of college for our sales program. Interest and enthusiasm are generally enough, because

they can always learn about the products and selling techniques as they go along."

Feron's, a racquet shop chain with stores in Connecticut, New York and New Jersey, looks for interest in racquet sports first and foremost. "We're looking for people who know how to play and know the game of tennis, and have a working knowledge of the other racquet sports," reports a spokesman. "Previous retail background always helps, of course, but we don't have any fixed educational background in mind for our sales people. It's a matter of knowing your way around racquet sports and being able to get along with people." The spokesman himself is a prime example of the tennis job switcher, having gone from a department manager and assistant buyer at Gimbel's to road selling for the Bancroft Sporting Goods Co. and then a stint at Herman's before joining the Feron's organization.

Tennis sales clerks at retail shops or sporting goods stores can expect to earn about $4.25 per hour, less than the average assistant teaching pro, but the figure rises with experience, and there's always the chance of a promotion into buying or store management.

MANUFACTURER'S REPRESENTATIVE: This is not the field for job hoppers to leap into bearing a smile, a passable forehand and a fancy to try their luck at peddling racquets for a while. Representing a manufacturer takes more than just a love of the game; it takes business sense and usually a business background.

"What we're looking for," advises a sales executive with a sports equipment firm "is someone with some college, preferably with a degree, and not necessarily a tennis enthusiast, but someone who wants to sell well." That's for starters. Although many manufacturers do hire some sales people right out of college, most job openings for sales reps call for professional salespeople. A tennis freak with experience in consumer package goods (nationally advertised items) could very well take a knack for the game into the wholesale equipment market, but without that selling experience, tennis mania doesn't count for much at most manufacturing companies.

What does a sales rep do? Sell. A specific sales territory is usually assigned to an individual and he or she has accounts (clubs, pro shops, sporting goods stores) in that sector on whom he makes sales calls regularly, checking that his company's line is prominently displayed and in sufficient stock. In some firms, the actual selling is supplemented with promotional work that can take the form of showing the company flag at tournaments or becoming involved in areas like junior development.

Salaries for sales reps vary widely, depending on base pay and commissions. On the average, a beginner can expect about $13,000 per year and, if all goes well, move up to $20,000 and above.

INDOOR CLUBS: The nicest way to get into indoor tennis is to own or go partners in a club, but if those are options open to you, then you don't need to be told about

how to get into tennis. For those with more ordinary incomes, the tennis boom has meant a surge in the construction of indoor facilities—and they all need employees. Apart from the teaching pros that all tennis clubs require, there are a handful of other jobs available.

"An indoor club is essentially a hotel with tennis courts instead of beds," observes a Connecticut businessman who operates three indoor facilities. And one key job that hotels and indoor centers have in common is that of the manager. This is one post where reverse sexism gives the hiring nod more often to women than to men. It's estimated that some 60 percent of indoor club managers are female and the reason, explains the Connecticut club owner, is that "most places are looking for a woman because so much of the day's play involves women and kids."

A manager's tasks divide roughly into three areas: daily routine operations, ancillary business and supervising. The daily operations entail opening up the club in the morning, making sure the courts are cleaned, keeping tabs on who has and hasn't paid for a court and making sure that the reservation phone desk is staffed. The ancillary business includes the pro shop (the manager often does buying and pricing), any vending machines in the building and, in the case of really large-scale indoor courts, keeping an eye on the on-premises restaurant. The third area, supervision, requires mostly that the manager watch how well the pro staff is doing its job. (Is one pro

impatient with beginners? Is another unable to deal with parents who want to know why Johnny's backhand hasn't improved much?)

A "people" person—someone who's loquacious, friendly and able to deal with new people easily—is the primary target of owners looking for club managers. Although some business background certainly helps, it's not a must. Some knowledge of the game, of course, is advisable: if you play, that's even better. The pay isn't terrific, hovering around the $7,500-a-year mark, but in a club's slow summer season some managers can handle two jobs to boost their incomes.

Clubs also need desk help, people to answer the phone and make court reservations, bookkeepers (at large clubs), babysitters and people to clean the courts (somebody has to do it, and more than one odd-jobber or high school student makes money that way).

RESORTS: If your idea of heaven is to frolic for a week in a warm place with lots of tennis courts and a seductive beach or mountain thrown in, how would it be to work at such a pleasure place year round? Resorts, like other service facilities, have a number of fixed jobs that require no knowledge of tennis at all—such as working in the restaurant or hotel, tending the grounds, managing a gift shop, etc. But there are certainly attractive positions available where a few tennis smarts will come in handy (and most resorts let employees use empty courts gratis during

their off hours, another plus).

To start at the top, anyone aspiring to be a resort executive will need substantial previous experience. The tennis director at a South Carolina resort says, "We're looking for guys who have good marketing backgrounds and who know how to reach the customer. They have to know how to make immediate sales and do it in a way that will keep the people coming back."

Beyond management and the teaching pro jobs already considered, there are opportunities at resorts in sales (virtually every resort with a court has a pro shop), maintenance, promotion and office work. "You can get into the lower-level areas without any background in tennis at all, if you've got a good head on your shoulders," maintains the assistant manager of a California resort.

To get into something like pro shop management, though, requires a genuine knowledge of tennis. "The people you find in pro shops," observes the Californian, "are tennis oriented. They're not necessarily good players, but they are familiar with brand names and have good heads for figures." (They're also mostly females.) Pay for managing or clerking in a pro shop can vary widely according to the resort and its location, anywhere from $6,500 a year on up.

Although the larger resorts usually retain outside agencies to handle their advertising, promotion and public relations, a lot of smaller places have their own staffs do these jobs. That often means a handful of people get involved in a number of areas.

"We look for people who can do a variety of tasks," says the marketing director for a Florida resort. "We seek creative people who can also roll up their sleeves and empty the trash after a tennis tournament or who can handle tournament tickets or tennis packages." Here, as in so much of the tennis business, "a love of the game and enthusiam" are the most sought-after qualities.

SPECIALIZED JOBS: Some jobs in the tennis world are either so limited or so specialized that it isn't really practical for a job hunter not already in that particular field to go hunting. Racquet stringing is one of these; so are fashion designing, writing, tournament promoting and organizing, court building and tennis club architecture. Unless you've already got some training in areas like these or are prepared to start at the bottom and spend perhaps years learning the business, the job prospects are bleak at best.

For anyone contemplating a job switch, there is a risk involved. But it's not impossible to start a new career in tennis. Enough people have—and are—doing it to prove old Citizen Helvetius wrong.

GETTING A GAME ON A BUSINESS TRIP

Even if you are not somehow involved in tennis through your business at home, you may still enjoy playing after hours when you are on the road. The hardest part is finding someone to play with.

Take heart. The tennis possibilities for the traveling businessman in most big cities today are better than ever. More indoor clubs are looking for transient business. More hotel chains are setting up arrangements with local clubs. Many downtown hotels are actually building courts right on the premises.

Not that things couldn't be a lot better. In this era of computer technology, nobody has yet come up with a nationwide system by which a "member" can dial a special number (it would be an 800 toll-free number), tell the central office when he intended to be in a particular city and when he was free to play, and let IBM do the rest. The end result would be that your computerized print-out would be waiting for you as soon as you check into your hotel, listing the name and telephone number of your playing partner(s), where your game is slated and maybe even a little casual description of his or her game—"likes to run around

backhand on return of serve. . . ."

Until such time, though, the degree to which you can work tennis into your business trips depends almost entirely on how much preliminary work you're willing to do on your own. The facilities are there, but you've got to apply a little strategy.

The best strategy can be summed up in two words: plan ahead. If you think the best way to pick up a tennis game in a strange city is to wait until you've checked into your hotel room and then start making calls to clubs in the area in the vague hope that somebody needs a fourth, you're probably the sort of person who would look for pizza in Peking. No. What you have to do is get something going before you arrive, especially if you're only going to be in a place for a few days at most.

It's not as difficult as you might think. The best thing to do, if you can, is to establish some sort of a tennis connection in each of the cities you regularly visit—someone you can write or phone on short notice and be pretty well assured that they'll be able to set up some games for you either at their club or at some public facility where you pay by the hour.

A good way to develop a network of such connections is to trade numbers and addresses with tennis players you meet on vacation. The idea here is that one hand washes the other; you'll fix them up when they come to your town and they'll do the same for you when the situation is reversed. Another way is to ask around your local club for the names of tennis-playing friends

or relatives in other cities.

Don't overlook your own company's resources. It may well be, for instance, that your company's branch office in, perhaps, Cleveland has purchased some indoor time or has a corporate membership in a local club. Find out about it. Probe your customers for suggestions and possibilities. And don't be shy about asking fellow employees in other cities to see what they can do for you. Ideally, the somebody you ask should be a couple of notches beneath you in the executive hierarchy—somebody who is ambitious and fearful, somebody who will understand, without having it spelled out for him, that the failure to secure you some good tennis may not be in the best interests of corporate harmony, if he knows what you mean.

In the event none of your efforts to secure a tennis connection is successful, then you have to think less in terms of people and more in terms of a place.

Several strategies present themselves. The surest way to slake your tennis appetite on a business trip is to stay at an actual tennis resort. The only problem is that most tennis resorts are not exactly next door to

the typical businessman's destination city.

A growing number of hotels—particularly in such warmer places as Phoenix, Miami and southern California—are not exactly tennis resorts, but they present a strong recreational orientation without making a mockery of the Puritan ethic. And several hotel chains have made ambitious attempts to beef up their tennis operations in non-resort destinations.

Staying at any of these places is not in itself a guarantee that you'll be able to work in some good tennis on your next trip. There's still the problem of finding other players.

The only sure-fire solution to the problem of finding suitable playing partners on the road is to take along your own partner—although it might be difficult for you to convince your wife that the only reason you're taking your secretary with you to Pittsburgh is her first-rate tennis game. Still, some executives do arrange their travel schedules to coincide with the travel schedules of colleagues with whom they play tennis at home.

But if you're traveling alone and you still would like to guarantee yourself some tennis time, the best thing to do is book some lesson time. Even if you're a very good player, it may well turn out, if you're good enough, that the pro might want to hit with you just for practice. Most teaching pros, too, once they get to know you, will give you names of people you can call for games, but you have to make the initial overtures, no one gives anything away

these days. Don't wait until the last minute. Some businessmen have lessons booked six months in advance.

There are other possibilities. In some areas, indoor clubs hold open round robins on certain nights of the week. Alas, it's not easy for the businessman on the move to learn of these opportunities. But a few minutes on the phone when you get to a particular place could give you an idea of what's available one way or the other.

And don't overlook public facilities in certain parts of the country. Of course, you run a risk. You may wind up spending two hours standing around in your tennis clothes while the local players treat you with such xenophobic disdain you want to burn down the clubhouse. On the other hand, you may luck out. A fourth may not show up, somebody may turn an ankle or another stray player may be looking for a hit. Before you know it, you've made your connection.

Tennis on the road may be difficult to arrange but, once you set things in motion, you may find yourself logging in even more court time than you do at home. In fact, many businessmen would no more leave their tennis racquets behind than their toothbrushes or razors when they go on a business trip.

One publishing executive puts it this way: "Even if I don't have anything set up in the way of a game, I always take my tennis gear with me when I make a business trip, particularly when I go to Europe. What I always do is ask around among the people

I'm seeing if anybody wants to play, and I usually connect.

"Last spring I went to Paris for talks with one of the biggest publishing executives in France. Somehow, we started talking about tennis, and I asked him if he wanted to play. He begged off but asked if I was interested in a game with somebody else. I said, 'Sure.' And do you know who that somebody else happened to be? The guy's wife."

Vive la France!

HOW TO MAKE TENNIS PART OF A MEETING OR CONVENTION

Remember the good old days when the only thing anybody had to worry about at a sales meeting or convention was making sure there was enough booze and a public address system that wouldn't go on the fritz when the company president was in the middle of telling everybody how great a year it was going to be, as long as everybody pulled together and worked extra hard?

Well, as anybody who is in the hotel or resort business will tell you, things have changed. Tennis has become an integral part of the recreation schedule of business meetings and conventions around the country, and a number of resorts and hotels have facilities that cater to such get-togethers. Many businessmen who are saddled with the duty of arranging the tennis program at their company's next large-scale function recoil at the prospect of setting it up. But you don't have to be a genius to coordinate a smoothly run tennis program. Then, again, you can't just wing it, either. You have to do some planning and leg work and, in some cases, you may have

to use a little imagination. What you don't want to do, at all costs, is wait until everyone has arrived at the resort before you start to plan the best way to accommodate all the tennis-minded people taking part in the meeting or convention.

CHOOSING THE RIGHT FACILITY: For starters, let's assume you've been asked to suggest some meeting or convention sites that are geared to handle tennis players in large numbers. Choose carefully. The fact that a resort or hotel has a dozen or so courts is no guarantee that their particular tennis program is going to meet your particular needs.

Make sure, for instance, that the resort doesn't have an ongoing clinic program that will monopolize the bulk of the tennis courts for all but the early morning and late evening hours. Check the ratio of rooms to courts. If you find a resort that has a ratio that's greater than 20 to 1, the chances are that court availability is going to be a problem. There could be mitigating factors, of course—such as a large golf program, for example, which could cut down on the number of potential tennis players.

Obviously, you will have to look into a variety of non-tennis areas to make sure the resort can handle whatever it is your company has to do, but that doesn't really concern us here. Suffice it to say that the greatest tennis facilities in the world aren't going to mean a thing to your company president if he is forced to give his annual talk inside the locker room of the tennis clubhouse.

KNOW WHO'S PLAYING: Once you've settled on a site, you should use whatever means you can summon to get an idea—even a rough one—of how many potential tennis players you're going to be dealing with at the meeting or convention. The best way is to send around a questionnaire to all the would-be company participants. Keep it brief. Find out, first of all, if they are interested in playing tennis during their "free" time at the meeting, and try to find out just what sort of tennis they'd prefer: instruction, tournaments or just free play. You might also ask them to rate themselves as A, B or C players—although that kind of classification can be misleading and is not as preferable as the new USTA rating system.

And don't forget to include with your questionnaire some information regarding the tennis dress requirements. Anytime large groups converge on a tennis site, there are invariably hassles about the "appropriate" tennis clothing. A simple note ahead of time about what's expected can avoid all that.

ARRANGING THE TENNIS PROGRAM: As soon as you have a fair idea of how many players you're going to have to accommodate, you're ready to start making plans in earnest. A lot of what you plan, of course, will depend on the schedule of events—that is, the amount of time available for tennis. Other considerations are the number of tennis-playing spouses and, of crucial importance, the number of players in relation to the number of available courts. It is obvious that if you have 150

tennis players and only one or two courts at your disposal, you are going to have trouble putting into effect any sort of meaningful program—unless you can convince the rank beginners in the group that there's nothing at all unusual about playing tennis with four people on each side of the net.

But working under the assumption that there are enough courts to give you some working margin, you have a number of options. One option is simply to let everyone fend for himself, letting the tennis staff make all the arrangements the same as they would do for any guests. The problem here is that throwing everything into the lap of the local talent might not strike some wise guy in your company as his idea of coordinating a tennis program and it may lead him to wonder if this is how you approach your responsibilities in the company.

A second option is to have the local staff arrange the sort of program used for large groups, whatever that might include —a reasonable enough prospect, except that who's to say how many of these programs have been staged successfully? Consider option two with care.

Which brings us to the third option: a reasonably varied program that you plan with the local tennis staff and tailor specifically to meet whatever tennis needs your particular group has. The elements of such a program might include the following:

1. *Daily instructional clinics:* A very good thing for spouses during those periods of the day when the company executives are closeted away, dealing with corporate affairs. Most resorts are equipped to give group lessons, but try to keep the number of participants down to no more than five or six per court. You may have to charge for the lessons, but you should be able to set up some sort of a reduced rate with the resident professional. If possible, try to set up separate clinics for beginners and intermediates, and if the resident pro tries to convince you that the clinics he runs are beneficial to players of all levels, tell him he's full of cat gut and stick to your guns.

2. *Tournament competition:* Tournaments can work out very nicely at conventions so long as you don't confuse yourself with the director of the U. S. Open and are content to keep things as simple as possible. Forget the standard single elimination type of tournaments; it's much too unwieldly. Besides, a substantial percentage of the tennis players at the typical business meeting or convention are beginners or early intermediates. You'll be better off with a round-robin style doubles tournament in which all players change partners after each match.

The best time to plan this sort of a round-robin tournament is along toward the end of the business proceedings, perhaps on a Saturday morning when there are no official events going on. The resorts will generally reserve a certain number of courts for you, but try not to let the number of people in the tournament get too large.

A veteran resort pro and arranger of many such tournaments, Ian Crookenden, does it this way. "If I have, say, 32 players

and plenty of courts, I'll split them up in groups of five or six, and each player will then play everybody in his group," he says. "Everybody then totals up the number of games he's won, and the four players with the highest totals meet in the finals. Where there are more people, we try to keep it to doubles—four people per court, each serving a game, then moving on to a new group of four. Again, the top four qualify for the final playoffs. That way we can see that everybody gets enough tennis to satisfy his recreational desires—to get enough exercise—and still come up with a bona fide champion."

Sounds simple—a mere matter of arranging partners as you would at a bridge party, perhaps. It doesn't always turn out to be so easy, though.

Some play tennis for the social fun and others play strictly for the competition so they can win, then go home and say, "I was the best at the convention." If you know who they are beforehand, you might find it best to set up two tournaments—a single or double elimination for the really serious players, a round robin for the rest.

At some meetings, there's also the question of whether wives—however good at tennis they may be—should play in the main draw or in a tournament of their own. Would it aggravate your boss—or your top customer—if your wife was to beat him in the tournament final? Could be. At any rate, wives in the past have generally been excluded from businessmen's tournaments. But that is changing as women achieve in business the near-parity they've already achieved in tennis. One option is to have both men's and women's tournaments, with spouses included in each.

FREE PLAY: Your involvement with the free-play part of your tennis program should depend primarily on how good a job the tennis staff at the resort does at moving people in and out of games. Some resorts, sad to say, are woefully lax in this crucial area, and you may end up having to set up your own game-arranging system.

Most intermediate and advanced players will probably want to set up their own twosomes and foursomes to escape the ineffable horror of having to play on the same court with a novice. So the biggest favor you can do for them is to post a sign-up sheet somewhere (have people list their names, room numbers and ratings) and let nature take its course. Where you're going to run into difficulties are with beginners and early intermediates who may feel too self-conscious about their games to scrounge anything up on their own.

Setting aside a couple of courts that cannot be reserved in advance but are, nonetheless, held for your company's use, is a good way to assure that those people who haven't been able to arrange games for themselves will have a chance to get in some tennis.

EXHIBITIONS: More and more resorts have hired name pros to lend their stature to the local tennis program. Frequently, the celebrity player is off somewhere playing in a tournament. But, if he's

available, it's not at all unreasonable to suggest that he or she put on a tennis exhibition for the benefit of your group. The exhibition shouldn't run you any extra money.

Of perhaps the most concern to a pro like Crookenden is a fear that many businessmen will attempt to crowd in too much tennis in a limited schedule. "They usually reserve one afternoon for tennis," he notes, "and somebody says, 'O.K., all those who want to play tennis, we've got the courts this afternoon.' And so they start at 1 or 2 o'clock and try to finish before the cocktail party at 6. The poor guys nearly kill themselves."

A far better way to handle things, Crookenden contends, is to schedule an hour or two of tennis each day, perhaps in the early morning or late afternoon.

"Tennis is just like any other exercise program," says Crookenden. "You ought to do it on a regular basis, instead of driving yourself till you reach the saturation point. But that's the way top businessmen do it—which explains, maybe, how they got where they are."

OFF-COURT TENNIS ACTIVITIES

When you are off the court and still find yourself unable to satiate your tennis appetite, there are many activities you can engage in to fill the gap. Instructive and entertaining tennis films are available, many at almost no cost. They are perfect for evening get-togethers among tennis-playing friends or for special events at your club. Or how about taking your own photos at a professional tournament?

Think of all the TV racquet games found in taverns, airports and anywhere else people are likely to sit for awhile. Many are available for your home sets as well. There are tennis games, some involving boards, some with darts and some with cards, that can be played at home. Finally, there are many kinds of useful gadgets and decorative objects you can easily make out of your used tennis equipment.

HOW TO BORROW AND ENJOY TENNIS FILMS

Have you ever wanted to take a private lesson from an expert such as Vic Braden or get some instruction tips from a touring pro or sit in the front row at a match between Jimmy Connors and Bjorn Borg? You can do any or all of these things without leaving the comfort and convenience of your own home—and you can do them at a cost that ranges from comparatively little to practically nothing. How? Through a tennis film program pioneered by the USTA and augmented by a number of tennis-oriented corporations and some of the nation's leading sports filmmakers.

If you're interested, the first step is to send a check for $2.50 along with the words "Film List" to the USTA's Education & Research Center at 729 Alexander Rd., Princeton, N.J. 08540. That'll get you a USTA booklet whose full title is "Tennis Film List," a catalog of about 120 of the finest tennis films made.

The best of modern-day instruction, the highlights of famous matches of the past, scenes of all-time greats in their prime —they're all there, ready and waiting for you to borrow on film as you would a book from a library. And the USTA booklet not only gives you their titles, but tells you what each film is about, what equipment you'll need to show it, where and how to go about ordering it and what, if anything, it will cost you.

The cost really is minimal. Indeed, many of these films—including some of the best—are available on a so-called "free-loan" basis. But you may have to pay a small fee to cover postage and handling and, in practically all cases, you'll at least have to pay for return shipping.

The credit belongs largely to the USTA which, through its Princeton center and 23 sectional and district film libraries, is the nation's largest distributor of free-loan tennis films. But while the USTA picks up much of the tab here, it also gets a big assist from such firms as Wilkinson Sword, Kemper Insurance, American Airlines and Volvo.

As for the rest of the free-loan films, they're brought to you mainly through the generosity (and public image-building) of commercial sponsors.

Because free-loan films are much in demand, as you might expect, it's best to order well in advance. The USTA recommends that you send in your request at least 90 days ahead of time to make sure you get the film you want exactly when you'd like to have it.

What happens if the free-loan films are all taken? Well, the cost goes up from there but not much. Of the films available through the USTA or commercial distributors that aren't free, most are offered for

rental for under $25 and many for as little as $6 to $12. Whichever you choose, it has to be one of the best buys in tennis.

It wasn't always so. In the old days, notes Eve Kraft, director of the USTA Education & Research Center, tennis films were used mainly as filler material at camps or resorts—shown to aspiring tennis players or some other captive audience on rainy days when there wasn't much else to do. The selection of available films was very small, and generally wasn't that good.

"But today with the growth of tennis," says Kraft, "the quality and quantity of tennis films has improved tremendously—especially on the instructional level. People can see the top professionals on the movie screen. They recognize them and respect them for their knowledge of the game. They can hear the professionals motivate and encourage students, telling them how they should practice properly and condition their bodies for maximum performance. Students can watch the films and then discuss them with their instructors. This can lead to a beneficial exchange of information between each student and the instructor."

Kraft also places great stress on the importance of non-instructional tennis films—those that can be shown for their pure entertainment value.

"Entertainment movies are important," she says, "because they bring the excitement of tennis tournaments, tennis personalities and tennis trends into a classroom or meeting hall. They help keep the sport alive at the grass roots level by sparking new interest in beginners, as well as allowing the old-timers to relive a particularly well-played point that may have had them standing and applauding in appreciation years ago."

Ron Holmberg, a leading coach and member of TENNIS Magazine's Instruction Advisory Board, notes that you can use these highlight films to improve your game —if you're attentive. "By watching match highlight films," he says, "you're not just limiting yourself to the basics of stroke production. You can also analyze player movement between shots, observe how the pros set up for a stroke and see their strategies put into action.

"Sometimes I'll stop a film when a student has a question or when I see something in the film that I want to point out. . . . Reinforcement of previous tennis lessons is a primary purpose in showing a tennis film. But you should also apply what you see during a good film to your practice session on the court afterward."

To do that, you have to be alert. It's often suggested by instructors that students take brief notes or simply remember key words and phrases from a film that can easily be recalled on the court later. Try to fix in your mind an image of the professional in the film executing a perfect stroke motion and visualize the scene again when you practice the shot. If grips and swings are demonstrated during the film, keep your racquet handy so if there's enough space in the viewing room, you can get up

and practice what you're seeing.

Tennis films, moreover, can be a godsend to non-tennis players who are somehow thrust into service as tennis instructors.

"In a lot of schools around the country," observes USTA film coordinator, Julia Rudy, "baseball and football coaches are being told to teach kids tennis. Good films can give these teachers a brief background on the basics of the game. They can provide some insight as to how the teacher should instruct his students to hit the basic shots—at the very least, getting them started on the right foot in learning and then teaching the sport."

If you are interested in obtaining a tennis film, Rudy reminds you to make sure you already have—or can easily obtain—the proper equipment to show the film.

"The 16-millimeter format is easily the most common," she says. "It's prevalent in commercial distribution and offers the widest choice of titles. If you or your group don't own a 16-millimeter projector, inquire about the possibility of renting one from a local photography store. You can often rent by the day, week or month, and at some stores a projectionist can also be hired to show the film you selected."

There are plenty of prints available, though, in 8-millimeter or Super 8 film—the kind that most people use in home movies. The USTA film list also includes titles available in Super 8 film loop and 35-millimeter filmstrips—and some even in videotape cassettes, which may well be the wave of the future.

But for now, films are what most of us will rely on. And remember that they're extremely fragile and very expensive to repair or replace. So treat them with care. There's somebody out there—maybe a future Jimmy Connors or Chris Evert Lloyd—waiting as eagerly as you did to get his or her hands on them.

HOW TO TAKE GOOD PHOTOS AT A TOURNAMENT

Part of the fun of attending a professional tennis tournament, especially one as big and prestigious as the U.S. Open, is the opportunity it gives you to take your own photographs of your favorite players on and off the court. The drama and excitement of major league tennis—the people and the pageantry, the big moments and the small —they're all there to be captured on film.

And the best part of it is that you don't have to be a professional photographer to get in on the action. All it takes is a little equipment, a little planning and a little luck and you can come home with enough self-made souvenirs to fill a photo album—with a few that are maybe even good enough to hang on your den or office wall.

The basic rules of tennis photography —in fact, all sports photography—are fairly simple, but they can never be over-emphasized.

1. Keep your camera ready at all times with your lens cap off, your film advanced and your shutter cocked; many times, it's a case of "now or never."

2. Unless you're an expert at light-meter readings, always stand with your back to the sun so there's always front-lighting on your subject.

3. Make certain you have a clear and unobstructed view of your subject; you don't want someone walking in front of you just as you click the shutter.

4. Be sure that your background is free of clutter; you don't want your subject to disappear into a sea of faces.

5. Attempt to frame your subject so that he or she turns up dead-center in the finished photograph.

Beyond that, the type of camera you use can be crucial. Many people, of course, own a fixed-focus, Instamatic-type camera, which is usually very good at doing what it was intended to do—take a close-up picture of a fairly stationary object under optimum lighting conditions.

If it's a candid shot of Chris and John Lloyd strolling the grounds that you want— or a shot of Jimmy Connors or Bjorn Borg or Martina Navratilova signing an autograph book for your son or daughter—or a shot of any of the players brushing elbows with your spouse as they enter or leave their locker room—a fixed-focus camera will do just fine. And you may find that, through the years, the photos you have taken with such a camera will become endowed with priceless memories.

But for sheer performance—to get pictures that you'll be proud to show to fellow shutterbugs—your best bet is probably a 35-millimeter single lens reflex camera.

"That's the kind that virtually all the pros use," says an accomplished photog-

rapher and design director. "With a single lens reflex, many of which are reasonably priced, you can adjust the shutter speed for fast action and you can add a telephoto lens for close-ups. I recommend a 135 or 200-millimeter lens."

If you're an amateur and it's real action you want, the best place to start your picture-taking at a huge complex like Flushing Meadow is out on one of the field courts. "The fences are low and right next to the sidelines, so you're right on top of the action," says another professional photographer. "Shooting from a fence on a field court is almost as good as sitting on the court."

Another expert recommends that you get a schedule of the day's matches, pick out one featuring players you want to photograph and arrive at the court well ahead of time to get a good location. The ideal place, if you can arrange it, is near the net on the opposite side of the court from the umpire's chair with the sun at your back.

"As the players warm up, so should you," says this expert. "Familiarize yourself with their styles. Note which shots they'll be hitting as they face you. On one side of the net, they'll be turning toward you when hitting forehands, on the other side they'll be pivoting in your direction for backhands. If the player turns away from you to hit, you shouldn't shoot. You want him to be facing in your direction."

Also, practice follow-focusing a few times—tracking the player with your camera as he moves for a shot, concentrating on keeping him in the center of your viewfinder. It's usually best to frame your photos vertically (turning the camera on its side) so you get close to a full figure of your subject and don't crop his legs and racquet arm out of the picture.

The key to getting a satisfying stop-action photograph is timing the click of your camera to the player's hit of the ball. If you are using a single lens reflex model, set the shutter speed at 1/500th of a second to avoid any blurring. As the player moves toward you to hit a shot, squeeze the shutter instead of jerking down on it so the camera doesn't jog. Squeeze so it clicks right at the hit.

To time your shot and the player's shot right, "look for small body signs that will tip you off to what kind of shot the player's going to hit," says one photographer. "That way you'll be ready for him when he attacks the ball."

"Most spectators think the professional photographer has the best seat in the house," says TENNIS staff photographer Stephen Szurlej, "but it just isn't so. Following a player through a lens provides only a limited view of the action. Don't think taking pictures is a way to see the match better. If you want to watch a match, you can do it best from a good seat instead of somewhere near the court."

For that reason, if for none other, sooner or later you'll be heading into the main stadium where the big stars are usually scheduled to play. You'll quickly find,

though, that even with a long telephoto lens, it's impossible to get close-up action photos from a stadium seat.

So instead of aiming for one player only, try to get a more interesting shot such as a wide-angle view of the court and the entire stadium. You can always catch the stars, if you wait long enough, on one of the practice courts where they work out before and after their matches.

Whatever you're doing—wherever you're doing it—it's also vitally important to be aware of what's going on around you and keep your eyes open to additional picture possibilities. Are there any former greats roaming among the crowds? A movie star or two? Get them quick—in an interesting pose, if you can—and it could be the one shot with which you can impress your non-tennis-playing friends.

If it's your first time out, though, try not to make a pest of yourself. In time, you'll learn what you can and can't do with impunity. And never forget that there are rules of etiquette for tennis photographers just as there are for tennis players. When you're shooting at courtside, for example, you should never use a flash, indoors or out, never use a motor drive and never shoot during a tie breaker.

You should also exercise discretion and common sense at all times so you don't aggravate either the pro players or the pro photographers. You're out there for fun; they're trying to make a living.

The type of film you'll be using will depend to a great extent on the type of camera you're using. But when it comes time to get your pictures developed you'll be better off if you've used color slide film. Color is what gives the impact of the moment, some believe. You can get color slides converted into either color or black-and-white prints, and slide film itself is often less grainy than print film.

Finally, there is one thing that all the experts agree on, and that is that you should take with you as much film as you can afford. "Shoot a lot," they say, "The only way you're going to learn is by making mistakes. No matter how much you bring, you'll still need more."

OFF-COURT RACQUET GAMES

If you're looking for a way to enliven a post-match party, or for something to keep the kids amused while you're out playing a couple of sets, why not try some racquet games.

TV RACQUET GAMES: These electronic gadgets won't do much for your errant backhand, but they're fun to play and some of them are almost harder to master than the real thing.

Attached to the antenna terminals of your TV set, the typical electronic game produces a playing area on your screen marked out like a tennis court (or a squash court, football field or jai alai fronton on some sophisticated models). Each player usually has a hand control that can move a racquet or player around the screen and alter the speed and spin of the ball each time it is hit. The fancier gadgets even have scoreboards and suitable sound effects.

First introduced around 1972, the early TV games offered a limited choice of sports and frequently ended up in the back of the closet after wearing out their welcomes. But the newer models are more challenging. Some have the sophistication of a small computer with plug-in devices

that allow you to indulge almost any sports fantasy in the privacy of your own home.

When TV tennis palls, you can don your green eyeshade and take on the neighbors at blackjack or throw a scarf around your neck and become the Red Baron. Such variety comes with a price, of course. You can pay almost $200 for your "entertainment system," but there are some very satisfactory models around for $40 or less in the discount stores.

And if a skeptical friend ever asks you why you bought one of these games, tell him you wanted to work on your hand-eye coordination, which may very well improve.

BOARD AND CARD GAMES: While TV tennis games aren't really portable, tennis board and card games are. If you take your children along with you to the courts, they can pass the time playing a tennis tabletop game. You can do the same while waiting for a court or while enjoying some refreshments with friends at your club or at home.

None of these games will do anything for your tennis skills, but some of them are fun to play, even for the hardened tennis aficionado, and a few are challenging enough to hold the attention of the most precocious child. Most games of this type can be obtained in local toy or department stores. If they don't have any, ask them to find out if some are available from the manufacturers they deal with.

You may decide to give tabletop tennis a try before investing in a board game. You can do so easily, assuming you have a deck

of cards somewhere in the house and a rudimentary knowledge of tennis.

Here's how it works. One deck of cards is used. The two players cut the deck and the high card denotes the server of the first game. After all the cards are shuffled, the server deals one card to his opponent and one card to himself, both face up.

The player with the higher card wins the first point, and scoring is the same as in a regular game. The dealer serves until the first game is over. After the first game, his opponent becomes the server (dealer). There is no need to change sides after every odd game, unless the sun and wind are so rough that the cards keep blinding you and blowing away.

The cards can't be any simpler than that, so let's spruce it up a bit. First, anytime the server deals an ace to himself or his opponent, that is termed an ace serve. The server wins this point. Anytime he serves a two to himself or his opponent, that is a double fault and the server loses the point.

In the event that the two cards match (e.g., server and receiver both get fours) that's a "let" and two showdown cards are dealt. The first goes to the receiver, who must say either "in" or "out." "In" means he thinks the next card going to the server will be less than the card he just received. "Out" means that the card going to the server will be greater than the first showdown card the receiver got. If the receiver guesses wrong, he loses it.

Thus, if the first showdown card is a three, it would be best for the receiver to call "out," because the chances are the next card will be higher than a three and he will win the point. But if the first card is a king, it would be wise to call "in." If either showdown card is an ace, the server wins the point. If either showdown card is a two, it's a double fault and the receiver wins the point.

MAKING USE OF YOUR OLD EQUIPMENT

BALL RETRIEVER: If you're like most tennis players, you probably have a closet full of dead tennis balls neatly coffined in their cans. No, don't rush off and throw them all out. Give the balls to the kids in your neighborhood and keep the cans. For about 15 minutes of your time and 20 cents' worth of adhesive tape, you can make a ball retriever that will come in very handy during your practice sessions. Here's how to do it:

1. With an ordinary can opener (the clamp-on kind or even electric if you have one), cut the bottoms neatly from seven or eight cans. Get rid of the bottoms immediately before someone cuts a hand.

2. Tape the cans together into a long tube using plastic-backed adhesive tape, electrician's tape or duct tape. Two-inch wide tape is best. Don't use masking tape; it's too weak for the job.

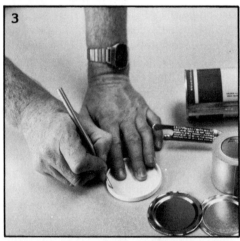

3. Using a sharp carpet knife or X-acto knife, cut a hole in the plastic lid of one can. The hole should be about one-quarter inch smaller than a tennis ball. Follow the crease in the lid for the best results.

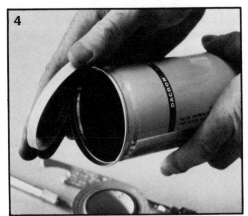

4. Attach the lid to the end of the tube with contact cement or epoxy glue. You may have to experiment a little since some glues contain solvents that may damage the plastic. Check the instructions first.

6. When you're ready to use the balls, turn the retriever upside down and the balls will roll out. To use your retriever to store tennis balls, place an uncut lid on the end of the filled tube.

5. Now your ball retriever is complete. Pick up the balls by pressing downward sharply so that they pop easily inside the plastic lid. You can retrieve as many as 20 balls with this gadget.

BALL-CAN LAMP: If you have empty ball cans you'd like to do something with, you might try making a lamp. For one lamp, all you need is one can, its plastic lid and a few dollars' worth of parts, obtainable at a hardware or electrical goods store. The only tools you'll require are an electric drill, a screwdriver and a small wrench. The parts that you'll need in addition to the ball can and the lid are: a light socket (twist or push switch—about $1); metal ceiling fixture cover (about $1.25); one 8½-inch length of three-eighths-inch threaded tube and a thin electrical nut (about $1), and about nine feet of dual wire with a plug attached ($1).

Assembling these components takes only a few minutes. Here's how:

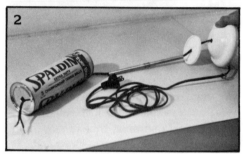

2. Thread the wire through all of the components starting with the nut, then the base, can cover, tube, ball can and light socket.

1. Put the plastic lid on the bottom of the can and drill a three-eighths-inch or slightly larger hole through can and lid.

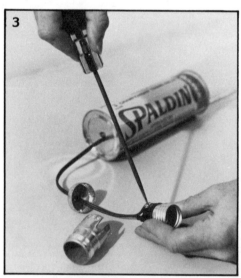

3. Strip the insulation from the ends of the wire and attach them to the screw terminals in the light socket. Reassemble the light socket.

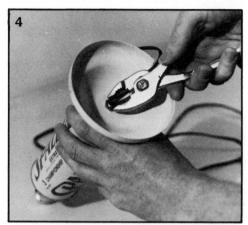

4. Screw one end of the tube into the bottom of the socket, push the components together and tighten the nut in the base.

5. Screw a 60-watt or smaller bulb into the socket and add a lampshade of the type that pushes onto the bulb (about $2 at a five-and-ten).

6. Plug the lamp in and switch it on. The unit is ideal for bedside, den or bar.

If you dislike the maker's logo on your lamp, you can easily spray the can with enamel paint or glue a piece of colored paper to fit around the can. One alternative might be to collect the autographs of top players on a white sheet of paper and then glue that around the can. A clear acrylic spray will protect the signatures.

BALL-CAN STORAGE RACK: Your old ball cans can also be put to good use as part of a racquet and practice-ball rack. You'll need four ball cans, a small piece of wood (five-eighths by 2 by 12 inches) as well as a few screws, nuts and bolts. The rack may be mounted to a plaster or sheetrock wall in one of your closets or in your den. It will hold two racquets and up to six practice balls.

1. Drill 10 holes in the support piece, according to the dimensions shown here, using a three-sixteenth-inch drill. Round the corners of the support, sand smooth and finish with paint or stain.

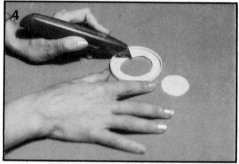

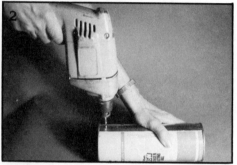

2. Using an ordinary can opener, cut the bottoms out of the four cans. Drill two three-sixteenth-inch holes near the top of the back of each can, three-quarters of an inch from the lip and one inch apart to match the support piece holes.

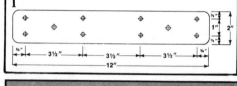

4. With a sharp knife, cut a hole slightly larger than your racquet grip in two of the plastic ball-can lids. Put them on the tops of the two outside cans, which will act as racquet holders with the handle inside the can.

3. Using one-inch long three-sixteenth-inch bolts, attach the cans to the support piece. Start the bolt head inside the can and use a nut and washer on the back side. Don't tighten the nuts too much or you may split the wood.

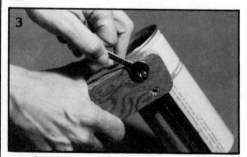

5. Using two No. 10 sheet metal screws and appropriate plastic wall fasteners, attach the rack to the wall. Put two plastic caps on the bottom of the two center cans for ball storage. The balls can be taken out by removing the caps.

BALL-CAN CUP DISPENSER: Need a handy and inexpensive way to store and dispense paper cups at your club's water fountain? One used ball can, a can-opener, a couple of pieces of strong wire and a few minutes of your time are all you'll need to make a dispenser that will store 36 seven-ounce plastic cups.

1. Take an empty ball can and cut out the bottom with a can opener. Use a can that is crimped at one or both ends.

3. Insert the plastic cups so that the bottoms of the cups protrude from the crimped end of the can. One can will hold up to 36 cups.

2. Twist a piece of wire around each end of the can and attach it vertically to the fence of your tennis court using the loose ends of the wire.

4. Put the plastic cover back on the top of the can. The cups can be removed one at a time by pulling downward.

BALL-CAN ORGANIZERS: Somewhere along the line, at least once in your life, you've probably said to yourself: "If I could just get organized. . ." Well, now you can. All it takes is four old ball cans, some contact paper, a clothespin and some glue.

What you do is put them together and, presto, what you have is a nifty desk organizer which, if you manage it right, can be your first step in creating order out of chaos.

1. Using tin scissors, cut your cans to varying heights and dispose of scraps immediately before someone gets a cut.

2. Cover the rim of each can and then the entire can with contact paper. Add your initials or your full name, if you like.

3. Place the cans together in an arrangement that pleases you and glue them together where they touch. Also, glue on your clothespin.

4. Fill 'er up with pens and pencils, scissors, rulers, whatever; add a note pad and some flowers, and, ah, how sweet it is!

TENNIS SHOE PLANTER: Remember the days when proud parents used to bronze baby's first shoes? If you do or if you're just into nostalgia, you can have your very own equivalent with a bronzed tennis shoe which does double duty as a memento and a flower pot.

So don't throw out your tired, your poor, your squashed sneakers. Instead, get a can of bronze spray paint and some attractive plastic flowers, and make a tennis shoe flower pot. Here's how:

1. Remove the laces from the shoes and wash off any dirt, oil or grease with a sponge and a good kitchen spray cleaner.

3. Spray the shoes with bronze paint. Repeat every 15 minutes until a rich coat is achieved. Three coats should be enough.

4. When the top is dry, spray the bottom and both sides of the shoelaces. When everything's dry, replace the laces and spray the entire shoe for the last time.

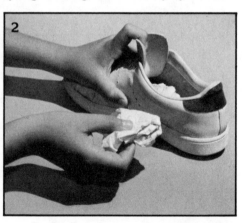

2. Stuff the toes of the shoes with newspaper to shape them and put the shoes on newspaper ready for painting.

5. Fill the shoe with dry dirt or sand. Poke plastic flowers into the sand for a pleasing arrangement. Say what you will, at least it will be something different!

RACQUET ASHTRAY STAND: If you are the kind of person who can never find an ashtray or whose ashtrays always seem to need emptying, here's one that's hard to lose and has the capacity to handle your Monday-night poker game. It's a unit that uses an old racquet as a stand and a ball can as the receptacle for the ashes.

To make one, you'll need a racquet and ball can, of course, plus a pressed wood base about 10 inches square, two one-quarter-inch, 4-inch long carriage bolts and one 2-inch wood screw. Proceed as follows:

1. Drill and countersink a one-quarter-inch hole in the center of the base. Also drill a three-sixteenth-inch hole in the butt of the racquet handle.

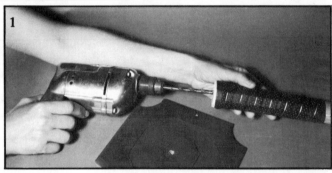

2. Halfway between the top and bottom of the tennis ball can, carefully drill a one-quarter-inch hole through opposite sides of the can.

3. Drill one-quarter-inch holes in the center of each side of the racquet frame, making sure the holes are exactly opposite each other.

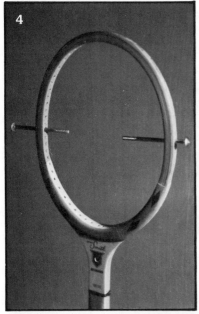

4. Insert a carriage bolt through the racquet frame on each side. These bolts will be used to suspend the can in the frame.

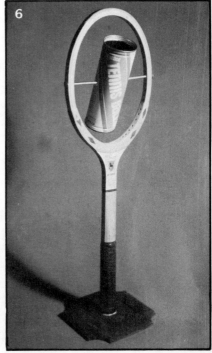

5. Attach the can to the carriage bolts and fasten with nuts inside the can. Tighten the nuts so the can may be rotated to empty the ashes.

6. Screw the base to the butt of the handle using the wood screw. When you stand the unit on its base, you'll have a completed ashtray.

RACQUET-COVER BALL-HOLDER: When you're practicing your serve, it can be bothersome to have to lean over repeatedly to pick up more balls. You could buy one of those tennis ball pick-up devices which also doubles as a holder and stand. But there's a simpler—and cheaper—way. A few minutes' work will turn an old racquet cover into a practice-ball holster so you can fire off your serves in rapid, gun-slinging fashion.

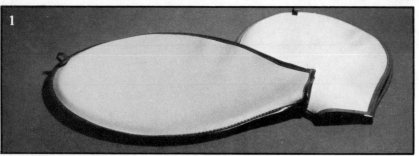

1. Dig out an old racquet cover from your closet. Most will hold about 12 balls, but one of the new oversized covers will take 18.

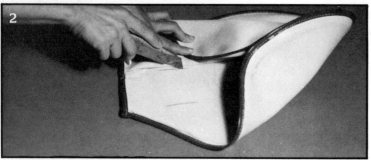

2. With a sharp knife, make two slits about two or three inches long and as far apart as possible near the throat opening.

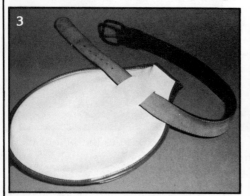

3. Take an old belt (wide leather ones are probably the best) and thread it through the two slits in the back of the cover.

4. Strap the holster around your waist, zipper partly closed, and fill with balls. Wear it on the side opposite your serving arm.

RACQUET PICTURE FRAME: An old tennis racquet can be converted into a frame for a portrait or, perhaps, a tennis photo. Hang it in your den or office to remind you of the good times you shared out on the court. Here's how you can turn the racquet into a picture frame.

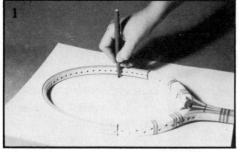

1. Remove the strings from the racquet and trace an outline of the inside of the racquet face on a piece of heavy cardboard or poster board.

2. Enlarge the tracing by one-quarter inch all around and cut out the enlarged shape. Attach the photo to the board with white glue or rubber cement.

3. Place the photo face down on the racquet frame and trim the shape, if necessary. Then tack or staple the cardboard to the racquet.

4. Insert two picture-hanging screw eyes into the frame at its widest point. Attach a wire to the eyes to hang the frame.

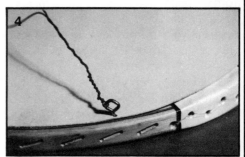

5. Nail a picture hook to your wall and hang the picture. You can angle the frame by using a second nail near the butt end of the racquet.

HOW TO SEW YOUR OWN RACQUET COVER

If you'd like something that's a little different from the usual racquet cover with a maker's name emblazoned across the front, you can sew your own in less than an hour. Anyone with minimal sewing skills can make this cover from half a yard of material. You can use a trim with a tennis motif or perhaps a trim that coordinates with one of your tennis outfits.

You'll need half a yard of sturdy 45-inch wide fabric (cotton duck, denim or vinyl), 1¼ yards of 1-inch wide trim, a 12-inch conventional zipper, a package of fold-over braid and suitable thread. Here's how to make your cover:

1. Lay the racquet head on your fabric and trace the outline twice for the two sides of the cover. Add one and one-quarter inches all around for depth and seam allowance.

2. Pin the trim to the zipper, mitering the bottom edge along the fold line to form a square. Stitch the trim to the zipper.

3. Mark a center line on the front of the cover. The line should be the length of the zipper plus one inch. Reinforce this opening by placing a line of stitches one-quarter inch outside it. Cut down the center line to within one-quarter inch of the lower end of that outside stitching. Fold the frayed cut edges back against the outside of the fabric along the stitching line.

4. Top-stitch the trimmed zipper to the racquet cover. On the inside of the cover, slipstitch the edges to the zipper tape.

5. With the two inside faces of the fabric together, stitch the front and back of the cover together. Then, apply the fold-over braid around the edge, turning under the raw edges at the neck.

Now you have a cover that will protect your racquet and look fashionable at the same time.

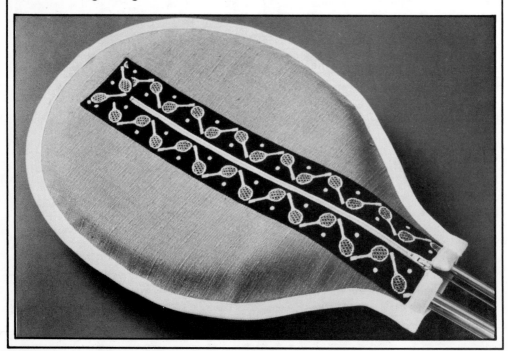

DIRECTORY OF ADDRESSES

Association of Tennis Professionals
319 Country Club Road
Box 402050
Garland, Tex. 75040
(214) 494-5991

International Tennis Federation
Barons Court, West Kensington
London W149EG, England

International Tennis Hall of Fame
Newport Casino
Newport, R.I. 02480
(401) 846-4567

National Tennis Association
P.O. Box 11097
919 North Michigan Ave.
Chicago, Ill. 60611
(312) 943-5933

Professional Tennis Registry—U.S.A.
1629 K St. N.W.
Suite 520
Washington, D.C. 20006
(800) 227-1548

Tennis Foundation of North America
200 Castlewood Court
North Palm Beach, Fla. 33408
(305) 848-1026

Tennis Grand Masters
Williamsburg Court
7710 Shawnee Run Road
Cincinnati, Ohio 45243
(513) 271-5506

U.S. Pro-Celebrity Tennis Association
12953 Marlboro St.
Los Angeles, Calif. 90049
(213) 394-0286

U.S. Professional Tennis Association
1620 Gulf of Mexico Drive
Longboat Key, Fla. 33548
(813) 388-3939

U.S. Racquet Stringers Association
P.O. Box 40
Del Mar, Calif. 92014
(714) 452-8602

U.S. Tennis Association
51 East 42nd St.
New York, N.Y. 10017
(212) 949-9112

USTA Education and Research Center
729 Alexander Road
Princeton, N.J. 08540
(609) 452-2580

(continued)

**U.S. Tennis Court and Track Builders
     Association**
1800 Pickwick Ave.
Glenview, Ill. 60025
(312) 724-7700

Women's Tennis Association
1604 Union St.
San Francisco, Calif. 94123
(415) 673-2018

World Championship Tennis
1990 First National Bank Building
Dallas, Tex. 75202
(214) 748-5828

The Rice Economies

For Sandy

The Rice Economies

*Technology and Development
in Asian Societies*

FRANCESCA BRAY

University of California Press

Berkeley · Los Angeles · London

University of California Press
Berkeley and Los Angeles, California

University of California Press, Ltd.
London, England

Library of Congress Cataloging-in-Publication Data

Bray, Francesca.
   The rice economies : technology and development in Asian societies /
Francesca Bray.
      p.   cm.
   Originally published: Oxford ; New York : Blackwell, 1986. With
a new pref.
   Includes bibliographical references and index.
   ISBN 0-520-08620-1
   1. Rice trade—Asia.   2. Asia—Economic conditions—1945–
3. Agriculture—Economic aspects—Asia.   I. Title.
HD9066.A7B73   1994
338.1'7318'095—dc20   93-41318
                                                                         CIP

Printed in the United States of America
9   8   7   6   5   4   3   2   1

Contents

Contents

Figures and tables

Figures

Tables

Chinese dynasties

Zhou:	1066–221 BC
Spring and Autumn period:	722–481 BC
Warring States:	*c.*403–221 BC
Qin:	221–206 BC
Han:	206 BC–AD 220
Three Kingdoms:	220–80
Six Dynasties:	222–589
Northern and Southern Dynasties:	317–589
Sui:	581–618
Tang:	618–907
Five Dynasties:	907–60
Northern Song:	960–1127
Southern Song:	1127–1279
Yuan:	1279–1368
Ming:	1368–1644
Qing:	1644–1911
Republic of China:	1911–49

Japanese eras

(There is little agreement as to the exact nomenclature and dates of the periods of Japanese history; the following is a rough guide.)

Jōmon:	To *c*.200 BC
Yayoi:	200 BC–AD 250
Kofun:	250–552
Yamato:	300–710
Asuka:	552–645
Nara:	645–794
Heian:	794–1185
Kamakura:	1185–1392
Muromachi:	1473–1568
Momoyama:	1568–1600
Tokugawa:	1600–1868
Modern:	1868 to date
Meiji:	1868–1912
Taisho:	1912–26
Shōwa	1926–

Preface

This book is a social history written from a materialist perspective. Starting from the assumption that one cannot understand the history of agrarian societies without a grasp of how the concrete conditions of agricultural production evolved, I trace the development of the technology of wet-rice agriculture in East and Southeast Asia from prehistoric to modern times, and link this development to social and economic change.

As a macroregion, East and Southeast Asia is as diverse as Braudel's Mediterranean (1972) or Chaudhuri's Indian Ocean (1990). The unity I attribute to these multifarious societies derives from their shared reliance on the same staple crop, rice, with its technical logic of development. From Burma to the Philippines and from Bali to Korea, rice is indisputably the most important food-grain in the economy. Unlike the rice regions of South Asia, where for climatic and / or topographical reasons effective water control is extremely difficult (Farmer 1981), in all the societies of East and Southeast Asia small-scale irrigation has been a crucial factor in the development of one of the most land- and labour-intensive farming systems in the world. This I contrast to a Western model that has taken quite the opposite direction.

In the case of the staple crop that feeds the population and fills the coffers of landowners and the state, the development of the social institutions which depend upon its supply is inseparable from the development of the agricultural system that produces the crop. Rice and wheat have quite different characteristics and requirements: farming systems based on these crops are presented with a different range of technical choices, and they experience different patterns of social and political development in consequence.

I start this study with an analysis of techniques and proceed to an analysis of social formations because I think this method can throw

new light on Asian history. The past two centuries of Western supremacy have promoted the view that there is only one trajectory of technical development that constitutes real progress. Inherent in this model
are capitalist criteria of efficiency consolidated during the Western
experience of industrialisation and agricultural development: increasing output and profits are produced through scale economies,
mechanisation and the progressive substitution of capital for labour.
We have internalised the emblems of progress found in this model: we
all learn at school that a tractor is more advanced than an iron plough,
which is more advanced than a hoe; a thousand-acre farm specialising
in wheat and run by three individuals is more efficient than a half-acre
farm growing sixteen different crops and taking up much of the labour
of a family of eight.

The Western attachment to teleology usually works in our own
favour: other societies come out as inferior, as failures. From Hegel and
Marx on, China, for example, has been stigmatised as a society which
failed to progress or to experience historical change until forcibly sub-
jected to Western influence. Even Joseph Needham's writings in *Science
and Civilisation in China* (to which I contributed [Bray, 1984]),
sinophile and critical of Western claims as they are, are inspired by the
essentially negative 'Needham question': until about 1500 China was
ahead of Europe in many branches of science and technology, so why
did China fail to develop capitalism, industrialisation and the scientific
revolution? Specialists and comparatists have debated the relative
importance of various 'inhibiting factors', as if capitalism was the
evolutionary goal of all healthy societies. The language of failure is
particularly salient in the work of economic historians, who do not
hesitate to speak of China from about 1000 to 1949 in terms of stagnation, involution or 'growth without development' (e.g., Elvin 1973;
Huang 1990). Yet as Perkins (1969) demonstrates, despite the natural
disasters and devastating wars that interrupted the otherwise steady
growth of a huge population, between 1000 and 1800 Chinese agriculture developed and expanded sufficiently rapidly to maintain, and
sometimes improve, overall living standards. These centuries of economic and social continuity require positive explanation—stability is
not something that can be taken for granted.

Here I am not concerned with Asia's 'failure' to be like the West,
though in Chapter 4 I do discuss how the organisation of labour and
investment between wet-rice agriculture and other productive sectors
evolved in ways that were unpropitious for industrial forms of organisation. My main concern is to provide materials for understanding
Asian societies, not as evolutionary failures or stagnating ponds of

surplus humanity, but as societies which work in different ways from
those of Europe, and to which our accustomed teleologies cannot use-
fully be applied. I consider the historical analysis of an absolutely fundamental technology, the technology of staple food production, an
important contribution to this endeavour. I also think it is a crucial factor in understanding how the Asian rice economies are evolving today.

I first started thinking about the specificity of wet-rice economies
during a year's fieldwork in Malaysia in 1976, when the discrepancies
between much of the development literature and my observations at
the village level set me reflecting on the different effects the Green
Revolution was having on the rice and wheat regions of Asia. My
ambitions to extend my hypothesis historically grew when I returned
from Malaysia to continue work on a general history of Chinese
agriculture. I noticed that in North China, where dry cereals were the
staple crops, a pattern of technological development and relations of
production rather similar to that of late medieval Western Europe
started to emerge in the early centuries A.D. It was characterised by the
formation of large estates that were centrally managed and heavily
dependent upon economies of scale, such as the use of animal-powered
machinery. The owners of these estates successfully resisted repeated
state efforts to disestablish them (Bray 1980). But nomadic invasions
and civil unrest pushed the political centre south to China's rice regions,
and although large-scale ownership of land persisted throughout
China's history, large-scale management became a thing of the past.
The Chinese state, whether out of benevolence or self-interest, traditionally supported the rights of the individual peasant against aristo-
cratic or gentry landowners. This position was easier to sustain when
rice cultivation was the mainstay of the economy because even though
land-ownership might be concentrated, small family farms predominated. Peasant farmers were easier to tax than the gentry, and the persistence of peasant farming must surely have been a factor in the
longevity of the Chinese empire. But what was it that allowed peasant
farming to survive in the teeth of gentry ambitions? Government
encouragement was not enough, as we can tell from what happened
during the early dynasties in North China. Unlike Gourou (1984:6),
who denies any determining influence of rice cultivation on the
societies in which it is practised, I feel sure that important reasons for
the survival of peasant farming must lie in the basic conditions of rice
production (Bray 1984).

Japanese historians have long used the notion of a rice-growing culture as a fundamental explanation of the specificities of Japanese society (Kanazawa 1971; Tamaki 1979). At the time when I was pursuing

fieldwork in Malaysia there were already strong advocates for sub-stituting a 'Japanese model' for the 'Western model' in the agricultural development of Asia's rice regions (Ishikawa 1967; Ishii 1978a). Since I first published this book in 1986, other Asian historians have started to explore the long-term demographic and economic characteristics peculiar to rice-based societies (Hayami and Tsubouchi 1990). But most economic history remains wedded to the Western bias of capitalist teleology, privileging labour productivity and profits in its interpretations. Today it seems to me that both the political and the environmental reasons for rejecting such values are overwhelming.

When I completed this book eight years ago I hoped it would serve a dual purpose. The first was to go beyond historical analyses of Asia as 'not-Europe'. Cultural and political historians have so far been among the most creative contributors to this project. But the material condi-tions of life should not be neglected in these analyses, for they are as fundamental in defining a society as religion or political ideas. New cri-teria are needed for evaluating systems of production as well as systems of thought. The study of technology in this book questions Western-biased criteria and models. I hope that soon there will be many more studies of productive technologies that diverge from Western norms, bringing original and stimulating perspectives to bear on the articula-tions between production and power, and transcending the language of involution, stagnation and failure.

My second purpose in writing this book was to take history through the present and into the future, to provide an analysis of the social and technical frameworks which Asian agricultural modernisation pro-grammes were and still are attempting to transform. At that time I felt that perhaps the most striking and pertinent feature common to Asia's rice economies, as described in both historical documents and contem-porary literature, was that although the ownership of land tended to become concentrated when methods were improved and production increased, economies of scale did not apply as in the Western model, and the basic unit of management remained the small family farm. I expected that this would make the Western-style modernisation of established wet-rice zones particularly difficult and contentious. This has indeed proved to be the case, even in wealthy and technically advanced countries, as recent literature on the deepening of Japan's agricultural crisis shows (Tweeten 1993).

There are, of course, certain rice-regions even in Asia where West-ern patterns occur. The Muda scheme in Malaysia, where processes of class differentiation have been so vividly described by Scott (1985), is one example. My explanation is that this pattern is most likely to occur

in areas, like Muda, where rice farming was introduced fairly recently and where fields were initially constructed on a large scale, so that there are few infrastructural barriers to plans involving large-scale mechanisation and farm consolidation. One might say that Muda's infrastructure is closer to those of Australia and California, where enormous rice fields constructed since the last world war, levelled by laser and sown from planes, use minimal labour to produce yields that are among the highest in the world. But long-established rice systems have proved extremely resistant to the transition to modern large-scale farming, which may perhaps prove to be a blessing, given the disastrous predicament of world agriculture today and the urgent need to adopt alternative strategies.

Eight years after this book was first published, I now see it as serving a third purpose. I was delighted to find that some of the most enthusiastic supporters of this work were ecologists and environmentalists working on sustainable development. Environmental concerns have started to penetrate even the international development agencies. Increasing numbers of people now question the Western farming model, which, as science and technology advance, is becoming even more wasteful and destructive of the environment and of rural life (Friedmann 1990). Ecologists tend to seek inspiration for viable alternatives from small groups as yet "untainted" by Western ideas and input, for instance horticulturists in Amazonia or upland farmers in the Yucatán. Yet it is extremely unlikely that their environmentally impeccable techniques could be extended to support large populations or that their farming methods could be transposed. Nor could they solve another of the most urgent problems of our times: how to improve the livelihood of the ever-growing numbers of rural poor.

According to the World Bank, 'the greatest numbers of the poor, including the very poorest, are found overwhelmingly in rural areas' (1990:33). Attempts to address this problem by modernising farming have usually just made things worse: cereal monoculture, mechanisation and expensive inputs marginalise poor farmers, displace labour and reduce alternative economic opportunities. Surely an obvious improvement is to encourage the development of agricultural systems which absorb labour and encourage economic diversification (Bray 1992; Bray forthcoming). The history of Asia's rice economies shows that even without chemicals and laboratory-bred seeds, intensive rice-farming has the potential to provide a lasting basis for a diversified rural economy, feeding and providing employment for large populations. I do not, of course, advocate that we try to convert Bangladesh into eighteenth-century Japan, or that we turn the clock back nine cen-

turies in China's Yangzi Delta. But I do think that Asian rice, as well as other farming systems where land and labour are or have been used intensively, should be carefully studied for indications as to how rural economies could best be revitalised to meet both environmental and humanitarian needs.

I am grateful to the British Academy and the Royal Society for financing a field trip to Malaysia in 1976–7, to the British Council and to the Universities' China Committee for supporting a study tour to China in 1980 and to the Leverhulme Trust for providing a most generous two-year fellowship in 1982–4, which enabled me to spend several months in Asia. The British Academy helped me again in 1982 with a Wolfson Fellowship which allowed me to spend several months in Paris working on archival material. Dr Joseph Needham and the East Asian History of Science Library (now the Needham Research Institute) in Cambridge provided me with unfailing support throughout.

It would be impossible to thank by name all those who have given me help and advice in this project. The villagers of Bunut Susu, and especially their *imam*, Encik Abdul Rahman bin Haji Suleiman, were its inspiration; it was through the kindness of the Kemubu Agricultural Development Authority staff and their economist, Puan Rohaini Zakaria, that I made their acquaintance. In Singapore I received generous help from the staff of the Institute for Southeast Asian Studies; in Kuala Lumpur from Wan Ahmad Radzi and Puan Fadillah Ibrahim and their families; in Kota Baru from Datuk Haji Yussuf Bangs, Encik Johan Arif and Robert and Pauline Whyte. In Penang the staff of the Centre for Policies Research kindly allowed me access to their invaluable collection. In Hong Kong I was given help and encouragement by, among others, Peter and Ei-Yoke Lisowski, Mr and Mrs P. L. Lam and George Hicks, who was most generous in providing material from his collection on the economies of Southeast Asia. In 1977 a visit to Taiwan was made fruitful through the good offices of the Joint Committee for Rural Reconstruction, and Professor T. T. Chang of the International Rice Research Institute gave me valuable assistance in the Philippines. A study tour of China in 1980 was arranged through the kindness of Academia Sinica; to that organisation, and to all the distinguished scholars of agricultural development and history who kindly spared time to discuss their work with an undistinguished foreigner, I am grateful. In Japan I must mention Professors Hayashi Takeshi, Kojima Reiitsu and Tada Hirokazu and their colleagues at the Institute of Developing Economies and Professors Ichimura Shinichi, Ishii Yoneo and Tsubouchi Yoshihiro of the Insti-

tute of Southeast Asian Studies in Kyōto, as well as Professors Katō Yuzo and Nakaoka Tetsurō and Drs Fujimoto Akimi and Christian Daniels, all of whom were kind enough to discuss my work with me. At the Centre National de la Recherche Scientifique in Paris, where I worked on the final stages of this book, I was fortunate in the encouragement of my directors, M. Lucien Bernot and M. Jacques Gernet. In Cambridge, Ben Farmer and Sir Joseph Hutchinson gave me much expert advice, and my colleagues at the Needham Research Institute, Gregory Blue and Timothy Brook, helped keep my feet on the Chinese ground. Sean Magee was my guardian angel at Basil Blackwell and Charlene Woodcock at the University of California Press. Without Sandy Robertson this book would never have been written, and my gratitude goes beyond words.

University of California, Santa Barbara
September 1993

Additional references

Braudel, Fernand (1972): *The Mediterranean and the Mediterranean World in the Age of Philip II*, Harper and Row, New York.

Bray, F. (1992): 'Population, agricultural intensification and economic diversification', in Lars O. Hansson and Britta Jungen (eds), *Human Responsibility and Global Change*, Institute of Human Ecology, University of Göteborg Press, Göteborg: 99–114.

—— (forthcoming): 'Rice economies and agricultural development', *Scientific American*.

Chaudhuri, K. N. (1990): *Asia before Europe: Economy and Civilisation of the Indian Ocean from the Rise of Islam to 1750*, Cambridge University Press, Cambridge and New York.

Friedmann, Harriet (1990): 'Family wheat farms and Third World diets: a paradoxical relationship between unwaged and waged labor', in Jane L. Collins and Martha Gimenez (eds), *Work without Wages: Domestic Labor and Self-Employment Within Capitalism*, State University of New York Press, Albany: 193–213.

Hayami, Akira and Yoshihiro Tsubouchi (eds) (1990): *Economic and Demographic Development in Rice Producing Societies*, Proceedings of the Tenth International Economic History Conference, Leuven University Press, Leuven.

Huang, Philip (1990): *The Peasant Family and Rural Development in the Yangzi Delta, 1350–1988*, Stanford University Press, Stanford, Calif.

Scott, James C. (1985): *Weapons of the Weak: Everyday Forms of Peasant Resistance*, Yale University Press, New Haven.

Tweeten, Luther, Cynthia L. Dishon, Wen S. Chern, Naraomi Imamura and Masaru Morishima (eds) (1993): *Japanese and American Agriculture: Tradition and Progress in Conflict*, Westview Press, Boulder, Colo.

World Bank (1990): *World Development Report 1990: Poverty*, Oxford University Press, New York.

Acknowledgements

The author and the publishers would like to thank the following for permission to use figures and tables from, or base figures and tables on, their own copyright material. Dr T. T. Chang, International Rice Research Institute, Manila, for figure 1.1, redrawn from his article 'The origin, evolution, dissemination and diversification of African and Asian Rices', *Euphytica* 1976; Routledge and Kegan Paul, London, for figure 2.3, from Hsiao-T'ung Fei, *Peasant Life in China: A Field Study of Country Life in the Yangtze Valley*; Professor Keiji Nagahara, Department of Economics, Hitotsubashi University, for figure 2.5, from Hideo Kuroda, 'Chūsei nōgyō jutsu no yōsō', in Nagahara and Yamaguchi (eds), *Nōgyō, nōsankako* (Nihon Hyoronsha, Tokyo, 1983; International Rice Research Institute, Manila, for figure 2.7, from R. Barker, 'Yield and fertiliser input', *IRRI*, 1978; Professor Shigeru Ishikawa, Aoyama University, Tokyo, for figure 3.1, from Ishikawa, *Economic Development in Asian Perspective* (Tokyo, 1967); Professor Yoneo Ishii, Centre for South East Asian Studies, Kyoto University, for figure 3.6, from Yoshiro Kaida, 'Irrigation and drainage: present and future', in Ishii (ed.), *Thailand: A Rice-Growing Society* (Hawaii UP, 1978); University of Malaya, Kuala Lumpur, Malaysia, for figure 4.2, from J. T. Purcal, *Rice Economy: Employment and Income in Malaysia* (East-West Center Press, Honolulu, 1972); Board of Trustees, Stanford University Press, for figure 5.1, from Thomas C. Smith, *The Agrarian Origins of Modern Japan* (Stanford UP, 1959); Dr Janice Stargardt, Cambridge Project on Ancient Civilization in South East Asia, for table 3.1, based on table 21 from Stargardt, *Satingpra I: The Environmental and Economic Archaeology of South Thailand* (Oxford and Singapore, 1983).

Map 1   East and Southeast Asia

Map 2   Central provinces of China

Map 3   States of peninsular Malaysia (showing Muda and Kemubu regions)

Introduction

Eurocentric models of historical change

European historical methodology has understandably been profoundly marked by the growth of capitalism, but it is doubtful to what extent models derived from Europe's highly specific experience are applicable to other parts of the world. Historians attempting to interpret Asian history find themselves wrestling with such intractable categories as 'feudalism' or 'peasants' which, despite their reassuring vagueness, rarely seem to fit the case exactly. Evading the issue entirely, one long-standing Western tradition recognises the essential 'otherness' of Asian societies by attributing to them a timelessness and unchanging quality encapsulated in the concept of the Asian Mode of Production. Others, recognising that all societies change eventually, and faced with the necessity of accounting for such awkward facts as the development of commerce and commodity production in pre-modern India and China, or industrialisation and the emergence of capitalism in Meiji Japan, have preferred to think of Asia as following basically the same path as Europe, but less successfully and less rapidly. Thus Marxist historians in China and Japan categorise a vast span of Chinese history (from about 200 BC to 1911 or 1949) as feudal, with 'sprouts of capitalism' emerging intermittently during the past four or five centuries but withering before they bore fruit (see Grove and Esherick 1980; Brook 1981). Non-Marxist historians too, especially when explaining the failure to develop capitalism (or the contrary in the case of Japan), usually measure off Asian societies point for point against a European model of development, to see where they are lacking (Elvin 1973; Tang 1979; Yamamura 1979; Jones 1981).

Both of these methods are essentially negative, the one denying the occurrence of any significant change, the other obscuring the specificity

of non-European societies. If we look only for what is typical of Europe, the significant features of a less familiar society may simply escape our notice. Over the last four centuries European society has been completely transformed, and advanced capitalism has accustomed us to a breakneck pace of change. By comparison it is not surprising that Asian societies seem to have stood still. Yet where adequate documents exist it is not difficult to show that in Asian societies too the forces of production were expanded and relations of production transformed – though not always in the way one might expect. The difficulty lies in accounting for the nature of such changes: if the dynamics of change differ from those we have identified as operating in European history, then it is not surprising that our traditional models fail adequately to interpret change in non-European societies, or even to acknowledge its existence.

While it is easy to appreciate that eurocentric models will generally prove inadequate to explain the evolution of non-European societies, it is not so easy to construct appropriate alternatives. One important obstacle is our failure (in the main) to recognise the relativity of our conception of technological progress. Changes in technology are clearly one key to explicating economic history, though of course there is considerable debate as to the exact degree to which technological development determines, affects, or is simply an expression of changes in the social formation. But what exactly constitutes technological development? Here all our doubts seem to evaporate. Philosophers like Gehlen (1965) and Habermas (1971) have pointed out the immanent connection between the contemporary evaluation of technology and the 'rationality' (in the Weberian sense) that prevails in capitalist society. To be more specific, in a society where relatively scarce and expensive wage-labour is the basis of production, technical progress is largely evaluated in terms of efficiency in replacing labour. Yet this highly specific model of technological advance is generally presumed to be universal in its application. Although one can easily envisage situations in which different criteria might apply, little attempt has been made to hypothesise alternative paths of technological development or to examine the social and economic implications of such differences.

If we consider the case of agriculture, we find that technological progress is generally construed as a sequence from primitive tools like digging-sticks or hoes to more complex instruments like ploughs or harrows, culminating in the mechanical sophistication of tractors, combine-harvesters and crop-spraying aeroplanes. To this one would add the application of scientific methods to such agricultural procedures as crop selection, nutrition and weeding, resulting in the laboratory breeding of new crop strains with desirable characteristics, and the

industrial production of chemical fertilisers, herbicides and pesticides. 'Progress' seems to lie chiefly in the increasingly efficient substitution of alternative forms of energy for human labour. Now labour-saving changes in agriculture have three possible effects: first, they may enable the same number of workers to bring larger areas of land under cultivation; secondly, they may enable the same area to be cultivated by fewer workers, thus liberating the surplus labour for some other employment; and thirdly, they may allow the same area of land to be more intensively cultivated without increasing the number of workers.

The first type of change is of particular importance where land is plentiful and labour scarce, as it has been in much of the New World; it is not surprising, for example, that it was in underpopulated Australia and the United States, as the world market for wheat expanded in the later nineteenth century, that the reaper-binder and the combine-harvester were developed (Jones 1979). The second type of change is important where labour is in high demand, scarce and expensive, as was the case in Europe in the early stages of the development of capitalism. As Boserup (1981: 99) says: 'There was usually keen competition for scarce labour [between agriculture and manufactures], and most often agriculture lost in this competition. Nothing could be more inappropriate than to characterise the European economy in this period as a labour surplus economy. On the contrary, one of the most serious problems in the period of pre-industrial urbanisation in Western and Central Europe was insufficiency of food production, due not to shortage of land, but to shortage of labour.' In fact in the early stages of the 'Agricultural Revolution' demands for labour generally grew, as cropping frequency increased and as techniques became more intensive in response to the greater demand for agricultural produce (Chambers 1967). At first the greater demand for agricultural labour could be accommodated by population increase, but as industrialisation advanced and the competition for labour grew, it became both necessary and (given advances in engineering and design) possible to develop labour-saving agricultural machinery such as the multiple-furrow plough, patent seed-drills, threshers and so on.

Changes of the third type are particularly valuable where land is in short supply; they do not necessarily displace labour but may increase its effectiveness by eliminating bottlenecks or performing tasks more thoroughly. The substitution for hoeing of deep ploughing with horses in nineteenth-century Japan, and the twentieth-century introduction of hand-tillers and transplanting machines are instances of this (see chapter 2).

But in similar situations of land shortage and abundant labour – such

as are characteristic of most regions where rice is intensively farmed – a fourth type of technical change is equally important, namely changes which increase both land productivity and labour demands. In areas such as the Yangzi Delta or Java, the introduction of high-yielding and quick-ripening crop varieties was extremely valuable because it not only increased the yields of a single crop but also permitted multi-cropping; by the same token it increased the number of operations and the quantity of labour required (which does not necessarily mean that the productivity of labour was reduced). Where rural populations are dense and opportunities for alternative employment few, technical changes which absorb labour and reduce agricultural underemployment are preferable to those which increase output at the cost of reducing the labour force. Advances of this fourth type, while frequently dependent upon highly skilled labour, do not necessarily require mechanical sophistication; indeed it is not unusual for agricultural implements to become simpler as cultivation techniques become more sophisticated and productivity rises (Boserup 1965).

Certain economists (Hayami and Ruttan 1979: 6) have characterised technological changes which produce the first or second effects just described as *labour-substitutes*, while those of the third and fourth type are essentially *land-substitutes*.

It is clear, then, that the development of agricultural techniques may take more than one direction, and that this will probably be significantly influenced by such factors as population density, demands for labour in other sectors, tenurial relations, or cropping patterns, to mention but a few. If technological changes are introduced rather than developing spontaneously, then it is crucial to ensure that they are of the appropriate type. Introducing labour-saving machinery in a poor country which is heavily overpopulated is bound to lead to economic problems and social upheavals, as the literature on contemporary development makes abundantly plain. Nevertheless, just as international banks and Third World governments alike have been dogged in their conviction that the development of heavy industry is an essential prerequisite for more general economic development (a belief which Lenin was perhaps justified in holding but which hardly applies to most nations today [Dumont 1983–4: passim]), so the majority of agricultural ministries and development agencies working in Asia have aimed at the 'modernisation' of local agriculture along lines with which, it is true, we are familiar from the experience of Western Europe and the New World, but which in many respects seem incompatible with prevailing conditions in East Asia and elsewhere.

An alternative model?

A significant difference between the technical development of Western grain-farming (described in appendix A) and Asian rice cultivation, which has important implications for socio-economic change, is that while wet-rice agriculture has enormous potential for increasing land productivity, most improvements are either scale-neutral and relatively cheap, or else they involve increasing not capital inputs but inputs of manual labour (see chapter 5). It has often been assumed that this implies a corresponding reduction in the productivity of labour, but this is not necessarily true. Where a transition from broadcast sowing to transplanting, or from single-to double-cropping is made, the increases in yield will certainly outstrip concomitant rises in labour inputs. The additional labour requirements are spread out over the year, and for most tasks household labour suffices to run a wet-rice smallholding. But even small farms will usually have to exchange or hire labour to cope with the bottlenecks of transplanting and harvesting, and farmers within a community will often agree to stagger planting and harvesting so that effective rotas for labour exchange or hire can be established; like the demands of irrigation, this is an important factor in creating a spirit of communality within rice communities (Liefrinck 1886; Embree 1946; Takahashi 1970; Bray and Robertson 1980) – which is not to say that individualism and conflict are absent, as we shall see in chapter 6.

The inconspicuous, low-cost nature of many improvements to wet-rice cultivation, and the association of highly productive techniques with a form of tenurial relations, namely smallholding, regarded by many as backward, have contributed to the image of Asian economies as historically stagnating and resistant to change. Yet there is an abundance of evidence to show that great progress has been made over the centuries in increasing the productivity of rice-land. Furthermore, the development of rice agriculture has often been accompanied by the growth of commercial cropping, trade and manufacture, as well as by significant changes in the relations of production.

The significance of a model of development for rice economies

There is good historical evidence to suggest that the dynamic underlying the development of the forces of production in wet-rice societies is very different from that manifest in the European transition from feudalism to capitalism. The model of technological and economic progress accepted

as generally valid is directly derived from the Western experience (see appendix A): it postulates the superior efficiency of large units of production, culminating in the rationality of modern capitalism. But in Asian agriculture the historical trend was towards not larger but smaller units of production – are we then to conclude that Asian agriculture stagnated or became increasingly inefficient as time went by? If we take as our yardstick the isolated examples of late nineteenth-century China or contemporary Java, with their dense and impoverished populations and cripplingly subdivided landholdings, we might perhaps be justified in such a conclusion. But a broader historical perspective forbids such a view. How would such an interpretation account for medieval China or eighteenth-century Japan, where changes in farming techniques did reduce the size of holdings but were accompanied by spectacular increases in agricultural productivity and in commercial and manufacturing activity? And how would we explain contemporary events in East and Southeast Asia, where the incursions of advanced capitalist technology have failed to modify basic patterns of land tenure and rural production?

The universal pretensions of our Western model of technological and economic progress have been strengthened by various scholars' claims to find 'feudal relations', 'sprouts of capitalism', or other elements of European social formations in non-European societies. But the recognition of these superficial resemblances often serves to obscure more fundamental and determinant differences. Reams of paper have been covered in the attempt to explain Song China's failure to develop capitalism, because historians have identified in Song society certain features believed to have contributed to the development of capitalism in Europe. If such phenomena as the high level of scientific and technical knowledge, the existence of a free market in land, or the advanced development of commercial institutions are taken in isolation from the relations of production, then the problem seems valid enough. But if we situate them in the context of Song China's economic base and the general dynamic of expansion of the forces of production, then we see that 'China's failure to develop capitalism' is simply a red herring, distracting us from a more thorough and fruitful examination of the specific characteristics of China's economic evolution. An obsession with classifying India as 'feudal' or 'non-feudal' has, as Mukhia (1981) shows, similarly diverted attention from India's specific path of historical development. Political scientists have identified Japan as the single nation in Asia to conform to the Western model of transition from feudalism to industrial capitalism, yet profound dissimilarities between Japanese and Western capitalism continue to puzzle them. Such mysteries are unlikely to be solved until it is recognised that the

superficial similarities between Japan and Europe mask differences deeply rooted in the productive forces.

Clearly the role of the technological base in determining overall social change must not be overestimated. A model based on technical dynamics alone cannot account for the political, institutional and external factors which have played such a crucial role in shaping the Asian nations. Yet despite their many cultural and political differences, I hope to show that societies which depend for their subsistence on wet-rice cultivation have in common a basic dynamic of technical evolution, which differs from the model of progress derived from the Western experience, and which imposes very different constraints upon social and economic development. A basic model of this nature serves an important purpose: it not only focuses our attention upon specific characteristics of non-Western societies but situates them in an evolutionary rather than a static framework. It should thus enable us to supersede the image of Asia as unchanging, as a Europe *manquée*, and help us to explicate the history of Asian societies in their own terms. Last but not least, it should provide fresh and perhaps constructive insights into contemporary processes of change in Asia.

The first three chapters of the book are an investigation of the technical means by which rice cultivation has been intensified and levels of land- and labour-productivity raised. The first chapter considers the potential of the rice-plant itself; the second looks at ways in which land use is developed by rice-farmers and the scope for rationalisation and mechanisation; the third is a study of water control, an essential feature of any developed rice technology. The fourth chapter makes a distinction between 'mechanical' technologies, like that of European agriculture, and 'skill-oriented' technologies such as rice cultivation; from this perspective it looks at rice cultivation as a basis for more general economic development and diversification, with particular reference to its links with petty commodity production and rural industrialisation. The fifth chapter considers the issues involved in the planned development of rice economies, taking as its point of departure a historical evaluation of the relative efficacy of capital and labour inputs in improving rice technology. Rice societies are a paradoxical combination of individualism and communalism, and the sixth chapter looks at how technological development affects relations of production; is a socialist reorganisation of rice production beneficial and stable, and to what extent has the impact of capitalism resulted in a shift towards capitalist farming and the differentiation of the peasantry?

1

The rice-plant: diversity and intensification

Rice is the staple food of almost half the population of the world, second only to wheat in its importance. The annual world rice harvest in 1981–2 came to over 400 million tonnes, from a cultivated area of about 145 million hectares (Swaminathan 1984: 65), while in 1978–9 world production of wheat was 450 million tonnes from 230 hectares (Fischer 1981: 249). Over the centuries rice has become an increasingly popular food not only in Asia but throughout the world, replacing tubers, millets and other food grains as the staple food in island Southeast Asia and parts of Europe, Africa and Latin America; it has become an increasingly important export crop in the USA and Australia. But the bulk of the world's rice crop is produced in monsoon Asia, the zone where it was first domesticated: 90% in monsoon Asia as a whole, and 64% in East and Southeast Asia alone (Swaminathan 1984: 65).[1] Despite a recent preference for bread and other wheat products among the wealthier classes, rice is by far the most widely consumed and cultivated crop in the Far East.[2]

This chapter will describe briefly the historical advance of rice cultivation through East and Southeast Asia, showing how the natural characteristics of the plant, its flexibility and enormous potential for breeding varieties suitable to almost any ecological or economic circumstance, permitted the increasingly intensive use of land and encouraged an ever greater number of both subsistence and commercial farmers to rely on it as their staple food.

The origins of Asian rice

The origins of domesticated Asian rice are still undetermined, but the distribution of wild rices (figure 1.1) suggests a centre, or centres, of

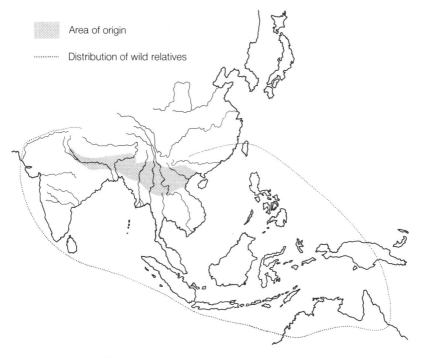

Figure 1.1　Area of origin of domesticated rice
(from Chang 1976a)

domestication somewhere in the piedmont zone of Assam, Upper Burma and Thailand, Southwest China and North Vietnam.[3] There is linguistic and ethnographic evidence to suggest that the earliest staple foods grown in monsoon Asia were tuber crops and millets, which were later superseded by rice (Kano 1946). The earliest archeological finds of domesticated rice to date come from China, from the site of Hemudu in Zhejiang province (near Ningbo in the Yangzi Delta). Excavations began in 1976 and are still continuing. The earliest stratum of Hemudu village, which is situated at the edge of a marsh, has been carbon-dated to about 5000 BC; the sheer volume of rice remains shows that the villagers were not proto-farmers but relied heavily on cultivated rice as a food supply even at that early date (Zhejiang CPAM 1976, 1978; Zhejiang Prov. Mus. 1978; You 1979).

A great number of Central and Southern Chinese neolithic sites of slightly later date contain remains of domesticated rice, among them several fourth millennium sites in the Yangzi Delta and further upstream, and a couple of sites in Guangdong which may date back to

2000 or 3000 BC (Yang 1978). There are also two early sites in North Thailand, Non Nok Tha and Ban Chiang (dated to about 5000 and 4500 BC respectively), which 'strongly suggest the presence of rice-farming in the northeastern Thai plateau prior to 4500 BC' (Gorman 1977: 433).[4] Gorman suggests that the domestication of rice began in naturally marshy areas in upland Southeast Asia about 9,000 years ago and that, as their skills improved, early rice-farmers were able to occupy non-marshy sites such as Ban Chiang and Non Nok Tha. Such a hypothesis seems consistent with the evidence from China and Thailand, and from Vietnam, where wet-rice cultivation was established in the Red River Delta by the mid-third millennium BC or perhaps earlier (Higham 1984). There is also linguistic evidence for a domestication of rice in the extended piedmont zone of Southeast Asia.[5]

India was for long believed to be the original centre of rice domestication, not only because of the varietal diversity of Indian rices (Vavilov 1949: 29), but also because until recently the supposed remains of rice from sites of the great Harappan civilisation were, at 1800 BC, the earliest known in the world (Vishnu-Mittre 1974). The Harappan 'rice' remains proved to be a misidentification however (Reed 1977: 918), and with the earliest Indian evidence now dated to about 1500 BC (Vishnu-Mittre 1977: 585), there is a clear case for giving preference to the Southeast Asian piedmont zone as the original home of domesticated rice.

Rice cultivation was probably a rather late introduction to Japan. The earliest evidence comes from sites in the southern island of Kyūshū which can be dated back to about 300–400 BC,[6] and from Kyūshū it spread gradually northwards, reaching the northern tip of Honshū before the Yayoi period ended in the mid-third century AD (Sahara, forthcoming; Tamaki and Hatade 1974: 58). Japanese rices are assumed to have originated in the Yangzi Delta, and there are three possible routes by which they might have reached Japan: overland through North China to Korea and then by sea; by sea from the Yangzi Delta to Korea and thence to Japan; or by sea from the Yangzi Delta directly to Kyūshū. The second hypothesis is currently favoured on the basis of associated tool typologies (Gina Barnes, pers. comm. 1984).

As we have seen, rice was cultivated from very early times on the mainland of Southeast Asia, but tuber crops or millets remained the staple crops of much of the Malay peninsula and Indonesian archipelago until rather late. The magnificent carvings of Borobudur (*c*.ninth century AD) depict millet but not rice, and rice seems to have been introduced to Java, not by land through Siam and then Malaya, but by sea from India during the later period of Hindu influence. Irrigated rice

appears to have been introduced to Java in medieval times (perhaps before the establishment of the kingdom of Majapahit in the thirteenth century), whence it spread gradually to the scattered communities of the Southern Malay peninsula, though dates for this are generally uncertain (Hill 1977: 20–7; van Setten 1979: 1–9). However the northern kingdoms of Malaya, Kedah and Kelantan, seem to have adopted wet-rice cultivation somewhat earlier, deriving their skills from the mainland Southeast Asian tradition (unlike the other Malay and Indonesian regions, which refer to wet-rice fields as *sawah*, the Northern Malays use the term *bendang*). Furthermore in early medieval times a sophisticated system of wet-rice cultivation flourished on the Songkla peninsula in Southern Thailand, an area which probably had close trade relations with the Cambodian state of Funan (Stargardt 1983).

Although rice was a relative late-comer to the outer fringes of the Far Eastern world, it always arrived to stay. Once people became accustomed to eating rice they were loath to change back to other foods, and once they had built rice-fields on their land they were understandably reluctant to abandon them. The adaptability of the rice-plant meant that its cultivation was not confined to well-watered river valleys or deltas: it could be grown on steep slopes cleared of virgin forest in Borneo, along deeply flooded river-banks in Burma and Bangladesh, or on salt-marshes won back from the sea along the China coast. Under such difficult conditions as these crops might be small, but where conditions were slightly more favourable rich harvests could be had, and most of the great civilisations of the Far East, the Chinese dynasties, the kingdoms of South India and Ceylon, the Angkorian empire, Srivijaya and many more, were founded on the wealth of their rice-fields. Let us look at the natural characteristics of the rice-plant which account for its historical popularity and success.

Natural characteristics of rice

Rice is by nature a swamp plant, and by far the greatest number of varieties are grown in standing water, but there are also dry rices which are grown on steeply sloping hillside fields (Freeman 1970; Geddes 1976; Hill 1977). Generally speaking, dry or hill rice varieties will not grow in wet fields, nor can wet rices be grown in upland fields, but some interchangeable varieties do exist. It has been suggested that dry-rice cultivation developed earlier than wet, on the grounds that the techniques involved are less complex (see Watabe 1977: 16), but most botanists reject this on morphological grounds (Grist 1975: 27). Hill rice can only be grown by systems of shifting cultivation and does not,

therefore, provide a suitable base for the development of complex
technical systems or of the related social and economic organisations,
and so our discussion will be confined to wet-rice systems.

Rice is an extremely adaptable plant, with an efficient system of air
passages connecting the roots and the shoot which enables it to grow in
dry upland soils, in irrigated fields, or along flooded river-beds. It is
largely self-pollinated, but cross-pollination does occur in degrees
varying between less than 1% and as much as 30% (Grist 1975: 72), and
a very large number of wild varieties exists.[7] The range of variation in
rice is so great that no internationally recognised system of classification
has yet been developed, although repeated attempts have been made ever
since the Rice Congress at Valencia in 1914 urged 'the formation of a
real botanical classification of the varieties of cultivated rice'.[8]

Among the Asian domesticated rices, *Oryza sativa*, two sub-species are
commonly distinguished, *indica* and *japonica*, both of which include
glutinous and non-glutinous varieties. A list of the most important
differences beween the sub-species is given by Grist (1975: 94). The
contrasts which most immediately strike the non-specialist are that *indica*
rices have longer, more slender grains which usually remain separate
when cooked, while *japonicas* have shorter, rounder and more translucent
grains which quickly become slightly sticky. The *indica/japonica* distinction was first drawn in the late 1920s by a group of Japanese botanists, on
the basis of morphology, hybrid sterility and geographic distribution. But
some Asian rices, notably those of Indonesia, do not seem to conform to
either category, and in 1958 a third sub-group named *javanica* was
proposed to designate the *bulu* and *gundil* varieties of Indonesia (Grist
1975: 93).

In China both *indica* and *japonica* varieties have been cultivated since
neolithic times (Bray 1984: 484). The earliest Chinese dictionary, the
Shuowen jiezi of AD 100, was the first work to contain the terms *geng* and
xian which have been used to designate *japonica* and *indica* rices in
Chinese ever since (ibid.: 487). Not surprisingly, the majority of rice
varieties grown in India are *indicas* and in Japan *japonicas*. Most rices
grown in the tropical zones belong to the *indica* and *javanica* groups,
which tend to have a fixed growth period. *Japonica* rices are highly
sensitive to photoperiod, or day-length, and do poorly in the short-day
tropics. They are, however, widely grown in North China, Korea and
Japan. Altitude is also an important factor: a study of cultivated rices in
Yunnan province in the Chinese foothills of the Himalayas showed that
indica varieties predominated up to 1,750 m and *japonica* varieties over
2,000 m, while in the zone between 1,750 and 2,000 m intermediate
varieties were found (Ding 1964).[9]

Rice (figure 1.2) has a number of advantages compared with many other food crops. First, it is very palatable, and is the only cereal which can simply be boiled and eaten without disintegrating into mush. Perhaps because of its flavour it has frequently been considered a luxury food: in medieval Japan peasants paid their dues to their lords in rice grown specially for this purpose, though they could afford to eat only millets themselves, and similarly in many parts of India today poor farmers sell their rice crops to the cities and buy cheaper grains for their own consumption.

The nutritional value of rice varies considerably according to type, environment and method of preparation, but generally speaking it is highly digestible and nutritious. Unmilled rice compares favourably with wheat and other cereals in its protein, fat, vitamin and mineral content, but unmilled or 'brown' rice has little sale outside the health-food stores of the West. It takes a long time to cook and is difficult to chew, and most rice-eaters prefer their rice to be not only hulled (removing the husk), but also milled and polished (removing all the coloured pericarp as bran). This leaves the grain white and shining. In polishing rice loses much of its nutritional value: highly polished rice contains only 7% protein, whereas rice that has simply been husked still contains nearly 10%.[10] Washing and cooking methods often deplete the nutrients further, and deficiency diseases such as beri-beri are not uncommon among consumers of rice too poor to supplement their diets with alternative sources of protein and vitamins. But just as Europeans traditionally regarded white bread as a luxury more desirable than brown, so most Asians wish their rice to be as highly polished as possible. The problem of nutritional deficiency has been exacerbated by the recent spread of efficient mechanised mills, for now almost all rice is highly polished, even in villages. Traditionally the Asian poor used their own hand-mills or bought inexpensive rice that was poorly polished and so they were, despite themselves, protected in some measure against deficiency diseases. They also garnished their rice with soy products, fish sauces and vegetables, which combined to make an impressively healthy diet compared with that consumed by the proletarians of urban or rural Europe (Fortune 1857: 42). So although modern analyses of the nutritional value of rice show it to be poorer in many respects than wheat, in fact many traditional Asian rice-based diets are nutritionally more than adequate.[11]

Rice is a relatively high-yielding crop even under adverse conditions. Provided the water supply is adequate, nitrogen-fixing organisms which occur naturally in the paddy-fields enable farmers to harvest up to 2 tonnes/hectare without applying any mineral fertilisers (Swaminathan

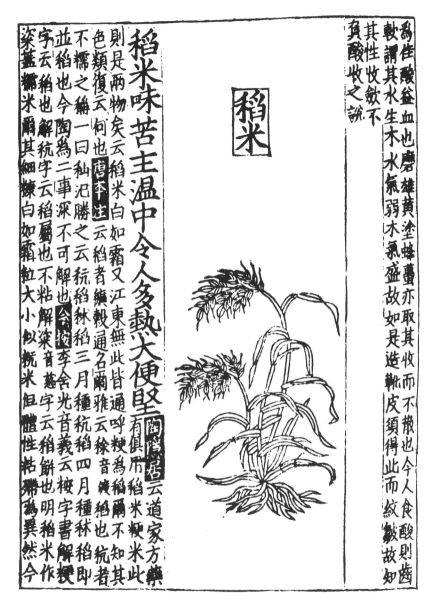

稻米

Figure 1.2   The rice-plant

(from a twelfth-century Chinese botanical work, the *Zhenglei bencao,* 1468 edn)

1984: 69). A very rough idea of the productivity of rice is given by the world production figures cited earlier, from which one can derive average annual yields of 1.95 t/ha for wheat and 2.75 t/ha for rice.[12] And this is not just a recent contrast. A map of one of the Gufukuji Temple's holdings in Kagawa prefecture, Japan, dating to 753, shows that dry fields were only one-quarter to one-third as productive as neighbouring rice-fields; even poor quality rice-fields yielded about one-third more grain than a dry field (Farris 1985: 107).

Of course yields may be much higher or much lower than those just mentioned. The highest rice yields in the world are in fact obtained in Australia (Grist 1975: 485), where as much as 7 t/ha may be had on fields which are sown with rice once every six or seven years, being used as pastures in the interim. In contrast, in parts of Malaysia where there is no irrigation and modern varieties and inputs cannot be used, subsistence farmers may get as little as 1.5 t/ha (pers. obs.).

But of special interest to farmers living on the margins of subsistence is that rice has a high yield to seed ratio. Wheat, barley and rye, the staple cereals of Northern Europe, bear heads with relatively few grains, say between 20 and 90; each plant will normally develop four or five tillers, giving a possible maximum of 400 or so grains per plant in all (Leonard and Martin 1963: 291). Theoretically, then, each seed-grain could produce 400 offspring. In reality, given the physiology of the plant and inefficient sowing techniques like broadcasting, in Europe up to the seventeenth or eighteenth century the ratio of crop to seed-grain averaged no more than 4 : 1 or 3 : 1, of which of course a high proportion had to be set aside as seed for the next crop (Slicher van Bath 1963: 382). A single panicle of rice may contain up to 500 grains, though 75 to 150 is more usual, and a well-watered plant on fertile soil can produce up to 50 tillers (Leonard and Martin 1963: 615); the number of grains produced from a single seed could thus easily average 2,000 in transplanted rice. Yield to seed ratios of 100 : 1 can be obtained even using such simple cultivation techniques as those practised in parts of Malaysia which have not seen the benefits of the 'Green Revolution' (pers. obs.; Hill 1977: 134). Setting aside one-fiftieth or one-hundredth of the rice harvest for seed-grain is much less of a hardship and a risk for subsistence farmers, then, than keeping enough wheat for sowing.

One reason why rice gives high annual yields is that it is often possible to grow two or even three crops a year in the same field. This does not mean that the annual yield is thereby doubled or tripled, but it will certainly be increased significantly. Alternatively, overall output can be increased by draining the rice-fields after the harvest and planting crops such as wheat, vegetables or tobacco. Since a crop of transplanted rice

may occupy the field for as little as two to three months, there is more scope for multi-cropping than when directly sown cereals like wheat, millet or maize are the main crop.

The possibilities of multi-cropping and the high yields of wet rice are consistent with very high land productivity, though this does depend on heavy inputs of labour. As a wet-rice farming system becomes more intensive the land's population-carrying capacity increases sharply, as do labour requirements. The intensification of rice-farming both permits and requires demographic increase. It is no coincidence that the most densely populated agricultural regions of the world, Java, the Tonkin Delta and the Lower Yangzi provinces of China, all have a centuries-long tradition of intensive wet-rice farming. No wheat-growing areas can sustain such numerous populations.

Rice-fields planted with a second crop generally give higher yields each season than those which are only single-cropped, thanks to the additional ploughing and manuring, and also to the beneficial effects of drying out the soil (Grist 1975: 44; Watabe 1967: 103). This fact is clearly appreciated by landowners in Northern Thailand, for example, who will often lend their rice-fields free to landless peasants in the dry season to grow soybeans or groundnuts (Bruneau 1980: 386). If the field is continuously planted with wet rice its fertility, unlike that of dry fields, will not diminish over time even if few or no fertilisers are used, for the nutrient content of the irrigation water, together with the nitrogenising power of the naturally occurring algae, are sufficient to maintain regular returns from traditional rice varieties. This is obviously an important consideration for a subsistence farmer.

So rice will allow poor farmers to produce reasonable yields from their land, at the cost, it is true, of heavy investments of labour, but without necessitating such capital outlays as the purchase of fertilisers. Another important consideration for subsistence farmers is the risks involved in production. If one may reap a hundredfold in a good year but three years out of four are bad, one's hold on life is bound to be precarious. Here again, rice offers significant advantages.

A very important risk-reducing factor in rice-growing is the enormous range of varieties available to farmers even in isolated areas. The number of cultivated varieties of *Triticum aestivum* (by far the most important of the six types of domesticated wheat) totals some 20,000 throughout the world (Feldman and Sears 1981: 98). There are about 120,000 cultivated varieties of Asian rice (Swaminathan 1984: 66). The great range of rice varieties derives in part from its natural propensity to diversify, but this propensity has been encouraged and channelled by the conscious intervention of rice farmers through the ages.

Rice-farmers usually grow several different varieties of rice in any one season, partly to provide for different requirements and partly as a means of minimising their risks. Different fields will suit different varieties depending on the soil, exposure or water supply. Late rains will mean that quick-ripening varieties must be planted instead of better-yielding slow-maturing rices. It is often desirable to rotate varieties to reduce the incidence of disease. Small quantities of special rice are required for ceremonies, while less desirable but sturdier varieties are grown for sale. Another very important factor which rice-farmers must take into account is timing: labour is in peak demand at transplanting and harvesting, water (also a limited commodity) at ploughing and just after transplanting. If a number of different varieties are planted, then the requirements of water and labour will be spread over a more manageable period. Thus an Iban family would commonly plant 15 or more varieties of rice (Freeman 1970: 188); Lüe farmers in Northern Thailand grow various types of glutinous rice for their own consumption and of non-glutinous rice for sale according to carefully calculated harvesting schedules (Moerman 1968: 150); and in eleventh-century Anhui (Central China) poor farmers grew large-grained *japonica* rices to pay their taxes, and *indicas* for their own consumption (Bray 1984: 491).

Rice-farmers, then, have traditionally used a wide range of varieties both as a policy to ensure subsistence and as a strategy to increase their income. Where rice is the main commodity, as in the Northern Thai village of Ban Ping, or in San-lin village in Central Taiwan, farmers wish to maximise their rice yields; indeed even today they will often make their financial calculations in terms not of cash – whose value to such farmers in a fluctuating market or inflationary economy appears highly unstable – but of rice (Moerman 1968: 153; Huang 1981: 44). Where other sources of income predominate, farmers wish to plant rice varieties which free the rice-fields sufficiently early for them to plant commercial crops such as tobacco, vegetables or sugar-cane, or varieties whose peak labour requirements will not clash with other activities such as the cultivation of cash crops in dry fields (e.g. Bruneau 1980: 407).

Since their requirements are so specific and varied, it is not surprising that rice-farmers have always devoted considerable attention to the development and maintenance of desirable strains according to a number of criteria such as yield, habitat, flavour, growth period and season, resistance to flood, drought and disease, glutinous or non-glutinous endosperm, and fragrance. There are black and red rices as well as white. 'Rouge-red rice is soft, fragrant and sweet, and when it is cooked it turns a uniform red in colour. It is one of the best of the late rices. One variety tolerates saline conditions and is ideal for brackish fields by lakes

or near river mouths', says the *Qun fang pu*, a seventeenth-century Chinese botanical work (Bray 1984: 494). Rices such as these were used to reclaim the swamp-lands of Hong Kong by migrant Chinese fleeing from the Mongols in the thirteenth and fourteenth centuries (Watson 1975: 30).

The 'glutinous' characteristic is one that has been much valued by Asian rice-farmers. 'Glutinous' varieties in fact contain no gluten; the stickiness of the cooked grain is generally assumed to result from the presence of dextrin and a little maltose as well as starch in the endosperm (Grist 1975: 100). Glutinous rice is highly valued as a ceremonial food and as the chief ingredient in rice 'wines' or beers. Cakes made of glutinous rice are exchanged at weddings and religious festivals all over Asia. In Malaya a large cake of glutinous rice, coloured brilliant red, yellow or purple and decorated with eggs and flowers, is offered to the bride as a symbol of fertility. In South China cakes of glutinous rice, wrapped in broad bamboo leaves and steamed, are exchanged on the day of the Dragon Boat Festival. Most Asians eat ordinary rice as their staple, but some mountain-dwellers prefer the glutinous kind, regarding it as more nutritious – if inclined to make the brain sluggish. In Northern Thailand this dietary distinction is seen by the local peasants as a mark of both ethnic and political identity: only effete southerners, soldiers or government officials, eat non-glutinous rice, and though local farmers grow the higher-yielding non-glutinous varieties for sale, they always take care to plant enough glutinous rice for their own consumption (Moerman 1968).

From the point of view of the cultivator, one of the most important differences between rice varieties is the ripening period, which may vary between 90 and 260 days. *Japonica* rices take a fixed period to ripen regardless of the date at which they are planted, but most *indicas* are photosensitive and will always flower at a particular date (Grist 1975: 84). It is therefore easier to breed quick-ripening varieties of *indica* than of *japonica*. Quick-ripening varieties are especially useful where the water supply is uncertain or insufficient. They also make multi-cropping possible, but they usually yield significantly less than medium-or long-term rices. The great exceptions, of course, are the recently developed 'high-yielding varieties' (HYVs) which have come to play such an important part in Asian rice production since the 1960s. These are derived from semi-dwarf mutants of *indica* rices; they are mostly quick-ripening, permitting double-or even triple-cropping, and they respond very positively to chemical fertilisers, often yielding more than half as much again as traditional varieties.

Where deep flooding rather than inadequate water is the problem, in

deltas or lakelands for example, the introduction of floating rices has sometimes proved effective. Floating rices are most extensively grown in the deltaic plains of Burma and Bangladesh; in Bangladesh they constitute almost one-quarter of the total rice crop (Oka 1975b: 279), and about 25 varieties are known (Grist 1975: 140). They are also important in the other flood-plains of Southeast Asia, and the introduction of floating rices to the Burma Delta at the end of the nineteenth century was one of the major agricultural innovations of the colonial period (Adas 1974: 130). And in pre-revolutionary Cambodia, although floating rice occupied only a small area (some 85,000 out of over 1 million hectares under rice), it had great economic significance, for unlike ordinary rices it was grown almost exclusively for sale. The crop was supposed to be very ancient in the Plaine des Lacs, but was only introduced to the south of Cambodia by French officials in the late nineteenth century (Delvert 1961: 329).

Yields of floating rice in Cochinchina generally were quite high: 2 t/ha as opposed to 1.8 t/ha in single-cropped and 2.6 t/ha in double-cropped fields (Henry and de Visme 1928: 52). In parts of Thailand floating rices will yield up to 5 t/ha if transplanted, even though no fertilisers are used; average yields in areas prone to flood are likely to be much lower, but at 2 t/ha still higher than non-floating rices in the same vicinity, which yield only 1.45 t/ha (Oka 1975b: 282). So far little attention has been devoted to breeding improved varieties of floating rice, despite their great potential importance, but work in this field is now in progress (ibid.: 284 ff).

Selection techniques

Since rice-farmers' requirements are so specific and vary so widely, it is not surprising that they have always devoted considerable attention to the development and maintenance of desirable strains. As cross-pollination does occur in varying degrees, and since wild rices are common in many of the areas where rice is cultivated, in the natural course of events one would expect rice cultivars to evolve and change continuously. Human selection has thus been crucial in maintaining desirable strains and selecting new cultivars. The techniques of rice-farming lend themselves particularly well to selection.

One of the simplest methods of improvement is to pick out the best panicles at harvest time and set them aside for seed-grain. This process was probably facilitated from very early times by the use of the reaping-knife. A small, flat knife with a curved blade, the reaping-knife is

held in the palm of the hand and the heads of grain are cut off just below the ear, one by one, by drawing the stem across the blade with the index finger (figure 1.3). Stone, shell and pottery reaping-knives are common in neolithic sites throughout China and Japan, and knives with small metal blades were used to harvest rice throughout much of Southeast Asia until very recently. Ethnographers have frequently linked this knife specifically with the cultivation of rice, for its use is often accorded ritual significance by rice-growers: Malay farmers, for instance, believed that since it was hidden in the palm of the hand, unlike the naked blade of the sickle it would not frighten away the 'rice soul', *semangat padi*, without which the seed-grain could not grow (Hill 1951: 70). But the reaping-knife is also used by Asian farmers growing foxtail and broomcorn millets (Fogg 1983; *Wang Zhen nongshu* 1313: 14/6b), the cultivation of which preceded that of rice in many parts of East and Southeast Asia. However, all the early domesticated cereals of the Far East, including rice, have large seed-heads or panicles, are naturally free-tillering and tend to ripen unevenly. In such circumstances it is not desirable to reap all the heads from a single plant simultaneously: it is better to gather the heads individually as they ripen, for which purpose a small knife is preferable to a sickle. And if each panicle is cut individually in this way, then it is easy for the farmer to pick out specially fine heads, or to select seed-grain from a plant which has ripened earlier than the rest and may thus produce quick-ripening offspring.

Transplanting is another stage of rice cultivation at which the farmer has a chance, not so much to select the best plants, as to eliminate sickly plants or mutants, and so maintain reasonably pure strains.

A third stage of possible control in traditional rice-farming occurs just before sowing, when the seed-grain, which has usually been stored in the ear as a protection against insects and mildew, is taken out and husked. It is then common practice to soak the seed briefly in order to separate out empty or rotten kernels and weed-seed. Sometimes clear water is used; in early and medieval China it was commonly believed that water obtained from melted snow was especially beneficial: 'It will immediately dissolve the hot properties of the grain so that the young shoots will be unusually handsome' (Song 1966: 11). Later on a brine solution was often used to test the seed:

First construct a bucket of 2 gallon capacity. (Separately prepare a fine-meshed bamboo basket slightly smaller than the bucket.) Put in 1 gallon of water and add salt. For ordinary rice use 120 ounces of salt, for glutinous rice use 100. Stir with a bamboo brush for five or six minutes until the salt has dissolved, then insert the basket into the bucket and gradually pour in 4 or 5 pints of seed, not too much at once. Skim off the empty kernels that float to the surface with a bamboo strainer.

Figure 1.3   Harvesting-knife, ketaman, *used in Kelantan*
(photo courtesy A. F. Robertson)

Repeat several times until no floating seeds remain, then draw out the basket, put it into another vat of water and rinse away the salt. (Zeng 1902: 1/18b)

In Malaya the strength of the brine was tested by floating a duck-egg in the water, and in post-revolutionary China a hen's egg was used to test a thin suspension of clay. Modern agronomists recommend specific concentrations of salt, ammonium sulphate or lime as more accurate than the folk methods just described (Bray 1984: 246). Even though the grain has already been selected at harvest the process of soaking is not superfluous, for there may be significant differences in speed of germination and in flowering time even between grains taken from the same ear, and the heavier grains can be relied upon to flower and set more quickly (Ding 1961: 310). This is of particular importance where quick-maturing varieties are being grown.

In the past it was usually peasant farmers who selected and developed new strains of rice and passed them from hand to hand. Specially successful varieties might sometimes travel great distances in this fashion: for example in seventeenth-century China a variety known as 'Henan early' was recorded as far away as South Fujian, perhaps 750 miles away (Ho 1959: 173).

An interesting example of the development of quick-ripening varieties is provided by the so-called 'Champa' rices. Champa was an Indochinese state to the south of Annam, known to the Chinese as early as the first century AD for having rices so precocious they could be cropped twice in one year (Bray 1984: 492). There is also archeological evidence that double-cropping was practised even earlier, in the Dong S'on period (Higham 1984: 105). By the sixth century the Annamese apparently possessed such a wide range of wet and dry, early and late varieties that they could grow rice all the year round, but the quick-ripening varieties gave very low yields while requiring just as much labour as the other sorts (Amano 1979: 193). They did, however, have very moderate water requirements: they would grow in poorly watered fields, did well as dry crops when grown in hilly regions and were generally highly resistant to drought. Many farmers must have grown them, if not as their main crop, at least as a form of insurance.

The Champa rices had spread northwards as far as South China by the medieval period, passing from farm to farm, for when the Song emperor Zhenzong decided to encourage their cultivation in the Lower Yangzi region he sent not to Annam but to Fujian province for 30,000 bushels of Champa seed; this was in AD 1012. The Champa rices, unlike those most popular in much of China at that time, were *indicas*, and at first they gave consistently lower yields than most traditional

Chinese varieties. But peasants quickly selected and developed higher-yielding varieties to grow in the well-watered lowland fields. By the end of the Song dynasty, some 250 years after their official introduction, later-ripening and more prolific Champa rices had been bred and soon the range was as wide as for any other type of rice.

Although it was the Song government which first introduced the Champa rices to the Yangzi Delta, it was through the efforts of individual peasant farmers that the best varieties of Champa rices were developed. In recent times, however, the breeding and even the choice of rice varieties has become increasingly a matter for officialdom.

The Japanese set up agricultural research stations where the best 'native' varieties were crossed to produce 'improved' varieties as early as the 1870s (Dore 1969: 98); these improved rices were distributed to local farmers, together with detailed instructions as to their cultivation, through the recently founded Agricultural Associations. In the early 1920s the Japanese authorities introduced high-yielding *japonica* rices to Taiwan to replace the local *indicas*, which they considered insipid (Huang 1981: 59). Many Taiwanese farmers adopted the new *japonica* rices enthusiastically, for as they were mostly exported to Japan they commanded almost double the price of local rices (Wang and Apthorpe 1974: 163), but Taiwanese consumers continued to prefer the *indicas*, which offered farmers the additional advantage of requiring fewer fertilisers. When the Japanese first occupied Taiwan in 1895, 1,365 varieties of rice, all *indicas*, were grown on the island. Today many farmers grow *japonicas* in the main season and *indicas* in the off-season, and a 1969 report stated that only 86 *indicas* and 53 *japonicas* were then grown on Taiwan (Huang 1981: 48). Seed of the *japonicas* is these days distributed through the Farmers' Associations; the villagers do not keep the *japonica* seed themselves as they say it will deteriorate. However they refuse to use the *indica* seed bred at the Agricultural Research Station. Instead they select their own, sharing out seed from high-yielding fields; they say that, like the native fowls, the original native rices will never degenerate (Wang and Apthorpe 1974: 163).

In China, in contrast to Japan and its colonies, the emphasis was on improving *indica* strains. Breeding programmes were first set up in the universities in Canton and Nanking in 1925, and in 1934 a national breeding programme and distribution service was set up by the National Agricultural Research Bureau (Shen 1951: 199). Traditional *indicas*, in China as elsewhere, are tall and have a tendency to lodge (that is, to fall over if wind or rain are too strong). The Chinese breeders concentrated on producing new varieties from semi-dwarf mutants, and had developed high-yielding types by the early 1960s, a few years before similar 'miracle

rices' were developed by the International Rice Research Institute (IRRI) in the Philippines (Harlan 1980: 307).

The Chinese and Japanese policy had been to select the best varieties available locally and to improve them through pure-line selection. IRRI, founded by the Ford and Rockefeller Foundations in 1960, was able to draw on the best available strains from many nations for its breeding programmes. The chief characteristics of the new heavy-yielding varieties (HYVs) are their short growing period, their pronounced response to chemical fertilisers and of course their high yields. The early HYVs had a number of shortcomings, chief among them being their lack of flavour, their inadaptability to local conditions and their vulnerability to disease. Since they were often grown as part of a 'technological package' which imposed virtual monoculture of a single variety over large areas (we shall discuss this further in chapter 4), such shortcomings were sometimes exacerbated to the point where yields were hardly greater or more reliable than those of the traditional varieties. But more careful attention to local testing and adjustment, and to breeding for reliability as well as simply high yields, has brought about enormous improvements:

IR36, a variety now grown on more than 10 million hectares of the world's rice land, is a result of this strategy. It resists four major rice diseases and four serious plant pests, including brown planthopper biotypes 1 and 2. It grows well in a variety of cultural environments, tolerates several adverse soil conditions, has grain of good quality and matures in 110 days, which enables farmers to harvest as many as three crops in one year on irrigated paddies. IR36 is the progeny of 13 different varieties from six nations. (Swaminathan 1984: 70)

Both insect pests and disease organisms show remarkable rapidity in adapting themselves to attack resistant varieties. It is often wild or primitive crop varieties which exhibit the greatest capacity for long-term resistance to pests and diseases, and a continuous supply of genetic material is necessary to ensure successful and sustained breeding programmes (Chang 1976b). Most Asian rice-growing nations started national collections of rice varieties in the 1930s, but these collections tended to concentrate on commercial varieties and to neglect the wild and primitive strains whose germ plasm is the most useful for breeding purposes. Only in the 1960s did IRRI's germ plasm centre start systematically collecting and classifying wild and cultivated rices from all over the world; by 1983 their collection included '63,000 Asian cultivars, 2,575 African rices, 1,100 wild rices and 680 varieties maintained to test genetic traits. Thousands of breeding lines with one or more desirable traits are also preserved' (Swaminathan 1984: 67).

IRRI has provided the world with many of its most successful rice

varieties in recent years, but research at national level is also producing interesting results. Most rice-breeding programmes are based on the technique of crossing selected parents to achieve a new variety which combines their desirable characteristics and which will, in principle, breed true. But since 1970 Chinese scientists, using male-sterile plants, have overcome the difficulties inherent in working with this mainly self-pollinated crop and have managed to produce hybrid rices (Harlan 1980: 302). These may eventually produce results as spectacular as those achieved with other hybrid crops like maize.

The drawback of hybrids is that while the first generation is more vigorous than either of its parents, subsequent generations quickly lose the desired characteristics. This means that the hybrid seed must be produced in laboratories, and that farmers must buy new supplies every year. In any case it is becoming generally true that rice-farmers no longer have any direct part in selection or breeding. If the improved variety they choose to grow is particularly stable, then they may be able to produce their own seed-grain at least for a few years; otherwise they have to purchase their seed from a Farmers' Association (Harriss 1977: 147). But many poorer farmers cannot afford this, and pleas have been made for the professional breeders to develop more stable varieties, as well as to consult more carefully with local farmers to take their requirements into account (Chambers 1977: 405). Plant-breeders today have at their disposal enormous resources which should enable them to produce the right variety for every situation, but given the time and expense involved it is possible they may choose to serve the peasant farmers' interests less well than their own. In any case it is clear that the number of rice varieties of which a late-twentieth-century rice-farmer disposes is far less than it would have been even thirty years ago. But the new varieties often combine the advantages of several traditional varieties, so in a sense the farmer's choice has not been reduced, but has become less direct.

In conclusion, we see that rice offers several significant advantages to the peasant farmer. Although we shall see in subsequent chapters that it is hard work to grow, generally requiring more labour than other crops, it is also the highest yielding of all cereals after maize, but has superior nutritional value (Huang 1981: 49). It is highly adaptable, can be grown under almost any conditions, does not necessarily require fertilisers (although it does respond well to their use) and will produce as many as three crops a year if there is sufficient water, without exhausting the fertility of the paddy field. The techniques of rice cultivation are such that farmers themselves have been able to select for desirable traits through the centuries, and so a very wide range of cultivars has been

developed. By keeping a range of varieties in stock the farmer can protect himself in fair measure against the risk of drought or flood, and can also increase his income, either by producing more rice, or by combining rice cultivation with more profitable activities like cash-cropping.

The distinctive feature of wet-rice cultivation is the degree of intensity with which land can be used. If quick-ripening varieties are used, as many as three crops of rice a year can be grown even by farmers who do not have access to chemical fertilisers, for the water supply provides nutrients naturally. This means that once rice cultivation is established in a region it will sustain population growth almost indefinitely. No other crop has such a great population-carrying capacity, and this is one of the factors to which we can attribute the success and popularity of rice. Although it is possible to increase yields even with traditional inputs alone, as we shall see in the next chapter the techniques of rice-farming are such that intensification is achieved, not through high levels of capital investment, but rather through using increased amounts of labour.

2

Paths of technical development

As societies develop and their populations grow, so too their agriculture expands and develops to produce more food, and eventually to support the growth of commerce, manufactures and industry. Increases in agricultural production may be achieved through expanding the area under cultivation or through improving the productivity of existing farm-land. Where land is freely available, where agricultural labour is scarce, or where more attractive employment than farming beckons, innovations in farming practice will tend to improve the productivity of labour. But if land is scarce and labour plentiful, then farmers will usually consider the productivity of land more important.

Asian rice cultivation is generally considered labour-intensive and technologically primitive compared to the advanced farming systems of the West today. It is certainly true that the historical development of Asian rice cultivation techniques has followed a very different pattern from that of European wheat cultivation (outlined in appendix A). In both cases, however, the long-term trend was the same: more grain was produced. But in Europe many of the most striking advances increased the productivity of human labour by substituting animals or machines, taking advantage of the essentially extensive nature of the farming system to introduce economies of scale. As we shall see in this chapter, by their nature the wet-rice systems of Asia respond positively to increases in the application of labour, but are not as susceptible as Western farming systems to capital-intensive economies of scale. Instead, highly sophisticated management skills were developed which brought about enormous improvements in rice yields.

This chapter explores the dynamics of wet-rice systems: the technical means by which increases in rice production may be achieved, and the inherent trend towards intensification of land-use and small-scale management.

Building new fields

Wet-rice fields have a great advantage over dry fields in that they tend to gain rather than lose fertility over the years. Swidden fields cut from the jungle will often produce very high yields of dry rice (and other crops) during the first year of cultivation, but their great fertility comes from the forest humus and the ashes of the felled trees, which are quickly washed away. During the second year much of the fertility is lost, and unless in exceptional circumstances it is unusual for farmers to cultivate their swidden fields for more than three years before moving on to clear new land. Of course most permanent dry fields retain some natural fertility over a much longer period, but manuring and fertilising are really crucial for growing cereals without irrigation, which is one reason why livestock play such an important role in most dry-grain farming systems.

Wet-rice yields are affected by the natural fertility of the soil to some extent, as well as by the soil structure. Heavy, alluvial soils with only slight acidity are most suitable for rice, while sandy soils give satisfactory yields only if they are heavily treated with organic matter (e.g. Grist 1975: 21). But in fact soil type is much less important than the water supply. 'Whether the land be good or poor, if the water is clear then the rice will be good', says the sixth-century Chinese agricultural treatise *Qimin yaoshu* (Bray 1984: 498). 'Water is the most important factor in rice-growing, the water-soil relationship largely determining the ability of the soil to develop its full potentiality for rice production' (Grist 1975: 20). The distinctive feature of wet-rice fields is that, whatever their original fertility, several years' continuous cultivation brings it up to a higher level which is then maintained almost indefinitely. This is because water seepage alters the chemical composition and structure of the different soil layers in a process known as *pozdolisation*.

The podzolisation of soils is caused by the influence of percolating water in conjunction with various organic acids. The latter help to dissolve some of the mineral compounds and to deflocculate the clay particles so that they may be carried down to the subsoil in colloidal suspension. The cultivation of rice requires that the land be kept under water during much of the year, and this irrigation water slowly but continually seeps from the surface horizons to the subsoils, carrying with it more or less colloidal clay and some compounds in solution. The addition of more or less organic manures, including a considerable amount of night-soil [the author is describing the Chinese case], helps to increase the podzolisation effect. Occasional liming of the soil tends to offset the leaching effect since lime helps to coagulate the clays and prevents their forming colloidal suspensions in the water.

Wherever it is possible to obtain water for irrigation, practically all the soils of

the important groups of South China are planted to rice. After formerly
well-drained upland soils have been used in this way for a period of several years,
their characteristics are changed, much of the red iron compounds are dissolved
and removed from the surface to the subsoil or into the river waters, and the soils
fade in colour until, after a long time, they are predominantly grey like the rice
lands of the alluvial plains . . . Practically every bit of land in South China which
will hold water and which can be irrigated is planted to rice for at least a part of
the time. The soils are worked and cultivated and fertilised until they become
well adapted to rice culture, regardless of their original characteristics. (Thorp
1937: 155)

This transformation requires years of hard work, in return for decades
if not centuries of stable yields. It is not surprising, then, that
rice-farmers often prefer to work existing fields more intensively rather
than opening up of new fields which, at least for the first few years,
will produce less than long-established ones (see Geertz 1963: 32).

But even a well-established paddy-field may eventually be overtaxed.
When quick-ripening new HYVs were introduced to Lombok (an island
off Bali) in the 1970s, three crops were grown annually instead of two,
and two of them were often rice. 'However, it seems that this
intensification of land use has meant that the limits for the stability of the
flooded field ecosystem have been transgressed: in the 1940s, one
hectare could yield four to five tons of rice in one harvest, in the 1970s
only three tons' (Gerdin 1982: 66).

Well before such limits are reached, overpopulation, inequality of land
distribution, or the dissemination of new techniques may lead rice-
farmers to overcome their aversion to opening up new fields. Perhaps
'build' is a more appropriate term than 'open up', when one considers the
engineering skills which are often required. Rice-fields come in an
astonishing and ingenious variety, from dizzying flights of terraces
perched high up on mountainsides, to dyked fields reclaimed from
marshes or the shores of the sea.

The rice-farmers of most ancient times grew their crops in natural
swamps. Several neolithic sites have been found in or near marshes (see
chapter 1). In pre-Indian Java rice was grown only in swamps (van Setten
1979: 33), as indeed it still is today in parts of the Malaysian state of
Pahang (Hill 1977: 160).

But natural marshes are limited in extent, and it is impossible to
control the depth of the water, an important factor in improving yields. A
rice-field should ideally be carefully levelled so that the depth of water is
uniform, and in the absence of modern engineering this severely restricts
field size. One Chinese agronomist, writing well after collectivisation and
communisation had begun, gives the optimal size of an irrigated

rice-field as under 0.1 hectare (Ding 1961: 294); a Japanese expert, pointing out that prewar the limit of a field's area in Japan was about 0.1 hectare, says that now with modern equipment this can be extended to 0.3–0.5 hectares (Kanazawa 1971: 15). This is minute compared with the wheat-fields of the American mid-West, where a single field may be several hundred hectares in size (Leonard and Martin 1963: 14).

To retain the water, low bunds (or little dykes – the French call them *diguettes*) usually less than 2 feet high are built round the carefully levelled field. Bunded fields are certainly of ancient origin. There is written evidence to show that poldered fields, technically more demanding than simple bunded fields (see p. 34) were already known in parts of the Yangzi Delta in the Spring and Autumn period (722–481 BC) (Bray 1984: 113), while clay models of bunded rice-fields are found in graves all over South China by the Han dynasty (206 BC–220 AD) (figure 2.1).

It is easier to construct level fields on land which is fairly flat to begin with, and most early wet-rice farmers settled in river valleys or deltaic plains, where natural rainfall could if necessary be supplemented as a water supply by streams or rivers. In peninsular Malaysia even today, the narrow coastal plains and river valleys are the only important wet-rice areas, though until recently much hill rice was also grown on swidden farms in the interior (Hill 1977: 173). In Thailand the historical spread of wet-rice cultivation can be traced from its earliest prehistoric roots in the river valleys and basins of the north, down to the central flood-plains where the kingdom of Ayutthaya (fourteenth to eighteenth centuries) was based, and eventually, in the nineteenth century, right to the marshy delta of the Chao Phraya around Bangkok (Ishii 1978b).

Moving from well-watered and well-drained valleys or plains to sloping hillsides or vulnerable flood-plains entailed the development of more sophisticated field types. First let us consider terraced fields. Terracing is essentially a means of levelling areas of soil so that hill-slopes may be cultivated. Agricultural terracing is a world-wide phenomenon,[1] and its purposes may be manifold. In some cases, as for example the presumably megalithic terraces (perhaps dating back to 2000 BC) of Gio-Linh in Quang-Tri province, North Vietnam, terraces were constructed as much for ritual or religious considerations as for agricultural purposes (Colani 1940; Wheatley 1965: 135). Sometimes people simply preferred to cultivate hillsides rather than valley floors for reasons of health. Agricultural terraces in the Cuzco region of Peru were also used for defence purposes (Donkin 1979), while the Shans of North Burma used their terraces as observation posts from which they could swoop down to levy tolls on passing travellers (Leach 1954). But most

Figure 2.1   Bunded field: clay model from a Han grave
Canton Museum

terraces had more prosaic functions: in China terraces are known as
'three-fold conservers', *san bao*, that is to say, they prevent erosion and
conserve soil moisture and nutrients, and in many cases crops grown on
terraced fields give yields several times higher than those grown in the
same area under normal conditions. Raikes (1967) has characterised
agricultural terracing as a form of proto-engineering for mitigating
climatic stress. Liefrinck (1886: 40) describes how the productivity of
irrigated terraces in Bali increases over the years as the irrigation water
brings fertile sediments down from the mountainside which accumulate
as a layer of rich topsoil. But the foremost advantage of wet-field
terracing is that the terrace walls retain the run-off water, enabling
irrigated crops to be grown on steep slopes which would otherwise have
to be planted with dry crops, or even left bare:

Terracing means cutting steps in the mountain to make fields. In mountainous
areas where there are few level places, apart from stretches of rock, precipices or
similarly barren areas, all the rest, wherever there is soil, from the valley bottom
right up to the dizzying peaks, can be split to make ledges where crops can be
grown. If stones and soil are in equal proportion then you must pile up the stones
in rows, encircling the soil to make a field. There are also mountains where the
slope is excessively steep, without even a foothold, at the very limits of cultivation
where men creep upwards bent close to the ground. There they pile up the soil
like ants, prepare the ground for sowing with hoes [because the fields are too
narrow to use ploughs], stepping carefully while they weed for fear of the chasm
at their side. Such fields are not stepped but mount like the rungs of a ladder,
hence their name of 'ladder fields'. If there is a source of water above the field,
then all kinds of rice may be grown. (*Wang Zhen nongshu*: 11/2b)

Not all terraces, however, scale the dizzying peaks. The origins of
agricultural terracing are far from clear,[2] but as Wheatley pertinently
says:

the virtual inseparability of rudimentary terracing from wet-padi cultivation is a
point to be borne in mind in any discussion of wet-field terracing in Asia.
Although the act of bunding may produce initially only insignificant inequalities
in the levels of fields, the potentiality is always present for increasing vertical
differentiation as cultivation laps against a zone of foothills or is pushed towards
the head of a valley. (1965: 132)

Such 'valley terraces', as Donkin calls them in contradistinction to
'cross-channel' and 'contour terraces', are common in rice-growing
areas of East and Southeast Asia, for example in Negri Sembilan in
Malaysia, and along the tributaries of the Upper Mekong in Yunnan,
where the difference in level between the fields at the edge of the stream
and those at the side of the valley can reach 30 feet or more (pers. obs.).

Woodard gives a description of the construction of low terraces in the Celebes, where he was cast ashore in 1793:

Many of the rice grounds are made on sloping lands, where the natives form little canals at about twenty yards distance from each other, in order to water the grounds. These divisions are levelled by carrying the higher part of the land to the lower, so as to form steps. This is performed by women and children, by means of small baskets. The land is overflowed six inches deep for about fourteen or sisteen [*sic*] days, when it becomes very moist. They then turn in about 20 bullocks, used to the employment, which are driven round the rice-fields to make the land poachy. The Malays term it *pruning*. This being done, they let the water in, which overflows it again, and renders the land fit for planting . . . (1805: 90)

Terraces on gentle slopes will usually be rather wide, with walls of earth, as in the Celebes, Yunnan and Negri Sembilan. Where slopes are steeper, the terrace wall must be faced with stone, and the fields are usually much narrower. Keesing distinguishes four types of terracing in Northern Luzon (1962: 312): the Lapanto-Bontoc type are faced with almost vertical stone walls to maximise the area of the field, while the South Kalinga terraces have stone walls capped with an inward lean of earth; the famous Ifugao terraces, which are commonly up to 20 feet in height and sometimes as much as 50, have stone walls more sloping than the two previous types, carefully sculpted to the terrain; the terraces of Tinguian, which are in the lowlands, do not have stone walls. All types are drained after the main crop to grow dry crops such as tubers or vegetables, and it is quite probable that rice cultivation in these terraces is a relatively late introduction.

Terraced fields can be built by single households or small groups of peasants, as was often the case in medieval China where impoverished farmers migrated from densely populated areas to carve a new living for themselves out of the mountainside. Terraced fields built in this way not only provided land for the landless, but also, since the newly opened land was often situated in inaccessible areas not inscribed on the land registers, they were generally not assessed for tax for some years at least (Li Jiannong 1957: 27). Often, however, the combined requirements of engineering the landscape and ensuring a reasonably equitable and efficient distribution of water have meant that large groups of farmers collaborated in constructing terrace systems. Wheatley, discussing the prehistoric stone terraces of Gio-Linh, describes complex systems of tanks and terraces, flumes and channels, bridges and causeways which were associated with objects such as menhirs and circular earth mounds presumably representing chthonic gods. This, he feels, suggests that the whole system was designed on the basis of a cult: 'the integral character of each of these systems is a sufficient indication that it did not develop piecemeal . . . [The units] were combined in such a way as to facilitate the management of an entire socio-economic unit, namely the territory and persons constituting a group of families or even a whole village' (1965: 136).

The *subak* irrigation systems of Bali offer a fascinating and well-documented study of how such organisations have worked in more recent times, though in this case on a secular basis. Liefrinck (1886) gives details of the *subak* under Dutch colonial rule, but points out that their organisation had remained essentially unchanged since pre-colonial days. Indeed *subak* groups still play an important role in Bali today (Geertz and Geertz 1975: 19 ff). Where a village becomes overpopulated, an enterprising group of villagers will form a society and select a suitable spot of uncleared land to build new terraces. Having obtained permission from the authorities to use the land, they hold a meeting to formulate the conditions of participation (usually the members of the *subak* share costs, labour and benefits equally), and when the season is suitable they construct the irrigation works and clear the land by collective effort. The land is then divided into individual holdings, which the original *subak* members can transmit to their heirs; cooperation between members remains the basis for maintenance and repairs (Liefrinck 1886: 7).

The terracing of rice-fields is a method of retaining water. But in many cases, when land is low-lying and the water-table high, it is more important to design fields so as to eliminate excess water. One of the most common forms is the poldered field, familiar to Europeans from Holland but also common in China, where it seems to have developed rather early. The first-century BC *Yue jue shu* refers to cultivated fields created amidst the flood near the ancient gate of Suzhou, a city in the Yangzi Delta (Bray 1984: 113), and Miao (1960: 140) quotes texts which indicate that poldered fields were being constructed in the area of Taihu Lake in Southern Jiangsu as early as the Spring and Autumn period (722–481 BC); Miao believes that poldered fields were quite common along the south bank of the Lower Yangzi until medieval times, probably linked to the flourishing of a local aristocracy, and various Tang dynasty (618–907) references describe powerful families in the Nanjing area reclaiming land along lake shores in this fashion. The Song writer Fan Chengda (1120–93) describes poldered fields with dykes several miles long, like great city walls, with rivers and canals inside and gates and sluices outside, which took extra water from the Yangzi in times of drought and were able to supply grain to neighbouring regions during famines (Bray 1984: 114).

Even when the dykes were much smaller, poldered fields were usually self-contained units, subdivided into separate fields with their own drainage channels; on the high dykes the farmers' houses were built and mulberries and other useful trees were planted (figure 2.2). Fei, an anthropologist native to Taihu Lake region, describes a village there in the 1930s which had about 1,500 inhabitants sharing 11 poldered fields, *yu tian*, about 180 hectares in all. Each unitary *yu tian* was subdivided into dozens of small plots (figure 2.3), and since the water came from the stream at the edge of the unit, the nearer a plot was to the centre the more difficult it was to supply and drain water. The levels of the plot therefore had to be graded like a dish, and to prevent the formation of a pool in the middle, the bunds between the plots were constructed parallel to the margin. In order to raise water from the stream outside into the outer plots, square-pallet chain-pumps (figure 2.4) were fixed at selected spots along the bank and the water was pumped into small channels which threaded between the plots, eventually depositing the water in a deep trench dug in the lowest part of the *yu tian*, from which it was then pumped back into the stream outside (Fei 1939: 156).

The construction of a variety of dyked fields is comprehensively described by the fourteenth-century Chinese agronomist Wang Zhen (*Wang Zhen nongshu*: ch. 11; see also Bray 1984: 113–23). Wang distinguished between two types, 'poldered fields', *yu tian*, which are built up above the level of the river or lake from layers of soil before being dyked, and 'encircled fields', *wei tian*, which are simply dyked; both of them may range in size, Wang says, between thousands of acres and a few acres (1313: 11/15b). Another way of reclaiming marshy land was to build 'strongbox fields', *gui tian*:

> In 'strongbox fields' the soil is built up into a dyke to protect the fields, as for 'encircled fields' but a bit smaller. On all four sides are placed escape conduits, and the shape is similar to a strong-box and is convenient to cultivate. If the area is very marshy then the fields should be of smaller size, built with firm dykes on higher ground so that the water outside cannot easily get in but the water inside can easily be pumped out with a chain-pump. The parts which remain under shallow water should be sown with quick-ripening yellow rice (which only takes 60 days from sowing to harvesting and thus is not endangered by floods) . . . This is an excellent method of reclaiming marshy land. (*Wang Zhen nongshu*: 11/17b)

Silt banks and eyots might also be dyked to make 'silt fields', *sha tian*, which were more easily irrigated and drained than fields on the land, as well as having rich and fertile soil well suited to all kinds of rice: 'their advantage over other fields lies in their freedom from drought and flood' (ibid.: 11/24b).

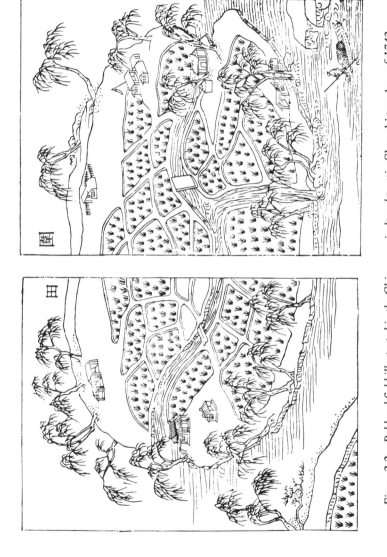

Figure 2.2   Poldered field illustrated in the Chinese agricultural treatise Shoushi tongkao of 1742

(ch. 14/5b)

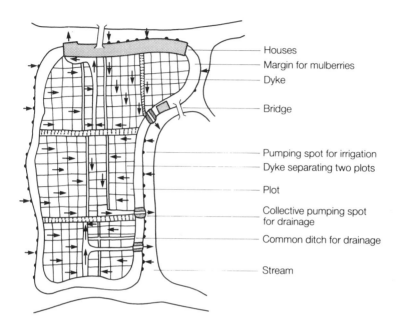

Houses
Margin for mulberries
Dyke

Bridge

Pumping spot for irrigation
Dyke separating two plots

Plot

Collective pumping spot
for drainage

Common ditch for drainage

Stream

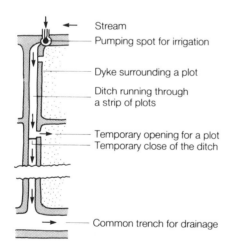

Stream
Pumping spot for irrigation

Dyke surrounding a plot

Ditch running through
a strip of plots

Temporary opening for a plot
Temporary close of the ditch

Common trench for drainage

Figure 2.3   Poldered field in the 1930s in the Yangzi Delta
(after Fei 1939)

Most dyked fields are extremely fertile, and in medieval China they spread rapidly from the Taihu Lake area of the Yangzi Delta to Hubei, Hunan, Guangdong and Guangxi. Most of the swampy lakes in the Yangzi Delta had already been turned into poldered fields by the twelfth century. By the mid-fourteenth century so much of the Dongting Lake in Hunan, which had acted as an overspill when the Yangzi was in spate, had been converted to dry land that there was severe danger of flooding, and the government forbade any further reclamation in the area (Li Jiannong 1957: 16). Today the practice continues to spread, and large areas of Lake Dian, the biggest lake in Yunnan, are being dyked and turned into fields.

If lake margins or river-banks were so marshy that the construction of dykes was impossible, in some parts of Asia floating fields were constructed. In China the usual method was to make a wooden frame which was thickly covered with fertile mud and dead water-weeds and tethered to the bank (*Chen Fu nongshu*: 1/2). The earliest literary reference to floating fields is in a sixth-century poem on the Yangzi River by the scholar Guo Pu:

> Covered with an emerald screen
> They drift, buoyed up by floating water-weeds.
> Without art the grains are sown,
> And fine rice-plants thrust up of their own accord.
>   (See Amano 1979: 175)

Floating rice-fields were to be found in several regions of South China, including the Yangzi and Lake Dian, as well as in Kasumigaura in Northeast Japan, Lake Inlé in Burma and Lake Dal in Kashmir (Bray 1984: 121).[3]

Finally there was the reclamation of saltlands from the sea. First a sea wall was built to cut off the projected fields from the tides, then a system of canals was constructed to leach out the salt with sweet water from a river. Initially salt-tolerant plants like barnyard millet (*Echinocloa crus-galli*) were sown to put the land in good heart, but after a few years the land was fit for any use. Wang (1313: 11/22a) refers to crops of rice and millet being grown in such fields, while a Japanese plan of reclaimed land, dating from 1300, shows that rice and wheat were grown as well as garden crops (Kuroda 1983: 61). In Japan 'salt dykes', *entei*, were first known from about the eighth century, when they were used in the construction of salt-pans, but it was not long before their scope for land reclamation was realised. Most of the early projects were only a qualified success, but by the eleventh to thirteenth century large-scale reclamation of this sort was common along the coasts of Honshū and Kyūshū. One

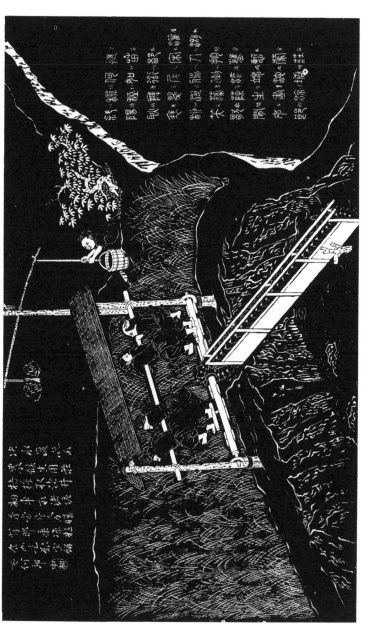

Figure 2.4 A square-pallet chain pump

(from a Qing edition of the *Gengzhi tu* (Agriculture and sericulture illustrated), perhaps copying the original Song illustrations of 1149)

project begun in 1238 in Aki (now Hiroshima) was subsequently referred
to as the 'thousand *chō* [1,000 ha] of Tomita estate' (Kuroda 1983: 63)
(figure 2.5). Such reclamation continued piecemeal right through
medieval times and into the Meiji period. In Okayama (Southwest
Honshū), for example, over 2,500 ha of rice-land were reclaimed in the
river delta between 1590 and 1690 (Beardsley et al. 1959: 52).

Along the coast of Central China, sea-walls had been built in early

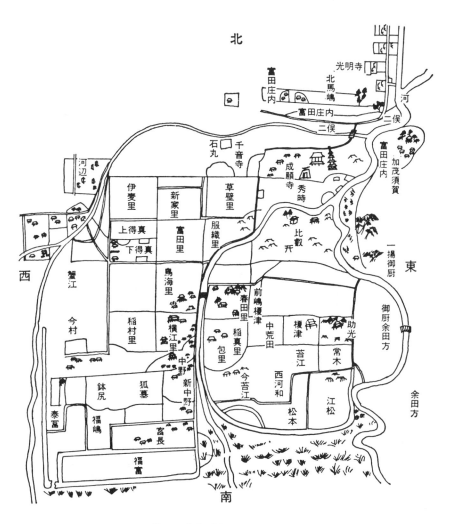

Figure 2.5   The Tomita estate
(from Kuroda 1983: 62)

medieval times which by the Song dynasty had fallen into disrepair. In 1026 the official Zhang Lun ordered the construction of several hundred miles of new sea-wall along the Jiangsu coast, and this project was brought to final fruition by the energetic statesman, poet and reformer Fan Zhongyan (1126–93). The local population were so grateful for the benefits brought by this scheme that many of them named their children Fan (Li Jiannong 1957: 15). Another great official benefactor was the Vietnamese mandarin Nguyên Công Trú, who administered two enormous projects for reclaiming salt-marshes, one in Annam (Thaibinh), and the other in Ninh-binh in the Red River Delta. These projects went under way in 1828, and the reclaimed land was distributed to groups of ten migrant households in lots of 100 *mâu* (1 *mâu* = 0.36 ha); the state also provided houses, buffaloes and ploughs. Over the next century the population of Thai-binh quadrupled, from 2,350 to over 10,000 tax payers, while the area of rice-fields increased from 19,000 to 24,000 *mâu* (Lê 1955: 39).

But not all such reclamation was officially sponsored. Watson (1975) describes how the founders of the Man clan, in flight from the Mongol invasion, arrived in the thirteenth century in what are now the New Territories of Hong Kong only to find that four other major lineage groups had already possessed themselves of all the best rice-land. Since they could fly no further, the Mans were obliged to occupy the only land left, a marshy, brackish area in the river delta draining into Deep Bay. The Mans built dykes with locks, enclosing the existing land and reclaiming extra land from the bay. The dykes retained the rain water and excluded salt water floods, and the locks were manipulated so as to minimise the salt content of the irrigation water. The process of reclamation was aided by the gradual geological uplift of Deep Bay and consequent silting up of the delta. In their 'new fields' the Mans grew one crop a year of special red rice highly resistant to salt. Although this rice gave only medium yields and was not considered of very high quality, the 'new fields' had the advantage of requiring no fertilisers and the red rice took very little labour. Nowadays the Mans have mostly given up farming for more lucrative pursuits, but the reclaimed salt marshes did provide them with an adequate if hardly bountiful living for over six centuries.

Although they were enterprises of considerable scale, requiring sophisticated design and organisation of manpower, these projects did not rely on heavy capital investment. This is an important feature of all the types of reclamation discussed. Most of the construction work involved shifting large quantities of earth, but this was done using such rudimentary equipment as baskets and shovels. Sometimes, as when

building terraced fields or small 'strongbox fields', it was enough for a few households to cooperate. Even large-scale projects set up by officials or by great landowners depended principally on organising the necessary corvée labour. The expenses for repairing a broken sea-wall on the Takada estate of Yamato (modern Nara) came to 10 bushels of hulled rice, of which 8 bushels consisted of provisions for the corvée workers (2 pecks a man-day for 200 man-days), and the rest for such equipment as the corvée workers did not provide themselves, namely wooden posts and straw mats for cladding (Kuroda 1983: 66).

The expansion of world rice markets during the colonial period triggered the reclamation of vast areas of land in Southeast Asia. Migrants from the north flooded into the Burmese Delta between 1850 and 1900 and cleared large tracts of forest for rice-fields, which they farmed using extensive techniques (table 2.1). Between 1850 and 1880 the average holding size in the Upper Delta rose from 2.6 ha to 3.8 ha, while around Rangoon it rose from 4 ha to over 12 ha. The increase in the size of farms often led to over-hasty cultivation and underproductive methods (Adas 1974: 59, 62).

Considerable areas were also opened up for rice in Cochinchina and the Bangkok Delta at the same period, but in these regions land could only be rendered suitable for cultivation through the provision of large-scale drainage networks; this was undertaken at considerable expense by the French and Thai governments (see chapter 3).

As the supply of unoccupied land that can easily be converted to productive rice cultivation has shrunk, the costs of reclamation have risen, and there has been a corresponding shift from expanding the cultivated area to improving yields (table 2.2).

Raising yields

Here a highly simplified account of wet-rice cultivation is perhaps called for. As a rule, the farming cycle begins with the monsoon rains. Once enough rain has fallen to soak and soften the soil, the main field is tilled. The rice seed may have been sown meanwhile in a special seed-bed for transplanting, or it may simply be sown broadcast in the main field after tilling is completed. The young seedlings grow in standing water, and if irrigation is available the depth of water will be adjusted to follow the growth of the plant. The crop may or may not be fertilised and weeded. Just before harvesting any remaining water is drained off and the soil is allowed to dry out as much as possible before the reapers set to work. The grain is then dried and stored, threshed or unthreshed depending

Table 2.1   Rice production in the Burmese Delta

	1855	1905/6
Rice exports	162,000 tons	2,000,000 tons
Price per 100 baskets	Rupiahs 45	Rupiahs 120
Cultivated rice area	280–320,000 ha	about 2,400,000 ha

Source: Adas 1974: 58

Table 2.2   Relative contributions of area and yield to total growth in rice production during the period 1955–73

	A	B	C
Burma	1.98	1.13	0.84
Cambodia	−1.04	−2.76	1.54
Indonesia	2.84	1.31	1.50
Japan	0.64	−0.88	1.55
Korea	4.09	0.55	3.52
Laos	3.48	1.61	1.75
Malaysia	5.91	3.97	1.86
Philippines	2.78	1.11	1.62
Taiwan	2.00	−0.15	2.15
Thailand	2.84	1.78	1.06
Vietnam	5.27	1.08	4.18

A: Annual growth rate of output (in %)
B: Change in output due to change in area (in %)
C: Change in output due to changes in yield (in %)

Source: ADB 1978: appendices I–4.5c/d

upon the variety and the harvesting technique. These are the basic steps of wet-rice cultivation.

We shall now discuss the modifications and elaborations by which Asian farmers have increased and stabilised their yields, leaving aside for the moment the question of water control, which deserves a chapter to itself.

One crucial factor in determining the choice of cultivation methods is the amount of land available. As one might expect, the simplest and least time-consuming methods of wet-rice cultivation are practised in regions where suitable land is abundant. Often such cultivation systems carry a high degree of risk, for the rice crop is left to grow more or less at the mercy of drought, flood or pests. The methods used to intensify rice cultivation generally stabilise yields as well as raising them.

There is often a marked contrast between the methods used in areas of high population density and sparsely inhabited regions of the same country. The twelfth-century Chinese writer Zhou Qufei records such a contrast with disapproval:

The farmers of Qinzhou [southernmost Guangdong] are very careless. When tilling they merely break up the clods, and the limit of their sowing techniques is to dibble in the seed. Nor do they transplant the rice seedlings. There is nothing more wasteful of seed! Furthermore, after sowing they neither weed nor irrigate, but simply leave Nature to take care of the crop. (Shiba 1970: 53)

As his standard of comparison Zhou had the rich and crowded regions of the Lower Yangzi, where rice was sown in meticulously ploughed and harrowed seed-beds, transplanted, irrigated, fertilised with a variety of manures and commercial fertilisers, and weeded and fed several times before harvesting. No wonder he was shocked by what he considered the laziness and improvidence of the southern barbarians. Marked contrasts existed between the Lower and Upper Yangzi provinces until heavy migration from the Delta to Hunan and Hubei in the sixteenth and seventeenth centuries imposed the use of more productive techniques (Rawski 1972). Similar differences existed between Upper and Lower Burma up to the early twentieth century, when migrants from the densely settled plain of Mandalay introduced some technical improvements to the Burmese Delta (Adas 1974: 129), and between Tonkin and Cochinchina during the French occupation of Vietnam (Henry and de Visme 1928: 52). Sometimes migrants raise cultivation standards by introducing improved techniques; this has been a guiding principle in such policies as the Indonesian *transmigrasi*, whereby landless farmers from Java and Bali are given a new start in underpopulated and underproductive islands like Sulawesi (Charras 1982; Mantra 1981: 134 ff). On the other hand, when they find themselves in areas where land is plentiful, migrants not infrequently abandon the laborious techniques necessary in overcrowded regions in favour of less demanding methods. This was what happened when the French opened up the land market in Cochinchina to rich French and Vietnamese: although the landowners employed highly skilled farmers from Tonkin as their labourers, the

cultivation methods used were far less intensive and productive than those of Tonkin (Robequain 1939: 96).

So many variations and combinations exist in wet rice cultivation techniques that an exhaustive examination would easily occupy a whole volume. An excellent study of historical and regional variation in Malaya (Hill 1977) gives an idea of the complexity of the subject. Here we shall simply mention a few of the more significant variations.

The least productive and reliable system of wet-rice cultivation systems is one where the fields are not accurately levelled or thoroughly tilled, the only supply of water is natural rainfall, the rice is sown broadcast, directly onto the fields, no fertilisers or manure are used, and the crop is not weeded or protected from pests. Such simple methods were to be found, for example, in large areas of Laos and Cambodia (Delvert 1961; Taillard 1972). A highly productive system would include careful water control, based on an adequate irrigation network; the fields would be accurately levelled, carefully tilled and manured; selected seed-grain would be sown in a separate seed-bed, to be transplanted into the main field in straight lines suitably spaced, the right amount of fertilisers would be applied and weeding would take place at frequent intervals, and herbicides and pesticides would be used to safeguard the crop. The success of the Green Revolution is premissed on such practices, but cultivation systems of comparable sophistication existed well before the 1960s, some of the earliest in parts of medieval China (Bray 1984: 597), and the most highly developed (which in many respects served as models for the agronomists of the Green Revolution) in early twentieth-century Japan and Taiwan (Dore 1969; Francks 1983; Ishikawa 1967: 59).

There are several discrete operations in wet-rice cultivation, each of which can be perfected separately or in combination – although in general all the operations will be at a similar level of sophistication. The question of seed selection and preparation has already been dealt with in chapter 1. Next comes the question of the seed-bed and sowing techniques. It is very wasteful to sow the seed directly in the main field, and the use of a separate seed-bed also permits more efficient and economical use of water and fertilisers. Here a medieval Chinese agronomist describes the preparation of the seed-bed:

In autumn or winter the seed-bed should be deeply ploughed two or three times so that it will be frozen by the snow and frost and the soil will be broken up fine. Cover it with rotted straw, dead leaves, cut weeds and dried-out roots and then burn them off so that the soil will be warm and quick. Early in the spring plough again two or three times, harrowing and turning the soil. Spread manure on the seed-bed.

The best manure is hemp waste, but hemp waste is difficult to use. It must be pounded fine and buried in a pit with burned manure. As when making yeast, wait for it to give off heat and sprout hairs, then spread it out and put the hot fertiliser from the centre to the sides and the cold from the sides to the centre, then heap it back in the pit. Repeat three or four times till it no longer gives off heat. It will then be ready for use. If it is not treated in this way it will burn and kill the young plants. Neither should you use night-soil, which rots the shoots and damages human hands and feet, producing sores that are difficult to heal. Best of all the fertilisers is a mixture of burned compost, singed pigs' bristles and coarse bran, rotted in a pit.

The seed-bed should be soaked and brought to a fine tilth, then sprinkled with chaff and compost. Trample them into the soil, rake the surface quite smooth, and then you can broadcast the seed. (*Chen Fu nongshu*: 5–6)

Nowadays the seed-bed is more likely to be prepared with a small rotary tiller, or even a tractor, and fertilised with chemical fertilisers, phosphates and nitrates. If the seedlings are to be tranplanted mechanically rather than by hand, then they may not even be sown in soil; instead specially treated paper is used, in sheets of a size which will fit directly into the mechanical transplanter. Transplanting takes place once the seedlings have grown to 20 or 25 cm, which may take one month or two depending on the variety. By thus reducing the period the rice-plants spend in the main field, the farmer may well be able to grow two or more crops where only one was possible before.

Transplanting also contributes to higher yields by strengthening the root system and encouraging tillering. If the plants are set in the ground in regular lines, then weeding and pest control are greatly facilitated. In China it appears that farmers tried to plant in straight lines, judging probably by eye, as early as the first century AD; this can be seen from numerous clay grave models depicting rice-fields.[4] Later methods became more sophisticated, involving the use of marker ropes, special 'seedling horses' (figure 2.6), or adjustable marking machines (Bray 1984: 279 ff). Straight lines also permitted the use of weeding hoes or, eventually, specially designed rotary weeders (apparently these were an eighteenth-century Japanese invention) which saved much painful bending (Bray 1984: 314 ff). Thus a switch from broadcasting to transplanting will easily increase yields by 40% (Grist 1975: 149).

The question of how the field is tilled is an interesting one, for it presents a striking contrast with the course of development in European agriculture, where increasingly powerful animal-drawn implements were developed to till as large an area as possible. The fundamental importance of animal traction in European agriculture was a crucial factor in the development of mechanisation. In the wet-rice regions of

馬　秧

Figure 2.6   A 'seedling-horse', yang ma, illustrated in the Nongzheng quanshu
(21/9a)

Asia, however, things developed rather differently. In underpopulated areas where land for rice and for grazing was plentiful and manpower was scarce, cattle were often used not to pull ploughs but simply to trample the fields to a good tilth; this was a common practice in parts of Malaya and Indonesia (Hill 1977; Woodard 1805). But the combined use of plough and harrow brings the soil to a much better consistency, and the simple but effective ploughs and harrows which are still in use in many parts of China were in use in the Canton and Tonkin area by the fourth century AD, as can be seen from surviving grave models (Bray 1984: 223). Very similar ploughs and harrows are to be found throughout East and Southeast Asia. Although they have frequently been dismissed as primitive by Westerners, in fact the shallow ploughing and thorough stirring of the soil into a thick smooth mud is exactly what is required for wet-rice cultivation. Deep ploughing may well break up the claypan below the mud which makes the rice-field impermeable, and the substitution of tractors for traditional ploughs requires much care (Berwick 1951). Where rice production is really intensive there is little land available for pasture; however manpower is abundant. Under these circumstances tilling methods frequently revert to what has been described as 'horticulture', that is to say farmers will till their fields with a variety of heavy iron hoes rather than with ploughs. Tokugawa Japan was a particularly conspicuous example; Ōgura Nagatsune depicts several hundreds of hoe types in his *Treatise of Useful Farm Tools* (*Nōgu Benri Ron*) of 1822. A few decades later, however, impressed by the superior efficiency of Western steel ploughs and deep tillage, Japanese agronomists were advocating a return to horse-ploughing, and in fact the horse-plough was widespread throughout Japan until the postwar period (Ishikawa 1981: 19). In other areas tractors or mechanical tillers have been substituted for more traditional ploughs, or for simple hoes. However it is well to remember that in wet-rice agriculture a simple tool such as the hand-hoe may well represent a more advanced technical stage than the more complex animal-drawn plough and harrow.

The choice of fertiliser also gives considerable scope for improving yields. Commercial nitrates and phosphates are an essential element of the Green Revolution package, and without them the HYVs often yield even less than traditional varieties, whereas with them they may yield more than twice as much (Yamada 1975: 184; Barker 1978: 66). But traditional varieties do not usually respond well to chemical fertilisers; they require the use of manure or other organic fertilisers. The simplest of fertilisers, used by almost all rice-farmers throughout history, are compost, manure and the ashes from the rice stubble, which is generally burned just before ploughing. Until ten years ago these were still the

chief fertilisers in use in Kelantan, Malaysia; since compost and manure were in very short supply, these were usually reserved for the seed-bed, while the burnt stubble was the only fertiliser used on the main field (Bray 1985). Burning the stubble has often been condemned as wasteful and ineffective, but in fact it is a good source of potassium and phosphates, and the heat serves the useful purpose of killing the eggs of insect pests.

Farmers in the densely populated areas of China were experimenting with new sources of fertiliser in medieval times. As well as piling the mud from the irrigation ditches onto the fields and ploughing in weeds and other types of green manure, Chinese farmers purchased commercial fertilisers such as oil-cake, fish-meal and the waste from making bean-curd. The expense was not usually begrudged, for these commercial fertilisers were very effective: a single finely pounded oil-cake would fertilise a sixth of an acre of rice seedlings (enough to transplant an area as much as 25 times the size) (*Shen Shih nongshu*: 236). A thriving trade in fertilisers developed in medieval China, not only in the more industrial fertilisers like oil-cake but also in lime and in mollusc shells (used for the lime content), river mud, silkworm waste and human manure, all of which were sometimes transported over considerable distances.

The introduction of chemical fertilisers has led to very significant increases in rice yields. In 1937 a member of the Chinese National Agricultural Research Bureau calculated on the basis of experimental results that national rice output could be increased by 30% if the correct amounts of nitrates, superphosphates and potassium were to be applied throughout the country. In fact chemical fertilisers were already in fairly widespread use, especially in the coastal provinces, but domestic production was insufficient and between 1928 and 1933 China was importing 100–150,000 tons of chemical fertilisers annually, although for rice cultivation alone the application of some 6 million tons would have been necessary to achieve the 30% increase (Shen 1951: 38).

But chemical fertilisers by themselves do not always produce higher yields. Modern rice varieties must also be available, as many traditional varieties respond poorly or even negatively to their application (figure 2.7). It was the dissemination of improved varieties in the early decades of this century which led to the development of the chemical fertiliser industry in Japan (Francks 1983: 79). The provision of adequate water also has a significant effect on the efficiency of chemical fertilisers, as experiments in different regions of India and in Japan show (Ishikawa 1967: 119). The rapid expansion of irrigation networks in the Japanese colonies of Taiwan and Korea in the 1920s and early 1930s allowed the dissemination of improved varieties and of chemical fertilisers, bringing

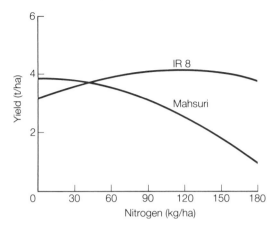

Figure 2.7   Response to nitrogen fertiliser
(from Barker 1978: 49)

average rice yields from about 1.5 t/ha to 2.5 t/ha by the mid-1930s (ibid.: 95).

Even under optimal conditions response to an increase in the amount of fertiliser applied is not linear, but reaches a level of maximum efficiency after which returns diminish; this level varies according to soil type, climatic conditions, rice variety and so on (Barker 1978: 49). In India from 1953 to 1963 the annual growth rate in the application of fertilisers was 19% and the annual increase in total agricultural output 2.5%; in Japan over the same period the annual increase in fertiliser application was only one-third as great at 5.8%, but the corresponding increase in agricultural production was one-third higher, at 3.3% (Ishikawa 1967: 106, table 2–7).

The point at which an increase in fertiliser application becomes uneconomic will be determined by the relative prices of fertilisers and of rice; for many Southeast Asian rice-farmers the oil crisis put chemical fertilisers almost completely out of reach for several years. By contrast, in Japan during the period 1965 to 1979, although the nominal value of fertiliser inputs more than doubled, in real terms it actually declined by 24% (Matsuda 1982: 441).

Weeding the rice may also contribute to significant increases in yields, for weeds not only deprive the rice plants of water and nutrients but also harbour pests and diseases. But weeding the rice-fields is very difficult unless the seedlings have been transplanted in regular lines, and often farmers preferred to invest their labour elsewhere rather than crawl through the mud. Labour-saving devices seem to have been developed as

early as the Song period in China's Yangzi Delta, probably because the spread of double-cropping greatly increased the amount of weeding necessary. The fourteenth-century agronomist Wang Zhen, who described a number of innovations in the hope that they would be widely disseminated, writes of a weeding device

> shaped like a wooden patten, a foot or so long and roughly three inches broad, spiked underneath with rows of a dozen or so nails . . . The farmer stirs together the mud and weeds between the rows of crops so that the weeds are buried in the mud . . . In certain areas I have seen farmers weeding their fields by hand, crawling between the crops on their hands and knees with the sun roasting their backs and the mud soaking their limbs – a truly pitiable fate, and so I have described the hand-harrow here in the hope that philanthropists may disseminate its use. (*Wang Zhen nongshu*: 13/28b)

These implements are still in use today, and are photographed in Hommel (1937: fig. 97). We have already referred to the rotary weeders invented in Japan. The great modern improvement in weeding has been brought about by the production of chemical herbicides, used in many areas before the Green Revolution and rendered all the more indispensable by the spread of double-cropping and chemical fertilisers (which of course fertilise the weeds as well as the crops).

Chemical pesticides are another important innovation, and one which is almost without historical precedent. True, in China at least, farmers used to mix their seed-grain with ashes, arsenic or aconite in order to prevent attacks by insects (Bray 1984: 250), but still the crop remained highly vulnerable to pests and blight. The helplessness felt by the farmers is well described in an eighteenth-century Chinese work on technology:

> There are two disasters that strike rice fields in the mountains, which can be counted neither as flood nor drought although their effect is intensified by either. The peasants accept these disasters as inevitable; although they weep and curse them there is nothing they can do. Alas, how bitter is such a fate! The first disaster strikes in mid-autumn, when the grain has started well, has flowered, and is just heading. Suddenly a cold spell strikes several nights running – what the locals call 'freezing the cassia flowers' – the rice panicles are blasted by the cold, shrivel, and turn black and mottled. This is known as the 'dark wind'. The other strikes in midsummer, in stifling humid weather when the hot air presses down on the land so that clouds form in the mountains. Frequently this produces rain, and its arrival coincides with a strong southerly wind which carries the rain back and forth with it. Such constantly changing weather, veering from wet to dry, affects the grain in the fields, for leaf-hoppers appear and, munching noisily, devour all the leaves completely. The peasants say these two disasters fall from the heavens. (*Suo shan nongpu*: 1/4; tr. Bray 1984: 505)

Table 2.3   Rice yields in East and Southeast Asia

Country	Year	Yield (t/ha of unhusked rice)	
Japan	1950	4.25[a]	
	1956	5.06[a]	
	1962	5.79[a†]	
	1965	4.58[b†]	
	1977	5.14[b†]	
Taiwan	1926	2.12	(native rice)[a]
		2.31	(improved rice)[a]
	1967	5.1⎫	(C. Taiwan)[a]
	1972	5.7⎭	
China (PRC)	1921–5	2.56	(E. Central)[a]
	1949	1.89[c]/2.16[d]	
	1957	2.69[c/d]	
	1968	3.16[c]	
	1978	3.98[e]	
	1981	4.32[e]	
	1983	5.07[e]	
South Korea	1955	2.7[f]	
	1965	3.1[f]	
	1974	3.7[f]	
Burma	av. 1963/7	1.62[g]	
	av. 1971/5	1.71[g]	
Indonesia	av. 1963/7	2.13[g]	
	wet-season av. 1963/7	6.01	(Bimas programme, Java)[h]
	wet-season av. 1963/7	3.38	(non-Bimas control, Java)[h]
	wet- and dry-season av. 1968/79	3.70	(Bimas)[h]
	wet- and dry-season av. 1968/79	4.85	(Bimas Baru using HYVs)[h]
	wet- and dry-season av. 1968/79	3.17	(Inmas: free choice of inputs)[h]
	av. 1970/4	2.61[g]	
Malaysia	av. 1950/5	1.92	(main season)[i]
	av. 1963/67	2.42	(main season)[i]
		2.75	(off-season irrigated)[i]
	av. 1971/5	2.73	(main season)[i]
		3.20	(off-season)[i]
Philippines	av. 1963/7	1.30[g]	
	av. 1971/5	1.59[g]	
Thailand	av. 1963/7	1.86[g]	
	av. 1970/4	1.88[g]	

Some measures could be taken to control pests even then; Chinese works advise running a bamboo comb through the plants to kill lurking insects, or sprinkling lime or tung oil on the plants. But it is only with the twentieth-century development of the chemical industry that truly effective pesticides have become available.

The foregoing processes aim to increase the yields of rice. Once the rice is ripe, it is still possible to increase the amount of grain available for consumption or sale by improving harvesting, processing and storage methods. Storage is a serious problem. Grain stored unthreshed, in the panicle, as is usually the case when reaping-knives and not sickles are used, may last for several years without spoiling. But farmers who have adopted double-cropping, new high-yielding varieties and the sickle have to thresh their grain before storing it, and complain that this type of rice keeps much less well (Bray 1985). Both large- and small-scale storage present enormous problems, and it has been said that even today more grain is lost in store than is lost by natural disasters; in some countries losses in storage are said to reach 50%, and 12% seems to be a reasonable average for most parts of South and Southeast Asia (Grist 1975: 401; Tani 1975).

Rice yields throughout Asia have risen steadily in the last few decades, with improvements in water supplies, better cultivation practices, the dissemination of improved varieties and increased use of chemical fertilisers and pesticides (table 2.3). The question arises as to whether they can be increased indefinitely. Economic considerations will evidently impose certain limits on the further improvement of irrigation networks or on farmers' ability to increase their use of fertilisers. But it seems that the limits of the soil and of the rice-plant have not yet been reached. If we consider the case of Japan, which has the highest yields anywhere in Asia, we find that from 1965 to 1977 yields increased at an average annual rate of 0.97%. This surely gives grounds for optimism.

Sources:
[a] Ishikawa 1981: 3, table I–1
[b] Matsuda 1982
[c] *Agricultural Yearbook of China 1980**
[d] Wiens 1980*
[e] OECD 1985
[f] Ban et al. 1980: 45
[g] ADB 1978: 346, appendix I–4.4
[h] Palmer 1977: 103
[i] Taylor 1981: 53, appendix, table 2. 1
[†] Ishikawa and Matsuda both take their figures from the Ministry of Agriculture's *Economic Survey;* the break in progress after 1962 seems improbable, especially given the figures for Taiwan. Perhaps Matsuda's figures are in fact for polished, not unhusked rice.
 * See Stone (1982) for an evaluation of these statistics.

Labour productivity and the mechanisation question

The productivity of labour can be increased through a variety of means. Fertilisers, herbicides and pesticides may all improve yields without raising labour requirements, indeed the use of herbicides and pesticides can release the farmer from hours of back-breaking labour. So too do improvements in the water supply, dealt with in chapter 3. Sometimes yields can be improved without any additional expenditure of capital or of labour, if work-patterns are reorganised so that labour is deployed more efficiently. According to studies carried out in Kelantan, Malaysia in 1973–4, an average of 203 eight-hour man-days per hectare were required in the off-season to produce 2.8 t/ha of rice (Fujimoto 1976a: 41; 1976b: 162). Although the greatest potential for increasing yields lay in the application of pesticides and fertilisers to the young seedlings, better *timing* of operations, it was found, would also improve yields by a far from insignificant amount, possibly totalling as much as 30% (Fujimoto 1977: 56).

The most obvious way of raising the productivity of human labour is to substitute some alternative form of energy. In Asian countries where pasture-land is scarce, draught animals may sometimes require almost as much labour for the provision of fodder as they save in the field. Water-power is another matter. The spread of water-raising equipment in medieval China must have brought about considerable savings in human labour (Needham 1965: 330–62; Li Jiannong 1957: 28–36).

The oldest piece of water-raising equipment was the swape or well-sweep (*shaduf* in Arabic), first known in Babylonia and Ancient Egypt and mentioned in a Chinese text of the fourth century BC; a hand-operated scoop-wheel which raised water into a flume was also in early use in China. The most typical Chinese and East Asian water-raising device was the square-pallet chain-pump, colloquially known as the 'dragon-backbone machine' (figure 2.4), which was in use by the second century AD. Though usually worked by human labour, it could also be geared up and turned by animal-or water-power, as an illustration from the seventeenth-century technical treatise *Tiangong kaiwu* shows (Needham 1965: 581–2). Water-wheels seem to have been a later introduction from the West, first illustrated in an agricultural treatise, the *Wang Zhen nongshu*, of 1313. But even though they contributed greatly to the spread of irrigation, compared to motorised pumps the efficiency of the traditional machinery was low. 'An ox would be able to irrigate, by turning a water-wheel, 0.3 *mu* [approx. 0.02 ha] in one hour; when operated by four labourers, only 0.1 *mu* per hour would

be possible, but when equipped with a 3 HP electric motor it would irrigate over ten times as much' (Vermeer 1977: 190).

Perhaps more efficient in their replacement of human labour were the water-powered hammers and mills which hulled and ground the grain (Needham 1965: 390–405). Water-powered trip-hammers were said by one first century Chinese writer to be one hundred times as efficient as the traditional pestle and mortar, and by the fourteenth century Wang Zhen tells us of huge water-mills which could mill enough grain daily for a thousand families (*Wang Zhen nongshu:* 19/10a-b). As in medieval Europe, many of the Chinese mills were owned by abbeys or monasteries, or by rich merchants, though the government made repeated attempts to control them so as to reduce their profits and lower the prices paid by the poorer citizens.

To return to irrigation, there is no doubt that the introduction of small diesel and electric pumps has revolutionised the lives of millions of rice-farmers. In the Saga Plain in Japan, for example, the installation of specially designed electric pump-sets reduced the labour requirements for irrigation from 70 man-days/ha in 1909 to 22 in 1932 (Ishikawa 1981: 16), and output per man-day increased from 12.6 to 25.3 kg of rice in the same period (Francks 1983: 259); the considerations governing the choice of electricity as the energy source, as well as the size and design of the pumps, were very carefully considered beforehand (ibid.: 210–45).

Since pumps increase the output of the land as well as reducing labour requirements, it is not surprising that unavailability or lack of capital seem to be almost the only obstacles to their adoption. Before 1949 few Chinese farmers had been wealthy enough to purchase pumps, but collectivisation permitted the rapid mechanisation of irrigation in most parts of China (though 'dragon backbones' are still in use in some poorer areas [Wertheim and Stiefel 1982: 30]). Although the figures are far from accurate, it seems that between 1949 and 1956 the number of HP of installed pumps quadrupled from 100,000 to 396,000, while the area irrigated by these pumps rose from 370,000 ha in 1954 to 883,000 ha in 1956; by 1965 it was claimed that over 7 million HP of pumps were installed, irrigating some 6.6 million ha of land (Vermeer 1977: 193, table 34).

The mechanisation of other processes in rice farming has, however, often met with both technical and social obstacles. Here we shall deal briefly with some of the technical problems encountered and their solution. The suggestion has often been put to me that the only real obstacles to the large-scale mechanisation of rice-farming must be social, since rice cultivation in the USA and Australia (and to some degree in

Southern Europe and Africa) is very highly mechanised indeed, to the point that in the USA the crop is often sown by plane and may require only five man-days per hectare in all. It is certainly true that in most Asian rice-growing regions high population densities, scattered holdings and acute shortage of capital do hinder easy rationalisation, though they can be counteracted to some extent by such institutional measures as land reform or the provision of rural credit. Dumont (1957: 150) points out that when a programme of land consolidation was implemented in Japan after the Second World War that of itself led to a 15% increase in production. And in Kelantan, Malaysia, where in the 1970s the Agricultural Development Authority made tractors available for hire at heavily subsidised rates, their use was quickly adopted by all but the poorest farmers, even though they often damaged the bunds separating the fields and impacted the soil (Bray and Robertson 1980).

There is an important natural obstacle to the adoption of heavy machinery in Asia, namely the paddy soils. The agronomist Grist explains (1975: 198):

Where land can be cultivated during the dry season and flooded in the wet season, or where a firm bottom or pan provided by heavy clay soil exists and water control is good, the machines and system of cultivation for paddy differ but little from those employed in cultivating a dryland cereal such as wheat, although the technique must be adjusted to conditions arising from imperfect water control. Soils of this description are found in the rice areas of the United States, the Guianas, Australia, and parts of Europe and Africa. It is in these countries, therefore, that paddy cultivation is highly mechanised. A great deal of paddy land in Asia is in deltas, coastal strips and along the banks of rivers; much of it is swamp and consists of clay silts, silts and silty sands – providing a deep 'mud' in which machine wheels cannot find adhesion, so that the flotation method appears to be the only one for heavy implements.

The demands of terrain and water control form a further obstacle to the use of large machines, for they often severely restrict field size. This is not simply a by-product of population pressure or partible inheritance: there is little that can be done, for instance, to broaden terraced fields on a steep slope. The intensive demands on skilled labour typical of rice cultivation are a further obstacle to the use of machinery. First, the high degree of skill required has made it difficult even to substitute hired labour for family labour, so that farms have tended to become smaller as methods become more intensive, and secondly, the more skilled and complex a human task is, the more difficult it is to design a machine that can perform it as well. For instance, where a farmer using a sickle finds no difficulty in cutting every panicle of rice in the field, a combine-harvester will miss a swathe round the edge and in the corners which,

especially in a small field, may make a substantial difference to the total yield. Corners are always a problem with machinery: farmers in Kelantan who hired tractors to plough their fields then had to till the corners themselves, using heavy iron hoes.

A subsistence farmer relying on family and exchange labour may not count the cost in man-hours of his rice crop, particularly if he has few opportunities to invest his labour elsewhere. But the introduction of double-cropping, the need to use hired labour, the possibility of increasing his income through cash-cropping or off-farm employment, all bring increasingly acute pressures to bear on his time and capacities. When double-cropping was introduced in Kelantan, rice-farming became a year-round occupation instead of occupying only six or seven months, and since large blocks of land were irrigated according to the same schedule, it became difficult for farmers to overcome the bottlenecks of transplanting and harvesting by exchanging labour. With barely one month between the harvesting of one crop and the planting of the next, pressure on labour became intense, and so most farmers who could afford to do so switched from buffalo-ploughs to tractors, despite the disadvantages mentioned earlier (Bray and Robertson 1980).

Experiments with the mechanisation of rice cultivation in Malaysia, as in most Asian countries which were once Western colonies, go back to the 1920s and 1930s, and were until recently based almost exclusively upon the modification of Western-style heavy machinery. Not surprisingly, such experiments were usually only a qualified success (e.g. Berwick 1951). The real breakthrough was to come from Japan.

Farm size in Japan had long been small: in 1910, 70% of farmers operated less than 1 hectare and only 3% operated more than 3 ha (Agric. Bureau 1910: 8), but land ownership was far less equally distributed. After the Second World War an extremely effective programme of land reform was implemented (Dore 1959). In 1945, 46% of Japan's total farm-land had been cultivated by tenants, but by 1950 the figure had dropped to 10% and it continued to fall thereafter (Ogura 1967: 70); it is important to note, however, that the total number of farms remained almost unchanged, at 5.4 million in 1908 and 5.2 million in 1970 (Tsuchiya 1976: 85). The Agricultural Land Law of 1961 prohibited farmers from acquiring holdings of over 3 ha. Since smallholding had been institutionalised, there would clearly be a market for appropriately small-scale machinery. As the economy recovered after the war and decentralised light industries started to expand, many of which used a putting-out system similar to that of Europe in its early phase of industrialisation, opportunities for commercial cropping and for part-time employment off or on the farm increased; moreover, these

occupations were more profitable than rice-farming. The traditional Japanese attachment to the family rice-farm, coupled with a costly government policy of rice-price subsidies, prevented farmers from abandoning rice cultivation, but they were anxious to have as much free time as possible to engage in more lucrative activities. They also had more capital to invest in their farms. Clearly the time was ripe for the mechanisation of rice-farming.

The principle obstacle to the rapid introduction of farm machinery was the lack of suitable equipment. Results from experimental farms in Japan generally showed that large-scale machinery as used in the West was not suitable for use in the typical tiny paddy-fields: even on cooperative farms where land consolidation had been carried out, although its use greatly improved the productivity of labour this often entailed a considerable reduction in rice yields (Tsuchiya 1976: 180). It took some time for suitable small-scale machinery to be perfected. The first item to be developed was the power-tiller, now a familiar sight all over the world. This first came into use in Japan in the 1950s, and by the 1960s had become a standard item of farm equipment. The Japanese Institute of Agricultural Machinery, one of whose duties is to test all new farm machinery on performance, durability and handling, tested over 400 models of power-tillers between 1955 and 1975 (Grist 1975: 233), and certainly played a key role in the more recent development of successful small-scale harvesters and (most difficult of all) transplanting machines.

Japanese agriculture mechanised rapidly. From 1955 to 1966 power-tillers were the main machines in use, and transplanters and small-scale reaper-binders were first introduced in about 1967 (Tsuchiya 1976: 186); their dissemination was rapid, following immediately on the perfection of efficient models. The transplanter was undoubtedly the greatest challenge. Although over one hundred models of various types had been developed in Taiwan alone by the early 1960s, none had given satisfactory results; by that time engineers in China as well as Taiwan were competing with the Japanese, and progress was speedy. More than ten efficient models were launched on the Japanese market in 1969, varying in price from $300 for a hand-operated machine to $1,000 for a pov·ered type (Grist 1975: 221). In 1970 only 1% of Japanese farmers owned a transplanter, but the figure had risen to 61% by 1979. Reaper-binders, which became common in the late 1960s, were gradually superseded after the mid-1970s by the more efficient combine-harvesters; in 1982, 55% of farmers owned reaper-binders, and 31% owned combine-harvesters (Matsuda 1982: 444). But the figures for ownership of farm machinery do not represent the full extent

of their use, for farmers in Japan tend to share their machines although very few rent them out for profit (ibid.: 450); the development of group and contract farming has also extended the use of machinery in recent years (Morio 1982).

The integrated mechanisation of rice cultivation, from ploughing to winnowing, has now been achieved in Japan, and since the process began in about 1955 there has been a transition from small- to medium-sized machinery. This was facilitated by a programme of land improvement whereby fields were regularised and enlarged and drainage improved; such improvements have been carried out on 43% of Japan's rice-land so far, but the very largest plots are no more than 0.3 ha in size, and the remaining 57% still consists of plots of less than 0.1 ha (Matsuda 1982: 447). A similar programme of land consolidation was initiated in Taiwan in 1962, but technical problems and corruption brought it to a halt in 1971 with only about 200,000 of Taiwan's 750,000 ha of arable land having been consolidated. As in Japan, the resulting fields were still tiny by Western standards. For example in San-lin in Central Taiwan field-size was doubled, yet this still only brought the average from 0.085 ha to 0.17 ha (Huang 1981: 121, 127).

The care and effort which have gone into designing appropriate machinery have ensured that yields in Japan have not suffered through its introduction: in fact, thanks to modern fertilisers and pesticides and improved water control, land productivity has continued its steady increase in Japan, rising by 12.2% between 1965 and 1977; labour productivity increased by 6.5% per annum over the same period, but although initially the price of machinery was low relative to rice prices, enabling many farmers to make this capital investment, from 1965 to 1977 the productivity of mechanical investment dropped rapidly, by 9.8% per annum (ibid.: 441).

Similar patterns of small-and medium-scale mechanisation have also occurred in South Korea, especially since the third Five-Year Plan of 1972–6 which set the modernisation of agricultural techniques as a priority (Ban et al. 1980: 71, 189), and in Taiwan, following an ambitious programme of land consolidation (Huang 1981: 121, 134). In both these countries, as in Japan, a rapid expansion of the economy and the growth of rural employment opportunities outside rice farming made farm mechanisation both possible and desirable. Much of the farm machinery has been imported from Japan, presenting problems of maintenance and repair (ibid.: 141).

Most Asian countries have experimented with Japanese power-tillers and threshers, but each region has specific technical requirements, which means that imported machinery may prove unsuitable, and in none

of the other rice-growing regions of Asia are economic conditions as favourable as in Japan, Taiwan and South Korea. In quite a few regions, for example the Muda Scheme in Malaysia (see chapter 3), large-scale machinery still predominates; it is usually owned by private entrepreneurs who keep hire-prices at their uppermost limit, beyond the means of poor farmers who are also deprived of the opportunity of hiring out their labour (MADA 1980). Although some progress has been made towards modifying large-scale machinery to suit the local conditions of the Muda region, for instance reducing the size of the tractors from 60–70 HP to 35–40 HP, the use of heavy combine-harvesters is still damaging fields and making deep ruts, causing difficulties for the new tractors. At the same time:

Virtually no progress has been made in the mechanisation of transplanting despite years of development effort undertaken by various government agencies in cooperation with Japanese scientists. Initial attempts centred around the development of transplanting attachments for four-wheel tractors . . . A number of 8-row prototypes were tested . . . but were eventually abandoned owing partly to the high rate of missing hills created by tractor tyres as well as manoeuvrability problems. (MADA 1980: 6)

Here is a clear case of inappropriate technology applied to one process impeding the development of appropriate technology for another.

Quite apart from technical difficulties, financial obstacles must be presumed to play an important role in discouraging mechanisation, at least in the 'free' economies. Although tractors, mechanical threshers and other machinery are usually explicitly incorporated in the Green Revolution package, figures indicate that while poorer farmers have eagerly adopted improved varieties and fertilisers, which raise yields and income, they have lagged significantly behind larger farmers in investment in all forms of mechanisation or labour-saving products like pesticides (Barker and Herdt 1978: 91). In countries like Java, Thailand and India few tractors are to be found at all.

In the socialist economies financial difficulties are more easily circumvented, as brigades or communes can make more economical use of capital equipment than individuals. Ideological considerations have led the Chinese government to pursue a variety of policies on agricultural mechanisation, emphasising the virtues now of the Russian *kolkhoz*, now of intermediate technology, now of Wheat Belt-style farms. But ecological factors have confined large-scale Western-style machinery largely to North China and Manchuria, and in the rest of China, especially in the rice regions, efforts have been concentrated on producing small-scale equipment similar to that used in Japan, if

somewhat heavier and sturdier (American RSID 1977: 151). Stavis (1978: 264) concludes that ideological pressures have in the main been overridden by a general pragmatic concern to improve rural living standards and increase production. Although supporting evidence is not yet available, it seems highly probable that the expansion and diversification of China's rural economy under the 'responsibility system' will lead to a rapid increase in small- and medium-scale mechanisation, as it did in Japan under similar circumstances. In a speech given in London in July 1985 He Kang, the Chinese Minister of Agriculture, said that from 1978 to 1984 the average annual increase of HP for farm machinery was 8.8%; this represents an emphasis on small machines, for in the year 1983–4, while the number of full-size tractors was expected to increase by 1.9% to 857,000, the number of power-tillers was expected to increase at ten times the rate, by 19.6%, to 3.3 million.

Japan has shown how the technical obstacles to mechanising rice-farming can be overcome. The most important achievement of small- and medium-scale mechanisation in Japan, Korea and Taiwan has been to reduce the labour requirements of rice cultivation and allow farmers more free time for more profitable alternative employment *without* exacerbating income differentials between rich and poor farmers and *without* depriving poorer farmers of opportunities for farm work. It has also been a significant factor in reducing the gap between rural and urban incomes, which is one reason why many economists consider the implications of the Japanese experience to be crucial for developing countries where land is scarce and labour plentiful.

3

Water Control

The chief objects of water control, as far as the rice farmer is concerned, are to reduce the risk of flood and drought, to ensure an adequate and regular supply of water which can be let in and out of the fields as required, and thus to increase the rice crops and even, if the water supply is sufficient, to allow the cultivation of more than a single crop a year. In dry areas where previously only low-yielding dry crops could be grown, or in flooded areas where farming was impossible, the introduction of water control means that new rice-fields can be constructed, increasing the arable area as well as intensifying production.

A comparison of the countries of monsoon Asia made by Ishikawa in the 1960s, based on statistics provided by the FAO and national government agencies, shows a clearly positive correlation between the irrigation ratio (the proportion of irrigated to total cropped area) and land productivity (the total cereal output per unit of cropped land) (1967: 74, chart 2–3). A study by UN(ECAFE)'s Bureau of Flood Control published in 1950 also shows that rice yields in those regions of Asia where water control systems do not exist are significantly lower than where water control is practised (figure 3.1). Japanese economists distinguish two landmarks in land productivity in Asia. The first is an average rice yield of about 2.3 t/ha, the second of about 3.8 t/ha (ibid.: 77). Amano (1954) estimates that the first level had been reached in China as early as the tenth century; Japan had reached it some time before the Meiji Restoration of 1868.[1] Ishikawa suggests that this first landmark in productivity can only be achieved where water control is practised (1967: 78; 1981: 30). The second level of 3.8 t/ha, reached by the 1950s in the deltas of the Yangzi, the Pearl and Red Rivers, and in Japan, seems to depend on more complex improvements over a large range of inputs which include not only water control but also improved crop varieties and fertilisers (ibid.: 122).[2] The crucial role of water control in raising rice yields is in any case clearly demonstrated.

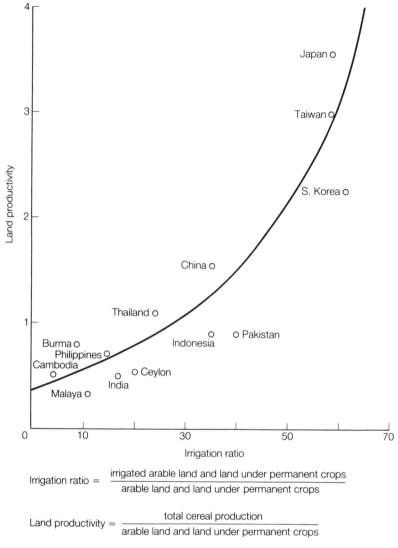

Irrigation ratio = $\dfrac{\text{irrigated arable land and land under permanent crops}}{\text{arable land and land under permanent crops}}$

Land productivity = $\dfrac{\text{total cereal production}}{\text{arable land and land under permanent crops}}$

Figure 3.1   Land productivity and irrigation ratio
(from Ishikawa 1967: 74)

Water control and institutions: the debate

Water control systems came in all sizes, from a single tank or well used by an individual farmer, to the vast irrigation networks of the Punjab and

the proposed Mekong Valley Project which was to have involved the cooperation of China, Laos, Cambodia and Vietnam. Since it is rare that the water supply in any system is adequate to meet all the requirements of all the users, strategies which minimise or resolve conflicts between users are an indispensable feature of water control systems. The larger the total system into which a particular water control unit is integrated, the wider the potential range of conflict. There are a number of ways in which conflicts between individuals, communities, regions or even nation states may be dealt with: sometimes a system has in-built technical safeguards, or technical efficacy may be improved to meet increasing demands, but more important (at first glance anyway) are the codes of customary rights and regulations, enforced through careful supervision, which sometimes prove difficult to incorporate into national legislation when the state (or Irrigation Authority) replaces the village elders as the ultimate arbiters of justice.

Many contemporary Asian states are investing heavily in water control projects in the hope of raising agricultural productivity and improving rural incomes. Their concern for their voters' prosperity reflects attitudes of earlier Asian rulers who wished to ensure their subjects' well-being for a variety of reasons: pure humanitarianism, the hope of suppressing the rebellious instincts which so often welled up after bad harvests, the desire to increase the volume of taxes, or the ritual duty of a monarch who symbolised the good fortune of his people. Other concerns also underlay the state construction of water control projects. The fourteenth-century rulers of Ayutthaya wished to link their capital city more directly to the sea, for reasons of strategy as well as trade (Tanabe) 1978), and trade was an important consideration in the construction of canals in Transbassac and Southern Thailand in the second to sixth centuries (Stargardt 1983: 199). Many waterways in China, though serving a secondary purpose for irrigation, were primarily designed to ensure efficient movement of the grain tax from the provinces to the capital and the frontiers (Eberhard 1965: 80; Twitchett 1970: 84; Huang 1974: 51), while a number of large-scale irrigation projects undertaken by successive Chinese governments were designed as settlement schemes for landless peasants (Bray 1980). In feudal Japan local lords built canals in part to ensure their political control over the area (Kelly 1982b: 14), while in nineteenth-century Siam the royal house established water control facilities in vast areas of the swampy Bangkok Delta to provide estates for impoverished nobles (Tanabe 1978).

In the nineteenth century Marx and Weber suggested that there were strong links between the technical and social demands of water control and the emergence of centralised, monolithic states in Asia, associating

such centralisation with the inhibiting of local initiative, with economic stagnation and with the development of a complex bureaucracy and social hierarchy which also impeded economic growth. Such hypotheses were subsequently elaborated by historians like Chi (1936) and Wittfogel (1931; 1957), who saw the necessity for centralised management of water resources as the key factor in determining the political and institutional forms of Asian societies. Chi in fact used the geographic expansion of state water control to explain a political and historical dynamism in Chinese society, but Wittfogel took Marx's notions of stagnation and repression further, postulating an equation between 'hydraulic society' and 'Oriental despotism'. Numerous subsequent studies have shown that centralisation and bureaucratic control are not necessarily concomitants of Asian water control systems, even when these are integrated into very large networks,[3] yet the concept of 'hydraulic societies' retains its fascination; it is interesting that, while repudiating Wittfogel's negative evaluation of the Chinese state, Needham too adheres to the idea that Chinese society was essentially organised around a monolithic 'feudal bureaucracy', derived in large part from the managerial requirements of predominantly large-scale water control (Needham 1974).

One of the main arguments that underlies such theories as 'Oriental despotism' and 'hydraulic societies' is that only a highly centralised state can mobilise sufficient capital and technical and administrative expertise to construct and run huge irrigation systems such as the Angkorian network described later in the chapter. It is certainly true that both Hindu and, later, Buddhist monarchs all over Southeast Asia saw it as part of their kingly role, an act of the highest religious merit, to donate generously from the royal treasuries to provide the necessary materials and funding (usually this meant stone, timber and the rice to feed corvée labourers). But kings were not the only instigators of such works. Temples, dignitaries, or even rich villagers often gave endowments to construct or maintain irrigation works on different scales. Such donations were usually recorded in inscriptions set, for example, in the wall of the tank thus financed; the stages of construction would be accompanied by religious rituals and the whole work consecrated upon completion (Stargardt 1983: 187).

Although the acquisition of religious merit was an important motive, we must not forget that it was usual for the builder of such a work to retain rights over the water which passed through it. In medieval Ceylon, for example, farmers paid something akin to a tithe to the owners of the tank which watered their fields. Since the provision of irrigation water improved yields, both farmer and donor stood to benefit materially, and if it was a monarch who was responsible for the improvement, he could

count on an increase in his tax revenues, paid as a proportion of the farmer's produce which, even during times of peace and prosperity, might amount to over one-fifth of the harvest.[4] Often kings would donate tanks to religious foundations; again this was an act of merit which increased the revenues of the monastery or temple. As Stargardt (1983: 197) rightly points out, Southeast Asian societies were equally aware of both the religious and the economic benefits to be derived from hydraulic works, and to regard either motive as predominant would be a distortion.

Turning to the Far East, the link between 'feudalism' and water control has also been insisted upon by Japanese historians, departing from the early twentieth-century Marxist analyses of Japanese history which take water and its control as an essential fourth factor of production (together with land, labour and capital) (see Kelly 1982a: 9). The organisational requirements and political potential of irrigation agriculture are seen by most Japanese historians, whatever their period of study or political persuasion, as crucial in determining the persistence of small-scale peasant agriculture (*shōnōsei*), the 'feudal' subordination of the individual to a hierarchical community (*hōkensei*) and the eventual emergence in early modern Japan, from previously more autonomous agricultural groupings, of the village as a corporate body (*kyōdōtai*) corresponding to the basic unit of irrigation (e.g. Kanazawa 1971: 13–16; Kelly 1982a: passim).

One reason why Japanese social scientists of every political hue take such a lively interest in water control is that it is seen even today as a key element in the agricultural modernisation debate, intimately related to the fate of Japanese rice farmers. The post-Second World War land reforms were closely linked with legislation reorganising irrigation management (the Land Improvement Law of 1949), and with heavy government investment in irrigation projects (Ogura 1967; Shimpo 1976; Kelly 1982a: 15). The mixed results did little to resolve the debate as to whether it was social and political factors which determined the technical organisation of irrigation and levels of agricultural production, or vice versa. Scholars such as Kanazawa (1971: 16) and his colleagues of the 'feudalist' persuasion believe, for example, that prewar irrigation management was largely determined by forms of land tenure and political control, and hold that radical legislative reforms were (and remain today) an indispensable precondition for technological improvement and the breaking-down of a crippling system of smallholder agriculture. On the other hand, Shinzawa Kagatō and his followers, who have been highly influential in shaping state policy, maintain that state investment in technological improvement can resolve the social contra-

dictions which hitherto impeded the rationalisation and modernisation of Japanese agriculture (Kelly 1982a: 22).

Much Japanese scholarship on water control focuses on the contradiction between common management of water and individual ownership of land. This preoccupation with the dialectic between communality and individualism, and the necessity for breaking traditional moulds, is to some extent historically determined in the case of Japan. In other parts of Asia different factors may be more important. The famous *subaks* or irrigation societies of Bali may be said to exhibit a degree of communal pressure towards individual participation similar to that of the Japanese irrigation groups, yet in the next-door island of Lombok, where regional rulers intervened much more directly in village life, popular participation in the running of the *subak* is small even in areas of Balinese population (Gerdin 1982: 71). Groslier (1979) points to the preponderantly ritual factors which determined the form of the elaborate irrigation networks of classical Angkor. Taking contemporary examples in Sri Lanka, Chambers (1980: 48), while allowing the importance of prevailing technological levels in shaping the organisation of water control, maintains that such features of a society's culture as the degree of hierarchy or egalitarianism are also major determinants.

The debate as to whether technological change determines social evolution or vice versa is implicit, if not explicit, in almost all works on modern development, and as it applies to the question of water control it is of special relevance to the rice economies of Asia today. Many national governments and international aid agencies are currently investing heavily in the construction of large-scale irrigation schemes in areas where water control was previously small-scale or even non-existent. Official planners have become ruefully aware of the social complexities and difficulties attendant upon such technical change, and the literature on water control has grown rapidly in consequence. Since the conflict of interests between individual and community, so meticulously documented in the Japanese studies, is common to all water control systems, most social science studies have focused mainly on the institutional features of water control, treating the technical features as secondary. But the classification of water control management according to criteria such as 'centralisation' or 'decentralisation' lends itself to ideological bias. Furthermore, at least in so far as wet-rice cultivation is concerned, it is undeniable that certain social and economic characteristics (such as the small scale of fields and farms, and the necessity for cooperation at various levels between the farmers in a single water control unit) are common to all the societies in question, whatever higher political or economic forms may prevail. It is also clear that these

characteristics are imposed by the technical requirements of irrigated rice cultivation.

A technical classification of water control systems

The technical concept of 'water control' (*shuili* in Chinese, *suiri* in Japanese, literally 'turning water to advantage') is perhaps peculiarly Asian.[5] It covers three interlinked categories: irrigation, drainage and flood control. Although Westerners usually connect rice principally with irrigation, in fact any or all of the three may be necessary for its successful cultivation, depending on topography and climate. Irrigation proper, the supplementing of an insufficient water supply, may be carried out on almost any scale from the individual household to a whole province or nation. Drainage, the removal of excess water, tends to require greater investments of labour and other resources, and cannot usually be carried out without the cooperation of a relatively large community or the intervention of a wealthy family or institution. Flood control along the great rivers of monsoon Asia requires enormous investments in construction and maintenance, but since it is literally a matter of life and death for thousands if not millions of their subjects, and often a matter of national survival as well, Asian monarchs have made it a primary concern since very early times.[6] While irrigation and drainage functions tend to be complementary, those of irrigation or drainage may well conflict with those of flood control, often with disastrous results. One thinks, for instance, of the peasants of North China breaching the Yellow River dykes to irrigate their wheat-fields (Needham 1971: 228), or of the rich landowners of Central China draining so much of the shore of the Dongting Lake to make dyked fields that the lake could no longer serve as a proper overspill for the Yangzi when it was in spate. Generally speaking, in the rice-growing regions of monsoon Asia irrigation and drainage systems were constructed independently of flood-control dykes and canals. Today, given the vastly increased financial and technical resources available, it is possible to construct water control systems integrating all three functions.

   In this chapter we shall follow a broad classification of water control systems based primarily on their functional and technical characteristics.[7] We shall demonstrate some of the important factors in their historical expansion and change, briefly linking institutional to technical forms, and considering the implications for contemporary development.

Gravity-fed irrigation networks

Many of the world's most impressive irrigation systems have been found in arid zones, hardly surprisingly, for in such areas, although subsistence agriculture may often be sustained without supplementing the meagre supply of rain water, it is only by providing extra water, and especially an assured and regular supply of water at the main growth period of the principal crops, that surpluses can be produced. The effect of irrigation is equally impressive for dry crops like wheat or cotton and for wet crops like rice or sugar-cane. The Sudan's Gezira Scheme allowed good cotton to be grown under almost desert conditions (Gaitskell 1959); the irrigation schemes of the Punjab have allowed abundant crops of wheat, cotton and rice to be grown (Dasgupta 1977; Farmer 1981); more anciently, irrigation water from the Yellow River and its tributaries gave rise to the intensive production of millet, wheat, sorghum and other cereals and in particular maintained a steadily high level of production in the Wei River valley, a naturally arid region in the northwest where Chang'an, the traditional capital of China, was located (Bray 1984).

Wet rice, like dry crops, flourishes under irrigation in arid zones, but a more regular and abundant supply of water is required if crop growth is to be maintained, especially where rainfall is not only low but irregular. Very often rainfall patterns differ significantly within a relatively small area, and irregularity, poor seasonal distribution and high evaporation are just as important obstacles to successful agriculture as low rainfall, which is why it is not unreasonable to speak of the 'dry zones' of Sri Lanka and South India, for example (Mendis 1977: 13; Farmer et al. 1977: 10). In these areas, as in other 'arid zones' of monsoon Asia, annual rainfall may vary by as much as one-third from good year to bad (Nakamura 1982: 8).

The rice-plant's maximum water requirements occur between flowering and ripening. Since the rice has to be sown during the rains, its period of maximum growth often extends into the dry season, rendering harvests precarious in the absence of irrigation. In Upper Burma, for example, the annual rainfall of 700–1,050 mm is barely sufficient to produce a rice crop (Stargardt 1983: 196). But if water can be regularly supplied to the fields during the dry period production can easily be doubled, and indeed sometimes double-cropping becomes possible as in the case of Angkor in the ninth to twelfth centuries, when the Khmer empire was at its height (Groslier 1974: 103; 1979: 174–8). Stargardt (1983: 119) computes the increase in rice production in the Satingpra peninsula in Southern Thailand as irrigation techniques developed from

the fourth to fourteenth century (table 3.1) and, if her computations are correct, the differences between fourth- and sixth-century production figures clearly show how irrigation could contribute to the growth of cities and elaborated economies. It is not simply the rise in average production, but the comparative reliability of irrigated rice crops, that permits such a leap from village to city, as Groslier says of the parallel stage in Khmer Cambodia (1974: 113): 'ce qui est certain, c'est que par rapport à l'ancienne économie de subsistance, on était passé à un système de production intensive et . . . dans toute la mesure du possible à l'abri des écarts du climat'. Ishikawa shows clearly that in Asia the productivity of rice, as well as of other crops, is directly correlated to the proportion of arable land which is irrigated (1967: 75) (figure 3.1).

It is important to remember, however, that, as Stargardt has shown (1983: 185–205), the vast and impressive irrigation systems characteristic of the Southeast Asian arid zones, those which supported the Pyū and Pagan dynasties of Upper Burma, the Pallava and Chola kings of South India and Ceylon, the kingdoms of Kediri and Majapahit in Java, and the Khmer empire in Cambodia, developed gradually from pre-existing small, local irrigation systems and, generally speaking, represented an increase in scale and sophistication of management rather than any great leap forward in technical expertise. Indeed they usually relied heavily for

Table 3.1   Rice production at Satingpra, fourth to fourteenth centuries

Century	area under rice (ha)	rice production (kg)
4th (pre-urban)	19,200	16,400,000
6th–9th (urban)	50,000	48,000,000
9th–13th (urban II[a])	130,000	130,000,000
9th–13th (urban II[b])	130,000	202,000,000
13th–14th (urban III[a])	37,000	35,200,000
13th–14th (urban III[b])	37,000	44,400,000

[a] Assuming single-cropping of long-season varieties.
[b] Assuming double-cropping of one long-season and one short-season traditional variety.
Source: based on Stargardt 1983: 119

their construction, maintenance and management on the contribution of villagers whose skills had been developed over centuries.

Ponds, tanks and reservoirs

The main evidence for both the early networks of tanks or ponds, and for the great irrigation systems of Southeast Asia, is archaeological, though some early inscriptions survive in Bali and Java (van Setten 1979: 33, 61) which refer to irrigation works or officers, while for South India there is considerable epigraphic evidence for the medieval period as to how revenues for irrigation works were raised, workers paid, rights allotted, and so on (Stargardt 1983: 186).

The typical dry-zone irrigation systems of Southeast Asia are situated in the valleys of small rivers or on the edges of the alluvial plains of great rivers like the Mekong of Chao Phraya (Stargardt 1983: 200–5). Sometimes rainwater was collected in small tanks sited on natural depressions or excavated in alluvial soils, as in early South India and Sri Lanka. Such tanks were widespread in Andhra Pradesh and Tamil Nadu; sluices in the earthen walls controlled the flow of water into distributary channels which led down the natural slope of the land to water the fields below (Stargardt 1983: 186). Similar tanks go back at least to the third century BC in Sri Lanka (Brohier 1934–5; cited Stargardt 1983: 190–1), where they may originally have been connected with Naga worship. Small tanks filled by rainfall or natural percolation from the high water-table were used for domestic as well as irrigation purposes. These small tanks, and field canals, originated in the fourth to sixth centuries in the Satingpra sites (see Stargardt 1983: 80–2); navigable canals were first dug in the sixth century (ibid.: 82).

It is not easy to enlarge rain-fed tanks much beyond the scale of a single household in zones where rainfall is in any case sparse, and very often such tanks dried out soon after the rains unless the water-table was high and rainfall was supplemented by percolation. But if a stream or small river is trapped or diverted much larger volumes of water can be stored. Spencer (1974: 86) says that the technique of damming a small valley with an earth barrier is Indian in origin, and is found in Southeast Asia only in zones of Indian influence (including the Cham region of Vietnam). In early Cambodia, the plains of Upper Burma, South India and Ceylon, larger streams and rivers could be trapped since the stronger earthen or stone dams were carefully designed to withstand water-pressure and were provided with sluice controls leading off into distributary channels.

Shifting the dam further downstream allowed the tank to be enlarged,

sometimes to enormous capacity. Leach (1961: 18) describes the village tanks of contemporary Sri Lanka as being about 7 feet in depth. 'Very roughly, the full tank covers much the same area of ground as the land below which it is capable of irrigating.' But where larger works were undertaken the dams or bunds were usually short relative to their capacity. The site would be carefully chosen to correspond to a natural depression, and as Stargardt points out 'the basic principle in the technology employed was to achieve an inverse ratio between the scale of bunding work and its effect' (1983: 192). The Mahendrataṭāka tank, built in the early seventh century by a Pallava king of South India, contained sufficient water to irrigate land almost 13 km away (Venkayya 1906: 203; cited Stargardt 1983: 188), and some South Indian tanks held enough supplies for 15 months, a necessity since their sources of supply could be extremely erratic (ibid.).

In mountain valleys the danger of rivers destroying their dams at the height of the rains meant that it was preferable to build a feeder canal rather than dam the river directly, diverting a more easily regulated portion of the river waters to fill the tank. Such works were common in Pyū (c.sixth- to eighth-century) and Pagan (mid-ninth- to late thirteenth-century) Burma, and could also attain enormous capacities. One Pagan royal tank irrigated about 15,000 ha, and several served areas of 7–10,000 ha (Stargardt 1983: 195).

Without doubt, however, the most impressive irrigation network in Southeast Asian history was that constructed around the capital of Angkor when the Khmers were at the height of their power in the ninth to twelfth centuries. At one point the Angkorian irrigation works supplied some 167,000 ha along the northern plain of the Tonlé Sap basin (Groslier 1979: 190). The city of Angkor was founded in the ninth century, on a sweep of fertile alluvial soil watered by numerous rivers and close to the rich fisheries of the Tonlé Sap. It also happened to be the geographical centre of the Khmer empire.[8] The 'hydraulic city' was developed under Indravarman (r. 877–89), who like Hindu rulers elsewhere in Southeast Asia strove to achieve the kingly virtues of Rāmā and to ensure the happiness and prosperity of his subjects, not only through his own spiritual perfection, but also by active intervention. The monarch was the 'Lord of the lords of the soil' (Groslier 1974: 114); as the Old Javanese version of the Rāmāyana has it:

> Care of the farmlands is always the king's responsibility
> For from these comes all the produce for the kingdom's welfare.
>
> (tr. van Setten 1979: 78)

The layout of Angkor was highly symbolic, for it was not a city in the European sense, but a political and ritual centre which interpreted the cosmos as a whole in terms of stone, soil and water. Thus as Groslier points out, to draw any distinction between *urbs* and *rus* in the case of Angkor would be wrong, for here *urbs* actually represents *rus* and nature, incorporating in itself the gods of fertility and the soil (1974: 111). The Khmer rivers and waterways, in the Angkorian philosophy, represented the triple course of the Ganges (Mekong means 'mother Ganges'), the temple which they surrounded represented the sacred mountain of Meru.

The early Khmer monarchs had inherited from the Funanese a huge network of canals which, as well as facilitating transport, drained and desalinated the northern plains between the Gulf of Siam and the Lower Mekong, and provided irrigation through a number of dams and tanks. Following the Hindu cosmological ideal, however, the tanks, canals, moats, temples and cities of Angkor were strictly geometrical in shape. The huge tanks, or *baray*, were not natural depressions but were built *above* or *below* the natural plain, to trap the waters of a small river. A double channel was dug around the site of the proposed *baray*, and some of the excavated soil was used to build the square retaining dyke between the channels, while the rest was used to fill in the stone monument or temple-mountain built in the centre of the *baray* (figure 3.2). The *baray* of Indravarman's capital, Lolei, was 300 ha in area and held at least 10 million cubic metres (Groslier 1974: 100). The clay and sand soils used to build the dyke formed an impermeable layer, preventing losses from seepage. The river water was fed into the *baray* through a series of dams and feeder canals. Since the natural slope of the land was northeast-southwest, the water moved naturally southwest through the distributary canals, and was let into the fields and led from one to another (the fields were square, and about 80 m across) by the simple expedient of making a small breach in the banks. The water supply from these huge reservoirs seems to have been sufficient to allow the Khmer to grow two crops of rice a year.

Being fed by gravity alone, the irrigation network was limited to an arc of between 30° and 45° below the *baray*, and the only way to expand the system was to build a new *baray* upstream. Each new king, therefore, founded a new temple with its associated *baray* and irrigation network, proceeding gradually northwards. It is not certain, though, that all the old systems remained operative and that the system expanded arithmetically with time, for the silt carried by the feeder canals tended to settle in the reservoirs. No cleaning was carried out, for this would have meant the enormous task of draining the whole *baray* (and depriving a whole district

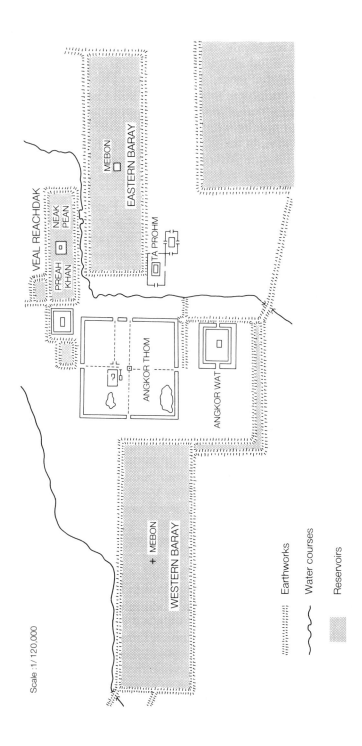

Scale :1/120,000

WESTERN BARAY

+ MEBON

VEAL REACHDAK

PREAH
KHAN

NEAK
PEAN

EASTERN BARAY

MEBON

TA PROHM

ANGKOR THOM

?

ANGKOR WAT

||||||||||| Earthworks

⌒ Water courses

▨ Reservoirs

Figure 3.2   General plan of Angkor
(based on Coédès 1948)

of crops for at least one season). As the *barays* silted up and the irrigation water carried less fertile silt into the fields rice yields would fall, and eventually – and suddenly – the water flow would cease altogether. Then the whole agricultural area dependent upon that *baray* had to be abandoned, for as the fields dried out a ferrous hard-pan formed which made the land irreversibly sterile.

The inbuilt obsolescence of the *barays* was probably a significant factor in the decline of Angkor from the fourteenth century. The Siamese conquered the Khmer capital in 1364, and thereafter continuous civil wars which lasted on and off for five centuries prevented any attempt at reconstruction of the Angkorian canals. Cambodia shifted back to the old zones of habitation in the north, and to the old agricultural techniques, which remain in use today. Rice yields are low, much land is left fallow and irrigation techniques are rudimentary or non-existent (Delvert 1961: 353). After the fourteenth-century Siamese invasion the Cambodians reverted to a subsistence economy, using extensive techniques where sometimes the rice-harvest gave only three times the amount of seed-grain. The population fell steadily, thanks to poverty and war, to an estimated 1 million in 1879 when the French moved in (ibid.: 425). The old agricultural heartlands around Angkor were soon overgrown by scrub (*veal*), except in the immediate vicinity of reservoirs and rivers, where the modern villages stand on ancient Angkorian sites (Groslier 1974: 105).

Much the same happened on the Satingpra peninsula in Southern Siam (closely linked by trade, culture and technology with the Mōn and Khmer empires across the South China Sea). Satingpra too was destroyed by the Siamese in the fourteenth century, at a time when it was probably already weakened economically by the deterioration of its irrigation network and consequent decline in agricultural production (Stargardt 1983: 36). Today aerial photographs show the faint outlines of the ancient square rice-fields, which had produced two crops of irrigated rice each year. They lie beneath the bunds of the modern strip-shaped fields in which a single crop of unirrigated rice is produced (ibid.: figs 37–9).

It was not always the case, however, that the fall of a kingdom meant a reversion to less intensive cultivation methods. Leach tells us that in Ceylon the large central reservoirs and feeder canals built and controlled by the state during the Sinhalese kingdom of Anurādhapura (*c.*second century BC to thirteenth century AD) fell into decay with the fall of the kingdom to be repaired very much in their ancient form under British rule. But village tanks in the same region, which had not always been linked to the larger systems, were constantly being built and repaired, and although very few can claim to have survived intact for more than a

few centuries, many have been constructed on sites where ancient tanks had previously stood (1961: 15 ff). In Burma too, parts of the Kyaukse irrigation works have functioned continuously for over two thousand years (Stargardt 1983: 197). So while a few ancient centralised systems created almost irreversible damage to the environment as they decayed, others were able to survive indefinitely in segmented form.[9]

It is also important to bear in mind the crucial contribution of local farmers and dignitaries to such hydraulic works, of whatever size. Without the funds, materials, labour, management skills and technical expertise provided locally, hydraulic works on whatever scale would have been impossible. As we have seen, the huge works of Angkor or medieval Ceylon and Burma simply applied tried and tested technical principles on a much larger scale than hitherto. They did not represent any intrinsic technical advance, which is why such systems were often able to survive for centuries in segmented and uncoordinated form long after the centralised state which had built them had disintegrated. Although the initiative for large irrigation schemes, as for other public works, may have come from high up, they depended for their success on close collaboration between state and village. In many of these societies, the titles given to villagers who acted as engineers or organisers of labour were of much earlier origin that the inscriptions which record their contribution.[10] The interpretation of such titles is often difficult, but village officers certainly appear to have included elders in charge of the construction of local irrigation works, surveyors of dams and officers in charge of maintenance (van Setten 1979: 60 ff). Royal officers, on the other hand, had the role of mobilising and, where necessary, arbitrating between different villages.[11] Usually it was the royal treasury which provided the rice rations during construction work for the locally levied corvée labourers, but once the work was complete, individual villages became responsible for the normal running and maintenance. Village committees, often elected for fixed periods (e.g. Stargardt 1983: 189 on South India, 196 on Burma), had the power to levy taxes on the irrigated land, part of which contributed to the royal revenues; the rest was used to pay labourers to clear out channels, to remove silt or repair bunds; carpenters and other craftsmen were paid to mend boats and sluices, and so on (Venkayya 1906; Stargardt 1983: section V passim). In some cases village labour was not paid, but each farmer contributed a certain amount of labour and materials during the dry season (e.g. in medieval Sri Lanka; Stargardt 1983: 192).

The level of local skills and knowledge which the medieval kingdoms of Southeast Asia could command was not inconsiderable:

The degree of expertise shown in levelling and aligning the bunds was very high and further exhibited in the excellent alignments followed by the canals – sometimes covering long distances and managing by means of tunnels to cross from one watershed to another. Excessive water pressures on the tank bunds were mitigated by the construction of high- and low-level paved sluices to regulate outflow and even by the introduction of further sophisticated devices such as valves and stone facings on the bunds. (Stargardt 1983: 192)

But these techniques, though sophisticated, had originally been developed by small communities and were therefore limited in potential. The great states of Southeast Asia were able to increase the scale of such works, but did not develop new technologies which would have enabled them to adapt to more challenging environments. The irrigation systems we have described were typical of upland valleys and plains, watered by small streams and rivers, in areas where natural rainfall was sparse and erratic; they were fed by natural gravitational flow. Thus the Khmers of Angkor were able to expand their irrigation network north of the Tonlé Sap and east of Angkor to the edge of the plains (Groslier 1974: 103), but their skills were not sufficient to master the meandering lower course of the Mekong. It was not until the colonial era that attempts to master the great rivers of Southeast Asia and to drain their deltas became feasible. The technologies and other skills and resources involved will be discussed further on in this section.

In the hilly regions of Southern and Central China, and in Japan, one of the most ancient forms of storing and redistributing water was a system based on small ponds which, like the small ponds or tanks of South Asia described earlier, supplied anything from a single farm to a small hamlet. But given the greater abundance and regularity of the natural rainfall in East Asia, the proportion of stored water to irrigated area could be much smaller, as low as 1: 5 instead of 1: 1:

On high land, identify the places where water accumulates and dig out ponds. Out of 10 *mu* [approx. 0.6 ha] of land you must be prepared to waste 2 or 3 *mu* for water storage. At the end of the spring when the rainy season comes heighten the banks and deepen and widen the interior. Strengthen the banks by planting mulberry or silkworm-thorns[12] to which buffalo may be tethered in the shade as their nature requires. Meanwhile the buffalo by trampling the banks will strengthen them, the mulberries will be well watered and grow into fine trees, and even in the dry season there will be sufficient water for irrigation, yet in heavy rains the tank will not overflow and harm the crops. (*Chen Fu nongshu*: 2)

Small ponds were constructed by rice-farmers throughout Central and Southern China at an early period, as can be seen from the large number

of clay models (figure 3.3) found in graves of the Later Han dynasty (AD 25–220). In Sichuan, the Yangzi region, Guangdong and Guizhou, as well as in the Tai kingdoms of Yunnan, individual farmers dug small ponds which served to grow lotuses and water-chestnuts and to raise fish and turtles, as well as to irrigate the rice-fields (Bray 1984: 110; Yangzi 1979: 59). A text of slightly earlier date than the grave models, relating to the provinces just north of the Yangzi, refers to much larger ponds, in fact reservoirs, covering an area of one or more *qing* (i.e. well over 50 ha);

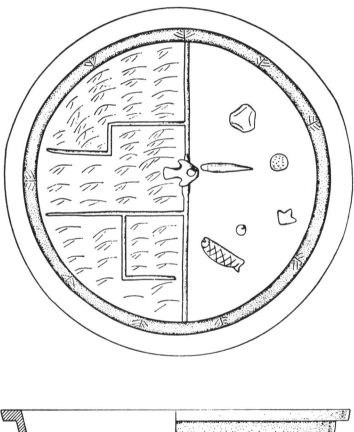

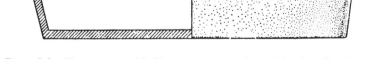

Figure 3.3   Han grave-model of irrigation pond and rice-field, from Guizhou (the right-hand section, the pond, contains fish, water-chestnuts and other aquatic plants)
(from *Wenwu* 1979: 5, fig. 17)

these, it says, would irrigate four times the area of rice-fields.[13] Such reservoirs had become common by the early Song dynasty (960–1127), and Ma Duanlin, a twelfth-century scholar, writes:

Along the Central and Southern Chinese coast there are reservoirs everywhere. Generally the lake lies higher than the rice fields, which in turn are higher than the river or sea. When there is a drought they release the lake water to irrigate the fields, and when it is too wet they drain off the water from the fields into the sea, so that there is never any natural disaster. (tr. Bray 1984: 110)

Large and small ponds are still important sources of irrigation water in many parts of Central and Southern China today (Gustafsson 1984: 144). In the Meiquan district of Hubei province, irrigation water is now supplied by one medium and 30 small reservoirs, and by 6,010 ponds; in all the irrigated area is about 8,000 ha, which shows how small the majority of the ponds must be (Nickum 1981).

Ponds are the most ancient type of irrigation supply in Japan. They were probably introduced from Korea in about the fifth century AD, together with new rice varieties and iron-tipped tools (Tsukuba 1980: 61; Kelly 1982a: 2). Tanaka (1983: 31–3) characterises these small ponds or reservoirs in which, according to archaeological evidence, the water was often retained by a simple dam of poles and logs, as typical of the economy of the Kofun period (third to sixth centuries AD). Recent archaeological excavations in the Nara Basin, however, indicate that 'saucer ponds' dug into the upper slopes, which could water a greater area by natural gravity flow and which were very common in early China, were extremely rare in Japan before the Kamakura era (1185–1392); only during the Tokugawa period did they come to predominate as a water supply for rice cultivation (Farris 1985: 96). A great deal has been written on the social organisation associated with pond irrigation in Japan (e.g. Tamaki 1979: 24–32), and we shall return to this in chapter 6. But as the feudal warrior class started building up their local bases and expanding the area of cultivated land under their control, larger irrigation networks based on small rivers and derivation canals became increasingly common. The proportion of land in Japan irrigated by ponds fell steadily, until by the turn of this century only one-fifth of the irrigated land in Japan was watered from ponds (Agric. Bureau 1910: 21). Today the proportion has fallen to one-sixth (Kelly 1982a: 3).

Nevertheless the Japanese still construct ponds for irrigation purposes where the terrain is suitable. Beardsley et al. point out in their study of Niiike in Southern Honshu, where as well as new canals a large pond was built to supplement the irrigation supply during the national programme of land improvement in the 1920s, that pond-water has the great

advantage that it does not need to be pumped up into the fields (1980 edn: 145). And the Japanese encouraged the construction of large numbers of storage ponds in Northwest Taiwan after they gained control of the island in 1895 (Wang and Apthorpe 1974: 33).[14]

More recently still, tank irrigation was introduced to the Khorat plateau of Northeast Thailand, using American capital and technical aid, during the 1950s. These tanks vary in size, irrigating on average a few hundred hectares. Because local ecological conditions and distribution requirements had been insufficiently studied, the tanks have not proved very successful (Kaida 1978: 223).

Contour canals

Another method of gravity-fed irrigation is typical of the low mountain ranges of East and Southeast Asia, where rainfall is often higher and more regular than in the neighbouring plains. Under such conditions it is not necessary to store the water seasonally in reservoirs so as to distribute it more evenly throughout the year. Instead the supply is perpetual. Water is diverted from mountain streams, springs or small rivers, and led (again by natural gravity flow) along a series of small contour canals, distributary channels and water pipes to the rice-fields. (It is desirable to water the fields from diversion canals rather than directly from the stream, as this facilitates control over the quantity, depth and speed of water available.) One of the earliest irrigation systems of this type is to be found in the Gio-linh highlands of Vietnam, which as we have already mentioned (p. 30) seems to have been designed according not only to technical criteria but also to ritual precepts. In the Hinduised cultures of medieval Java and Bali cosmological principles also played an important role in spatial organisation. Round a mother village four more villages would be grouped, on the corners of a square based on the cardinal points. The group of five villages formed a unit called *mancapat*, which sometimes was extended to include the eight compass directions (van Setten 1979: 58–9). But despite their cosmological sensitivities, topographical and tenurial complexities did not permit the Balinese and Javanese to construct their irrigation works according to the strict symmetries of Angkor; indeed the intricacies of Balinese waterworks are more reminiscent of interwoven spiders' webs.[15]

Irrigation systems based on exactly the same principles as the Balinese *subak*, if slightly less complex, are common in North and Northeast Thailand, Southern and Southwest China and the Philippines. The Funanese had built terraced rice-fields in the northern hills of their Cambodian domain well before they were conquered by the Khmers in

the late sixth century (Groslier 1974: 97). While the Lao have traditionally preferred to grow rice along river-banks in the flat plains, the White Tai of the Laos hills, descended from Chinese soldiers who intermarried with Tai women in about 1600 after a campaign along the northern border between Laos and Tonkin, brought with them agricultural and engineering skills which generally impressed French diplomat de Reinach: 'Ils savent admirablement tirer parti des ressources du sol. Par d'ingénieux canaux établis à flanc de coteau, ils amènent les eaux nécessaires à l'irrigation de leurs rizières de montagne; ils savent également capter les sources *souvent fort éloignées* pour les employer au même usage' (1952: 205).

Such systems rely on very simple tools but sophisticated design. Most rivers in the steep mountain valleys of the area are fast-flowing, prone to flooding and difficult to control. The Minangkabau rice-farmers of North Sumatra and Malaya built mud and brushwood dams across smaller streams in their territory during the wet season (Hill 1977: 132), but since the dams had no sluices, control over the supply to the fields was limited and there was always the danger that in heavy spate the stream would burst the barrier. A more effective solution is to build contour canals which water the terraced rice-fields from above. Since the stream is captured higher up, the dam does not have to be particularly high or strong, provided the gradient of the conduits is carefully regulated; for this the Balinese use a simple type of water-level (*geganjing*) 'employed with remarkable skill' (Liefrinck 1886: 50). Small dams might simply consist of a few tree-trunks laid at such an angle as to force water into the conduit, while larger ones are made of stones held together in bamboo baskets or gabions.[16]

The complex layout of conduits, check-ponds to trap silt, sluices and overflows, tunnels and aqueducts found in Balinese *subaks* is described in detail by Liefrinck (1886). Though the tools and materials used are simple, the design is by no means so. Considerable natural obstacles have to be overcome: for example it is not uncommon for water to be taken by tunnels up to a mile long under a ridge, or led by a stone or wooden aqueduct across a valley or into another watershed.

Such technology must be of ancient origin in Asia. Many of its elements are first described and illustrated in the *Wang Zhen nongshu* (ch.18), and Wang's notes often contain excerpts from much earlier writers. For instance Du Shi, a high official of the Han dynasty (fl. *c.*25–57 AD) and the inventor of the first Chinese water-wheel, had already alluded to the bamboo pipes which Wang describes and illustrates (figure 3.4): hollowed bamboos, joined end to end, were used to bring water from mountain springs or streams, across valleys, slopes or

Figure 3.4   Bamboo aqueduct
(*Wang Zhen nongshu*: 18/20a)

level ground, to fields which were often a considerable distance away. Wang also shows a wooden aqueduct or flume (figure 3.5), again used to transport water over long distances. If a village was at a distance from any water source, Wang says (ibid.: 18/21b), all the families would join forces to construct such a flume. As long as the source was a spring high above the village, the water would run down all by itself as was its nature, but if it came from a low-lying pond or ditch then it would have to be pumped up into the flume. These flumes, Wang says, crossed valleys on stilts and went in tunnels through spurs of high land. Sometimes, especially if the gradient was steep, the water would be full of mud and silt by the time it ran into the fields, in which case if would be filtered through a fine-meshed bamboo basket (ibid.: 18/35b).

Where water distribution is as complex as in these systems of valley irrigation, numerous social problems also have to be taken into account. The Balinese *subak*, as explained earlier, does not correspond to the social unit of the village but comprises a group of individual farmers whose fields are watered from the same source. Sometimes potential conflict between *subaks* can be eliminated by technical means: where a conduit borders on another *subak*'s ground, for instance, an underground tunnel can be built to prevent water theft; or two conduits coming from different sources may cross, in which case an aqueduct or tunnel can be constructed. While the *subak* members regulate their internal affairs according to their own very strict rules, in the case of disputes between *subak* organisations over rights to land and water, government officials will be called in to mediate; in pre-colonial times these were court posts (Liefrinck 1886: 11 ff; van Setten 1979: 45).

The irrigation system of Mandalay was also constructed with simple tools but sophisticated skills.[17] First built by the Burmese kings, it was subsequently repaired by the British and is still in use today, though over the centuries some of the smaller canals have fallen into disuse, only to be replaced much later by other canals following almost the same bed. Like the Balinese, the Burmese are well aware of the importance of building their canals and conduits at the right gradient, which varies according to soil type, the upper and lower limits being imposed by the necessity of preventing both silting-up and erosion. It is necessary to obtain a flow from the canals which will provide the fields with a total of about 2 m depth of water over the four months' growth period of the rice. A device called the *khaichein*, a graduated board to which a plumb-line is attached, is used to calculate the gradient during the construction of the canals, and the speed of flow and weight of water is measured by floating cups along the stream. The canals, main, feeder and derivation, are worked and maintained by the state, but the small channels, ditches and

Figure 3.5   Wooden flume
(*Nongzheng quanshu*: 17/20b)

drains are the responsibility of the local farmers under the direction of a canal chief, elected by the villagers, who organises corvée labour for maintenance: for every acre of field a farmer must repair 50 feet of bank along both sides of the channel.

Systems of similar antiquity and durability operate in parts of Thailand. In the Chiangmai valley and other valleys of North Thailand, the dams are called *fai* and the contour canals *muang*. There are 'many small-scale traditional systems which are operated and maintained by villagers . . . Accounts of the ancient Chiengmai irrigation systems given in the book *The Laws of King Mengraaj, King of Lannothai*, written in 1292, are sketchy and incomplete but are still apt descriptions of the irrigation works as they exist today' (Potter 1976: 81). Irrigation was essential to the economic viability of the early states of North Thailand, hence the provision of a legal code for water management, but the traditional networks were, and still are, organised and maintained without direct government intervention (Moerman 1968: 51). Although irrigation administrators were appointed only with state approval, like their subordinates they had to be chosen by the villagers, and this remains largely true today even of the irrigation canals of recent construction financed by the government. The traditional *fai* and *muang* networks cannot be expanded beyond limits imposed by rainfall and topography. If it is wished to bring more land under irrigation then integrated headworks systems must be constructed. The new irrigation networks are also gravity-fed systems with weirs and contour canals, but because they are constructed of more modern and expensive materials (concrete rather than brushwood and gabions), the main weirs and water-gates are built and maintained by government workmen instead of villagers (Potter 1976: 83). 'But even in [these] large-scale state-backed irrigation systems the terminal network beyond the lateral channels employs the old *muang*, and the organisation for operation and maintenance has changed little . . . In their form, and in the engineering principles involved, the smale-scale, traditional *fai* and *muang* systems and the larger gravity irrigation systems can be considered similar' (Kaida 1978: 211) (figure 3.6).

Bacdayan documents a case in Northern Luzon where the new dam and contour canals necessary to expand the existing irrigation system in the 1950s were planned, designed and constructed by the local people without any outside help: 'this remarkable engineering feat . . . was made possible only through the people's detailed familiarity with the territory through years of hunting and foraging' (1980: 179).

In Japan it seems that contour-canal irrigation began to develop in the medieval period, gradually surpassing village-based pond irrigation in

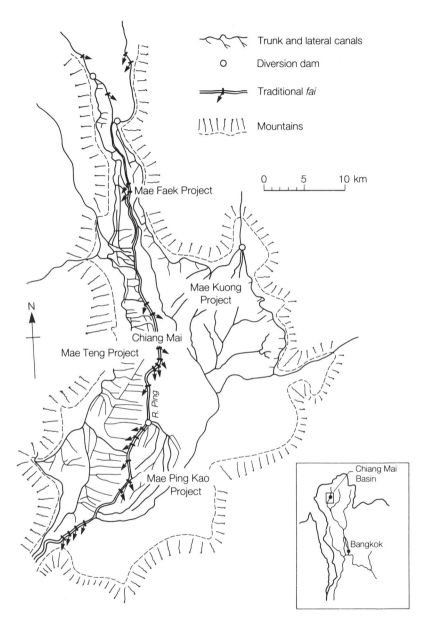

Figure 3.6   Irrigation systems in the Chieng Mai Basin
(from Kaida 1978: 212)

importance as the power of the court nobility waned and local warrior chiefs gained increasing economic and social control over the countryside. Irrigation networks spread from small mountain basins to the larger river plains as the warrior chiefs' ambitions grew: new technology made flood control and canal construction possible even along larger rivers by the fourteenth and fifteenth centuries (Kelly 1982a: 2), and these irrigation networks were improved and added to continuously over the centuries (table 3.2; also Shimpo 1976: ch. 1). A

*Table 3.2   Main canals along the Aka River (Northeast Honshū)
in the Tokugawa period*

	Period of construction	Estimated area served
Daihōji	unknown	40 ha
Gokamura	unknown	200 ha
Sankason	unknown	40 ha
Shōryūjigawa	c.1609	4,100 ha
Shida	c.1610?	510 ha
Nakagawa	c.1615	3,000 ha
Inaba	1607–22; 1689–92	1,150 ha
Kumaide	1661?	40 ha
Etchū	1703–4	40 ha
Ōgawa	1706	260 ha
Tenpō	1831–8	50 ha

Source: Kelly 1982b: 18

major drawback of this type of irrigation, however, is that the water supply is limited, being confined to a single river system (and Japanese rivers are not the mighty giants of the mainland). As the area irrigated by any one network grew, water shortages became endemic, and increasingly strict and complex regulations became necessary to prevent open conflict between different groups of users (see chapter 6). The Japanese traditional networks, like those of Southeast Asia, have survived and expanded over the centuries, and in many cases it has been possible to incorporate them into modernised irrigation systems, solving the problem of water shortage by the construction of a large concrete dam at

the head of the central system. But in such cases, although the consequent technical changes required in irrigation methods have not been enormous, the regulations governing water allocation, which had often remained unchanged for centuries, required considerable modification. In the case of the irrigation network in Shiwa (Northeast Honshū), which was first developed in the early seventeenth century following the establishment of the Tokugawa shogunate, a codification of the irrigation rules was recorded in 1672 and, apart from one minor adjustment in 1895, these remained in effect until the opening of the new Sannōkai dam in 1952 (Kelly 1982a: 55; Shimpo 1976: 21 ff).

Institutional difficulties frequently arise because the modernisation and extension of water control facilities threatens the delicate balance of rights and obligations between water-users. It may even be that farmers oppose certain forms of technical improvement rather than sacrifice their place in the traditional hierarchy established in Japan over centuries of wrangling and rivalry:

As one follows the route of the [Twelve-Gō] canal [in Niiike, Okayama] and its branches today, one comes across a few control and diversion structures of recent date and modern aspect standing side with very humble, primitive arrangements. Prefectural loans have helped to build [two] concrete water gates ... [between which] sections of concrete or rock retaining walls alternate with heavy piles or stakes interwoven with bamboo strips to support the banks. Some diversion ditches that water the fields in the vicinity are no more than holes in the bank. At other places there are crude diversion devices made of piles of submerged rocks and pine trunks laid across the canal, of calculated thickness and depth beneath the surface to control the amount of water diverted. These simple arrangements are readily displaced by accident or high water, and their reinstallation becomes a matter of sometimes acrimonious arbitration; it is difficult to replace them with more precisely measured modern devices, not only because of the expense involved, but because of jealous fears that one side or other will come out on the short end. (Beardsley et al., 1980 edn: 148)

Perhaps the most venerable and impressive of all irrigation networks based on contour-canals is to be found in China, in the Chengdu Basin of Sichuan, where the Min River, a tributary of the Yangzi, flows swiftly down into the plain from the sheer foothills of the Tibetan plateau. The Guanxian irrigation works were started under the direction of Li Bing, who was appointed Governor of Sichuan in 250 BC; he died in about 240 BC and the scheme was completed under his son, Li Ergang, some ten years later. Needham calls Guanxian 'one of the greatest of Chinese engineering operations which, now 2,200 years old, is still in use and makes the deepest impression on all who visit it today. The Guanxian irrigation system made it possible for an area of some 40 by 50 miles to

support a population of about five million people, most of them engaged in farming, and free from the dangers of drought and flood. It can be compared only with the ancient works of the Nile' (1971: 288).

Li Bing tamed the tumultuous floodwaters of the Min with a device of great elegance and simplicity: at the point where the Min reaches the plain, he divided the river into two huge feeder canals by means of a division-head of piled stones called the Fish Snout (figure 3.7). One feeder canal serves only for irrigation, the other also acts as a flood channel. The flow of water into the irrigation canal is regulated by means of dykes and connected spillways so that when the floodwaters rise above the level of safety they automatically spill off into the flood channel.

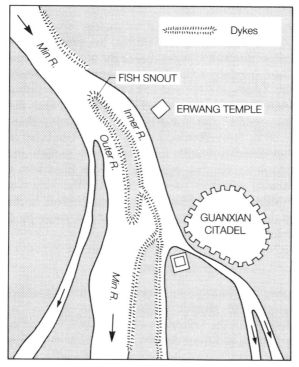

Figure 3.7   The Fish Snout at Dujiangyan
(after Wuhan 1979: 68)

Each year there is a cycle of operations corresponding to the flow of water . . . Throughout the centuries, the advice of Li Bing to clear out the beds and keep the dykes and spillways low has been faithfully followed, and if it has been

possible to preserve the system so closely as he left it, this is partly because the river is not extremely silt-laden, and partly because its annual fluctuations have permitted incessant and effective maintenance. Every year, about mid-October, the annual repairs begin. A long row of wooden tripods is placed across the outer feeder canal at its inlet and covered with bamboo matting plastered with mud to form a cofferdam, thus diverting all the flow into the inner canal. The bed of the outer canal is then excavated very actively to a predetermined depth, and any necessary repairs to the division-heads are carried out with the aid of gabions. About mid-February, the stockade-dam is removed and re-erected at the intake of the inner canal, so that all water flows to the right, and similar maintenance of the inner system is effected. On the 5th of April, the ceremonial removal of the cofferdam marks the opening of the irrigation system and gives opportunity for a general celebration, even in these days of slide-rules and plans for power-stations. (Needham 1971: 293)

It is significant that the original technology used to construct the Guanxian works, while cheap and simple, has proved effective enough not only to allow for gradual expansion of the network over two millennia but also to render largely redundant more modern irrigation technology and materials. Between 1949 and 1959 the area under irrigation almost doubled, from half a million to 930,000 acres, and the Irrigation Authority envisaged an eventual irrigated area of no less than 4.4 million acres (ibid.: 289). Nevertheless, when I visited Guanxian in 1980, the works still remained essentially unchanged both in form and construction. Wooden posts, bamboo mats and gabions filled with stones were still the essential materials used to maintain the Fish Snout and to control the water flow; the only obvious concession to the twentieth century was that the inner bank of the river just above its division had now been reinforced with concrete.

'Creek' irrigation[18]

The tank, pond and contour-canal systems we have described so far are basically designed to provide irrigation alone; this means they can generally supplement the seasonal water shortages without necessitating recourse to pumps or lifting devices: gravity-flow is sufficient. But in areas such as the great river deltas, where the land is flat and swampy and the flow of water sluggish, drainage becomes as important as irrigation. In deltaic areas where the water-flow is very slow, 'creeks' serve not only as irrigation channels and drainage ditches but also as storage for the water. Since the land has no natural slope which will allow the water to run from field to field inside an irrigation unit, all fields must take their supply of water directly from the creeks. This means that an intricate network of waterways must be developed to serve all the fields – usually

each network will take its water directly from a river and discharge it into the same river further downstream – and a rather high proportion of the surface area is occupied by waterways rather than fields. To ensure adequate supplies of water it is necessary to dredge the bed of the main river as well as the creeks, and dykes have to be built around the fields to prevent flooding. Of course since the creeks are below the level of the land, it is necessary to raise the water into the fields by pumps or other devices.

It is not usually possible for individual peasants or even groups of farmers to construct the large, complex and coordinated networks of ditches and channels that will convert deltaic flood-plains to fertile rice-fields. Not surprisingly, this 'creek' irrigation as the Japanese call it was a relatively late development which depended on considerable investment by very wealthy landowners or even the state.

This can clearly be seen in the Chinese case of the Yangzi, or Jiangnan, Delta. Although the inland areas of the Delta had become an important agricultural region in Tang times (seventh to ninth centuries), the marshy coastal zones could not easily be occupied unless extensive hydraulic works were carried out to prevent flooding and salinisation, and for this new hydraulic techniques had to be developed as well as administrative skills.

As mentioned in appendix B, by the eleventh century the Song state was under considerable pressure to increase agricultural production in the Yangzi area, and the high fertility of the land already reclaimed by wealthy landowners from lakesides and river-banks probably gave impetus to the official policy of deltaic reclamation which began in the early Song. The techniques of constructing dyked and poldered fields had already been mastered (chapter 2), but the design and maintenance of intricate water networks still presented problems. The Song *Dynastic History* for 1158 tells us that in previous times creeks had been opened up in great numbers joining the Taihu Lake to nearby rivers or to the sea, but that now they had all silted up because the troops in charge of their maintenance had been withdrawn, and the peasants' fields had in consequence become submerged. The estimated cost to restore them to their former state was more than 3.3 million man-days, an equal number of strings of cash and over 100,000 bushels of grain. Thereafter, 24 creeks were opened up between the Taihu Lake and the Yangzi, and 12 more were opened up directly to the sea; according to the statesman Fan Zhongyan some 6,000 or 7,000 farmer-soldiers[19] were settled in the Suzhou area specially to maintain the system and prevent flooding (Nishioka 1981: 127). Large areas, then, were already being reclaimed during the Song (e.g. Elvin 1978: 81 on the Ningbo region).

This is reflected in the agricultural treatises of the time, which devote long sections to dyking fields, to water management and to water-raising devices. The square-pallet chain-pump had been known in China for over a thousand years, as had many other water-lifting devices like the *noria* or 'Persian wheel', and the swape or well-sweep, but their use spread rapidly during the Song (Needham 1965: 530 ff; Li Jiannong 1957: 28 ff). The Song also saw the publication of five works specially devoted to water control, *shuili*; during the 90 years of the ensuing Yuan dynasty (1279–1368) nine works on water control were published; during the three centuries of the Ming dynasty (1368–1644) no less than 81 works on water control are known to have been produced (Shen Baixian 1979: table 5.1, pp. 517 ff). While the spread of water-pumps demonstrates that there must have been a steady expansion of creek-irrigated fields, the explosion of books on water control proves the keen interest taken by government officials and the landowning class alike in this subject.

As we have already said, cooperation across the board was necessary to reclaim and maintain large tracts of swampy land at the mouths of large rivers. Only the state had sufficient resources and authority to organise and finance the dredging of the main rivers, using corvée labour to carry out the work.[20] During the early Ming (up to about 1500) the dredging of creeks and repairing of dykes was organised by local landowners, most of whom resided on their land at that period. The labour was provided by their tenants and was levied according to the length of their land bordering on the creeks and dykes. Landlords also organised collective drainage, a practice which remained necessary until the adoption of pumping-machines in the twentieth century. So in the Song and early Ming state authorities, landowners and peasant farmers all cooperated to keep the fertile dyked fields in working order. As the saying went: 'If Suzhou and Taihu Lake have a good harvest, then all China will be well-fed' (cited Nishioka 1981: 150).

But the Song and early Ming were periods of unprecedented economic expansion, and as the monetary economy advanced two phenomena developed which necessitated radical changes in the management of creek irrigation in the Yangzi Delta. The first was the growth of a class of absentee 'gentry' landowners, who by the later Ming greatly outnumbered resident landlords. These gentry landlords, thanks to their position as bureaucrats, had sufficient income to acquire much larger amounts of land than the resident landlords, whose incomes were restricted to their rents. A would-be reforming official writing in the mid-sixteenth century took as a standard case a landlord owning 1000 *mu* (approximately 60 ha), and thus having at least 100 tenants on his

land (Hamashima 1980: 87). However these tenants were not available as corvée labourers for the maintenance of local irrigation works, because as bureaucrats the gentry landlords were exempted from all corvée responsibilities. Furthermore, as the economy of the Yangzi Delta became increasingly commercialised and the relative price of rice fell, peasant farmers relied more and more on commercial crops (such as cotton) and on small-scale commodity production to earn cash with which to pay their rent, formerly often payable in kind.[21] The slack season for rice cultivation had been the time when irrigation work was carried out, but it was no longer a slack season as far as peasant farmers were concerned, and they stood to lose heavily if they were obliged to give up their time to irrigation repairs. The burden on the independent peasants, and on the tenants of the remaining resident landlords, was increased by the non-participation of gentry landlords in corvée labour schemes.

In order to prevent the total deterioration of the creek irrigation networks and to diminish popular resentment and antagonism towards the gentry, Ming officials worked out a series of reform measures. First, the privilege of corvée exemption was denied in as many cases as possible. Secondly, a landowner's corvée responsibilities were calculated not according to the length of land beside the waterways, as hitherto, but according to the total area, a much more equitable arrangement now that the concentration of land-ownership was increasing. And finally, not only were gentry landlords obliged to provide corvée labour by sending their tenants to join in maintenance work, but the government guaranteed the tenants some compensation for their work, issuing them with ration cards for rice which they then claimed from their landlord; in case of default, the tenant was allowed to deduct double the amount from his rent. Needless to say, reforms of this kind were fiercely opposed by the gentry landlords, but Geng Ju, the official who proposed them in this particular form, managed to put them into effect in the region under his jurisdiction in the early seventeenth century. They were then gradually adopted throughout the Delta region, and continued to provide a model up to the twentieth century.

It is interesting that in the village near Shanghai described by Fei in the 1930s drainage of the dyked *yu* fields was still carried out with communal labour. With the entrenchment over the centuries of absentee landlordism, tenants had in fact gained rights of permanent tenancy approximating to ownership, and so the labour contributions were calculated on the basis of farm size (Fei 1939: 172). No technical changes had taken place in the system of creek irrigation until the very recent introduction of small modern pumping machines, which at the

time that Fei carried out his study was presenting the villagers with considerable organisational problems. The advantages offered by collectivisation in such circumstances are obvious.

In Japan creek irrigation is confined to the few flat deltas, most notably the Saga Plain in Kyūshū, which has been the focus of intensive study by Japanese scholars, since it is considered to be the region which had the most advanced rice-growing technology in the 1920s and 1930s. Traditional creek irrigation was firmly established in the Saga Plain in the mid-Tokugawa period, when the local *daimyō* family, the Nabeshima, carried out extensive improvements to the local canal network (Francks 1983: 102). Irrigation and drainage were extremely arduous tasks, relying on constant use of man-powered water-wheels similar to the Chinese square-pallet chain-pumps; Saga farmers hired labourers to man the pumps in the high season (Kelly 1982a: 34). 'Rationalisation' began in the 1920s, as the development of mining and industries in Kyūshū attracted the labourers away from agriculture. In response to the resulting severe labour shortage, which coincided with a boom in rice prices, local government officials and prefectural Farmers' Associations, *nōkai*, working in consultation with the farmers, began to investigate suitable methods of mechanising pumping. After several experiments which failed, a suitable small electric pump was developed which could cover units of between 5 and 20 ha (Francks 1983: 119), usually consisting of plots belonging to a number of farmers. The pumps were operated jointly by the cultivators of the fields they served, so that each individual farmer might participate in several pump groups. The households in each pumping unit were responsible for providing the labour required to set up the new pumping facilities, but the local Irrigation Society or *kumiaia* bore all the capital costs of installation and management, and was responsible for the initial designing of the infrastructure. The installation of the electric pumps reduced labour inputs for irrigation from 70 man-days/ha in 1909 to 22 man-days/ha in 1938 (Ishikawa 1981: 16, table 1–3).

In Tonkin, where the danger of flooding was acute, the few modern irrigation works constructed under French colonial rule were akin to creeks: 'des canaux 'bas', qui peuvent à l'occasion servir au drainage et qui ne risquent point d'inonder les rizières environnantes' (Gourou 1936: 105). These new irrigation facilities regularised the supply of water, but in the absence of mechanical pumps the labour requirements were no less than those of the traditional irrigation networks: in a good field about 11 man-days were necessary, using a swape, to provide 10 cm of water (the optimal depth for growing rice-plants) for 1 ha of land, and much more time was required on most land (ibid.: 103). But most of the

Tonkin Delta had been under intensive rice cultivation for centuries; the dykes which prevented the Red River from flooding were very ancient, and had been reinforced and properly organised as early as the Trân dynasty in the thirteenth century; a programme of canal-building was initiated in the fifteenth century, while sea-walls were used to reclaim the salt-flats from the fourteenth century, and especially large areas were reclaimed under the direction of Nguyên Công Trú in the early nineteenth century (ibid.: 130, 135, 207). By the time the French took over Tonkin there was little scope left for reclaiming land or extending water control (Robequain 1939: 249). In Cochinchina, in the Mekong Delta, however, the situation was quite different.

Cochinchina was practically uninhabited when the French arrived, but it clearly had great potential for development as a rice-exporting region.[22] The French invested heavily in water control from 1870 on, setting up a system of primary, secondary and tertiary canals, and the area under rice cultivation increased fourfold between 1880 and 1937 (table 3.3). To

Table 3.3   Rice in French Cochinchina

	1880	1900	1937	Increase 1880–1937 (%)
Cultivated area (ha)	522,000	1,175,000	2,200,000	421
Exports from Saigon (tonnes)	284,000	747,000	1,548,000	545
Pop. of Cochinchina	1,679,000	2,937,000	4,484,000	267

Source: Robequain 1939: 243

recoup the costs, large concessions of land were made to 'Europeans' (many of whom were in fact naturalised Annamites), as well as to companies. To get the land off their hands quickly the government sold at low prices and in large units, many rice estates being between 500 and 1,000 ha in size (Robequain 1939: 96); in 1930 some 120 French *colons* held around 100,000 ha of land between them (ibid.: 214). The labour force consisted mainly of migrants from the Northern provinces of Tonkin and Annam, who were taken on as tenants under a bailiff, and given lots of about 10 ha (Brocheux 1971: 149).

Although the investment in water control considerably increased rice

production in Cochinchina, cultivation methods were extensive and yields lower than the fertility of the soil and the abundance of water might have led one to expect.[23] Most of the migrants came from regions where intensive cultivation techniques were practised, but when they took up their tenancies most of them were destitute and had to rely on the landlord to provide tools, draft animals and seed-grain, as well as loans of rice and money; their lots of 10 ha were immense compared with the farms of Tonkin, where the population density was such that a majority of peasants owned less than 0.2 ha (Gourou 1936: 360), and the shortage of labour in Cochinchina meant that even if tenants had been in a position to hire or exchange labour there simply was not enough available to practise intensive methods. In fact, given the prevalence of absentee landlordism and the poverty of the migrant peasants, landown-ers found it easier to make their money by usury than by high farming: 'Ces fermiers sans ressources, souvent instables et inquiets, reçoivent des propriétaires des avances en argent et en grains. C'est sur l'intérêt de ces prêts *autant et plus que* sur l'amélioration progressive des rizières que compte le propriétaire' (Feyssal 1934: 18; my emphasis). Even with low rice yields, the landowners did extremely well: the investment in canal-building in Cochinchina cost about 48 piastres/ha and gave a return of over 40% (Henry and de Visme 1928: 58). The peasants, on the other hand, did badly: not only were they debt-ridden and harassed by frequent bad harvests,[24] but furthermore poor seed-selection and cultivation methods meant the rice produced was of low quality. Indochinese rice found difficulty competing with Thai and Burmese rices on international markets, and this led to a severe crisis during the Depression (Henry and de Visme 1928; Henry 1932).

The Lower Delta of Siam too had remained almost uninhabited until it was developed to produce rice for export in the late nineteenth century, when creek-style waterways and poldered fields were constructed in large numbers. Under natural conditions the Delta is not only uninhabited but uninhabitable: in the rainy season the whole area of a million hectares is submerged, and in the dry season the mud parches and cracks and 'desert conditions prevail on a large scale. People cannot even find enough water to drink' (Takaya 1978: 187). The hardships suffered by early migrants to the region are vividly described by Hanks (1972). But although the Delta presents few attractions as a human habitation, it is an ideal natural habitat for rice, being almost uniformly flat and subject each year to very gradual flooding, the waters eventually reaching a depth of about 1 m – in fact the Delta is by far the most favourable natural environment for rice in the whole of Thailand (Takaya 1978: 181).

The Siamese state had been exporting rice grown in the northern regions to Malacca and elsewhere since the sixteenth century. Until the mid-nineteenth century all international trade from Siam, including that of rice, was in the hands of the king, who obtained the rice as a tax in kind on agricultural produce – the *akon* tax or tithe (Ishii 1978b: 32). But with the signing of the Bowring Treaty between Britain and Siam in 1855 the royal trade monopoly came to an end, with especially important implications for the rice trade: 'Through this treaty, rice exports were liberalised and grew rapidly in response to the increasing demand on the international rice market; accompanying this, rice production expanded sharply, particularly in the young Delta' (ibid.: 39).

Canals to provide rapid and efficient transport between the inland regions and the Gulf of Siam had first been constructed through the Delta region in the Ayutthya period, but in order to open the Delta up and to provide irrigation and drainage for rice cultivation it was necessary to expand the network considerably. While the corvée system had provided the labour force for such work in earlier periods, from the mid-nineteenth century a more reliable and productive work-force of Chinese immigrants was employed (Tanabe 1978: 49). This cost vast sums of money: for instance the construction of the 27 km Mahasawat canal required a total investment of 88,120 baht, most of which was provided by Rama IV, who then (for the first time in Siamese history) claimed ownership of the land bordering the canal (some 2,500 ha), which he granted to his sons and daughters to use as rice-land. It was supposed to be cultivated by corvée peasants, *bao phrai*, or debt-slaves, *that*. Other canals were financed by nobles or wealthy Chinese, who also claimed possession of land along the banks (ibid.: 154). But much of the land remained uncultivated, and that which was brought under cultivation was underproductive: it was not until the sytem of corvée and debt slavery began to disintegrate in the late nineteenth century that the Delta began to realise its agricultural potential. In 1877 the government published a document entitled 'The Regulation of Canal Excavation' in which the wastefulness and underproductivity of the old ownership system was criticised; a new policy had been introduced in the 1870s whereby migrant free peasants were encouraged to contribute their labour or capital to the construction of new canals, in return for which they were granted ownership of a tract of land constituting a household farm, together with tax concessions; they also had to pay a canal fee for the irrigation water (ibid.: 58 ff). As a result of these institutional changes, large tracts of the Delta were swiftly brought under cultivation in the 1870s and 1880s, but as the productivity and thus the value of the land rose, the peasants began to lose their relatively privileged status. Not

only did a lively market in land grow up and the pawning and mortgaging
of their land by peasants become frequent, but the government changed
its policy of undertaking canal construction as public works. Instead it
gave concessions to wealthy nobles, Chinese, or companies, who made
their profit by selling the land:

> In 1888 the Siam Canals, Land and Irrigation Company, whose shareholders
> were royalty and Chinese, began construction of a canal system and land
> reclamation in a vast tract of wasteland in the delta flat region to the northeast of
> Bangkok. In this famous Rangsit canal system, the government contract
> recognised that all unowned land within forty *sen* (sixteen hundred metres) on
> either side of the new canals would become the possession of the company from
> the time of construction. In this way the company was able to sell huge areas of
> land to royalty, noble officials, and peasants.
>
> The Rangsit canal system comprised a trunk canal, the Rangsit canal, and a
> lattice of several tens of canals. The Rangsit canal differed from the conventional
> canals in having lock gates at either end at the junction with the rivers, through
> which the water level could be controlled and the drainage and irrigation
> function raised. And the project was not only epoch-making in its technological
> aspects; historically it was greatly significant in the process of disorganisation of
> the old system, marking the affirmation of landownership of the adjoining lands
> that led to the development of an extensive new landlord-tenant system aimed at
> the collection of landrent. (Tanabe 1978: 65)

Here is a clear instance of the way in which technological advance can
disrupt social organisation.

It is interesting that although otherwise the rice economy of Malaya
was generally much later in its development than that of Siam, the
northern kingdom of Kedah became a rice-exporter at an early date, and
it was not long before the *raja* initiated land reclamation schemes to
expand production.[25]

The Portuguese traveller Pires had mentioned as early as 1512 that
Kedah had rice in quantities, but rice only became an important export
crop after the founding of the East India Company settlement at Penang
seriously threatened Kedah's control over trade in the region. The ruler
decided to ensure his wealth through a new form of trade: the export of
Kedah rice to Penang and other ports. The capital, which had hitherto
been situated on the estuary of the Muda River, was moved inland to
Alor Setar, on the flat, flooded plains which are the heart of the Muda
scheme today. By 1785 Kedah's total rice exports amounted to 80,000
piculs (over 10,000 tons), and by 1821 she was exporting that amount to
Penang alone. Migrants from Patani in Southern Siam and from the
Indonesian islands had started reclaiming swampland in the Muda plain
for paddy-fields in the sixteenth and seventeenth centuries, and a

proportion of their crop went to the ruling class as tax. To increase their rice revenues the Kedah rulers were prepared to construct canals, which served the dual purpose of draining the swampy land and of facilitating transport of the tax rice. The first canal was built in 1664–5, an extension was constructed in 1738 and two further canals had been built by 1816, thus providing a large area of the Muda plain with the basic infrastructure for the colonisation of padi-land. These early canals were built with corvée labour, *krah*, and although the settlers had rights of usufruct over the land they opened up, its ownership remained vested in the state. The state thus incurred very few costs for this early reclamation programme, but derived considerable benefits. After a period of disruption following the Siamese invasion of 1821, the Kedah rulers were anxious to encourage the peasants who had fled to return and new migrants to settle in the region. In 1885 the Prime Minister built a main north-south drainage canal 20 miles long, at a cost of $250,000 Straits Settlement dollars; several more followed before indirect British rule was imposed in 1909, and by 1915 Kedah had a network of 250 km of drainage canals.

This network, together with a certain amount of gravity-fed irrigation provided by temporary brushwood dams across the rivers, permitted the cultivation of a single crop of padi in the main season. In the 1960s a major plan was drawn up to double the area of rice cultivation and to provide sufficient water for double-cropping throughout the scheme. The increase in the water supply was to be achieved principally through the construction of two large dams providing gravity-fed irrigation, thus transforming the Muda plain from an area of predominantly creek irrigation (or 'controlled drainage irrigation') to one of predominantly gravity-flow irrigation (Taylor 1981: 41, table 2.6):

The construction of infrastructural facilities took place between 1966 and 1970, at a cost of $245 million [Malaysian] ($2,550 per ha). The principal infrastructural components were the Muda and Pudu dams and their associated reservoirs, connected by a 6.8 km tunnel; a conveyance system comprising an existing river channel, a diversion barrage, 115 km of main conveyance channels, and several regulators; an internal network comprising 965 km of primary and secondary distribution canals spaced from 1.2 to 2.0 km apart, 865 km of drainage channels, 770 km of laterite surface road, and many minor structures; and a 100 km coastal embankment to control tidal intrusion and enable drainage outflow from the scheme. The Muda scheme is designed to receive about one-third of its water supply from streamflow, rainfall, and the Muda and Pudu reservoirs respectively. (Taylor 1981: 44)

The scheme now covers an area of 96,000 ha. Management is provided by a special body, the Muda Agricultural Development

Authority (MADA), set up in 1970. Compared with other water control schemes in Malaysia, the Muda scheme has performed well: double-cropping and the adoption of new varieties and modern inputs are almost universal, and by 1975–6 mean annual yields of padi had risen to 7.66 t/ha, compared to 3.63 t/ha in the Kemubu irrigation scheme (see below), and 1.12 t/ha in Pahang, where water control facilities are more or less non-existent (ibid.: 43). The land consolidation which accompanied the extension of the canal infrastructure in the Muda area has facilitated mechanisation, and even large-scale mechanisation, on the scheme (Jegatheesan 1980), and the rapid commercialisation of padi production, with the increasing capital requirements which this entails, is believed by a number of observers to have set in train the differentiation of the Muda peasantry and the emergence of capitalist farming (de Koninck 1978; Gibbons et al. 1980; Lim et al. 1981: p 2). This will be discussed at greater length in chapter 6.

Pump irrigation schemes

In areas where the land is flat and the water-table low, drainage presents few problems. However the provision of irrigation water has, in the past, been next to impossible. The only exception was well irrigation.

Before the dissemination of artesian and diesel pumps which made them an attractive alternative to the capturing of surface water, wells were more typical of dry regions than of high rainfall areas.[26] In regions where there was a long dry season, as in medieval Ceylon, these limited sources of irrigation water, serving individual farmers or small groups, might stand in direct contrast to vast and complex gravity-fed irrigation networks whose growth and decay often seemed symbolic of the states which constructed them.

Typically an individual farmer digs a well on his own land and uses it only for his own purposes. If the water-table is low, then animal power or diesel pumps may be necessary to raise the water to ground level, and the necessary capital investment may limit the use of wells to richer farmers and landlords, unless the state provides loans or subsidies (Vaidyanathan 1983: 18). Networks centred on wells seldom attain the size of irrigation networks served by rivers or other types of surface water.[27]

Pasternak (1972a: 27–34; 1972b: 205) describes the social changes which occurred when the government installed pumps in a Taiwanese village in the mid-1950s. Previously the villagers had relied on an integrated irrigation system, run by an elected irrigation association. As pressures on the supplies and the demand for water grew, sharp conflicts became endemic and the irrigation association played a crucial role in

arbitrating over disputes. Once the new pumps were installed and came to constitute the chief source of irrigation water, the role of the irrigation association dwindled and real authority developed upon 'natural groups consisting of the twenty-five farmers who drew water from a single pump' (ibid.).

The invention of powerful mechanical pumps has permitted the development of irrigation facilities where none were possible before. This is the case of the Kelantan plain on the east coast of peninsular Malaysia. Rice cultivation techniques which were advanced compared to the rest of Malaya, by which transplanted wet rice was grown in fields bunded to retain the rainwater, were probably introduced from Siam in about the sixteenth century, but the shortage of water meant that only one crop could be grown a year. Furthermore in many places the water was not sufficient to grow even one crop of wet rice: instead dry rice was grown by various methods (Hill 1951; Dobby 1957). It is notable that wet-rice land was valued according to its elevation, which determined the amount of available water and so, to a great extent, land productivity: low-lying land, *tanah dalam*, was the most productive, intermediate land, *tanah serderhana*, gave lower yields of wet rice, while high land, *tanah darat*, could only be used for dry rice (Bray and Robertson 1980: 226). Despite their industry and skill, Kelantanese farmers could only obtain low yields of wet rice, averaging about 230 *gantang*/acre (1.5 t/ha); dry-rice yields were often as low as 150 *gantang*/acre (less than 1 t/ha), and their harvests were extremely vulnerable to drought (Haynes 1932: 14; Baker 1936: 20; Fedn of Malaya 1953: 84).

The first small irrigation schemes in Kelantan were set up in the 1930s under the newly formed Department of Irrigation and Drainage, but they could only be established in a few specially favourable areas (Haynes 1933: 13; Moubray 1937: 23). No significant progress had been made by the early 1950s, when the Rice Production Committee received numerous complaints about the uncertainty of the water supply and the unsatisfactory arrangements for its control (Fedn of Malaya 1953: 87). However in 1967–73 the federal government invested about $75 million Malaysian ($3,770 per ha) in infrastructural work to create the Kemubu irrigation scheme, of about 19,000 ha, which together with four smaller schemes totalling some 12,500 ha is now managed by the Kemubu Agricultural Development Authority (KADA), created in 1973. The water is all pumped from the Kelantan River:

The Kemubu Scheme infrastructure involves the Kemubu pumphouse with five diesel pumps, each having an hydraulic capacity of 250 cusecs; two private-sector pumps with a capacity of 275 cusecs; 374 km of irrigation canals, almost

one-half of which are tertiaries; 344 km of drainage channels and a variety of structures to control and facilitate the movement of water within the irrigation distribution system, including tertiary offtakes that are gated and equipped with measuring devices (although not all function properly). The scheme has an irrigation canal density of about 18m per ha and is designed so that each tertiary offtake serves an irrigation unit of about 20 ha. Prior to the current phase of upgrading irrigation facilities in Malaysia's large-scale schemes, the irrigation infrastructure in Kemubu was probably the most extensive in Malaysia. The many micro-undulations in the scheme's topography, however, make timely and equitable distribution of irrigation water throughout the scheme area difficult. (Taylor 1981: 45)

Double-cropping is now possible in most of the Kelantan plain, and although yields are still much lower than in the Muda area, averaging only 3.63 t/ha in 1975–6 (ibid.: 43), most farming families now have an assured subsistence – indeed 50–65% of families market padi in varying amounts (Shand and Mohd. Ariff 1983: 241). But average yields still do not exceed 2.5 t/ha even in the main season, and often drop sharply in the off-season if, as is not infrequently the case, there are difficulties with the irrigation. Despite a substantial increase of 36% in the Guaranteed Minimum Price of padi in 1980, in the following year there was a 35% drop in average padi output per farm, from 4.3 to 2.8 t (ibid.: 177). This can be attributed partly to a preference for more remunerative off-farm employment, and partly to the difficulties farmers often experience if they do try to produce two crops of padi a year. The improved varieties grown in Kelantan do not mature particularly fast, and in consequence the official irrigation schedule is so intensive that farmers often fall behind in their operations and have to miss a season. Or they may be obliged to miss a season if there is a pump failure (Bray and Robertson 1980: 234). The uniformity imposed by the schedule no longer allows the labour bottlenecks of transplanting and harvesting to be avoided through staggered timing and labour exchange, and family labour must therefore be supplemented with hired labour. Three-quarters of Kemubu padi farmers felt they had suffered from labour shortage in 1981, and two-thirds hired extra labour to cope, thus reducing their already meagre profit-margins; for a number of reasons, mechanisation does not seem to offer the solution at present (Shand and Mohd. Ariff 1983: 105; 119 ff).

Another problem Kemubu farmers have had to face is the change in value of their land. While formerly low-lying land was the most valuable, now it is often so waterlogged that it can only be cultivated in the off-season, if at all. Large areas of dry land formerly used for growing rubber, fruit, tobacco or vegetables, which are relatively profitable

sources of income, now lie below the water-table and must be used instead as poor-quality rice-land (Bray and Robertson 1980: 232). The reduced opportunities for generating farm income from crops other than rice was a contributing factor in the drop of overall incomes of 12% between 1979 and 1980, from $3236 to $2862 Malaysian (Shand and Mohd. Ariff 1983: 221). It is hardly surprising that young people in Kelantan prefer almost any employment to padi farming, and as they leave the region in search of work more and more rice-land lies fallow.

Each tertiary offtake in the Kemubu scheme serves an irrigation unit of about 20 ha, and in the absence of a proper network of quaternary channels, the majority of fields receive their water from neighbouring fields rather than directly from an irrigation channel (Taylor 1981: 163). Generally, the nearer a field is to a secondary irrigation channel, the higher its yields, and the value of land is changing accordingly (Bray and Robertson 1980: 232). Farmers often express frustration at the impossibility of controlling water effectively at terminal level – not to mention the much wider problem of pump failure: the total area of over 19,000 ha is served by only seven pumps, each of which thus supplies over 2,500 ha (ibid.: 164). A programme of terminal-level improvement is envisaged by KADA; in the meantime, groups of farmers often cooperate to dig small irrigation channels to provide a better supply to their fields (pers. obs.).

A rather different problem presented itself at first in the Muda scheme and in other Malaysian schemes. At the outset MADA staff experienced serious difficulties in enlisting the support of the Muda farmers in irrigation work. Conflicts over water between individuals or groups of farmers were frequent and sometimes fatal (Afifuddin 1978: 277), and it was feared that the lack of traditional village cooperative organisations would constitute a serious stumbling-block to development. Discussing similar problems in the nearby Krian irrigation scheme, Horii suggests that this is in large part attributable to the lack of any native experience of irrigation organisation; 'the weakness and immaturity of self-governing organisation and village solidarity in traditional Malay society were probably largely responsible for the problems associated with rice irrigation in the country' (1981: 36).

While Horii's explanation does carry certain condescending overtones of the Japanocentric concept of 'tightly structured and loosely-structured societies', it is certainly true that where farmers have no previous experience of water control they tend to remain indifferent to the struggles of technicians and administrators trying to increase the efficiency of a new scheme. Studies of state irrigation schemes in Thailand refer to the 'minimal' level of peasant participation and to local

farmers' lack of both knowledge and enthusiasm (Kaida 1978: 223, 231). This does not seem particularly surprising, however loosely or tightly the society may be structured, if the scheme is a completely new implantation. One might expect that the problems would be greatest where new, modern pump-irrigation schemes were installed rather than where pre-existing gravity-flow or other types of network were expanded and modernised. But of course it is not unknown for officialdom to encounter local obstructiveness when attempts are made to introduce innovations into a 'tightly-structured' society with long experience of water control, as we saw earlier in the case of Niiike in Japan. And speaking of Northern Thailand which has, as we have seen, a long tradition of local-level water control, Wijeyewardene maintains that 'both government and farmers consider the provision of irrigation water a duty of the state' (1973: 99).

On balance, however, it seems that local experience is to be valued rather than distrusted. Discussing China, Vermeer points out that certain regions 'had a long-standing experience in managing and distributing the scarce and often unreliable river water supply for irrigation. This experience, both in management and in irrigation techniques, is not easily taught. Examples that are quite illustrative have been given in China of the differences between old irrigation districts and newly-established ones in the successful use of irrigation facilities' (1977: 133). In their efforts to overcome local ignorance and inertia, governments have sometimes resorted to bringing in skilled outsiders to inject a little knowledge and enthusiasm. In the sixteenth and seventeenth centuries, Ming and Qing officials brought farmers skilled in irrigation methods from the Yangzi Delta up to Zhili (the area around Peking) to teach intensive rice-farming methods to the northerners who had been settled on newly constructed irrigation schemes in the province (Brook 1982: 684). Ecological conditions were against them, however, notably the danger of salinisation; similar attempts to establish wet-rice cultivation in North China since the establishment of the People's Republic have also met with very limited success (Vermeer 1977: 165, 233). Similarly successive Indonesian governments have encouraged Balinese and Javanese rice-farmers to migrate to the Outer Islands where their skills in water control and intensive cultivation methods would set a good example to less industrious local farmers (p. 44 above). The success of this particular policy is difficult to gauge. An alternative is to set up an institutional framework which encourages, or even compels, local farmers to participate actively in irrigation groups which meet the precise technical demands of the system, as happened in Taiwan in the 1950s (Ishikawa 1981: 62).

But the flexibility and good sense of the farmers themselves should not be underestimated. The Muda scheme is a case in point: despite their initial gloom, MADA officials were delighted to find that 'after a faltering start, the peasantry manifested high resiliency and ability to adapt, improve and innovate. This was very much a result of increased economic incentives and the formation of a new, workable organisational framework [the Farmers' Associations, which provide a forum for discussion between officials and farmers in Malaysia]. As a result, the infrastructure even though absent at the critical tertiary levels was made to work productively although at levels below its potential' (Afifuddin 1978: 289).

Patterns of growth and change

Let us now propose a few generalisations on historical trends in the evolution of water control systems. For a start, these Asian systems display a surprising degree of technical and institutional continuity.

Asian rice cultivation seems to have begun in naturally marshy areas and spread rapidly into regions where rainfall was sufficient to grow a crop in small bunded fields. From there it was but a step to the construction of small-scale gravity-flow irrigation networks like the pond-fed or canal-fed systems typical of the hills of East and Southeast Asia. The skills and techniques involved could be developed to a high degree of sophistication which could easily be applied to larger-scale works based on the same technical principles, the huge tank-fed irrigation networks of medieval Ceylon and Angkor, for instance, or the *fai* and *muang* (dam and contour canal) networks which ensured the economic survival of the early states of Northern Thailand. Small communal units could be integrated into larger networks, or basic techniques applied to constructing works on a larger scale, the chief difference being that as networks grew in size and complexity, management usually diverged so that two distinct levels appeared. First, there was a local level of irrigation officers, usually chosen by their villages, though sometimes the posts were hereditary; they were responsible for regular maintenance and management, the labour and materials being provided by the farmers who benefited from the water. Secondly, there were state officers appointed at national level, who were responsible for coordination, for the organisation of large-scale construction projects (which were often financed by the central state), for the maintenance of the primary waterways and for arbitration in disputes between localities.

As water control systems become larger and more complex, the higher

administrative levels acquire an increasingly dominant role. In cases such as the development of networks of tank-and-canal irrigation in medieval Ceylon and Burma, this process was in fact reversible: the technical and financial requirements remained divisible so that, when centralised control of the hydraulic network disintegrated, elements of the system (in this case village tanks) could still survive independently. But some types of water control system cannot be subdivided. The combined irrigation-and-drainage networks which we have considered under the heading of 'creek irrigation' depend for their efficacy on intricate and extensive canal networks which spread excess water over a sufficiently wide area to prevent deep flooding and to allow control by pumping. 'Creek irrigation' networks are not subdivisible below a certain size requiring considerable capital investment and coordinated organisation. In China, where the state had a long-standing tradition of investment in agricultural projects, the first systems of creek irrigation were established in the Yangzi Delta in medieval times; in Tokugawa Japan it was feudal lords anxious to secure their personal economic base who financed creek irrigation projects in the few deltaic plains. But the huge, marshy flood-plains of the Mekong and Chao Praya had to await the mid-nineteenth century growth of international rice markets before they were drained and opened up to rice-farmers, often at considerable expense.

Since the late nineteenth century the governments of almost all Asian states have taken an increasingly active role in expanding and developing national water control facilities. It is often supposed that 'modern' hydraulic works represent a qualitative break with 'traditional' systems, but this is an exaggerated point of view. It is true that certain types of hydraulic network, for example the *fai* and *muang* networks of Northern Thailand, cannot be expanded by traditional means beyond certain limits imposed by rainfall and topography, but the old network of dams and contour canals requires little modification to be incorporated into a new, expanded network served by modern headworks (Kaida 1978: 211). In the Malaysian state of Kedah, the famous new Muda irrigation scheme represents the extension and improvement of an infrastructure of drainage canals initiated by the Sultan in 1664 and subsequently developed by private interests. Similarly in China and Japan a great number of modern hydraulic networks represent the coordination and integration of smaller traditional networks, often supplemented by the construction of one or more large reservoirs or headworks (Gustafsson 1984: 144); it has been calculated that 70.9% of ponds and reservoirs and 73.7% of the river irrigation systems which existed in Japan in the 1960s had been constructed before the Meiji Restoration of 1868 (Francks 1983: 32).

Apart from changes in size, hydraulic networks have also changed in construction materials and design. Most simple networks were constructed largely of earthworks, wood and gabions, and brick was also used in India (Tada, forthcoming), but in the larger systems it was not unusual for stone to replace the earthworks, for instance in the Hinduised states of Southeast Asia. In China in the Ming dynasty (1368–1644) a large number of earthen dykes and other hydraulic works, which had required yearly maintenance by a large labour force, were rebuilt in stone (Yangzi Region 1979: 165). Nowadays concrete is largely replacing earth and stone in structures such as dams and water-gates, as well as being used for the lining of canals (e.g. VanderMeer 1980: 227). Although the installation and maintenance costs of concrete channels are not necessarily less than those of earthen channels, the concrete lining prevents loss of water through seepage and can contribute to significantly higher yields of rice (Taylor 1981: 157). In the near future polyester flumes reinforced with fibreglass may prove even more effective (ibid.: 188).

The design of water control systems has been continuously improving over the centuries, although naturally always subject to constraints imposed by environment and materials. Again it is difficult to draw a hard and fast line between 'traditional' and 'modern'. The application of Western science has not necessarily transformed the field overnight. Although theories of hydraulics were sufficiently advanced to constitute one of the subjects studied by engineers in Europe by the late eighteenth and early ninteenth centuries, their application even today has to be tempered by experience and adapted to local environment and resources (Tada, forthcoming). The importance of the 'human element' in water control cannot be underestimated but is impossible to quantify (Levine 1980). Discussing water control in the People's Republic of China, for example, Gustafsson points out that most Western-designed water control is very wasteful, since water is usually considered by Westerners to be an abundant and free commodity; this leads to a preoccupation with the installation of sophisticated 'hardware' and a neglect of local social organisation and the consequent management requirements (1984: 128). On the other hand, while Chinese administrators from the Song dynasty (tenth century) onwards failed to develop a mathematically derived science of hydraulics, they devoted considerable thought to the political and social as well as technical and fiscal factors involved in the effective management of water control systems (Shen et al. 1979).

Many practical design features – effective locks, sluices and valves, for example, retaining dams which are short relative to their capacity, and complex networks of overspill and feeder canals – have been in existence

for centuries (Stargardt 1983: 192; Needham 1971: passim), and frequently modern schemes have largely incorporated the pre-existing infrastructure, although sometimes the potential scope of modern technical improvements has been limited by traditional social rivalries, as in the case of Niiike in Japan, mentioned earlier. On the other hand, in the very same district of Niiike, improvements in engineering technology made possible a complete remodelling of the canal network and field layout, enormously improving the irrigation facilities and cutting down on wastage of arable land (Beardsley et al. 1980 edn: 135).

One area in which undeniable technical advances have been made in the twentieth century is in the raising of water. Many gravity-flow systems were so designed that no water-raising was necessary to irrigate the fields, but 'creek irrigation' cannot work unless the water is raised by pumps or some other device, and many new irrigation networks are entirely dependent on powerful electric pumps which pump water up into the feeder canals from low-lying rivers (often the earlier lack of irrigation in these places was largely due to the difficulty of raising sufficient water in the absence of mechanised water-raising technology, as for instance in many parts of Malaya). The earliest water-raising devices of East and Southeast Asia were probably swapes, still in common use in Tonkin in the 1930s (Gourou 1936: 103), and even found in some parts of Japan in the 1950s (Beardsley et al. 1980 edn: 145). More effective than swapes are the wooden foot-pumps, square-pallet chain-pumps, which can raise water to a height of up to 5 m (Needham 1965: 339). These first appeared in China almost two millennia ago, and continue in use in certain areas today. But the first motor-pumps were introduced into the Yangzi Delta in the late 1920s, an innovation which greatly eased labour demands, though it presented considerable organisational problems as the *raison d'être* of the communal pumping groups was destroyed (Fei 1939: 172). The adoption of small electric irrigation pumps by the farmers of the Saga plain in Japan also entailed considerable institutional reorganisation (Francks 1983: ch. 7), but cut labour requirements by as much as two-thirds (Ishikawa 1981: 16). In many recently constructed irrigation schemes central pump-houses serve very large areas: in the Kemubu scheme in Malaysia seven centrally located pumps are designed to irrigate a total of 19,000 ha (although tests have shown that in practice they operate at only about 72% of their original design capacity) (Taylor 1981: 164). The adoption of improved pumping machinery can revolutionise farming efficiency by allowing more effective use of water, in some cases providing extra water and so permitting more intensive cropping patterns, for example the introduction of double-cropping on most Malaysian irrigation schemes,

in others enabling a more effective timing of water use, as in the development of 'rotation irrigation' in Taiwan (VanderMeer 1980). It is also important to note that the effectiveness of fertilisers is greatly increased when a controlled water supply is assured.

We have seen how historically water control systems have spread from easily mastered environments to meet more and more difficult technical challenges, requiring greater investments of labour and capital, and higher levels of management expertise. In the last century developments in water control have been a major factor in increasing rice production in most countries in monsoon Asia.

In China and Japan water control facilities were already highly developed at an early stage,[28] and the scope for increasing the area, at least in the heartlands, has therefore been relatively limited. Buck (1937: 187) shows how extensive water control facilities were in the rice-growing provinces of China by the 1930s (figure 3.8). Although the irrigated area in China was expanded by some 13 million ha between 1965 and 1975, most of this was in North and Northwest China, and in Central Asia. Even so, there was still some scope for expansion in the south: the area under water control along the Yangzi was expanded from 4 million ha in 1949 to 10 million in 1974 (Vermeer 1977: 187–8).

In Japan by the end of the nineteenth century there were few possibilities for expanding the area of rice under water control, and the government turned its attention instead to the colonies of Taiwan and Korea. When the Japanese took over Taiwan in 1895 the percentage of irrigated arable was 36.6%; by 1946 it was 69.6%; a maximum of 77.6% was attained in 1966, but since then the proportion has fallen somewhat, reaching 52% in 1973 (Shen et al. 1979: 209–10). After the Japanese annexed Korea in 1910, their efforts at first were concentrated on rehabilitating existing water control systems, but from 1920 new systems were constructed too. Between 1920 and 1933 the irrigated area was expanded by 165,000 ha, and over a similar period rice yields increased from 1.7 to 2.5 t/ha (Wade 1982: 24–5). This effort was continued after the war. The irrigated area in South Korea was expanded from 350,000 ha (28% of the total padi area) in 1952, to 585,000 ha (46%) in 1974 (Ban et al. 1980: 95).

In Thailand, as we have seen, gravity-fed irrigation was an early development in the north, but the reclamation of the flood plains did not begin until the late nineteenth century. Since then the central government has continued its efforts to improve water control facilities, and the total irrigated area has increased from 608,000 ha in 1917 to 1,824,000 ha in 1967 (Motooka 1978: 311), of which 1,445,000 ha are state projects (Wijeyewardene 1973: 95). In 1917, 592,000 ha were

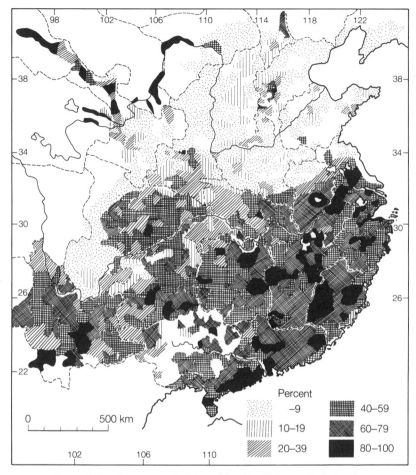

Figure 3.8   Percentage of cultivated land in China under irrigation
(from Buck 1937:187)

under irrigation in the Bangkok Delta and 16,000 ha in Northern
Thailand; by 1967 these figures had increased to 1,408,000 ha and
172,000 ha respectively (Motooka 1978: 311).

In Indonesia, water control was already highly developed in the Inner
Islands of Java, Madura and Bali before the Dutch took power, but
almost non-existent in the Outer Islands. The Dutch invested heavily in
improving the networks of Java. It has been estimated that between 1880
and 1939 they spent 250 million guilders on water control (Geertz 1963:

145), both on improving existing networks and on expanding the irrigated area. In Pasuruan Residency alone, 58 waterworks were constructed between 1856 and 1868 (Elson 1978: 11). Since independence further heavy investments have been made to rehabilitate and improve water control facilities in Java, but success has been hampered by the lack of appropriate local-level organisations (Birowo and Hansen 1981: 19).

The Dutch also planned reclamation schemes in the swamplands of the Outer Islands, in particular in Kalimantan, in the 1920s, with a view to providing rice-land for migrants (the transmigration scheme referred to earlier), but the projects were overambitious and the areas reclaimed remained limited. Further plans, even more ambitious in the areas involved though perhaps more realistic in the technology required, have been drawn up at various stages under the post-independence Five-Year Plans: for example in 1967 a plan was made to reclaim 5 million ha of saline swamp in Kalimantan over a period of 15 years; since then pilot projects have been carried out and the plan reduced to 250,000 ha (Hanson 1981: 222).

In fact today much of the land in monsoon Asia which is naturally suited to water control has already been brought into use, so that the continued expansion of water control facilities has now reached a point of diminishing returns, where the costs of construction are high and the corresponding improvements in production relatively low. The stage has been reached in several countries where expanding the area under water control has become a less rewarding exercise than improving facilities already in existence (e.g. Taylor 1981: 137, 187; Kaida 1978: 236). And although there is certainly scope in many existing systems for improvements in the 'hardware', especially at the terminal level (i.e. the supply to individual fields), where wastage of water tends to be particularly high (Taylor 1981: 188), it is widely agreed that the greatest scope for increasing the effectiveness of water control now lies in the improvement of management: working out better scheduling, adjusting terminal-level supplies, reducing the size of management units, encouraging positive participation by local farmers, reducing tension and conflicts between users, and so on (Taylor 1981: 188; Kaida 1978: 230 ff; Vermeer 1977: 131 ff).

The importance of involving local farmers directly in decision- making and planning is clearly shown by examples from Japan, Taiwan and Korea. Building on their own traditions and experience, the Japanese introduced the equivalent of their own irrigation associations, *suiri kumiai*, to both their colonies, where they have flourished and developed along very similar lines:

The Irrigation Associations bring together farmers under the same irrigation system to organise and operate it themselves, employing staff who (at least in principle) are responsible to farmers' representatives, and dividing up the operating and maintenance expenses between themselves. Such a form provides for effective liaison between staff and farmers, and disciplines the staff to operate the system effectively through the mechanisms of accountability of staff to farmers. (Wade 1982: 9)

Decentralisation of water management is an important means of increasing the efficiency and equity of water distribution, as the contrasting cases of Meiquan in the People's Republic of China and Dhabi Kalan in Haryana, India demonstrate (Nickum 1980; Vander-Velde 1980: 259). Indeed it is widely acknowledged that the lack of decentralisation on the sub-continent adversely affects the efficiency of water control projects (Vaidyanathan 1983: 76–85). But successful decentralisation often presupposes skills and knowledge, as well as a willingness to cooperate, on the part of local farmers. These are more likely to be found where irrigation or water control associations were already in operation, that is to say, where water control facilities were already in existence. Thus improvements to the traditional irrigation systems of Northern Thailand involve certain modifications to the traditional irrigation organisations, but can rely upon their support and are generally successful, whereas the introduction of completely new water control facilities to Northeastern Thailand has aroused the local farmers, innocent of any experience of water control, to nothing more than apathy and indifference; even on the technical level, the schemes must be judged only partially successful. The mandarin approach to water control can be highly counterproductive. Instructing and involving local farmers so that new or enlarged schemes can function more efficiently may be no easy task, but it is perhaps the most urgent problem now facing agricultural planners (Afifuddin 1977; Tamaki 1977; Chambers 1980; Vaidyanathan 1983).

4

Rice and the wider economy

The specific technical and organisational requirements of rice cultivation have a pervading influence on the rural economy as a whole, which is manifested at a number of levels. The relatively inflexible ratio of irrigated to non-irrigated land will influence crop choices, for example, while the demands of operating an irrigation system will determine the timing of all agricultural operations, as well as the organisation of labour within the community as a whole. The intensive but intermittent labour requirements of rice cultivation have the effect of tying large numbers of skilled workers to the land, at the same time leaving considerable scope for investing surplus household labour in commercial cropping or petty commodity production. This chapter will examine how the specificities of rice cultivation affect the development of other types of economic activity.

'Skill-oriented' and 'mechanical' technologies

There is a significant divergence between the evolution of agricultural systems like those of Northern Europe and North America, which emphasise the importance of increasing the productivity of labour (see appendix A), and of those like the rice economies of Asia, which stress raising the productivity of land. These distinct processes involve distinct types of technical change: in the first, labour is the scarce or costly resource and there is a historical trend towards the subsition of machinery for labour; in the second, there is an increase in the use of skilled manual labour accompanied by the development of managerial skills, and in effect labour is substituted for land.

For purposes of easy reference it would be useful if one could make a simple terminological distinction between these two types of technical

change, and indeed between the two types of technology which they engender. A contrast between 'technical' and 'technological' change (i.e. change based on the one hand on the development of low-capital labour and management skills, and on the other of the development of capital-intensive equipment and machinery) might have seemed appropriate, given the common vernacular usage of 'technique' as skilled performance and 'technology' as sophisticated equipment, were it not for a generally accepted convention among economists and other specialists that 'techniques' are in fact constituent elements of a technology, though how far a 'technology' extends beyond being simply a combination of related techniques is subject to much debate. Unfortunately 'nothing better indicates the underdeveloped state of technological studies than the basic disagreements over fundamental terms' (Layton 1977: 198). Some of the difficulties inherent in attempting to define or subdivide such a vague and complex notion as 'technology' are outlined by Rapp (1985: 128–9). Mitcham (1978) proposes a functional typology, distinguishing technology-as-object (apparatus, tools, machines), technology-as-knowledge (skills, rules, theories), technology-as-process (invention, design, making, using) and technology-as-volition (will, motive, need, intention); the first two categories might at first appear to provide the distinction sought here, but closer inspection shows that they are not in fact appropriate. Economists have described technical change which involves no new capital investment in equipment (for example organisational improvement) as *disembodied* technical change, and that which does require new investment in plant and equipment as *embodied* (Freeman 1977: 227), but it does not follow that one can contrast 'embodied' and 'disembodied' technologies, and as the contrast focuses on the presence or absence of capital in a single instance rather than on long-term characteristics, it too seems inadequate for present purposes.

In the absence of any more appropriate terminology and in order to avoid clumsy circumlocution, it is proposed here to use the terms 'skill-oriented' and 'mechanical' to denote respectively technologies which tend towards the development and intensive use of human skills, both practical and managerial, and technologies which favour the development of equipment and machinery as a substitute for human labour. Technological trends in Asian rice economies would then be characterised as 'skill-oriented', and those in modern Western agriculture as 'mechanical'. Of course the distinction does not imply that managerial and practical skills are absent from 'mechanical' technologies, nor that the development of 'skill-oriented' technologies precludes the use of complex equipment, including labour-substituting machinery. But as chapter 2 showed, there are often considerable technical

difficulties in developing suitable machinery to substitute for highly skilled labour; furthermore if the principal requirement is to raise the productivity of land, the benefits of mechanisation may be restricted to equipment which eliminates bottlenecks and permits the intensification of land and labour use.

Any technical innovation in agriculture is likely to provoke shifts in the allocation of resources which will benefit certain social groups to the disadvantage of others. The capital-intensive nature of most agricultural innovations in early modern Europe encouraged a polarisation of rural society into entrepreneurial farmers and landless labourers. One of the advantages of a 'skill-oriented' agricultural system such as wet-rice cultivation, which provides little scope for economies of scale and depends far less upon capital investment, should be that technological advance does not promote economic inequalities to the same extent.

The new inputs typical of many phases of development in rice agriculture are *divisible*, that is to say, new seed or improved fertilisers can be bought in any quantity according to the farmer's inclination or financial situation. Innovation is thus within the scope of farmers of all income groups. Often organisational improvements or a more careful carrying out of operations can make important contributions to increasing output without requiring any increase in capital outlay at all.

Since in a 'skill-oriented' technology like rice cultivation efficiency depends less upon the range of equipment than on the quality of labour, and since economies of scale do not operate as they do, for example, in the European case described in appendix A, a skilled and experienced smallholder or tenant farmer is in just as good a position to raise the productivity of his land as a wealthy landlord[1] (see chapter 5). Indeed as productivity rises, the costs of adequately supervising the many tasks involved in wet-rice farming become prohibitive: inspecting an irrigated field for weeds is almost as onerous as weeding it oneself.

So although prices of land rise as production is intensified and yields increase, and although there are often very high rates of tenancy in areas where wet rice is intensively farmed, the difficulties of effective supervision mean that landlords find little or no economic advantage in evicting their tenants to run large, centrally managed estates. Instead they generally prefer to leave their tenants to manage their small farms independently, shouldering all or part of the risks of production. Thus, contrary to the pattern set by the development of the 'mechanical' technology of Northwest Europe, in wet-rice societies there has been little trend towards the consolidation of landholding and the polarisation of rural society into managerial farms and landless labourers. Units of management remain small, usually at the scale of the family farm (table

Table 4.1   Farm sizes in Asia

		Farm size (ha)	Wet-rice area (ha)
Japan	1960[a]	1.00	0.56
	1978[a]	1.15	0.64
Korea	1965[b]	0.91	
	1979[b]	1.02	
Taiwan	1965[c]	1.05	
	1979[c]	1.02	
Java	1969/70[d]		0.8
Central Java	1971/2[e]	0.5	0.5
Thailand (Rai Rot)	1972[d]		6.0
Philippines (Laguna)	1966[d]		2.2
	1975[d]		2.2
Malaysia (Kelantan)	1971/2[e]	0.9	
Sri Lanka	1972/3[d]	0.8	

Sources:
[a] Hou and Yu 1982: 131
[b] ibid.: 206
[c] ibid.: 611
[d] Taylor 1981: 89
[e] IRRI 1978: 8–9

4.1), and the producers are not separated from control of the means of production (see chapter 6, and appendices B and C for the historical cases of China and Japan). The small-scale independent management units controlling land and skills are, however, inextricably linked into much larger-scale cooperative units for the management of water and the redistribution of labour. The paradox between the individual and the communal nature of rice cultivation has frequently been remarked upon by Japanese social scientists (e.g. Kanazawa 1971; Tamaki 1979).

The specificity of wet-rice agriculture

Wet-rice cultivation shapes and divides a landscape decisively, imposing a technical, economic and linguistic distinction between wet and dry.

Flying over Kelantan [Malaysia], one is immediately struck by the contrast between the wide tracts of flat green riceland with the irrigation channels glinting in the sun, and the distinct patches of dark wooded land which hide the homesteads from view. Near the coast the sea of ricefields is most extensive, the islands of woodland becoming larger and more contiguous as one flies westward, until they finally merge into dense jungle. The distinction between riceland (*bendang*) and village land (*kampong*) is determined primarily by the elevation of the land. The low-lying areas, usually with moist heavy soils, are suitable for rice farming and not much else; land which is even a few feet higher is comparatively dry and safe from floods, providing a natural place to build houses, plant trees for shade and protection from the wind, and grow vegetables, spices and fruit. This distinction between padi fields and village land (respectively 57% and 35% of the land area) looms large in the life of Kelantanese communities. *Bendang*, or padi fields, provide the staple rice necessary for subsistence; no individual *kampong* crop is necessary to physical survival, but together these two types of land provide a varied diet and a source of cash income. (Bray and Robertson 1980: 217)

The same distinction and complementarity are found in all rice-growing regions. Rice-fields which are undrained and permanently waterlogged are suitable for very few other crops apart from semi-aquatics like taro, ginger, indigo and sugar cane (Bray 1984: 112). On the whole dry and wet land are not interchangeable, and rice-farmers must make a long-term choice as to the proportion of land to be allotted primarily to rice and that given over to other crops. The concentrated periods of heavy labour requirements are also a determining factor.

Some crops compete with rice for land, labour and water, and cases where rice-farmers have given up producing their subsistence requirements to turn their wet-fields over entirely to commercial crops, though comparatively rare, are not unknown. In fifteenth-century Fujian province, China, many farmers chose to devote their wet-fields principally to sugar, which fetched a high price on the export market, and to buy their rice from other provinces (Rawski 1972). And in nineteenth-century Java the 'Culture System' produced intense competition between sugar-cane and rice, for land, irrigation-water and labour. As a result localities where the sugar quota was high tended to produce only a single crop of rice a year; at the same time rice production intensified in localities where little sugar was grown, and such areas supplemented the food needs of the sugar districts.[2]

Of course the farmer's choice as to how to allocate his resources will be determined by the demands of the market as well as by technological constraints, and in fact a fair degree of technical flexibility is possible. In the Japanese village of Niiike, studied by Beardsley and Hall, rice was grown only for subsistence until the 1930s, and cotton was the most important economic crop, grown in hillside fields throughout the area:

The farmers of Niiike have shifted in recent years to an increasing emphasis upon paddy farming for a number of reasons, among them the increased importance of cash-crop farming, the collapse of the market for locally grown cotton, and the improvement of hitherto marshy paddy land ... Cotton was [formerly] a major product of the Okayama Plain, where some of Japan's largest spinning mills had been built after the Meiji Restoration. The mills later turned to the cheaper and more plentiful cotton imported from the United States and southern Asia. The market for domestic cotton thus declined sharply after 1910. The Niiike farmers turned to raising mat rush, the basic material for the covering of floor mats. A swamp plant, this rush could be grown as a second crop even in hard-to-drain paddy fields. Intensive use of chemical fertilisers began about the same time. [With the programme of rice-land improvements of 1925 to 1930] household labour was needed now in the paddy fields or could be profitably employed in weaving the mat rush into *tatami* covers. Gradually cultivation of the hillside dry fields was abandoned, and pine trees were planted ... Niiike became a paddy farming village. All parts of the valley floor low enough to lead water are utilised for paddy. (Beardsley and Hall et al. 1980 edn: 134–6)

Greater flexibility in the redeployment of limited land and labour resources can sometimes be achieved through mechanisation, and the possibility of mechanising certain agricultural operations has recently permitted many Asian farmers to make the transition from subsistence to commercial cropping. To take two examples from Thailand, the introduction of tractors permitted the Lüe farmers of Ban Ping in the north to open up a large area of new fields in a nearby flood-plain for the commercial production of non-glutinous rice, although they continued to use the plough in the home fields where they grew glutinous rice for their own consumption. The case of the Ban Ping farmers is interesting, as they were very quick to adopt tractor ploughing but continued it only for a few years, to clear the new land and also to till it quickly at a period before local water control networks had been constructed which eliminated seasonal flooding. The Lüe farmers preferred using ploughs to tractors, partly because ploughs are said to give higher yields, and they only used the tractors for a brief period; nevertheless tractors were an essential element in the transition to commercial rice-cropping (Moerman 1968).

Nearby, in the Chiengmai Basin, rice-farmers wishing to supplement their incomes turned not to commercial rice production but to the cultivation of dryland crops, opening up new fields on higher land where they grew groundnuts, garlic, chilli and maize. But in order to free enough household labour for such enterprises they too started using machinery for certain rice-growing operations (Bruneau 1980: 426).

Fields that can be drained can be used for other crops. An early

Chinese description of drainage techniques is given in the *Wang Zhen nongshu*:

High fields are tilled early. In the eighth month they are ploughed dry [that is, without waiting for rain or irrigation as is usual before ploughing] to parch the soil and then sown with wheat or barley. The method of ploughing is as follows: they throw up a ridge to make lynchets, and the area between two lynchets forms a drain. Once the section has been tilled they split the lynchets crosswise and let the water drain from the ditches; this is known as a 'waist drain'. Once the wheat or barley has been harvested they level the lynchets and drains to accumulate the water in the field which they then plough deeply. This is vulgarly called a twice-ripe field. (*Wang Zhen nongshu*: 2/5b, tr. Bray 1984: 111)

The climate in China's Yangzi valley was sufficiently warm to allow the alternation of summer rice with winter barley or wheat, and this double-cropping system spread rapidly after the fall of the Northern Song dynasty to the Mongols in 1127. A twelfth-century work says:

After the fall of the Northern Song many refugees from the Northwest came to the Yangzi area, the Delta, the region of the Dongting Lake and the Southeast coast, and at the beginning of the Shaoxing reign (1131–63) the price of a bushel of wheat reached 12,000 cash. The farmers benefited greatly, for the profits were double those of growing rice. Furthermore, tenants paid rent only on the autumn crop, so that all the profits from growing wheat went to the tenant household. Everyone competed to grow the spring-ripening crop, which could be seen everywhere in no less profusion than to the north of the Huai River. (*Ji le bian*, tr. Bray 1984: 465)

Further south in China barley was preferred to wheat as it matured earlier and was better adapted to humid conditions and poorly drained land (Shen 1951: 208). In South Japan wheat, barley and naked barley (collectively known as *sanbaku*) were the most common second crops in drained rice-fields. The incentive to convert undrained fields, *shitsuden*, into drained fields, *kanden*, was provided by access to the commercial markets which developed during the Tokugawa and Meiji periods (Francks 1983: 59, 108), and later *kanden* expanded further as the development of pumping equipment made it possible to drain low-lying fields (Ishikawa 1981: 43).

Uniformity and systemic change

The constraints of efficient labour use and water control impose a degree of technical uniformity and cohesion on rice-farmers, as well as requiring cooperation between them. All the farmers within a single irrigation unit will have to fill and empty their fields at the same time, which means they

will have to plant varieties with a similar ripening period. They will usually cooperate on the maintenance of their joint irrigation channels, and will also be obliged to cooperate in order to fulfil their labour requirements during the periods of peak demand.

It has been pointed out that if rice-farmers had restricted their farm size to the area which they could manage with family labour alone, they would often not have been able to produce enough for their own subsistence (Wong 1971). To some extent such problems could be mitigated by spreading one's efforts over several different plots and by planting a number of rice varieties. Lewis (1971: 49) describes the tactics of Filipino farmers in the lowland *barrio* of Buyon, all of whom grew early and late, glutinous and non-glutinous rices in the same season, in order to split up fields and the timing of operations and so spread out their labour requirements; thus one household could cope alone with several plots amounting to over an acre where it would have been unable to manage a single field of the same area. In most rice-growing societies, however, farmers supplemented their family labour through labour exchange or, much less frequently, labour hire.

Labour exchange systems have been found in almost every society where rice is grown. Some regions have formal, permanent labour-exchange societies, in others arrangements may be *ad hoc*, or several kinds of arrangement may co-exist. In Kelantan, Malaysia, for instance, two systems of communal labour co-existed until very recently. For *berderau*, exchange labour proper, a group of friends, relatives or neighbours would get together to plant rice on a rota basis, 10 or 12 families in a group. These groups were of long duration, as the advantages of having one's field planted first had to be rotated among the members of the group over several years. *Pinjaman*, literally 'borrowing', was a system more akin to hiring labour: a farmer would provide a good meal for a day's work, and was under no obligation to work in the other farmers' fields (Bray and Robertson 1980). In Japanese villages exchange labour for transplanting was called *kattari* or *yui*; there too the *kattari* group was formed of about a dozen families on a permanent basis. There were also a number of other types of cooperative group, covering activities from repairing irrigation channels to organising funerals (Embree 1946: 99); a similar range of cooperative groups was to be found in Korean villages (Reed 1977: 19).

Many exchange organisations are based on simple proximity, but in Southwest China, 'far from being confined to the village, the exchange of labour is commonly practised among different localities. Since such transactions, based as they are on reciprocity, really constitute a credit system, some form of security is needed, and this is provided by ties of

kinship. Thus we find that exchange of services among relatives is considered most desirable' (Fei and Chang 1948: 64). It is perhaps not surprising that in a strongly patrilineal society like that of China cooperation between kin is preferred, whereas in Malaya, where descent groups are bilateral and the word for 'kinsman' and 'friend' is the same, the choice is not so obvious. In other cultures still other criteria may apply. In the Madras area of India exchange labour is confined to members of the same caste (Nakamura 1972: 161).

It is important to bear in mind that exchanging labour does not increase the amount of labour available, but redistributes it so that it can be deployed to best effect. It seems that labour exchange is usually confined to rice farming alone, and does not extend to cash crops, for which extra labour is hired if necessary (e.g. Potter 1976: 42). In Tokugawa Japan the institution of labour hire developed as the rural economy expanded and diversified, but was in large part confined to commercial crops and rural manufactures (Smith 1959: ch. 8). But in Tonkin labour hire had a completely different nature and origins. French colonial rule put paid to what few rural industries there were and laid a heavy stress on rice monoculture. The introduction of monetary taxes (which as usual laid a far heavier burden on the poor than on the rich), together with rapid population growth, had led by the 1930s to the development of a landless labouring class, who found their only employment in rice-farming, and consequently to the disappearance of cooperative organisations (Popkin 1979: 155; Fforde 1983: 56).

Another almost ubiquitous form of cooperation in rice-growing areas, at least where water control of any sophistication is practised, is represented by the various irrigation groups and associations referred to in chapter 3. Irrigation associations are not necessarily egalitarian, although it has been alleged that the communal nature of water control in rice-growing societies counteracts the tendency towards economic polarisation inherent in the private ownership of land (see Kelly 1982b: 12). But although hierarchies do exist in irrigation societies and the least powerful members are often unashamedly exploited (see chapter 6), all the farmers however humble do belong to the group.

Communal organisations such as labour-exchange groups and irrigation societies greatly reinforce the technical uniformity and cohesion imposed on rice-growing societies by the physical demands of rice cultivation. They often prove a highly effective, rapid and acceptable channel for popularising innovations and standardising techniques. The sharing and reinforcement of skills and resources is especially important where a single technical change entails a transformation of the whole system, as is frequently the case in rice cultivation. Changes in rice

cultivation come not singly but in 'packages'; in fact one might characterise such change as systemic: new varieties allow double-cropping but require more water and fertilisers, as well as an intensification of labour use which transforms previous patterns of organisation. Let us take as an instance what happened in Kelantan, Malaysia when an irrigation scheme was constructed by the Kemubu Agricultural Development Authority (KADA) to permit double-cropping of rice.[3]

Each irrigation unit serves over 20 ha. The water is supplied by KADA for a charge of M$25 per hectare per annum, according to a very strict timetable calculated for each district every season. Sufficient water has to be supplied to soften the soil for ploughing, and after transplanting there must be 15 cm of water standing in the fields during the period of maximum growth. It is also advisable to change the water in the padi-fields every week or so.

Every season KADA issues a timetable to each district prescribing the exact day on which each operation is to begin and finish (figure 4.1). It is necessary to follow this timetable almost without deviation if two crops are to be grown successfully. In particular, if transplanting is not completed on time, then the crop is likely to fail through lack of water. If the timetable is to be adhered to, then the farmers must set to ploughing and sowing almost as soon as they have finished harvesting. In the old days the month or two after the harvest was a time of rest and celebration, with feasts, plays, dancing, kite-flying and other amusements, and even now the farmers feel they deserve a rest after the harvest. But there is no time allowed for resting under the new system, and so it happens that the farmers begin to lag behind the new timetable, one season by only a few days, the next by a few days more, until eventually they have to forfeit a whole season. In Bunut Susu, the village I was studying, half the farmers lost the monsoon season of 1976–7.

It is essentially the presence or absence of water which determines which land can or must be used for rice, and over which period of the year. It is instructive to see what happens when the water-level changes as it did in Kelantan. Before the construction of the KADA irrigation scheme permitting the double-cropping of rice (see chapter 3), poorly drained land, although it produced the highest yields of rice, was usually left idle in the dry season; slightly higher land, especially where soils were sandy, would produce good crops of vegetables or tobacco.

The old varieties of rice cannot be grown in double-cropped fields because their growth period is too long. Over the past five years a number of new, high-yielding varieties have been introduced, mostly by KADA, though some of the most popular varieties were in fact found by

Figure 4.1   KADA timetable for rice cultivation
(photo courtesy A. F. Robertson)

the farmers themselves. Under favourable conditions the new varieties give much higher yields than the old. In some parts of the KADA area the average yield is as much as 5 t/ha, but the highest yields reported for Bunut Susu, which had problems with its water supply, were 3.75 t/ha, and on poorly drained or dry soils yields of less than 2 t/ha were usual.

KADA recommends the use of 7.5 bags of chemical fertiliser per hectare each season, and almost invariably the farmers comply. In 1977 it cost M$135 to fertilise one hectare. A disadvantage of chemical fertilisers is that they encourage the growth of weeds, and regular weeding of the standing crop is now often necessary.

The new varieties ripen at five months. As soon as double-cropping and the new, looser-grained varieties were introduced, the farmers of Bunut Susu gave up the use of the reaping-knife and started harvesting with sickles. Instead of cutting the stems halfway down and storing the rice in bundles to be threshed as required, the farmers now cut the stems at ground-level and thresh the grain immediately into wooden tubs. The new method of harvesting means that all the rice, ripe, over-ripe and under-ripe, is cut at once, but the sickle is much quicker than the reaping-knife. Previously it might have taken a month to harvest all the rice grown on one farm, and reaping was all done with family labour. Now most farmers hire three or four men to help, and five men can easily harvest a hectare in five or six days. Most farmers also hire tractors now to prepare their fields in the short time available between the two crops.

This has led to a transformation in the organisation of labour. In the old days borrowing and exchanging labour were possible because, although the tasks had to be carried out quickly on individual farms, they could be staggered throughout the village. But now the irrigation timetable requires that the same tasks be completed throughout a large area in a short space of time, and so the peak demands for labour are much more intense. In the old days nobody hired labour, but now many people hire themselves out at transplanting and harvesting time for the equivalent of about M$38 per hectare of work. Many elderly people who no longer farm, or women or young men who do not own padi land, hire themselves out at these times, as do poorer farmers who otherwise would find it difficult to meet the expense of purchasing inputs. The owners of larger padi farms now usually work only on their own land.

Monoculture and markets

Rice-land can be cropped extremely intensively, producing higher total outputs than any other type of grain-land. In a commune in Central

China a rotation of two crops of rice followed by one of wheat produced a total of 20 t/ha (Wertheim and Stiefel 1982: 28); in the central islands of Indonesia it is also common to grow two crops of rice followed by some other crop, and the annual output of rice may reach 8 to 10 t/ha (e.g. Gerdin 1982: 66). The output of rice has been enhanced by recent improvements in technology, but the intensive use of rice-land is nothing new. A late seventeenth-century Chinese work, *New Descriptions of Guangdong Province*, says:

[The inhabitants of Southern Guangdong and Annam] produce more grain than they can eat, so they carry it in great wains to the fairs of Hengzhou [modern Nanning, on the border of Guangxi and Vietnam], where it is bought by merchants who ship it down the Wu, Man and Tan rivers to Canton . . . The reason for the abundance of grain is that the climate in these southern regions is so warm that the land produces three crops in a single year . . . They grow two crops of rice in the early fields and then plant brassicas to make oil or indigo for dyeing, or grow turmeric or barley, rape or sweet potatoes. Once the main-field crops have been harvested they soak the straw in sea-water and burn it for the salt. On flat hills and ridges reeds, sugar cane, cotton, hemp, beans, aromatic herbs, fruits and melons are grown in profusion. The people are all extremely industrious and devote themselves so diligently to their farming that truly no patch of land is wasted and no hands are ever idle. (*Guangdong xinyu*: 371, tr. Bray 1984: 509)

But despite its great potential productivity, too heavy a dependence upon rice cultivation alone is not advisable. Expounding his concept of 'agricultural involution', based on a historical study of Indonesia, Geertz (1963) suggested that it was possible to absorb extra labour generated by population growth through the intensification of rice cultivation, thus providing the whole community with a small, if often inadequate, livelihood. In fact, despite its potential for responding positively to increases in labour inputs, the intensification of rice monoculture is a far less efficacious way of absorbing labour and generating extra income than is economic diversification.[4] There are a number of possible improvements which eliminate bottlenecks and spread the labour requirements for rice cultivation more evenly over the year (figure 4.2), yet underemployment in areas of rice monoculture tends to be high (table 4.2) even though there may still be acute labour shortages at peak periods (e.g. Shand and Mohd. Ariff 1983: 102). While it is possible to relieve such shortages through mechanisation, this only exacerbates the problem of overall employment in rice cultivation, and tends to cause economic inequalities by depriving the poorer farmers and the landless of opportunities to hire out their labour.[5] Only where circumstances are particularly favourable to rice-farmers, for example in postwar Japan

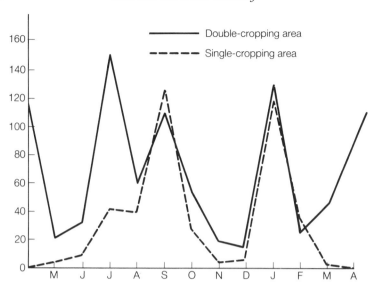

*Figure 4.2   Labour inputs in single- and double-cropping areas in Province Wellesley,
Malaysia*
(after Purcal 1972: 22, 71)

*Table 4.2   Underemployment in single- and double-cropping rice areas in
Province Wellesley, Malaysia*

Months:	M (%)	J (%)	J (%)	A (%)	S (%)	O (%)	N (%)	D (%)	J (%)	F (%)	M (%)	A (%)	Average (%)
Double-cropping area	52	38	2	23	35	27	33	44	7	52	43	43	33
Single-cropping area	64	40	8	8	24	36	37	45	−3	50	60	61	36

Source: Purcal 1972: 26, 76

where rice prices have been high and input costs low, is specialisation in
rice monoculture profitable and relatively secure from fluctuations in
world grain and oil prices. Where rice monoculture is imposed upon
farmers despite relatively unfavourable conditions, acute problems
frequently result.

Grain markets depend upon adequate means of bulk transport, and
especially of water transport. In the Mediterranean, where every city had

easy access to the sea, control of the grain trade had become the key to political power by the time of the Greeks and Phoenicians. The vast land-mass of East Asia, with its tangles of mountain ranges, is not so easy of access; even today one of the chief obstacles to China's economic development remains the lack of adequate transport networks. If Asian states have always taken such an active interest in encouraging agricultural production within their territories, this must be due in part to the difficulties of supplementing local food supplies from abroad.

By the tenth or eleventh century Song China already had a huge volume of inter-regional trade in rice, concentrated mainly along the Grand Canal, the Yangzi and other large southern rivers, and the east coast.[6] Private grain-ships plying the Grand Canal could often carry 1,000 piculs (approximately 7,000 hectolitres), while certain ocean-going junks had double that capacity (Shiba 1970: 73). The main centres of the regional rice-trade were the great Yangzi river-ports, Hangzhou, Nanjing and Wuchang. Rice was commercially produced in almost every southern province of China, and was sold not only to the cities but also to rural areas which had difficulty in meeting their own needs, either because they were unsuited to rice production, or because of a poor harvest, or because they had turned to the production of more lucrative commercial crops. In the twelfth century the mountainous district of Huizhou in Fujian sold tea, lacquer, paper and wood to the Yangzi Delta in exchange for rice. The Song long-distance rice-trade was extensive, and was an important factor in encouraging the expansion of rice production in many areas such as the Canton region, which by the thirteenth century was exporting rice to Champa and other foreign parts (ibid.: 63).

But this lively response to markets was only possible where water transport was available, and Shiba makes the point that 'at the periphery of the commercialised system, there remained a number of localised, discrete and self-sufficient marketing systems' (ibid.: 67). This has been true of China throughout her history. Rawski's (1972) study of Fujian and Hunan in the sixteenth to eighteenth centuries clearly demonstrates the ready response of Chinese farmers to market stimuli such as price rises, but this was conditional on access to transport, so that it was not uncommon, as indeed it still is not today, to find flourishing trade centres separated from self-sufficient backwaters by a single ridge of mountains.

It has often been said that the growth of commerce, and of the rice-trade, in Tokugawa Japan was largely due to the *sankin kōtai* system 'whereby feudal lords were required to spend six months of every year in the capital and the other six months in their fiefs. The passage of the lords and their many retainers from distant parts of the country led to

improvements in the road system and to the development of commercial facilities for them along the way, while keeping the more remote parts of the country in communication with the capital and other urban centres' (Francks 1983: 50).

But easy access to transport and markets often tempted farmers into more profitable ventures than rice production, to the disapproval of officials concerned with forestalling food shortages. A thirteenth-century Chinese official, Fang Dazong, complained that certain districts in Fujian had almost given up cultivating ordinary rice in favour of sugar-cane or glutinous rice for wine-making, whereas in the most productive regions of the province '[the authorities] have forbidden the cultivation of glutinous rice, the manufacture of wine from it, the growing of oranges, and the excavation of ponds for the rearing of fish. The reason for this ban is the desire that no inch of land should be uncultivated, and no grain of rice uneaten. If regions which produce a surplus of rice take such precautions, how much more should those whose harvests cannot supply half their needs' (Shiba 1970: 54).

Governments were not easily able to restrict a farmer's choice, however, even by obliging him to pay taxes in kind. Even in Song China many farmers chose or found it necessary to purchase rice in order to pay their taxes (ibid.: 56).

The principal rice-producing region of China in Song times was Jiangsu in the Yangzi Delta, but by the 1720s it had become a net importer of rice, buying it not only from the provinces of the Central Yangzi but also from Shandong and Taiwan. By that time the Canton region too had switched from exporting rice abroad to importing it from the neighbouring province of Guangxi (Chuan and Kraus 1975: 59, 65, 71). Areas of intensive rice cultivation tended, if they had access to other markets, to diversify into the production of more profitable commodities, while hitherto underdeveloped areas found an incentive to step up their rice production in order to fill the gap.

In a stimulating article on the indirect effects of colonial capitalism on monsoon Asia, Baker (1981) describes the resulting shift in inter-regional economic links. At first it was the long-settled, densely populated areas of intensive agriculture which supplied food to the new areas of colonial industrial or semi-industrial production, most of which were in sparsely populated regions where there were few obstacles to claiming land and establishing plantations or factories:

The planters moved into the hills of central Ceylon, upper Malaya, outer Indonesia and Annam, and spread out estates of tea, rubber, coffee, and spices. The peasants were pushed out into the hitherto relatively vacant parts of India,

Malaya, and Indochina to grow cotton, sugar, indigo, tobacco, and oilseeds, and onto the marginal lands of Java in order to accommodate sugar . . . Initially [the demand for food] was satisfied by the established agricultural systems in the long-settled densely populated areas. Tonkin sent food into Annam; India exported rice to Ceylon and to the Straits; Java exported to the Outer Islands. But before the end of the nineteenth century, this situation had substantially changed. The west also helped to open up new areas of food production within the southeast Asian region . . . the most important and spectacular expansion came through the opening up of the lower reaches of the Irrawaddy, Chao Phraya, and Mekong river basins . . . Roughly fourteen million acres were newly planted with rice in mainland southeast Asia in little over half a century. (Baker 1981: 332)

The colonial powers played an important role in providing infrastructure for the opening up of new land, constructing canals which served the dual purpose of draining marshy areas so that they became cultivable and providing easy access by water so that the produce could be shipped out. But much of the labour force for this expansion of food production came from the 'ancient' areas (East India, South China, Tonkin, Java), as did the technical skills and a great deal of the capital. In return the 'ancient' areas received an inflow of remittance money and, eventually, large quantities of grain. 'In the late 1920s, Burma, Thailand, and Indochina were producing about 9.4 million metric tons of cleaned rice (or equivalent) a year, and exporting about 5.4 million tons of this total. Indonesia, Malaya, and Ceylon together produced 3.9 million tons and imported another 1.6 million, while China and India were importing about a million tons apiece' (ibid.: 338).

These new areas of rice monoculture were, however, extremely vulnerable, as were the rice regions of Taiwan and Korea developed by the Japanese in the early decades of this century to supply their home market with cheap rice. Farmers in such areas had not developed any alternative sources of income. When the Depression hit Asia and the demand for rice suddenly contracted, in Southeast Asia the resulting surpluses of rice made for a devastating fall in prices, severe impoverishment, communal strife, and a stagnation of the rural economy which in Burma and Thailand lasted until well into the 1950s (ibid.: 341, 346). Japan had made a particular effort to step up rice production in her colonies as well as in Japan after the urban Rice Riots of 1918, but unfortunately the rise in production coincided with the Depression and a consequent decline in per capita rice consumption in Japan. In 1931 exports to Japan accounted for about half the total rice production in both Korea and Taiwan, and for 15% of Japan's total consumption, but from 1933 Japan introduced strict import controls (Ogura 1980: 167).

However the situation of Taiwanese and Korean rice-farmers soon picked up as Japan launched into full-scale war (Wade 1982: 25).

The problems associated with over-reliance on rice monoculture were amply demonstrated in China during the 1960s and early 1970s, when everyone was urged to 'take grain as the key link'. To encourage self-sufficiency government grain supplies to areas which had formerly specialised in cash crops such as cotton were cut off. Not only did this policy have a drastic effect on the output of non-cereal crops, but the use of unsuitable land for the intensive production of irrigated rice and other grains was often quite counterproductive (Lardy 1984a). The recent trends towards agricultural specialisation and renewed government efforts to redistribute grain between provinces have led both to increases in grain yields and to improved levels of consumption (Lardy 1984b).

In Malaysia too the government has in effect forced rice monoculture on farmers in certain areas, most notably in the Kemubu and Muda regions. The construction and extension of irrigation networks in these areas, together with the introduction of double-cropping, is part of an effort to achieve national self-sufficiency in rice. But new patterns of land use and the more intensive labour requirements of double-cropping have effectively precluded economic diversification in these regions. In 1974–5 Malaysia succeeded in supplying 93% of its national rice requirements (Mokhtar 1978: 119), but the demand for rice is relatively inelastic, particularly as many better-off Malaysians are now turning to wheat products, and so a rice-farmer's potential for increasing his income by selling more rice is limited.

Considering the Muda region, traditionally a monoculture area, where holdings are relatively large, mechanisation is advanced and the labour force is fully commercialised, Bell (1978) saw few opportunities for improving rice-farmers' incomes. The intense economic specialisation of the region meant that there were few opportunities for off-farm employment, and the technical demands imposed by the irrigation scheme allowed no possibility of switching from rice to high-value crops. Recent increases in government support prices have benefited large farmers more than small, for profit elasticity is very high with respect to land, for which the factor coefficient is nearly 1.0 (Mokhtar 1978: 125). The outcome foreseen by Bell was a rural exodus and the concentration of landholding accompanied by increasing mechanisation of rice production, and more recent evidence tends to support his predictions (Muhd. Ikmal 1985).

The situation in the Kemubu region is somewhat different, for Kelantan has a long tradition of economic diversification (table 4.3). Rice-farmers supplemented their incomes by growing vegetables,

Table 4.3   Non-padi income as proportion of net padi income in
KADA and MADA (1979/80)

Tenurial group	Full tenants (%)	Part tenants (%)	Owner-operators (%)
KADA	144	77	60
MADA	49	25	26

Source: From official sources.

tobacco, rubber or coconuts, by local and long-distance trade and, of especial importance, by seasonal migration. The transformation of much good dry-crop land into mediocre irrigated land has considerably restricted opportunities for non-rice cropping. Since the income from dry land is frequently double or triple that from double-cropped rice-land, the prices of the remaining dry land have shot up and much wooded land has recently been cleared for vegetable gardens or orchards (Bray and Robertson 1980: 237). Perhaps more serious than the encroachment of irrigated on dry land are the new patterns of labour inputs demanded by double-cropping, which often require a farmer to make a choice between growing rice and supplementing his income through other activities. Shand and Mohd. Ariff (1983: 171) suggest that in Kelantan the introduction of double-cropping has restricted the freedom of farmers and their families to take up sustained off-farm employment, while its positive impact on agricultural underemployment has been modest, since this still amounts to over 25%. While Shand and Ariff (ibid.: 253) see mechanisation as a possible solution enabling farmers to earn more off-farm income while still producing padi for sale, other official sources point out that the labour absorption consequent upon the introduction of double-cropping in Kemubu, although low, is still higher than it has been in Muda; they say that for reasons of equity further mechanisation in Kelantan would be very undesirable. At the same time they severely criticise the emphasis on monoculture, blaming the Malaysian government for sacrificing Kelantan's regional needs to national objectives.

Economic diversification

The possibilities for increasing employment and incomes and for generating wealth lie not so much in maximising the production of rice as

in using intensive rice cultivation as a basis for economic diversification. The resource and management requirements of rice cultivation generally mesh extremely well both with commercial cropping and with small-scale manufacturing activities.

Rice lends itself to productive combinations, such as the centuries-old system of rice, fish and silk production typical of certain regions of East China and South Japan, which is in fact a self-sustaining ecosystem (Fei 1939; Ishikawa 1981: 46): mulberry trees are grown on high land, often along the banks of the rice-fields (figure 4.3); silkworm droppings are used as powerful fertilisers for the rice; fish live in the irrigation channels as well as the rice-fields, nibbling away the water-weeds and eating the larvae of insect pests as well as being fed with the silkworm moultings. Often the farmers raise ducks in the rice-fields too, in which case some of the fish will enliven the diet of the ducks rather than that of the farmers.

The importance of vegetable gardens and orchards in the Kelantan rural economy has already been mentioned. Since almost every household, however poor, owns a house-plot, the income from garden produce plays an important role in poorer households, especially those with no other agricultural land to their name. In a study carried out in Java in 1972/3, Stoler (1981) found that poor households cultivated their garden plots far more intensively than households with access to other land, but tended to concentrate on production for their own consumption rather than for sale. Wealthier households had a much more entrepreneurial attitude towards their gardens.

In another Javanese village, Mizuno (1985) found that half of all the farmers and one-third of the labourers were engaged in part-time production of coconut sugar. Even though the adoption of rice double-cropping has increased opportunities for labour hire, many households prefer sugar to rice production: although it requires an initial cash outlay to lease the trees and several hours' labour daily to tap the trees and boil down the sap, sugar production 'has the great advantage of providing a secure daily cash income' (ibid.: 32).

In Java, as in Malaysia, rice cultivation is not in itself a profitable occupation. It provides a degree of security, but all farming households, whether they own land, rent it, or hire out their labour, derive the major part of their income not from rice but from other part-time occupations. This is not entirely surprising in regions where the pressure on land is so acute that very few households have large enough rice-farms even to supply their domestic needs. Since the population in Java averages 660 per sq. km,[7] this is true of the majority of Javanese households (Mizuno 1985: 1, 34), and almost all of them resort to what White (1976: 280)

Figure 4.3   Picking mulberry leaves to feed silkworms, illustrated in the Song work
Gengzhi tu
(Agriculture and sericulture illustrated) (Qing edition of 1886)

calls 'occupational multiplicity' simply to survive (see also, for example, Mantra 1981; Montgomery 1981).

Even in more prosperous economies it is rare to find that rice production is profitable in itself (see chapter 5); nevertheless it still serves as a basis for more profitable diversification. Taiwanese rice-farmers realise little or no profit on double-cropped rice, yet they continue to cultivate their rice-land, apparently because: '(1) "it is a resource that must be used", (2) it [is] a source of food, specifically rice, (3) taxes levied on it [have] to be paid, and (4) additional taxes [are] imposed if it [is] not cultivated' (Gallin and Gallin 1982: 218). Interviews with part-time farmers in Northeast Japan indicated that their refusal to give up rice cultivation stemmed from (1) a sense of responsibility, both spiritual and proprietorial, (2) their emotional attachment to the land, and (3) a need for security. As a consequence the men often took full-time work in the vicinity but left the farm in charge of the women, who diversified their incomes by growing fruit and vegetables, and especially a highly profitable species of mushroom, as well as rice (Shimpo 1976: 45, 72).

Petty commodity production and rural industrialisation

In the 'skill-oriented' technology of wet-rice cultivation increases in agricultural production are generally achieved through an intensification of land productivity rather than an expansion of the cultivated area, and it is the skilled application of large amounts of labour that counts rather than capital investment or the introduction of machinery. The required equipment is simple, and labour is most frequently supplied by the household or community involved. The technical requirements of wet-rice cultivation have consistently placed a high premium on the application of skilled labour, and given only low returns on investment in capital equipment or the expansion of production units (see chapter 5).

Wet-rice agriculture can support higher population densities than most other agricultural systems, and this has been extremely important in shaping more general patterns of economic development. Before the Industrial Revolution such countries as China could be considered technically and economically in advance of Europe. Boserup points out that for reasons of transport facilities, markets, access to labour and so on, it was only in densely populated areas that commercialisation and manufactures were feasible at that time, and 'the main advantage of a dense population, i.e., the better possibilities to create infrastructure, seems to have outbalanced the disadvantage of a less favourable ratio between population and natural resources' (1981: 129). Changes in the

medieval Yangzi Delta (see appendix B) show clearly how density of population and economic advance may go hand in hand. Nevertheless, the generalised economic growth of medieval China did not lead to capitalism and industrialisation as in Europe, partly because the demands of intensive rice cultivation and multi-cropping placed heavy constraints on the availability of labour.

In industrialising Northern Europe (see appendix A) agricultural development led to a polarisation of rural society into large farmers and a landless labour force. Although much manufacturing in the early stages was rural- rather than urban-based, even those who combined the occupations, eking out their agricultural wages with Smith's famous 'pin-money', belonged to a potentially mobile labour force, for as labourers rather than tenants they had no direct stake in the land they farmed. If higher wages could be had elsewhere, or in another form of employment, then there was nothing to tie them to the land. It was the existence of this type of labour force that provided a basis for increasing occupational specialisation, the development of more concentrated production and eventually the large-scale mechanisation of industry. On the other hand the experience of medieval China, as of early modern Japan (see appendices B and C), strongly suggests a link between the intensification of wet-rice production and the growth and entrenchment of part-time petty commodity production, which continues to flourish even today.

The organisation of resources typical of a 'skill-oriented' technology such as intensive rice-farming dovetails very neatly with petty commodity production, which requires very little capital to set up a family enterprise, and absorbs surplus labour without depriving the farm of workers at times of peak demand. It can be expanded, diversified or contracted to meet market demands, but the combination with the rice-farm guarantees the family's subsistence. The products can be conveniently conveyed to local or national markets by merchants, who pay the villagers for their labour and often provide raw materials as well as information on the state of the market. Since the owners of the enterprise also supply the labour, rural manufactures of this type sometimes prove more competitive than larger urban industries: the case of the silk industry in eighteenth-century Japan comes to mind. Japanese entrepreneurs turned increasingly to the countryside for cheap labour, and highly developed putting-out systems were evolved, taking advantage of household labour that was only partly absorbed by the demands of agriculture. By the late Tokugawa period a large proportion of households in the more advanced regions of Japan were engaged in some form of commercial manufacturing (Francks 1983: 51).

In Song and Ming China, as in Tokugawa and early Meiji Japan, there was almost no centrally organised, large-scale, capital-intensive industry. The market was supplied by petty commodity producers, and visitors from early capitalist Europe were generally impressed by the high levels of consumption that they found at all social levels. But the successful and durable system of intensive rice-farming combined with petty commodity production effectively inhibited indigenous technical and social changes of the type prerequisite for mechanisation and industrialisation.

As capitalist industry flourished in the West, it rapidly outstripped the manufactures of Asia in efficiency and levels of production. Most Asian nations, as soon as the opportunity arose, endeavoured to develop their own capitalist industries; Japan is the first and to date the most successful example. Yet it is striking how deeply Japanese industry has been and remains rooted in the countryside. The improvements in rice agriculture during the Meiji period spread labour requirements more evenly over the year and thus did not prevent younger sons or daughters from taking up by-employment or working at home (Francks 1983: 57). In 1884, 77% of Japanese factories were situated in rural areas, and more than half in 1892 (Umemura 1970). Much of the rural industrial labour force consisted of village women, often young girls on short-term contracts of three or four years, whose families received their wages while they themselves were given only board and lodging and a little pocket-money (Boserup 1981: 167). While the chemical and machine industries were concentrated in the towns, textile and ceramics manufactures and metal-working factories were mostly to be found in rural areas, and the majority of these establishments employed fewer than 20 people (Francks 1983: 53, table 3.1).

In Japan today, centralised capitalist industry still relies heavily on the putting-out system, and many farming families are involved in the production of components for large companies such as Mitsubishi or Sony. Although they may need to use high-cost and sophisticated equipment, and although the product is an element in capitalist industry, the workers are still part-time farmers who control their own labour, not industrial proletarians. Of course an increasing number of rural Japanese now work full-time in industrial jobs, but they still belong to households whose patterns of economic organisation are determined to a large extent by the family farm (Shimpo 1976).

In Southeast Asia, where recent development policies have resulted in a widespread intensification of rice production, again rural petty commodity production has accompanied the expansion and commercialisation of agriculture. The nature of such enterprises varies widely, but usually reflects the prevailing level of national prosperity. The goods

produced may require almost no investment of skills, material or technology, or (as in the case of Japan) they may be almost as sophisticated as urban manufactures. In Central Luzon village women weave straw hats for sale (Takahashi 1970), and in Sumatra men produce iron hoes and other tools for the national market while their wives run the rice-farms and work as dress-makers (Kahn 1980).

In the Sumatran village studied by Kahn, the villagers produced rice only for consumption and relied on the sale of cash-crops and locally produced goods for all their other needs. Their village speciality was steelware, sold locally to pedlars and small merchants who redistributed it throughout the province. The small steel workshops relied entirely for raw materials on scrap steel, and the more expensive equipment like anvils was usually purchased second-hand. Most workshop-owners employed two, or sometimes three, hired labourers. The running costs and profits were divided into equal shares, one going to each worker and one to the workshop. The owner of the workshop thus extracted a small surplus from his workers (Kahn 1980: ch. 5).

Kahn demonstrates clearly the symbiotic relationship between petty commodity production and rice cultivation in Indonesia. While the economic enterprises typical of rural commodity production in monsoon Asia cannot be classed as capitalist, they are highly dependent on fluctuations in the world as well as in the national economy. Thus increased demand for peasant-produced commodities during Indonesia's period of economic isolation from 1958 to 1965 led to a rapid expansion of steel-smithing: enterprises increased both in number and in scale. But the subsequent opening up of the economy and the crippling inflation of the mid-1960s, epitomised in rocketing rice prices (600 *rupiahs* for 10 litres in Jakarta in 1963, 48,000 *rupiahs* in 1966), led to the temporary collapse of rural manufacturing enterprises. Farmers stopped engaging in commodity production and turned back to cultivating their rice-land in order to secure their subsistence. When the economy began to recover, petty commodity production expanded again, and since it was so much more profitable than rice-farming, many farmers no longer cared to produce enough rice even for their own subsistence (ibid.: 195–8).

At a higher level of economic reward, the spectacular expansion of rural-based industry in Taiwan over the last two decades is based in large part on family enterprises: in 1971 three-quarters of the industrial and commercial establishments located in the rural areas of Taiwan were small family businesses with fewer than ten workers (Gallin and Gallin 1982). Again the development of rural industries has been closely meshed with rice cultivation. In 1956 the only factory in the village of Xin

Xing studied by the Gallins was a brickworks. Most of the farmers devoted themselves principally to intensive rice cultivation. The lack of agricultural machinery and of rural industries meant that there were very few opportunities for local off-farm employment, and those who succumbed to the lure of higher manufacturing wages (some 15% of the local population) were obliged to migrate to distant cities. 95% of local incomes came from farming and agricultural labour.

By 1979 the situation had completely changed. Farmers had been able to adopt new technology enabling them to overcome labour shortages and change their patterns of land use. They either diversified into profitable cash-crops or worked part-time in remunerative off-farm activities, although they did not give up cultivating their rice fields. Over 30 labour-intensive manufactures had been established locally, ranging in size from large textile or furniture factories to family workshops doing piece-work. 85% of local incomes was now derived from off-farm activities, although about 83% of the local households still farmed. Significantly the growth of local industry had led a number of former migrants to return.

In Taiwan in the 1960s and 1970s large numbers of industries moved to the countryside in search of cheaper labour and raw materials. By 1971, 50% of industrial and commercial establishments and 55% of manufacturing establishments were located in rural areas. As a result, between 1952 and 1972 the average real income of farming households doubled, although remaining significantly lower than urban incomes (Gallin and Gallin 1982: 239).

In China a significant increase in rural incomes has been achieved since 1978 through the simple expedient of raising agricultural prices (see chapter 5), and the introduction of the 'responsibility system' led to a spurt in overall agricultural production. But many economists doubt that there is much potential for further growth in agricultural output (e.g. Lardy 1984b: 864). The fostering of rural manufactures, even at the level of petty commodity production, seems vital if differentials between urban and rural incomes are to be reduced, as present economic policies recognise:

[The] historical 'scissors' gap between agricultural and industrial prices cannot be closed overnight and its existence has provided a way of concentrating agricultural accumulation in the hands of the state. The major mechanism has been the high profit made on light industrial products manufactured using agricultural raw materials. (Dong Furen 1982, quoted Watson 1984: 86)

Since about two-thirds of China's light industrial products are sold in rural areas (Watson 1984: 86), it is only by involving the rural labour

force in their production that the 'scissors' effect can be counteracted. Although many brigades set up small factories in the 1960s and 1970s, it was acknowledged that there were serious problems involved in management, providing incentives, responding to market needs, acquiring plant and raw materials, and distributing the goods efficiently. The new economic policies expressly encourage economic diversification and decentralisation, but as yet figures on public and private investment in rural-based industries, their production levels and profits, are hard to come by. In an initial burst of post-Maoist euphoria, the authorities in Chen Village in Guangdong simply parcelled out all the brigade factories to the highest bidders, regardless of their antecedents or qualifications (Chan et al. 1984: 273). If such excesses and carelessness can be avoided in the future, given the abundance of labour and raw materials and the new levels of rural accumulation, there seems no reason why local industrialisation should not go hand-in-hand with overall rural growth in China as it has in Taiwan and Japan.

5

Development

'Development' is a subject so complex that it has generated its own branches of economics and sociology. This chapter is not intended to provide comprehensive treatment, descriptive or prescriptive, of development in Asia's rice economies.[1] Instead, after raising some of the general issues likely to affect rural development in these economies, it concentrates on the technical means by which growth may be promoted (institutional means such as land reform and collectivisation will be dealt with in chapter 6). In the past growth in Asia's rice economies has followed a very different pattern from agricultural development in the West, particularly where the balance between labour and capital is concerned. The highly specific characteristics and tolerances of wet-rice cultivation are factors which should be borne in mind by development planners.

It has often been asserted that traditional patterns of agriculture in Asia have been brutally disrupted, first by the impact, whether direct or indirect, of capitalism and world markets, and then, directly, by modernisation programmes, and in particular by the so-called Green Revolution with its associated package of New Technology. The intrusion of capital, the necessity to purchase inputs and to sell grain for cash, especially in areas of subsistence economy, were expected to offset the benefits resulting from increased output by causing profound changes in the relations of production, enriching wealthy farmers and emmiserating the poor. It is certainly true that the Green Revolution, with its heavy reliance on such capital inputs as chemical fertilisers, irrigation infrastructure and farm machinery, has highlighted many of the problems involved in developing the means of production. Questions of both equity and efficiency have arisen, and the social or technical desirability of differing degrees of agricultural mechanisation, the possible emergence of capitalist farming and differentiation of Asian

peasantries, are intricately linked to the roles of capital and labour in producing technical change. It must be recognised that the capital requirements of the New Technology and of participation in national and international markets, like the unprecedented degree of centralised planning and grass-roots level intervention which are typical of the Green Revolution, have marked a new era in Asian rice-farming. Yet it would be rash to say that they have caused a complete rupture and brought about a radical transformation in the nature of Asian rice technology. The heritage of centuries is not so easily overcome.

Some basic issues

The stated aim of almost all development programmes is 'growth'. In the case of agriculture, 'growth' may mean increasing overall agricultural output, increasing its value and/or increasing rural incomes. Considerations of equity, the redistribution of wealth and the eradication of poverty have to be balanced against requirements for absolute increases in output and rapid rates of growth, investments in capital goods and international expertise must be weighed against investments in education or the encouragement of local enterprise.

These days agricultural development in Asia is usually seen as a major economic priority to be tackled at national level. Most Asian states have an explicitly formulated agricultural development programme, for which they rely heavily on international expertise and finance. Centralised planning has played an increasingly important role in development of late, but although the Five-Year Plan as such is a twentieth-century phenonenon, development planning and government intervention in economic activities, and especially in agriculture, have a long pedigree in East and certain parts of Southeast Asia. Where the state derives the bulk of its income directly from agricultural production it has a clear interest in agricultural development.

As appendix B shows, in eleventh-century Song China the state put into action a well-coordinated programme of agricultural development: it introduced new varieties, popularised double-cropping through the distribution of new seeds and of leaflets on cultivation techniques, invested heavily in water control and provided peasant farmers with financial aid. Nor was this period unique. One of the most influential agricultural works ever published in China was the *Complete Treatise on Agricultural Administration* (*Nongzheng quanshu*) of 1639, written by the statesman and one-time Prime Minister Xu Guangqi; this contained lengthy sections on systems of colonisation, land distribution, water

rights and credit as well as famine relief, all based on Xu's long experience as a high-ranking official and on a vast range of earlier writings on agricultural administration and improvement (Bray 1984: 64). Xu was one of a long line of Chinese administrators who attempted to popularise wet-rice cultivation in China's northern provinces (Brook 1982; on famine relief see Will 1980).

Vietnamese rulers too invested in water control and land reclamation projects, and provided peasant farmers with financial aid. The medieval empires of Angkor and Ceylon constructed huge irrigation systems dependent on centralised management. While the rulers of Tokugawa Japan largely confined their intervention to issuing exhortatory edicts, it was recognised that agriculture was the foundation of the economy; the urgent attention subsequently paid to industrialisation has never blinded Japanese statesmen to the economic (and of course political) importance of agriculture, and ever since 1870 Japan has made systematic efforts to achieve balanced sectoral development.

Until recently modern development plans all too frequently excluded the possibility of including the farmers themselves among the planners, but the innumerable difficulties encountered in imposing change from above have lately made many development experts sensitive to the importance of whole-hearted grass-roots participation. Historical examples show clearly how important the contribution of farmers has been to sustaining or even initiating growth. In China since 1949 this has been an ideological tenet: the active participation of farmers in advancing agricultural technology was for many years declared to be even more crucial to success than scientific research and development; more recently, rural demands have been instrumental in effecting a complete reshaping of rural institutions, and indeed of national economic policy. Such attitudes are perhaps to be expected in a socialist country, but a stress on popular participation and greater decentralisation is becoming current now in many other Asian countries (e.g. Afifuddin 1977; Tamaki 1977).

Today planned development has reached unprecedented levels of sophistication and expenditure, and frequently transcends national boundaries. A programme to increase rice production may depend on technical expertise from IRRI, chemical fertilisers and machinery supplied by multi-national conglomerates, oil at prices dictated by OPEC, and credit – and consequently strongly worded advice – extended by the World Bank. All this, together with conflicts of interest between political parties, rich landowners and poor peasants, town and country, the industrial and the agricultural sector, is bound to affect not simply the nature of development programmes but even perceptions of

the issues involved. To cite one well-known instance, the problems of rural Java were perceived by Sukarno's administration as an agrarian question; land reform was believed to be the answer, but since it was clearly going to be a slow and difficult process, and since Sukarno had repudiated foreign aid, immediate efforts were concentrated on rural extension work. In 1964/5, despite shortages of fertiliser, the short-lived Demas (Mass Demonstration) Project resulted in yield increases of between 40% and 140% (Palmer 1977: 26). After the political turmoil of 1965, however, Indonesia was welcomed back into the international economic fold. Anxious to impress its foreign creditors, Suharto's government reassessed the rural problem as primarily one of backward technology, and it brought in multi-national corporations to raise rice yields with advanced technology. This proved very profitable to the corporations but less so to Javanese farmers: fertiliser imports rose from $34.6 million in 1964 to $290.5 million in January-June 1974, while yields on the farms which had adopted the new Bimas (Mass Guidance) technology, although higher than on the non-Bimas controls, seldom surpassed the levels achieved on the Demas farms in 1964/5 (Palmer 1977: 192, 104).

Everyone agrees that rural Asia faces severe problems, but not everyone agrees on their precise nature. Even overpopulation is a relative concept (Grigg 1980). Mao maintained that China would benefit from population growth because labour could be substituted for capital; China's population policy was subsequently completely reversed, but the reorganisation of management under the 'responsibility system' seems likely to produce demands for a further reconsideration. Most of Asia's other rice regions also have extremely high population densities (table 5.1), average farm sizes are very small, and in most regions rural underemployment is common and the marginal productivity of labour very low.

Rural poverty is recognised as probably the most pressing problem Asia faces, but again interpretations vary. Poverty can be absolute or relative. For a majority of Asian farmers it is absolute: their basic needs are not met, their incomes are tiny (table 5.2) and indebtedness is high (ILO 1977). Whether their lot has been improving or not as a result of recent development programmes can again be disputed: in a recent conversation between two economists, both experts on current events in Indonesia, one maintained that the poorest Javanese peasants had experienced a steady increase in real income over the last five years, the other that in fact even in absolute terms their incomes had fallen significantly. And then there is the gap between rich and poor farmers: does the introduction of new technology and increased commoditisation

Development

Table 5.1   Population densities in Asia

China (PRC)	1968/70[a]	763 persons/km² arable land
C. and S. Chinese communes	1979[b]	1,666 persons/km² arable land
Vietnamese communes	1980[c]	1,400–2,000 households/ km² wet-rice land
Japan	1968/70[a]	1,887 persons/km² arable land
S. Korea	1968/70[a]	1,408 persons/km² arable land
Indonesia	1975[d]	731 persons/km² arable land
Java and Madura	1977[e]	660 persons/km² arable land
C. Java	1977[e]	1,090 persons/km² arable land
Lombok	1930[f]	1,200 persons/km² wet-rice land
	1971[f]	2,500 persons/km² wet-rice land
Malaysia	1975[d]	202 persons/km² arable land
Thailand	1975[d]	268 persons/km² arable land
Philippines	1975[d]	563 persons/km² arable land

Sources:
[a] Ban et al. 1980: 17
[b] Wertheim and Stiefel 1982
[c] Fforde 1984
[d] Taylor 1981: 6
[e] Mizuno 1985
[f] Gerdin 1982: 63

Table 5.2   Income shares of decile groups in Asia

| | Entire economy | | Rural areas | |
	Poorest 40%	Richest 20%	Poorest 40%	Richest 20%
Malaysia 1970	11.6	56.0	12.4	45.7
Philippines 1971	11.6	53.8	13.3	51.0
Sri Lanka 1973	15.1	45.9	17.0	42.7
Bangladesh 1963/4	18.0	44.5	18.5	43.0

Source: IRRI 1977: 20

widen or narrow it? It is well established that wealthy farmers almost
always do better out of technological change than the poor or landless, if
only because they have access to credit on more favourable terms. But
obviously much depends on previous agrarian conditions, on the nature

of the new technology and on the way in which it is introduced. The case of Japan is poles apart from that of Java.

The gap between rural and urban incomes is an acute problem in Asia. According to one estimate, '415 million people or about 40 per cent of the total population representing the developing market economies of Asia lived in conditions of absolute poverty in 1969 and about 355 million (85 per cent) of these were found in rural areas'; despite overall economic growth in a number of these countries, the Asian Development Bank felt that the problem had worsened considerably during the 1970s (ADB 1977: 61, 63). South Korea has been a notable exception: there government pricing policies and technical advances brought agricultural incomes to just above urban levels in 1975, though this was a short-lived achievement (Ensor 1985: 69).[2] In Korea the rapid expansion of the industrial sector has permitted the absorption of a large quantity of surplus rural labour and contributed significantly to maintaining rural living standards; the rural population fell from 58% of the total population in 1959 to 38% in 1975 (Lee 1979: 57). In other Asian countries such as Thailand, Malaysia and the Philippines there has also been a high rate of out-migration from the countryside, but there the rate of industrial and economic growth has not been sufficient to provide jobs for the majority of the rural poor, and landlessness and underemployment are widespread (ILO 1977).

Some progress has been made in narrowing the urban-rural gap where it has been possible to diversify rural production and integrate rural labour into the national economy through agricultural diversification, the production of commercial crops and, above all, the expansion of rural manufactures and industries. Japan and Taiwan are the outstanding examples (e.g. Shimpo 1976; Gallin and Gallin 1982), and China is making increasingly successful efforts in that direction. But the success of such policies presupposes the existence of well-developed consumer markets, at home or abroad, as well as the provision of transport facilities and the availability of equipment and raw materials. Off-farm incomes in poor countries like Indonesia, and even in high-growth economies like Malaysia, are seldom sufficient to raise farmers above the poverty-line (e.g. Kahn 1980; Shand and Mohd. Ariff 1983: 248).

Rice-farming today is not generally a profitable occupation in itself, particularly if expensive commercial inputs are used. Part of the reason is that staple food cereals, and indeed agricultural products in general, suffer from severe underpricing relative to industrial goods, including such essential inputs as chemical fertilisers. Governments bent on industrialisation are usually more than willing to subsidise this process by keeping domestic food-prices low, and the now common institution of

the Guaranteed Minimum Price (GMP) may well leave the double-cropping rice-farmer little better off than if he had spent half the year idle. A government study conducted in Taiwan in 1971/2 showed that a rice-farmer could make US$50–70 per hectare on his first crop, but suffered a net loss on the second (Huang 1981: 115). In response to increasing rural discontent and illegal migration to the cities, China recently decided to shift the urban-rural economic balance by drastic repricing: between 1978 and 1982 average procurement prices for all agricultural products rose by 41.6%, and grain procurement prices rose by 48.9%; this raised annual grain production over the same period from 304 to 353 million tonnes (OECD 1985: 45, 16), an increase which can only have been welcome given China's demographic conditions.

In Japan, on the other hand, a politically powerful rice-farmers' lobby has ensured that rice cultivation has been kept profitable through costly government subsidies. But one undesirable result of subsidies familiar to anyone from the EEC is overproduction: in contrast to the situation in China, the Japanese population is not growing, and furthermore wheat products are becoming increasingly popular. While rice prices before the Second World War were based on calculations of the costs of production, since 1946 support prices have been designed to reduce the gap between industrial and agricultural incomes, and the government has calculated family labour costs not on the basis of agricultural labourers' wages but on the average wages of manufacturing workers. This has resulted in heavy financial loss to the government as well as high levels of overproduction (Ogura 1980: 208). Japan now has a mountain of rice so expensive that it is quite uncompetitive on world markets, selling at double the price of imported grain (ibid.: 219). Some *saké* brewers now import Japanese varieties of rice grown in the USA. Far from encouraging further increases in rice production, Japanese policy-makers' prime concern is how to persuade rice-farmers to switch to other crops (e.g. Ogura 1980), not an easy task given the traditional reverence for rice and the technical difficulties of transforming rice-fields.

In Malaysia higher rice prices have failed to stimulate production. Despite an increase in the GMP of 36% in 1981, there was a 35% drop in rice production in the KADA region that year (Shand and Mohd. Ariff 1983: 177). Young Malaysians refuse to become rice-farmers; they would rather leave the land they inherit idle and find jobs in the towns. The rural poor of countries like Thailand, Java and the Philippines are usually less fortunate: non-agricultural jobs are scarce and the struggle to gain access to farm-land, even as a labourer, is becoming increasingly acute (Hart and Huq 1982).

A further drawback to price manipulations as a means of increasing

rural incomes is that they often increase inequalities *between* farmers, since farmers with larger marketable surpluses will benefit more from higher prices than those who are obliged to use most of the rice they produce for their own consumption. Even in the case of South Korea, conspicuous for its lack of inequality between farmers, it has been argued that high agricultural support prices 'tended to have a regressive influence on income distribution' (Lee 1979: 43, quoting Hasan 1976: 53).

Equity and increased production frequently impose conflicting demands on development planners, and problems of production are usually easier to solve, both technically and politically. The Malaysian government has repeatedly stated its commitment to combating rural poverty, particularly among rice-farmers (most of whom are Malays). But at the same time it is aiming to achieve self-sufficiency in rice, a need the more urgently felt after a world shortage in the early 1970s when cheap imports from Thailand were for a while virtually unobtainable. It seems unlikely that Malaysia will ever achieve complete self-sufficiency in rice, but through heavy investment in double-cropping and irrigation, particularly in MADA and KADA, domestic production had come to fulfil 85% of national requirements by 1980 (Min. of Finance 1980: 105). The criticism has been made by several economists, however, that by forcing farmers into rice monoculture so as to maximise national production the government has increased their economic vulnerability and reduced their real incomes, in effect sacrificing regional development to national objectives (e.g. Bell 1978; Taylor 1981: 186).

Labour and capital

The first three chapters discussed trends in the technical development of the basic resources, or factors of production, in wet-rice cultivation: the biological adaptation and improvement of the plant itself; the development of the productivity of the land upon which it is grown; and the perfection of control over the water supply. Here the relative potential of labour and capital for bringing about such improvements will be explored.

There are of course considerable problems inherent in the use of the term 'capital', which can take on a range of meanings that not only denote financial assets, equipment and infrastructure, but can also be extended to include a labour force and its quality, as for example when a nation's educational system is described as contributing to its human capital. Since I am concerned here with historical as well as contempor-

ary situations, including both subsistence and commercialised economies and the transition to capitalised farming, in order to avoid confusion I shall define my terms as follows.

The term *capital* is used to denote financial assets which can be accumulated or invested in expanding the means of production. *Capital goods* are durables acquired through the investment of capital and include, for example, draft animals and farm machinery or equipment which is purchased rather than home-made. *Capital inputs*, as well as capital goods, would also include commercial fertilisers, purchased seed-stock, cash rents, land tax and irrigation fees, as well as the *hiring* of labour. Rents in kind, the use of family or exchange labour, and taxes paid in labour or in kind would not come under this heading. *Technical infrastructure* includes such constructions as irrigation works, terraced fields or transport networks, which may be achieved either through capital investment or simply through the organisation of labour. In the former case the necessary raw materials will be purchased and the labour force (usually) paid for its work; in the latter, materials may be locally available free or they may be contributed by a benefactor or by the beneficiaries of the work, and the labour will be levied or donated. It seems to me particularly important to draw these distinctions given recent trends towards centralised agricultural development planning in both the socialist and the capitalist nations of Asia. In the capitalist nations development strategies have been principally based on the investment of large amounts of capital in infrastructural projects and in the dissemination of new technology, whereas socialist governments have not infrequently preferred to substitute labour for capital where possible, especially in the construction of infrastructure.

Given the importance of central economic planning in Asian economic development today, it is crucial to pay close attention to the relative efficacy of labour and of capital under different circumstances. The amounts of both labour and capital available for use in agriculture are not independent variables: agricultural production cannot be isolated from the national economy as a whole, especially when labour supplies and levels of capital accumulation are to be taken into account. But here for the sake of clarity agriculture will be treated independently of other sectors of the economy.

The historical experience: the predominance of labour and the 'Japanese model'

It would hardly be accurate to characterise Asian rice-based economies, even before the advent of Western capitalism, as subsistence economies

in which capital played little or no role. Many were commercialised, some (such as medieval China and Tokugawa Japan) to quite a high degree. Nevertheless, the nature of the inputs required to raise output in wet-rice cultivation was such that capital played a subordinate role to labour in developing the forces of production.

The historical material shows clearly how over time Asian systems of wet-rice cultivation became progressively more intensive in their use of labour, while relying on relatively low levels of capital investment. In large part this is because the general trend in technical development has been towards the concentration of resources on raising the productivity of land. Although total labour requirements vary from region to region, depending upon soils, climate, water supply and so on, it can be shown that broadly speaking yields of wet rice correlate positively with labour inputs (Ishikawa 1981: 2, 22) (table 5.3).

Table 5.3   Rice yields and labour inputs

	Yields (t/ha)	Human labour inputs (man-days/ha)
Japan 1950	4.25	255
1956	5.07	229
1962	5.79	190
S. Korea 1960	3.27	139
Taiwan 1926	2.11	96
1967	5.1	113
1972	5.7	125
E. China 1921–5	2.56	146
Java 1969–70	3.5	360
Thailand (Nong Sarai) 1972	2.0	83
Philippines C. Luzon 1966	2.2	60
1970	2.7	71
1974	2.2	82
Laguna 1966	2.5	88
1975	3.5	105
India Madras 1956	2.25	216
W. Bengal (Hoogly) 1956	1.80	133
(24-Parganas) 1956	1.54	103

Sources: Ishikawa 1981: 3; Taylor 1981: 89

Rice yields are also directly related to the efficacy of management of the water supply, and until very recently this imposed restrictions on the size of wet-rice fields and was an important barrier to mechanical rationalisation of the European type. Given the large investment in labour and time required to develop a productive rice-field, there was instead a strong incentive to evolve land-saving skills, skills which were both technical and managerial. Effective supervision of such skilled work is highly demanding, and as rice cultivation systems became more productive there was a marked tendency for units of management to become smaller rather than larger, usually taking the form of family farms supplying the bulk of their own labour.

The Asian wet-rice economies were often characterised by a high level of investment in the form of such technical infrastructure as irrigation works, but at least until the colonial period these used only a small proportion of liquid capital, relying instead on voluntary or enforced labour contributions and the donation by state or local beneficiaries of construction materials.

As to capital inputs, many of the new inputs characteristic of early periods of development in Asian rice agriculture were *divisible*, that is to say, extra labour, new seed or improved fertilisers could be bought in any quantity according to the farmer's needs, inclination or financial situation. Often organisational improvements or a more careful carrying out of operations would make important contributions to increasing output while requiring no increase in capital outlay at all. Innovation was thus within the scope of farmers of all income groups.

An early example of divisible inputs is to be found in the case of medieval China. The expansion of agricultural output in medieval South China was brought about by the introduction of quick-ripening and drought-resistant rice varieties, permitting the development of multiple cropping and an increase in the rice-growing area; by the development of local irrigation and water control facilities; by an increase in the application of fertilisers, mainly industrial by-products such as bean-cake; and by the spread of improved rice cultivation techniques, described in such works as the *Chen Fu nongshu* (1149) and *Wang Zhen nongshu* (1313). These are all what Ishikawa (1981: 36) calls 'labour-using technological factors', that is to say, higher yields are obtained through a new technology requiring increased labour inputs. Describing similar developments in Tokugawa Japan, Smith says of commercial fertilisers:

Insofar as they replaced natural fertilisers they saved an enormous amount of labour. They drastically reduced and might entirely eliminate the work of cutting

and hauling grass from the mountainside, then trampling it into the ploughed and flooded fields; moreover, this labour was saved at the planting when the work load reached its annual peak and time and human energy were most precious. How great was the potential for saving at this season may be judged from the fact that in the seventeenth century about ten man-days per *tan* [bushel] of paddy were spent in cutting grass and composting fields prior to planting. But this is only part of the story. Multiple-cropping was a common result – indeed often the chief aim – of the adoption of commercial fertilisers; and insofar as it was, the new fertilisers added more labour to farming than they saved, though it should be noted that the addition came mostly at a time when employment was otherwise slack. (1959: 101)

In fact, as Smith points out later (1959: 142 ff), there were four principal technical elements in Tokugawa agriculture, namely commercial fertilisers, a new type of thresher (the *semba-koki*), multiple cropping and crop diversification (in response to market demands) which, while increasing a farmer's total labour requirements, spread them out evenly over the year (figure 5.1). The steady reduction in the gap between the size of large and small farms, which by the late Tokugawa period were approaching uniform family size, is also significant in this context.

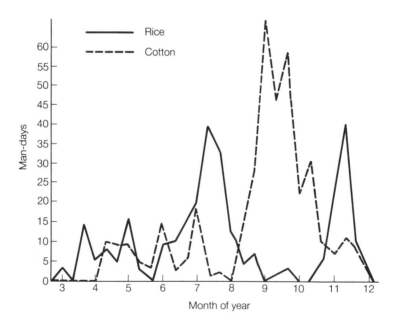

Figure 5.1   Labour demands on a holding in Shinshū in 1823
(from Smith 1959: 143)

One might be tempted to attribute this type of technological development, in the case of medieval China at least, to historical necessity: the lack of capital for investment in, or the lack of scientific knowledge for production of, labour-saving devices such as farm machinery or chemical herbicides. But it is in fact intrinsic to the technical trends in wet-rice cultivation examined in previous chapters. The new inputs which made possible the surge in agricultural productivity in Song China and Tokugawa Japan form a very similar package to that being promoted in Asia today under various Green Revolution policies. The 'New Technology' is frequently seen as a package requiring heavy and unaccustomed capital investment on the part of traditional farmers, forcing a shift towards the commercialisation of agriculture and a consequent emmiseration of poor peasants who must borrow in order to obtain the necessary capital (e.g. de Koninck 1978). As mentioned above, such capital inputs as commercial fertilisers had in fact been a crucial factor in agricultural improvement in both medieval China and Tokugawa Japan. Problems of transport and distribution meant that their cost was a significant item even then in a peasant farmer's accounts, especially since prices were not infrequently fixed at high levels by merchant monopolies:

Although farm income was highly variable costs were relatively rigid. The prices of the commodities the peasant bought were controlled, within certain limits, by powerful merchant guilds that exercised local monopolies with government sanction. Since the peasant sold either in a free market, or in one positively rigged against him and in favour of monopoly merchants to whom he was required by law to sell, he was periodically caught in a cost-price squeeze. The squeeze was more frequent and tighter moreover by virtue of the fact that a single item, fertiliser, accounted for a very high percentage of his cash expenditures; for one item could be more easily controlled than several, and this particular item was one for which the peasant could not reduce his purchases without suffering an immediate and sharp decline in income. (Smith 1959: 159)

Commercial fertilisers were a very heavy item of expenditure in the budgets of Tokugawa farmers. They accounted for over one-half of the total cash expenditure of one eighteenth-century mixed rice and cotton farm in Settsu province (in the relatively advanced region of the Kinai, near Ōsaka), and it seems that this was by no means atypical (ibid.: 82).

So capital inputs, at least in the form of commercial fertilisers, did play an important part in agricultural development in pre-modern China and Japan. On the other hand the switch to multiple cropping and the diversification of crop choice, though largely dependent upon the use of commercial fertilisers (and also new, improved crop varieties), necessitated no increase in capital inputs unless it became necessary to hire labour.

While there definitely was a growth in the free agricultural labour market in Tokugawa Japan (as opposed to various sorts of bonded labour), it was mainly hired by larger holdings to help with such commercial activities as silkworm-breeding or brewing (Smith 1959: ch. 8; Nakamura 1959). Slow demographic growth and a steady expansion of trade and industry in both urban and rural areas not only pushed up wages but also, by the eighteenth century, brought about severe labour shortages in agriculture which the central and provincial governments attempted in vain to curb.[3] High wages must have been a contributing factor in maintaining the majority of holdings in Tokugawa Japan at the size of a family farm, where the bottlenecks of transplanting and harvesting could be overcome through exchanging labour with neighbouring families. However the lack of any major labour-saving inventions or innovations in agriculture (apart from the thresher mentioned earlier), even on large farms where labour costs were a considerable drain on the budget, sustains the point that the investment of skilled labour was more profitable in wet-rice agriculture than that of labour-saving capital goods.

The value that was placed on the quality rather than the quantity of labour can be seen in the following passage, in which a seventeenth-century Chinese landowner exhorts his heirs to choose their tenants with care:

There is a proverb which says, 'It is better to have good tenants than good land', and this is a very accurate statement ... There are three advantages in having good tenants, namely that they are on time with ploughing and sowing, they are energetic in fertilising, and they are resourceful in conserving every drop of water. The men of old used to say: 'The most important thing in agriculture is doing everything at the proper season.' ... With diligence like this, one *mou* may yield the produce of two. Without the land being extended or the acreage increased, the tenant will have a surplus and the landlord too will profit by it. In the conservation and use of water, everything depends on speed and timing. Damming up the waters, waiting, and then releasing them, all have to be done at the proper time. Only good and experienced farmers know about this. (*Hengchan suoyan* by Zhang Ying, tr. Beattie 1979: 146)

Zhang Ying goes on to stress the crucial importance of adequate irrigation networks in producing good rice crops and maintaining an income from rents, and urges his descendants: 'When it comes to constructing ponds and building dykes, you must supervise the matter in person' (ibid.: 148): clearly the tenants themselves were expected to provide both tools and materials (tamped earth, shovels and baskets in the main) as well as the labour force.[4] Improvements in water control were one of the most important contributory factors in the growth of agricultural production in pre-modern China and Japan. Here, capital

investment was at a minimum, while the initial labour requirements were very high, and skills and knowledge were thereafter required in order to profit fully by these infrastructural improvements.

Although accurate cost-accounting for farm management in pre-modern China and Japan is no easy matter,[5] it is fair to assume that the purchase of new seeds and fertilisers, the construction of water control systems, and so on, yielded reasonable economic returns in the majority of cases, given the remarkable and rapid expansion of the economy as a whole. Just as important, one can deduce that although many of the improvements were 'labour-using', nevertheless labour productivity in rice agriculture did not fall: the spread of agricultural specialisation and of multiple cropping, and the growth of rural manufactures and other income-generating activities, in conjunction with slow demographic increase,[6] show that labour productivity in agriculture must have risen quite significantly; and while the improvements in rice cultivation absorbed larger amounts of labour, they did not cause insuperable bottlenecks, nor did they preclude the possibility of combining rice cultivation with other economic activities.

In an important essay on labour absorption in Asian agriculture, Ishikawa (1981: 1–149) maintains that increased labour inputs are essential to combat underemployment and raise incomes in rural Asia. The historical case of Japan is particularly important in this context, especially as it is the only Asian country for which accurate calculations of long-term changes in labour inputs can be given.[7] From the early Tokugawa period (*c.*1600) up until the commencement of agricultural mechanisation in the late 1950s both rice yields and per hectare labour inputs increased steadily (table 5.4). Since many South and Southeast

Table 5.4   Rice yields and labour inputs in Japan

	Rice yields (t/ha)	Rice labour inputs (man-days/ha)	Total labour inputs (man-days/ha)
1874	2.36	278	353
1880	2.53	275	375
1890	3.04	271	393
1900	2.87	267	397
1910	3.08	251	398
1920	3.94	235	384
1930	3.92	211	357
1940	3.74	206	359
1950	4.13	256	394
1960	4.99	214	345
1970	5.75	146	235

Source: Ishikawa 1981: 42

Asian agricultural systems, at least prior to the innovations of the Green Revolution, were at a level of technological organisation and development of resources comparable to that obtaining in Japan before the Meiji reforms of the 1870s and 1880s, the possibility of following a 'Japanese model' of agricultural development has of late gained quite wide popularity among economists and planning agencies. Perhaps the clearest exposition of the model is presented by Ogura (1967; see also Ishikawa 1967: 59).

The 'Japanese model' differs from most Western-derived development strategies in that it is based on improvement in the application of human skills rather than the substitution of machinery for labour, and requires a low level of capital investment. The three principal features derived from Japan's historical experience are: (i) the intensification of land use relying on such inputs as fertilisers, improved varieties and better techniques; (ii) the modest level of capital required; and (iii) the small scale and easily divisible nature of the improvements, appropriate to the prevailing levels of technical development and patterns of agricultural organisation.

As Ishikawa points out, however, there are two levels of success which may be achieved by increasing labour inputs. The first, typified by China up to 1954, Korea up to the same period, and by India and other Asian countries today, shows a marked increase in yields but a diminution in farm size and almost no improvement in farm income (1967: 78): in this case technical improvement perpetuates subsistence-level agriculture, and while this allows for demographic growth it cannot improve rural living standards, nor can it contribute to the general development of the national economy. But in the case of Meiji Japan a higher level of improvement was achieved, where farm incomes and the *productivity of labour* increased. Ogura and other economists suggest that this was what allowed Japanese agriculture not only to finance its own development but also to accumulate capital which contributed to the growth of the industrial sector (see also Geertz 1963; Ishikawa 1967: ch. 4). As Ishikawa (1981) repeatedly stresses, if the economies of the poorer Asian countries are to improve, it is crucial not simply to increase agricultural output through an increase in labour and other inputs, but also to maintain, and preferably increase, the marginal productivity of labour. There are some inputs which are more likely to achieve this effect than others (1981: 40).

Choice of technological inputs

One can make a clear distinction between two types of technology in rice

agriculture: (i) *biochemical* technology, which denotes improved rice varieties, fertilisers and pesticides; these can be considered land substitutes since they increase yields; and (ii) *mechanical* technology which substitutes for labour. Some inputs may save both land and labour, for example chemical herbicides or mechanical pump-sets. Usually a rational choice can be made as to which type of input should be invested in to produce the greatest improvements under particular circumstances.

The higher a country's latitude, the shorter the growing season for rice. In the Yangzi valley the season is about 120 days, and a single crop of rice alternated with wheat or barley had been standard cropping practice for centuries. As from 1956 quicker-ripening rice varieties were disseminated and efforts were made to double-crop rice over an area of 2.3 million ha in Central China. But in the absence of mechanisation acute labour shortages were experienced during the busy season, and results on the whole were poor. The lack of pump-sets for irrigation was one of the chief problems; another was the overlap between harvesting and threshing the first rice crop and tilling the fields and transplanting the second. From the mid-1960s a major effort was made to mechanise these processes, and the double-cropping of rice then became feasible (Ishikawa 1981: 52, 107).

In lower latitudes the growing season is longer. In Taiwan at the turn of the century, when the Japanese decided to develop rice production, the major constraint on the introduction of double-cropping was not the short growing period or the lack of mechanisation but insufficient water. Under Japanese rule the Taiwanese irrigation network was greatly expanded and improved, and the process was only discontinued in 1933 when rice prices in Japan fell sharply. After the Second World War there was less investment in the expansion of the irrigation network, but this was compensated for by improvements in water conservation and management (ibid.: 62). The cultivation of two crops of rice followed by a third crop of maize, potatoes, soy, tobacco or vegetables is now widespread in Taiwan (Food and Fertiliser Centre 1974).

Where water supplies are inadequate rice yields will always be low. At this stage the improvement of water supplies will in itself increase yields more than the introduction of improved varieties and fertilisers, since adequate water is a prerequisite for the efficient use of biochemical inputs. The development of water control facilities not only stabilises and raises rice yields but also permits greater cropping frequency. The efficiency of large-scale irrigation projects as opposed to various types of low-level improvement has to be considered in such cases (e.g. Taylor 1981: 121–75; Ishikawa 1967: 131–53).

Improvements in water control nowadays require considerable capital

investment, but the biochemical inputs typical of the Green Revolution package, namely HYVs, fertilisers and pesticides, are, like the innovations of Tokugawa and Meiji Japan, both divisible and labour-using, and so they are likely to prove accessible and beneficial to farmers at all income levels. Mechanical inputs tend to be indivisible or 'lumpy': either one buys a whole thresher or no thresher at all. But the costs can be split if they are purchased by groups or cooperatives, or hired. And when it enables farmers to intensify their cropping practices then mechanical technology, like biochemical inputs, can absorb rather than displace agricultural labour: this is characteristic of such items as pump-sets, threshers and drying machines, but not always of tillers and tractors (Ishikawa 1981: 70).

It seems to be especially difficult to raise the marginal productivity of agriculture without resorting to mechanisation in cases where labour use is already intensive and skills highly developed. A survey carried out in North Arcot (Tamil Nadu, India) by IRRI (1975) showed that in 1981 of the extra labour necessitated by the cultivation of high-yielding as opposed to traditional varieties (232 as opposed to 175 days), 60% was required for extra weeding and plant protection and 40% for harvesting and processing; at the same time the new varieties yielded 4.0 t/ha as opposed to 2.9 t/ha. Here, then, labour inputs rose by 33% and yields by 38%, showing a slight increase in labour productivity. But in Sidoarjo (East Java), the same survey showed that while labour inputs rose by 8%, from 256 to 276 man-days/ha, yields rose by only 6%, from 4.5 to 4.8 t/ha. On the other hand, in Subang (West Java), where the introduction of the new varieties led to the replacement of the reaping-knife by the sickle, yields rose by 30%, from 3.0 to 3.9 t/ha, and labour inputs fell by over 9%, from 170 to 154 man-days/ha, a rise in labour productivity which might seem to denote a signal improvement for the peasants. But while the replacement of the reaping-knife by the sickle may hardly strike the reader as a radical shift to advanced technology, the reallocation of labour involved has had considerable social repercussions, mainly due to the inequalities in access to land and in labour opportunities prevailing in Javanese society (Palmer 1977: 145; Collier 1981). Similar disruptions have resulted from the mechanisation of farming in the Muda region in Malaysia, and more especially from the introduction, not of sickles, but of combine-harvesters (Lim et al. 1980: 65; de Koninck 1981: 12). Indeed they are typical of regions where opportunities for off-farm employment are scarce, and this includes even relatively affluent rice regions where monoculture prevails, for in such cases the labour productivity of a few farmers can be increased only at the cost of unemployment to others.

Capital investment

The dissemination of the 'New Technology', with its heavy reliance on capital inputs such as chemical fertilisers and new pressures on traditional forms of labour organisation, has marked an important shift in the balance between labour and capital. Capital investment by the state has increased enormously, as has that made by the private sector and by farmers themselves. Let us first look at the ways in which the state may invest in rice agriculture so as to encourage increased output and, to a greater or lesser extent, relieve the financial burden on the farmers themselves.

The state has several areas in which it may invest to foster agricultural growth. The first is technical infrastructure: land reclamation; the provision of transport facilities; and most importantly water control, an essential prerequisite for the efficient development of rice cultivation. As we saw in chapter 3, Asian states traditionally met most of the costs of constructing large-scale water control networks with conscripted labour, but under the pressures of colonialism and the expansion of world rice markets hired labour was increasingly substituted in a number of regions from the mid-nineteenth century. Now that reclamation and irrigation schemes are designed by professional engineers, and specialised plant is available which can carry out such work much more quickly and effectively than coolies with shovels, and expensive equipment like sluice-dams and central pumping-stations are part of the designs, hydraulic projects have become extremely capital-intensive. At 1979 prices it was projected that the future costs of irrigation development in Asia as a whole would be between $3,055 and $3,975 per hectare, and already the cost of constructing new projects in parts of Malaysia was as high as $5,465 per hectare (Taylor 1981: 180).

Malaysia is perhaps an extreme case, where the state has undertaken sole responsibility for investment in infrastructural construction, relying entirely upon capital investment to achieve it. China on the other hand has continued to use labour in the process of capital formation, keeping cash costs to a minimum. Up to 1957 state-organised labour used outside the community mobilised 5 to 10 million peasants a year; from 1957 responsibility for their wages fell upon their commune. 'According to the latest data, nowadays 17 million people, or about 5% of China's total agricultural labour force, work all-year-round in regular agricultural capital construction teams under the [prefecture] or commune' (Vermeer 1977: 63). The PLA played an important role in large projects, for example undertaking 49% of the earth-work and 73% of the concrete-work on the Jinjiang (Middle Yangzi) Project (ibid.: 105). Most labour

and capital for local-level projects was provided not by the central government but by the province, prefecture or commune. It is interesting that since 1979 state investment in hydraulic works has fallen from 3,496 million *yuan* (1979) to 1,774 million *yuan* (1982), but to compensate the government is trying to negotiate contracts with households or work-teams which stipulate the contribution of a certain number of unpaid work-days for capital investment in agricultural projects (OECD 1985: 48, 50).

It is not only the socialist regimes of Asia which require local-level participation in the provision of technical infrastructure. Ever since the Meiji period the Japanese government has required both the prefectures and the benefiting farmers to meet a substantial proportion of the costs, often as much as 25% each (Ishikawa 1967: 143). Under such arrangements new projects would require the approval of at least two-thirds of the landowners involved, which often proved a considerable obstacle to innovation (Shimpo 1976: 18). (In Japan, as elsewhere, the irrigation fees paid by farmers are intended to meet some of the running costs rather than to recoup initial expenditure.)

In South Korea many small-scale infrastructural projects have been organised locally under the New Community Movement (*Saemaul Undong*), launched by President Park in 1971. Over the first decade, 'approximately 70% of the total resources required for these projects was contributed by rural people in the form of donations of labour, land, and recently even cash. In this respect, the managerial capabilities of the Saemaul leaders must be given special credit' (Whang 1981: 15). Or, to put it another way, 'local self-help projects require considerable uncompensated labour and often the contribution of other scarce resources by villagers, while in many cases benefits are intangible or deferred for many months or even years' (Brandt 1980: 277).

When it comes to capital inputs, especially fertilisers, and capital goods such as tilling, harvesting and processing machinery, state investment or subsidy can take a number of forms. The government can establish national industries to supply these products, it can import them, or it can rely on the private sector to import or produce them. Generally imported products cost more than locally produced goods, and the private sector charges more than the public. If it is left to the private sector to supply the capital inputs, the cost to the farmer will be high unless state subsidies are applied at various levels. Let us take fertilisers and tractors as illustrations.

In Indonesia after 1966 the value of fertiliser imports rose steeply, from $34.6 million in 1964 to $290.5 million in January–June 1974; meanwhile government subsidies on fertilisers rose from 1,000 million

rupiahs in 1964 to 5,700 million *rupiahs* in 1967–8, but then fell to 2,250 million *rupiahs* in 1969 and to 714 million *rupiahs* in 1970 (Palmer 1977: 172, 192). The original subsidy level was set so that the price of 1 kg of urea would be equal to that of 1 kg of milled rice, but the balance was soon upset since the oil crisis sent fertiliser prices up at a time when the government was keeping rice prices low (ibid.: 54).[8] Despite the financial difficulties facing the farmers, however, the application of chemical fertilisers increased from 3.5 kg/ha in 1960/1 to 26.3 kg/ha in 1973/4 (ADB 1978: 416), largely because government regulations obliged farmers to grow the new HYVs which, unlike traditional varieties, cannot be grown without chemical fertilisers (Loekman 1982).

In China green manures, nightsoil and other organic fertilisers have continued to play an important role in maintaining soil fertility; although the amounts used are impossible to quantify, they have been described as 'enormous' (American Delegation 1977: 200), but the proportion of chemical fertilisers used has been growing continuously. Organic manures are usually locally produced and distributed. Until about 1958 most chemical fertilisers were imported, but domestic production began to take off in the late 1950s, helped by the setting-up of innumerable small-scale local plants producing mainly urea; this development was possible thanks to the wide distribution of coal deposits in China (ibid.: 154). While fertiliser imports stayed at between 1 and 2 million tonnes between 1969 and 1979, domestic production shot up from 1.4 million to over 12.3 million tonnes over the same period (Stone 1982: 236). In 1973 small-scale plants accounted for 60% of national production. Since 1980 the Ministry for the Chemical Industry has been reorganising and amalgamating small plants, and state investment has dropped (OECD 1985: 52).

Under the commune system the costs of fertilisers, as of all other production expenses, were met by the production team or brigade, which derived its income from selling its produce and products to the state (e.g. Aziz 1978: 57). Under the 'responsibility system' there are several ways in which production may be organised.[9] Probably the most widespread is 'contracting everything to the household' (*baogan daohu*), under which arrangement the household is responsible for all investment in production, as it also is under 'contracting output to the household' (*baochan daohu*); under specialised contracting for grain production the contracting unit is a work-group and fertilisers and other inputs are purchased with internal credit coupons issued at the beginning of each year to the group, to the cash value of its output target (Walker 1984: 787; Watson 1984: 95, 93).

Turning to the case of tractors, two government projects in Malaysia

offer an interesting contrast. On the Muda scheme (MADA) in Kedah the mechanisation of ploughing developed rapidly through the 1960s. 40% of ploughing was mechanised by 1966 and 94% by 1970; double-cropping of rice was introduced in 1969. MADA is a relatively prosperous rice region, and in the late 1960s some farmers began to invest in power-tillers and even in four-wheel tractors; a majority, however, hired large tractors from private contractors to plough their fields. The contracting industry was extremely competitive; average ploughing costs fell from M$77–87 per ha in 1965 to M$65 (for two passes) in 1970. Contracting was entirely in private hands; the Farmers' Associations did not provide tractor hire as one of their services. Some 300 to 400 private business contractors were in operation in MADA in the mid-1970s. But after the introduction of double-cropping, farmers with larger than average holdings (regardless of their tenurial status) invested in power-tillers, the number of which rose from 580 in 1970 to about 3,500 in 1976; the mean farm size of tiller-owners was 3.15 ha, compared to the average MADA farm of 1.6 ha. Not only did the purchasers use their tillers on their own farms, they also undertook contract ploughing (on an average of 18 ha per season in 1976), thus competing with the businessmen who owned the large tractors and eventually ousting many from the market (MADA 1980).

In contrast, on the Kemubu scheme (KADA) in Kelantan, a region characterised by generalised poverty, there are a few commercial firms which provide tractor-hire services, but almost no tillage machines are owned by farmers. The overwhelming majority of tractors (over 100 large tractors in 1982) are owned by KADA and hired out through the local Farmers' Associations. By keeping hire prices extremely low (at only M$26 per hour in 1982) KADA effectively cuts out any competition from the private sector (Abdullah Hussein, pers. comm. 1982). Even so, many farmers still rely on buffalo ploughs, largely for financial reasons (Bray 1987). In 1980/1, 21% used animals for all or part of the tillage of their fields, and in 1981/2 the figure rose to 35% (Shand and Mohd. Ariff 1983: 119). The overall degree of mechanisation is thus much lower than on the Muda scheme, despite the state subsidies.

Another area in which the state can invest in order to encourage agricultural growth is the provision of credit facilities. Formerly if farmers needed cash they would turn to their landlords or to money-lenders, pledging their next harvest or their land as collateral. Many Asian states have legislated against such transactions, which all too frequently plunged families into irredeemable misery. It is not easy to eradicate money-lending, however: a poor peasant who has urgent need of cash and little chance of persuading the local bank that he is

credit-worthy may well turn to a money-lender in desperation. But Asian governments have made conscientious efforts to supply credit on favourable terms and on a reasonably egalitarian basis for investment in agriculture, and to foster organisations which count the provision of credit facilities among their functions. Agricultural banks, cooperatives and Farmers' Associations are all willing to provide loans and savings facilities to farmers, but there are certain drawbacks for both sides. Poor farmers often find it difficult or impossible to obtain credit from official sources, from banks because they have little security, and from cooperatives or FAs because these are frequently dominated by the wealthier farmers who tend to monopolise credit facilities (e.g. ILO 1977). On the other side, farmers feel much less obligation towards impersonal institutions than towards known individuals, and of course it is more difficult for such institutions to enforce repayment than for a landlord or money-lender, for governments are honour-bound not to foreclose on mortgages and expel farmers from their land. Malaysian officials frequently complained to me of the high levels of default on debts; in the Philippines farmers repay money-lenders, but not the government which is helping them to buy their land (Mangahas et al. 1976).

While Asian governments are investing heavily in promoting agricultural production, the rice-farmers' cash disbursements are also increasing. Whereas formerly many subsistence farmers were obliged to enter the market to obtain cash to pay their taxes (see chapter 6), now they also need cash to purchase inputs. In theory it is possible to remain aloof from such pressures, cultivating old-fashioned varieties by traditional methods. But even where governments do not impose regulations enforcing the adoption of new technology, as was the case recently in Java (Loekman 1982) or earlier this century in Japan and its colonies (Dore 1969: 104; Ban et al. 1980: 164), the systemic nature of change in rice cultivation systems exerts heavy pressure to conform. A farmer whose land is incorporated into an irrigation scheme designed to permit double-cropping, for instance, will no longer be able to plant traditional slow-ripening varieties in his fields (Bray and Robertson 1980). He is therefore obliged, at the very least, to purchase improved seeds and fertilisers. In areas where cropping frequency increases, old patterns of labour input will change: the hiring or purchase of machinery may become necessary, and labour exchange gives way to labour hire. Farmers who are struggling to break even, especially tenant farmers, will seek to minimise their costs by using only family labour on their own farm, but will be anxious to supplement their income by hiring out their labour to others (e.g. Takahashi 1970: 105), while farmers with capital to

invest may prefer to lease or purchase machines rather than hire labour. Overall, the introduction of the New Technology has brought a fall in the proportion of total labour inputs supplied by household rather than hired labour (table 5.5).

Table 5.5   Proportion of hired labour used in rice production

	Total labour (man-days/ha)	Family labour (%)	Hired labour (%)
Indonesia			
Java 1969/70	360	22	78
Philippines			
Laguna 1966	88	42	58
1975	106	20	80
C. Luzon 1970	71	39	61
1974	82	33	67
C. Taiwan 1967	113	69	31
1972	125	62	38

Source: Taylor 1981: 89

Productivity of labour and capital

In the past it appears that increases in rice yields in Asia were always dependent upon an increase in labour-inputs, but were considerably enhanced by the improvement of techniques and by the use of better varieties and of more fertilisers. When such improved inputs were used, as in medieval China and in Tokugawa and Meiji Japan, labour productivity rose as well as the productivity of land, and generalised economic growth was possible; when they were not, as in colonial Tonkin and Java, labour productivity fell and emmiseration resulted. To what extent has this pattern been modified by recent changes in technology, and how has the increased importance of capital inputs affected the productivity of capital and of labour?

In recent years rice yields have risen throughout Asia. This has in the main been attributed to the dissemination of the New Technology, and in particular of 'land-saving' biochemical technology. The divisible nature of biochemical technology has allowed its almost universal adoption, indeed in certain places an inverse ratio has been found between farm size and the adoption rate of biochemical inputs (Fujimoto 1983: 126; Palmer 1977: 82). On small farms biochemical inputs are in general the principal capital outlay, and household labour is very

intensively used; hired labour, and even the hiring of machinery, is kept to a minimum.[10] This reduction in capital investment does not reduce yields – on the contrary, rice yields per hectare often increase as the size of farm decreases (Gibbons et al. 1980: 128) – but it does have an adverse effect on profits and on the productivity of household labour.

To take the case of China, where for many years it was contended that labour could and should be widely substituted for capital: between 1957 and 1975 the productivity of agricultural labour, reckoned in output-value per man-day, fell by between 15% and 36% (T. Rawski 1979: 119; see also Watson 1984: 87, table 1). The fall occurred despite considerable improvements in water control and fertiliser use over the period. These technical improvements in fact raised production costs steeply, since agricultural prices remained low while industrial prices were high. The gross income from agricultural production over this period grew by only 80%, and production costs increased by 130%; thus returns to capital investment in agriculture also declined (Watson 1984: 85). But this was largely a result of pricing policies: in terms of absolute output, labour productivity did at least remain more or less stable, for while the total agricultural labour force grew by 50% between 1957 and 1975, so too did grain output (ibid.: 88).

To remedy the stagnation in labour productivity and stimulate agricultural growth, China's economists at first advocated a policy of mechanisation. But from the outset doubts were expressed in many quarters as to the wisdom of displacing agricultural labour when rural underemployment was such a serious problem. Large-scale agricultural mechanisation has been confined to a few regions like the Manchurian provinces; elsewhere investment in mechanisation has been aimed principally at eliminating bottlenecks so as to permit increased cropping intensity and the diversification of economic activities (see chapter 2). It is noteworthy, however, that the spectacular gains in output since the adoption of the 'responsibility system' are apparently due mainly to the renewed energy which Chinese farmers are pouring into their land. Yields of all crops have increased significantly, and rice yields went from a national average of 4.0 t/ha in 1978 to 5.1 t/ha in 1983, up by over 25%; during the same time output per head of total population in the rich rice-growing central and eastern regions increased by 16% and 25% respectively (Watson 1984: 805, 808). How much of this is due to improved management and longer hours, and how much to greater investment in improved inputs, is difficult to say, for now that management and accounting have been decentralised, figures for levels of household investment will not be easy to estimate. Nevertheless, the overall pace of agricultural growth and the rapid diversification into

commercial and industrial crops as well as other economic activities indicates that, as in medieval China and Tokugawa Japan, the productivity of labour must also be rising at a good pace.

Under certain circumstances Chinese farmers are now even allowed to hire labour, though only in limited amounts, to supplement that which the household alone can supply. Although the hiring of labour represents an additional production cost, the size of farm is an important determinant of the profitability of rice-farming, so that labour hire can be a very worthwhile investment if sufficient land is available. A study undertaken in 1977/8 in Province Wellesley, Malaysia, showed that the factor coefficients of increase in income for land, total labour and fertilisers were 0.54, 0.26 and 0.16 respectively, so that an increase of 10% in the land farmed would theoretically result in an increase of over 5% in income, an increase in 10% of fertiliser use in under 2% (Fujimoto 1983: 141). (In the Muda region the factor coefficient for land was in the order of 1.0 [Mokhtar 1978: 125].) Although returns to total labour are seen, at least in this case, to be at an intermediate level between land and fertiliser, it is the hiring of labour which enables a farmer to cultivate larger areas and so make larger profits. The division of a given area of land into very small farms will produce higher yields and a greater total output, but also higher total consumption and much lower profits for the farmers. In Province Wellesley, where almost equal amounts of household and hired labour are used by rice-farmers, the level of profits was such that household labour earnings were slightly above the average for casual labour, but in the poorer and more densely populated state of Kelantan, where farms are smaller and almost all labour is provided by the household, household labour earnings are in fact negative.[11] This is indeed the vicious circle of subsistence production deplored by Ishikawa.

Even in countries like Japan, where yields are high, technology is advanced and farmers enjoy relatively high incomes, rice-farming itself is an unprofitable occupation; it is the complementary activities from which Japanese rice-farmers derive their comfortable incomes. In 1979 only 15% made a profit from rice-farming as such, namely those who cultivated over 1 ha of rice-land (Matsuda 1982: 449), and this despite the extremely high rice support prices and low cost of fertilisers in Japan.[12] In part the low profits may be ascribed to overinvestment in machinery. Labour hire has been uncommon, expensive, and limited by legal restrictions in Japan since the land reforms (Ogura 1980: 465), and every stage of rice cultivation has now been effectively mechanised. But while land productivity (measured in terms of output per hectare) has increased steadily, if quite slowly, at a rate of 0.97% per annum between

1965 and 1977, and labour productivity has increased spectacularly at 6.5% per annum, returns to capital invested in machinery have dropped steeply by 9.8% per annum; meanwhile returns to capital invested in fertiliser have increased by 0.77% per annum (Matsuda 1982: 441).

While the rapid increase in labour productivity is highly desirable, it could have been achieved at much lower capital costs if farmers had been willing to share or hire machinery rather than buy it outright. The overinvestment in labour-substituting rather than land-substituting mechanisation has led to discrepancies in profitability between small and large farms, i.e. the appearance of scale economies, which were absent in Japan in the prewar period, when most increases in production were effected with scale-neutral improvements such as water control and biochemical technology (ibid.: 443). That sizeable increases in labour productivity as well as output can be achieved without resorting to wide-scale mechanisation can be seen from the example of South Korea, where the mechanisation of rice-farming has been later and much slower than in Japan[13] (table 5.6). One of the important if non-quantifiable factors contributing to the rapid development of Korean agriculture has been a marked improvement in expertise, both in the education level of farmers and in the quality of extension services (Ban et al. 1980: 111).

Table 5.6   Mechanisation in Korea and Japan

| | Korea | | | | Japan | | | |
| | 1964 | 1979 | | 1962 | | 1978 | |
		A	B	A	B	A	B
Power tillers	653	236,000	9.2	1,414,000	4.1	3,168,000	1.5
Tractors	376,000 HP	2,000	—	11,000	—	1,096,000	4.3
Transplanters	—	2,400	—	—	—	1,601,000	3.0
Threshers	14,610						
Harvesters		12,500	—	—	—	2,450,000	1.9

A: Total number
B: Number of households per machine

Sources: Hou and Yu 1982: 198; Ban et al. 1980: 75

Expertise and participation

In the case of a crop like rice, the intensification of production is a

systemic process and is therefore heavily dependent upon the skills, experience and active involvement of the broad mass of rice-farmers. Successful scientific research and development (R & D) should therefore aim to integrate the ideas and suggestions of the farmers themselves with the results from experimental stations, encouraging the active participation of the farmers in agricultural improvement.

R & D is frequently regarded as a process by which the results of specialised scientific research are popularised through extension work, and the potential contribution of the target farmers may well be underrated. Yet such research activites as crop breeding were practised by peasant farmers for millennia before falling into the hands of the scientists. The high-yielding varieties of rice developed in Meiji Japan were bred by farmers. The most famous and widely adopted was called *Shinriki* (power of the gods), and was bred in Hyōgo, near Ōsaka, by a local farmer in 1877. Its appearance coincided with a growth in official extension services which greatly improved communications between agricultural regions, permitting its rapid adoption in most of Southern Honshū (Francks 1983: 61). At the same period Japanese farmers were also trying to develop improved farm equipment and machinery, working in active cooperation with local manufacturers (Ishikawa 1981: 164). Many of the technological advances of the period were in fact due to research and experiments carried out by the farmers themselves. The same is true of modern China. Wertheim and Stiefel report a not untypical case of individual initiative from Northern Hubei, where a commune director was determined to develop the double-cropping of rice in a region where it had never previously been practised for climatic reasons. Experimenting through the 1960s and 1970s, he and his colleagues succeeded in breeding appropriate rice varieties, and rice double-cropping subsequently became common throughout the district, with the addition of a winter crop of wheat or rapeseed; in 1978 an experimental plot gave a total yield of 20 t/ha (1982: 28).

Just as important as incorporating grass-roots contributions into R & D is engaging popular support for innovation. The extent of popular participation in agricultural development depends to a large extent on how innovation is advocated or imposed, and by whom. Not surprisingly, farmers tend to be suspicious of official intervention and respond more positively to the example of successful peers. One thinks of the centuries-old Chinese policy of using 'master farmers' as disseminators of improved techniques. Many rice-growing cultures have a long tradition of village officers meeting regularly to decide on technical matters such as the distribution of scarce resources like water and labour, and the technical cohesion imposed by the requirements of intensive rice

cultivation often helps to smooth the path of innovation. The extension of technical information through the help of cultivating landlords in Meiji Japan is described in appendix C.

Wertheim and Stiefel maintain that successes in both production and distribution in China have depended in large part upon the rate of true popular participation, fostered by emphasis on the 'mass line' (1982: 135, 87). This permitted all levels of planners, administrators, experts and farmers to contribute to the gradual formulation of appropriate development strategies through a process of feed-back. Perhaps the most dramatic example of popular contribution to the economy in China is the official adoption of the various forms of the 'responsibility system' in Document 75, issued in 1980, in which the government was obliged to recognise a *fait accompli* and incorporate the complexities of a system evolved by the masses themselves into official economic policy (Watson 1984: 90).

The New Community Movement (*Saemaul Undong*) launched in Korea in 1971 has depended for its success on a number of elements familiar from earlier Chinese experience, including (as well as the charismatic leadership provided by President Park himself) mass participation under the leadership of educated and dedicated members of the local community (e.g. Whang 1981). Again a key feature has been the integration of local experience with centralised expertise: 'detailed information about the reasons for success or failure in the case of specific projects does in fact flow back up through bureaucratic channels, and problems are discussed and solutions proposed at every level of the hierarchy' (Brandt 1980: 278).

The crucial importance of popular involvement in running water control systems effectively has already been mentioned in chapter 3. Lack of active support can prove disastrous, as in Central Luzon, where the villagers will hardly participate at all in maintaining irrigation systems; they leave it entirely to the irrigation authority and take water from the system whenever it suits them, cheerfully disregarding their neighbours' needs; 'a sort of anarchy prevails' (Takahashi 1970: 52). But the cohesive nature of rice farming technology requires cooperation, not anarchy, if decent yields are to be achieved: one farmer flouting the water regulations can damage the crops of all the farmers in the same irrigation block.

The potential contribution of popular participation is well illustrated by the case of the Demas (Mass Demonstration) programme carried out in Java in 1964/5. At this time there were few funds available for subsidising new technology; instead the programme relied almost exclusively on extension work carried out by young and dedicated

officers living in the villages and working in close consultation with the farmers. Despite prevailing shortages of fertilisers, yield increases of between 40% and 140% were achieved. Such levels were seldom attained by farmers under the later Bimas (Mass Guidance) programme, which was imposed upon the farmers through government regulations; the new extension officers did not feel the need to fraternise with the farmers, and their advice was not always enthusiastically received (Palmer 1977: 192, 104; Loekman 1982).

In rice-cultivating societies technical choices and management decisions are in the hands not of a few landlords but of vast numbers of family farmers. The higher the levels of rural education and training, the more likely farmers are to be receptive to advanced techniques, as the examples of the East Asian nations show. Whatever the excellence of existing extension services, active grass-roots support is more likely to emerge where the farmers feel they have some personal control over what is happening, and where innovation by individuals is the result not of half-hearted submission to remote authority but of an active and informed commitment to change.

6

Peasant, landlord and state: changes in relations of production

Asian rural societies have usually been characterised, at least until very recently, as 'peasant societies'. If we accept the loose definition of peasants as rural producers with a degree of independent control over their resources, who produce for their own consumption and sometimes also for sale, relying principally if not exclusively upon household labour,[1] then the rice economies studied here certainly developed over time into peasant economies. The progressive development of Asian wet-rice technology was linked with the intensification of skilled labour inputs and a reduction in farm size. This tended to improve the position of the farmer vis-à-vis landowners, although intensive rice agriculture was rarely unassociated with tenancy. The potential for economic diversification, using household labour and low levels of capital investment, gave farmers further scope for individualistic entrepreneurial activity. Yet there was an inherent tension in rice-growing societies between individualism and the spirit of communality required to keep irrigation networks functioning smoothly.

Conflict, cooperation and control

In order to ensure access to water and labour, even the most privileged members of rice-growing societies have traditionally been obliged to cooperate closely with their fellow-farmers. On the other hand where essential resources are in short supply — labour and land for instance — conflicts inevitably arise. To some extent such organisations as irrigation societies and labour exchange groups have the effect of reducing social inequalities and promoting communal harmony; nevertheless, social and economic hierarchies are to be found in all village societies where there is pressure on resources.

Lê (1955: 225) refers to the institutionalised hierarchy which existed within the traditional Vietnamese commune. Communal land was distributed regularly by the village notables (mandarins, officials, examiners and old men) among the members of the commune, but not on an egalitarian basis: each member's allotment corresponded to his status, determined by his social rank, titles and seniority. Despite constant legislation during the eighteenth-century Trịnh dynasty to ensure their equitable distribution, communal lands were in fact largely concentrated in the hands of the notables. In 1860 the Nguyên rulers of Tonkin again attempted to reform the inequalities of the commune: all rich landlords were ordered to give one-third of their property to the village as communal land, and the sale and pawning of communal land was forbidden. It was to be redistributed equally between all villagers every three years. But in spite of this legislation the notables retained their power: the poorer peasants were either kept in ignorance of the reforms or were afraid to incur the enmity of the notables. Central government had little direct control over the notables' administration of the villages, and the growing problems of inequality, exacerbated by overpopulation and frequent natural disasters, resulted in frequent popular uprisings, which government attempts at repression and administrative reform were powerless to quell (ibid.: 360).

Once feudal relations began to decline in Tokugawa Japan (see appendix C), village hierarchies became somewhat less marked in that the traditional elites lived elsewhere and did not participate directly in village life (Kelly 1982b: 27). But as the economy grew, differences between rich and poor peasants, landlords and tenants, became more apparent. In Shiwa village in the twentieth century, the rich owned the land near the main irrigation canal: this land had higher yields and lower labour requirements, as well as privileged access to water in times of shortage (Shimpo 1976: 12). Not surprisingly these rich farmers bitterly opposed the construction of a new dam and irrigation network, which threatened to shatter the traditional hierarchy of privilege.

Customary regulations help keep such traditional systems for the allocation of resources working smoothly at village level, but when communities are contending for these resources, especially for water, then a higher authority has to be brought in as arbiter.

Where the wider political structure is undeveloped, communities will often subsist more or less in isolation, relying on kinship and customary law to maintain order. The Laotian villages described by Taillard (1972) were limited in size to seventy or eighty members, linked by ties of kinship or friendship, and their irrigation units were never big enough to overlap village boundaries.

In certain cases the size of the community is actually defined by the capacity of the water source. The surface area of the tank in the Ceylonese village of Pul Eliya studied by Leach corresponded exactly to the area of rice-field it could irrigate, in this case about 60 ha (1961: 18). As a social unit Ceylonese villages were very tightly bound: all the members of one village would belong to a single *variga* category, and endogamy within the *variga* was expected (ibid.: 23). The village community was still more closely bound by the necessity to cooperate in production and to decide jointly on the allocation of resources, under the direction of the irrigation headman, the Vel Vidāne, who mediated between villagers and government. Every year a decision had to be taken, in view of the current level of the irrigation tank and the likely rainfall in the coming months, as to what area of fields was to be cultivated. The traditional tenure system was based on the ideal of fair shares for all: 'The *ideal* system is functionally perfect. Everything fits together like a jigsaw puzzle, the technology of irrigation, the technology of rice-growing and the egalitarian ideology of village politics' (ibid.: 177). But although the allocation of individual strips of land theoretically gave every villager equal rights to water, the actual and the ideal arrangements were not identical. However villagers were also engaged in cooperative labour which 'follows a pattern which is antithetic to that of landown-ership, and the rewarding of labour has the effect of counterbalancing the unequal distribution of primary title' (ibid.: 241).

Tamaki (1979: 24–33) describes a somewhat similar social system in early Japan: the irrigation ponds of the Yamato kingdom in Western Japan (AD 300–710) (see chapter 3) were of a size to irrigate enough land to feed 10 to 20 families, which thus was the size of a typical hamlet. Again, all the households would meet in May to discuss the prospects for rain, and to decide on the area of padi that could be cultivated and the proportion of their fields which each member was entitled to plant with irrigated rice. Any infraction of these rules was punishable by expulsion from the community.

[But] there is a threshold of complexity in irrigation systems at which cooperation must give way to coordination; at which those served by the systems relinquish their decision-making power and their direct role in settling disputes. Authority and responsibility for these vital functions are then transferred to managerial structures of one sort or another. This is not to say that cooperation is then absent, but rather that it is no longer the dominant pattern of operation. The transfer to managerial coordination is not simply dependent on the size of the irrigated area. It is also – and more directly – dependent on the number of farmers drawing water *from a single source*. Where so many farmers are involved that face-to-face relations break down, management of some kind becomes

necessary. Otherwise the system may be disrupted by constant conflict, and much of the community may be deprived of water. (Pasternak 1972: 194)

The most voluminous literature on water rights and customs deals with Japan, and there is an admirable analytical summary in Kelly (1982a).[2] Irrigation rights are seen by many Japanese scholars as a natural response to the conflicts which arise between irrigation communities; because they are the product of specific historical and geographical circumstances they are not considered to be rational or widely applicable (ibid.: 19, 21, etc.).

In general, the nearer a farmer's land is to the source of irrigation, the greater his advantage. Farmers with land at the side of the main channel will have better access to water than those with land at the end of a minor channel; those upstream are better off than those downstream. Traditional agreements as to water rights are not infrequently the outcome of bloody disputes, and such apparent improvements as the building of a new dam may completely disrupt the traditional hierarchies; hence the fierce opposition which such projects often encounter (e.g. Shimpo 1976).

There is political power to be gained through mediating conflicts, whether inter-or intra-communal. Within the community, the irrigation headman is usually elected, although sometimes the appointment must be officially ratified by the government. The post usually goes to one of the wealthier members of the community. It may be short-term or permanent, and rarely does the headman receive more than token remuneration, but in terms of prestige and power the rewards are great. The allocation of water rights often served landlords or gentry as a means of protecting their class (or perhaps 'group') interests. This seems to have been the case in Tokugawa Japan, and Furushima (1954: 202; cited Kelly 1982a: 17) argues that even in the 1930s, when former tenants had acquired titles to land, irrigation customs continued to favour the former landlord elite households. But this may have been only a regional phenomenon. Writing of Northeastern Japan in the late Tokugawa period, Kelly (1982b: 192, 212) maintains that there is very little evidence for landlords or domain officials having exercised much direct authority in controlling water use. Waswo (1977) describes how Meiji and Shōwa improvements in water control, often initiated by landlords, had the eventual effect of reducing their influence within village society. And Kitamura (1950; cited Kelly 1982a: 13) actually maintains that irrigation customs were an obstacle to the consolidation of landlord power, since they tended to encourage tenancy on large holdings and did not favour owner-operation on a large scale.

In China too, Morita believes that there was a gradual decline in landlord participation in water control during the Qing dynasty (1644–1911) and subsequent Republican period, and that the irrigation groups were taken over by independent farmers. 'He attributed this to the increasing dispersal of landlord holdings; landlords were thus less knowledgeable about local water-control conditions and arrangements in all the areas of their holdings and more able to avoid levies and assessments for repairs and operation/maintenance' (Kelly 1982a: 62). This view is supported by Hamashima's study of the Yangzi Delta (1980). The evidence suggests, then, that the increase in absentee landlordism favoured the greater autonomy of tenant smallholders.

When it comes to mediating between whole communities in conflict, a higher level of political intervention is necessary, and the rewards are correspondingly greater. Tamaki (1979) describes how the Kamakura feudal state (1185–1392) had its power base in the upland valleys of Japan, watered by small gravity irrigation networks similar to those of Southeast Asia. Such a system could irrigate larger areas than the Yamato ponds mentioned earlier, areas large enough to establish feudal estates (*shōen*). In their constant search for greater power, the warring feudal lords turned in the fifteenth century to the marshy alluvial plains, where they constructed canals and opened up large areas for cultivation. A powerful feudal lord would have control over a whole plain and would covet possession of others as a sure way of increasing his economic and political power. This was the beginning of the so-called Warring States period. Since farmers were obliged to spend much of their time fighting, it is not surprising that levels of agricultural production were low when the Tokugawa shogunate was established in 1600.

Even the most powerful and bureaucratic centralised state can hardly hope to subdue all the rivalries and enmities which arise over competition for water. It is even more tricky than solving the land problem. In Japan (Kelly 1982a: 21) groups of individual farmers, and not landlords, are now the chief antagonists, and conflicts over water distribution remain unsolved all over the country. Recently a new source of tension has become common:

LIDs [Local Irrigation Departments] in most of the major rice-growing areas have been faced in the 1970s with an increasing concentration of water demands in the field preparation/transplanting period, already the period of highest water volume demand. This has been due in part to mechanisation, which shortens considerably the spring work period, and also to the spread of monovariety cultivation . . . It is compounded by the trend toward part-time farming. Spring Sundays are moments of feverish activity in most areas, and the water difficulties

often experienced on those days are nicknamed 'Sunday droughts' by the farmers. As a consequence of these factors, LIDs face mounting shortages and strain on network facilities during this spring peak period. (Kelly 1982a: 46)

Vaidyanathan (1983: 76–85) lists the difficulties encountered in running the large state-managed irrigation systems of India, where sheer scale often precludes the flexibility required to deal with local conflicts. In China it seems that the efficiency of water control has increased steadily since 1965 (Gustafsson 1984: 136). The Constitution provides that water areas and water flows be owned by the state (ibid.: 153), and the 150 large irrigation districts of over 20,000 ha, as well as the medium districts of 667 to 20,000 ha, have a professional body of management established by the government. Integrated smaller systems drawing on several different sources, like the Meiquan district in Hubei studied by Nickum (1981) which depended on a combination of small reservoirs and ponds, have the flexibility to cope with drought relying entirely on their own resources. Irrigation systems which share a source such as a medium-size river are more likely to find themselves in competition with other areas, and an increasing problem in China today is the competition for water between the countryside and the cities, and between the industrial and agricultural sectors. The recent introduction of the 'responsibility system', which divides up irrigation tasks and allocations not between production brigades but between individual households, has led to much confusion over water rights (Gustafsson 1984: 140).

Historical changes in relations of production

The contrast between the evolution of wet-rice economies and the Northwest European model of agricultural development is very striking if one considers the social effects of the development of the productive forces.

'Feudal' relations and frontier zones

In rice-growing areas where cultivation techniques were undeveloped and extensive, one often finds relations of production which share certain features with those of feudal Europe. Since the land's productivity and thus its population-carrying capacity are low, control over labour is crucial to the dominant class. The peasant producers have access to land only through establishing tributary relations with a member of this dominant class, and there is no market through which producers might acquire proprietary rights in land.

Discussing conditions in Europe, historians have pointed out that one important characteristic of classic feudalism is that the nature of political relations and of the process of extraction is such as seriously to inhibit development of the factors of production (Kula 1970: Ch. 3; Brenner 1982: 34–40). The economic cake is thus limited, and any gain by one class is necessarily at the expense of another. All European observers remarked that in Malaya peasants were loath to produce any more than their basic subsistence requirements for fear of the rapacity of the rulers. The ultimate rights to all land were vested in the rajas (Clifford 1895: 114; Downs 1967: 117). A peasant had rights of usufruct over all the wet-rice land he was able to keep under cultivation ('living land', *tanah hidup*), but although he could pass these rights on to his heirs he could neither buy nor sell land. To maintain his usufructuary rights he was obliged not only to pay fees in kind on the produce of his land but also to perform corvée labour or *krah* for the local raja. The usual levy on rice-land consisted of a tithe (Ooi 1966: 178), and there were additional levies on fruit-trees and other produce. Some scholars suggest that since access to manpower was such an important asset, the Malay rulers were obliged to refrain from exploiting their subjects so ruthlessly that they fled their territories (Lim 1977: 4), but usually the *krah* system was shamelessly abused to support a whole ruling class:

In theory, apparently, the Krah was an order issued by the Ruler to the people, conveyed on a sealed paper, which must be instantly obeyed, whatever its nature. In practice, however, every relative of the Ruler and every person who can boast a drop of blood of the Rulers, reserves to himself the right to Krah whenever opportunity offers, according to his ability to enforce obedience to his orders, by which means the wants of the upper classes are supplied free of cost by the labour of the country people, who are forever working out some Krah or other ... (Graham 1904: 16)

The peasants in Java were in a still more insecure position, for they did not even benefit from permanent rights of usufruct over their rice-land: each year the village chief redistributed the wet-rice fields among the villagers, so that (as on many medieval European manors) nobody cultivated the same field two years running. Only to dryland fields did usufructuary rules similar to those of Malaya apply (Raffles 1817: I, 151).

Although the institutions of the Angkorian empire were bureaucratic rather than feudal in character, many officials were rewarded for their services with fiefs 'provided with fields and cultivators', and it has been suggested that the cultivators had a status similar to that of European serfs (see Sahai 1970: 144).

Tenurial relations in early Tokugawa Japan also strongly resembled

Western feudalism; peasant farmers acquired improved tenurial status and greater independence as agricultural methods improved and the economy expanded and diversified (appendix C).

As a general rule, given the importance of individual skills and experience in developed rice technology, it seems improbable that serfdom was ever compatible with intensive rice cultivation (Erkes 1953). In his discussion of the concept of 'hydraulic societies' Eberhard argues that 'there was a clear correlation between irrigation and tenancy' (1965: 87). Little is known of tenurial conditions in China's rice-growing regions before the Song, but although many Japanese scholars maintain that the large estates amassed during that period were feudal in nature,[3] others such as Lewin (1973) affirm that there is no evidence whatsoever for the existence of feudal institutions in the Song. By far the largest category of landholders registered in the early Song were independent smallholders, followed by the category known as 'farmers tilling land half their own', *ban zi geng nong*, that is, farmers who leased in extra land to make ends meet: such farmers clearly could not have been serfs (Bray 1984: 605).

It is likely, however, that conditions in China's frontier regions were less favourable. Wherever the population was sparse it was possible for rich men to lay claim to huge tracts of land, unhampered by official intervention. Labour was in short supply, but as economic alternatives were non-existent, the unfortunate farmers working on these estates found themselves with few privileges and a great many obligations (Golas 1980: 305). However when Fujianese migrants opened up land in Taiwan in the eighteenth century, constructing irrigation networks in order to grow rice intensively, there was no question of feudal relations between landowners and their tenants; in fact Taiwan's tenurial system was directly evolved from the system of three-level ownership (see appendix B) then prevailing in Fujian (Meskill 1979: 47).

In nineteenth-century Indochina and Siam we find a contrast between the traditional population centres, where intensive wet-rice production was practised, and the technically underdeveloped frontier zones of Cochinchina and the Chao Phraya Delta, or Bangkok Plain, then in a phase of rapid expansion. In the regions of intensive rice cultivation the relations between landlord and tenant did not include labour services or other forms of control over personal freedom. But in the frontier zones, where land was plentiful but labour scarce, migrant farmers reverted to relatively primitive, land-extensive techniques (Tanabe 1978: 42); furthermore the forms of appropriation in these areas presented many similarities to those of feudal Europe. Although Scott (1976: 67) has described the colonisation of Indochina as an example of the growth of

capitalist labour relations (in contrast to the situation in Tonkin and Annam), 'capitalist' seems an inappropriate label for a situation where the landless poor worked small individual plots on the estates of large landowners to whom they owed labour dues, political allegiance and a variety of demeaning services (Brocheux 1971; Popkin 1979: 181).

One of the reasons why peasants in frontier zones are so vulnerable to feudal-type exploitation is their inability to participate directly in markets. They are obliged to rely on rice monoculture and have little or no opportunity to diversify their economic activities or even to sell their rice directly. This ensures their economic subjugation to the owners of the land. In Cochinchina the powerful landowners exerted their rule in opposition to state policy, but during the early stages of the reclamation of the Bangkok Plain in the 1860s and 1870s, the Siamese kings institutionalised a system of 'feudal' relations such as by then had disintegrated further inland: large grants of land were made to financially distressed members of the royal family and noble officials, the labour to be largely supplied by corvée peasants, *bao phrai*, or by debt slaves (Tanabe 1978: 55). The intention behind this policy was to expand rice production in the Delta to supply the growing demand for rice in China and other Asian countries. But the government was soon obliged to recognise that the large noble estates were not in fact as productive as peasant smallholdings. In 1877 a new policy was introduced which encouraged landless peasant migrants from the crowded north to reclaim unoccupied rice-land along the newly excavated canals of the Delta and to work it independently, in return for the payment of land-tax and irrigation dues directly to the state (ibid.: 62).

The Siamese rulers were not alone in recognising the pernicious effects on productivity of 'feudal' relations of production and the relative advantages of independent peasant farming. Raffles roundly blamed the extortions of the Javanese chiefs for the poor state of the country's agriculture (1817: I, 151), and during their brief occupation in 1811–16 the British governors abolished feudal dues and land allotments in many regions, redistributing land among the villagers and commuting all former dues into a land-tax based on a proportion of the average produce of the field (ibid.: 158). Immediate improvements were reported both in the industry of the Javanese peasants and in the crime rate. It is not clear whether these early nineteenth-century modifications in tenurial relations were directly responsible for the subsequent intensification of Javanese rice cultivation, or whether they merely facilitated an inevitable response to the reduction in the wet-rice area imposed by the Dutch introduction of the Culture System. Geertz (1963) argues that the obligation to cultivate sugar on part of their rice-land forced Javanese

peasants to adopt more intensive rice-cultivation techniques in order to survive. But Elson (1978) has pointed out that in fact rice cultivation techniques were more advanced and productive in the areas where little sugar was grown and thus more resources could be devoted to the rice crop. It was the non-sugar regions, Elson says, which produced surpluses of rice which were sold to those rice-farmers who also worked as wage-labourers on the sugar estates. In Elson's view, then, the intensification of rice cultivation in the non-sugar areas can be seen as a response to market demands.

Smallholder economies: expansion and stagnation

Wet-rice cultivation is not, like the farming system of Northwest Europe, subject to economies of scale, nor does it respond positively to the centralisation of management. It is therefore not surprising to find that in both medieval China and Tokugawa Japan, as new techniques were applied and land productivity rose, the position of tenants vis-à-vis their landlords improved: they acquired more managerial and economic independence, and tenurial contracts were modified in their favour (appendices B and C). The development of intensive rice production gave rise to long-term economic expansion and diversification, and although the ownership of land was concentrated in relatively few hands, the household rather than the estate was the basic unit of both agricultural and commodity production.

In China and Japan it seems that technological development gradually led to modifications in tenurial relations, whereas in the cases of Siam and Java the state took an active role in imposing tenurial change expressly to favour increased production. In the Malay States the British introduced a system of land registration which protected peasant rights, and in Kelantan the acreage under padi rose from 66,000 acres in 1911 to 207,000 in 1925 (Bishop 1912: iv; Shaw 1926: xiii). As the Malayan population grew and the supply of new arable land diminished, tenancy rates increased, but the relations between landlord and tenant were usually of a redistributive rather than of an exploitative nature; they generally remain so today despite the increased commercialisation of agriculture (Bray and Robertson 1980; Horii 1981; Fujimoto 1983). On the East Coast sharecropping contracts prevail, while cash rents are more common on the West Coast, but most contracts are between kin, indeed often between parents and children, and they are flexible and relatively generous. The landlords are frequently older people, sometimes too poor

or ill to farm the land themselves, more often older relatives of their tenants, renting them land as a way of starting them out on the ladder towards ownership. Pure tenants are most commonly young people who as yet have acquired no land of their own.[4] Owner-tenants are older householders with growing families. Tenancy is a means of matching land and labour within a community so that resources are not wasted.

Initially the transition from subsistence to commercial production in wet-rice economies appears to increase the value of skilled labour and to sustain a general expansion of the economy, as in medieval China and Tokugawa Japan. But eventually a point of crisis may be reached. Once the population grows beyond certain limits, pressure on land reaches a point where returns to labour begin to diminish, and the rural population becomes increasingly impoverished. The competition for land enables landlords to impose heavier burdens on their tenants, and in addition, as more and more mouths have to be fed off the same area of land, rents which once seemed fair become extortionate.

The difficulties faced by the poorer peasants are especially acute where rice monoculture prevails and there are few opportunities for profitable alternative employment. In several instances the policies of colonial governments, anxious to extract agricultural taxes from their new subjects but loath to invest in the colonies, led to a rapid degradation of rural conditions. Geertz's account of what happened in Java is well known. The small island of Lombok, off the tip of Bali, also suffered severely.[5] Lombok was taken over by the Dutch from the Balinese in 1894. Although Balinese rule had not been especially lenient rice exports had flourished then. They continued to grow under the Dutch, but peasants were now obliged to sell much of their produce in order to pay cash taxes on irrigated land which amounted to 20% of the crop in 1914–20, over 15% in 1930–40 and over 25% in 1940–50. The Dutch government made little or no attempt to develop local industries or to promote the cultivation of alternative crops; however it did invest in irrigation improvements (though the farmers themselves also had to contribute to these, being liable for up to one month a year in corvée duties).

During the colonial period the population increased steadily at a rate of between 1.3% and 2% per annum; the extension of the cultivated area did not keep pace. 'The decline in the total ration of *sawah* [rice-land] per capita during the colonial period is to some extent counterbalanced by the extension of permanent irrigation facilities, which allow for a more stable and therefore higher output. The impact of irrigation extension should not be overestimated, however, since the best irrigation opportunities were probably exploited before the Dutch takeover.'

Although the irrigated land per capita doubled from 0.047 ha in 1900 to 0.086 ha in 1940, the total of irrigated plus rain-fed rice-land dropped from 0.131 ha to 0.123 ha in the same period, and had fallen as low as 0.066 ha by 1971; in the most productive region, Western Lombok, the total fell from 0.083 ha in 1930 to 0.040 ha in 1971 (Gerdin 1982: 63).

The Dutch government introduced a system of land registration which gave peasants legal possession, rather than inalienable usufructuary rights, to the land they cultivated. This meant they were also registered as tax-payers, and land could now be freely bought, pawned or sold. Although certain forms of tenancy and wage-labour had existed in pre-colonial times, in the 1890s most peasants still had hereditary rights of production. Even in the 1970s, peasants still regarded ownership of rice-land as the primary economic resource, but official statistics showed that by now one-third of the population of Lombok owned no land at all, and 67% of all holdings (owned, not cultivated) were under 1 ha in size; in certain areas the figures for landlessness reached over 70% (Gerdin 1982: 84–5). This is not to say that none of the landless had access to land as tenants, but the landowners' positions had been considerably strengthened: rents were 50% higher than in the 1940s, preference was given as tenants to those who had land of their own, the length of tenancies had decreased and various forms of wage-labour were replacing tenancy (ibid.: 92).

Similar disruptions were caused by the French colonial government in Tonkin and Annam. Before the advent of the French 'the great mass of peasant households cultivated their own plots, which they held either as private land, or as part of the allocation of communal land; the role of landlordism was insignificant, and the largest landowner in the commune was usually the commune itself' (Fforde 1983: 24). French researchers of the 1920s and 1930s believed that tenancy and wage-labour in the pre-colonial period were almost unknown (Henry 1932: 113; Gourou 1936: 360). Rice production was the basis of the economy: trade and commodity production were not highly developed, and were not regarded as profitable (Fforde 1983: 41, 104). The introduction of monetary taxes by the French (who also turned a blind eye to corruption for private ends of the communal system of land allocation) brought about significant changes: 'Higher and monetised taxes forced peasants to borrow funds from their patrons in the communes. *In the absence of resources with which to increase commodity output* this was the only way in which average producers in wet-rice areas facing demographic saturation could obtain the necessary funds' (ibid.: 9; my emphasis). There was a rapid change from 'a rural social structure ... based primarily upon small peasant cultivators of their "own" land, to one based upon a

mixture of heavily indebted and rackrented tenants and a poverty-stricken landless rural proletariat' (ibid.: 45).

Egalitarianism or differentiation: the impact of capitalism

There are two principal schools of thought as to what happens to peasant economies under the impact of developing capitalism. The first is that increasing commoditisation and commercialisation lead to the gradual disappearance of family farming and the differentiation of the peasantry into a small class of capitalist farmers (or an agrarian bourgeoisie) and a large class of landless agricultural labourers.[6] The second is that the peasant economy survives, in articulation with the capitalist mode of production, largely because peasants are able to supply goods more cheaply than capitalist producers.[7] To say that there is disagreement as to the precise definition of capitalist farming is an understatement. The question has not yet been resolved for Europe (e.g. Cooper 1978; see also Brenner 1982), let alone for Asia.[8] Perhaps the most useful definition is that a capitalist farm is one that relies principally upon wage-labour and accumulates surplus value by this means (see, e.g., Sen 1975: ch. 7).

The introduction of money taxes to Asia's rice regions had effects which were anything but benign. But significantly, even though landlessness increased under such conditions, the transition to capitalist relations of production, whereby landowners evict their tenants in order to run large, consolidated farms using cheap wage-labour, did not generally occur. This seems surprising, especially in the case of Java where export crops like sugar and coffee were grown on capitalist plantations alongside the rice-fields,[9] until we remember the considerable technical obstacles to such a transformation. In the Philippines also, the two systems of capitalist and smallholding farming co-existed: the Spanish government made large grants of land to religious foundations and wealthy entrepreneurs, and the *haciendas* which produced export crops were run with hired labour, but those which grew rice were operated either through direct leaseholdings to peasant farmers, or through the *inquilinato* system, by which an agent leased the land and sub-let it in small parcels to sharecroppers (Ofreneo 1980: 10). In nineteenth-century Siam too, capitalist commercial plantations co-existed with smallholder rice-farming (Tanabe 1978: 42).

One cannot account for this by pleading the absence of international markets or of commercial inputs, as chapters 4 and 5 have shown. Even

today, wet-rice economies still prove remarkably resistant to the transition to capitalist farming.

The egalitarian, redistributive aspects of Asian rice economies have been highlighted in a number of studies. Leach (1961) describes how the *ideal*, if not the real, allocation of land and water in a Ceylonese tank village is based on the principle of fair shares for all; Fujimoto's study (1983) of economic relations between Malaysian rice-farmers leads him to conclude that they are not intended to maximise the personal gains of the landowner but permit a more equitable sharing of income among kinsfolk and friends. Perhaps the most influential spokesmen for the redistributive nature of wet-rice economies have been Geertz (1963) and Scott (1976), with their concepts of 'shared poverty' and 'moral economy'.

In his study of the Javanese colonial economy Geertz put forward the view that social and economic differences in village society were kept to a minimum by a variety of redistributive means such as labour-sharing, tenancy relations, public feasts and so on, so that even the poorest were assured of survival through the largesse of those somewhat richer than themselves. These practices had the effect of inhibiting economic differentiation, reinforcing existing relations of production. Geertz's concept of 'shared poverty' has been criticised on a number of grounds. Alexander and Alexander (1982) say that it obscures important elements of social stratification in colonial Java, for instance ignoring the large number of landless already noted by Raffles; furthermore, they say, 'redistributive' practices such as group harvesting actually contribute to economic differentials, since kin and neighbours are rewarded at a much higher rate than landless peasants or outsiders. The Alexanders feel that accepting the concept of 'shared poverty' leads to a misinterpretation of the Green Revolution, since the New Technology does not in fact require a rejection of traditional attitudes towards wealth and profit, but rather has changed the balance of economic advantage. Elson (1978) too criticises Geertz for attributing an exaggerated homogeneity to traditional Javanese society. Other studies suggest that redistributive work-spreading today does not operate throughout the economic strata of Javanese rural society but is most common among poor farmers who have no cash to hire labour (Gerdin 1982: 68).

Scott's argument, based on his studies of late colonial Vietnam and Burma, is not that economic differentiation and exploitation were largely absent from village life, but that there was a general consensus among rich and poor alike that everyone had a right to survival. Poor tenants and other clients of rich landowners would seldom have the opportunity to cross the poverty line, for normally high rents and rates of interest would

claim most of their income; but what remained would be sufficient for subsistence under normal conditions, and it was accepted by landlords as well as tenants that in case of a poor harvest or some other crisis rents would be lowered or even abolished, loans would be made, and the charity of the rich would ensure the survival of the poorest. Since the poor were concerned with subsistence rather than with profits, social stability could be maintained over long periods. However if once the poor suspected that their minimal requirements for survival were threatened, they became ripe for rebellion.

This view of class and economic relations between Southeast Asian peasants was quickly countered by Popkin (1979) in another study of Vietnam. Popkin argues that Scott's view of rural institutions is over-romanticised and that Asian peasants are primarily motivated by individual economic and political gain. Benevolence towards others comes not so much from principles of equity as from the controls imposed by other members of society, and significant inequalities are to be found between individuals within a community.

Both Scott and Popkin have been criticised for over-generalisation (e.g. Peletz 1983). It has been pointed out that Scott's area of study in Northern Vietnam had a long history of high population density, so that one might naturally expect social constraints on economic behaviour to be well developed there, while Popkin's material comes mainly from the frontier zone of Cochinchina, where social norms had not yet been established which might curb rampant individualism.

The debate as to the existence of a 'moral economy' is in many ways paralleled by interpretations of the Chinese lineage or clan. While an eleventh-century document on the administration of the Fan clan estate in the Yangzi Delta expressly forbids the land to be rented out to members of the clan (Twitchett 1960: 11), in the frontier zones of the south single-lineage villages were in the majority, and the leasing of land to members of the lineage was thus inevitable. Here the lineages were powerful solidarity groups, which fiercely protected the rights of their members against outsiders. Freedman (1958, 1966) believes that lineages developed in China's frontier zones in response to competition for land and water; in unity lay strength, and a cohesive lineage group could more easily undertake irrigation works for rice cultivation and protect its assets against other lineages than could communities of individuals without such strong ties. Freedman argues that a significant reason for the greater strength of lineages in South China than in the north or centre was the need for cooperation to establish irrigated rice cultivation.[10] But cooperation did not lead to egalitarianism. There was a considerable status gap between the highest and lowest members of a

lineage, although '... the contrast between high and low status reinforced the integrity of the lineage. It may be that in a popular sense the poor were exploited by the rich, but even as they were exploited they enjoyed privileges important enough to make their continued residence worthwhile' (1958: 127). It was better to be a minor member of a strong lineage than a slightly more important member of a weak one which had fewer resources at its disposal.

Land and landlessness

It was believed by many that the recent exposure to capitalist markets and the introduction of the New Technology would lead to the differentiation of the peasantry into rich managerial farmers and landless labourers. As was mentioned in chapter 5, wealthier farmers do have better access to credit and to other inputs which should allow them to make more efficient use of their resources, and it was felt that many poorer farmers, especially tenants, becoming indebted through the necessity to purchase costly modern inputs, would eventually have to sell their land and work as hired labourers. But despite the commercialisation consequent on the recent widespread adoption of the New Technology, and the increase in the number of landless, capitalist relations of production have seldom emerged: large farmer-operators are the exception, and the basic unit of production remains the family farm.

One rare example of what might be called capitalist farming is to be found in the Muda region of Malaysia, where holdings were traditionally rather large, and where environmental conditions have favoured large-scale mechanisation of rice-farming (see chapter 2). A number (as yet very small, and not necessarily increasing) of Malay and Chinese entrepreneurs operate holdings of 7.5 to 30 ha (Muhd. Ikmal 1985: 28). This has led to the displacement of agricultural labourers by machines, and to a consequent fall in agricultural wages and the marginalisation of small farmers, suggesting to many (e.g. de Koninck 1981; Lim et al. 1981) that this is a case of incipient capitalist farming. But it is a new phenomenon and little studied; as yet the number of large farms seems to be insignificant: 28 farms out of perhaps 50,000 were found to be larger than 7.5 ha (Muhd. Ikmal 1985). Furthermore it has been suggested (ibid.: 89) that the capitalist interpretation fails to take account of the relationship between the farm unit and the family life-cycle, for apparently the family is still the basic operational unit even on Muda's largest farms.[11]

Despite the numerous inequalities to be found in rural Asia, the

'skill-oriented' nature of intensive rice cultivation does oblige the upper strata of village societies to give the poorer members direct access to land. Access to land, and direct control of production, whether as owners or tenants, are thus guaranteed to a far greater number of farmers than in a 'mechanical' technology where economies of scale operate. On the other hand there is no doubt that the number of landless in Asia's rice regions has increased in recent years, and that their plight has worsened. To what extent is this a direct result of the introduction of the New Technology, rather than a historical phenomenon exacerbated by demographic increase?

Markets in land are certainly nothing new. While an owner's profits from rice-land may be low, it is nevertheless an excellent long-term security and a source of prestige, hence the lively market in land in most regions where intensive rice cultivation has been practised. Most tenants' dearest ambition is to save enough to buy some rice-land, though how many actually succeed is difficult to say, since most studies are synchronic and do not take into account the domestic cycle, whereby children first work on their parents' farm for nothing, then take on the task as their parents' tenant, inherit a little land on marriage, save enough to buy more, and eventually lend or rent land out to their own children or other tenants.

Since Chayanov's study of the Russian peasantry (1966, first published in Russia in 1925), it has become evident that such cyclical patterns of domestic development are fundamental to an understanding of the structure of rural society (Shanin 1972; Harriss 1982). Their importance, for instance, in determining the nature of tenurial contracts in contemporary Malaysia is clear (Bray and Robertson 1980; Horii 1981). In a village-level study of late Tokugawa Japan, Smith (1977) qualifies the general rise in rural living standards (Hanley and Yamamura 1977) by emphasising that this secular increase is an aggregate of constant fluctuations at the level of intensely competing individual households attempting to match their labour and land resources.

Statistics on landlessness generally are not easy to interpret, since in many cases those classified as landless are actually tenant farmers although they own no land. For instance in Korea in 1945, before the land reform, the number of households without any access to land even as tenants was estimated at less than 3% (Lee 1979: 51); 50% of farming households *owned* no land, but *access* to land was much more evenly distributed. This was also true in China in the 1930s (Buck 1937), as it is today in Malaysia (Shand and Mohd. Ariff 1983: 25).

The constant efforts of the Vietnamese state to set limits to the concentration of land have already been referred to. In China, by

maintaining accurate land registers, the government was able to keep track of the growth of large estates and even to impose upper limits on the size of holdings. On several occasions it simply confiscated land above a certain limit and redistributed it to landless peasants. Under the Public Fields Law (*Gongtian fa*) of 1260, for example, the state compulsorily purchased one-third of the land of all families owning over 100 *mu* in the six prefectures around Taihu Lake in the Yangzi Delta; an upper limit of 100 *mu* (about 6 ha), even in such a rich and productive region, hardly seems excessive. But in any case large estates seldom survived for long in China's economically advanced areas, where the risks and rewards of entrepreneurial activity ensured a rapid turnover (Bray 1984: 607).

Such situations, where entrepreneurial opportunities (even on a modest scale) abound, provide the means for many smallholders to grow rich and buy land; conversely, they invariably produce a number of poor, marginalised and landless peasants. Landlessness occurred not only in medieval China but in Tokugawa Japan as the rural economy expanded and diversified (Smith 1959). Once the Japanese invaders had been repulsed in 1597, a reform of the land-tax laws in Korea allowed for rapid advances in agricultural technology (in particular the expansion of irrigation and the spread of double-cropping of rice and wheat), agricultural diversification (tobacco and ginseng became important exports to China) and the growth of a class of rich peasants. Inevitably, it also resulted in the dispossession of many other peasants (Lee 1984: 227). One may then consider that marginalisation and landlessness are not simply a product of capitalism, but a historical phenomenon, though the introduction of the New Technology has probably resulted in the dispossession of a higher proportion of the rural population.

There is no doubt that landlessness is an increasingly severe problem in such rice-growing regions as Java, Bali and Lombok, where the population is extremely dense. In Java now most landless are in fact obliged to seek employment outside agriculture, for small and medium landholders are preferred as labourers to the landless or to migrants on account of their reliability and skills; this despite the fact that landholders command wages up to 30% higher (Hart and Huq 1982). But despite the increasing marginalisation of the landless, Java is a striking example of the tenacity of smallholder farming in rice agriculture. It is a moot point as to whether increasing landlessness in Java should be attributed principally to the adoption of the New Technology, for it is clear that since the early nineteenth century there has been a steady and long-term growth in landlessness, due largely to population increase. Certainly demographic growth rather than technological change was the key factor

in the increasing rates of tenancy in Java from 1900 on (Palmer 1977: 131).

There can be no doubt, however, that where pressure on land is acute those working as wage-labourers, whether full- or part-time, have been dealt a heavy blow by the introduction of farm machinery, motorised rice-mills, chemical herbicides and other labour-saving devices, although it must be said that the effect has been compounded by population growth. On the Indonesian island of Lombok the introduction of new HYVs has resulted in a doubling of the labour productivity of cultivators, partly because yields are higher, but also because there has been no corresponding rise in agricultural wages, so that the cultivators can retain a higher proportion of the crop. Landless labourers have fewer opportunities for agricultural employment and now find it almost impossible to get access to land through tenancy, partly as a result of tenants' recent efforts to avoid undue exploitation by landlords in the face of technological changes. Fixed rent tenancy, *majeg* (payable in kind after the harvest), had in any case been in steady decline throughout this century, while landowners' use of wage-labour increased, but Gerdin believes that the New Technology has dealt the final blow:

During 1975–76, there was uncertainty as to how to handle *majeg* agreements. The tenants refrained from cultivating HYVs during the wet season so that the land-owners would not demand higher deliveries of rice [rent was only paid on the main crop, the off-season crop being retained by the tenant]. However, tenants sometimes grew a secondary crop of HYV, since they would get all of this crop. In 1978, there were virtually no *majeg* agreements in the area. If landowners rent their land nowadays, they usually do so on agreements for cultivation during one season (around four months) only. Land rent usually has to be paid in cash beforehand, which makes it more than likely that land is leased to well-to-do peasants rather than to landless workers. (1982: 136)

Yet in Kelantan, Malaysia, the introduction of the New Technology occasioned renegotiations of rental contracts which were not infrequently to the benefit of tenants rather than landlords (Bray and Robertson 1980). But Kelantan is a region of labour shortage rather than labour surplus, and the growth of the Malaysian national economy still provides plenty of alternatives to agricultural work. In Lombok, as in Java and Bali, not only is there no expanding sector of the economy to absorb the surplus labour, but traditional petty commodity production is declining rapidly, faced with competition from cheap imports (Gerdin 1982: 137). In Java too it is notorious that the introduction of the New Technology has led to discriminatory wages and fewer opportunities of profitable employment for the poor, thus increasing rural differentiation

(White 1976). To some extent this is the result of the political changes which took place after the fall of Sukarno in 1965, which deprived the poorer members of Indonesian society of most of their participatory rights.

In chapter 5 it was shown that although small farms can often outdo larger farms in terms of absolute land productivity, profit margins are usually in direct relation to farm size. Access to land is just as important as its ownership; in fact ownership may actually be an economic liability (Fujimoto 1983: 129). The system of 'three owners of a single plot', *yitian sanzhu*, was introduced to Taiwan by Fujianese colonists in the early eighteenth century. The chief owner, *dazu*, paid taxes to the government and received rent from the minor owner, *xiaozu*. During the eighteenth century the minor owner acquired most of the attributes of full ownership, notably the right to sell the land or to sub-let it to tenants, *dianren*, who were often poor migrants. 'The parcels available were often quite large (5 *jia*[12] was a standard size in portions of the Upper Valley [in Central Taiwan]) and came with houses, sheds, stables, seedbeds, gardens, bamboo palisades, and tools. Three-year leases were customary and could be had for a small rent deposit and a rent of about half the crop' (Meskill 1979: 49). The *xioazu* cleared about 10 to 20 taels of silver per *jia* of land rented out, but the after-tax income of the actual owner of the land, the *dazu*, was only 5 taels per *jia* (ibid.).

In his study of Malaysia in the 1970s Fujimoto says: 'From the static economic point of view, it was clearly shown that tenancy *per se* did not harm but improved the cost-return relations on individual farms. In other words, tenancy appeared to provide access to one of the most important production factors, land, at lower cost than the ownership of land' (1983: 220).

Where the economy has been successfully diversified, rice prices are low in relation to other products and the profits to be made through rice cultivation are less than those made through commercial cropping, petty commodity production or other non-agricultural work (as is the case in most of East Asia today); in such a case farmers do not regard the acquisition of extra rice-land as a priority once they have enough for their own subsistence, nor are they prepared to invest heavily in improving their rice-farms if easier profits can be made elsewhere (see chapter 4). Nakamura believes that in the Meiji period most savings from the Japanese agricultural sector were not reinvested in agriculture but were transferred to more profitable sectors (1966: 137). Mizuno points out that while the better-off peasants in Java today owe their prosperity to the Green Revolution improvements in and commercialisation of rice-farming, they invest the surplus thus accumulated in non-agricultural

activities. Well-to-do Malaysian farmers often invest in profitable equipment such as rice-mills (pers. obs.). In Korea, the initial government emphasis on investing so as to increase basic agricultural productivity has now shifted towards the promotion of higher incomes through diversification (Brandt 1980: 277). In China the new economic policies allow farmers to choose how they will use the rest of their land once they have fulfilled the grain quota, and it seems that the area devoted to grain has fallen significantly, despite its increased price both for quota and on the free market; this, the eminent economist Chen Yun declared at a special meeting of the Chinese Communist Party in September 1985, could result in grain shortages leading to social disorder (*Guardian*, 24 September 1985).

In areas such as Java and the Muda region of Malaysia, where the chief profits are to be made through rice-farming, it seems that those who have no access to land at all are becoming more numerous and find themselves in an increasingly difficult position because of the new technology. They rely entirely on wage-labour for their living, and the advance of mechanisation has reduced opportunities for labouring and consequently brought down wages; furthermore farmers often prefer to hire other farmers as labourers, since this guarantees a certain degree of skill and experience. In fact what seems to be happening in areas like Muda and Java is that the truly landless are being displaced from agriculture, while larger farmers draw their (part-time) labour force from those with farms which have dwindled to below subsistence size because of increased competition for land. This development is largely a result of pre-existing institutional inequalities, not in land ownership, but in access to land. 'Under the economic and institutional conditions prevailing in [Northwest Malaysia and Northern Sumatra], the possibility to reproduce and increase capital is a direct function of a farmer's capacity to hire labour which, in turn, is largely a function of his farm size and tenure. However ... the farm benefits, although distributed very unequally, are still such that they do not allow for a caricatural classification of tenurial groups nor for a clear distinction of operators versus landless labourers' (Gibbons et al. 1980: 21).

'Land to the tiller'

The examples of Japan, Taiwan and Korea demonstrate even more clearly the desirability of reducing institutional inequalities. They also show that the intensification of rice production and general expansion of the rural economy are in no way incompatible with the predominance of family smallholdings, even in a capitalist national economy. In rice-

growing societies family farms do not simply survive the competition with capitalist farms, as Kautsky predicted (Banaji 1980), for it seems that capitalist rice-farming is unlikely to develop at all, even in such an advanced economy as Japan.[13] This makes a strong case in favour of populist land reform of the 'land-to-the-tiller' type as a prerequisite for rural growth in the rice regions.

In Japan and Taiwan land reforms had immediate positive effects, rapidly reducing tenancy to very low levels, increasing farmers' incomes and freeing them from the necessity to produce enough rice for the payment of rent, and thus encouraging saving and reinvestment in agriculture as well as the diversification of agricultural production (see appendix C on Japan, Mao [1982] on Taiwan). In Korea the process was more confused and the impact somewhat delayed:

The politics of Korea's land reform efforts in the 1945–52 period is as complex and confusing as most of what was going on in that period. American combat officers with no prior experience in Korea understandably made less than ideal administrators during the first years of Liberation from Japanese rule. Koreans, with no recent experience in running their own government, weren't much of an improvement. (Ban et al. 1980: 283)

Yet, partly through government intervention, partly through private negotiations between landowners and their tenants, the percentage of full tenancy fell from 49% in 1945 to 5% in 1964 (ibid.:286). Nevertheless, agricultural growth was slow during this period, for reasons which are not entirely clear. In Korea, although to a slighter extent than in Japan and Taiwan, there has been a gradual convergence of farm size to the 0.5–2.0 ha range (Ban et al. 1980: 295; appendix C; Mao 1982: 737), accompanied by diversification of the sources of farm income and a marked increase in rural prosperity.

Institutional inequalities in access to land are recognised throughout Southeast Asia as a significant obstacle to rural development. In Malaysia the desirability of land reform has been much debated (e.g. Gibbons et al. 1980; Fujimoto 1983), but no concrete legislation has ever been proposed. In Indonesia agrarian laws were passed in 1960 and 1961 which set upper limits both on ownership and on the leasing-in of land, but implementation proved extremely difficult and led to considerable unrest. 'The change in government in 1966 was a special setback for land reform since agitation for reform had come to be regarded as within the province of communist politics . . . Today land reform has been largely forgotten under an avalanche of rice intensification programmes which scarcely touch upon the topics of farm size and ownership' (Palmer 1977: 135). In the Philippines the mildest of land reforms were proposed, but

again implementation proved almost impossible because of the fierce opposition of landowners (Mangahas et al. 1976; Wurfel 1977; Tadem 1978):

> Philippine agrarian reform has already produced an increase in rural conflict since 1973. That conflict will escalate as reform moves into small landholdings (that is, below 24 ha), because landlord resistance will rise, and will spread most rapidly if the reform slows . . . because of tenant frustration. Some of the recent literature has warned that the Philippine agrarian scene is inherently explosive. (Wurfel 1977: 39)

An additional threat to Philippine peasants is the government's recent policy of granting huge areas of land to contractors to set up 'corporate farms', run with wage-labour. Although export crops occupy the larger part of many such farms, the contractors are also encouraged to devote part of their land to rice production. One such farm, established in Davao del Norte in 1977, was 549 ha in size, and the 34 peasant farmers who had originally opened up the land for cultivation were evicted and gaoled when the title-holder took possession (Tadem 1978: 56). The corporate farming programme was initiated in 1974. By late 1977, 84 such farms had been set up, requiring heavy capital investment in land development and equipment; efficiency and productive levels were low, even by Philippine standards (ibid.). Another government approach was to encourage group rice-farming, 'voluntary groupings of small individually cultivated farms of approximately equal productive capacities into larger units, the aggregate area treated and operated as a single farm' (Ofreneo 1980: 72). Production of rice on such farms was reported as being 75% above average, but as of 1980 very few groups had been formed.

Even in Japan, Taiwan and Korea it is doubtful if land reform could have been successfully carried out except with the backing of outside forces. In Japan before the Second World War the landlord class had effectively blocked all attempts at legislation to help tenants, and it was the Americans who instigated land reform in 1945 (see Dore 1959; appendix C). In Korea too the American occupation forces played an important role; furthermore the defeat of the Japanese colonial government, and the weakening of the political power of Korean landlords, many of whom had been collaborators with the Japanese, reduced the potential opposition to reforms (Ban et al. 1980: 288). In Taiwan the government which initiated land reform consisted of mainlanders who had no loyalty to the traditional Taiwanese landlord class, and who based their legislation on Sun Yat-sen's Principle of Equalisation of Land Rights (Mao 1982: 724).

Group farming

It must be said that rapid rural development in these three countries has still not been successful in eliminating the gap between rural and urban incomes. The lag in agricultural profits is not infrequently attributed to diseconomies in management which the rigidity of the present land laws makes it difficult to transcend, and it is not rare to find the persistence of smallholding deplored as backward and an obstacle to further growth (Moon 1982: 205). In Taiwan amendments are in fact being made to the land laws so as to 'promote land use efficiency' (Mao 1982: 751).

In all three countries various forms of group and cooperative farming are to be found, some still at the experimental stage, and some more successful than others. In Korea cooperation between farmers is largely confined to the traditional practice of group transplanting, but in the late 1960s the government introduced a Joint Rice Farming programme, under which 5 to 10 ha were to be farmed by the 10 to 15 cultivators who owned the land. The idea was that operations would be carried out jointly, but private ownership would be retained, and each farmer would receive the harvest from his own plot (Reed 1979: 29) The programme has not been a great success, for it seems that 'whatever benefits might accrue to joint farm members, they are not seen by the majority of farmers as great enough to offset their perceived costs of participation' (ibid.: 33); the persistence of joint farming in Korea is completely dependent on constant official supervision.

One reason for the lack of success of joint farming in Korea so far must be the relatively low levels of mechanisation. In Taiwan the mechanisation of rice-farming is more advanced, and in 1975 71% of farms were under 1 ha in size (Hong 1979: 52). The Joint Commission for Rural Reconstruction started a pilot programme for joint rice-farming in 1964, whereby blocks of 12–15 ha of rice-land were farmed as a single unit. The programme has proved especially successful among farmers in their thirties and forties, mostly full-time farmers. In 1971, 617 working units were organised to farm 11,290 ha of rice-land, with the participation of 15,345 farmers; by 1976 the figures had risen to 4,306 units, 107,392 ha and 144,336 farmers; during this period yields were 10% to 14% higher than in control areas, production costs were 10% to 15% lower and profits from rice-farming 20% to 45% higher (ibid.: 62). Hong felt that joint cultivation, appropriate as it was to present social and technical conditions in rural Taiwan, might be only a temporary phenomenon, if farm incomes rose and the price of farm machinery declined; but he felt that in such a case, a return to individual

farming might well prove a long-term obstacle to rural development (ibid.: 64).

Various types of joint farming are also found in Japan, including organisations for the joint use of machinery (the most common), group cultivation organisations, cooperatives and contract farming organisations (Kubo 1979; appendix C). Some Japanese agricultural specialists believe that group farming is only a transient phenomenon and predict that it will eventually be replaced either by independently viable family farms or by capitalist large-scale farming. Others (Ogura 1980; appendix C) see sophisticated forms of group farming as the main hope of Japanese agriculture.

Socialist land reform

The socialisation of Chinese agriculture was a gradual process, conducted with the active support of the majority of farmers:

Chinese peasants were not expected to exhibit self-sacrificing altruism in their embrace of socialism. Nor were they expected to shed very quickly their age-old preoccupations and beliefs in favour of ideological attachment to Marxism-Leninism. They were, on the contrary, expected to be willing to cooperate with social and economic change insofar, and only insofar, as they were convinced that change might benefit themselves. (Shue 1980: 326)

Mutual Aid Teams and cooperatives were not totally alien concepts to most Chinese peasants, for in several respects they were 'intrinsically very much akin to the traditional rural cooperative practices which had widespread existence in many parts of China [and especially in the rice regions] long before the advent of Communism' (Wong 1979b: 99). The course of land reform in China, the rise and fall of the communes and the recent rise of the 'responsibility system' are briefly described in appendix B.

In Vietnam, traditional communal institutions, retained even during the colonial period, resumed much of their former significance as the Vietminh established their political dominance, even before the formal passing of the Land Reform Law in December 1953 (Fforde 1983: 46; Moise 1983). In fact in the rural areas under Vietminh control, a large proportion of land was reallocated before the Land Reform Law was passed, between 1945 and 1953 (Fforde 1984: 10).

Cooperativisation occurred in 1959–60. It appears that coercion was generally absent, and the rapid movement of peasants into 'lower-level' producer cooperatives resulted from perceptions of the balance of material benefits and costs. The steady trends from then until the 1970s were for, first, a transition

from 'lower-level' to 'higher-level' cooperatives (this was largely completed by the late 1960s) and, second, an amalgamation of cooperatives. Whereas the earliest cooperatives were well below commune level, with an average membership of ca. 50 families, by the late 1970s the clear target was to have cooperatives coterminous with communes. By that time a typical commune would possess around 250–350 ha of wet-rice land and ca. 5,000 families. Agriculture remained dominated by rice monoculture. Such strikingly high population densities were permitted by the adoption of double rice-cropping and the growing of a third crop of non-rice staples where and when possible. (ibid.: 11)

But as in China collective agriculture on the commune scale presented numerous problems, and it seems that by the mid-1970s, despite a reaffirmation by the central government of its commitment to the collectivist principle, most communes' Management Committees were largely non-functional. Such collective economic activity as there was, was controlled by the work brigades (ibid.: 14). By the late 1970s it was clear that the communes were performing well below expectation, and at the 6th Plenum of August 1979 a fundamental change in policy took place. Agricultural production was to be organised through 'output contracts' signed between cooperatives and their member households, a system similar in almost every respect to the Chinese 'responsibility system' which emerged at almost the same time:

[The output contracts] effectively gave an area of land to the [cooperator] in return for a fixed delivery of output to the cooperative. Collective control was maintained by the stipulation that certain parts of the production process (water supply, pest control, etc.) should be the responsibility of the cooperative. The rest, including most importantly the harvest, were to be carried out by the cooperator. (ibid.: 17)

In Vietnam, as in China, the new policy seems to be a *post facto* official recognition of a grass-roots movement. In both countries there has been a striking increase in agricultural output as a result of the reorganisation of production.

In his 1967 analysis of the economics of Asian agriculture, Ishikawa made what seems at first sight a paradoxical suggestion that one should

treat collective farm agriculture as a variant of peasant agriculture. This is because the present form of collective farm in Mainland China is still substantially a cooperative of individual peasant farms, and the technical foundation of these collective farms does not seem to have changed fundamentally from that in the peasant farm agriculture. (1967: 19)

Recent events bear out Ishikawa's view; nevertheless the role of communal organisation in such aspects of rice production as water

control and the use of machinery remains essential. It may be that the current emphasis on the farming household as the basic production unit will shift back to higher levels of organisation in the future, as the balance shifts towards economic diversification, with consequent pressures (as in Japan and Taiwan) to increase the productivity of labour in rice-farming.

Once rice cultivation techniques reach a certain level of intensification, the family farm comes to predominate as the basic unit of production. It shows a remarkable historical resilience: in China family rice-farms gradually ousted other forms of organisation in medieval times, served as a basis for a flourishing and diverse economy for several centuries, and survived not only the demographic pressures and economic deterioration of the period from 1800 to 1949 but also the rise and fall of the People's Communes. In the other countries of monsoon Asia too, the household farm has persisted as the basic unit of agricultural production despite significant changes in other levels of economic and productive relations: the rise of advanced socialism in China and Vietnam, and of advanced capitalism in Japan. The persistence of this form of production in the face of significant historical change can largely be accounted for by the 'skill-oriented' nature of rice-growing technology, but it is not by any means unique to Asia's rice economies. It is a common feature of most agricultural systems where the intensification of labour use is the principal means of increasing output, for instance those of Mediterranean Europe (Duby 1962; Zangheri 1969; Mottura and Pugliese 1980).

At the same time there is in wet-rice agriculture an essential tension, a dialectical relation, between the individual and the community, imposed by the technical requirements of intensive rice cultivation, and the balance between the two is constantly shifting. It seems that the commune is too large for the satisfactory management of rice production, but at the same time the individual family farm is too small to stand alone. Looking at recent development, one might almost speak of a convergence between forms of management in East Asia's socialist and capitalist nations, towards dual-level management.

By combining individual access to land with the sharing of water and of capital resources, the productivity of rice-farming can be increased to levels where it provides a secure basis for economic diversification and rural growth, even where pressure on land is high and average farm sizes small. It is not the ownership of land as such which permits such development, so much as access to land, and the guaranteed right to a fair proportion of its product. Unfortunately political conditions in most of Asia are not such as to allow of appropriate institutional change, nor are demographic trends likely to ease the acute pressure on land. In fact

the conditions of tenancy will certainly deteriorate further, and the number of landless will continue to increase, although it is unlikely that capitalist farming and a true differentiation of the peasantry will result. In countries where the vast majority of the population is rural, policies of urban industrialisation can do little to improve the situation. Under such conditions, encouraging the development of rural-based, low-capital industries will not prove such a way to wealth as it has done in East Asia, but in the absence of political solutions it can at least provide more opportunities for marginal farmers and the landless to engage in profitable employment.

APPENDIX A:

The Western model

This commonly accepted model of agricultural development derives from the historical experience of Northwestern Europe (in particular the Netherlands and Britain where 'high farming', scientific methods and mechanisation made especially rapid progress) and of the grain-belts of the New World. In several respects it is a construct or an abstraction – there are those, for instance, who would question the very existence of 'capitalist farming' in Europe (e.g. Cooper 1978) – which amalgamates elements from different historical periods or geographic regions to form a coherent picture of increasing efficiency: the rationalisation of landholdings into large units of management goes hand in hand with the development of farm machinery, a reduction in the labour force and an increase in capital inputs (ranging from drainage systems to chemical fertilisers). Economies of scale are the keynote. The potency of this model's attraction can be seen from the alacrity with which it was adopted by the leaders of socialist states: communisation and tractorisation were accepted as the *sine qua non* of modern agriculture.[1]

If we look more closely at some of the factors which affected agricultural development in Europe, it is apparent that the path followed was closely related to the conditions of production specific to this region. Northern Europe has a short growing season, and the staple cereals, wheat, barley and rye, bear heads with relatively few grains – at best a few dozen, compared with the hundred or more grains in a panicle of rice or millet – and often a single head on each plant. This may seem a trivial point, but it affects yields and means that a much higher proportion of the harvested crop must be kept for seed-grain.[2] The climate of Northern Europe does not permit more intensive cultivation than three grain crops in two years, but even this is a very recent development which depends on the use of fertilisers and scientific crop rotations. Before the

seventeenth century the commonest method of fertilising grain-fields was to pasture livestock on the fallows; thus corn could only be grown one year in every two or three.[3] Under these conditions, the farming system of North Europe used land extensively and could not support high population densities. The size of a family subsistence holding was necessarily large: a feudal manse in the ninth century was often as big as 40 hectares (Slicher van Bath 1963: 42; Mukhia 1981: 278).

Livestock played a crucial role in this farming system. First they were the chief source of manure, and the right to fold the village flocks on one's fallow was hotly contested in medieval times.[4] Since yields were so low, draught animals were essential, for it was impossible to till sufficient land for subsistence by manpower alone. Though in some regions plough-teams consisted only of a pair or two of oxen, in heavier soils between eight and a dozen oxen might be needed for a team, and records from the French imperial estates in Carolingian times show that from an early date feudal landholders relied on their villeins to supply not only manpower but also a large proportion of the animal traction necessary for working the demesne (Duby 1962: 206; Slicher van Bath 1963: 67).

In the absence of scientific crop-breeding methods and inorganic fertilisers there was little scope for improving the productivity of land. '[This] could only be achieved in unusually favourable circumstances, namely, when the land could be more heavily manured or more cattle could be kept than was usual on the average farm. If cattle and manure were lacking, the possibility of increased production was practically non-existent' (Slicher van Bath 1963: 18). One way of increasing yields, provided draught animals were available, was simply to bring more land under the plough. A great deal of new land was cleared and brought under cultivation in the eleventh and twelfth centuries as population pressures increased, though it has been suggested that much of it had to be abandoned after a few decades as its fertility was rapidly exhausted (Bloch 1931; Abel 1935; Duby 1962; Neveux 1975). Improved farming techniques, also dependent upon increased use of human and animal labour, were an important factor in raising and maintaining land productivity: several ploughings and careful harrowing could improve germination rates and keep down weeds, contributing to higher yields and permitting the fields to be cropped more frequently. Modifications in both bovine and equine harness, which started to gain currency in Europe in the ninth and tenth centuries (Chaunu 1979), may have contributed to improved farming practice, facilitating, for example, the replacement of the light scratch-plough or ard by the heavy but more efficacious mouldboard plough. It appears that the admittedly slight increase in grain yields between the ninth and thirteenth centuries was

largely due to such factors as a more intensive working of the soil (Duby 1962: 193).

Where draught animals and heavy equipment like turn-ploughs and harrows play such a crucial role in agricultural production, it is clear that large farms, which can afford more animals and equipment and can organise their use more efficiently, will have a significant advantage over small holdings. Generally speaking, the larger the farm in medieval Europe, the more likely it was to produce a surplus. Manorial demesnes had varied enormously in size, the area of arable land varying from as little as 5 hectares to as much as 250 hectares (Slicher van Bath 1963: 44). But by the twelfth or thirteenth century urbanisation was providing an expanding market for agricultural produce, and many territorial lords, conscious that large consolidated estates were more profitable and easier to manage than scattered smallholdings, had begun to 'withdraw their demesne land from the village farms, to consolidate, enclose, and cultivate them in separate ownership' (Ernle 1972: 38). The transition to private ownership of land was directly related to the superior economic performance of large farms, for under feudal relations it was extremely difficult for the farmer to increase the quantity of land, or labour, at his disposal. By the twelfth and thirteenth centuries villeinage was dying out in many parts of Northern Europe: the peasants were freed from their feudal obligations but in many cases lost some or all of the land to which they had previously had hereditary rights, and were thus obliged to join the swelling ranks of wage-labourers.

The gulf between subsistence smallholders and successful farmers continued to grow throughout late medieval times. Rises in the price of land were, as one might expect, accompanied by increasing rates of tenancy, and the tenants that landlords preferred were not smallholders but well-to-do farmers who could afford to invest in animals and equipment, 'small capitalists' like the English yeomen, whose profit margins were higher and who could afford to pay decent rents (Duby 1962; Moore 1967). This was a period of land-hunger and widespread enclosures, during which many peasants found themselves unable to survive as independent farmers and were obliged to sell their labour.

Capitalist relations in agriculture were already apparent in many parts of Northwest Europe before the fifteenth century, by which time markets in both land and labour were well developed. Though agricultural technology was still at a primitive stage, the social relations necessary for the foundation of a 'modern', mechanised agriculture already obtained, even though the technical expertise was still lacking. Especially in the Netherlands and Britain, farming methods improved notably in the seventeenth and eighteenth centuries, and land productivity rose

accordingly. As effective drainage, scientific crop rotations and other improvements characteristic of 'high farming' were adopted, farmers continued to add to the size of their holdings wherever possible (all the agricultural experts were agreed that only large farms were efficient), and the labour force required on individual farms increased correspondingly.[5]

Throughout its development, the dynamic of the agricultural system of Northwest Europe was the superior performance of large, centrally managed units of production. Under such conditions, an immediate consequence of the expansion of the forces of production was the polarisation of rural society into farmer-managers and wage-labourers. This also had implications for wider patterns of economic development: because very few rural labourers had land of their own, they constituted a relatively mobile labour force, large numbers of whom sought work in the towns, facilitating the development of urban-based industries. Although many of these began as small workshops, run almost like a family enterprise, there were no obstacles to recruiting extra labour and increasing the size of the enterprise, and of course it was in the more sizeable units that mechanisation and the Industrial Revolution had their roots:

Machinery can seldom be used with success to abridge the labour of an individual; more time would be lost on its construction than could be saved by its application. It is only really useful when it acts on great masses, when a single machine can assist the work of thousands . . . It is not called into use by a scarcity of men, but by the facility with which they may be brought to work in masses. (Ravenstone 1824, quoted in Marx 1976: I, 566)

Ever since the beginning of the 'Agricultural Revolution' in the seventeenth century, farmers in Northwest Europe had cherished the hope of substituting machines for at least part of their labour force, which as we mentioned earlier was relatively expensive during this period of conflicting claims for labour. But the agricultural tasks to be performed were complex, and the relatively simple skills of the early engineers were not adequate to the task. Many unsuccessful attempts were made to produce agricultural machines in the seventeenth and eighteenth centuries, and the need for such machines was felt more acutely as time passed. By the early nineteenth century engineers had at their disposal both the specialised materials and the expertise required to develop machines for agriculture (Fussell 1952). The first successful mechanical threshers came on the market in the 1830s, and agricultural labourers rioted all over England as they saw their livelihood threatened on a large scale (Hobsbawm and Rudé 1968). Reapers, combine-

harvesters, mechanical drills and horse-hoes followed. By the 1960s the proportion of the British workforce involved in agriculture had dropped from its 1800 figure of over a quarter to nearer 3.5 per cent (Mitchell 1974: 660), and by 1970 it had dropped by a further quarter to 2.7 per cent (Fream 1977: xxxii).

APPENDIX B:

The historical experience of China

The case of Southern China illustrates some of the more general changes in the economy and in relations of production which may accompany the development of rice agriculture. The most striking period of development of Southern Chinese agriculture began in the Song dynasty (960–1279), when the government initiated a series of development policies so sweeping in scope and result that they may well be compared to the so-called 'Green Revolution' of contemporary Asia (Elvin 1973; Bray 1979). The economic centre of China had first begun to shift from the northern plains (where dry grains, millets and wheat, were the main crops) down to the Yangzi rice-growing region during the eighth and ninth centuries. Fear of the Khitan and other nomadic invaders drove thousands of peasants to abandon their land in the north, and by the Song dynasty the greater part of the population lived in the southern provinces.[1] The Chinese government was faced with the double problem of feeding an increased population on a greatly reduced area, and of maintaining large armies to protect its borders.[2]

It was clearly necessary to increase agricultural production in the southern provinces, and the government undertook a series of measures to improve farming methods and yields. One of the most famous was the introduction to the Yangzi Delta in 1012 of new varieties of quick-ripening rices from Champa in Vietnam (see chapter 1). This transformed production patterns, allowing double-cropping of rice or the alternation of summer rice and winter wheat. Seeds of the new varieties were distributed to farmers through the district *yamens*, and written instructions on their cultivation methods were circulated. These were presumably intended not for the peasants themselves, most of whom would be illiterate,[3] but for the Song equivalent of an agricultural extension officer: 'master farmers', *nong shi*, were local farmers chosen for their skill and experience to fill a minor official post which carried the

duty of improving agricultural techniques in their village. They were to instruct their peers not only in new techniques such as improved sowing and fertilising methods or crop choices, but also in the organisation of mutual aid and so on. It was presumably these 'master farmers' who channelled to ordinary peasants the information contained in the agricultural books commissioned and printed on government order, which contained information on better cropping practices, new tools, machines, fertilisers and irrigation methods (*Wang Zhen nongshu*; Bray 1984: 55 ff). As well as providing information, seeds and often such infrastructural support as new irrigation networks, the Song government introduced financial incentives to invest in agricultural improvement, including loans to farmers at low interest rates, lower levels of taxation and tax rebates on newly reclaimed land (Golas 1980).

While the role of the government was crucial in stimulating agricultural development in Southern China in its initial stages, perhaps its chief success was the degree to which the rural population recognised the merits of the new technology and were willing to experiment and improve on their own initiative. There was some early resistance to innovation: for instance, some peasants objected to double-cropping because they feared the extra work involved would not be justified by the increase in yields, while landlords feared that it would erode the fertility of their soils; as more commercial fertilisers became available and varieties improved, these objections were silenced. Peasants bred locally new and improved varieties of rice and other crops, some of which travelled from hand to hand over vast distances. Landlord and lineage associations reclaimed lakeside marshes, building dyked and poldered fields, while land-hungry peasants opened up hillside terraces or migrated to the wide, fertile plains of the sparsely populated Middle Yangzi, taking with them improved seeds and advanced technology.

The Song 'Green Revolution' had its roots in the most populous, agriculturally and economically advanced areas of China, the Lower Yangzi provinces of Jiangsu and Zhejiang and the coastal province of Fujian. By the fourteenth century the changes had gained momentum and the new technology was spreading to less developed areas, until by the eighteenth century it had reached even such remote provinces as Yunnan in the far southwest.

The innovations brought about a rapid upsurge in agricultural productivity in Song China. Improved yields and the multi-cropping of staple grains produced unprecedented surpluses, and as a result it was possible for commercial cropping and rural industry to develop on a scale hitherto unknown. Rice was exchanged for charcoal, tea, oil, wine and other locally produced goods at the village markets which sprang up all

over the country, while a vigorous national trade in these and other commodities permitted intensive regional specialisation (Shiba 1970; Elvin 1973). Suzhou, near Shanghai, had already become a centre of specialised silk production by the twelfth century, and the local farmers devoted themselves entirely to raising silkworms and producing silk thread; rice they bought on the market. Another important commercial crop was sugar, which was especially popular in Fujian, Sichuan and Guangdong; in certain areas of twelfth-century Sichuan as many as 40% of the peasants were engaged in growing sugar-cane (*Tangshuang pu*: 3a). Sugar had totally supplanted rice in several districts of Fujian by the fifteenth century, and was exported not only to other provinces of China but also throughout Southeast Asia (Rawski 1972: 48). Other commercial crops included tea, vegetables, fruit, timber, oil-seeds, dyes and fibre crops, bamboos and (after 1500) tobacco. These were almost invariably produced by peasant farmers, though some landlords did possess large orchards or plantations (Shiba 1970).

There was also a very marked increase in manufacturing, most of which took the form of 'cottage industries'. The farmer's wife had traditionally been responsible for spinning and weaving, not only for her family's use but also to pay that part of the tax dues which was levied in cloth. The silk industry in pre-Song times had been small and predominantly urban-based, under official control, but during the Song it expanded rapidly, especially in the southeastern provinces and Sichuan. Some areas specialised in rearing silkworms or growing mulberry leaves, others in weaving a particular type of silk cloth. Much of the weaving was done in peasant households: brokers provided the silk thread, paid the women for their work and marketed the cloth (Shiba 1970: 111). The cotton industry, which first became important in the fourteenth and fifteenth centuries, was run along similar lines: there was a national market for raw cotton, which peasant women bought from traders at local markets, span and wove, and then sold back again. Other industries included paper-making, the production of lacquer wares, metal goods, charcoal, and comestibles such as wines, spirits, bean-curd, sauces and pickles. Again, almost all production was on a household scale, and most of the producers were farming families.

It has already been pointed out that wet-rice cultivation is not, like the farming system of Northwest Europe, subject to economies of scale, nor does it respond positively to the centralisation of management. It is therefore not surprising to find that as new techniques were applied in China and land productivity rose, the position of tenants vis-à-vis their landlords improved: they acquired more managerial and economic independence, and tenurial contracts were modified in their favour.

There were no legal obstacles to the sale of land in medieval China, and when the Song improvements brought about an increase in the value of land, many wealthy people invested in landed property and large estates were amassed. But these were not the consolidated, centrally managed holdings with which we are familiar from post-feudal Europe: they were almost invariably subdivided into small parcels leased to peasant farmers. Although a few consolidated holdings were established in areas of low population density, even in the early Song widely dispersed estates were typical of areas such as the Yangzi Delta; by the end of the Song few consolidated holdings survived (Golas 1980: 304).

During the Southern Song (1127–1279) all three forms of rental agreement known in later periods, namely sharecropping, fixed rent in kind and fixed rent in cash, are known to have existed. Significantly sharecropping[4] seems already to have been in decline in Southern China: fixed rents paid in grain were common on the large dispersed estates of the Lower Yangzi, where supervision costs on sharecropping would have been disproportionately high (Golas 1980: 308; McDermott 1978: 208). By the fourteenth and fifteenth centuries tenants in Fujian and most other parts of Central and Southern China always paid their rents as a fixed quantity, and the landlord played no part at all, even supervisory, in the process of production (Rawski 1972: 18). As cultivation techniques became more complex and the supervision of tenants more onerous, landlords took less and less direct interest in the way their land was farmed, and tenants acquired rights to greater security of tenure or even, eventually, to permanent tenancy. So secure were the rights of tenants in fifteenth century Fujian that, on payment of a fee called 'manured soil money', *fei tu yin*, the tenant received transferable and negotiable cultivation rights over the topsoil, and could sub-let or sell his rights without the landlord's consent. This system of 'two owners of a single field', *yi tian liang zhu*, was common in many parts of China right up until 1949 (Fei 1939; Rawski 1972: 190). The tenant had very strong customary rights, and often the landlord could only raise rents if the tenant agreed. Permanent tenancy rights were widespread in China even during the poverty-stricken 1930s (Myers 1982: 40).

Through the centuries there were considerable fluctuations in the distribution of landholding in China, but generally the majority of holdings in the economically advanced rice areas were either those of medium landowners, averaging 6 hectares or so (a minute area compared with the advanced farms of eighteenth- or nineteenth-century Britain, or even the size of a feudal manse), or of smallholders or part-tenants. In the eleventh century the latter constituted over 50 per cent of the registered population of Southern China and held a quarter of the land

(Golas 1980: 303). In the seventeenth-century Yangzi Delta really large landowners were rare and probably three-quarters of the land was owned by medium landowners or smallholders (Huang 1974: 158). Though landlessness did occur, and became more frequent as population growth increased the pressure on land, most peasants eventually acquired access to land at least as a tenant, and under the system of fixed rents, skilled tenant farmers could hope to save enough to buy some land of their own (Myers 1982). Fei (1939: 177) reports that even in a crowded twentieth-century village near Shanghai he met no one who had been landless all his life. Thus there was no proletarianisation of labour, and the basic unit of production remained the family smallholding.

The expansion of agricultural production appears to have kept pace with population growth in China until about 1800 when, for a number of reasons, the situation began to deteriorate rapidly. Landlords were affected as well as tenants, who quite commonly withheld payment of rent temporarily or even permanently if harvests were bad. Absentee landlords had few institutional forms of redress against defaulting tenants in China; as a last resort they would hire bands of strongmen to recuperate the rents due to them. Moore (1967: 180) and Ash (1976: 43) see this simply as evidence of the ferocity of landlord exploitation, but it also offers proof of their financial desperation and their relative helplessness in the face of village solidarity.[5]

Significantly, even though landlessness increased under such conditions, the transition to capitalist relations of production, whereby landowners evict their tenants in order to run large, consolidated farms using cheap wage-labour, did not occur in China. In fact it can even be shown that despite the huge growth of the population and the rather small increase in arable land between 1700 and the 1930s, the land tenure situation did not worsen (Myers 1982: 43).

Land reform under the People's Republic first took the form of simple redistribution: land, livestock and other capital assets were taken from the landlords and 'rich peasants' and redistributed among the 'middle' and 'lower peasants'. There were no absolute criteria for these categorisations, but in general 'rich peasants' had more land than they could cultivate with family labour alone and so they hired extra hands, 'middle peasants' worked their land themselves, and poor peasants had little or no land and had to hire out their labour. According to surveys made in the 1930s, full tenancy was not very widespread in the northern provinces, and was most widespread in the rice-growing regions of the centre, east and southeast (Myers 1982: 40). But even in the rice regions poor peasants in fact benefited only marginally from land reform since the amount of resources available for redistribution, that is to say owned

by landlords and rich peasants, in fact formed a relatively small proportion of the land and a very small proportion of the other capital assets (Wong 1973). It was only with collectivisation that the gap between poor and middle peasants was closed.

In the twenty years following the formation of the People's Communes in 1958–9, while wheat production rose by 180%, rice production rose by only 107%.[6] Wong argues that while the Mutual Aid Teams (which derived from pre-existing peasants' cooperative organisations and were the first stage in the process of collectivisation) were the optimally sized unit for efficient agricultural production and decision-making, the Agricultural Producers' Cooperatives (the second stage in collectivisation) 'had clearly reached the limit of an optimum size beyond which productivity growth could not be further increased ... It can thus be seen that the decision to collectivise Chinese agriculture could only be rationalised on macroeconomic and ideological grounds!' (1982: 6). It is perhaps significant that Wong's studies were carried out in Guangdong, a region of rice multi-cropping.

In regions such as Manchuria, the large-scale mechanisation of wheat and maize production permitted by the reorganisation of land use has proved successful. But the chief advantage offered by the reorganisation of agriculture in rice-growing areas lay not so much in land consolidation or mechanisation as in the communal purchase of electric or diesel pumps for water control. One of the advantages is that while these pumps free humans and animals from the concentrated drudgery of irrigation work, they also often increase the frequency of cropping and the area of irrigated land, thus absorbing labour more evenly over the year rather than simply displacing it (T. Rawski 1979: 85).

But this particular advance in irrigation technology corresponds to a rather low level of social organisation, namely , the brigade or commune. Where major irrigation networks are concerned the improvements have often been rather minor, largely because the responsibility for organising water control is decentralised, and competition for the scarce resource between communes, districts and even provinces has continued unabated (Gustaffson 1984: 129). So much for Wittfogel's notions of the all-embracing powers devolving to the centralised, totalitarian state. The latest shift towards decollectivisation under the 'responsibility system' is, not surprisingly, proving particularly advantageous in areas where intensive rice cultivation is combined with the production of commercial crops or livestock (Dumont 1984).

The recent liberalisation of agricultural production under the 'responsibility system', combined with large increases in prices for agricultural products, rapidly led to an impressive increase in crop

production (see chapter 5), and to greater diversification into the cultivation of industrial and other economic crops, and rural industrialisation (see chapter 4). There has been a significant and welcome reduction in the gap between urban and rural incomes as a result. A new problem is now surfacing, however. During the sixties and early seventies 'grain was taken as the key link' and regional self-sufficiency was given priority, a policy which often resulted in inefficient use of local resources and reduced yields even of food-grains. Now the low price of food-grains relative to other agricultural products has led many peasants to reduce the proportion of their plots used for grain to the strict minimum required to fulfil the official quota, and there are fears in some quarters that this will eventually lead to national grain shortages. At a special conference of the Chinese Communist Party held in mid-September 1985, the veteran economic planner Chen Yun complained: 'Some peasants are no longer interested in growing grain. They are not even interested in raising pigs and vegetables because in their opinion there can be no prosperity without engaging in industry' (Bonavia and Lee 1985).

APPENDIX C:

The Japanese experience

An interesting example of the way in which a long-established tradition of rice-cultivation can affect economic patterns is to be found in Japan. It has often been claimed that Japan is the unique example of an Asian state which has followed the European path from feudalism to industrial capitalism. As Japan was the first, and for a long time the only Asian nation to threaten Western domination of the world market in manufactured goods, it is not surprising that many people have tried to explain Japan's success in terms of its basic similarity to Europe. It has even been suggested that over the two centuries leading up to Japan's early phase of modernisation, tenurial relations underwent basically similar changes to those which preceded the Industrial Revolution in England (Yamamura 1979), though since farms, that is units of management, became generally larger in England as they became smaller in Japan, one might question exactly where the similarity lies. But many Japanese economists, equally familiar with their own economy and with those of neighbouring East and Southeast Asian countries (which once formed part of the 'Greater Co-Prosperity Sphere' and now are seen as crucial trading partners), see significant parallels not between Japan and Europe but between the rice-growing economies of this region. Agriculture in these countries uses both land and labour intensively, and many of their common problems derive from this fact. In the case of Japan the problems have been encapsulated in the term *shōnōsei*, 'smallholder system', which is regarded by many Japanese today as a burdensome relic of an agrarian past which they believe to have been significantly shaped by the development of irrigated rice cultivation.

Tokugawa Japan underwent an agricultural and economic expansion in many respects similar to that of Song China, indeed many agricultural innovations were probably based on Chinese precedent (Furushima 1963). In an effort to consolidate their power and increase their

revenues, the first Tokugawa rulers organised cadastral surveys to tighten their control over the land-tax, and encouraged agricultural development and the expansion of manufacturing. They opened up communications networks and promoted agricultural innovation as well as the development of industry and commerce, promulgating edicts urging the peasants to work harder, drink less, engage in handicrafts and so on. Treatises on improved farming methods were published, such as the *Nōgyō Zensho* of 1697 and the later *Nōgu Benri Ron*; these were based on their authors' wide experience and intensive practical research in Japan itself, though their debt to the great Chinese treatises is immediately apparent. These works were widely read by Japanese farmers, some of who went on to write their own agricultural tracts.

In Japan, before the agricultural improvements and commercial development of the Tokugawa period (1600–1868), rural society consisted of landowning families and various categories of bondsmen. Some (the *genin*) were hereditary or indentured servants who lived with the landowner's family, but the majority were in a category more akin to the serfs of medieval Europe. These serfs had a number of regional names, the most common being *nago* (Smith 1959: ch. 5). The *nago* lived separately from the landowner but depended on him not only for land and loans of tools and animals, but often (since their allotments of land were small and unproductive) for food (Yamamura 1979: 285). The landowner's status vis-à-vis his *nago* was that of 'master', *oyakata*; he guaranteed their survival in return for labour services. *Nago* had only customary rights to their land (the landowner was legally responsible for paying the land-tax, though in fact a *nago* might be obliged to make the payment, in his landlord's name), and were thus not considered to be proper members of the village community. They had no rights to common land or water, and could not hold office or participate in the village assembly (Smith 1959: 10, 25).

But whereas Japanese peasants had previously produced rice chiefly to pay their taxes and feudal dues, and had themselves subsisted on the produce of their dryland fields (buckwheat and barley), the technical improvements under the Tokugawa allowed them to start to extend the cultivation of irrigated crops to produce rice both for their own consumption and for the market. The number of rice varieties increased dramatically; one record gives 177 names for rice in the early seventeenth century and 2,363 by the mid-nineteenth century, while a nineteenth-century agricultural diary states that between 1808 and 1866 the breeding of improved rice varieties permitted an extension of the growing period by 17 days (Smith 1959: 95). New irrigation works were built on official and private initiative, and new tools and fertilisers

became widely available. As in Song China, there was a rapid increase in the production of commercial crops. Cotton-farming in the Kinai is perhaps the best-known example, but in the mountains of Honshū sericulture became important, and sugar-cane was widely grown in Kyūshū and the islands (Smith 1959; Furushima 1963; Hauser 1974).

As agriculture progressed in Tokugawa Japan, so too the economy expanded in other spheres. The basic unit of production, as in China, was the individual household, responsible for the management of its landholding and supplementing its income by cottage industries such as the weaving of silk or cotton, wine-brewing, or the manufacture of bean-curd or pickles. The rapid expansion of textile and other commodity production was based largely upon the increased participation of peasant families in manufacturing on a household scale. Some highly specialised industries, such as the silk-brocade manufactures of Kyōto, now found they had serious rivals in the villages, where labour costs were rated on a very different scale. As in medieval China, the scope for direct investment in production was severely restricted, but there were fortunes to be made as merchants or middlemen, providing the link between local producers and the national market. A class of village entrepreneurs emerged, capable of challenging their urban counterparts (Yamamura 1979: 291), but despite the rapid growth of petty commodity production and inter-regional trade there were few instances of what we should recognise as capitalist development either in manufacturing or in agriculture.

The expansion of the rural economy was accompanied by marked changes in relations of production. The social and legal status of the dependent rural classes improved rapidly. The servant classes decreased in number while the lower echelons of the landholding class grew, and tenants who had previously been obliged to provide their landlords with various free labour-services acquired a far greater measure of economic independence. With the expansion of agricultural production and the growth of non-agricultural sources of income, labour became a marketable commodity. Hereditary servants on the large feudal farms gradually acquired greater freedom, until at last the transition to wage labour was complete; under these conditions tenants too demanded payment for any work undertaken on the landlord's farm.

The increase in labour costs made the large holdings of the formerly privileged landowners uneconomic. They could no longer compete effectively with smallholdings for 'since the one type of holding was prone to buy and the other to sell labour, the competitive positions of the two as farming units ... were drastically altered. Circumstances now favoured the family-size farm and strongly penalised any larger unit'

(Smith 1959: 125). But it was not merely the growth of a market in labour which led to the demise of the old feudal system. As Smith remarks (ibid.: 92), most technological innovations of the period tended to strengthen the solidarity of the household farm. Technical improvements in rice cultivation, being closely related to the intensification of skilled labour inputs, tended to increase the tenants' degree of independence from his landlord.

During the eighteenth century there was a shift from rents paid in kind to fixed cash rents, and throughout the nineteenth century rents actually fell (Yamamura 1979: 297). But despite falling rental shares landlords continued to lease their land to tenants, and their incomes 'tended to rise, because the total value of output was larger when tenant farmers worked the land than when hired labour cultivated commercial crops for the landholders' (ibid.: 298). The gradual improvement of tenant status continued in Japan through the nineteenth and early twentieth centuries, when landlords found to their dismay that their investments in irrigation and other improvements, by increasing their tenants' financial security, brought them not more but less respect and influence in the village (Waswo 1977).

The *shōnōsei* tradition of family farming made many Western innovations in agriculture quite unsuitable for adoption in Japan. In the late nineteenth century, the period of the Meiji Restoration, Western agronomy and agricultural technology were greatly admired in Japan: officials and students were sent abroad to study, and foreigners were hired as advisers by the newly established Ministry of Agriculture. Many Western breeding techniques and some new crop varieties proved successful and were widely adopted, but Western machinery and farming methods often proved quite unsuitable. After 1880 the government decided to emphasise 'improvements within the framework of Japanese agriculture, by developing new strains of traditional crops, and by diffusing more widely the best practices of particular [Japanese] regions' (Dore 1969: 99). It was not simply that peasant farmers were incapable of adapting to the new Western technology, rather, Western technology and centralisation of management, though appropriate to capitalist farming, were fundamentally unsuited to wet-rice production. A number of capitalist entrepreneurs set up as farmers in Japan in the late nineteenth century, and those who ran livestock farms or grew industrial crops often prospered – indeed wealthy farmers producing industrial crops on large farms, using wage-labour drawn from neighbouring rice-farms, were not uncommon even in the eighteenth century (Yamamura 1979: 299) – but capitalist entrepreneurs who set up in rice-farming invariably failed (Dore 1969: 110).

In Meiji Japan the resident, cultivating landlords (*tezukuri jinushi*) were often instrumental in improving the agricultural methods of their tenants. These well-educated farmers were in the vanguard of technological advance (Waswo 1977: 33, 38). Francks argues that one reason for the success of the *tezukuri jinushi* was 'a function of their role as village leaders, hence their contact with the outside world and their participation in and leadership of agricultural societies, discussion groups and so on ... the need for access to such non-market information sources was characteristic of the new technology of this period' (1983: 66). But their role as village leaders also enabled them to improve their tenants' performance as well as their own:

> It was an accepted part of the landlords' role that they supervise their tenants' farming – as an old saying put it: 'The trail made by landlords [through their tenants' fields] is the best fertiliser yet devised'. Given the authority landlords possessed, simply commanding their tenants to change farming techniques was often sufficient. Where innovations required greater labour or involved some degree of risk, however, economic incentives were important. A landlord in Gifu Prefecture promised to cover all losses if the advice he gave his tenants on ways to increase yields proved unsuccessful. Others gave prizes of money or tools to tenants who produced superior crops. (Waswo 1977: 39)

These landlords were active members of the local community, farming part of their land but renting the rest to tenants with whose methods they were intimately familiar and over whom they exerted both social and economic influence, such tenurial relations being quite typical of intensive rice cultivation. But although their role as instigators of technical change brought them immediate financial rewards in the form of increased rents, in the long run it undermined their position in rural society: the increased security experienced by tenants as a result of the innovations reduced their economic dependence upon their landlords, who thus lost much of their influence (Waswo 1977: 5).

But the Japanese government was ready to take over the responsibility of promoting innovation among small farmers. For this it relied not only on trained extension officers but also sometimes on police enforcement. Farmers in Japan and the Japanese colonies resented what Japanese historians sometimes refer to (in allusion to Frederick the Great) as 'extension by the sabre method', and clashes with agricultural officials or with the police were frequent, but in general the ingrained respect of peasants for their superiors prevailed: 'the incidence of compliant submission [can] be inferred from the fact that the improvements recommended did in fact become standard practice' (Dore 1969: 104).

An official report of 1910 stated that tenancy in Japan was then on the increase, and that in 1908 full-and part-tenants together constituted

66% of all farmers (Ag. Bureau 1910: 9). Increasing landlordism was in part a response to the Meiji tax reforms of 1870 which fixed land taxes at about 9% of the gross value of the land (Nakamura 1966: 160). While tenants' incomes were largely unaffected, landlords' incomes rose, and their profits were mostly invested outside agriculture in, for example, the national banks or in government bonds.

It had always been felt by Japanese statesmen that fostering agriculture was not only to the economic benefit of the state but also to its political and moral advantage. In the Meiji period these beliefs were encapsulated in the philosophy of *Nōhon shugi* (literally 'agrarian fundamentalism'): 'The principal *Nōhon shugi* beliefs included a faith in agricultural economics, an affirmation of rural communalism, and a conviction that farming was indispensable to those qualities that made the nation unique' (Havens 1974: 8). 'The ethics textbooks used in the national school system after November 1936 conferred official recognition on agrarianism as a major source of civic virtue' (ibid.: 11). In its official, bureaucratic form, *Nōhon shugi* justified a number of government programmes intended to improve agricultural productivity as a necessary part of industrial expansion. These programmes generally kept rice prices low and did not contribute to the well-being of tenants, but they held a great appeal for landowners.

Conditions for tenants and smallholders gradually deteriorated as Japan invested ever more resources in industrialisation, and their plight grew especially serious after the great crash of 1929; popular forms of *Nōhon shugi* took on anti-establishment overtones and led to several political incidents. Throughout the 1920s and 1930s landlord-tenant relations grew steadily worse, but no attempts at legislation to improve the position of tenants could be effective, for the political role of the landlord class was much too strong (Ogura 1967). A successful policy for defusing popular resentment was found in the state-supported schemes for the agricultural colonisation of Manchuria, introduced in the 1930s under the ideological influence of a private schoolmaster, Katō Kanji, whose nationalistic and expansionist ideas managed to fuse popular and bureaucratic *Nōhon shugi* (Havens 1974: 11). The colonisation of Manchuria was a crucial element in Japan's preparations for war.

By the end of the war Japan's economy was in ruins. In 1945, 46% of Japan's farmland was cultivated by tenants, most of whom were then on the brink of starvation. General MacArthur, the chief of the American occupation forces, was determined to reconstruct Japan as a healthy democracy, and the political opposition of the landlord class cut no ice with him. In 1945 the Americans set in motion Japan's First Land Reform. This provided that any farmland exceeding 5 ha leased by a

resident landlord, and all farmland leased by an absentee landlord, should be surrendered to the tenants at the latters' request within five years; that the system of rent in kind should be completely replaced with that of rent in cash; and that contracts could not be cancelled without the approval of the Agricultural Land Commission. Adjustments were made in 1946 during the Second Land Reform which went still further: the government was to buy up all absentee landlords' land and all resident landlords' land over 1 ha (4 ha in Hokkaido), which was to be sold to tenant farmers within two years of the promulgation of the law. It is estimated that 80% of tenanted land, totalling 2 million ha, fell under this provision (Ogura 1967: 145). By 1950 tenancy had fallen to 10%, and continued to fall thereafter (ibid.: 70), since the reform relieved former tenants of the heavy burden of rent which had hampered capital accumulation and limited agricultural diversification and the growth of commodity production.

Independent smallholding was thus institutionalised in Japan.[1] Since the 1950s, sustained by heavy government investment in irrigation, R & D and other development programmes, and more particularly by the rice price support policies mentioned in chapter 5, Japanese rice-farming technology has advanced steadily and has now reached the stage of integral mechanisation (see chapter 2). Increased rice yields have provided farmers with the financial basis for the successful diversification of agricultural production, and they have become increasingly prosperous. Although a large part of their income is derived from other economic activities, to the point where many of them have become part-time farmers,[2] they have not abandoned or converted their rice-fields: apart from their deep-rooted emotional attachment to rice-farming (Shimpo 1976: 45), rice production is heavily subsidised and continues to be lucrative, to the farmers, if not to the national economy. In some regions rice-farming is still expanding (ibid.: xxvi).

Compared to most other Asian nations Japan's development of agriculture appears outstandingly successful, and indeed has often been invoked as a model. But it is not without its problems. The economic inefficiencies of over-investment in capital goods, especially machinery, have been mentioned in chapters 2 and 5; rice production is at present only economically viable on farms where the rice area exceeds 1 ha (Matsuda 1982: 449). Given the increasingly heavy dependence of Japanese farmers on expensive machinery, Shimpo (1976: ch. 5) sees as a solution either the concentration of holdings into 'American-style' large, mechanised farms, or the survival of family farms owning machinery in common and working together as 'cooperative villages'.

Farmers' organisations for the joint use of machinery became common

in the 1960s and are still in existence today. But the increase in part-time farming has caused organisational problems within these groups, as well as making it difficult for many farms to manage with family labour alone. For instance in the Yamaguchi City area in 1975, of 5,925 farmers all but 520 were part-time (Morio 1982). Such circumstances provide an opportunity for small groups of four or five what one might call 'professional farmers' to offer their services as contract farmers. They jointly hire or purchase larger-scale machinery and contract individually to other farmers for various stages of rice production, hoping eventually to contract for the full process, in which case they will have complete control of management over the land in question. Such organisations are described by Morio as being highly profit-oriented. But although from 1972 to 1976 the number of contract farming groups increased nationwide from 2,481 to 3,493, and in Yamaguchi from 42 to 58, the area of land under full contract was not large: in the organisation studied by Morio the four individual members had full contracts on only 11.0 ha of rice-land by 1978, a figure which had fluctuated continuously over the previous five years (Morio 1982: table 5).

Another serious problem is that heavy subsidies have resulted in overproduction of rice and constitute a heavy financial burden to the government, which is in no position to alienate the farming lobby. Many observers feel that Japanese agriculture faces a bleak future, having reached the limits of development. Many economists believe that the present organisation of rice production should be changed and greater emphasis given to diversification, for example into wheat and animal husbandry. The influential agricultural economist and adviser Ogura sees a reform of the agricultural structure as the only hope for survival, short of the disbanding of smallholder farming through government purchase. In the Japanese tradition, Ogura believes that 'the marriage of man and land is spiritually essential for the existence of a nation' (1980: 587). He feels that the necessary agrarian reforms should have as their objectives not only a higher degree of self-sufficiency in all foods, but also a reduction in the gap between rural and urban incomes, increased social justice and the strengthening of grass-roots organisations. The policies adopted should aim to foster viable family farms and cooperation between them, in part through legal reforms to ensure the inheritance of land by a single person (ibid.: 596–642).

The chief problems of Japanese agriculture today seem largely to be caused through Japanese farmers' reluctance to abandon growing rice. It was through the development of rice that Japan was able to achieve rapid industrialisation and spectacular growth in all sectors. Has rice-farming now outlived its usefulness?

Notes

Chapter 1 The rice-plant: diversity and intensification

1 There are two families of domesticated rice, the African rices (*Oryza glaberrima* L.) and the Asian rices (*Oryza sativa*), but the African rices are not cultivated outside that continent. Although the African and Asian rices are generally supposed to derive from a common ancestor (Chang 1976a), African rices had no influence on the development of the Asian species and so will not be discussed further.

2 In the People's Republic of China in 1977, 45% of the total food-grain production was rice and 14% was wheat (Barker, Sisler and Rose 1982: 166). The total figure also includes coarse grains such as millets, sorghum and barley, pulses, soybeans, tubers and maize, some of which would be used as animal feed rather than directly for human consumption.

3 More detailed treatment is given in Chang (1976a) and Bray (1984: 481–7); Bray (1984: 29–47) discusses the possible causes and processes of plant domestication, especially as they apply to East and Southeast Asia.

4 There are, however, many difficulties associated with these dates (Reed 1977: 911–17; Muhly 1981: 134).

5 The names of rice in the ancient Southern Chinese Wu language (*i'nuân*), in Annamese (*n'êp*), Cham (*ñióp*), Sedang (*ñ'ian*) and Japanese (*ine*) are all closely related phonetically (Sasaki 1971: 288), indicating a common origin. In his study of Austro-Thai words in Chinese, Benedict (1967: 316) notes that they include a number of terms for rice, including cooked rice, as well as words associated with rice cultivation such as plough, pestle and mortar, seed, sow and winnow. Benedict and several other Western scholars suggest that the Thai originally came from the region of the Yangzi Delta and migrated south and west, but Chinese ethnographers believe that they originated in the border region of Yunnan, North Thailand and Burma.

6 The date of transition from the earliest Japanese neolithic culture, the Jōmon, to the Yayoi is usually put at about 300 BC to coincide with a transition in pottery styles. However it has been suggested (Sahara, forthcoming) that a better criterion than pottery styles would be the transition from a hunter-gathering economy to food production.

7 Wild species of rice 'include the 18 wild-growing taxa in the genus *Oryza* which can be considered as valid species . . . Because of human disturbances of their adapted habitats, many wild forms have receded from cultivated sites. Some wild species are rapidly becoming extinct' (Chang 1976b: 5).

8 Grist (1975: 101) describes some of the more useful classification systems based on morphology and other criteria.

9 The process of differentiation between *indica* and *japonica* rices is still not clearly understood; see Oka (1975a: 25), Bray (1984: 488) for an account of the literature.

10 These figures are taken from Grist (1975: 451); Whyte (1974: 38) gives slightly lower figures.

11 But it is interesting to note that while rice consumption is increasing in popularity outside Asia, in many Asian countries wheat products such as bread are now considered higher-status foods and are beginning to replace rice as the staple among well-to-do members of the population.

12 In countries like Japan, China, Taiwan and Korea, where rice-farming methods are very intensive, the gap is even wider; see Ishikawa (1967: 70, table 2–2).

Chapter 2   Paths of technical development

1 The most famous examples are probably the rice-terraces of Bali, the stone-walled terraces of Peru in which the Incas grew irrigated maize, the serried rows of the Ifugao terraces in Northern Luzon in the Philippines, and the terraced rice-fields of Southern China. But agricultural terracing is also to be found throughout Latin America, around the Mediterranean, in the Middle East, the Himalayan kingdoms, hilly regions of South and Southeast Asia, Japan, Korea and many parts of Africa. There are irrigated and dry terraces, terraces for growing rice, maize, millets, potatoes and beans, shallow and steep terraces, stone-buttressed and earth-walled terraces, in fact terraces of every kind.

2 See Bray (1984: 124) for a summary of the major arguments, diffusionist or otherwise.

3 The floating fields of Lake Dal in Kashmir and of the Mexican lakes are generally used for growing vegetables rather than cereals.

4 Chen (1977), referring to Chinese works of the second and third centuries BC, affirms that transplanting in China must have begun even earlier.

Chapter 3   Water control

1 There is a widely held view that Japanese agriculture 'took off' from relatively low levels of production during the Meiji period. Ogura estimates that rice production doubled, from 3.75 million tons to 7.8 million between 1868 and 1912 (1980: 147), while Ohkawa and Rosovsky (1960) calculate that the agricultural growth rate during the same period was as high as 2.3% per annum. However study of the preceding Tokugawa period shows that

between the 1680s and the 1879s rice yields rose from 1.3 to 1.6 *koku/tan* (from about 2.5 to 3 t/ha), i.e. by about 23% (Nakamura 1966: 137), while the early Meiji statistics on land acreage and productivity, compiled for tax puposes, were recognised by the Meiji officials themselves to be underestimated; in fact a growth rate of 0.8–1.2% per annum for the Meiji period seems more realistic (ibid.). Government statistics also show that between 1920 and 1960, while agricultural output did increase significantly in some regions (i.e. by about 30% in Tōhoku), in other areas progress was very slight (nearer 7% in Kinki and Kyūshū) (Tsuchiya 1976: 46–55).

2 The fact that the Chinese national average yield in the 1930s was still only 2.74 t/ha (Ishikawa 1967: 77; see also Amano 1954: 87), and thus had hardly risen since a thousand years previously, does seem to confirm that modern scientifically developed inputs are necessary to raise productivity above the first landmark. However we must bear in mind that (i) considerable regional and temporal fluctuations occurred in China over the period, the Song and early Ming being a period of rather generalised economic expansion, the late Ming one of decline, the nineteenth century one of severe depression; and therefore (ii) agricultural conditions in China in the 1920s and 1930s were not necessarily representative of the highest technical and economic levels achieved.

3 The literature is too vast to attempt to list it fully. One of the earliest and most circumstantial attacks on Wittfogel's equation between irrigation and centralised political control is to be found in Leach (1961). An excellent critique of the Chinese case is in Eberhard (1965: 74 ff). A more recent evaluation of the debate is in Steward (1980).

4 See Stargardt (1983: 196) on Burma under Pagan rule; the rate there increased in times of war. In many important cases such as Angkorian Cambodia, no record of the level of taxation has survived (Sahai 1970: 113 ff). Thirteenth century documents from South India show that there the water-taxes increased progressively for up to three or four years after construction was completed, as productivity gradually rose; thereafter they were reduced, but as they were proportional to the crop harvested, the overall revenue was still augmented (Venkayya 1906).

5 And also very ancient in origin; it is used in the *Lüshi chunqiu*, a Chinese work of political economy dating from 239 BC.

6 The spectacular nature of such works as the Yellow River dykes in the North China Plain, representing centuries of unremitting struggle and a vast expense of human labour and technical resources, has – together with some impressive instances of state-organised irrigation and drainage which we shall discuss below – provided much of the raw material for theories of 'hydraulic bureaucracies' and 'Oriental despotism'.

7 For much more sophisticated and comprehensive treatment of the climatic, topographic, hydrological and other technical factors involved, see such works as Vaidyanathan (1983), Stargardt (1983), or Gustafsson (1984). Spencer (1974) gives a clear and helpful list of the twenty different techniques of water control known to him from Southeast Asia. The usual

Japanese classification distinguished three main forms of irrigation in Japan: 'river irrigation' (gravity-flow branching canals with intakes along rivers), 'pond irrigation' (canal networks from storage ponds typically fed by hillside run-off and/or off-season diversion from rivers), and 'creek irrigation' (networks of improved natural ditches in the few flat deltas of Japan) (Kelly 1982a: 29). Nishiyama (1959) has applied the same three categories to China: 'river irrigation' he says was confined to the Yellow River system in the north, but in Central China 'pond irrigation' was common, while the flat and swampy lands of the Lower Yangzi relied on a system of drainage and irrigation akin to 'creek irrigation'. This classification, however, does not cover various types of irrigation found in South China, nor those typical of Southeast Asia. Ishikawa (1981) proposes an interesting classification of Asian agricultural systems based on water use rather than water control.

8 The following account is based on Groslier (1974, 1979). The Khmers had conquered the Funanese and taken over the northern plains of Cambodia in the late sixth century, but moved their capital to Angkor only in *c*.800. As we shall see, the form of the Cambodian 'hydraulic city', as well as its siting in the centre of the empire, was of great religious significance.

9 Nakamura (1982) points out, however, that the supplementary water provided by local storage systems is not always sufficient, at least in South India and Sri Lanka, to provide for widespread irrigated cropping, though it does provide a buffer against rainfall deficits.

10 Most of the titles of irrigation officers recorded in the inscriptions of the Javanese kingdoms of Kediri (1078–1222) and Majapahit (1293-*c*.1520) are non-Sanskritic, which points to very early origins (van Setten 1979: 60 ff).

11 Stargardt (1983: 270, n. 64) points out that epigraphic and manuscript sources provide striking similarities between the respective roles of royal officers and village organisations in South India, Burma and Bali.

12 The leaves of both these trees are used to feed silkworms. Here we have a good example of the diversification possible within an economy based on wet-rice cultivation; the author was writing of the Lower Yangzi during a period of rapid commercialisation and growth.

13 This passage comes from the Chinese work *Huainanzi* of about 120 BC, quoted in Wuhan 1979: 144.

14 But only the small duck-ponds are privately owned by individual households; the irrigation ponds, like irrigation channels, belong to the Irrigation Authority (i.e. the state) which allocates water rights in return for fees calculated on the basis of the amount of land owned (ibid.: 54).

15 In certain parts of Java, however, it seems that the old *mancapat* system has been revived for the purpose of solving problems attendant upon contemporary developments in irrigation (van Setten 1979: 58).

16 A common irrigation device throughout East and Southeast Asia. Their use in Chinese hydraulic works is described in Needham (1971: 293–5).

17 This account is based on a course of seminars given at the Collège de France in 1980–1 by M. Lucien Bernot.

18 The Japanese term; Taylor (1981: 27) calls it 'controlled drainage irrigation'.

19 The Chinese government took an active role in land clearance and reclamation throughout the imperial era. Settlement schemes were usually in border areas or underpopulated regions. Whether military or civilian, they had an important dual function: first, an influx of Chinese settlers into areas whose political allegiance was often uncertain had a stabilising effect; and second, the new agricultural colonies served as overspill areas for refugees and landless peasants from areas of dense population. Land was cleared, irrigation was often provided and colonists were offered food, seed-grain, animals and implements either as outright gifts or on credit, while for several years they were not required to pay taxes. It is notable that agricultural colonies and state farms still play an important role in the People's Republic today (Bray 1984: 95).

20 This account is based principally on the excellent study by Hamashima (1980).

21 This is a problem commonly associated with the commercialisation of subsistence economies in Asia today, and will be discussed further in chapter 4.

22 As well as for other tropical crops like rubber; see Chesneaux (1971) on the range of colonial exploitation in Vietnam.

23 Yields averaged 1.8 t/ha on single-cropped fields and 2.6 t/ha on double-cropped; these figures were in fact marginally higher than those for Tonkin or Annam, where the adverse effects of extreme subdivision of holdings and seasonal water shortages took their toll, even though cultivation methods were much more intensive (Henry and de Visme 1928: 52).

24 The canals provided only drainage, not true irrigation, so that rice cultivation was confined to the wet season; natural disasters, whether flood or drought, reduced average annual yields by about 25% (ibid.: 52).

25 This account is base on Afifuddin (1978: ch. 2).

26 Common in North China, Central Asia, South India and Northeastern Ceylon (Nakamura 1982: 5). Sometimes wells are linked in a very sophisticated fashion to conduct water over long distances from points where water is more easily accessible (Goblot 1979).

27 In Northeast China, where wells were the most usual source of water for irrigation, even cooperative wells provided water for only 25 to 30 *mu* (1.5 to 2 ha) (Gamble 1954: 155). In South India a single well irrigates on average 1.2 ha of rice-land (Bandara 1977: 95).

28 It is not easy to compile statistics on the areas involved, but the number and names of projects undertaken are easier to find, e.g. Furushima (1956: 229) on Japan from 1551 to 1867, and Perkins (1969: 333 ff) on China; the latter also attempts to deduce acreages.

Chapter 4   Rice and the wider economy

1 Contemporary studies in rice-growing regions of Southeast Asia consistently demonstrate that tenant farmers tend to farm more carefully and achieve higher yields than landowners (e.g. Gibbons et al. 1980: 122; Bray and Robertson 1980).

2 This interpretation is given by Elson (1978), who suggests that Geertz's concept of 'involution' requires revision in the light of the complementary nature of nineteenth-century regional economies in Java.

3 What follows is based on the field-notes which I compiled in 1976–7, plus some additional information acquired in interviews and conversations on subsequent visits.

4 In a study of the Green Revolution in Java, Montgomery (1981) affirms that it is improvements in rice cultivation which offer the greatest hopes of profitable labour absorption, but this would require very heavy investments in irrigation and land improvement which the Indonesian government is unlikely to find attractive.

5 On the concepts of agricultural underemployment and 'disguised unemployment' see, for example, Sen (1975), Stewart (1977) and Ishikawa (1981: 90 ff).

6 International exports were banned at this time, for the war against the northern nomads made it vital to ensure adequate supplies for the Chinese army (Shiba 1970: 50).

7 These figures were calculated by Mizuno from the *Statistical Pocketbook of Indonesia* 1977–8.

Chapter 5   Development

1 The recent work by Barker, Herdt and Rose (1985), which unfortunately appeared too late to be made use of here, treats contemporary development in Asia's rice economies in detail.

2 Lee (1979: 32) points out that deficiencies in sampling techniques, etc., throw doubt on this claim, but acknowledges a significant increase in rural incomes in the decade up to 1974, citing for example the IBRD study which estimated that between 1963 and 1972 there was an annual growth of real wages in manufacturing of 7.2%, the corresponding figure for agricultural wages being 6.5%.

3 Mainly by forbidding immigration to Edo or migration from one lord's jurisdiction to another (Smith 1959: 111).

4 See also chapter 3 and Hamashima (1980) on water control projects in the Yangzi Delta.

5 Especially in the case of China; see for example Beattie (1979: 135). Much more material is available for Japan, where farmers' ledgers, accounts and diaries survive, and farm budgets are cited in the reports of Tokugawa administrators (Furushima 1963; Smith 1959: 81; Toya 1949: 59; Yamazaki 1961).

6 Although the Chinese bureaucracy kept records of population figures from very early times their accuracy is often suspect. Among other problems of interpretation, under-registration was common since the population records were the basis of tax registers. However it does seem that during the two-and-a-half mainly peaceful and prosperous centuries of Ming rule (1368–1644) population growth was steady but linear, rather than exponen-

tial as it was to become later (Ho 1959: 23). In the case of Tokugawa Japan, it can be shown that although agricultural output expanded greatly between 1600 and the mid-nineteenth century, between 1720 and 1868 the population was nearly static (Smith 1977: 5).

7 Though even here it is only possible from the 1930s (Ishikawa 1981: 13).

8 An obvious solution would have been for Indonesia to use its own considerable oil resources to produce fertilisers domestically on a large scale. At the ASEAN summit held in Bali in 1976 it was decided to establish a urea plant in North Sumatra as one of four ASEAN industrial projects, and this plant opened in early 1984 (*Asia Yearbook 1984*:108).

9 For some idea of the variation, see Gray and Gray 1983; for a theoretical justification, see Lin Zili 1983.

10 An exception is to be found where labour hire is used among farmers of equally low economic status as a redistributive measure, for example in the *barrios* of Central Luzon studied by Takahashi, where landlords ruthlessly collected their debts out of the tenants' rice crops but did not touch their other income: under these conditions it was understood among tenant farmers that they would all hire labour from each other, minimising the use of household labour; furthermore, when they were obliged to use family labour they would pay themselves wages (1970: 141, 61).

11 Low yields were a significant factor in the low profitability of rice-farming in Kelantan, and Fujimoto suggests that there was clear scope for increasing incomes through a much more intensive use of fertilisers (1983: 147).

12 Fertiliser costs as a proportion of total rice production costs dropped from 29.65 in 1965 to 13.5 in 1979 (Matsuda 1982: 441).

13 In Korea mechanisation of rice-farming was until very recently chiefly restricted to such machinery as pumps, mills and threshers (Ban et al. 1980: 75), which allow the intensification of cropping and can thus be considered as land-substitutes. Even after a government drive to promote mechanisation under the Third Five-Year Plan (1972–6) there was still only 1 power-tiller to 29 families (ibid.: 190).

Chapter 6 Peasant, landlord and state: changes in relations of production

1 The terms 'peasant', 'peasantry' and 'peasant economy' have been defined in a number of ways; the common factors are that peasants are essentially household producers, and that they are subordinate to other classes within the state, to which they generally owe some form of tribute. Whether or not the concept of a specific 'peasant economy' (first formulated by Chayanov) has real analytical usefulness is much debated (e.g. Harriss 1982: 23–6).

2 One reason why Japanese social scientists and historians have devoted so much attention to the subject is that they feel that the small size of Japanese farms entails their high level of dependence upon communal irrigation and increasingly outdated 'irrigation customs', *suiri kankō*, which are regarded as a potent institutional obstacle to change.

3 As they undoubtedly were in Japan until the seventeenth century; see Grove and Esherick (1980) for a summary of the Chinese debate.
4 Men and women both own and inherit land, either in equal shares according to the traditional Malay *adat* laws, or in the proportion of 2 : 1 if Islamic law is followed. Parents usually give their children some of their share on marriage; the rest is inherited on the parent's death.
5 The following account is based on the meticulous account by Gerdin (1982).
6 A list of key texts can be found in Harriss (1982).
7 This is the argument put forward by Kautsky (Banaji 1980), and it applies very well on the whole to labour-intensive forms of agriculture.
8 See for example Muhammad Ikmal (1985: ch. 2) and Kahn (1980).
9 What Boeke (1955) termed a 'dualistic economy'.
10 Potter (1970) also believes that the strongest lineages emerged in rice-producing frontier zones, far from government control, where the only limits to the reclamation and irrigation of rice land were those imposed by competing lineages. However Pasternak (1969; 1972b), citing evidence from Taiwan, says that lineages were only established once the frontier zones had already been opened up; Meskill's (1979) study of the colonisation of Taiwan supports this view.
11 Of course many of the huge mechanised farms of the North American grain belt are also family enterprises.
12 The *jia* was a variable unit, but was standardised by the Japanese in 1895 at 0.9025 ha.
13 Although the postwar land reforms did constitute an obstacle to the large-scale concentration of management for some time, the Japanese government is now anxious to encourage various forms of rationalised and larger-scale farming.

Appendix A The western model

1 In the USSR the virtues of 'rationalisation' were at first accepted without question, but it has subsequently become widely acknowledged that small private plots are much more productive than the *kolkhoz* (e.g. Wädekin 1975; Kerblay 1980).
2 Seed : yield ratios for wheat, barley and rye in Northern Europe in medieval times averaged 1 : 3 or 1 : 4 (Slicher van Bath 1963: 238); before the twelfth century 1 : 1.6 or 1 : 2 was more common (Mukhia 1981: 297). Although under modern conditions returns for wheat average 1 : 10 or more (Purseglove 1972: 294), at 3 to 4 t/ha the highest yields are still only about half the best yields of 7 t/ha which can be obtained for rice (Grist 1975: 485; Aziz 1978: 36).
3 The Romans had been familiar with green manures and the fertilising power of leguminous crops like vetch and alfalfa, but these did not gain any popularity in Northern Europe until the seventeenth and eighteenth centuries. Edible pulses such as peas and beans, appreciated for their high and reliable yields, first appear in rotations in the thirteenth and fourteenth centuries (Duby 1962: 183).

4 The rights to *vaine pâture* were still under dispute in France at the time of the Revolution (Moore 1967: 71).
5 Many improvements of the so-called Agricultural Revolution, such as scientific rotations (which increased the intensity of cropping) or more careful weeding, were labour-intensive (Chambers 1967: 112; Mingay 1977: 10).

Appendix B The historical experience of China

1 Song population figures are quoted in numbers of households rather than individuals. The census of 1080, taken before the population had been driven south by nomadic invaders, put the population at 14.5 million households, of which 10 million lived in the southern provinces. By 1173, when Northern China was under foreign rule, the total population of both North and South China was 18.75 million households, of which 12 million lived in the south (Lewin 1973: 45).
2 Golas (1980: 295) estimates that the total area of cultivated land in about 1100 was 7 million *qing* (1 *qing* = approx. 6 ha), while the figure for 755, though probably overestimated, stood at 14 million *qing*, or roughly double the amount.
3 Illiterate, that is, by the standards of the educated elite. The level of functional literacy in pre-modern China, even in the countryside, seems to have been rather high (E. Rawski 1979: 13–17).
4 Often regarded by economists as a contract which minimises risks but stifles entrepreneurial ambitions (see Bray and Robertson 1980).
5 Similarly, while Geertz's description (1963) of the Javanese system as one of 'shared poverty' has been rejected on the grounds that clear divisions existed between village rich and poor, nonetheless landlords as well as tenants suffered reductions in income as the economy declined.
6 Based on the figures from the *Agricultural Yearbook of China 1980* given in Stone (1982: 212–13).

Appendix C The Japanese experience

1 Between 1908 and 1970 the number of farms remained more or less constant, at just over 5 million, as did the average size. But during this period the number of farms in the middle range of 1.0 to 2.0 ha increased, showing a convergence towards medium-sized farms relying almost exclusively on family labour (Tsuchiya 1976: 85).
2 There has been a marked decentralisation of industry since 1945, providing opportunities for farming families to engage in commodity production: 'Since World War II there have been a number of instances of the formation of production regions in economically retarded farming areas where there had been no ways whereby local farmers could supplement their income. In

these cases, industries were attracted to the regions in question by a number of factors: relative stagnation in the agricultural sector combined with the creation of a labour surplus by mechanisation and rationalisation; the need to obtain cash to purchase farm machinery, agricultural chemicals and fertilisers; discontent of workers with the instability of being a migrant worker on construction projects far from home; and the desire of the local people to have the entire family work together at home' (Yamazaki 1980: 18).

References

ADB (Asian Development Bank) (1978): *Rural Asia: Challenge and Opportunity*, Praeger, New York and London.

Abel, W. (1935): *Agrarkrisen und Agrarkonjunktur in Mitteleuropa vom 13. bis zum 19. Jahrhundert*, Paul Parey, Berlin; tr. as *Agricultural Fluctuations in Europe*, Methuen, London, 1980.

Adas, Michael (1974): *The Burma Delta: Economic Development and Social Change on an Asian Rice Frontier, 1852–1941*, University of Wisconsin Press, Madison.

Afifuddin bin Haji Omar (1977): *Irrigation Structures and Local Peasant Organisation*, MADA, Alor Setar.

—— (1978): 'Peasants, institutions, and development in Malaysia: the political economy of development in the Muda region', MADA Monograph no. 36, Alor Setar (PhD diss., Cornell University).

Agricultural Bureau (1910): *Outlines of Agriculture in Japan*, Dept of Ag. and Commerce, Tokyo.

Alexander, Jennifer and Paul (1982): 'Shared poverty as ideology: agrarian relationships in colonial Java', *Man* 17, 4: 597–619.

Amano Motonosuke (1954): 'Chūgoku nōgyō no tenkai' [The development of Chinese agriculture], part 2 [3rd to 20th centuries], *Ajia Kenkyū* 1954, 2: 68–92.

—— (1979) *Chūgoku nōgyōshi kenkyū* [Researches into Chinese agricultural history], Ryukei Press, Tokyo (1st edn 1962).

American Rural Small-Scale Industry Delegation (1977): *Rural Small-Scale Industry in the People's Republic of China*, University of California Press, Berkeley.

Ash, Robert (1976): *Land Tenure in Pre-Revolutionary China: Kiangsu Province in the 1920s and 1930s*, Research Notes and Studies no. 1, Contemporary China Institute, SOAS, London.

Asia Yearbook 1984, Far Eastern Economic Review, Hong Kong.

Assoc. of the Japanese Agric. Science Societies (1975): *Rice in Asia*, University of Tokyo Press, Tokyo.

Aziz, Sartaj (1978): *Rural Development: Learning from China*, Macmillan, London.

Bacdayan, Albert S. (1980): 'Mountain irrigators in the Philippines', in Coward (1980): 172–85.

Baker, A. C., MCS, British Adviser, Kelantan (1936): *Annual Report on the Social and Economic Progress of the People of Kelantan for the Year 1935*, Cheong Fatt Press, Kelantan.

Baker, C. (1981): 'Economic reorganisation and the slump in South and Southeast Asia', *Comparative Studies in Social and Economic History* 23, 3: 325–49.

Ban, Sung Hwan, Pal Yong Moon and Dwight H. Perkins (1980): *Rural Development*, Studies in the Modernisation of the Republic of Korea: 1945–1975, Harvard University Press, Cambridge, Mass.

Banaji, Janius (1980): 'Summary of selected parts of Kautsky's *The Agrarian Question*', in Howard Newby and Frederick H. Buttel (eds), *The Rural Sociology of the Advanced Societies: Critical Perspectives*, Croom Helm London: 38–82.

Bandara, C. M. Madduma (1977): 'The prospects of recycling subsurface water for supplementary irrigation in the Dry Zone', in S. W. R. de A. Samarasinghe (ed.): *Agriculture in the Peasant Sector of Sri Lanka*, Peradeniya Ceylon Studies Seminar, Colombo: 87–99.

Barker, Randolph (1978): 'Yield and fertiliser input', in IRRI (1978): 35–66.

Barker, Randolph and Robert W. Herdt (1978): 'Equity implication of technology changes', in IRRI (1978): 83–108.

Barker, Randolph, Robert W. Herdt and Beth Rose (1985): *The Rice Economy of Asia*, Resources for the Future, Washington DC.

Barker, Randolph, Radha Sinha and Beth Rose (eds) (1982): *The Chinese Agricultural Economy*, Westview Press, Boulder, Colo; Croom Helm, London.

Barker, Randolph, Daniel G. Sisler and Beth Rose (1982): 'Prospects for growth in grain production', in Barker et al. (1982): 163–81.

Beardsley, R. K., J. W. Hall and R. E. Wade (1959): *Village Japan*, Phoenix Books, U. Chicago Press, Chicago and London; section on irrigation coops. repr. in Coward (1980): 127–52.

Beattie, Hilary J. (1979): *Land and Lineage in China: A Study of T'ung-ch'eng County, Anhwei, in the Ming and Ch'ing Dynasties*, Cambridge University Press, Cambridge.

Bell, Clive (1978): 'The future of rice padi monoculture in Malaysia', paper given in the *Symposium on the Viability of the Village in Contemporary Society*, Amer. Assoc. for the Advancement of Science, Washington, DC.

Benedict, P. K. (1967): 'Austro-Thai Studies, 3: Austro-Thai and Chinese', *Behavior Science Notebooks* 2: 275–336.

Berwick, E. J. H. (1951): 'Wet padi mechanical cultivation experiments, Kelantan, season 1950–51', *Malayan Agric. Journal* 34: 166–84.

Birowo, Achmad T. and Gary E. Hansen (1981): 'Agricultural and rural development: an overview', in Hansen (1981): 1–27.

Bishop, J. E., Acting British Adviser (1912): *Kelantan Administrative Report for the Year 1911*, Government Printing Office, Kuala Lumpur.

Bloch, Marc (1931): *Les caractères originaux de l'histoire rurale française*, Colin, Paris.

Boeke, J. H. (1955): *Economie van Indonesie*, H. D. Tjeek Willink, Haarlem.

Bonavia, David and Mary Lee (1985): 'Chen's last stand', *Far Eastern Economic Review* 3 October: 10–12.

Boserup, E. (1965): *The Conditions of Agricultural Growth: The Economics of Agrarian Change under Population Pressure*, Allen and Unwin, London.

—— (1981): *Population and Technology*, Basil Blackwell, Oxford.

Brandt, Vincent (1980): 'Local government and rural development', in Ban et al.: 260–82.

Bray, F. (1979): 'The Green Revolution: a new perspective', *Modern Asian Studies* 13, 4: 681–8.

—— (1980): 'Agricultural development and agrarian change in Han China', *Early China* 5: 1–13.

—— (1984): *Agriculture*, Vol. VI Part 2 in Joseph Needham, *Science and Civilisation in China*, Cambridge University Press, Cambridge.

—— (1987) 'Evolution in padi farming in Kelantan', in *Ouvrage collectif dédié à Lucien Bernot*, CNRS, Paris.

Bray, F. and A. F. Robertson (1980): 'Sharecropping in Kelantan, Malaysia', in G. Dalton (ed.), *Papers in Economic Anthropology* 3, JAI Press, Greenwich Conn.

Brenner, Robert (1982): 'Agrarian class structure and economic development in pre-industrial Europe: the agrarian roots of European capitalism', *Past and Present* 97: 16–114.

Brocheux, Pierre (1971): 'Les grands diên chu de la Cochinchine occidentale pendant la période coloniale', in Chesneaux et al. (1971): 147–63.

Brohier, R. L. (1934–5): *Ancient Irrigation Works in Ceylon*, 3 vols, Govt Press, Colombo.

Brook, T. (1981): 'The merchant network in 16th century China', *J. Economic and Social History of the Orient* 24, 2: 165–214.

—— (1982): 'The spread of rice cultivation and rice technology into the Hebei region in the Ming and Qing', in Li Guohao et al. (eds), *Explorations in the History of Science and Technology in China*, Chinese Classics Publishing House, Shanghai: 659–90.

Bruneau, Michel (1980): *L'organisation de l'espace dans le Nord de la Thaïlande*, Atelier Réproduction des Thèses, Université de Lille III (PhD diss., Paris IV, 1977).

Buck, J. L. (ed.) (1937): *Land Utilisation in China*, Commercial Press, Shanghai.

Buddenhagen, I. W. and G. J. Persley (eds) (1978): *Rice in Africa*, Academic Press, London.

Chambers, J. D. (1967): 'Enclosure and labour supply in the Industrial Revolution', in E. L. Jones (ed.), *Agriculture and Economic Growth in England 1650–1815*, Methuen, London: 94–127.

Chambers, Robert (1977): 'Challenges for rural research and development', in Farmer (1977): 398–412.

—— (1980): 'Basic concepts in the organisation of irrigation', in Coward (1980): 28–50.

Chan, Anita, Richard Madsen and Jonathan Unger (1984): *Chen Village: The Recent History of a Peasant Community in Mao's China*, University of California Press, Berkeley.

Chang, T. T. (1976a): 'The origin, evolution, cultivation, dissemination and diversification of Asian and African rices', *Euphytica* 25: 425–41.

—— (1976b): *Manual on Genetic Conservation of Rice Germ Plasm for Evaluation and Utilisation*, IRRI, Los Baños.

Charras, Muriel (1982): *De la forêt maléfique à l'herbe divine; la transmigration en Indonésie: les Balinais à Sulawesi*, Maison des Sciences de l'Homme, Paris.

Chaunu, Pierre (1979): *European Expansion in the Later Middle Ages*, North Holland Publishing Company, Amsterdam.

Chayanov, A. V. (1966): *The Theory of Peasant Economy*, Richard M. Irwin, Homewood, Ill. (1st Russian edn 1925).

Chen Fu nongshu [Agricultural Treatise, by Chen Fu], 1st edn 1149; repr. Zhonghua, Beijing, 1956.

Chen Liangzuo (1977): 'Woguo shuidao zaipei di jixiang jishu zhi fazhan ji qi zhongyaoxing' [The development of certain Chinese wet-rice cultivation techniques and their importance], *Shihuo yuekan* 7, 11: 537–46.

Chesneaux, J. (1971): 'L'implantation géographique des intérêts coloniaux au Vietnam et ses rapports avec l'économie traditionelle', in Chesneaux et al. (1971): 74–88.

Chesneaux, Jean, Georges Boudarel and Daniel Hémery (eds) (1971): *Tradition et révolution au Vietnam*, Editions Anthropos, Paris.

Chi, Ch'ao-ting (1936): *Key Economic Areas in Chinese History*, 2nd edn Paragon Reprint Corp., New York, 1963.

Chuan, Han-sheng and Richard A. Kraus (1975): *Mid-Ch'ing Rice Markets: An Essay in Price History*, East Asian Research Center, Harvard University Press, Cambridge, Mass.

Chūgoku Suirishi Kenkyūkai (ed.) (1981): *Chūgoku Suirishi Ronshū* [Collected essays on the history of water control in China], Kokusho Press, Tokyo.

Clifford, Sir Hugh (1895): 'Expedition to Trengganu and Kelantan', *Journal of the Malay Branch of the Royal Asiatic Society*, 34, 1 (May 1961): xi-162.

Coédès, G. (1948): *Les états hindouisés d'Indochine et d'Indonésie*, Brocard, Paris.

Colani, Madeleine (1940): *Emploi de la pierre en des temps reculés: Annam-Indonésie-Assam*, Publ. des Amis du Vieux Hué, Hanoi.

Collier, William L. (1981): 'Agricultural evolution in Java', in Hansen (1981): 147–73.

Condominas, G. and C. Gaudillot (*c.*1960): *Plaine de Vientiane: étude socio-économique*, Rapport d'études, 2 vol., Bureau pour le Développement de la Protection Agricole, Paris.

Cooper, J. P. (1978): 'In search of agrarian capitalism', *Past and Present* 80: 20–65.

Coward, J. Walter, Jr. (ed) (1980): *Irrigation and Agricultural Development in Asia: Perspectives from the Social Sciences*, Cornell University Press, Ithaca, NY.

Dasgupta, Biplab (1977): *Agrarian Change and the New Technology in India*, UNRISD, Geneva.

Davidson, J. (1975): 'Recent archaeological activity in Vietnam', *J. Hong Kong Arch. Society* 6: 80–100.

Delvert, Jean (1961): *Le paysan cambodgien*, Mouton, Paris/The Hague.

Ding Ying (ed.) (1961): *Zhongguo shuidao zaipei xue* [The cultivation of wet rice in China], Agriculture Press, Beijing.

—— (1964): 'Zhongguo shuidao pinzhong di shengtai leixing ji qi yu shengchan fazhan di guanxi' [An ecological classification of Chinese wet-rice varieties and their relation to the development of production], *Zhongguo nongye kexue* [Chinese Agronomy], no. 10.

Dobby, E. H. G. (1957): 'Padi landscapes of Malaya: Kelantan', *Malay J. of Tropical Agriculture* 10: i-42.

Dong Furen (1982): 'Relationship between accumulation and consumption', in Xu Dixin et al., *China's Search for Economic Growth*, New World Press, Beijing.

Donkin, R. A. (1979): *Agricultural Terracing in the Aboriginal New World*, University of Arizona Press, Tucson.

Dore, Ronald (1959): *Land Reform in Japan*, Oxford University Press, London.

—— (1969): 'Agricultural improvement in Japan 1870–1900', in E. L. Jones and S. J. Woolf (eds), *Agricultural Change and Economic Development: The Historical Problems*, Methuen, London.

Downs, Richard (1967): 'A Kelantanese village of Malaya', in Julian H. Steward (ed.), *Contemporary Change in Traditional Societies*, Vol. 2, *Asian Rural Societies*, University of Illinois Press, Urbana: 105–86.

Duby, G. (1962): *L'économie rurale et la vie des campagnes dans l'Occident médiéval*, 2 vols, Aubier, Paris.

Dumont, René (1957): *Types of Rural Economy*, Methuen, London.

—— (1983): *Albanie, Pologne, Nicaragua (Finis les lendemains qui chantent, vol. 1)*, Seuil, Paris.

—— (1984): *La Chine décollectivise (Finis les lendemains qui chantent, vol. 2)*, Seuil, Paris.

Eberhard, W. (1965): *Conquerors and Rulers: Social Forces in Medieval China*, Brill, Leiden.

Elson, R. E. (1978): 'The cultivation system and 'Agricultural Involution''', CSEAS Working Paper no. 14, Monash University.

Elvin, Mark (1973): *The Pattern of the Chinese Past*, Eyre Methuen, London.

—— (1978): 'Chinese cities since the Sung dynasty', in Abrams and Wrigley (eds), *Towns in Societies*, Cambridge University Press, Cambridge: 79–89.

Embree, J. F. (1946): *A Japanese Village: Suye Mura*, Kegan Paul, Trench and Trubner, London.

Ensor, Paul (1985): 'Loneliness is not the farmers' only problem', *Far Eastern Economic Review*, 18 July 1985: 69–71.

Erkes, E. (1953): *Die Entwicklung der chinesischen Gesellschaft von der Urzeit bis zur Gegenwart*, Proceedings of the Leipzig Academy of Science 100, 4, Akademie-Verlag, Berlin.

Ernle, Lord [R. E. Prothero] (1972): *English Farming Past and Present*, Benjamin Blom, New York (1st edn London, 1917).

Farmer, B. H. (ed) (1977): *Green Revolution? Technology and Change in Rice-Growing Areas of Tamil Nadu and Sri Lanka*, Macmillan, London.

—— (1981): 'The 'Green Revolution' in South Asia', *Geography* 66, 3: 202–7.

Farmer, B. H. et al. (1977): 'Setting the stage', in Farmer (1977): 7–19.

Farris, William Wayne (1985): *Population, Disease, and Land in Early Japan*, Harvard University Press, Cambridge, Mass.

Federation of Malaya (1953): *Report of the Rice Production Committee*, Kuala Lumpur.

Fei, Hsiao-t'ung (1939): *Peasant Life in China: A Field Study of Country Life in the Yangtze Valley*, Routledge, London.

Fei, Hsiao-t'ung & Chang Chih-i (1948): *Earthbound China: A Study of Rural Economy in Yunnan*, Routledge & Kegan Paul, London.

Feldman, M. and E. R. Sears (1981): 'The wild gene resources of wheat', *Scientific American* 1: 98–109.

Feyssal, P. de (1934): *L'endettement agraire en Cochinchine*, Hanoi.

Fforde, Adam (1983): 'The historical background to agricultural collectivisation in North Vietnam: the changing role of 'corporate' economic power', Birkbeck Discussion Paper no. 148, University of London.

—— (1984): 'Specific aspects of the collectivisation of wet-rice cultivation – reflections on Vietnamese experience', Birkbeck Discussion Paper no. 159, University of London.

Fischer, R. A. (1981): 'Development in wheat agronomy', in L. T. Evans and W. J. Peacock (eds), *Wheat Science – Today and Tomorrow*, Cambridge University Press, Cambridge: 249–70.

Fogg, Wayne (1983): 'The domestication of *Setaria italica* (L.) Beauv., a study of the process and origin of cereal agriculture in China', in D. Keightley (ed.), *The Origins of Chinese Civilisation*, University of California Press, Berkeley: 95–115.

Food and Fertiliser Technology Centre (1974): *Multiple Cropping Systems in Taiwan*, Taipei.

Forest, Alain (1980): *Le Cambodge et la colonisation française: histoire d'une colonisation sans heurts*, L'Harmattan, Paris.

Fortune, Robert (1857): *A Residence among the Chinese*, John Murray, London.

Francks, Penelope (1983): *Technology and Agricultural Development in Pre-War Japan*, Yale University Press, New Haven, Conn.

Fream, W. (1977): *Elements of Agriculture*, 15th edn, ed. D. H. Robinson, revised and metricated by N. F. McCann, John Murray, London.

Freedman, Maurice (1958): *Lineage Organisation in Southeastern China*, University of London, Athlone Press (repr. 1970).

—— (1966): *Chinese Lineage and Society: Fukien and Kwangtung*, University of London, Athlone Press (repr. 1971).

Freeman, C. (1977): 'Economics of research and development', in Spiegel-Rösing and Price (1977): 223–76.

Freeman, D. (1970): *Report on the Iban*, University of London, Athlone Press (1st edn Sarawak, 1955).

Fujimoto, Akimi (1976a): 'Rice operation and labour input among Malay peasants in Kelantan', *Japanese J. of Tropical Agriculture* 20, 1: 35–44.

—— (1976b): 'An economic analysis of peasant rice farming in Kelantan, Malaysia', *South East Asian Studies* 14, 2: 159–76.

—— (1977: 'The effects of farming techniques on rice yields: a case study in Kelantan Malaysia', *Kajian Ekonomi Malaysia* XIV, 1: 51–8.

—— (1983): *Income Sharing among Malay Peasants: A Study of Land Tenure and Rice Production*, Singapore University Press, Singapore.

Furushima Toshio (1954): 'Suiri shihai to nōgyō nōson shakai kenkei' [Control of irrigation and relations of agriculture and farming villages], in Ōtani Seizō (ed.), *Nōchi kaikaku*: I, 175–204.

—— (1956): *Nihon nōgyōshi* [A history of Japanese agriculture], Iwanami Zensho, Tokyo.

—— (1963): *Kinsei Nihon nōgyō no tenkai* [Agricultural development in the Tokugawa period], University of Tokyo Press, Tokyo.

Fussell, G. E. (1952): *The Farmer's Tools: 1500–1900*, Andrew Melrose, London.

Gaitskell, Arthur (1959): *Gezira: A Study of Development in the Sudan*, Faber and Faber, London.

Gallin, Bernard and Rita S. Gallin (1982): 'Socioeconomic life in rural Taiwan: twenty years of development and change', *Modern China* 8, 2: 205–46.

Gamble, Sidney D. (1954): *Ting Hsien: A North China Rural Community*, Stanford University Press, Stanford, Calif.

Geddes, W. R. (1976): *Migrants of the Mountains: The Cultural Ecology of the Blue Miao (Hmong Njua) of Thailand*, Clarendon Press, Oxford.

Geertz, C. (1963): *Agricultural Involution: The Processes of Ecological Change in Indonesia*, University of California Press, Berkeley.

Geertz, H. and C. Geertz (1975): *Kinship in Bali*, University of Chicago Press, Chicago.

Gehlen, Arnold (1965): 'Anthropologische Ansicht der Technik', in Hans Freyer et al. (ed.), *Technik im technischen Zeitalter*, Düsseldorf.

Gerdin, Ingela (1982): *The Unknown Balinese: Land, Labour and Inequality in Lombok*, Gothenburg Studies in Social Anthropology 4, Gothenburg.

Gibbons, David S., Rodolphe de Koninck and Ibrahim Hasan (1980): *Agricultural Modernisation, Poverty and Inequality: The Distributional Impact of the Green Revolution on Areas of Malaysia and Indonesia*, Gower Publ. Co., Westmead, Hampshire.

Goblot, Henri (1979): *Les qanats: une technique d'acquisition de l'eau*, Mouton, Paris.

Golas, Peter J. (1980): 'Rural China in the Song', *J. of Asian Studies* 39, 2: 291–325.

Gorman, C. (1977): '*A priori* models and Thai prehistory: beginnings of agriculture', in C. A. Reed (ed.), *Origins of Agriculture*, Mouton, The Hague: 321–55.

Gourou, Pierre (1936): *Les paysans du delta tonkinois: étude de géographie humaine*, Mémoires de l'Ecole Française d'Extrême-Orient, Paris.

—— (1984): *Riz et civilisation*, Fayard, Paris.

Graham, W. A., H.S.M.'s Resident and Adviser (Siamese and Malay States) (1904): *Report on the State of Kelantan for the Year August 1903 to August 1904*, Bangkok.

Gray, Jack and Maisie (1983): 'China's new agricultural revolution', in Stephan Feuchtwang and Athar Hussain (eds), *The Chinese Economic Reforms*, Croom Helm, London: 151–84.

Grigg, D. B. (1980): *Population Growth and Agrarian Change: An Historical Perspective*, Cambridge University Press, Cambridge.

Grist, D. H. (1975): *Rice*, Longman, London (5th edn).

Groslier, B. P. (1974): 'Agriculture et religion dans l'Empire angkorien', *Etudes rurales* 53–6: *Agriculture et sociétés en Asie du Sud-Est*: 95–117.

—— (1979): 'La cité hydraulique angkorienne: exploitation ou surexploitation du sol', *Bull. de l'Ecole Française d'Extrême-Orient* LVXI: 161–202.

Grove, Linda and Joseph W. Esherick (1980): 'From feudalism to capitalism: Japanese scholarship on the transformation of Chinese rural society', *Modern China* 6, 4: 397–438.

Guangdong xinyu [New descriptions of Guangdong Province], by Qu Dajun, 1st ed. late seventeenth century, repr. Zhonghua, Hong Kong, 1974.

Gustafsson, J. E. (1984): *Water Resources Development in the People's Republic of China*, Royal Inst. of Technology, Dept of Land Improvement and Drainage, Stockholm.

Habermas, Jürgen (1971): *Towards a Rational Society*, Heinemann, London.

Hamashima, Atsutoshi (1980): 'The organisation of water control in the Kiangnan Delta in the Ming period', *Acta Asiatica* 38: 69–92.

Hanks, Lucien M. (1972): *Rice and Man: Agricultural Ecology in Southeast Asia*, Aldine Atherton, Chicago and New York.

Hanley, Susan B. and Kozo Yamamura (1977): *Economic and Demographic Change in Preindustrial Japan, 1600–1868*, Princeton University Press, Princeton, NJ.

Hansen, Gary E. (ed.) (1981): *Agriculture and Rural Development in Indonesia*, Westview Press, Boulder, Colo.

Hanson, Arthur J. (1981): 'Transmigration and regional land development', in Hansen (1981): 219–35.

Harlan, Jack R. (1980): 'Plant breeding and genetics', in Leo A. Orleans (ed.), *Science in Contemporary China*, Stanford University Press, Stanford, Calif.: 295–312.

Harriss, John (1977): 'Pahalagama: a case study of agricultural change in a frontier community', in Farmer (1977): 143–54.

—— (ed.) (1982): *Rural Development: Theories of Peasant Economy and Agrarian Change*, Hutchinson University Library, London.

Hart, Gillian and Saiful Huq (1982): 'Labour and agrarian change in Java and Bangladesh', preliminary report for the ILO, Dept of Economics, Boston University.

Hasan, P. (1976): *Korea: Problems and Issues in a Rapidly Growing Economy*, Johns Hopkins Press, Baltimore, Md.

Hauser, William B. (1974): *Economic Institutional Change in Tokugawa Japan: Ōsaka and the Kinai Cotton Trade*, Cambridge University Press, Cambridge.

Havens, Thomas R. H. (1974): *Farm and Nation in Modern Japan: Agrarian Nationalism, 1870–1940*, Princeton University Press, Princeton, NJ.

Hayami, Yujiro and Vernon W. Ruttan (1979): 'Agricultural growth in four countries', in Y.Hayami, V. W. Ruttan and H. M. Southworth (eds), *Agricultural Growth in Japan, Taiwan, Korea and the Philippines*, University Press of Hawaii, Honolulu: 3–26.

Haynes, A. S., MCS, British Adviser, Kelantan (1932): *Kelantan Administrative Report for the Year 1931*, Al-Asasiyah Press, Kelantan.

—— (1933): *Annual Report on the Social and Economic Progress of the People of Kelantan for the Year 1932*, Al-Asasiyah Press, Kelantan.

Henry, Yves (1932): *Economie agricole de l'Indochine*, Gouvernement Général de l'Indochine, Hanoi.

Henry, Yves and Maurice de Visme (1928): *Documents de démographie et riziculture en Indochine*, 2 vols, Gouvernement Général de l'Indochine, publ. by the *Bull. économique d'Indochine*, Hanoi.

Higham, C. F. W. (1984): 'Prehistoric rice cultivation in Southeast Asia', *Scientific American* 250, 4: 100–07.

Hill, A. H. (1951): 'Kelantan padi planting', *J. of the Malay Branch of the Royal Asiatic Society* 24, 1: 56–76.

Hill, R. D. (1977): *Rice in Malaya: A Study in Historical Geography*, Oxford University Press, Kuala Lumpur.

Ho, Ping-ti (1959): *Studies on the Population of China, 1368–1953*, Harvard University Press, Cambridge, Mass.

Hobsbawm, E. and G. Rudé (1968): *Captain Swing*, Pantheon, New York.

Hommel, R. P. (1937): *China at Work*, Bucks County Historical Society, Doylestown, Pa; repr. MIT Press, Cambridge, Mass., 1969.

Hong Pi-feng (1979): 'An outline of group farming experience in Taiwan', in Wong (1979a): 51–65.

Horii, Kenzo (1981): *Rice Economy and Land Tenure in West Malaysia: A Comparative Study of Eight Villages*, IDE Occasional Papers no. 18, Institute of Developing Economies, Tokyo.

Hou, Chi-ming and Tzong-shian Yu (eds) (1982): *Agricultural Development in China, Japan and Korea*, Academia Sinica, Taipei.

Huang, R. (1974): *Taxation and Government Finance in Sixteenth Century Ming China*, Cambridge University Press, Cambridge.

Huang, Shu-min (1981): *Agricultural Degradation: Changing Community Systems in Rural Taiwan*, University Press of America, Washington, DC.

ILO (1977): *Poverty and Landlessness in Rural Asia*, Geneva.

IRRI (1975): *Changes in Rice Farming in Selected Areas of Asia*, Vol. 1, Los Baños.

—— (1978): *Changes in Rice Farming in Selected Areas of Asia*, Vol. 2, Los Baños.

Ishii, Yoneo (ed.) (1978a): *Thailand: A Rice-Growing Society*, University Press of Hawaii, Honolulu.

—— (1978b): 'History and rice-growing', in Ishii (1978a): 15–39.

Ishikawa, Shigeru (1967): *Economic Development in Asian Perspective*, Kinokuniya Bookstore, Tokyo.

—— (1981): *Essays on Technology, Employment and Institutions in Economic Development: Comparative Asian Experience*, Kinokuniya Bookstore, Tokyo.

Japanese Academy (1980): *Meiji mae Nihon nōgyō gijutsu shi* [A history of Japanese agricultural technology before the Meiji Restoration], Noma Scientific and Medical Research Materials, Tokyo (1st edn 1964).

Jegatheesan, S. (1980): *Progress and Problems of Rice Mechanisation in Peninsular Malaysia*, MADA, Alor Setar.

Jones, E. L. (1981): *The European Miracle: Environment, Economies and Geopolitics in the History of Europe and Asia*, Cambridge University Press, Cambridge.

Jones, L. J. (1979): 'The early history of mechanical harvesting', *History of Technology* 4: 101–48.

Kahn, J. S. (1980): *Minangkabau Social Formations: Indonesian Peasants in the World Economy*, Cambridge University Press, Cambridge.

Kaida, Yoshihiro (1978): 'Irrigation and drainage: present and future', in Ishii (1978a): 205–45.

Kanazawa Natsuki (1971): *Inasaku nōgyō no ronri* [The logic of rice cultivation], Tokyo University Press, Tokyo.

Kano Tadao (1946): 'Cereals cultivated in Indonesia' [in Japanese], *Ethnology and Prehistoric Studies of Southeast Asia* 1: 278–95.

Keesing, Felix M. (1962): *The Ethnohistory of Northern Luzon*, Stanford University Press, Stanford, Calif.

Kelly, William W. (1982a): *Irrigation Management in Japan: A Critical Review of Japanese Social Science Research*, Cornell University East Asian Papers no. 30, Ithaca, NY.

—— (1982b): *Water Control in Tokugawa Japan: Irrigation Organisation in a Japanese River Basin, 1600–1870*, Cornell University East Asian Papers no. 31, Ithaca, NY.

Kerblay, Basile (1980): 'Peasant family economy in the USSR today', in E. J. Hobsbawm, Witold Kula, Ashok Mitra, K. N. Raj and Ignacy Sachs (eds), *Peasants in History: Essays in Honour of Daniel Thorner*, Sameeksha Trust, Oxford University Press, Calcutta: 69–82.

Kitamura Toshio (1950): *Nihon kangai suiri kanko no shiteki kenkyū – sōron hen* [Historical research on Japanese irrigation customs: general volume], Iwanami shoten, Tokyo.

de Koninck, Rodolphe (1978): 'A quoi sert la révolution verte? Notes sur la Malaysia et l'Indonésie', in Gordon P. Means (ed.), *The Past in Southeast Asia's Present*, Canadian Council for Southeast Asian Studies, Ottowa: 87–101.

—— (1981): 'Of rice, men, women and machines', paper presented at the Universiti Kebangsaan, Bangi, Selangor, Malaysia, 16–18 March.

Kubo, Yoshiharu (1979): 'The cooperative farming system in the mixed farming areas of Hokkaido, Japan', in Wong (1979a): 3–13.

238 *References*

Kula, Witold (1970): *Théorie économique du système féodal: pour un modèle de l'économie polonaise 16e-18e siècles*, Mouton, Paris (1st Polish edn 1962).

Kuroda Hideo (1983): 'Chūsei nōgyō gijutsu no yōsō' [Aspects of medieval agricultural technology], in Nagahara and Yamaguchi (1983): 43–76.

Kyuma, Kazutake (1978): 'Climate and rice-growing', in Ishii (1978a): 164–70.

Lardy, Nicholas R. (1984a): *Agriculture in China's Modern Economic Development*, Cambridge University Press, Cambridge.

—— (1984b): 'Consumption and living standards in China, 1978–83', *China Quarterly* 100: 849–65.

Layton, E. (1977): 'Conditions of technological development', in Spiegel-Rösing and Price (1977): 197–222.

Lê Thành Khôi (1955): *Le Viêt-nam, histoire et civilisation*, Edns de Minuit, Paris.

Leach, E. R. (1954): *Political Systems of Highland Burma: A Study of Kachin Social Structures*, LSE Monographs on Soc. Anth. no. 44, Athlone Press, London.

—— (1961): *Pul Eliya, a Village in Ceylon: A Study of Land Tenure and Kinship*, Cambridge University Press, Cambridge.

Lee, Eddy (1979): 'Egalitarian peasant farming and rural development: the case of South Korea', in Dharam Ghai, Azizur Rahman Khan, Eddy Lee and Samir Radwani (eds), *Agrarian Systems and Rural Development*, ILO/WEP Study, Macmillan, London: 24–71.

Lee, Ki-baik (1984): *A New History of Korea*, Ilchokak, Seoul.

Leonard, W. H. and J. H. Martin (1963): *Cereal Crops*, Macmillan, New York.

Levine, Gilbert (1980): 'The relationship of design, operation and management', in Coward (1980): 51–62.

Lewin, Günter (1973): *Die erste fünfzig Jahre der Song-Dynastie in China*, Akademie-Verlag, Berlin.

Lewis, Henry T. (1971): *Ilocano Rice Farmers: A Comparative Study of Two Philippine Barrios*, University of Hawaii Press, Honolulu.

Li Jiannong (1957): *Song Yuan Ming jingji shigao* [A draft economic history of the Song, Yuan and Ming dynasties], Sanlian Press, Beijing.

Liefrinck, F. A. (1886): 'Rice cultivation in Northern Bali', in J. van Baal (ed.) (1969), *Bali, Further Studies in Life, Thought and Ritual, Selected Studies on Indonesia* Vol. 8, W. van der Hoeve, The Hague: 1–74.

Lim Teck Ghee (1977): *Peasants and their Agricultural Economy in Colonial Malaya 1874–1941*, Oxford University Press, Kuala Lumpur.

Lim Teck Ghee, D. S. Gibbons, G. R. Elliston and Shukur Kassim (1981): *Land Tenure in the Muda Irrigation Area: Final Report*, part 1: *Methodology*; part 2: *Findings*, Centre for Policy Research, Universiti Sains Malaysia, Penang.

Lim Teck Ghee, D. S. Gibbons and Shukur Kassim (1980): 'Accumulation of padi land in the Muda region: some findings and thoughts on their implications for the peasantry and development', paper presented at the Universiti Kebangsaan, Bangi, Selangor, Malaysia, 26–9 May.

Lin Zili (1983): 'On the contract system of responsibility linked to production – a new form of cooperative economy in China's socialist agriculture', *Social Sciences in China* 1: 53–104.

Loekman Soetrisno (1982): 'The consequences of agricultural modernisation in

Java: experiences from below', paper presented at the conference on *Village-Level Modernisation: Livelihoods, Resources and Cultural Continuity*, ISEAS, Singapore, 21–4 June.

MADA (1980): 'Progress and present status of mechanisation in Muda', paper presented at the MARDI National Rice Conference, Selangor, Malaysia.

Mangahas, Mahar, Virginia A. Miralao and Romana P. de los Reyes, with the assistance of Normando de Leon (1976): *Tenants, Lessees, Owners: Welfare Implications of Tenure Change*, Ateneo de Manila University Press, Quezon City.

Mantra, Ida Bagus (1981): *Population Movement in Wet Rice Communities*, Gadjah Mada University Press, Yogyakarta, Indonesia.

Mao, Yu-kang (1982): 'Land reform and agricultural development in Taiwan', in Hou and Yu (1982): 723–58.

Maruyama, Eizo (1975): 'Rice cultivation and water balance in South-East Asia', in Assoc. Japanese Ag. Sci. Socs (1975): 225–47.

Marx, Karl (1976): *Capital*, Penguin, Harmondsworth.

Matsuda, Toshiro (1982): 'Recent developments of rice technology in Japan: an economic analysis', in Nōdai Research Institute (1982): 440–62.

McDermott, J. P. (1978): 'Land tenure and rural control in the Liangche region during the Southern Sung', PhD thesis, University of Cambridge.

Mendis, M. W. J. G. (1977): 'Spatial considerations in the economic development of the Mahaweli region', in S. W. R. de A. Samarasinghe (ed.), *Agriculture in the Peasant Sector of Sri Lanka*, Ceylon Studies Seminar, Peradeniya, Colombo: 13–20.

Meskill, Joanna Menzel (1979): *A Chinese Pioneer Family: The Lins of Wu-feng, Taiwan, 1729–1895*, Princeton University Press, Princeton, NJ.

Miao Qiyu (1960): 'Wu Yueh Qian Shi zai Taihu diju di yutian zhidu he shuili xitong' [The poldered fields regulation of Master Qian of Wu and Yueh in the Taihu Lake area and the classification of water control], *Agricultural History Research Anuual*, Beijing, 2: 139–58.

Mingay, G. E. (1977): *The Agricultural Revolution: Changes in Agriculture 1650–1880*, A. and C. Black, London.

Ministry of Finance, Malaysia (1980): *Economic Report 1980/81*, National Printing Dept, Kuala Lumpur.

Mitcham, Carl (1978): 'Types of Technology', *Research in Philosophy and Technology* 1.

Mitchell, B. R. (1974): 'Statistical Appendix', in C. Cipolla (ed.) (1976), *The Fontana Economic History of Europe, Contemporary Economies*, volume 2, Collins, London: 625–755.

Mizuno, Koichi (1978): 'The social organisation of rice-growing villages', in Ishii (1978a): 83–115.

Mizuno, Masami (1985): *Population Pressure and Peasant Occupations in Rural Central Java*, Occasional Papers no. 4, Centre of Southeast Asian Studies, University of Kent at Canterbury.

Moerman, M. (1968): *Agricultural Change and Peasant Choice in a Thai Village*, University of California Press, Berkeley.

240 *References*

Moise, Edwin E. (1983): *Land Reform in China and Vietnam*, University of North Carolina Press, Chapel Hill.

Mokhtar Tamin (1978): 'Rice self-sufficiency in West Malaysia: microeconomic implications', PhD thesis, Stanford University, Stanford, Calif.

Montgomery, Roger (1981): 'Employment generation within the agricultural sector', in Hansen (1981): 99–114.

Moon, Pal Yong (1982): 'Problems of organising joint utilisation of farm machinery in Korea's smallholding system', in Hou and Yu (1982): 195–228.

Moore, Barrington (1967): *Social Origins of Dictatorship and Democracy*, Penguin, Harmondsworth.

Morio, Mese (1982): 'Joint rice farming in Japan', in Nōdai Research Inst. (1982): 464–83.

Morita Akira (1974): *Shindai suirishi kenkyū* [Research on the history of water management in the Qing period], Aki shobo, Tokyo.

Motooka, Takeshi (1978): 'Rice exports and the expansion of cultivation', in Ishii (1978a): 272–334.

Mottura, G. and E. Pugliese (1980): 'Capitalism in agriculture and capitalistic agriculture', in F. H. Buttel and H. Newby (eds), *The Rural Sociology of the Advanced Societies*, Croom Helm, London: 171–99.

Moubray, G. A. de C., MCS, British Adviser, Kelantan (1937): *Annual Report on the Social and Economic Progress of the People of Kelantan for the Year 1936*, Cheong Fatt Press, Kelantan.

Muhammad Ikmal Said (1985): *The Evolution of Large Paddy Farms in the Muda Area, Kedah*, Siri Monograph no. 8, Centre for Policies Research, Universiti Sains Malaysia, Penang.

Muhly, J. D. (1981): 'The origins of agriculture and technology – West or East Asia? Summary of a conference on *The Origin of Agriculture and Technology*, Aarhus, Denmark, Nov. 21–25, 1978', *Technology and Culture* 22, 1: 125–45.

Mukhia, Harbans (1981): 'Was there feudalism in Indian history?' *Journal of Peasant Studies* 8, 3: 273–310.

Myers, Ramon H. (1982): 'Land property rights and agricultural development in modern China', in Barker et al. (1982): 37–47.

Nagahara Keiji and Yamaguchi Keiji (eds) (1983): *Nōgyō, nosankako* [Agriculture and agricultural processing], *Social History of Japanese Technology* I, Nihon Hyoronsha, Tokyo.

Nakamura, Hisashi (1972): 'Village community and paddy agriculture in South India', *Developing Economies* 10, 2: 141–65.

—— (1982): *Studies in Socio-Cultural Change in Rural Villages in Tiruchirapalli District, Tamilnadu, India*, no. 5, Institute for the Study of Languages and Cultures of Asia and Africa, Tokyo.

Nakamura, James I. (1966): *Agricultural Production and the Economic Development of Japan 1873–1922*, Princeton University Press, Princeton, NJ.

Nakamura Satoru (1959, 1960): 'Bakumatsuki Senshū ni okeru nōminsō no bunkai – Nihon shihonshugi seiritsu no kiso katei no kyūmei' [The disintegration of the peasantry in late Tokugawa Izumi: search for underlying processes of the rise of Japanese capitalism], *Rekishigaku kenkyū* 236 (Dec.

1959): 13–28; 237 (Jan. 1960): 29–34 [Abstract in Sumiya and Taira (1979: 100)].

Needham, Joseph (1974): 'The nature of Chinese society: a technical interpretation', University of Hong Kong Gazette XXIII, 5 part 2.

Needham, Joseph and Wang Ling (1965): *Science and Civilisation in China*, Vol. IV, part 2: *Mechanical Engineering*, Cambridge University Press, Cambridge.

Needham, Joseph, Lu Gwei-Djen and Wang Ling (1971): *Science and Civilisation in China*, Vol. IV, part 3: *Civil Engineering and Nautics*, Cambridge University Press, Cambridge.

Neveux, H. (1975): 'Déclin et reprise: la fluctuation biséculaire 1330–1560', in E. Le Roy Ladurie (ed.), *L'âge classique des paysans, Histoire de la France rurale* Vol. II, Seuil, Paris.

Nickum, James E. (1980): 'Local water management in the People's Republic of China', in Coward (1980): 289–98.

—— (1981): *Water Management Organisation in the People's Republic of China*, Sharpe, New York.

Nishioka Hiroaki (1981): 'Sōdai Sushū ni okeru urato kanri to kakoda kōchiku' [The management of creeks and construction of dyked fields in Suzhou in the Song dynasty], in Chūgoku Suirishi (1981): 121–54.

Nishiyama Buichi (1959): 'Chūgoku ni okeru suito nōgyō no hattatsu' [The development of wet-rice cultivation in China], *Nōgyō Sōgo Kenkyū* 3, 1: 135–9.

Nōdai Research Institute (1982): *Proceedings of a Seminar on Agricultural Research and Education in Asia, 26–31 October 1981*, Tokyo University of Agriculture.

Nōgu benri ron [Treatise on useful farm tools], by Ōgura Nagatsune, 1st edn 1822.

Nōgyō zensho [Collected writings on agriculture], by Miyazaki Yasusada, 1st edn 1697.

Nongzheng quanshu [Complete treatise on agricultural administration], by Xu Guangqi, 1st edn 1639; re-ed. with commentaries by Shi Shenghan, 2 vols, Guji Press, Shanghai, 1979.

OECD (1985): *Agriculture in China: Prospects for Production and Trade*, Paris.

Ofreneo, Réné E. (1980): *Capitalism in Philippine Agriculture*, Foundation for Nationalist Studies, Quezon City.

Ogura, Takekazu (ed.) (1967): *Agricultural Development in Modern Japan*, Fuji Publishing Co., Tokyo.

—— (1980): *Can Japanese Agriculture Survive?*, Agricultural Policy Research Centre, Tokyo.

Ohkawa, Kazushi and Henry Rosovsky (1960): 'The role of agriculture in modern Japanese economic development', *Economic Development and Cultural Change* 9, 1 part 2: 43–67.

Oka, Hiko-ichi (1975a): 'The origins of cultivated rice and its adaptive evolution', in Assoc. Japanese Ag. Sci. Socs. (1975): 21–34.

—— (1975b) 'Floating rice, an ecotype adapted to deep-water paddies – a review from the viewpoint of breeding', in Assoc. Japanese Ag. Sci. Socs. (1975): 277–87.

Ooi Jin-bee (1966): 'Some aspects of peasant farming in Malaya', *Tijdschrift voor economische en sociale geographie*, The Hague, 56, 5: 170–85.

Palmer, Ingrid (1977): *The New Rice in Indonesia*, UNRISD, Geneva.

Pasternak, Burton (1969): 'The role of the frontier in Chinese lineage development', *Journal of Asian Studies* 28: 551–61.

—— (1972a): 'The sociology of irrigation: two Taiwanese villages', in W. E. Willmott (ed.), *Economic Organisation in Chinese Society*, Stanford University Press, Stanford, Calif.: 193–214.

—— (1972b): *Kinship and Community in Two Chinese Villages*, Stanford University Press, Stanford, Calif.

Peletz, Michael G. (1983): 'Moral and political economies in rural Southeast Asia', *Journal of Comparative Studies in Society and History* 25, 4: 731–9.

Perkins, Dwight H. (1969): *Agricultural Development in China, 1368–1968*, Edinburgh University Press, Edinburgh.

Popkin, Samuel L. (1979): *The Rational Peasant: The Political Economy of Rural Society in Vietnam*, University of California Press, Berkeley.

Potter, Jack M. (1970): 'Land and lineage in traditional China', in M. Freedman (ed.), *Family and Kinship in Chinese Society*, Stanford University Press, Stanford, Calif.: 121–38.

—— (1976): *Thai Peasant Social Structure*, University of Chicago Press, Chicago.

Purcal, J.T.(1972): *Rice Economy: Employment and Income in Malaysia*, East-West Centre Press, Honolulu.

Purseglove, J. W. (1972): *Tropical Crops: Monocotyledons*, Longman, London.

RID (Royal Irrigation Dept of Thailand) (1957): *The Greater Chao Phraya Project*, Bangkok.

Raffles, Thomas Stamford (1817): *The History of Java*, 2 vols, London; repr. Oxford University Press, Kuala Lumpur, 1978.

Raikes, R. (1967): *Water, Weather and Prehistory*, London.

Rapp, Friedrich (1985): 'The philosophy of technology: a review', *Interdisciplinary Science Reviews* 10, 2: 126–39.

Ravenstone, Piercy (1824): *Thoughts on the Funding System and its Effects*, London.

Rawski, Evelyn Sakakida (1972): *Agricultural Change and the Peasant Economy of South China*, Harvard University Press, Cambridge, Mass.

—— (1979): *Education and Popular Literacy in Ch'ing China*, University of Michigan Press, Ann Arbor.

Rawski, Thomas G. (1979): *Economic Growth and Employment in China*, World Bank/Oxford University Press, London.

Reed, C. A. (1977): 'Origins of agriculture: discussion and some conclusions', in C. A. Reed (ed.), *Origins of Agriculture*, Mouton, The Hague: 879–956.

Reed, Edward (1979): 'Two approaches to cooperation in rice production in South Korea', in Wong (1979a): 14–36.

de Reinach, Lucien (1952): *Le Laos*, 2nd edn, Guilmoto, Paris.

Robequain, Charles (1939): *L'évolution économique de l'Indochine française*, Centre d'Etudes de Politique Etrangère, P. Hartmann, Paris.

Sahai, Sachchidanand (1970): *Les institutions politiques et l'organisation administrative du Cambodge ancien (VIe – XIIIe siècles)*, Publn de l'Ecole Française d'Extrême-Orient vol. LXXV, Adrien-Maisonneuve, Paris.

Sahara Makoto (forthcoming): 'Recent research on the Yayoi culture'.

Salomon, Jean-Jacques (1984): 'What is technology? The issue of its origins and definitions', *History and Technology* 1, 2: 113–56.

Sasaki Komei (1971): *Inasaku izen* [Before rice cultivation], NHK Books, Tokyo.

Scott, James C. (1976): *The Moral Economy of the Peasant: Rebellion and Subsistence in Southeast Asia*, Yale University Press, New Haven, Conn.

Sen, Amartya (1975): *Employment, Technology and Development*, Clarendon Press, Oxford.

Shand, R. T. and Mohd Ariff Hussein (1983): *A Socio-Economic Analysis of the Kemubu Project*, Part II, Universiti Pertanian Malaysia, Serdang.

Shanin, Teodor (1972): *The Awkward Class: Political Sociology of Peasantry in a Developing Society, Russia 1910–1925*, Clarendon Press, Oxford.

Shaw, G. E., Acting British Adviser (1926); *Kelantan Administrative Report for the Year 1925*, Government Printing Office, Singapore.

Shen Baixian, Zhang Guangcai et al. (1979): *Zhonghua shuili shi* [A history of water control in China], Commercial Press, Taipei.

Shen, T. H. (1951): *Agricultural Resources of China*, Cornell University Press, Ithaca, NY.

Shenshi nongshu [Treatise on agriculture by Master Shen], mid-seventeenth century, repr. in Chhen Hengli and Wang Dacan, *Bunongshu yanjiu* [Researches on the Agricultural treatise by Master Shen and its expanded (eighteenth-century) version], Zhonghua Press, Peking, 1958.

Shiba Yoshinobu (tr. and ed. Mark Elvin) (1970): *Commerce and Society in Sung China*, Michigan University Press, Ann Arbor.

Shimpo, Mitsuro (1976): *Three Decades in Shiwa: Economic Development and Social Change in a Japanese Farming Community*, University of British Columbia Press, Vancouver.

Shue, Vivienne (1980): *Peasant China in Transition: The Dynamics of Development towards Socialism*, University of California Press, Berkeley.

Slicher van Bath, B. H. (1963): *The Agrarian History of Western Europe AD 500–1850*, Edward Arnold, London.

Smith, Thomas C. (1959): *The Agrarian Origins of Modern Japan*, Stanford University Press, Stanford, Calif.

Smith, Thomas C. (with Robert Y. Eng and Robert T. Lundy) (1977): *Nakahara: Family Farming and Population in a Japanese Village, 1717–1830*, Stanford University Press, Stanford, Calif.

Song Yingxing (tr. E.-T. Z. Sun and S.-C. Sun) (1966): *T'ien-kung k'ai-wu: Chinese Technology in the Seventeenth Century*, Pennsylvania State University Press, University Park and London (1st Chinese edn 1637).

Speare, Alden (1981): 'Rural and urban migration: a national overview', in Hansen (1981): 202–18.

Spencer, J. E. (1974): 'La maîtrise de l'eau en Asie du Sud-Est', *Etudes rurales* 53–6: *Agriculture et societe en Asie du Sud-Est*: 73–94.

Spiegel-Rösing, Ina and Derek de Solla Price (eds) (1977): *Science, Technology and Society: A Cross-Disciplinary Perspective*, Sage Publications, London.

Stargardt, Janice (1983): *Satingpra I: The Environmental and Economic Archaeology of South Thailand*, Studies in Southeast Asian Archaeology I, Inst. of Southeast Asian Studies (Singapore), BAR International Series 158, Oxford.

Stavis, Benedict (1978): *The Politics of Agricultural Mechanisation in China*, Cornell University Press, Ithaca, NY.

Steward, Julian H. (1980): 'Initiation of a research trend: Wittfogel's irrigation hypothesis', in G. L. Ulman (ed.) (1980), *Society and History: Essays in Honor of K. A. Wittfogel*, Morton, New York.

Stewart, Frances (1977): *Technology and Underdevelopment*, Macmillan, London.

Stoler, Anne L. (1981): 'Garden use and household economy in Java', in Hansen (1981): 242–54.

Stone, Bruce (1982): 'The use of agricultural statistics: some national aggregate examples and current state of the art', in Barker et al. (1982): 205–46.

Sumiya, Mikio and Koji Taira (eds) (1979): *An Outline of Japanese Economic History 1603–1940: Major Works and Research Findings*, University of Tokyo Press, Tokyo.

Suo shan nongpu [A survey of the agriculture of Shuttle Mountain] by Liu Yingtang, 1st edn 1717, repr. Agriculture Press, Beijing, 1960.

Swaminathan, M. S. (1984): 'Rice', *Scientific American* 250, 1: 62–71.

Tada, Hirokazu (forthcoming): 'British engineers' apprenticeship in irrigation technology: the restoration of old canals in North India, 1810–1840s'.

Tadem, Eduardo (1978): 'Peasant land rights and the Philippine corporate farming program', *Philippine Social Sciences and Humanities Revue* 42, 1–4: 56–76.

Taillard, Christian (1972): 'Introduction à l'étude des berges de la Nan Ngum et du Mekong', *Asie du Sud-Est et Monde Insulindien* 3, 2: 195–233.

Takahashi, Akira (1970); *Land and Peasants in Central Luzon*, East-West Center Press, Honolulu.

Takaya, Yoshikazu (1978): 'Landform and rice-growing', in Ishii (1978a): 171–91.

Tamaki, Akira (1977): *The Development Theory of Irrigation Agriculture*, Special Papers no.7, Institute of Developing Economies, Tokyo.

—— (1979): *Mizu no shisō* [The philosophy of water], Ronso, Tokyo.

Tamaki Akira and Hatade Isao (1974): *Fūdo: daichi to ningen no rekishi* [Climate: the earth and human history], Heibonsha, Tokyo.

Tanabe, Shigeharu (1978): 'Land reclamation in the Chao Phraya Delta', in Ishii (1978a): 40–83.

Tanaka Yoshiaki (1983): 'Kodai nōgyō no gijutsu to tenkai' [The techniques and development of ancient agriculture], in Nagahara and Yamaguchi (1983): 7–42.

Tang, Anthony M. (1979): 'China's agricultural legacy', *Economic Development and Cultural Change* 28, 1: 1–22.

Tangshuang pu [Monograph on sugar], by Wang Shao; 1st edn 1154, repr. Beijing, 1956.

Tani, Tatsuo (1975): 'General status of rice storage in Southeast Asia', in Assoc. of Japanese Ag. Sci. Socs. (1975): 514–22.

Taylor, Donald C. (1981): *The Economics of Malaysian Paddy Production and Irrigation*, The Agriculture Development Council, Bangkok.

Thorp, James (1937): 'Soils', in Buck (1937): 130–61.

Toya Toshiyuki (1949): *Kinsei nōgyō keiei shi ron* [The history of farm management in the Tokugawa period], Tokyo (see Smith 1959: 81).

Tsuchiya, Keizo (1976): *Productivity and Technological Progress in Japanese Agriculture*, University of Tokyo Press, Tokyo.

Tsukuba Hisaharu (1980): 'Inasaku' [Rice cultivation], in Japanese Academy (1980): 29–126.

Twitchett, D. C. (1960): 'Documents on clan administration I: The rules of administration of the charitable estate of the Fan Clan', *Asia Major* 8, 1: 1–35.

—— (1970): *Financial Administration under the T'ang Dynasty*, 2nd edn, Cambridge University Press, Cambridge.

UN (ECAFE) (1950): *Flood Damage and Flood Control Activities in Asia and the Far East*, Flood Control Series no. 1, Bangkok.

Umemura, Mataji (1970): 'Agriculture and labour supply in the Meiji era', in Kazushi Ohkawa, Bruce F. Johnston and Hiromitsu Kaneda (eds), *Agriculture and Economic Growth*, Princeton University Press, Princeton, NJ: 21–6.

Vaidyanathan, A. (1983): *Water Control Institutions and Agriculture: A Comparative Perspective*, Working Paper no. 178, Centre for Development Studies, Trivandra, Kerala.

VanderMeer, Canute (1980): 'Changing local patterns in a Taiwanese irrigation system', in Coward (1980): 225–62.

Vander Velde, Edward J, (1980): 'Local consequences of a large-scale irrigation system in India', in Coward (1980): 299–328.

van Setten van der Meer, N. C. (1979): *Sawah Cultivation in Ancient Java*, Oriental Monographs no. 22, ANU Press, Canberra.

Vavilov, N. I. (1949): *The Origin, Variety, Immunity and Breeding of Cultivated Plants*, tr. K. Starr Chester, *Chronica Botanica* vol. 13, Waltham, Mass.

Venkayya, V. (1906): 'Irrigation in Southern India in ancient times', *Archaeological Survey of India, Annual Report 1903–4*, Calcutta: 205–11.

Vermeer, E. B. (1977): *Water Conservancy and Irrigation in China: Social, Economic and Agro-Technical Aspects*, Leiden University Press, Leiden.

Vishnu-Mittre (1974): 'The beginnings of agriculture: palaeobotanical evidence from India', in J. Hutchinson (ed.), *Evolutionary Studies on World Crops: Diversity and Change in the Indian Subcontinent*, Cambridge University Press, Cambridge: 3–33.

—— (1977) 'Changing economy in ancient India', in C. A. Reed (ed.), *The Origins of Agriculture*, Mouton, The Hague: 569–88.

Wade, Robert (1982): *Irrigation and Agricultural Politics in South Korea*, Westview Press, Boulder, Colo.

Wädekin, Karl-Eugen (1975): 'The Soviet *kolkhoz*: vehicle of cooperative farming or of control and transfer of capital resources', in Peter Dorner (ed.),

Cooperative and Commune: Group Farming in the Economic Development of Agriculture, University of Wisconsin Press, Madison: 95–116.

Walker, Kenneth R. (1984): 'Chinese agriculture during the period of readjustment, 1978–83', *China Quarterly* 100: 783–812.

Wang, S. H. and R. Apthorpe (1974): *Rice Farming in Taiwan: Three Village Studies*, Institute of Ethnology, Academia Sinica, Taipei.

Wang Zhen nongshu [Treatise on agriculture], by Wang Zhen, 1st edn 1313, Imperial edition 1783, Beijing (also modern repr. Nongye Press, Beijing, 1981).

Waswo, A. (1977): *Japanese Landlords: The Decline of a Rural Elite*, University of California Press, Berkeley.

Watabe, Tadayo (1967): *Glutinous Rice in Northern Thailand*, Monograph of the Centre of Southeast Asian Studies, Kyoto University, University Press of Hawaii, Honolulu.

—— (1977): *Ine no rōdo* [Rice road], NHK, Tokyo.

—— (1978): 'The development of rice cultivation', in Ishii (1978a): 3–14.

Watson, Andrew (1984): 'Agriculture looks for 'shoes that fit'', in Neville Maxwell and Bruce Macfarlane (eds), *China's Changed Road to Development*, Pergamon, Oxford: 83–108.

Watson, J. L. (1975): *Emigration and the Chinese Lineage: The Mans in Hong Kong and London*, University of California Press, Berkeley.

Wertheim, W. F. and M. Stiefel (1982): *Production, Equality and Participation in Rural China*, UNRISD, Geneva.

Whang, In-Joung (1981): *Management of Rural Change in Korea: the Saemaul Undong*, Seoul National University Press, Seoul.

Wheatley, Paul (1965): 'Agricultural terracing', *Pacific Viewpoint* 6: 123–44.

White, Benjamin (1976): 'Population, involution and employment in rural Java', *Development and Change* 7: 267–90.

Whyte, R. O. (1974): *Rural Nutrition in Monsoon Asia*, Oxford University Press, Kuala Lumpur.

Wiens, Thomas (1980): 'Agricultural statistics in the People's Republic of China', in A. Eckstein (ed.), *Quantitative Measures of China's Economic Output*, University of Michigan Press, Ann Arbor.

Wijeyewardene, Gehan (1973): 'Hydraulic society in contemporary Thailand', in Robert Ho and E. C. Chapman (eds), *Studies of Contemporary Thailand*, ANU Press, Canberra: 89–110.

Will, Pierre-Etienne (1980): *Bureaucratie et famine en Chine au 18e siècle*, Mouton/EHESS, Paris.

Wittfogel, Karl (1931): *Wirtschaft und Gesellschaft Chinas: Versuch der wissenschaftlischen Analyse einer grossen asiatischen Agrargesellschaft*, Hirschfeld, Leipzig.

—— (1957): *Oriental Despotism: A Study in Total Power*, Yale University Press, New Haven, Conn.

Wong, John (1971): 'Peasant economic behaviour: the case of traditional agricultural cooperation in China', *Developing Economies* 9, 3.

—— (1973): *Land Reform in the People's Republic of China: Institutional Transformations in Agriculture*, Praeger, New York.

—— (ed.) (1979a): *Group Farming in Asia*, Singapore University Press, Singapore.

—— (1979b): 'The group farming system in China: ideology versus pragmatism', in Wong (1979a): 89–103.

—— (1982): *Labour Mobilisation in the Chinese Commune System: A Perspective from Guangdong*, ILO-ARTEP, Bangkok.

Woodard, David (1805): *The Narrative of Captain David Woodard and Four Seamen, who lost their ship while in a boat at sea, and surrendered themselves up to the Malays in the Island of Celebes*, 2nd edn, Johnson, London.

Wuhan Hydroelectric Institute (1979): *Zhongguo shuili shigao* [A brief history of water control in China], 2 vols, Hydroelectric Press, Beijing.

Wurfel, David (1977): 'Philippine agrarian policy today: implementation and political impact', ISEAS Occasional Paper no. 46, Singapore.

Yamada, Noboru (1975): 'Technical problems of rice production in tropical Asia', in Assoc. Japanese Ag. Sci. Socs. (1975): 170–201.

Yamamura, Kozo (1979): 'Pre-industrial landholding patterns in Japan and England', in Albert M. Craig (ed.), *Japan: a Comparative View*, Princeton University Press, Princeton, NJ.

Yamazaki, Mitsuru (1980): *Japan's Community-Based Industries: A Case-Study of Small Industry*, Asian Productivity Organisation, Tokyo.

Yamazaki Ryūzō (1961): 'Settsu mensaku nōson ni okeru ichi funō keiei no bunseki' [Farm management in cotton-growing villages of Settsu: the case of a rich peasant household], in idem, *Jinushisei seiritsuki no nōgyō kōzō* [Early landlordism and the structure of agriculture], Aoki Shoten, Tokyo: 130–238 (abstract in Sumiya and Taira 1979: 102).

Yang Shiting (1978): 'On the remains of cultivated rice discovered at Shixia, Guangdong' [in Chinese], *Wenwu* 7: 23–8.

Yangzi Region Planning Commission (1979): *Changjiang shuili shilüe* [A brief history of water control in the Yangzi], Irrigation and Hydroelectricity Press, Beijing.

You Xiuling (1979): 'A preliminary discussion of the origins, diversification and dissemination of rice cultivation in China, based on the archaeological rice remains from Hemudu' [in Chinese], *Acta Agronomica Sinica* 5, 3: 1–10.

Zangheri, R. (1969): 'The historical relationship between agricultural and economic development in Italy', in E. L. Jones & S. J. Woolf (eds), *Agrarian Change and Economic Development: The Historical Problems*, Methuen, London: 23–39.

Zeng Xiangxu (1902): *Nongxue zuanyao* [The essentials of agronomy], Sichuan, China.

Zhejiang CPAM (1976): 'Reconnaissance of the neolithic site at Hemudu in Yuyao County, Zhejiang Province' [in Chinese], *Wenwu* 8: 6–27.

—— (1978): 'First season excavations at Hemudu, Yuyao County, Zhejiang Province' [in Chinese], *Kaogu xuebao* 1: 39–94.

Zhejiang Provincial Museum (1978): 'A study and identification of the animal and plant remains unearthed at Hemudu' [in Chinese], *Kaogu xuebao* 1: 95–107.

Glossary

bendang: wet-rice field (Malay, used in Northern Malay States)

bund: low earthen dyke around a wet-rice field

conduit: a channel through which water is conveyed

corvée labour: free labour services owed by the individual to his feudal superior or to the state

cusec: cubic metres per second (measure of water-flow)

dibble: to sow seeds individually in pockets in the soil

extension: technical instruction given to farmers by officers directly or indirectly involved in R & D

flume: an inclined channel for conveying water

GMP: 'guaranteed minimum price'

gabion: a bamboo basket filled with stones, used in the construction of dams, weirs, etc.

Green Revolution: technological 'package' of agricultural improvements first introduced to Asian countries in the 1960s

HYV: high-yielding variety

hard-pan or clay-pan: the hard, impervious layer of ferrous soil which forms under the top layer of mud in a wet-rice field and prevents seepage

IRRI: International Rice Research Institute (Los Banos, Philippines)

KADA: Kemubu Agricultural Development Authority (Kemubu Irrigation Scheme, Kelantan, Malaysia)

kampong: village, or the dry land upon which a village stands (Malay)

krah: corvée labour (Malay)

kumiai: Japanese cooperative groups, especially *suiri kumiai*, irrigation associations

lodge: to bend and fall, of cereals with weak or over-long stems

MADA: Muda Agricultural Development Authority (Muda Irrigation Scheme, Kedah, Malaysia)

New Technology: the 'package' associated with the Green Revolution, including HYVs, chemical fertilisers, etc.

night-soil: human faeces, widely used as manure in East Asia

nōkai: Japanese farmers' associations

noria or 'Persian wheel': a large wheel with buckets around the rim used to raise water

padi/paddy: general term for growing or unhusked rice (Malay in origin)

panicle: a multiple-branching inflorescence, or seed-head, as in rice, millet

pericarp: the tough membrane surrounding the inner grain

polder: large earthen dyke used to encircle land and so to reclaim it from marshes or lakes

square-pallet chain-pump: a small wooden water-pump, often portable, operated with the feet

R & D: Research and Development

reaping-knife: small shafted knife used for cutting individual panicles of rice

sawah: wet-rice field (Malay, used in peninsula and archipelago)

sluice: a device for letting water in or out

subak: Balinese irrigation society

swape: a well-sweep, a bucket on a pivoted pole used for raising water

swidden: shifting cultivation, slash-and-burn agriculture

tank: a small reservoir

tillering: the growth of multiple shoots around the main stem of a plant

Index

agricultural planning, 141–3, 148
agricultural prices, 102, 137, 138, 146, 147, 208–9, 217
Angkor, 72–5, 142, 176; cosmological principles of hydraulic city 72; double-cropping, 73; inbuilt obsolescence of technology, 75; reversion to single-cropping, 75
Annam: rice multicropping, 22; tenurial conditions 181–2
Asiatic Mode of Production, 1, 65
Ayutthaya, 30; canal construction, 64

Bali: irrigation canals, 80; *subak*, 34, 67, 83; terraces, 32
Bowring Treaty, 97
Burma: autonomy of village tanks, 76; canal construction methods, 83; expansion of rice area, 42; extensive cultivation in Delta, 44; 'moral economy', 183; rainfall, 69; tanks, 72

capital inputs, 96, 140–1, 148, 152, 158–63
capital productivity, 147–66
capitalist farming, 140, 182, 185, 191, 194, 198, 200
capitalist relations, 1, 6; *see also* economic differentiation; polarisation
Celebes, 33
Ceylon, *see* Sri Lanka
China (*see also* Yangzi Delta): agricultural development, 141–2, 150, 203–9; agricultural prices, 146, 208–9; aqueducts, 81–3; capitalist relations, 6; commercial crops, 93, 117, 127, 128, 205, 209; communes, 160, 195, 208; construction projects, 158–9; contour

canals, 81–3; corvée labour, 92; crop pests, 51; domestication of rice, 9; double-cropping, 119, 203; expansion of water control, 109; extensive cultivation in remote provinces, 44; fertilisers, 49, 160; grain monoculture, 130, 209; grain production, 146, 208; Guanxian irrigation works, 88–90; irrigation management, 91–4, 104, 107, 112, 208; labour exchange, 120–1; labour hire, 165; labour inputs, 158, 164; labour productivity, 164; land reclamation, 39, 204; land reform, 194, 207–8; landlessness, 186, 207; landlords, 92, 153, 174, 206; landowning, 92, 187, 206; lineages, 184–5; mechanisation, 156, 208; multicropping, 125; ponds, 77–9; 'responsibility system', 138, 160, 164, 168, 195, 208–9; rice breeding, 22–4, 167, 204; rice trade, 127, 128, 204; rural industrialisation, 138–9, 205, 209; sea-walls, 41; seed-bed preparation, 45; settlement schemes, 64, 91, 104; small-scale mechanisation, 61; Song 'Green Revolution', 141–2, 150, 203–5; state investment, 141, 159, 160; state role in irrigation administration, 93, 208; tenurial relations, 174, 177, 205–8; terraces, 32, 33; transplanting, 46; transport canals, 64; water control, 208; water-raising technology, 54, 92; weeding techniques, 51; wheat, 119; yields, 63, 125, 164, 167
Cochinchina: creek irrigation, 95; expansion of rice area, 42; extensive cultivation, 44;

DATE DUE
